Handbook of
Psychotherapies with Children and Families

Issues in Clinical Child Psychology

Series Editors: **Michael C. Roberts**, *University of Kansas—Lawrence, Kansas*
Lizette Peterson, *University of Missouri—Columbia, Missouri*

A Continuation Order Plan is available for this series. A continuation order will bring delivery of each
new volume immediately upon publication. Volumes are billed only upon actual shipment. For further
information please contact the publisher.

Handbook of
Psychotherapies with Children and Families

Edited by

Sandra W. Russ

Case Western Reserve University
Cleveland, Ohio

and

Thomas H. Ollendick

Virginia Polytechnic Institute and State University
Blacksburg, Virginia

Kluwer Academic / Plenum Publishers
New York, Boston, Dordrecht, London, Moscow

Library of Congress Cataloging-in-Publication Data

Handbook of psychotherapies with children and families / edited by
  Sandra W. Russ and Thomas H. Ollendick.
       p.   cm. -- (Issues in clinical child psychology)
    Includes bibliographical references and index.
    ISBN 0-306-46098-X
    1. Child psychotherapy. 2. Family psychotherapy. I. Russ,
  Sandra Walker. II. Ollendick, Thomas H. III. Series.
    [DNLM: 1. Psychotherapy--methods--Adolescence. 2. Psychotherapy-
  -methods--Child. 3. Family Therapy--methods.   WS 350.2 H23589
  1999]
  RJ504.H3619 1999
  618.92'8914--dc21
  DNLM/DLC
  for Library of Congress   99-40702
                                                                   CIP

ISBN: 0-306-46098-X

© 1999 Kluwer Academic / Plenum Publishers
233 Spring Street, New York, N.Y. 10013

10 9 8 7 6 5 4 3 2

A C.I.P. record for this book is available from the Library of Congress

Printed in the United States of America

To all of the children and adolescents who have so richly
informed us throughout our development as researchers,
teachers, and clinicians. They have helped us to evaluate,
reexamine, transform our thoughts, beliefs and actions,
and to grow as mental health professionals.

Contributors

Anne Marie Albano, Child Study Center, NYU School of Medicine, New York, New York 10016

Catherine E. Barton, School of Education, Boston College, Chestnut Hill, Massachusetts 02467

Timothy A. Cavell, Department of Educational Psychology, Texas A & M University, College Station, Texas 77843-4225

Dante Cicchetti, Mt. Hope Family Center, University of Rochester, Rochester, New York 14608

Michael F. Detweiler, Department of Psychology, West Virginia University, Morgantown, West Virginia 26506

Raymond DiGiuseppe, Psychology Department, St. John's University, Jamaica, New York 11439

Dennis Drotar, School of Medicine, Case Western Reserve University, Cleveland, Ohio 44106-6038

Joseph A. Durlak, Department of Psychiatry, Loyola University of Chicago, Chicago, Illinois 60626

Cynthia R. Ellis, Munroe-Meyer Institute for Genetics and Rehabilitation, University of Nebraska Medical Center, Omaha, Nebraska 68198

Sheila M. Eyberg, Department of Clinical and Health Psychology, University of Florida, Gainesville, Florida 32610

Robert D. Felner, Department of Education, University of Rhode Island, Kingston, Rhode Island 02881

Peter Fonagy, The Anna Freud Centre, London NW3 5SD, England; Sub-Department of Clinical Health Psychology, University College London, London WC1E 6BT, England; and Child and Family Center for Outcomes Research and Effectiveness, Menninger Foundation, Topeka, Kansas 66601

Constance J. Fournier, Division of Educational Psychology, University of Missouri, St. Louis, Missouri 63110

Ned L. Gaylin, Department of Family Studies, University of Maryland, College Park, Maryland 20742

Scott W. Henggeler, Family Services Research Center, Department of Psychiatry and Behavioral Sciences, Medical University of South Carolina, Charleston, South Carolina 29425-0742

Kimberly A. Howard, School of Education, Boston College, Chestnut Hill, Massachusetts 02467

Alan Hudson, Department of Psychology and Intellectual Disability Studies, Royal Melbourne Institute of Technology, Bundoora 3083, Australia

Jan N. Hughes, Department of Educational Psychology, Texas A & M University, College Station, Texas 77843-4225

Philip C. Kendall, Department of Psychology, Temple University, Philadelphia, Pennsylvania 19122

Susan M. Knell, Meridia Behavioral Medicine, Cleveland, Ohio 44124

April Dawn Koontz, Clinical Child Psychology Program, University of Kansas, Lawrence, Kansas 66045

Amy L. Krain, Department of Psychology, Temple University, Philadelphia, Pennsylvania 19122

Chris Kratochvil, Department of Psychiatry, Creighton University, Lincoln, Nebraska 68178

William M. Kurtines, Child and Family Psychosocial Research Center, Florida International University, Miami, Florida 33199

Stan Kutcher, Department of Psychiatry, Dallhousie University, Halifax, Nova Scotia B3H 3J5, Canada

Kathleen L. Lemanek, Department of Psychology, Columbus Children's Hospital, Columbus, Ohio 43205

Richard M. Lerner, Eliot-Pearson Department of Child Development, Tufts University, Medford, Massachusetts 02155

Cindy Ellen Li, Psychology Department, St. John's University, Jamaica, New York 11439

Susan Logsdon-Conradsen, Department of Psychiatry, School of Medicine, Emory University, Atlanta, Georgia 30322

John S. March, Departments of Psychiatry and Psychology, Duke University Medical Center, Durham, North Carolina 27710

Kate A. McGlinchey, Department of Psychology, Loyola University of Chicago, Chicago, Illinois 60626

Robert J. McMahon, Department of Psychology, University of Washington, Seattle, Washington 98195-1525

Stanley B. Messer, Graduate School of Applied and Professional Psychology, Rutgers University, Piscataway, New Jersey 08855-0819

Linda Monaco, Department of Clinical and Health Psychology, University of Florida, Gainesville, Florida 32610

Donna Moreau, New York State Psychiatric Institute, New York, New York 10032

Laura Mufson, New York State Psychiatric Institute, New York, New York 10032

William C. Nichols, The Nichols Group, Inc., Watkinsville, Georgia 30677-4212

Thomas H. Ollendick, Child Study Center, Virginia Polytechnic Institute and State University, Blacksburg, Virginia 24061-0355

William A. Rae, Department of Educational Psychology, Texas A & M University, College Station, Texas 77843-4225

Jeff Randall, Family Services Research Center, Department of Psychiatry and Behavioral Sciences, Medical University of South Carolina, Charleston, South Carolina 29425-0742

Arista Rayfield, Department of Pediatrics, University of Kansas Medical Center, Kansas City, Kansas 66160

Sharon Reiter, Department of Psychiatry, University of Toronto, Sunnybrook Hospital, Toronto, Ontario M4N 3M5, Canada

Arthur L. Robin, Department of Psychiatry and Behavioral Neurosciences, Wayne State University, Detroit, Michigan 48202

Sandra W. Russ, Psychology Department, Case Western Reserve University, Cleveland, Ohio 44106-7123

Robert L. Russell, Department of Psychology, Loyola University Chicago, Chicago, Illinois 60626

Stephen R. Shirk, Department of Psychology, University of Denver, Denver, Colorado 80208

Patricia T. Siegel, Department of Psychiatry and Behavioral Neurosciences, Wayne State University, Detroit, Michigan 48202

Wendy K. Silverman, Child and Family Psychosocial Research Center, Florida International University, Miami, Florida 33199

Nirbhay N. Singh, Medical College of Virginia of Virginia Commonwealth University, Richmond, Virginia 23298

Sheree L. Toth, Mt. Hope Family Center, University of Rochester, Rochester, New York 14608

Mary E. Walsh, School of Education, Boston College, Chestnut Hill, Massachusetts 02467

C. Seth Warren, Graduate School of Applied and Professional Psychology, Rutgers University, Piscataway, New Jersey 08855-0819

Preface

The aim of this book on psychotherapies with children and families is to present a comprehensive overview of the current array of intervention approaches in the child mental health field. There is a focus on the integration of theory, research, and practice throughout the book. The book proceeds from the more global presentations of basic theoretical approaches to applications of these approaches with specific problems and populations. It then presents more integrated intervention approaches and overviews of the research literature. One of the unique features of this book is its focus on future directions for each approach, both in clinical practice and in research. A second unique feature is its structured format across diverse approaches with a focus on empirical validation of approaches. Another innovation is the presentation of interventions that integrate major components of different theoretical approaches. Thus, the book reflects the current trends in the field of interventions with specific problems and populations, empirical validation of the approach, and the integration of treatment approaches.

There are five major sections in this book. Part I consists of four chapters that address a variety of issues related to child psychotherapy. Chapter 1 by the editors examines the historical roots of child psychotherapy and explores current trends in the treatment of diverse child disorders. It emphasizes the movement to "treatments that work" and sets the stage for the chapters that follow. Chapter 2, by Toth and Cicchetti, reviews state-of-the-art concepts of developmental psychopathology and its importance for treatment of children and adolescents. Chapter 3 examines an equally important dimension to effective child treatment, namely, the social and contextual forces that inform child treatment. Our basic premise is that children and adolescents are embedded in these contexts and that their behavior, adaptive as well as maladaptive, cannot be separated from it. This chapter by Howard, Barton, Walsh, and Lerner discusses the importance of these forces. Rae and Fournier, in Chapter 4, explore legal and ethical issues related to interventions with children and their families.

Part II covers the basic theoretical approaches to child and family therapy. The purpose of this section is to present the major theoretical approaches to intervention with children and families that are in use today. A main theme of each chapter is empirical validation of the effectiveness of the treatment. To ensure a uniform presentation, each chapter discusses the theoretical overview of the approach, history of the approach, assessment and case formulation, description of intervention procedures and mechanisms of change, research evidence that supports the approach for specific problems and populations, utilizing the approach within a managed care framework, and suggestions for future research and practice.

After Part II's look at basic theoretical approaches, Part III examines these approaches in more depth by illustrating their applicability with diverse child and adolescent disorders. Basically, we have identified treatments that intersect with specific disorders. In our reading of the literature, we have identified procedures for specific problems/disorders that "work." That is, our emphasis in this section is on the efficacy and effectiveness of specific procedures for specific problems. In effect, we want to illustrate in this section that specific treatments are more efficacious with certain problems and that we have made progress in the pursuit of identifying such treatments. Many of the chapters in this section are based on psychosocial treatment protocols reviewed and funded by NIMH and the proposed contributors, for the most part, are experts in their respective areas. As noted by the title of this section, empirically validated procedures are highlighted. Each author discusses the basic approach utilized, description of the problem/disorder, description of the procedures to be used, major mechanisms of change, research support for efficacy, case examples, and future research, with attention to managed care.

Part IV presents empirically validated interventions that integrate specific components of different theoretical orientations. Shirk's introductory chapter in this section provides a conceptual framework for thinking about integrated treatment strategies. In general, these are not "theoretically pure" approaches, but rather are a pragmatic mix of different aspects of various approaches. All of the chapters are examples of integrated treatment approaches with specific populations. Because many of these integrative approaches are new, and often innovative, the amount of empirical validation of the approach demonstrates promise in intervening effectively with specific populations of children. Each author discusses, where relevant, theoretical overview of the approach, description of intervention procedures and mechanisms of change, specific problems and populations, research support for efficacy, case examples, and future research, with attention to managed care.

Finally, Part V addresses issues related to research in psychotherapy, including an overview of psychotherapy research, process issues, and outcome issues. It concludes with an Epilogue written by the editors. In this epilogue, we attempt to "pull together" much of what our contributors have offered and to project the status and future of child psychotherapy for the next century.

In sum, this book is a compendium of theory, research, and practice for the field of child and adolescent psychotherapy. The text is diverse and attempts to illustrate various psychotherapy modalities. One of the strengths of this handbook is the quality of the authors who have contributed chapters. They are leaders in the field, and many of them are innovators in the area of research and/or practice. After a careful review of each of these chapters, we conclude that the future of intervention research and practice is in good hands.

—S.W.R. and T.H.O.

Acknowledgments

We greatly appreciate the excellent scholarship offered here by our contributors. The time and intellectual energy that they dedicated to this project is reflected in the outstanding quality of their work.

We also want to thank Michael Roberts for initiating this volume for Kluwer Academic/Plenum Publishers. His guidance has greatly contributed to the project.

Mariclaire Cloutier, Senior Editor at Kluwer Academic/Plenum Publishers has very effectively worked with the management of this volume. Cathy Jewell and the editorial staff have been a pleasure to work with.

We express special appreciation to Gail Gangidine at Case Western Reserve University for her assistance in typing and correspondence and to Cindy Koziol at Virginia Polytechnic Institute for her assistance of the indexes as well as for correspondence. Their invaluable help is much appreciated.

On a personal note: Tom Ollendick thanks his children, Laurie Kristine and Kathleen Marie and grandchild, Braden Thomas. They have greatly inspired me over the years and have been the source of much joy, contentment, and reinforcement.

Sandra Russ thanks her husband Thomas Brugger, for his continual support and encouragement over the years.

Contents

Part IV. Integrative Approaches

Handbook of
Psychotherapies with Children and Families

Part I

Overview of Issues

1

Psychotherapy with Children and Families
Historical Traditions and Current Trends

THOMAS H. OLLENDICK and SANDRA W. RUSS

Psychotherapy with children and families consists of a variety of theoretical approaches and techniques in various forms and constellations, most of which include the child, the child's family, and the broader social and cultural context in which the child exists. Over the years, several theoretical approaches have been espoused; collectively, they weave a rich tapestry that reflects the evolution of child psychotherapy. These theoretical approaches, along with a host of practical realities that are present when working with children, have guided the development of the field of child psychotherapy as it is practiced at this time.

We are at a crucial juncture in the field of intervention (prevention and treatment) with children and their families. There is a strong movement toward developing and identifying effective interventions and in generating empirical support for their use in clinical practice (see Special Issues of the *Journal of Abnormal Child Psychology,* Volume 32, No. 1, 1998, and the *Journal of Clinical Child Psychology,* Volume 27, No. 2, 1998). In addition, the realities of managed care demand short-term treatment or, in the least, thorough justification of long-term approaches (Rodwin, 1995). As a result, a number of somewhat contradictory trends have emerged in recent years. This first chapter in our edited book will provide a brief history of the field of child psychotherapy and the forces that helped shape it. The histories will be brief because they are elaborated on in more detail in various chapters throughout this book. Following this brief foray into historical movements, we will turn our attention to current issues and trends in the field.

THOMAS H. OLLENDICK • Child Study Center, Virginia Polytechnic Institute and State University, Blacksburg, Virginia 24061-0355.   **SANDRA W. RUSS** • Psychology Department, Case Western Reserve University, Cleveland, Ohio 44106-7123.

Handbook of Psychotherapies with Children and Families, edited by Russ and Ollendick. Kluwer Academic/Plenum Publishers, New York, 1999.

HISTORY OF CHILD AND FAMILY INTERVENTIONS

As is often pointed out, the first "case" for clinical psychology was a child who was seen at Lightner Witmer's Clinic at the University of Pennsylvania in 1896 (Witmer, 1909). This young boy was a poor speller and would probably be considered to possess a learning disorder today. Indeed, most of the cases at the clinic were children with academic difficulties (Ross, 1959). At about the same time as these developments in the United States, in Austria Sigmund Freud described the treatment of Little Hans (S. Freud, 1909/1955), a young boy suffering from severe phobia. And in 1908, Clifford Beers founded the mental hygiene movement that led to the establishment of child guidance clinics throughout the United States (Rie, 1974). The Judge Baker Foundation, begun in 1917, was the first setting to use a treatment-oriented approach to working with children with emotional problems (Ross, 1959). In the 1920s, the focus on children with emotional problems and parent–child relationships increased.

During the 1920s, the observations and experiments of behaviorally oriented psychologists were paralleled by early attempts at behavioral treatments of problems in children (Wolman, Egan, & Ross, 1978). As a result, the application of behavioral principles to the problems of children has a long and rich tradition. However, the focus on children as a specific population with unique needs was not always recognized (Ollendick & Cerny, 1981). A tradition that began with the treatment of childhood fears, as evident in the early work of Mary Cover Jones (1924a,b), quickly changed its focus to the treatment of adult behavior disorders. Although occasional reports dealing with the treatment of child behavior disorders appeared in the literature, it was not until operant techniques were used to treat dysfunctional behavior in severely disturbed children (e.g., Ferster & DeMeyer, 1962; Wolf, Risley, & Mees, 1964) that behavior therapy with children drew wide acclaim. Following these early and seminal reports, behavior therapists and researchers refocused their interests and attention on the problems of children and the environments that nurtured those children, namely, families, schools, and other environmental contexts.

The psychoanalytic movement's influence on child treatment emerged in the 1930s. Hug-Hellmuth (1921, 1924), A. Freud (1927), and Burlingham (1932) are credited with adapting psychoanalytic techniques to, and for, children. Anna Freud and Melanie Klein developed many of the important methodological innovations for working with children, although Anna Freud was more influential in the United States (Tuma & Russ, 1993). Play was used as a form of communication and to substitute for free association. In general, the therapist was more responsive and gratifying to the child than the therapist would be with adults and the child therapist actively worked to develop a positive attachment (A. Freud, 1946). A. Freud's approach was more conservative in its interpretation of play and unconscious conflicts than was Klein's, and it gave more attention to ego defenses. A. Freud also stressed working with the family (Tuma & Russ, 1993). The psychoanalytic approach evolved into the psychodynamic approach (Fonagy & Moran, 1990). Psychodynamic therapists, in turn, base their interventions and techniques on psychoanalytic principles, but therapy is shorter, less frequent (once a week rather than four or five times a week), has more focused and immediate goals, and is more flexible in incorporating a variety of therapeutic techniques (Tuma & Russ, 1993).

Play remains a core part of the therapy process. The use of play in therapy and in child development is a great legacy of the psychoanalytic tradition (Kessler, 1988).

An alternative to the psychoanalytic approach emerged in the 1940s with an emphasis on nondirective communication with the child. Published in 1947, Virginia Axline's classic book, *Play Therapy*, presented a client-centered approach to working with children. Client-centered therapy with children is based on the principle that children have the ability to resolve their conflicts and overcome their problems in a therapeutic setting (Ellinwood & Raskin, 1993). The requirements of a therapeutic setting are that the therapist be empathic, congruent, and convey unconditional positive regard to the child.

As noted earlier, behavioral approaches with children witnessed a reemergence in the 1960s as an alternative to psychoanalytic, psychodynamic, and client-centered approaches. In the main, early behavioral approaches were based on classical, instrumental, and vicarious conditioning principles. These principles suggest that behavior is determined by the interaction of organismic and environmental forces. In a very general fashion, organismic variables are those that occur "within the skin" of an individual, and environmental variables are those that occur outside an individual. Genetic factors, constitutional factors, and past learning experiences are three major types of organismic variables that help determine behavior (Ollendick & Cerny, 1981). Genetic and/or innate factors include those variables associated with both normal and aberrant genetic transmission. Constitutional variables are usually conceptualized as those contributions to development that are biologically based and occur between conception and birth. This class of variables includes anatomical anomalies that occur because of maternal malnutrition or illness, drug-induced defects, or injuries sustained during the birth process itself. They might also include certain biologically based predispositions to behavior, such as temperamental characteristics. Finally, past learning (whether associated with classical, instrumental, or vicarious conditioning processes) is also considered an organismic variable because the results of previous learning experiences have been incorporated into the child's behavioral repertoire, which is unique to that individual. In contrast to organismic variables, environmental or ecological variables refer to those conditions that exist outside of the organism. This class of behavioral determinants includes not only changes in the physical environment but also changes in the social and cultural environment. The attitudes and behaviors that caregivers model for their children and the reactions of parents, family, teachers, and peers to the behavior of children are all potent factors in determining children's behaviors. Moreover, these environmental factors are frequently found to interact with organismic variables resulting in complex behavioral patterns. Rarely are behavioral problems determined solely by either organismic or environmental variables. Rather, both types of variables need to be taken into consideration if treatment programs are to be effective. Attention to organismic and environmental variables may help account for the popularity of broad-based behavioral interventions since the 1960s (Ollendick & Cerny, 1981). Social learning theory approaches to treatment, including those espoused by Bandura and his colleagues (Bandura, 1969, 1977; Bandura & Walters, 1963), are reflective of these developments. These relatively new approaches distinguish themselves from other models of behavior by acknowledging the role of cognitive variables in learning and the concept of reciprocal determinism in shaping behavior. According to this perspective, children both shape and are shaped by their environments. They are not passive responders to stimuli that impinge on them. They are active participants in their environments, and in designing them.

Psychodynamic, client-centered, and behavioral approaches were, for the most part, individually oriented approaches. Even though the family and school were part of the treatment process in varying degrees, the basic conceptualization was individualistic and child-focused. Family therapy approaches brought interactional processes into the picture (Everett & Volgy, 1993). Treatment involved the entire family, often with a focus on interactional processes and the role of the child in the family system. Family therapy approaches view children's behavior problems as a symptom of dysfunctional family life and the goal of treatment is to improve family functioning (Herbert, 1998).

The field of child psychotherapy expanded rapidly in the 1960s and 1970s. As Freedheim and Russ (1992) pointed out, no one approach dominated the scene, with the exception of the work with severely and moderately retarded persons for whom advancements in behavior modification therapy were most beneficial (Finch & Kendall, 1979; Ollendick & Cerny, 1981).

CHANGING CONTEXT

In the 1980s and 1990s, there was a sea change in the field of child psychotherapy. Several factors contributed to this changing state. First, the move to managed care changed the climate within which child and family psychotherapists worked. There is now a focus on short-term approaches and efficient treatment strategies. There is an increasing need for *effectiveness* and *efficiency* demanded by third-party payers (Koocher & D'Angelo, 1992). Second, the stress on empirically supported treatments—on treatments that are proven to work—has caused all conscientious therapists to reevaluate their practice by reviewing the scientific evidence for treatment effectiveness. Third, the growing awareness in the field about cultural and contextual variables, such as socioeconomic factors, ethnic minority background, and stability of family environment, has resulted in an increased sophistication in choosing among treatment approaches.

As we look back on the theoretical roots of the field of child and family psychotherapies, we can see the integration of principles and techniques in current research and practice. The field has become more sophisticated and, at the same time, more specialized. Current trends reflect the past and the changing contexts for the field as a whole.

CURRENT TRENDS IN CHILD AND FAMILY INTERVENTION

Current trends in the field of child psychotherapy reflect increasing sophistication and specialization in research and practice. The major trends in child psychotherapy today are (1) use of a developmental framework, (2) call for empirically validated or empirically supported treatments, (3) focus on specific problems and populations, (4) integration of treatment approaches, and (5) the importance of situational and contextual factors in planning and implementing intervention.

The use of a developmental framework in conceptualizing childhood disorders and treatment has become increasingly evident in recent years. However, we should hasten to assert that a developmental perspective has always been a hallmark of clinical work with children. For example, psychoanalytic and psychodynamic approaches have long striven to return the child to normal developmental pathways (A. Freud, 1965; Palmer, 1970; Shirk & Russell, 1996). Recently, however, there are new elements in the developmental framework that make it more salient for clinical practice. Campbell (1998), for instance, has emphasized research efforts that apply concepts and findings from normal development to the understanding of developmental processes in at-risk populations. A developmental approach also involves early recognition of pathognomonic signs and the awareness that numerous factors can cause and maintain psychopathology (Vernberg, 1998). In short, it has been recommended that interventions with children should be based on research findings in child development (Vernberg, Routh, & Koocher, 1992).

In the 1980s, the impact of a developmental psychopathology framework was felt and has become dominant in conceptualizing childhood disorders (Lease & Ollendick, in press; Sroufe & Rutter, 1984). A developmental psychopathology perspective incorporates general systems theory principles and considers multiple contributors and multiple outcomes in interaction with one another. Sroufe and Rutter (1984, p.18) have defined developmental psychopathology as the study of "the origins and course of individual patterns of behavioral maladaptation, whatever the age of onset, whatever the causes, whatever the transformations in behavioral manifestation, and however complex the course of the developmental pattern may be." In short, the developmental psychopathology approach is concerned with the origin and time course of a given disorder, its varying manifestations with development, its precursors and sequelae, and its relation to nondisordered patterns of behavior.

Protective processes and variables that place children at risk are viewed in the context of each other rather than in isolation (Cicchetti & Rogosch, 1996) and an organizational perspective is taken on development. Although this conceptualization of disorder is a rich one, the implications for child treatment of a developmental psychopathology perspective are just beginning to be articulated (Toth & Cicchetti, this volume). Much work in this realm remains to be accomplished.

A second trend is the emphasis on defining and using evidence-based treatments in clinical practice. There is a strong, healthy movement to obtain empirical support for the various treatment approaches—although the support for the approaches is variable and incomplete at this time. This movement toward empirically supported treatments is not without controversy, however. Central to this controversy is whether all forms of child and family psychotherapy should be submitted to the same rules of evidence and, assuming they should, the degree of evidentiary support necessary to conclude that a treatment possesses efficacy (i.e., reduces symptoms, increases functioning) as well as effectiveness (i.e., clinical utility). As noted by Lonigan, Elbert, and Johnson (1998) in the introduction to the Special Issue on Empirically Supported Treatments published in the *Journal of Clinical Child Psychology*, efficacy studies are aimed at establishing whether a particular intervention works under tightly controlled experimental conditions (i.e., clinical trials in research settings), whereas effectiveness studies are directed at establishing how well a particular intervention works under the conditions in which treatment is typically offered (i.e., in clinical practice). It seems to us that all forms of child and family psychotherapy should be subject to the same rules of evidence and that both types of support are necessary, with the latter building on the former. Recent reviews have shown that effective treatments exist for a variety of childhood disorders, including depressive disorders (Kaslow & Thompson, 1998), phobias and anxiety disorders (Ollendick & King, 1998), autism (Rogers, 1998), oppositional defiant disorder and conduct disorder (Brestan & Eyberg, 1998), attention deficit hyperactivity disorder (Pelham, Wheeler, & Chronis, 1998), and a variety of less frequently observed disorders (Kazdin & Weisz, 1998).

Recent research in child psychotherapy has followed research guidelines developed in the 1970s and 1980s (Kazdin, 1990). As a result, the research has become more focused and methodologically sophisticated. The technique of meta-analysis has enabled the field to arrive at a systematic evaluation and interpretation of outcome studies. In this approach, a common effect size (ES) metric is applied to a collection of treatment outcome studies, permitting a pooling of findings across the various studies. In most meta-analyses, the ES is the difference between the posttreatment (more rarely follow-up) means for treated and untreated children on some outcome measure of interest, divided by the standard deviation of the measure (see Weisz & Hawley, 1998). Computing the ES mean for any treatment group versus the control group comparison typically involves averaging ES values across the multiple outcome measures used in the study. By pooling these average ES values across studies, meta-analyses can generate estimates of overall treatment impact; compare outcomes among theoretically meaningful subsets of studies; and test child, therapist, and therapy characteristics that may moderate treatment outcome. Results of these meta-analyses have contributed to the field in that they offer evidence that psychotherapy is more effective than no treatment with children. Collectively, these meta-analytic findings indicate that the average child in treatment scored higher on outcome measures than did 76 to 81% of children in a control group (Kazdin & Kendall, 1998; Kazdin & Weisz, 1998). Although there is some evidence that behavioral and cognitive–behavioral therapies fare somewhat better than psychoanalytic, psychodynamic, and client-centered therapies in these analyses, limited support is evident for all therapies, including family therapy. This conclusion is more encouraging than conclusions based on global reviews conducted in the 1950s and 1960s, which appeared to suggest that treatments for children were largely ineffective.

Weisz and Weiss (1989, 1993) pointed out that most of the research studies in the meta-analytic reviews involved controlled laboratory interventions (i.e., efficacy studies). In many of these studies, children were recruited for treatment and were not clinic-referred; samples were homogeneous; there was a focal problem; therapy focused on the target problem; therapists were trained in the specific treatment approaches to be used; and the therapy relied primarily on "manualized" techniques. In essence, this was good research that followed many of the methodological guidelines for adequate research design. On the other hand, Weisz and Weiss (1993) cautioned that evidence for the effectiveness of psychotherapy is based on studies that are not typical of conventional clinical practice. Thus, the findings may not be generalizable to clinical work in applied settings.

The results of the meta-analytic reviews point to the need for specificity and precision in research. Weisz and Weiss (1993) concluded that the studies that showed positive results tended to "zoom in" on a specific problem with careful planning of the intervention. Behavioral and cognitive–behavioral approaches tended to fit these criteria better than psychoanalytic, psychodynamic, and client-centered approaches. In a similar vein, Freedheim and Russ (1983, 1992) stated early on that we needed to become very specific with these more traditional approaches and ask, "Which specific interventions affect which specific cognitive, personality, and affective processes? How are these processes related to behavior and practical clinical criteria?" (1983, p. 988). Recently, Shirk and Russell (1996) have also called for similar targeting of specific cognitive, affective, and interpersonal processes in child therapy.

Shirk and Russell (1996) identified major cognitive, emotional, and personality processes that are involved in change in psychotherapy. By focusing research questions on specific cognitive, affective, and personality processes, we can learn more about mechanisms underlying developmental processes and child psychopathology (Russ, 1998; Shirk & Russell, 1996). Specificity would also enable us to investigate which interventions facilitate the development of these processes and which do not.

The focus on specificity in research is consistent with the third trend of refining interventions for specific problems and populations of children. Schaefer and Millman (1977) recognized this trend early on. This practice grew out of Barrett, Hampe, and Miller's (1978) call for greater specificity in psychotherapy research. Their oft-quoted conclusion that the question in psychotherapy research should not be "Does psychotherapy work?" but rather "Which set of procedures is effective when applied to what kinds of patients with which sets of problems and practiced by which sorts of therapists?" (p. 428) led to more specific research and practice.

As child psychotherapy research has become more specific, so too has child psychotherapy practice. The move within many clinical settings to have specialty clinics for different diagnostic groups, such as childhood depression and anxiety disorders, reflects this change. Kazdin (1990) pointed out that many current reviews focus on specific areas of child dysfunction and treatment options for specific purposes.

For example, Parent–Child Interaction Therapy (PCIT) for oppositional children (see Rayfield, Monaco, & Eyberg, this volume) is a specific treatment approach developed for young noncompliant children. Principles of cognitive–behavioral therapy and of play therapy have been applied to this particular group of children. PCIT is a specific type of parent management training for preschool-age children that targets the parent–child relationship. Unique issues that arise with this specific group can be worked with and integrated into the treatment to develop the optimal treatment approach.

Gil's work with abused children is an example of adapting play therapy techniques to a specific population. She stressed the importance of the therapist being an active participant in the play and actively facilitating self-expression by using techniques such as presenting the child with cartoon figures in different situations with the child filling in the words or pulling secrets from a secrets bag. For many abused children, posttraumatic play is repetitive, devoid of pleasure, and can remain fixed (Gil, 1991). Gil intervenes in this repetitive play by making verbal statements, having the child take a specific role, or encouraging the child to differentiate between the traumatic event and current reality in terms of safety and what has been learned. The goal of interrupting the play is to generate alternatives that can lead to a sense of control, help feelings be expressed, and orient the child toward the future.

A fourth important trend in child psychotherapy is the integration of different theoretical approaches, specific techniques, or both from different schools of therapy. Kazdin (1990) pointed out that the field of child psychotherapy needs to consider combining treatment approaches if optimal results are to be obtained. Because there are so many children with multiple disorders, with a host of etiological factors involved, we need to use the most appropriate combination of intervention techniques. Also, the need for short-term intervention pushes therapists to search for optimal interventions.

Wachtel's (1977) sophisticated approach to integrating psychodynamic and behavioral techniques in a complementary way with adults should apply to the child psychotherapy area as well. For example, the therapist might decide to use both insight and problem solving approaches. Actually, this integration has always been true in child psychotherapy because working with children and families forces one to be pragmatic and to do what works (Russ, 1998). A number of integrated approaches are presented in Part III of this volume.

In a Special Issue of the *Journal of Clinical Child Psychology* (Volume 27, No. 1, 1998) on Developmentally Based Integrated Psychotherapy with Children: Emerging Models, innovative treatment approaches that integrated different theoretical perspectives and intervention techniques were presented.

For example, Knell's (this volume) cognitive–behavioral play therapy is based on cognitive–behavioral principles, but also integrates more traditional forms of play therapy. She weaves together change mechanisms from cognitive–behavioral approaches and psychodynamic play therapy. One benefit of this approach is that it can "speed up" the psychotherapy process.

Also, in the Special Issue, Shirk described a cognitive–interpersonal framework in targeting changes in interpersonal schema. Shirk defined interpersonal schema as referring to expectations about others' probable responses to the self. Within this cognitive–interpersonal framework, based on attachment theory, he presented a model of intervention that integrates relational, representational, and emotional components of child functioning. The therapeutic relationship is a crucial change process in schema transformation.

In her introductory comments to the Special Issue, Russ (1998) identified a dilemma that we face in developing integrated psychotherapy approaches, however. On the one hand, we know from the child psychotherapy outcome literature and from Weisz and Weiss's (1993) conclusions from their meta-analysis of child therapy outcome studies that those interventions that "zoom in" (to use Weisz and Weiss's term) on a particular problem in a focused way, with clear guidelines for psychotherapy, are most likely to demonstrate treatment efficacy. On the other hand, when we integrate different approaches and techniques, we lose that precision, at least in the beginning stages of model development. However, what we lose in precision we may gain in beneficial outcomes. Hypothetically, as we would be using the most effective change mechanisms from two or more approaches for different problems and populations, we might expect our integrated approaches to be synergistically effective. Quite obviously, we need time for this experimentation with different combinations of treatment to occur. However, such integrated approaches will need to be put to the test of science and not allowed to rest on their respective laurels. After all, it is possible that integrated approaches will be less effective than those from which they are derived. The combination of elements may prove volatile rather than therapeutic.

Finally, the field is becoming increasingly aware of the importance of situational and contextual factors in child development and in intervention. The complex interaction of these variables has been emphasized in the developmental psychopathology framework (Cicchetti & Rogosch, 1996). Campbell (1998) emphasized the importance of family and social environmental factors in understanding developmental processes. The importance of understanding cultural factors in working with ethnic minority groups is an important principle. The knowledge base about intervention with minority children is fragmented and the literatures regarding service delivery, social contexts, and specific problems are separate and distinct (Vraniak & Pickett, 1993). A comprehensive framework needs to be developed. There are some efforts in this area (Vraniak & Pickett, 1993), but there needs to be more empirically based guidelines about how to best intervene in different cultures and contexts.

The organization of this book is based on these important trends in the field. First, the conceptual frameworks of developmental psychopathology and social and contextual paradigms are presented. Then, each of the major theoretical approaches upon which our current research and practice are based is reviewed. Part III presents empirically supported approaches with children who have a variety of specific problems or disorders. Part IV presents approaches that successfully integrate elements from different theoretical approaches. This organization, in a sense, reflects the evolution of the field of child and family intervention. The field is at an exciting juncture, with a strong foundation based on its historical roots. Although many issues confront us, the future of child and family psychotherapy is a bright one. There is reason for optimism in the years ahead.

REFERENCES

Axline, V. M. (1947). *Play therapy*. Boston: Houghton Mifflin.
Bandura, A. (1969). *Principles of behavior modification*. New York: Holt, Rinehart & Winston.
Bandura, A. (1977). *Social learning theory*. Englewood Cliffs, NJ: Prentice–Hall.
Bandura, A., & Walters, R.H. (1963). *Social learning and personality development*. New York: Holt, Rinehart & Winston.
Barrett, C., Hampe, T. E., & Miller, L. (1978). Research on child psychotherapy. In S. Garfield & A. Bergin (Eds.), *Handbook of psychotherapy and behavior change* (pp. 411–435). New York: Wiley.
Brestan, E. V., & Eyberg, S. M. (1998). Effective psychosocial treatments of conduct-disordered children and adolescents: 29 years, 82 studies, and 5,272 kids. *Journal of Clinical Child Psychology, 27,* 179–188.
Burlingham, D. (1932). Child analysis and the mother. *Psychoanalytic Quarterly, 4,* 69–92.
Campbell, S. (1998). Developmental perspectives. In T. Ollendick & M. Hersen (Eds.), *Handbook of child psychopathology* (3rd ed., pp. 3–35). New York: Plenum Press.
Cicchetti, P., & Rogosch, F. A. (1996). Equifinality and multifinality in developmental psychopathology: Special Issue of *Development and Psychopathology, 8*(4), 597–600.
Ellinwood, C., & Raskin, N. (1993). Client-centered humanistic psychotherapy. In T. Kratochwill & R. Morris (Eds.)., *Handbook of psychotherapy with children and adolescents* (pp. 258–280). Boston: Allyn & Bacon.

Everett, C., & Volgy, S. (1993). Treating the child in systemic family therapy. In T. Kratochwill & R. Morris (Eds.), *Handbook of psychotherapy with children and adolescents* (pp. 247–257). Boston: Allyn & Bacon.

Ferster, C. B., & DeMeyer, M. K. (1962). A method for the experimental analysis of the behavior of autistic children. *American Journal of Orthopsychiatry, 32,* 89–98.

Finch, A., & Kendall, P. (Eds.). (1979). *Clinical treatment and research in child psychopathology.* New York: Spectrum.

Fonagy, P., & Mevau, G. S. (1990). Studies on the efficacy of psychoanalysis. *Journal of Consulting and Clinical Psychology, 58,* 684–694.

Freedheim, D. K., & Russ, S. W. (1983). Psychotherapy with children. In C. E. Walker & M. E. Roberts (Eds.), *Handbook of clinical child psychology* (pp. 978–994). New York: Wiley.

Freedheim, D. K., & Russ, S. W. (1992). Psychotherapy with children. In C. E. Walker & M. E. Roberts (Eds.), *Handbook of clinical child psychology* (2nd ed., pp. 765–780). New York: Wiley.

Freud, A. (1927). Four lectures on child analysis. In *The writings of Anna Freud* (Vol. 1, pp. 3–69). New York: International Universities Press.

Freud, A. (1946). *The psychoanalytic treatment of children.* New York: International Universities Press.

Freud, A. (1965). *The writings of Anna Freud* (Vol. 6). New York: International Universities Press.

Freud, S. (1955). Analysis of phobia in a five-year-old boy. In *Collected papers* (Vol. X, pp. 149–289). London: Hogarth Press. (Original work published 1909)

Gil, E. (1991). *The healing power of play.* New York: Guilford Press.

Herbert, M. (1998). Family treatment. In T. Ollendick & M. Hersen (Eds.), *Handbook of child psychopathology* (3rd ed., pp. 557–579). New York: Plenum Press.

Hug-Hellmuth, H. (1921). On the technique of child-analysis. *International Journal of Psychoanalysis, 2,* 287–305.

Hug-Hellmuth, H. (1924). *New paths to the understanding of youth.* Leipzig: Franz Deuticki.

Jones, M. C. (1924a). The elimination of children's fears. *Journal of Experimental Psychology, 7,* 382–390.

Jones, M. C. (1924b). A laboratory study of fear: The case of Peter. *Journal of Genetic Psychology, 31,* 308–315.

Kaslow, N. J., & Thompson, M. P. (1998). Applying the criteria for empirically supported treatments to studies of psychosocial interventions for child and adolescent depression. *Journal of Clinical Child Psychology, 27,* 146–155.

Kazdin, A. E. (1990). Psychotherapy for children and adolescents. In M. R. Rosenzweig & L. W. Porter (Eds.), *Annual review of psychology* (pp. 21–54). Palo Alto, CA: Annual Review.

Kazdin, A. E., & Kendall, P. C. (1998). Current progress and future plans for developing effective treatments: Comments and perspectives. *Journal of Clinical Child Psychology, 27,* 216–225.

Kazdin, A. E., & Weisz, J. R. (1998). Identifying and developing empirically supported child and adolescent treatments. *Journal of Consulting and Clinical Psychology, 66,* 19–36.

Kessler, J. (1988). *Psychopathology of childhood.* Prentice-Hall.

Koocher, G., & D'Angelo, E. J. (1992). Evolution of practice in child psychotherapy. In D. K. Freedheim (Ed.), *History of psychotherapy* (pp. 457–492). Washington, DC: American Psychological Association.

Lease, C. A., & Ollendick, T. H. (in press). Development and psychopathology. In A. S. Bellack & M. Hersen (Eds.), *Psychopathology in adulthood: An advanced textbook.* New York: Pergamon Press.

Lonigan, C. J., Elbert, J. C., & Johnson, S. B. (1998). Empirically supported psychosocial interventions for children: An overview. *Journal of Clinical Child Psychology, 27,* 138–145.

Ollendick, T. H., & Cerny, J. A. (1981). *Clinical behavior therapy with children.* New York: Plenum Press.

Ollendick, T. H., & King, N. J. (1998). Empirically supported treatments for children with phobic and anxiety disorders. *Journal of Clinical Child Psychology, 27,* 156–166.

Palmer, J. (1970). *The psychological assessment of children.* New York: Wiley.

Pelham, W.E., Jr., Wheeler, T., & Chronis, A. (1998). Empirically supported treatments for attention deficit hyperactivity disorder. *Journal of Clinical Child Psychology, 27,* 189–204.

Rie, H. (Ed.). (1974). *Perspectives in child psychopathology* (Vol. 3). Minneapolis: University of Minneapolis Press.

Rodwin, M. C. (1995). Conflicts in managed care. *New England Journal of Medicine, 332,* 604–607.

Rogers, S. J. (1998). Empirically supported comprehensive treatments for young children with autism. *Journal of Clinical Child Psychology, 27,* 167–178.

Ross, A. (1959). *The practice of clinical child psychology.* New York: Grune & Stratton.

Russ, S. (1998). Introductory comments to special section on developmentally based integrated psychotherapy with children: Emerging models. *Journal of Clinical Child Psychology, 27,* 2–3.

Schaefer, C., & Millman, H. (1977). *Therapies for children.* San Francisco: Jossey-Bass.

Shirk, S. R., & Russell, R. (1996). *Change processes in child psychotherapy: Revitalizing treatment and research.* New York: Guilford Press.

Sroufe, L. A., & Rutter, M. (1984). The domain of developmental psychopathology. *Child Development, 55,* 17–29.

Tuma, J., & Russ, S. W. (1993). Psychoanalytic psychotherapy with children. In T. Kratochwill & R. Morris (Eds.), *Handbook of psychotherapy with children and adolescents* (pp. 131–161). Boston: Allyn & Bacon.

Vernberg, E. (1998). Developmentally based psychotherapies: Comments and observations. *Journal of Clinical Child Psychology, 27,* 46–48.

Vernberg, E., Routh, D., & Koocher, G. (1992). The future of psychotherapy with children. *Psychotherapy, 29,* 72–80.

Vraniak, D., & Pickett, S. (1993). Improving interventions with American ethnic minority children: Recurrent and recalcitrant challenges. In T. Kratochwill & R. Morris (Eds.), *Handbook of psychotherapy with children and adolescents* (pp. 502–540). Boston: Allyn & Bacon.

Wachtel, P. (1977). *Psychoanalysis and behavior therapy: Toward an integration.* New York: Basic Books.

Weisz, J. R., & Hawley, K. M. (1998). Finding, evaluating, refining, and applying empirically supported treatments for children and adolescents. *Journal of Clinical Child Psychology, 27,* 205–215.

Weisz, J.R., & Weiss, B. (1989). Assessing the effects of clinical-based psychotherapy with children and adolescents. *Journal of Consulting and Clinical Psychology, 57,* 741–746.

Weisz, J., & Weiss, B. (1993). *Effects of psychotherapy with children and adolescents.* Newbury Park, CA: Sage.

Witmer, L. (1909). Clinical psychology. *Psychological Clinic, 1,* 1–9.

Wolf, M., Risley, T., & Mees, H. (1964). Application of operant conditioning procedures to the behaviour problems of an autistic child. *Behavior Research and Therapy, 1,* 305–312.

Wolman, B., Egan, T.,& Ross, A. (Eds.). (1978). *Handbook of treatment of mental disorders in childhood and adolescence.* Englewood Cliffs, NJ. Prentice–Hall.

2

Developmental Psychopathology and Child Psychotherapy

SHEREE L. TOTH and DANTE CICCHETTI

INTRODUCTION

Although it might be assumed that logical connections exist between the provision of psychotherapeutic interventions to children and adolescents and developmental theory and research, far too few bridges have been forged between these areas of knowledge (Cicchetti & Toth, 1992; Cicchetti, Toth, & Bush, 1988; Noam, 1992; Shirk, 1988a, Shirk & Russell, 1996). Because nondevelopmental adult-derived classification guidelines have historically been applied to formulating diagnoses of the mental disorders of childhood, it is not surprising that adevelopmental approaches to intervention, frequently drawn from the adult literature, often have been the norm when providing interventions to children and adolescents. The perpetuation of the "developmental uniformity myth" (Kendall, Lerner, & Craighead, 1984) to interventions for children, wherein it is assumed that mental disorders manifest themselves similarly regardless of age and therefore do not require therapeutic techniques that are sensitive to developmental change, has impeded efforts to provide theoretically guided and developmentally appropriate services to children and adolescents. Further, decision-making regarding what constitutes an action that is in a child's best interest cannot be made adequately unless the child's level of functioning across an array of developmental domains (e.g., cognition, emotion, language) and the concomitant capacity to comprehend the meaning of certain events are considered. Moreover, different incidents can

SHEREE L. TOTH and DANTE CICCHETTI • Mt. Hope Family Center, University of Rochester, Rochester, New York 14608.

Handbook of Psychotherapies with Children and Families, edited by Russ and Ollendick. Kluwer Academic/Plenum Publishers, New York, 1999.

have different meanings depending on when they occur in the developmental period. The individual's history, temperament, and current supports and resources all play a role in helping a child to construct an "individual" meaning from a given event, thereby further contributing to the overall impact on the child.

Fortunately, an increased dialogue among theorists, basic researchers, and professionals interested in providing developmentally guided prevention and intervention to children and adolescents has occurred in recent years. A major impetus to this process has emanated from the field of developmental psychopathology, an approach that advocates the importance of an active, bidirectional interchange between theoreticians and researchers in normal and pathological development (Cicchetti, 1984, 1990; Cicchetti & Toth, 1991; Rutter, 1986). As a growing number of research investigations have illustrated how the study of the interface between normal and abnormal development is mutually enriching for scientists of each persuasion, the application of findings conceptualized within the developmental psychopathology genre to intervention efforts has similarly increased. In fact, in recognition of the field's importance, the Institute of Medicine (1994) report on reducing risks for mental disorders via preventive intervention highlighted developmental psychopathology as one of four core sciences considered to be necessary for advancing prevention and intervention efforts for children and adolescents.

In this chapter, we bring a developmental psychopathology perspective to bear on elucidating a number of issues that are of relevance to the prevention and treatment of childhood disorders. We begin by describing the field of developmental psychopathology and examining some of its major tenets, along with the implications of these principles for intervention approaches with children and adolescents. Perspectives on intervention that are informed by a developmental psychopathology framework are then discussed. We conclude the chapter by providing recommendations that we believe could facilitate the incorporation of a developmental psychopathology perspective into interventions for children and adolescents.

Parameters of Developmental Psychopathology

Developmental psychopathology has emerged as a new interdisciplinary science only within the past several decades (Cicchetti, 1984, 1993; Rutter & Garmezy, 1983). Its application to the prevention and treatment of childhood disorders has been an even more recent phenomenon (Cicchetti & Toth, 1992a, Toth & Cicchetti, 1993). However, throughout its evolution into an increasingly established scientific discipline, the goal of integrating often disparate fields of study into an interdisciplinary perspective that will inform efforts to prevent and ameliorate maladaptation and psychopathology across the life span has been articulated (Cicchetti, 1989; Cicchetti & Toth, 1992b; Sroufe & Rutter, 1984). Despite its relatively recent ascendance, many of the roots and tenets of developmental psychopathology are grounded in the historical writings of some of the great theoretical systematizers from a variety of disciplines, including embryology, epidemiology, genetics, the neurosciences, philosophy, psychoanalysis, psychiatry, and psychology (Cicchetti, 1990). Developmental psychopathology has offered a common language and method for organizing these diverse and rich traditions, as well as for facilitating dialogue between basic and applied researchers, and, relatedly, toward reducing the schism that has separated developmental researchers and practitioners (Cicchetti & Toth, 1998).

Organizational Perspective on Development

Although developmental psychopathology is not characterized by the adherence to a single theoretical approach, the organizational perspective on development provides a powerful theoretical framework for conceptualizing the intricacies of the life span perspective on risk and psychopathology, as well as on normal ontogenesis (Cicchetti, 1993, Sroufe, 1990). The organizational perspective focuses on the quality of integration both within and among the psychological and biological systems of the individual. This attention to variations in the quality of integration provides the framework on which developmental psychopathologists characterize developmental status. Moreover, the organizational perspective addresses how development occurs, specifically identifying a progression of qualitative reorganizations within and among the biological, psychological, and social systems that proceed through differentiation and subsequent hierarchical integration (Werner, 1948).

In accord with the organizational perspective, development is not viewed as consisting of a series of tasks that need to be accomplished and that subsequently decrease in importance. Rather, development is conceived as being comprised of a number of age- and stage-relevant tasks. Although the salience of these tasks may wane in relation to newly emerging issues, the tasks remain important to adaptation over time (Cicchetti, 1993). A hierarchical picture of adaptation emerges in which the successful resolution of an early stage-salient issue increases the probability of subsequent successful adjustment (Sroufe & Rutter, 1984). As each new stage-salient issue comes to the fore, opportunities for growth and consolidation, as well as challenges associated with new vulnerabilities, arise. Thus, an ever-changing model of development in which newly formed competencies or maladaptations may emerge throughout the life course and transact with the individual's prior developmental organization is proffered (Cicchetti & Tucker, 1994). Although early adaptation probabilistically portends future functioning, the possibility of developmental divergence and discontinuity is recognized in this dynamic model (see our discussion on self-organization later in this chapter for elaboration). Because stage-salient issues also entail reciprocal roles for caregivers, parental influence can either enhance or impede a child's successful resolution of stage-salient issues (see Cicchetti, Rogosch, & Toth, 1998).

To more fully elaborate the principles that undergird developmental psychopathology, we turn next to an explication of the tenets of the discipline. Additionally, we examine the implications of each tenet for psychotherapy with children and adolescents. This presentation of principles is not addressed in any presumed order of importance, nor is it meant to be an all-inclusive list. Rather, we describe those underlying principles that we view as especially relevant to intervention efforts.

TENETS OF DEVELOPMENTAL PSYCHOPATHOLOGY AND
IMPLICATIONS FOR INTERVENTION

Normal and Abnormal

A basic premise that is reflected in the writings of many early theoreticians and that has guided work within developmental psychopathology involves the criticality of understanding the boundary between normality and pathology (Rutter & Garmezy, 1983). As such, it has been reasoned that one can learn more about the normal functioning of individuals by studying pathology and, similarly, more about pathology by examining normality (see Cicchetti, 1990; Kaplan, 1966; and Overton & Horowitz, 1991, for an in-depth discussion). Because all pathology can be viewed as a distortion, disturbance, or degeneration of normal functioning, in order to comprehend psychopathology, the normal functioning with which psychopathology is compared must be fully grasped. Thus, a core aspect of a developmental psychopathology perspective lies in its focus on both normal and abnormal, adaptive and maladaptive developmental processes (Cicchetti, 1984, 1990; Rutter, 1986; Rutter & Garmezy, 1983; Sroufe, 1990; Sroufe & Rutter, 1984). Moreover, even before a psychopathological disorder is diagnosable, certain pathways may signal adaptational failures in normal development that warn of likely future pathology (Cicchetti & Rogosch, 1996b; Cicchetti, Rogosch, & Toth, 1997; Sroufe, 1989).

When providing interventions to children, focusing on the interface between normality and pathology is especially important, as characteristics and/or behaviors may be "normal" at one period of development, but abnormal at another. The understanding of age-appropriate functioning across all developmental domains (e.g., cognitive, socioemotional, linguistic, neurobiological) thus becomes critical to intervention efforts. Unfortunately, clinical training programs often focus on "abnormality" to the exclusion of providing future therapists with a grounding in developmental theory (see, for discussion, Cicchetti & Toth, 1991). This misguided focus can result in the fostering of therapists who lack sufficient knowledge regarding the course of development to adequately determine what is or is not psychopathological in children who are referred for services. Moreover, an inadequate understanding of children's developmental organization can result in the provision of interventions and/or the interpretation of child functioning that misses the central role that competence in various domains of development exerts. The failure to consider the impact of a child's developmental organization may result in faulty conclusions about the kinds of intervention to utilize or may misjudge children's abilities to derive benefit from a chosen intervention.

Transcendence of Disciplinary Boundaries

Theory, research, and intervention efforts conceived within a developmental psychopathology perspective strive to unify the many contributions to the study of high-risk and disordered individuals that emanate from diverse fields of inquiry, including psychiatry, psychology, cognitive science, the neurosciences, genetics, physiology, cultural anthropology, sociology, epidemiology, statistics, and psychometrics (see Cicchetti & Cohen, 1995a,b). The principles of developmental psychopathology provide a conceptual scaffolding that can facilitate a needed multidisciplinary integration, as well as an increased synergy between research and practice. Such a broad and integrative approach is a necessity because developmental psychopathologists maintain that in order to understand functioning and to intervene when necessary, a comprehensive evaluation of biological, psychological, social, and contextual factors must be conducted. An interdisciplinary approach also increases the likelihood of identifying different pathways by which the same developmental outcome may be achieved (Cicchetti & Rogosch, 1996b; Robins & Rutter, 1990; Sroufe, 1989, 1997). In practice, this requires an appreciation for the developmental transformations and reorganizations that occur over time, an analysis of the risk and protective factors and mechanisms at the individual, familial, and environmental levels, the investigation of how emergent functions, competencies, and developmental tasks modify the expression of a disorder or lead to new symptoms and difficulties, and the recognition that a given stress or underlying mechanism may culminate in different biological and psychological difficulties, depending on when in the developmental period a stress occurred (Cicchetti & Aber, 1986; Cicchetti & Lynch, 1993; IOM, 1989, 1994). To achieve these lofty goals, developmental psychopathologists must transcend traditional disciplinary boundaries to move to a process level understanding of normal and abnormal developmental trajectories.

With respect to the importance of this principle for intervention, the criticality of training young professionals so that they become more sensitive and receptive to the importance of cross-disciplinary collaborations is underscored. It is highly unlikely that any one individual will ever have the skills necessary to conduct the complex and integrative assessments of the various psychological, biological, and social-environmental influences on functioning and to apply this knowledge to the design and conduct of intervention strategies. Cicchetti and Toth (1991) provide recommendations for the components of training programs that will result in individuals who are prepared to collaborate on multidisciplinary research projects and who will be able to apply such findings to programs of intervention.

Risk and Psychopathology

Despite the key role of "psychopathology" in the field of developmental psychopathology, it is erroneous to assume that studies conceived within this genre must be conducted on individuals who are already manifesting a mental disorder. Rather, developmental psychopathologists are as interested in individuals who are considered to be at high risk for the development of pathology, even when they do not manifest a disorder over time. Developmental psychopathologists similarly stress the importance of understanding the functioning of individuals who, after having diverged onto a deviant developmental pathway, resume more positive functioning and attain adequate adaptation (Cicchetti & Rogosch, 1997; Richters & Cicchetti, 1993). Finally, developmental psychopathologists are committed to understanding pathways to competent adaptation despite exposure to adversity (Cicchetti & Garmezy, 1993; Masten, Best, & Garmezy, 1990; Rutter, 1990).

These varied foci possess important implications for the development and provision of prevention, as well as of intervention strategies. By articulating the processes that protect high risk individuals from developing psychopathology, therapies can be designed to incorporate potential protective factors into programs of intervention. A number of interventions conceived within a developmental psychopathology tradition have utilized such an approach. For example, emanating from the area of attachment theory, Lieberman, Weston, and Pawl (1991) provided Infant–Parent Psychotherapy to high-risk mother–infant dyads with the goal of facilitating the development of secure attachment relationships. These investigators found that dyads receiving the intervention evidenced improvements in child, mother, and dyadic functioning. Similarly, in their preventive intervention for children with a depressed parent, Beardslee and colleagues (Beardslee et al., 1997) drew on existing research that revealed that children who felt responsible for parental depressive illness were the most likely to be adversely affected. Accordingly, Beardslee et al. (1997) developed educationally based programs that sought to dispel erroneous assumptions regarding the causes of parental depression. Intervention strategies such as these have benefited considerably from an incorporation of the findings of investigations that have elucidated contributions to adaptive as well as to atypical development.

Diversity in Process and Outcome

As developmentalists have gained increased knowledge about the diversity inherent in development, it has become clear that the same rules of normal development do not necessarily apply to all children and families (e.g., see Baldwin, Baldwin, & Cole, 1990). Consequently, diversity in process and outcome are considered to be hallmarks of the developmental psychopathology perspective. Both continuities and discontinuities are likely across the course of development (Rutter, 1989). As such, behavioral patterns not evident in the early years of life may emerge in later years. Biological and psychological propensities, in interaction with new social fields such as the classroom or peer group, may impact on developmental processes across the life course (Kellam & Rebok, 1992). Moreover, individual's may move in and out of conditions of psychopathology and normality across the life span (Zigler & Glick, 1986).

In trying to understand the variability that emerges across the life span, the principles of equifinality and multifinality, derived from general systems theory, are relevant (Cicchetti & Rogosch, 1996a,b; von Bertalanffy, 1968). Equifinality refers to the observation that the same outcome may result from a diversity of pathways (see Sroufe, 1989). Singular pathways to a given disorder are expected to be rare rather than the norm. In contrast to equifinality, multifinality suggests that varied outcomes eventuate from a common starting point. Thus, a particular experience of adversity cannot be viewed as contributing to a similar, or even to any, psychopathological outcome in all persons.

A number of investigators have examined disorders that serve as useful illustrations of the construct of equifinality. For example, research has shown that there are multiple contributors to conduct-disordered outcomes among individuals who carry this diagnosis (Cicchetti & Richters, 1993). Sroufe (1989) also reported on work that has adopted a developmental approach to attention deficit hyperactivity disorder in which he discussed two pathways to the disorder, one primarily biological in nature and the other consisting predominantly of caregiver influences. Finally, Neumann, Grimes, Walker, and Baum (1995) examined differing developmental pathways to schizophrenia. Specifically, the behavior problems that predated schizophrenia were found to vary in their developmental course, with some problems reflecting an insidious but consistent escalation across childhood, while others manifested more precipitous increases in adolescence. A third subgroup of children was identified that evidenced more pronounced behavior problems that increased with age and that exhibited more neuromotor anomalies in the early years of life (cf. Walker, 1994).

With respect to multifinality, in her book Deviant Children Grown Up, Robins (1966) reported on a follow-up of children who had conduct disorder in childhood. Robins found some continuity in functioning, with a group of conduct disordered youngsters evidencing Antisocial Personality Disorder in adulthood. However, other children diagnosed with conduct disorder in childhood went on to develop schizophrenia and other disorders and still other children who had met criteria for conduct disorder during childhood did not evidence any disorder in adulthood. Moreover, variability among conduct disordered children with respect to the features of their disturbance as well as with respect to its course has been noted (Goldsmith & Gottesman, 1994; Richters & Cicchetti, 1993). Similarly, studies of the sequelae of maltreatment have consistently revealed diversity in process and outcome, despite similarities in the occurrence of abuse (cf. Cicchetti & Toth, 1995). In discussing depressive disorder during childhood, Harrington, Rutter, and Fombonne (1996) concluded that there are several different kinds of depressive syndromes in children, with some being related to depressive disorders in adulthood and others better conceptualized as components of another psychopathological problem. Examinations of the functioning of children who were at one time depressed and subsequently resumed nondisordered functioning also would be informative. It might be possible to identify core aspects of functioning that have remained stable, but that no longer culminate in depression because of compensatory factors within the individual and/or in the environment (Cicchetti et al., 1997). Such research might reveal that certain functioning characteristics that were once causally related to the development of a depressive disorder in an earlier environment can become positively adaptive in a new environment.

In view of findings and hypotheses such as these, it is disconcerting that beliefs in the continuity of functioning both prior to and during the provision of therapy have historically been embraced by the therapeutic community. In a seminal paper, Kiesler (1966) challenged the assumption of patient, therapist, and treatment homogeneity, wherein it was believed that at the beginning of treatment patients were more similar than dissimilar and that therefore patients who received the same treatment should evidence commensurate improvement. Despite cautionary statements such as Kiesler's regarding the fallacy of assuming continuity in the need for or response to treatment, many interventions continue to be driven by diagnostic considerations, frequently being informed by group- rather than individual-level data. Continuity and discontinuity of disordered behavior, as well as the existence of multiple pathways that may contribute to outcome, underscore the importance of conducting comprehensive and detailed assessments of functioning in children who are referred for services. Moreover, throughout treatment, evaluations that are structured to be sensitive to possible divergences from more expected trajectories must be implemented in order for therapists to be responsive not only to continuity, but also to discontinuity in functioning. It is only when psychotherapists are cognizant of the possible diversity in etiology, process, and outcome within similar diagnostic categories that the provision of interventions will be sufficiently responsive to the varying needs of children referred for services.

Self-Organization and Development

A principle of importance to developmental psychopathology is that individuals exert an active role in directing the course of their development. Although more distal historical factors and current influences are important to the process of development, individual choice and self-organization have increasingly been viewed as exerting critical influences on development (Cicchetti & Rogosch, 1997; Cicchetti & Tucker, 1994). Early experience and prior levels of adaptation neither doom the individual to continued maladaptive functioning nor inoculate the individual from future problems in functioning. Moreover, because not only can biological factors impact on psychological processes, but also because psychological experiences can modify brain structure, functioning, and organization (Cicchetti & Tucker, 1994; Eisenberg, 1995), developmental plasticity can be brought about by both biological and psychological self-organization (Cicchetti & Tucker, 1994). Thus, for example, the fact that most maltreated children evidence at least some self-righting tendencies in the face of extreme adversity attests to the strong biological and psychological strivings toward resilience that virtually all humans and living organisms possess (Cicchetti & Rogosch, 1997; Waddington, 1957). In contrast, the absence of such resilient self-strivings in some maltreated children attests to the deleterious and pernicious impact that traumatic experiences can exert on biological and psychological developmental processes.

Of relevance for the process of psychotherapy is the conclusion that change in the developmental course is always possible as a function of new experiences and reorganizations, in conjunction with the individual's active self-organizing strivings for adaptation. Moreover, it may be during transitional turning points or sensitive periods of development that the ontogenetic process is most susceptible, positively or negatively, to the individual's self-organizational strivings.

In psychotherapy, then, periods of developmental transition may represent times during which interventions can be most successfully provided. Additionally, it follows that stressors that may result in dysregulation for the individual similarly may serve as markers of periods during which intervention is likely to be the most effective. For example, if an adolescent presents with self-pathology that manifests itself through intense and turbulent relationships with others, then it may be following the ending of a relationship when the individual is likely to be most responsive to examining the historical and current issues involved with relationship difficulties and the role that self issues have exerted on their history of relationships. At times, it even may be useful to generate a state of disequilibrium in order to provide an opportunity for an intervention to facilitate the attainment of a higher level of organization (Futterweit & Ruff, 1993).

Contextual Influences

Although historically more closely associated with developmental psychology than with developmental psychopathology (cf. Lerner & Kaufman, 1985; Vygotsky, 1978), developmental psychopathologists are devoting more attention toward the issue of context (see Cicchetti & Aber, 1998). The impetus for an increased emphasis on context has emerged because of the fact that research on childhood psychopathology has traditionally failed to incorporate a unifying theoretical orientation regarding the role of contextual effects (Boyce et al., 1998). In fact, when contextual influences on childhood psychopathology have been considered, "context" has most typically been defined as consisting of a single setting, most often the family (Boyce et al., 1998).

More recently, a number of investigations framed within a developmental psychopathology conceptualization have found that outcome and course of adaptation or maladaptation varies as a function of contextual influences. For example, Sroufe (1997) observed that in a well-staffed summer camp setting, children who had exhibited serious conduct problems in their schools evidenced very little aggressive behavior. Similarly, Cicchetti et al. (1998) found that the adaptation of toddlers with mothers with depressive disorders varied as a function of the presence or absence of accompanying contextual stressors in the microsystem. Specifically, maternal depressive diagnosis predicted insecure attachments, whereas intra-familial contextual stressors predicted toddler externalizing symptomatology. Findings such as these hearken to an ecological (Bronfenbrenner, 1979) or an ecological–transactional model of development (Cicchetti & Lynch, 1993), where various levels of an individual's ecology are seen as exerting influences on development.

The importance of context in child outcome must be considered during the course of diagnosis of disorder as well as throughout the provision of intervention. In fact, Jensen and Hoagwood (1997) maintain that understanding the range of children's functioning in relation to their environments is essential before one can infer that a given behavior is adaptive or maladaptive. In accord with such a position, Hoagwood, Jensen, Petti, and Burns (1996) present a conceptual model that can be used to guide the assessment of children within their environments across a varied range of outcomes. According to the model of Hoagwood et al. (1996), symptoms and diagnoses are not sufficient to portray children's mental health outcomes. Rather, these authors emphasize the importance of capturing the influences of cognitive and social functioning, peer and family relationships, the nature of the child's school, neighborhood, and home environments, and cultural and societal contexts. The necessity of attending to the transactions among these variables over time also is emphasized by Hoagwood and her colleagues.

A consideration of contextual influences on child psychopathology is especially important because children, unlike adults, have less opportunity to select their environments. Because social environments may facilitate or undermine treatment gains (Luthar, 1995), it is critical to involve individuals in the child's social world, such as parents, siblings, teachers, and peers, in the treatment process. Additionally, because environments are currently more accessible and receptive to modification than are genetic factors that may contribute to various susceptibilities to mental disorders, we must not fail to capitalize on the power of contextual influences in promoting or impeding child development. Although genetic interventions may become feasible at some point, in the foreseeable future contextual interventions will most likely continue to be regarded as the most effective way of addressing many childhood mental disorders (Boyce et al., 1998). Moreover, because childhood (and adult) psychopathology is polygenetically transmitted (i.e., multiple genes and the environment are necessary and sufficient for psychopathology to occur), interventions targeted at a single gene are unlikely to be effective in addressing the transacting genetic and environmental influences that eventuate in childhood psychopathology.

Cultural Considerations

In a related yet different vein from that associated with contextual influences, culture also emerges as an important consideration in examining the relevance of developmental psychopathology for intervention. In fact, some theorists have cautioned that developmental psychopathology must strive to avoid becoming a monocultural science (see Cicchetti, 1993; Cicchetti & Toth, 1998; Spencer & Dupree, 1996). Although the influence of culture has been acknowledged in various ecological systems (Bronfenbrenner & Crouter, 1983), it has only recently been considered integral to a comprehensive understanding of psychopathology (cf. Hoagwood & Jensen, 1997).

In fact, reviews of even normal child development research reveal a pattern of neglect with regard to cultural factors (Garcia Coll, 1990; McLoyd, 1990; McLoyd & Randolph, 1984, 1985). Specifically, according to Garcia Coll and her colleagues (Garcia Coll et al., 1996), research with minority children has suffered from the following: (1) a paucity of longitudinal investigations of normal development in minority children, (2) an emphasis on outcome versus process, (3) failure to attend to intragroup variability, (4) disregard for the diversity inherent in many minority group categorizations used, and (5) minimization of the effects of issues such as racism, prejudice, discrimination, and segregation on development. Such egregious omissions not only hamper our knowledge about the development of minority children, but also compromise our understanding of and theories about children more broadly. Ogbu (1981) argued that "the research model of dominant group developmentalists is ethnocentric. . . . It decontextualizes competencies from the realities of life" (p. 425).

Given that our knowledge of atypical child development is less advanced than our knowledge of normal development, and in view of the fact that an interplay must exist between normal and abnormal development, it is not surprising that our understanding of development in children of color is very limited. Consequently, our approaches to intervention with minority children and families have been severely hampered. Such a narrow perspective endangers children and families, as interventions that are not sensitive to cultural influences may result not only in the provision of ineffective intervention, but also in the perpetuation of stereotypes regarding family functioning.

Because proponents of a developmental psychopathology perspective recognize the importance of diversity within groups, this approach has increasingly been used to voice the necessity of understanding intraindividual as well as between group differences (Cicchetti, 1993; Richters, 1997). Therefore, the underpinnings of developmental psychopathology can serve to help guide investigations into development in minority children and resultant findings can be applied to the development and evaluation of intervention strategies for minority children and families. We currently know that sensitivity to varied developmental trajectories as well as to diverse parenting practices evident in minority families must be incorporated into our interventions if treatment is to be appropriate and effective.

A number of investigations possess relevance to the role of culture and psychotherapy.

In a longitudinal follow-up of children residing in high- and low-risk families, Baldwin et al. (1990) found that successful high risk families were found to be more restrictive and authoritarian in their parenting than were successful low risk families. Because many of the families studied by Baldwin and his colleagues (1990) were African American, these findings possess important implications for evaluating and providing intervention to families who are considered to be at high risk for the emergence of child psychopathology. The assumption that parenting in these families should mirror what is considered to be "appropriate" parenting in nonrisk families may result in very erroneous conclusions and actions. In observations of inner-city families over a period of 5 years, Burton (1995) concluded that even assuming consistency in well-accepted developmental stages of childhood can be invalid for children growing up in urban ghettos. For example, African-American teenagers do not experience adolescence as a period of transition between childhood and adulthood in the same way that mainstream youth do for a number of reasons, including relatively narrow age differences between family members, blurring of intergenerational boundaries, and the tendency for African-American youth to expedite their transition to adulthood by their assumptions of a shorter life span. Similarly, Garcia Coll and Vasquez Garcia (1996) caution against generalizing certain mainstream assumptions, such as the belief that being a teenage parent is maladaptive, to all cultures. Rather, in discussing competence in Puerto Rican adolescent mothers, Garcia Coll and Vasquez Garcia (1996) emphasize the importance of considering motivational, contextual, and life-span components of various societies before labeling behavior as adaptive or maladaptive. Moreover, because, for example, autonomy is not valued by Puerto Rican society (Garcia Coll & Vasquez Garcia, 1996), models of stage salient issues also need to be sensitive to culture.

Examples such as these underscore the importance of understanding and taking into account cultural issues when providing interventions to children who may diverge from assumptions derived from the mainstream, often monocultural developmental literature. It is clear that much more progress with respect to providing culturally sensitive interventions can be made as knowledge on development in normal as well as disordered minority children is incorporated into programs of intervention and, subsequently, evaluated.

Informing Developmental Theory

In addition to its applicability to guiding and contributing to the evaluation of interventions for children and adolescents, a developmental psychopathology perspective may facilitate the testing of claims of extant developmental theories (Cicchetti & Toth, 1992b; Kellam & Rebok, 1992; Koretz, 1991). Kellam and Rebok (1992) highlight the value of intervention for informing developmental theory. Specifically, in their discussion of preventive interventions, they conclude that preventive mental health trials may "contribute to the empirical basis for theory construction, particularly in regard to life-course development, socialization, and psychopathogenesis" (p. 163). For example, if an intervention targeted at reducing aggression in grade school is subsequently related to a reduction in delinquency, then evidence that early aggressive behavior is a contributor to a developmental pathway culminating in delinquency has been obtained (Kellam & Rebok, 1992). Additionally, Kellam and Rebok (1992) maintain that preventive trials can provide knowledge on the malleability of various components of the developmental model being studied when different types of intervention are provided. Thus, important information can be garnered on how best to intervene in the process of development so as to stem a psychopathological process.

Now that some of the core concepts that undergird developmental psychopathology have been presented and their relevance for clinical practice explicated, we next address linkages between developmental psychopathology and intervention.

PERSPECTIVES ON INTERVENTION

The Role of Theoretical Assumptions in Guiding Intervention

In applying a developmental psychopathology approach to intervention, a number of areas emerge as warranting consideration. We believe that these issues span various risk conditions and disorders, as well as possess relevance for diverse theoretical approaches and techniques that are utilized during the provision of child and family psychotherapy. In fact, we maintain that in the absence of a developmental perspective, many validated and potentially rich intervention strategies may not be as effective as they might be were they more sensitive to principles of developmental psychopathology.

To begin, Sroufe's (1997) discussion of a "developmental model" as opposed to a classic "medical model" possesses significant implications for understanding how underlying theoretical assumptions can guide conceptualizations of disorder and, consequently, of the intervention strategies that are utilized. In accord with the classic medical model, disorders are typically conceived as discrete entities that arise from single endogenous pathogens. Although this simple model has become outmoded in much of medicine (Rutter, 1996), Sroufe (1997) maintains that its influence continues to be felt in the implicit assumptions that guide "description and conceptualization of disorder itself, in the nature of research questions that are given priority (centered on endogenous factors), and in how research findings are interpreted" (p. 252). Although Sroufe (1997) acknowledges that even in a medical model, environmental factors may be recognized as exerting some influence on the etiology and course of disorder, he argues that, most typically, core etiological contributors are seen as residing in neurophysiological pathology, regardless of whether they are caused by genetic defects or environmental pathogens.

Conversely, in accord with a developmental perspective, behavior is seen as resulting from a combination of genes, environment, the history of prior adaptation, and current experience (Sroufe & Egeland, 1991). Stated simply, a developmental model of disturbance results in different approaches to assessment and treatment than that embodied by a medical model. Rather than seeking main effect causes of disorder and assuming that a particular treatment will be equally effective for similar symptom presentations, developmentalists ask queries such as

"How do individual children get off track? When going off track, what deviating track is a particular child likely to take? What influences tend to maintain them on the track they are on, and what would be required to bring them back to a more serviceable developmental pathway?" (Sroufe, 1997, p. 258).

Clearly, the answers to these questions versus a quest for a single endogenous disease pathogen dictate very different approaches to assessment and intervention. Despite similarity in symptom profiles, a developmental model suggests that, if followed longitudinally, diverse outcomes of disorder may emerge for different children. For example, the course of early onset versus "adolescent limited" antisocial behavior has been investigated (Moffitt, Caspi, Dickson, Silva, & Stanton, 1996). Moffitt et al. (1996) found that the prognosis for children evidencing early onset symptoms is much worse than for those exhibiting symptoms beginning in adolescence. If assessed only during adolescence, without knowledge of prior development and likely varied outcome, treatment approaches would most likely be similar for both early onset and adolescent limited profiles. Such a perspective would erroneously treat children traveling along diverse pathways the same and might exacerbate rather than ameliorate the symptoms of the child with the less severe prognosis. The interventions required to get one child "back on track" would necessarily be very different from those likely to be effective with the other child, depending on whether the condition was of early onset or an adolescent limited type. For example, using some of the more restrictive intervention strategies designed to address an entrenched conduct disorder might actually exacerbate the problems of an adolescent who had no prior difficulties and who may be in the midst of a more transitory phase of rebellion. Helping parents to understand these differences in trajectories and the reasons for recommendations of varied treatment strategies also are likely to be integral to intervention effectiveness.

In contemplating the implications of a hierarchical model of development for intervention, questions arise regarding the way in which intervention should proceed. Similarly to research in clinical neurology and developmental psychobiology, where studies on recovery of function following an insult have been shown to follow a sequential appearance of competencies that is consistent with that observed during ontogeny (i.e., from simple to complex; from lower to higher brain centers; see Denny-Brown, Twitchell, & Saenz-Arroyo, 1949; Sherrington, 1906; Teitelbaum, 1977), it might be that the achievement of competent functioning on stage-salient developmental issues that had been unsuccessfully resolved would follow the same emergence as that observed during normal development. If so, then important conclusions could be drawn regarding the identification of precursors to recovered functioning in children and adolescents who have a psychiatric disorder and such information could be incorporated into the psychotherapeutic arena.

Specifically, the issue of whether later stage-salient issues can be reworked positively without addressing earlier issues becomes a critical question. For example, is it possible to help an individual gain a positive sense of self without addressing the origins of a self-view that may have derived from an insecure attachment to his or her caregiver? Conversely, might it be possible that attention to a current salient issue could reverberate to earlier issues, resulting in an overall reorganization of early issues as well, with a related decision not to intervene on earlier issues? Because the concept of hierarchical integration posits that early issues become coordinated with later issues, one might argue that a similar reverse process would occur wherein earlier issues could benefit from positive resolution of currently salient developmental issues.

Work on attachment and parenting is of relevance to this point. For example, van den Boom (1994) sought to promote secure attachments in well functioning mothers and their infants who were drawn from lower socioeconomic backgrounds and who were selected for intervention because of their negative emotionality. A skills-training format that emphasized the acquisition of maternal sensitive responsiveness was utilized. Interestingly, although this intervention did not seek to modify maternal representations of infants, it was effective not only in enhancing maternal responsiveness and stimulation and in improving child sociability and cognitive sophistication, but also in promoting secure attachment relationships. These findings are interpreted as suggesting that maternal sensitivity is causally related to infant attachment security (van den Boom, 1994). Importantly, however, these results also are consistent with what might be expected to occur in accord with a hierarchical model of development if maternal sensitivity is a precursor of secure attachment. We are not aware of any research data that can directly speak to the role of hierarchical integration and intervention, although findings such as those of van den Boom possess implications for when and how interventions might best be targeted.

Prevention as Intervention

Developmental psychopathologists are as interested in preventing as they are in ameliorating psychopathology. Because developmental psychopathologists are invested in charting the course of development even before an actual psychiatric disturbance may become manifested, research in this field holds much relevance for application to the prevention and treatment of high-risk psychopathological conditions. In fact, Sroufe and Rutter (1984) stated: "[B]y thoroughly understanding factors that pull subjects toward or away from increased risk at various age periods, one not only acquires a deeper understanding of development *but one also gains valuable information for primary prevention*" (p.19, italics added). Also, once a disorder has emerged, an understanding of the mechanisms that contributed to the maladaptive outcome can be applied to its remediation.

A hierarchical model of development also lends considerable credence to opportunities afforded by preventive efforts. Such a perspective holds that interventions may be optimally effective if targeted at emergent skills rather than at those already consolidated. Rather than waiting until a psychopathological process has crystallized to the point of meeting diagnostic criteria, it might be much more beneficial to the child to identify and strive to right precursors of a maladaptive process. For example, interventions might be more effectively targeted at the time that a potentially pathology-inducing insult occurs, rather than assuming a "wait and see" approach to determining whether or not intervention is needed. Such situations often emerge with respect to sexual abuse, where immediate negative sequelae may not be evident (Kendall-Tackett, Williams, & Finkelhor, 1993), but where future difficulties often emerge. Knowledge of early developmental deviations and their link with subsequent psychopathology also could be used to prevent the emergence of full blown psychopathology, thereby decreasing both time and money expended in the treatment of more severe clinical conditions (Carnegie Task Force on Meeting the Needs of Young Children, 1994; Hamburg, 1992; IOM, 1989, 1994). Moreover, the targeting of preventive efforts at key areas prior to the emergence of a mental disorder requires an understanding of adaptive components of development so that their emergence can be facilitated. A focus on the "promotion of wellness" (Cowen, 1994) may suggest that broad-based "intervention" be instituted even in the absence of any subclinical signs of an incipient disease process. Large scale programs that are provided to all children in naturalistic settings such as schools might be very cost effective, as they can be incorporated into ongoing curricula. Once an intervention has been ended, a developmental perspective also suggests that the provision of "booster" interventions during times of developmental transitions might result in sustained positive outcomes. The utilization of booster interventions may support previously consolidated gains and help these earlier competencies to continue to be integrated into emerging issues, even during periods of disequilibration.

Developmental Considerations and Intervention

At least partially as an outgrowth of a developmental psychopathology perspective, those interested in understanding atypical development and in applying this knowledge to the prevention and remediation of psychopathology have become increasingly sensitive to the developmental dimensions of treatment. Psychotherapists, for example, have become more cognizant of the fact that no particular treatment is likely to be effective throughout the life course. Moreover, even children of similar ages cannot be viewed as a unitary group. Noam (1992), in discussing developmentally informed interventions for adolescents, emphasizes that adolescents' world views are defined by the meaning systems that they use to understand themselves, their peers, and their parents. Accordingly, Noam advocates that different methods of therapy must be provided that account for differences in symptoms, cognition, and patterns of recovery from illness. In order to provide effective psychotherapeutic interventions, an in-depth understanding of each individual's developmental organization is necessary. This is especially critical in childhood, a period during which developmental transformations and reorganizations are much more rapid than those seen in adulthood.

Attention to factors such as when during the developmental course and why a disorder occurred, how long it continues, and what precursors to the disordered functioning could be identified all require a developmental approach to ensure that prevention and intervention strategies are appropriately timed and guided. In fact, the developmental timing of an intervention may be even more important than its content. Minimally, the effect of an intervention will be enhanced or inhibited in relation to its sensitivity and responsivity to factors associated with the developmental period during which the intervention is provided. Similarly, interventions may need to take into consideration the developmental period during which a pathology-inducing insult occurred, even if the actual referral for treatment occurs years later. For example, in cases of sexual abuse that may have occurred when a child was preverbal, the utilization of verbally mediated intervention strategies may not be as effective as more experiential approaches such as play therapy because the memory of the abuse may not have ever been encoded verbally (see Cicchetti & Toth, 1998). To provide another example, in instances of childhood depression, the developmental period during which a stressor occurred that may have contributed to the initiation of an affective disorder must be considered. If a child suffered the loss of a parent during toddlerhood, a period when individuation and autonomy are central, then the loss of the parent may have ramifications that are more significant than they would have been if the loss had occurred in later childhood. Issues such as these must be considered when deciding how best to intervene because different approaches may be dictated by the knowledge of when in development a negative trajectory that culminated in disorder started.

In addition to factors related to where in the developmental course the initiation of a pathological process may have occurred, an understanding of children's developmental competencies also is necessary. Shirk (1988b) discusses the role of development in children's ability to benefit from psychotherapeutic interpretations. Specifically, developmental domains such as causal reasoning, emotion understanding, self-understanding, and language ability all must be understood and attended to when providing interventions to children and adolescents. Failing to consider children's developmental competencies can lead to the misinterpretation of behaviors both within and outside of the therapeutic context, as well as to the utilization of psychotherapeutic techniques that are inappropriate for the child's developmental level. Moreover, because various risk or psychopathological conditions may be associated with developmental perturbations and/or lags, age alone cannot be used to judge a child's ability to benefit from a given intervention. For example, maltreated children have been found to evidence decreased internal-state language for physiological states and negative affect (Beeghly & Cicchetti, 1994). Although it is unclear whether these lags represent actual language deficits or, rather, an adaptive response to monitoring language that might upset a maltreating caregiver, the implications of these differences must be considered in the provision of child psychotherapy. Therefore, trying to utilize normative guidelines to determine whether a maltreated child could benefit from a given verbally mediated intervention might result in erroneous conclusions. Research also has shown that maltreated children evidence dysfunctions and perturbations in their self-systems, typically presenting as having less positive self-views (Toth, Cicchetti, Macfie, & Emde, 1997). It may be that self-system deficits limit the kinds of interventions that can be provided to maltreated children. In fact, we would argue that very time-limited interventions that do not consider relationship issues as integral to psychotherapeutic change are likely to be ineffective in working with youngsters who suffer from self-system pathology. Issues such as these must be considered when determining which interventions are likely to be beneficial. In view of their importance for the provision of psychotherapy, we briefly present research in several illustrative areas of development that possess implications for therapy.

Causal Reasoning

Generally, there is a consensus that a primary goal of psychotherapy is to help a child construct a new understanding of the internal or external issues that may be contributing to behavioral problems that led to a referral for therapy. Such understanding is thought to occur through the therapist's use of interpretations.

However, the fact that such techniques are only as effective as the child's ability to understand the interpretive process is not as widely discussed. In considering developmental aspects of a child's capacity to understand and thereby profit from interpretive statements, a number of dimensions of interpretations must be considered, including: internal versus external, past versus present, and conscious versus unconscious (Shirk, 1988b).

Evidence suggests that the degree to which children believe they are responsible for an outcome versus the belief that outcomes are the result of forces beyond their control becomes more psychological and less situational with increasing age (Shirk, 1988b). Therefore, a therapeutic intervention that seeks to help a child understand a given event as related to internal, nonobservable sources is likely to be ineffective for a preschool or kindergarten age child. Rather, therapeutic interventions for young children need to be concretized to help the children grasp the relevance of a given statement or discussion to an actual situation in their lives. Expecting the child to, for example, generalize the premise embodied in a fictional story (e.g., the angry elephant) to instances when they themselves have been angry may be expecting reasoning processes that exceed actual developmental capabilities.

The temporal dimension of interpretations also must be considered when providing intervention to children, as prior to middle childhood children have difficulty linking past events with current emotions and/or behavior. Therefore, with young children interventions that focus on current concomitants of affect or behavior are likely to be the most effective means of bringing about increased understanding and change (Shirk, 1988b).

The conscious–unconscious dimension of statements also must be considered in evaluating the developmental appropriateness of child therapies. In general, unconscious explanations of behavior are difficult for children to understand. Thus, if two available explanations of behavior are feasible, prior to adolescence most children will reject unconscious explanations in favor of the more overtly evident cause (Shirk, 1988b). For example, trying to convince young children that they took a piece of candy because they were angry at their sibling versus they took the candy because they like cherry licorice might prove to be an uphill battle, depending on the child's level of cognitive development. Such child behavior in therapy may be confused with "resistance" or "denial" but, in actuality, is more likely to be a function of cognitive developmental constraints.

In addition to the child's ability to understand and make use of interpretive statements, the nature of the relationship between the child and therapist and the child's understanding of social relationships also is important to therapeutic effectiveness. Therefore, knowledge of the child's understanding of social situations is critical to the implementation of a successful plan of intervention.

Because some forms of abstract reasoning are not present until formal operations emerge during adolescence, social skills programs that are not sensitive to children's level of social reasoning and that require children to generate hypothetical situations, to consider various responses and to envision how others might react to their responses, and to imagine alternative outcomes based on how hypothetical situations are handled may be beyond the reasoning abilities of young children (Weisz, 1997). Developmental constraints in a child's ability to recognize the perspectives of others on activities, events, and oneself also may lead to limitations in the effectiveness of interventions that require children to consider situations from the perspective of others (Weisz, 1997). For example, an intervention that requires a child to reflect on how a given action affects others is likely to depend on the level of development with respect to social perspective taking that the child has attained (Selman, 1980). Thus, therapists must factor developmental constraints on such capacities into the design of interventions.

Emotion Understanding

Research on emotion understanding during childhood has generally concluded that, as children mature, their understanding of emotion becomes increasingly complex, with a shift from reliance on external to more internally mediated explanations (Nannis, 1988). Additionally, in contrast to primary emotions such as happiness, anger, sadness, and fear, self-conscious emotions such as shame, guilt, and pride emerge only during the preschool years with the growth of self-understanding (Campos, Barrett, Lamb, Goldsmith, & Sternberg, 1983; Lewis, Alessandri, & Sullivan, 1992). Because of limitations in their social cognitive skills, young children may generalize self-conscious emotions to situations that are inappropriate, thereby resulting in feelings such as guilt or shame in situations for which they have no control or responsibility.

With respect to an ability to consider multiple feelings, young children cannot articulate the experience of two feelings simultaneously (Harris, 1989; Harter, 1977, 1983a). Additionally, children typically are able to understand multiple emotions based on sequential experiences before they grasp multiple feelings based on simultaneous occurrences. Younger children's understanding of emotion also tends to be more bound by contextual cues.

Differences in the ability to distinguish between different emotions also have been found to occur with development. At approximately 2–3 years of age, children begin to talk about emotions and their causes, using words such as *sad*, *mad*, *happy*, and *scared* (Bretherton, Fritz, Zahn-Waxler, & Ridgeway, 1986). Three-year-olds also can accurately differentiate between situations designed to evoke these emotions (c.f. Levine, 1995). However, young children are less accurate at distinguishing between anger and sadness (Trabasso, Stein, & Johnson, 1981). In fact, research has found that children do not reliably identify stories designed to evoke anger until after age 5 and that it is not until 6½ years of age that they are able to identify stories designed to evoke sadness (cf. Smiley & Huttenlocher, 1989). Findings such as these, however, do not necessarily mean that young children do not understand the difference between anger and sadness. Rather, more recent research has revealed that issues such as the outcome of an event with respect to goal reinstatement (e.g., the child got his bicycle back versus he will never get his bicycle back) and outcome as consisting of an aversive condition (e.g., Jane's mad because she has to stay in the house and she doesn't want to) versus a loss (e.g., Jane's sad because she wants to play outside but she can't) predicted children's emotion choices (Levine, 1995). Kindergarten children were more likely to attribute anger when they believed a goal could be reinstated and when they focused on what brought about an undesirable situation. They were more likely to attribute sadness when they felt goal reinstatement was impossible and focused on the losses that would ensue.

A number of studies also have compared how children understand emotions in themselves versus in others. Interestingly, there appears to be a positivity bias operative with respect to children's assessments of how they think they personally would feel (Harter, 1990). Moreover, younger children have been found to be less likely to attribute negative emotions to themselves than older children, suggesting that the conceptualization of one's own emotional experience may be related to the anticipation of one's ability to cope with distressing feelings (Saarni, Mumme, & Campos, 1998). Specifically, younger children may not want to think about themselves in emotionally distressing situations because they fear they might start to feel that way and that they will become overwhelmed.

It is critical that such developmental aspects of emotion understanding be considered when providing intervention so as to avoid confusion for the child and frustration for the therapist. Issues such as the number of simultaneously occurring emotions that can be processed may possess important implications for whether or not a therapist tries to help a child address conflicting emotions (e.g., I love my sister but I'm angry at her). Moreover, helping the child to articulate the context within which various emotional reactions occur can provide a helpful perspective on why the child may be focusing on an angry versus a sad response. The failure to consider developmental correlates of emotion understanding may lead to ineffective interventions that are limited by realistic developmental constraints rather than by a more psychologically mediated explanation.

Self-Understanding

Changes in the content, organization, and structure of self-understanding occur over the course of development. A number of researchers have proffered that self-understanding begins with a focus on more physical external attributes and evolves to more internal, psychological constructs (Damon & Hart, 1982, 1988; Harter, 1983b,1998; Rosenberg, 1986). Advances in the accuracy of children's self-assessments also occur with increasing age, with middle childhood coinciding with the ability to incorporate the opinions and evaluations of significant others (Harter, 1988). In addition to changes in the content of self-concept, with increasing age self-referent beliefs also become more consolidated, differentiated, and hierarchically integrated (Thompson, 1990). For example, although preschoolers tend to make self-evaluative judgments without trying to integrate the judgments into a broad self-concept, older school-age children try to find consistency among diverse self-attributes, and adolescents try to organize these self-referent beliefs into a more abstract self-representational system (Damon & Hart, 1982). With increasing age, the evaluations of others become more integral to shaping the child's self-perceptions and, therefore, older children are likely to be more sensitive and responsive to the evaluative comments of others.

Of course, a child's individual history must be considered, as always, when trying to make conclusions about his or her developmental capacities. For example, maltreated children have been found to overrate their abilities in the early years of life, but to underrate their actual competencies beginning at around age 8 or 9, a time when the self begins to consolidate and when social comparison processes emerge in the child's repertoire (Vondra, Barnett, & Cicchetti, 1989). These findings suggest that, unlike conclusions reported for normally developing children who tend to be more sensitive and responsive to the evaluations of others with increased age, maltreated children may be less likely to incorporate the views of others (e.g., teachers) into their self-concepts. In fact, this view is consistent with theorizing in the area of attachment theory, where it has been argued that maltreatment results in the development of "closed" representational models wherein children tend to generalize earlier experiences into situations involving new relationship partners (see Cicchetti & Toth, 1995; Crittenden, 1990, for an elaboration). Such a stance decreases the likelihood that potentially corrective relationship experiences will occur. In the therapeutic arena, intervention efforts for children who are operating with closed models of relationships will need to be especially intensive. Moreover, the importance of intervening early so as to prevent the closure of representational models is underscored (Toth & Cicchetti, 1993).

In view of the findings on self-understanding, some theorists have argued that prior to adolescence children do not possess the introspective capacities needed to experience intrapsychic conflict and therefore lack a desire to change (Harter, 1988). If so, then interventions may need to be didactic in nature, targeting potential determinants of self-esteem, rather than trying to help children gain an understanding of issues that may be contributing to their low self-esteem. Similar arguments have been offered by Greenberg, Pyszczynski, and Solomon (1995), who have hypothesized that encouragement of the acquisition of skills and achievements may, as a secondary outcome, lead to more stable and higher self-esteem. Moreover, because the approval of significant others may be less likely to influence young children, the motivation for change derived from the desire to "please" the therapist is likely to be less evident with preschoolers.

Language Ability

Developmental variations in children's abilities to encode and decode language also need to be considered when providing child therapy (Weisz, 1997). Limitations in encoding skills (e.g., difficulty providing verbal labels for affective states) can restrict a child's ability to share inner thoughts and feelings, thereby impeding the therapist's ability to provide an intervention that is consistent with the child's inner state. For example, both cognitive–behavioral and psychodynamic interventions for anxiety disorder may require a child to describe his or her anxiety in terms of physiological arousal (e.g., My heart pounds and I get all sweaty") and psychological state (e.g., "I feel like everyone is looking at me and waiting for me to screw up and I'll be humiliated in front of them all"). If children's encoding abilities are too limited to allow for such descriptions, then they may be unable to provide therapists with sufficiently detailed information to help the therapist understand the nature of their anxiety (Weisz, 1997). Decoding constraints also may hinder a child's ability to understand comments being made by the therapist, thereby limiting any potential gains that might occur. Manualized therapies that are reliant on language are especially problematic in this regard, as they may preclude therapists from flexibly adjusting language so as to be in sync with children's capabilities (Weisz, 1997). Finally, developmental differences in children's abilities to use inner speech to guide behavior are likely to result in differences in children's responsivity to therapies that use language in efforts to increase self-control (Weisz, 1997).

The Developmental Course of Illness

Issues related to the developmental course of illnesses also possess implications for intervention. Because, as previously discussed, various pathways may lead to similar outcomes and, conversely, a similar pathway may lead to diversity in outcome, it is important that clinicians utilize appropriately varied treatment strategies. For example, children's developmental histories, stage in the life cycle, their current functioning and developmental organization across psychological and biological domains, and the characteristics that define a given disorder all must be factored into the process of treatment planning. Likewise, interventions should be directed at a range of developmental domains (e.g., cognition, language, emotion, representation) rather than assuming that a given form of psychopathology can be addressed by focusing exclusively on a single domain of development. This perspective holds true even for conditions that might be considered the outgrowth of a predominantly biological insult or characteristic, as maladaptation in one domain is likely to affect functioning in other domains. Thus, interventions must address the broader matrix of causal influences and sequelae if successful and sustained progress is to occur.

In considering the influence of the course of illness on the type of intervention that is provided, Post (1992) suggests that different interventions are likely to be more or less effective at various points during the illness. Specifically, Post argues that in treating mood disorders, psychodynamic therapies may be more effective when provided for an initial depressive episode, whereas recurrent episodes might be more responsive to behavioral and cognitive techniques of therapy. This premise is based on findings of behavioral sensitization and electrophysiological kindling in individuals with histories of repeated mood disorders. Post further maintains that because most psychodynamic therapeutic techniques require the reworking of cortical control using the limbic and cortically based representational memory systems, depressed patients with hypoactive cortical systems may not be amenable to such insight-oriented therapies. Finally, Post (1992) believes that different pharmacological interventions are differentially effective during various stages of disease evolution. Although based on research with adults that he conceptualized within a developmental perspective, Post's findings are compelling to consider with children because he utilizes a developmental perspective when describing aspects of the progression, course, and treatment of mental illness. Because developmental changes during childhood can be quite rapid, continual evaluation of therapeutic strategies as they relate to the developmental process, as well as with regard to the course of illness, must be conducted.

Although focusing on the provision of intervention, we believe that a developmental psychopathology perspective can be equally applied to questions of whether or not to intervene. In fact, the assumption that intervention can do no harm has been questioned (Rutter, 1981). Thomas (1979) stresses the importance of understanding development so as not to intervene unnecessarily or in an iatrogenic manner. According to Thomas, the provision of intervention to one component of a complex system contains a significant risk of leading to unforeseen negative consequences in other parts of the system. Because children rarely seek treatment, but rather are referred by parents or teachers who are invested in seeing that a change process is initiated, it is especially important that therapists consider the implications of their interventions with children. Moreover, depending on the context within which intervention is being provided, the initiation of services may result in disequilibrium in the family system. For example, this is often the case when child maltreatment has occurred. In such instances, the provision of psychotherapy to a child in the absence of interventions with the family may result in placing the child in a more detrimental situation if the parents are unable to accept and support the changes that therapy is bringing about (Toth & Cicchetti, 1993).

SUMMARY AND RECOMMENDATIONS

In this chapter we have proposed a developmental psychopathology framework as an integrative approach that can be directed toward developing and evaluating interventions for children and adolescents. As we have stressed throughout, a developmental psychopathology perspective holds considerable promise not only for informing intervention efforts, but also for being incorporated into the design and evaluation of preventive efforts. To date, we believe that developmental thinking has been more clearly evident in programs of prevention than it has in more traditional child therapies. Because one of the premises embodied by developmental psychopathology advocates a reduction of the schisms between normality and abnormality, biology and psychology, and research and practice, an increased integration among these areas can improve our understanding of risk conditions and mental disorders and, consequently, of prevention and intervention. However, before the full extent of this potential can be realized, we believe that the field of developmental psychopathology must continue to evolve. Moreover, individuals currently providing treatment to children and adolescents must increase their receptivity to the premises of a developmental psychopathology approach.

Relatedly, it is critical that dialogue between developmental psychopathologists and developmentalists of other persuasions continue in order to prevent a premature compartmentalization of the issues that we must confront. Throughout history, there has been a call for a cross-fertilization of developmental psychology and other areas of psychology with other disciplines (Cicchetti, 1990; Gottesman, 1974; Hinde, 1992). Discussions of training in applied developmental and developmental psychopathology have similarly called for a broad-based, multi- and interdisciplinary approach (Cicchetti & Toth, 1991; Fisher et al., 1993). Such goals also are consistent with the consensus that has emerged on the importance of incorporating a sensitivity to cultural pluralism and racial/ethnic diversity into training programs. The comprehensive agenda embodied by such a perspective is critical to developing well-grounded interventions for diverse populations of children and adolescents.

The realization of the exciting potential that developmental psychopathology holds for informing and evaluating intervention efforts also requires enhanced fidelity between the complexity of theoretical models that are proffered and the measurement and data-analytic strategies that are utilized in our investigations (Richters, 1997). Relatedly, clinical and research efforts must not focus exclusively on group-level information but, rather, must examine processes that underlie functioning in different individuals. The presence of equifinality and multifinality in development suggests that we must increasingly strive to understand the multiplicity of processes and outcomes that exist at the level of the individual as opposed to adopting the prevailing variable-oriented approaches (cf. Bergman & Magnusson, 1997). It is clear that intervention strategies can best be informed by data derived from investigations that were designed to capture the differential pathways to adaptation and maladaptation (Cicchetti & Rogosch, 1996b). For example, it may become increasingly possible to identify patients who are provided with a certain type of intervention based not simply on their diagnosis, but on their individual developmental organization. Issues such as the individual's degree of introspectiveness versus a tendency to externalize responsibility for outcome could play an important role in the kind of intervention that a therapist chooses to provide, and, consequently, in the effectiveness of intervention.

As we have emphasized throughout this chapter, developmental correlates must be factored into the design and implementation of prevention and intervention services. Similarly, in evaluating the effectiveness of services, a developmental perspective is necessary. Just as the concomitants of a risk or pathological process may vary as a function of the developmental period during which a given event occurred, so ,too, may the effectiveness of therapy depend on the sensitivity of the approach to developmental considerations. Because research is increasingly demonstrating varied consequences of disorders at different periods of ontogenesis, the design and targeting of intervention toward the sequelae associated with specific developmental issues is a promising direction to pursue in the provision of intervention.

The role of developmental transitions in the emergence or remediation of a psychopathological process also underscores the importance of devising service continuua for children and adolescents. Because developmental transitions provide challenges as well as opportunities for growth, the utilization of periods of change and reorganization as therapeutic ports of entry is likely to result in more effective and enduring psychotherapeutic benefits. Of course, such a perspective requires a departure from a more status quo approach to the delivery of mental health services, whereby payment is rendered in response to a circumscribed and specific mental disorder. Unless administrators in the service delivery system recognize the criticality of not only addressing psychopathology, but also of preventing the emergence of disorders and of promoting wellness (cf. Cowen, 1994), the costs for the provision of services to mentally ill children will continue to exceed what might be achieved if intervention were initiated earlier in the developmental process. To adequately achieve the necessary comprehensive service delivery system, the historical compartmentalization among mental health, special education, and social welfare systems also must be reexamined. Because the nature of childhood psychopathology cuts across discrete areas typically associated with various service systems, a coordinated system of intervention must be developed.

Finally, if the goals and promises expressed in this chapter are to be achieved, then efforts to improve the dissemination of research findings on childhood psychopathology and its treatment must be undertaken. In a follow-up to the National Institute of Mental Health plan for research on child and adolescent mental health disorders (NIMH, 1990), a "report card" was issued to assess progress during the 5-year period following the articulation of goals. Of concern was the conclusion that the National Institute of Mental Health had not yet taken the sufficient steps to educate the public about the nature and impact of child and adolescent mental disorders (Leckman et al., 1995). This conclusion about the paucity of information on the magnitude of the problem of childhood psychopathology underscores the lack of information being provided on the treatment and effectiveness of various interventions for disorders of childhood and adolescence. Such failure possesses far-reaching implications for the future availability of funding for research and intervention efforts. Thus, as professionals invested in fostering the welfare of vulnerable youth, we must intensify our efforts to conduct investigations into the etiology, course, and outcome of childhood disorders, both when developmentally appropriate interventions are provided, as well as in their absence. Moreover, such information must be channeled into the public and policy domains if sufficient and necessary commitment to addressing the needs of our children is to be achieved.

In summary, we have acquired a great deal of knowledge regarding normal and atypical development in recent years that is relevant to the provision and evaluation of psychotherapy to children and adolescents. It is critical that ongoing dialogues continue and burgeon between those conducting research and those providing intervention. Moreover, we applaud John Weisz's call for the necessity of "transporting" treatments that have been found to be effective in laboratory settings into "real world" clinical facilities (Weisz, Weiss, & Donnenberg, 1992). In many ways, we are at a crossroads in the provision of child psychotherapy and, as stated by Shirk and Russell (1996), "This critical period could determine whether traditional child psychotherapy continues to thrive or whether it is relegated to the archives of treatment history" (p. ix). We believe that the introduction of a developmental psychopathology perspective into traditional child psychotherapy can serve to revitalize and invigorate this venerable form of treatment with children and adolescents.

ACKNOWLEDGMENT
We acknowledge the support of a grant and scientific MERIT award from the Prevention Research Branch (MH45027) of the National Institute of Mental Health.

REFERENCES

Baldwin, A., Baldwin, C., & Cole, R. (1990). Stress-resistant families and stress-resistant children. In J. Rolf, A. Masten, D. Cicchetti, K. Nuechterlein, & S. Weintraub (Eds.), *Risk and protective factors in the development of psychopathology* (pp. 257–280). New York: Cambridge University Press.

Beardslee, W. R., Versage, E. M., Wright, E. J., Salt, P., Rothberg, P. C., Drezner, K., & Gladstone, T. R. G. (1997). Examination of preventive interventions for families with depression: Evidence of change. *Development and Psychopathology, 9,* 109–130.

Beeghly, M., & Cicchetti, D. (1994). Child maltreatment, attachment and the self system: Emergence of an internal state lexicon in toddlers at high social risk. *Development and Psychopathology, 6,* 5–30.

Bergman, L. R., & Magnusson, D. (1997). A person-oriented approach in research on developmental psychopathology. *Development and Psychopathology, 9,* 291–319.

Boyce, W. T., Frank, E., Jensen, P. S., Kessler, R. C., Nelson, C. A., & Steinberg, L. (1998). Social context in developmental psychopathology: Recommendations for future research from the MacArthur network on psychopathology and development. In D. Cicchetti & J.L. Aber (Eds.), Developmental psychopathology and contextualism [Special Issue]. *Development and Psychopathology, 10*(2), 143–164.

Bretherton, I., Fritz, J., Zahn-Waxler, C., & Ridgeway, D. (1986). Learning to talk about emotion: A functionalist perspective. *Child Development, 57*, 530–548.

Bronfenbrenner, U. (1979). *The ecology of human development: Experiments by nature and design.* Cambridge, MA: Harvard University Press.

Bronfenbrenner, U., & Crouter, A. C. (1983). The evolution of environmental models in developmental research. In W. Kessen (Ed.), P. H. Mussen (Ser. Ed.), *Handbook of child psychology: Vol. 1. History, theory, and methods* (4th ed., pp. 357–414). New York: Wiley.

Burton, L. M. (1995). The timing of childbearing, family structure, and the role of responsibilities of aging black women. In E. M. Hetherington & E. A. Blechman (Eds.). *Stress, coping, and resiliency in children and families* (pp. 55–171). Hillsdale, NJ: Erlbaum.

Campos, J., Barrett, K. C., Lamb, M., Goldsmith, H. H., & Sternberg, C. (1983). Socioemotional development. In M. Haith & J. Campos (Eds.), *Handbook of child psychology: Vol. 2. Infancy and developmental psychology* (pp. 783–915). New York: Wiley.

Carnegie Task Force on Meeting the Needs of Young Children. (1994). *Starting points: Meeting the needs of our youngest children.* New York: Carnegie Corporation.

Cicchetti, D. (1984). The emergence of developmental psychopathology. *Child Development, 55*, 1–7.

Cicchetti, D. (1989). Developmental psychopathology: Past, present, and future. In D. Cicchetti (Ed.), *Rochester Symposium on Developmental Psychopathology: Vol. 1. The emergence of a discipline* (pp. 1–12). Hillsdale, NJ: Erlbaum.

Cicchetti, D. (1990). An historical perspective on the discipline of developmental psychopathology. In J. Rolf, A. Masten, D. Cicchetti, K. Nuechterlein, & S. Weintraub (Eds.), *Risk and protective factors in the development of psychopathology* (pp. 2–28). New York: Cambridge University Press.

Cicchetti, D. (1993). Developmental psychopathology: Reactions, reflections, projections. *Developmental Review, 13*, 471–502.

Cicchetti, D., & Aber, J. L. (1986). Early precursors to later depression: An organizational perspective. In L. Lipsitt & C. Rovee-Collier (Eds.), *Advances in infancy* (Vol. 4, pp. 81–137). Norwood, NJ: Ablex.

Cicchetti, D., & Aber, J. L. (Eds.). (1998). Special Issue: Developmental psychopathology and contextualism. *Development and Psychopathology, 10*(2).

Cicchetti, D., & Cohen, D. (Eds.). (1995a). *Developmental psychopathology, Vol. 1. Theory and method.* New York: Wiley.

Cicchetti, D., & Cohen, D. (Eds.). (1995b). *Developmental psychopathology, Vol. 2. Risk, disorder, and adaptation.* New York: Wiley.

Cicchetti, D., & Garmezy, N. (Eds.). (1993). Special Issue: Milestones in the development of resilience. *Development and Psychopathology, 5*(4), 497–774.

Cicchetti, D., & Lynch, M. (1993). Toward an ecological/transactional model of community violence and child maltreatment: Consequences for children's development. Psychiatry, 56, 96–118.

Cicchetti, D., & Richters, J. E. (1993). Developmental considerations in the investigation of conduct disorder. *Development and Psychopathology, 5*, 331–344.

Cicchetti, D., & Rogosch, F. A. (1996a). Special Issue: Developmental pathways. *Development and Psychopathology, 8*(4), 597–896.

Cicchetti, D., & Rogosch, F. A. (1996b). Equifinality and multifinality in developmental psychopathology: Special Issue of *Development and Psychopathology, 8*(4), 597–600.

Cicchetti, D., & Rogosch, F. A. (1997). The role of self-organization in the promotion of resilience in maltreated children. Development and Psychopathology, 9(4), 799–817.

Cicchetti, D., Rogosch, F. A., & Toth, S. L. (1997). Ontogenesis, depressotypic organization, and the depressive spectrum. In S. S. Luthar, J. Burack, D. Cicchetti, & J. Weisz (Eds.), *Developmental psychopathology: Perspectives on adjustment, risk, and disorder* (pp. 273–313). New York: Cambridge University Press.

Cicchetti, D., Rogosch, F. A., & Toth, S. L. (1998). Maternal depressive disorder and contextual risk: Contributions to the development of attachment insecurity and behavior problems in toddlerhood. *Development and Psychopathology, 10*(2), 283–300.

Cicchetti, D., & Toth, S. L. (1991). The making of a developmental psychopathologist. In J. Cantor, C. Spiker, & L. Lipsitt (Eds.), *Child behavior and development: Training for diversity* (pp. 34–72). Norwood, NJ: Ablex.

Cicchetti, D., & Toth, S. L. (Eds.). (1992a). Special Issue: Developmental approaches to prevention and intervention. *Development and Psychopathology, 4*(4), 489–728.

Cicchetti, D., & Toth, S. L. (1992b). The role of developmental theory in prevention and intervention. *Development and Psychopathology, 4*(4), 489–494.

Cicchetti, D., & Toth, S. L. (1995). A developmental psychopathology perspective on child abuse and neglect. *Journal of the American Academy of Child and Adolescent Psychiatry, 34*, 541–565.

Cicchetti, D., & Toth, S. L. (1998). Perspectives on research and practice in developmental psychopathology. In I. Sigel & A. Renninger (Eds.), *Child psychology in practice: Vol. 4.* In W. Damon (Ser. Ed.), *Handbook of child psychology, 5th ed.* (pp. 479–583). New York: Wiley.

Cicchetti, D., & Toth, S. L. (1998). Risk, trauma, and processes of memory. *Development and Psychopathology, 10*(4), 589–898.

Cicchetti, D., Toth, S. L., & Bush, M. (1988). Developmental psychopathology and incompetence in childhood: Suggestions for intervention. In B. Lahey & A. Kazdin (Eds.), *Advances in clinical child psychology* (pp. 1–71) New York: Plenum Press

Cicchetti, D., & Tucker, D. (1994). Development and self-regulatory structures of the mind. *Development and Psychopathology, 6*, 533–549.

Cowen, E. L. (1994). The enhancement of psychological wellness. *American Journal of Community Psychology, 22*, 149–179.

Crittenden, P. M. (1990). Internal representational models of attachment relationships. *Infant Mental Health Journal, 11*, 259–277.

Damon, W., & Hart, D. (1982). The development of self-understanding from infancy through adolescence. *Child Development, 53*, 841–864.

Damon, W., & Hart, D. (1988). *Self-understanding in childhood and adolescence.* New York: Cambridge University Press.

Denny-Brown, D., Twitchell, T. E., & Saenz-Arroyo, I. (1949). The nature of spasticity resulting from cerebral lesions. *Transaction of the American Neurological Association, 74*, 108–113.

Eisenberg, L. (1995). The social construction of the human brain. *American Journal of Psychiatry, 152*, 1563–1575.

Fisher, C. B., Murray, J., Dill, J.,Hagen, J., Hogan, M., Lerner, R., Rebok, G., Sigel, I., Sostek, A., Smyer, M., Spencer, M., & Wilcox, B. (1993). The national conference on graduate education in the applications of developmental science. *Journal of Applied Developmental Psychology, 14*, 1–10.

Futterweit, L. R., & Ruff, H. A. (1993). Principles of development: Implications for early intervention. *Journal of Applied Developmental Psychology, 14*, 153–173.

Garcia Coll, C. (1990). Developmental outcome of minority infants. A process oriented look into our beginnings. *Child Development, 61*, 270–289.

Garcia Coll, C., Lamberty, G., Jenkins, R., McAdoo, H. P., Crnic, K., Wasik, B. H., & Vasquez Garcia, H. (1996). An integrative model for the study of developmental competencies in minority children. *Child Development, 67*, 1891–1914.

Garcia Coll, C., & Vasquez Garcia, H. (1996). Definitions of competence during adolescence: Lessons from Puerto Rican adolescent mothers. In D. Cicchetti & S. L. Toth (Eds.), *Rochester Symposium on Developmental Psychopathology: Vol. 7. Adolescence: Opportunities and challenges* (pp. 283–308). Rochester, NY: University of Rochester Press.

Goldsmith, H. H., & Gottesman, I. (1994). Developmental psychopathology of antisocial behavior: Inserting genes into its ontogenesis and epigenesis. In C. Nelson (Ed.), *Threats to optimal development: The Minnesota Symposia on Child Psychology* (pp. 69–104). Minneapolis: University of Minnesota Press.

Gottesman, I. I. (1974). Developmental genetics and ontogenetic psychology: Overdue detente and propositions from a matchmaker. In A. Pick (Ed.), *Minnesota Symposium on Child Psychology* (pp. 55–80). Minneapolis: University of Minnesota Press.

Greenberg, J., Pyszczynski, T., & Solomon, S. (1995). Toward a dual-motive depth psychology of self and social behavior. In M.H. Kernis (Ed.), *Efficacy, agency, and self-esteem* (pp. 233–260). Newbury Park, CA: Sage.

Hamburg, D. A. (1992). *Today's children: Creating a future for a generation in crisis.* New York: Times Books.

Harrington, R., Rutter, M., & Fombonne, E. (1996). Developmental pathways in depression: Multiple meanings, antecedents, and endpoints. *Development and Psychopathology, 8*, 601–616.

Harris, P. (1989). *Children and emotion.* Oxford: Blackwell.

Harter, S. (1977). A cognitive-developmental approach to children's expression of conflicting feelings and a technique to facilitate such expression in play therapy. *Journal of Consulting and Clinical Psychology, 45,* 417–432.

Harter, S. (1983a). Cognitive-developmental considerations in the conduct of play therapy. In C. Schaefer & K. O'Connor (Eds.), *Handbook of play therapy* (pp. 95–127). New York: Wiley.

Harter, S. (1983b). Developmental perspectives on the self system. In E. M. Hetherington (Ed.), *Handbook of child psychology* (Vol. 4, pp. 275–386). New York: Wiley.

Harter, S. (1988). Developmental and dynamic changes in the nature of the self-concept: Implications for child psychotherapy. In S. Shirk (Ed.), *Cognitive development and child psychotherapy* (pp. 119–160). New York: Plenum Press.

Harter, S. (1990). Developmental differences in the nature of self-representations: Implications for the understanding, assessment, and treatment of maladaptive behavior. Cognitive Therapy and Research, 14, 113–142.

Harter, S. (1998). The development of self-representations. In W. Damon (Ser. Ed.), N. Eisenberg (Vol. Ed.), *Handbook of child psychology: Vol. 4. Social, emotional, and personality development* (5th ed., pp. 553–617). New York: Wiley.

Hinde, R. (1992). Developmental psychology in the context of other behavioral sciences. *Developmental Psychology, 28,* 1018–1029.

Hoagwood, K., & Jensen, P. S. (1997). Developmental psychopathology and the notion of culture: Introduction to the special section on "The fusion of cultural horizons: Cultural influences on the assessment of psychopathology in children and adolescents." *Applied Developmental Science, 1*(3), 108–112.

Hoagwood, K., Jensen, P. S., Petti, T., & Burns, B. J. (1996). Outcomes of mental health care for children and adolescents: I. A comprehensive conceptual model. Journal of the American Academy of Child and Adolescent Psychiatry, 35(8), 1055–1063.

Institute of Medicine (1989). *Research on children and adolescents with mental, behavioral, and developmental disorders.* Washington, DC: National Academy Press.

Institute of Medicine (1994). *Reducing risks for mental disorders: Frontiers for preventive intervention research.* Washington, DC: National Academy Press.

Jensen, P. S., & Hoagwood, K. (1997). The book of names: DSM-IV in context. *Development and Psychopathology, (9)*2, 231–249.

Kaplan, B. (1966). The study of language in psychiatry: The comparative developmental approach and its application to symbolization and language in psychopathology. In S. Arieti (Ed.), *American handbook of psychiatry* (pp. 659–688). New York: Basic Books.

Kellam, S. G., & Rebok, G. W. (1992). Building developmental and etiological theory through epidemiologically based preventive intervention trials. In J. McCord & R. E. Tremblay (Eds.), *Preventing antisocial behavior: Interventions from birth through adolescence* (pp. 162–195). New York: Guilford Press.

Kendall, P., Lerner, R., & Craighead, W. (1984). Human development and intervention in child psychopathology. *Child Development, 55,* 71–82.

Kendall-Tackett, K. A., Williams, L. M., & Finkelhor, D. (1993). Impact of sexual abuse on children: A review and synthesis of recent empirical studies. *Psychological Bulletin*, 113, 164–180.

Kiesler, D. (1966). Some myths of psychotherapy research and search for a paradigm. *Psychology Bulletin*, 65, 110–136.

Koretz, D. (1991). Prevention-centered science in mental health. *American Journal of Community Psychology, 19,* 453–458.

Leckman, J., Elliott, G., Bromet, E., Campbell, M., Cicchetti, D., Cohen, D., Conger, J., Coyle, J., Earls, F., Feldman, R., Green, M., Hamburg, B., Kazdin, A., Offord, D., Purpura, D., Solnit, A., & Solomon, F. (1995). Report card on the national plan for research on child and adolescent disorders: The midway point. *Archives of General Psychiatry, 52,* 715–723.

Lerner, R. M., & Kaufman, M. B. (1985). The concept of development in contextualism. Developmental *Review, 5,* 309–333.

Levine, L. J. (1995). Young children's understanding of the causes of anger and sadness. *Child Development, 66,* 697–709.

Lewis, M., Alessandri, S., & Sullivan, M. (1992). Differences in shame and pride as a function of children's gender and task difficulty. *Child Development, 63,* 630–638.

Lieberman, A. F., Weston, D., & Pawl, J. H. (1991). Preventive intervention and outcome with anxiously attached dyads. *Child Development, 62,* 199–209.

Luthar, S. (1995). Social competence in the school setting: Prospective cross-domain associations among inner-city teens. *Child Development, 66*, 416–429.

Masten, A., Best, K., & Garmezy, N. (1990). Resilience and development: Contributions from the study of children who overcome adversity. *Development and Psychopathology, 2*, 425–444.

McLoyd, V. (1990). The impact of economic hardship on Black families and children: Psychological distress, parenting, and socioemotional development. *Child Development, 61*, 311–346.

McLoyd, V., & Randolph, S. (1984). The conduct and publication of research on Afro-American children: A content analysis. *Human Development, 27*, 65–75.

McLoyd, V., & Randolph, S. (1985). Secular trends in the study of Afro-American children: A review of *Child Development*. In A. . Smuts & J. . Hagen (Eds.), History and research in child development. *Monographs of the Society for Research in Child Development, 50*(4–5, Serial No. 211).

Moffitt, T., Caspi, A., Dickson, N., Silva, P., & Stanton, W. (1996). Childhood-onset versus adolescent-onset antisocial conduct problems in males: Natural history from ages 3 to 18. In *Development and Psychopathology, 8*, 399–424.

Nannis, E. D. (1988). A cognitive-developmental view of emotional understanding and its implications of child psychotherapy. In S. Shirk (Ed.), *Cognitive development and child psychotherapy* (pp. 91–115). New York: Plenum Press.

National Institute of Mental Health (1990). *National plan for research on child and adolescent mental disorders: A report requested by the U.S. Congress submitted by the National Advisory Mental Health Council*. Rockville, MD: US Department of Health and Human Services, Alcohol, Drug Abuse, and Mental Health Administration. US Department of Health and Human Services Publication 90-1683.

Neumann, C., Grimes, K., Walker, E., & Baum, K. (1995). Developmental pathways to schizophrenia: Behavioral subtypes. *Journal of Abnormal Psychology, 104*, 558–566.

Noam, G. (1992). Development as the aim of clinical intervention. *Development and Psychopathology, 4*, 679–696.

Ogbu, J. U. (1981). Origins of human competence: A cultural-ecological perspective. *Child Development, 52*, 413–429.

Overton, W., & Horowitz, H. (1991). Developmental psychopathology: Integration and differentiations. In D. Cicchetti & S. L. Toth (Eds.), *Rochester Symposium on Developmental Psychopathology: Vol. 3. Models and integrations* (pp. 1–42). Rochester, NY: University of Rochester Press.

Post, R. (1992). Transduction of psychosocial stress into the neurobiology of recurrent affective disorder. *American Journal of Psychiatry, 149*, 999–1010.

Richters, J. E. (1997). The Hubble hypothesis and the developmentalist's dilemma. *Development and Psychopathology, 9*, 193–229.

Richters, J. E., & Cicchetti, D. (1993). Mark Twain meets DSM-III-R: Conduct disorder, development, and the concept of harmful dysfunction. *Development and Psychopathology, 5*, 5–29.

Robins, L. (1966). Deviant children grown up. Baltimore: Williams & Wilkins.

Robins, L., & Rutter, M. (Eds.). (1990). *Straight and devious pathways from childhood to adulthood*. New York: Cambridge University Press.

Rosenberg, M. (1986). Self-concept from middle childhood through adolescence. In J. Suls & A. G. Greenwald (Eds.), *Psychological perspectives on the self* (Vol. 3, pp. 107–136). Hillsdale, NJ: Erlbaum.

Rutter, M. (1981). Stress, coping and development: Some issues and some questions. *Journal of Child Psychology and Psychiatry, 22*, 324–356.

Rutter, M. (1986). Child psychiatry: Looking 30 years ahead. *Journal of Child Psychology and Psychiatry, 27*, 803–840.

Rutter, M. (1989). Pathways from childhood to adult life. *Journal of Child Psychology and Psychiatry, 30*, 23–51.

Rutter, M. (1990). Psychosocial resilience and protective mechanisms. In J. Rolf, A.S. Masten, D. Cicchetti, K. H. Nuechterlein, & S. Weintraub (Eds.), *Risk and protective factors in the development of psychopathology* (pp. 181–214). New York: Cambridge University Press.

Rutter, M. (1996). Developmental psychopathology: Concepts and prospects. In M. Lenzenweger & J. Haugaard (Eds.) *Frontiers of developmental psychopathology* (pp. 209–237). New York: Oxford University Press.

Rutter, M., & Garmezy, N. (1983). Developmental psychopathology. In E. M. Hetherington (Ed.), *Socialization, personality and social development* (pp. 775–911). New York: Wiley.

Saarni, C., Mumme, D., & Campos, J. (1998). Emotional development: Action, communication, and understanding. In N. Eisenberg (Ed.), *Handbook of child psychology* (5th ed): *Vol. 3. Social, emotional, and personality development* (pp. 237–309). New York: Wiley.

Selman, R. (1980). *The growth of interpersonal understanding: Developmental and clinical analyses.* New York: Academic Press.

Sherrington, C. (1906). *The integrative action of the nervous system.* New York: Scribner's.

Shirk, S. (Ed.) (1988a). *Cognitive development and child psychotherapy.* New York: Plenum Press.

Shirk, S. (1988b). Casual reasoning and children's comprehension of therapeutic interpretations. In S. Shirk (Ed.), Cognitive development and child psychotherapy (pp. 53–90). New York: Plenum Press.

Shirk, S., & Russell, R. (1996). *Change processes in child psychotherapy.* New York: Guilford Press.

Smiley, P. A., & Huttenlocher, J. (1989). Young children's acquisition of emotion concepts. In C. Saarni & P. L. Harris (Eds.), Childrens' understanding of emotion (pp. 27–49). Cambridge, MA: Harvard University Press.

Spencer, M. B., & Dupree, D. (1996). African American youths' ecocultural challenges and psychosocial opportunities: An alternative analysis of problem behavior outcomes. In D. Cicchetti & S. L. Toth (Eds.), *Rochester Symposium on Developmental Psychopathology: Vol. 7. Adolescence: Opportunities and challenges* (pp. 259–282). Rochester, NY: University of Rochester Press.

Sroufe, L. A. (1989). Pathways to adaptation and maladaptation: Psychopathology as developmental deviation. In D. Cicchetti (Ed.), *Rochester Symposium on Developmental Psychopathology: Vol. 1. The emergence of a discipline* (pp. 13–40). Hillsdale, NJ: Erlbaum.

Sroufe, L. A. (1990). An organizational perspective on the self. In D. Cicchetti & M. Beeghly (Eds.), *The self in transition: Infancy to childhood* (pp. 281–307). Chicago: University of Chicago Press.

Sroufe, L. A. (1997). Psychopathology as an outcome of development. *Development and Psychopathology, 9*, 251–268.

Sroufe, L. A., & Egeland, B. (1991). Illustrations of person and environment interaction from a longitudinal study. In T. Wachs & R. Plomin (Eds.), *Conceptualization and measurement of organism–environment interaction* (pp. 68–84). Washington, DC: American Psychological Association.

Sroufe, L. A., & Rutter, M. (1984). The domain of developmental psychopathology. *Child Development, 55*, 17–29.

Teitelbaum, P. (1977). Levels of integration of the operant. In W. K. Horig & J. Staddon (Eds.), *Handbook of operant behavior* (pp. 7–27). Englewood Cliffs, NJ: Prentice–Hall.

Thomas, L. (1979). On meddling. In *The medusa and the snail: More notes of a biology watcher* (pp. 110–111). New York: Viking Press.

Thompson, R. (1990). Emotions and self-regulation. In R. Thompson (Ed.), *Nebraska Symposium on Motivation: Vol. 36. Socioemotional development* (pp. 367–467). Lincoln: University of Nebraska Press.

Toth, S. L., & Cicchetti, D. (1993). Child maltreatment: Where do we go from here in our treatment of victims? In D. Cicchetti & S. L. Toth (Eds.), *Child abuse, child development, and social policy* (pp. 399–438). Norwood, NJ: Ablex.

Toth, S. L., Cicchetti, D., Macfie, J., & Emde, R. N. (1997). Representations of self and other in the narratives of neglected, physically abused, and sexually abused preschoolers. *Development and Psychopathology, 9*(4), 781–796.

Trabasso, T., Stein, N. L., & Johnson, L. R. (1981). Children's knowledge of events: A casual analysis of story structure. In G. Bower (Ed.), *Learning and motivation* (Vol. 15, pp. 237–282). New York: Academic Press.

van den Boom, D. C. (1994). The influence of temperament and mothering on attachment and exploration: An experimental manipulation of sensitive responsiveness among lower-class mothers with irritable infants. *Child Development, 65*, 1457–1477.

von Bertalanffy, L. (1968). *General systems theory.* New York: Braziller.

Vondra, J., Barnett, D., & Cicchetti, D. (1989). Perceived and actual competence among maltreated and comparison school children. *Development and Psychopathology, 1*, 237–255.

Vygotsky, L. S. (1978). *Mind in society.* Cambridge, MA: Harvard University Press.

Waddington, C. H. (1957). *The strategy of genes.* London: Allen & Unwin.

Walker, E. (1994). The developmentally moderated expression of the neuropathology underlying schizophrenia. *Schizophrenia Bulletin, 20*, 453–480.

Weisz, J. R. (1997). Effects of interventions for child and adolescent psychological dysfunction: Relevance of context, developmental factors, and individual differences. In S. S. Luthar, J. Burack, D.

Cicchetti, & J. R. Weisz (Eds.), *Developmental psychopathology: Perspectives on adjustment, risk, and disorder* (pp. 3–22). New York: Cambridge University Press.

Weisz, J. R., Weiss, B., & Donenberg, G. R. (1992). The lab versus the clinic: Effects of child and adolescent psychotherapy. *American Psychologist, 47,* 1578–1585

Werner, H. (1948). *Comparative psychology of mental development.* New York: International Universities Press.

Zigler, E., & Glick, M. (1986). *A developmental approach to adult psychopathology.* New York: Wiley.

3

Social and Contextual Issues in Interventions with Children and Families

KIMBERLY A. HOWARD, CATHERINE E. BARTON,
MARY E. WALSH, and RICHARD M. LERNER

Children and families face unprecedented challenges to their health, positive development, and—most basically—survival. They are confronted by problems of poor nutrition, drug and alcohol abuse, unsafe sex, violence, school failure, underachievement, school dropout, crime, teenage pregnancy and parenting, and lack of job preparedness (Carnegie Corporation of New York, 1995; Dryfoos, 1990; Johnston, O'Malley, & Bachman, 1996; United States Department of Health and Human Services, 1996). In addition, there are challenges to their health (e.g., lack of immunizations, inadequate screening for disabilities, insufficient prenatal care, and lack of sufficient infant and childhood medical services) (Hamburg, 1992; Huston, 1991). Moreover, one-fifth of our nation's youth are poor and face the sequelae of persistent and pervasive poverty (Center for the Study of Social Policy, 1995; Huston, 1991; Huston, McLoyd, & García Coll, 1994; Schorr, 1988, 1997). Feelings of despair and hopelessness may often pervade the lives of youth whose parents have lived in poverty and see themselves as having little opportunity to do better, that is, to have a life marked by societal respect, achievement, and opportunity (Lerner, 1993a,b, 1995; McKinney, Abrams, Terry, & Lerner, 1994; Schorr, 1988, 1997).

The scope and severity of these challenges demand the continued development of effective and efficient intervention strategies. Effective interventions, however, do not exist apart from the people who are the focus of the interventions.

KIMBERLY A. HOWARD, CATHERINE E. BARTON, and MARY E. WALSH • School of Education, Boston College, Chestnut Hill, Massachusetts 02467.   RICHARD M. LERNER • Eliot-Pearson Department of Child Development, Tufts University, Medford, Massachusetts 02155.

Handbook of Psychotherapies with Children and Families, edited by Russ and Ollendick.
Kluwer Academic/Plenum Publishers, New York, 1999.

When designing and implementing an intervention, it is important to consider the nature of the population that the intervention is intended to help. Indeed, no intervention will be successful if it is not tailored to the needs of, and seen as relevant and necessary by, the individuals and the population in question (Dryfoos, 1990; Hamburg, 1992; Lerner & Barton, in press; Lerner, Walsh, & Howard, 1998).

Making the intervention task more complex is the fact that children and families are not isolated entities; they exist within a cultural context and a temporal (historical) context, and have different features of diversity associated with them. The key contextual issue in developing and implementing interventions with children and families involves taking a contextualized view of the population and considering the relationships between individuals and context in order to develop, choose, and enact appropriate and effective interventions with them (Ollendick & King, 1991).

Given the unprecedented need for effective interventions, on the one hand, and the complexity of person–context relationship that shapes all human development on the other, it is clear that a theory linking person and context in a dynamic manner is essential for our attempt to both understand and enhance human functioning. Numerous instances of such theories have evolved over the past 20 years (Ollendick, 1998). In the present chapter we will draw on past work (Lerner, 1995; Lerner et al., 1998; Walsh, 1992) to present one instance of such developmental systems theories—developmental contextualism—as a framework for understanding the social and contextual embeddedness of interventions with children and families. Accordingly, we will begin with a brief overview of developmental contextualism and then discuss its implications for the development and use of intervention strategies with children and families.

AN OVERVIEW OF DEVELOPMENTAL CONTEXTUALISM

Developmental contextualism is a perspective on human development that takes an integrative approach to the multiple levels of organization presumed to comprise the nature of human life; that is, to the "fused" (Tobach & Greenberg, 1984) and changing relations among the biological, psychological, and social contextual levels that comprise the process of developmental change. Rather than approach variables from these levels of analysis in either a reductionistic or a parallel-processing way, the developmental contextual view rests on the idea that variables from these levels of analysis are dynamically interactive—that they are reciprocally influential over the course of human ontogeny. In other words, variables operating at the biological level of functioning (e.g., a person born with a physical handicap) will dynamically interact with variables from the other levels (e.g., with the development of psychological well-being and self-efficacy, and the support and feedback received from the peer group). From this perspective, humans are both products and producers of their own development (Lerner, 1982; Lerner & Busch-Rossnagel, 1981).

Change and Relative Plasticity

The concept that is central in developmental contextualism is that changing, *reciprocal relations* (or dynamic interactions) between individuals and the multiple contexts within which they live comprise the essential process of human development (Lerner, 1986; Lerner & Kauffman, 1985). Accordingly, developmental contextualism stresses that the focus of developmental understanding must be on systematic *change* (Ford & Lerner, 1992). This focus is required because of the belief that the potential for change exists across the life span (e.g., Baltes, 1987). Although it is also assumed that systemic change is not limitless (e.g., it is constrained both by past developments and by contemporary contextual conditions), developmental contextualism stresses that *relative plasticity* exists across life (Lerner, 1984). That is, humans have the capacity to change across life, if variables dynamically interact in their life in such a way that promotes this developmental change. The resilient behavior in children and adolescents provides a concrete instance of such plasticity (Masten, 1989; Werner, 1990, 1995).

Relative plasticity has important implications for the application of developmental science to the problems of human behavior and development. For instance, the presence of relative plasticity legitimates a proactive search across the life span for characteristics of people and of their contexts that, together, can influence the design of policies and programs that promote positive development (Birkel, Lerner, & Smyer, 1989; Fisher & Lerner, 1994; Lerner & Hood, 1986).

Relationism and the Integration of Levels of Organization

From a developmental contextual perspective, human behavior is both biological and social (Featherman & Lerner, 1985; Tobach & Schneirla, 1968). In fact, no form of life as we know it comes into existence independent of other life. No animal lives in total isolation from others of its species across its entire life span (Tobach, 1981; Tobach & Schneirla, 1968). Biological survival requires meeting demands of the environment or, as we note later, attaining a goodness of fit (Chess & Thomas, 1984; Lerner & Lerner, 1983, 1989; Thomas & Chess, 1977) with the context. Because this environment is populated by other members of one's species, adjustment to (or fit with) these other organisms is a requirement of survival (Tobach & Schneirla, 1968).

Both behavioral and emotional problems involve a malfunctioning of the human psychosocial system (Magnusson & Öhman, 1987). Thus, the development of such problems involves the emergence of nonadaptive, nonfit, or inadequate characteristics in this psychosocial system. Indeed, from a developmental contextual perspective, behavioral/emotional problems exist and develop when, and only when, an inadequate relation exists between psychological and social functioning, that is, between an individual and his or her context. It is a malfunctional person–context relation that defines problematic behavior and development; and it is from the changing nature of this relation—occurring normatively or through remedial, preventative, or enhancing interventions—that either healthy/positive or maladaptive, and hence negative, nonfit, or problematic behaviors develop (Sameroff, 1989).

Relationism and integration have a clear implications for unilevel theories of development and for approaches to intervention that emphasize a similarly unilevel (e.g., a psychogenic or biogenic) orientation to etiology or "treatment." At best, such approaches are severely limited, and inevitably provide a nonveridical depiction of development, reflecting their focus on what are essentially main effects embedded in higher-order interactions (e.g., see Walsten, 1990). At worst, such approaches are neither valid nor useful. Accordingly neither biogenic theories or interventions (e.g., ones based on genetic reductionistic conceptions such as behavioral genetics or sociobiology; Freedman, 1979; Plomin, 1986; Rowe, 1994; Wilson, 1975), psychogenic theories or interventions (e.g., behavioristic or functional analysis models; Baer, 1970, 1976; Bijou, 1976; Bijou & Baer, 1961; Skinner, 1938), nor sociogenic theories or interventions (e.g., "social mold" conceptions of socialization; e.g., Homans, 1961; and see Hartup, 1978, for a review) provide adequate frames for understanding or addressing problems of human development. Interventions based on such theories are insufficiently attentive to the potential plasticity that exists in the human development system, and thus the multiple levels of this system that provide "points of entry" for useful interventions (Birkel et al., 1989; Lerner, 1984, 1995).

Developmental contextualism moves beyond simplistic division of sources of development into nature-related and nurture-related variables or processes. Instead, developmental contextualism sees multiple levels of organization that exist within the ecology of human development as part of an inextricably fused developmental system, one that affords formulation of a rich and multilevel array of strategies for developmental interventions into the life course (e.g., see the chapters in Lerner, 1998).

Historical Embeddedness and Temporality

The relational units of analysis of concern in developmental contextualism are considered "change units" (Lerner, 1991). The change component of these units derives from the ideas that all levels of organization involved in human development are embedded in history, that is, they are integrated with historical change (Elder, 1980; Elder, Modell, & Parke, 1993). History—change over time—is incessant and continuous, and it is a level of organization that is fused with all other levels. This linkage means that change is a necessary—an inevitable—feature of variables from all levels of organization (Baltes, 1987; Lerner, 1984); in addition, this linkage means that the structure, as well as the function, of variables changes over time.

Because historical change is continuous, temporality is infused in all levels of organization. This infusion may be associated with different patterns of continuity and discontinuity across people. The potential array of such patterns has implications for understanding the importance of human diversity, as well as the design and implementation of interventions into the course of human development.

The Limits of Generalizability, Diversity, and Individual Differences

The temporality of the changing relations among levels of organization means that changes that are seen within one historical period (or time of measurement), and/or with one set of instances of variables from the multiple levels of the ecology of human development, may not be seen at other points in time (Baltes, Reese, & Nesselroade, 1977; Bronfenbrenner, 1979; Valsiner, 1998). What is seen in one data set may be only an instance of what does or what could exist. Accordingly, developmental contextualism focuses on diversity—of people, of relations, of settings, and of times of measurement (Lerner, 1991, 1995, 1996).

Individual differences within and across all levels of organization are seen as having core, substantive significance in understanding human development (Baltes et al., 1977; Lerner, 1991, 1995, 1996) and for designing interventions that fit specific needs and characteristics of diverse groups toward which such efforts may be directed. Indeed, diversity is the exemplary illustration of the presence of relative plasticity in human development (Lerner, 1984). Moreover, by inferring that it is possible to generalize from across-person variation that exists within time to within-person variation across time, diversity constitutes the best evidence of the potential for change in the states and conditions of human life (Brim & Kagan, 1980). It underscores the belief that interventions can make a difference in human development.

The major assumptive dimensions of developmental contextualism—systematic change and relative plasticity; relationism and integration; embeddedness and temporality; generalizability limits and diversity—are intertwined facets of a common conceptual core. And, as is also the case with levels of organization that are integrated to form the substance of developmental change, the assumptive dimensions reflect the essential features of superordinate developmental systems views of human development (Ford & Lerner, 1992). As is the case with the several defining features of the life-span developmental perspective, which—according to Baltes (1987)—need to be considered as an integrated whole, the assumptive dimensions of developmental contextualism need to be appreciated simultaneously. Such appreciation is required to understand the breadth, scope, and implications for research and application of this conceptual framework.

Finally, we should emphasize that this relational, developmental contextual view is compatible with those of other developmentalists studying either clinical problems in childhood and adolescence and/or developmental psychopathology (e.g., Cicchetti, 1984, 1987; Magnusson, 1988; Magnusson & Öhman, 1987; Super, 1987; Wapner & Demick, 1988). To illustrate, Cicchetti (1987), writing about psychopathology during human infant development, notes that

> it is inappropriate to focus on discrete symptomatology to infer the presence of nascent or incipient infant psychopathology. Rather, disorders in infancy are best conceptualized as relational psychopathologies, that is, as consequences of dysfunction in the parent–child–environment system. (p. 837)

A similar stress on the relational and developmental contextual character of psychopathology is made by Super (1987), who considers "disorders of development as a class of phenomena that reveal something of the nature of our children and also of the nature of the worlds we make for them" (p. 2). Indeed, he notes that

> the settings, customs, and psychology of caretakers not only regulate the healthy emergence of human potential, they also shape the possibilities of disorder. At every stage of the etiology, expression, course, intervention, and final outcome of developmental problems, human culture structures the experience and adjusts the odds. (p. 7)

In a corresponding vein, Öhman and Magnusson (1987) indicate that

> any disease must be understood as resulting from a multiplicity of causal events spanning observational levels from biochemistry to sociology. Thus, any single-factor, linear causal model is unrealistic

for understanding disease in general, and mental disorders in particular. Instead, multiple interacting causal factors that often change in their effect over time must be postulated. (p. 18)

(See also Magnusson, 1988; Magnusson & Allen, 1983; Super & Harkness, 1982, 1986.)

Given, then, the prominence of ideas pertinent to a developmental contextual perspective for understanding development across the life span and, for present purposes, the pertinence of this perspective for conceptualizing the social and contextual issues in interventions with children and families, it is useful to discuss the clinical application of this perspective.

CLINICAL INTERVENTIONS USING A DEVELOPMENTAL CONTEXTUAL PERSPECTIVE

With its emphasis on the relations among the individual, the family unit, and the broader cultural and societal contexts in which they live, and on the diversity of people and settings, developmental contextualism provides a useful frame for understanding the social and contextual issues involved in interventions with children and families. Specifically, developmental contextualism encourages the clinician to include the following considerations in his or her work with individuals and family groups: (1) an understanding that an individual's development level is one aspect of context that has significant implications for intervention; (2) a specification of the impact of various levels of social, cultural, and ecological contexts on behavior; (3) the recognition of the role of strengths and assets in addition to presenting problems; and (4) the utilization of multiple levels of assessment and intervention. The following sections of this chapter will explore these four principles for clinical work of using a developmental contextual perspective. Specifically, it will apply the aforementioned concepts of this theory to clinical work with children and families and will provide a framework for understanding the social and contextual issues relevant to developing and applying appropriate interventions.

Development as Context

Within a developmental contextual perspective, an individual's developmental level is crucial to the understanding of his or her current difficulties. This perspective requires a consideration of the meaning of behaviors at different developmental periods, for behaviors that are "normal" at one age may be "abnormal" at another (Campbell, 1989; Ollendick & King, 1991; Sroufe, 1990; Sroufe & Rutter, 1984). For instance, enuresis is not uncommon in 3- and 4-year-olds but is unusual for a 10-year-old. Knowing the child's developmental period may aid one in more thoroughly assessing the factors contributing to this behavior. Because 10-year-olds are expected to have good bladder control, we know that enuresis at this age is a more severe problem than that same behavior exhibited by a 3-year-old. An appreciation of the developmental context of this behavior results in a different type of clinical intervention.

Consideration of developmental level is also useful in family work. Consider, for instance, a set of parents who feel that their two children do not offer sufficient help with household chores. It would be important to determine what behaviors are expected of the children by the parents and to compare those expectations with behaviors that are appropriate for the developmental level of the children. If one considers the developmental levels of the children, one may find that these children are not, in fact, being "defiant and lazy," but that the behaviors expected of them are more complex than they are capable of at that point in their development. Achenbach (1990) points out that

> to improve our understanding of maladaptive behavior, it is helpful to view it in relation to normative sequences and achievements for particular ages. When this is done it is evident that many behavioral and emotional problems for which professional help is sought are not qualitatively different from those that most individuals display to some degree at some time in their lives. (p. 4)

A developmental perspective, therefore, encourages clinicians to consider not only what is abnormal behavior or development, but what is normal as well. An understanding of healthy development and the factors that contribute to both positive and negative outcomes contributes to our understanding of psychopathology (Cicchetti & Garmezy, 1993; Sroufe, 1990; Sroufe & Rutter, 1984). As the two examples listed above demonstrate, an appreciation of the developmental context in which problems occur aids one in better recognizing atypical development (as with the 10-year-old enuretic boy) as well as developmentally appropriate problems (as with the two overburdened boys).

The influence of development on the interpretation of behaviors is particularly evident in the area of cognitive development (Campbell, 1989). For example, if a 5-year-old whose grandfather has passed away says that he wants "to go where grandpa is," the clinician interprets the child's wish quite differently than a similar wish expressed by a 14-year-old. The clinician recognizes that the 14-year-old has a more mature concept of the meaning of death, requiring a different kind of clinical response. The behavior may look similar, but its meaning is much different at these two developmental periods. Similar behaviors displayed at various points across the life span may have very different implications because they are embedded in a distinct and specific developmental milieu (Lerner *et. al.,* 1998; Ollendick & King, 1991). The wish to be reunited with one's grandparent is less concerning when embedded in the developmental milieu of the 5-year-old than when embedded in that of an adolescent. "In short, the accurate assessment of behaviors requires an understanding of appropriate and inappropriate, adaptive and maladaptive, and expected and unexpected behaviors/skills/abilities throughout an individual's development" (Lerner *et. al.,* 1998).

Moreover, using such a perspective when working with families requires a consideration of the developmental periods and life tasks of *all* family members, not just those of the children. Developmental contextualism tells us that while childhood is the period of the most noticeable human development, development nevertheless continues to occur throughout the life span (Lerner, 1984). A life-span orientation requires that one understand how these levels and life tasks may be aiding/conflicting with those of other members. Consider a family in which the

parents are at a point in their lives where they are reevaluating the relative importance of work and family. They have decided that they want their family to take
precedence over their work life and wish to make up for "lost time." At the same
time, their teenage son is at a point where he is trying to prove his independence
from his parents. Because he is striving to separate from his parents, he is inclined
to resist their efforts for closeness. While the parents feel that their son is being difficult and oppositional, the son feels that his parents are suffocating him and not
letting him do his own thing. In this example, the life tasks of the parents and the
son are dissonant and are causing considerable family conflict. When understood
as a poor fit between the parental and teenage life tasks, the labels of "difficult,"
"oppositional," and "suffocating" are removed. In the place of these rigid labels, a
developmental interpretation of the problem would lead to a better understanding
of the current emotional needs of both the parents and the son (e.g., see Grotevant
& Cooper, 1986, 1988).

An appreciation of the developmental context of a particular behavior or
problem also provides guidance in the choice of interventions used by clinicians
(Campbell, 1989; Ollendick & King, 1991). For instance, understanding the cognitive–developmental level of a 4-year-old, one would not be likely to use cognitive–behavioral reframing strategies during treatment. Clinicians must plan
interventions that are appropriate for children at their current developmental
level. Similarly, it is a widely understood phenomenon that older children can experience a greater number of differentiated emotions than a younger child. The
child's developing ability to experience and identify emotions will guide practitioners in developing appropriate interventions. Similarly, family treatment may
take different forms depending on the age of the children. With very young children, the clinician may wish to see the parents alone and then assign homework
that the parents would later do with their children.

Development in Relation to Context

A developmental contextualist framework involves not only a focus on development, but also development in relation to context. This framework challenges
clinicians to shift from a static focus on classification of the symptoms of psychopathology to a more dynamic orientation in which psychopathology and family dysfunction are viewed as products of the relationship between developmental
level of individual family members and specific environments, including the family itself. The dominant diagnostic system now used by most clinicians, DSM-IV
(American Psychiatric Association, 1994), classifies problem behavior in terms of
characteristic features of disorders at a single point in time, accounting for neither
the development of the disorder nor the context in which it occurs (Achenbach,
1990; Cowan, 1988; Ollendick & King, 1991). To the contrary, while it "does not
claim that every category of disorder represents a mental illness, its classification
system has its conceptual roots in the medical model of psychopathology, with its
assumption that psychopathology is a disease located somewhere in the patient"
(Cowan, 1988, p. 7).

Within a developmental contextualist framework, the problem behavior is not
located "within the child" (e.g., the child "has" a conduct disorder), but rather is
viewed as a disturbance in the relationship or a "lack of fit" between the child and

the settings that impact him or her (Chess & Thomas, 1984; Lerner & Lerner, 1989). Rather than a focus on "fixing the child," developmental contextualism requires the clinician to address the fit or match between the child and the contexts that surround the child (e.g., family, school, community, culture). Similarly, a lack of fit between a particular family and the societal or cultural environment in which they are living may be causing, exacerbating, or contributing to troublesome family interactions/relationships.

From this perspective, behavior is inexplicable when considered in isolation from the context in which it occurs. As an example, consider a 5-year-old boy exhibiting behaviors characteristic of separation anxiety, that is, manifesting distress when away from his parents, worrying that he may get hurt if not with his parents, and refusing to sleep apart from his parents. An acontextual explanation may conclude that this behavior, while typical of a 2-year-old, is abnormal for a 5-year-old. However, if this child is living in a violent neighborhood where physical danger is a daily reality, the behaviors that he is exhibiting are not "abnormal" nor are they unexpected. From a contextualist perspective, it becomes clear that he has very real reasons for fearing separation—reasons that could easily be overlooked were one to ignore the environmental conditions under which he is living.

Consider also a mother who refuses to come to school to meet with her son's nurse and teacher. The young boy is having considerable learning difficulties and the teacher and nurse suspect that he may have a learning disability. The nurse has tried several times to encourage the mother to come meet with her, but to no avail. The professionals at the school who are involved in this case cannot understand why this mother is seemingly ignoring her son's learning problems. When viewed acontextually, such behavior may seem to reflect low maternal concern for the well-being of her son. If, however, we learn that the family members are undocumented immigrants and that the mother fears that visiting her son's school may lead to detection, being reported to the Immigration and Naturalization Service, and eventual deportation of her and her family, this behavior becomes understandable. No longer would we label her neglectful and unconcerned with her son's welfare. Instead we would understand the fear she may be experiencing and deem her response as expected and natural.

To be understood appropriately and completely, the child's behavior in the first example and the mother's in the second one would need to be considered as a function of their respective contexts. From a developmental contextualist perspective, clinicians will be most effective in their work with children and families when they understand and approach problem behavior in terms of a lack of fit between child or family and context.

Just as a developmental contextual approach recognizes that there may be a lack of fit between individual or family and context, it also acknowledges that behaviors that are adaptive in or "fit" a particular context may be maladaptive or harmful in another context (Ollendick & King, 1991). For instance, consider a child who is living in a "tough" neighborhood where aggressive behavior is valued by children and adolescents and expected of them by their peers. In such a neighborhood environment, the frequent demonstration and use of such behavior may be important to the child's survival, but this behavior may be maladaptive in the school environment. If one intervenes to change the maladaptive behavior witnessed at school without understanding the adaptability of this same behavior in the neighborhood, one could be doing this child a disservice. While the child no longer exhibits aggressive behavior at school, he or she is now disadvantaged on the streets. An accurate assessment of a child's difficulties requires an understanding of the child within his or her contexts and his or her "problematic" behaviors within these contexts. In this example, the behavior of the child "fit" his neighborhood context, but did not "fit" well with his school context. Similarly, the intervention that appears to be successful in the school environment becomes an impediment in other contexts.

The "goodness of fit" notion implies that an intervention should work to enhance the "fit" of child and context (Chess & Thomas, 1984; Lerner & Barton, in press; Thomas & Chess, 1977). The problem does not lie solely in the environment or solely within the child. Problems result from a lack of fit between the individual and the context. Using a developmental contextual perspective, a clinician will gather information on the child's context to better understand the factors influencing and reinforcing the problem behavior.

Consider also a single-parent family in which the mother works two jobs to support her children. The oldest child, Marie, assumes responsibility for her younger siblings when their mother is working. Marie must be at home in the afternoon and evening to baby-sit the children, feed them dinner, put them to bed, get their lunches ready for the next day, and then clean up the house before she can do her homework or go to bed. Marie enjoys this responsibility, but finds that she has little time and energy left at the end of the day to devote to her studies. Consequently, her grades are slipping at school. Marie's role in this example may "fit" well with the current circumstances of the family, but may not fit well with her role as a high school student. An acontextual intervention may include requiring Marie to stay after school for help with her homework and extra tutoring in several subjects. This intervention, however, would not fit her home responsibilities and could result in many undesirable ramifications for Marie's family, e.g., her younger siblings being left home unattended while Marie gets tutoring and their mother works. To truly understand Marie's situation, one would need to consider all of the contexts in which she finds herself. Similarly, only interventions that address the varied contexts in which Marie has responsibilities would be appropriate and effective for both Marie and her family.

Children and families exist not only within their immediate contexts, but also within a specific historical moment. The concept of temporality suggests that at different historical moments the person–context or family–context relation could have different meanings, i.e., what is considered "normal" changes over time. Consider the popular maxim "Spare the rod and spoil the child." Forty years ago this was the dominant approach to child-rearing used in many U.S. communities. To deviate from such practices was deemed "abnormal" and lax parenting. Through recent history, however, the dominant view of proper parenting behavior has changed. Today, using "the rod" could be interpreted as abusive behavior and could lead to an intervention by child welfare officers. While the behavior remains the same, i.e., corporal punishment, the historical time has changed, and with it the popular opinion of what constitutes appropriate discipline.

The concept of temporality also argues for examining "tried and true" interventions such as individual counseling. Humans are embedded in the historical time in which they live. Not only do individuals change over time, but changes also occur in the wider society. Systems of assessment and intervention must be reevaluated to ensure that earlier models, developed in earlier historical moments, remain relevant and effective in the current time period.

For example, the earlier exclusive reliance on individual psychotherapy has begun to give way to increased emphasis on prevention measures and group interventions. New models of treatment have begun to emerge, e.g., group and family counseling and psychoeducational intervention. There is an increased emphasis on providing services through community schools. As our culture and needs change, so do our modes of intervention.

In a similar manner, the types of problems presented to clinicians today are often different from those one would have found in past decades. While syndromes similar to what is now called attention deficit hyperactivity disorder have been discussed since the 1860s, the symptoms that have defined the syndrome have changed. In the 1960s, the emphasis was on "hyperactivity," whereas today hyperactivity is only one aspect of the disorder, one that is not even necessary for diagnosis (Barkley, 1990).

Multiple Levels of the Environment

The implicit suggestion in many of the above examples is that a child's and a family's context is not unidimensional. Children exist within a family, a peer group, a school system, a community, a culture, and a specific period in history. Families also exist within these varied contexts. Similarly, the *problems* of children and families are not unidimensional. In fact, their development is affected by experiences at the multiple levels of the environment, that is, the inner biological, the individual/psychological, the social relational, the sociocultural, and the ecological levels of organization. As explained earlier in this chapter, these levels of experience are inextricably embedded in one another. An event that occurs at one level of experience impacts and is impacted by the conditions at the other levels of organization; in other words, they exhibit dynamic interactionism (Lerner, 1984).

Given the reciprocal relations among these multiple levels of experience and environment, accurate assessment requires integrating information about the child and/or family from multiple perspectives. For instance, when trying to understand the "acting out" behavior exhibited by a 12-year-old girl at school, one would want to know what nutritional/health needs the child and family may have, what psychological issues are being confronted by each family member, and what is the quality of the family relationships as well as the peer relationships of the girl. Also of interest would be the economic and social situations of the family. Exploring the levels of experience of the 12-year-old girl in question, we may find that the behavior problem exhibited at school is not the only difficulty experienced by her. We may learn as well that her father is an alcoholic and her mother is clinically depressed, creating a situation in which neither parent has the emotional resources available to give to her. We may also find that given their respective problems, neither parent is currently working, so the family rarely has enough money to eat regular and nutritious meals. In addition, this family is black in a predominantly white neighborhood and is being harassed by neighbors.

Without assessing the child's problem at the multiple levels of her environments, one may use an intervention that inadequately addresses all of her needs.

If one focused solely on the "acting out" behavior, one might use a behavioral reward type of intervention in which behavioral goals were set up for her and she was rewarded for reaching each goal. Such an intervention will have minimal effectiveness for a girl who is hungry, has poor peer and familial relationships, and fears for her safety in the neighborhood. Before effective intervention(s) can be applied, one must explore the realities of this girl's situation at many levels.

While it is easy to advocate for multilevel assessments such as the one described in the example of the 12-year-old girl, conducting such thorough assessments is often quite challenging. Before such an exploration can be done, a clinician must do two things. First, one must understand in which capacities one is competent to assess and intervene based on one's professional training. Most clinicians will be able to effectively assess the status of youth and families at the individual-psychological and the social-relational levels. Some may even be sensitive to many issues facing children and families at the sociocultural and ecological levels of the environment. Second, one must recognize that there are many areas in which one may not be competent to assess functioning, and must therefore consult with professionals from other disciplines, such as nursing, education, and law. A developmental contextual perspective makes it clear that a truly comprehensive assessment on all of the individual's or family's levels of experience may very well require multiple professionals, for many of these environmental levels lie outside of the expertise and training of clinicians. Indeed, Cowen (1984) states that

> although most mental health professionals are knowledgeable about the nature and assessment of human adjustment, they are not Renaissance persons with exhaustive knowledge of complex feeder-domains such as education, sociology, environmental planning, economics, family relations, architecture, public health, epidemiology, and social ecology, which contain significant knowledge about factors that relate to human adjustment. (p. 487)

Once we begin to view the problems experienced by our nation's youth and families as multidimensional, it becomes obvious that most of these problems do not fit into neat boxes that parallel the expertise and interest of the professions. Indeed, they often cut across professional and disciplinary boundaries. The resulting situation requires that clinicians be prepared and willing to engage in interprofessional collaboration; that is, they consult with other professionals who are trained to assess the functioning of individuals and families from the necessary perspectives. This requires flexibility in one's role and a willingness to work collaboratively with others for the good of children and families (Brabeck, Walsh, Kenny, & Comilang, 1997). Indeed, Schneider (1996) argues that psychology, and we would add, clinicians, "need(s) to eliminate some of the boxes we have put ourselves into. This means removing the walls within psychology and between our discipline and several others" (p. 715). This is a difficult task, but one necessary for thorough, multilevel assessment.

Just as a developmental contextual perspective requires one to conduct a multiple-level assessment, it but also requires multiple-level interventions. Within this framework, psychotherapeutic interventions are expanded to include multiple levels of organization (e.g., biological, sociohistorical, cultural, psychological). Accordingly, this will result in a shift in the clinician's orientation from a typical unilevel approach to intervention strategies involving all of the multiple levels of organization relevant to the youth or family problem in question (Lerner et al., 1998). A multilevel intervention approach in the example of the 12-year-old girl might include providing her with two good meals while she is at school (the biological level), a behavior modification program to address her inappropriate behavior at school (the individual-psychological level), social skills training (the social-relational level), treatment for her parents (her social-relational level), and employment counseling for her parents (the sociocultural level).

It is also important to note that a child's development does not occur at an even rate across the levels of organization. Therefore, an unevenness in strengths and weaknesses may be observed. It is possible for a child to be reading and doing other academic tasks at an age-appropriate level, but to be lagging behind his or her peers in developing age-appropriate social skills. By focusing on weaknesses only, one falls into a deficit model that focuses only on the child and his or her "abnormal" behaviors without considering contextual factors. A developmental contextual approach considers the child within his or her contexts and identifies strengths as well as deficits. This approach utilizes an optimization framework, focusing and building on strengths to maximize a child's full development. For instance, the child who is working at age-appropriate levels in school but lacks social skills could be included in group projects in the classroom that include children of varying academic abilities. This child may be able to slowly make social progress as he or she helps others in the group successfully complete the project. Assessing the child's functioning at his or her various levels of organization allows one to identify and build on existing strengths and skills. Working collaboratively with individuals in other professions affords one the opportunity to identify strengths in areas outside of one's expertise. Indeed,

> behaviors and abilities of clients that are viewed by one profession as strengths and assets may not even be noted by those in another profession. Collaboration across professions allows for the rich pattern of strengths and assets to be seen and capitalized upon by those in other professions. (Walsh, Brabeck, & Howard, 1997, p. 10)

Plasticity and Resilience

The malleability of the interconnectedness among levels of organization within the developmental system (i.e., plasticity) is evident in the research on resilience. The resilience literature clearly demonstrates that children have "self-righting tendencies that move children toward normal development under all but the most persistent adverse circumstances" (Werner, 1990, p. 112). In her research of Hawaiian children and youth, Werner (1990) identified three areas of protective factors that may contribute to a child's resilience. These include attributes of their disposition that are received positively by others (e.g., an easy temperament and intelligence), encouragement by family members to develop trust, autonomy, and initiative, and external support systems and role models (p. 111). These protective factors are found at various levels of organization, e.g., dispositional attributes are characteristics of the child and so are found at the individual/psychological level while family encouragement of certain behaviors and positive role models are located at the social-relational level of organization. Resilience in the face of hardships, then, is the result of the impact of both contextual and organismic characteristics on the individual's current functioning. However, as the literature on risk and prevention demonstrates, contextual and organismic factors do not interact in an additive or linear manner, but in a multiplicative way (Sameroff, 1996). It is therefore imperative that a clinician appreciate the complex and continually changing interplay between the individual and his or her contexts when one is engaging in clinical, systems, or policy interventions.

Perhaps most importantly, the concept of plasticity provides "hope" to clinicians. It implies that interventions are not fruitless endeavors; that poorly functioning individuals are not doomed to remain poorly functioning if an intervention can be developed that addresses a strength. While it is true that development may be constrained by past development and current contextual conditions, plasticity implies that humans do have the potential for change across the life span (Lerner, 1984). Clinicians can help to remove the constraining aspects of the child's context. To optimize the effects of an intervention, the clinician must address the contextual constraints at all levels of organization. For example, a homeless child who acts out in school requires a more complex diagnosis than that provided by the diagnostic label "conduct disorder," and a treatment plan more comprehensive than that offered by a unilevel intervention such as "insight-oriented therapy," or "pharmacological treatment" (Walsh, 1992; Walsh & Buckley, 1994). Just as comprehensive, multilevel assessments require input from professionals in many fields of expertise, so, too, do the interventions that result from such assessments. It may often be the case that psychologists, counselors, guidance counselors, parent aides, teachers, nurses, and lawyers will need to form partnerships and collaborate with one another and with the families they help in order to be most effective. It is imperative, however, that every effort is made to develop interventions that are coordinated and comprehensive. It has too often been the case that what was intended to be a comprehensive effort was, in fact, uncoordinated, disjointed, and fragmented care (Lerner, 1995; Schorr, 1988, 1997). Walsh et al. (1997) assert that

> such collaboration requires the dynamic interaction of each of the professions involved with the client in contrast to what sometimes masquerades unwittingly as a collaborative effort, that is, a set of treatment plans collected into a single sheaf of papers and summarized by a case manager. (p. 5)

The concept of multiple levels of organization, then, implies not only multiple levels of assessment and intervention by clinicians, but also collaboration among professionals. For instance, in the example of the homeless boy who acts out in school, one might have the school nurse assess his nutritional and physical needs, the teacher assess his educational needs, the school psychologist explore his emotional needs, and his parents report on his behavior outside of school and the social and economic stressors placed on them as a family. Such a collaboration would lead to a more holistic understanding of this boy's needs than would a simple diagnosis of "conduct disorder." Accordingly, the resulting intervention would also be holistic in nature, involving many of the collaborators.

Therefore, the interconnectedness of the levels of organization, or plasticity, has four significant implications for our work with children and families. First, plasticity gives us faith in the ability of people to change regardless of age. While certain types of change may be more easily accomplished at specific points in human development, change at any age can and does continue to be possible (Lerner, 1984). Second, interventions will be most successful when all of the levels at which a person or family is having difficulties are addressed. By removing as many obstacles as possible and encouraging skill-building in areas of difficulty, one will be most effective in promoting positive youth and family development. Third, when it is impossible to address the difficulties experienced at each level of organization by clients, it is still possible to promote positive change by utilizing existing strengths and skills. In fact, an intervention can occur at any level, and given the interconnectedness of the levels, will help to promote growth in other levels. This point should not, however, be used to circumvent a comprehensive, multilevel assessment and intervention. Our nation's youth and families deserve and need our maximum efforts whenever possible.

Finally, psychologists, child and family advocates, and all clinicians must broaden their definition of "intervention." Interventions need not always be at the individual, family, or group level. They may not, in fact, be what is typically defined as "clinical." The interconnectedness of the levels of organization implies that a change at any level of the environment will be felt at and have implications for the other levels. Therefore, systems and policy changes are also legitimate, and often times necessary interventions in efforts to improve the lives of the nation's children, youth, and families. Similarly, the research that informs systems and policy changes and direct clinical interventions must be recognized as essential to our intervention efforts.

The Need for Collaborative Research and Outreach

To be successful, these endeavors require more than collaboration across disciplines. In addition, two other types of collaboration are necessary. First, collaboration across *levels* of professions is essential. That is, colleagues in the research, policy, and intervention communities must plan and implement their activities in a synthesized manner in order to successfully develop and extend this vision. All components of this collaboration must be understood as equally valuable, indeed as equally essential. The collaborative activities of colleagues in university extension and outreach; in program design and delivery; in elementary, middle (or junior high), and high schools; in policy development and analysis; and in academic research are vital to the success of this new agenda for science and outreach for children, adolescents, parents, and their contexts, for example, their extended families, their schools, their workplaces, and their communities (Brabeck et al., 1998; Weissbourd, 1996).

Second, given the contextual embeddedness of these synthetic research and outreach activities, collaboration must occur with the people we are trying both to understand and to serve. Without incorporation of the perspective of the community into our work—without the community's sense of ownership, of value, and of meaning for these endeavors—research and outreach activities cannot be adequately integrated into the lives we are studying.

Thus, from a developmental contextual perspective, research that "parachutes" into the community from the heights of the academy (i.e., that is done in a community without collaboration with the members of the community) is flawed fatally in regard to its ability to understand the process of human development. This is the case because human development does not happen at the general level (Lerner, 1988, 1991); it does not occur in a manner necessarily generalizable across diverse people and contexts (Bibace & Walsh, 1979). Development happens in particular communities, and it involves the attempts of specific children and families to relate to the physical, personal, social, and institutional situations found in their communities. Without bringing the perspective of the community into the "plan" for research, then, the scholar may fail to address the correct problems of human development—the ones involved in the actual lives of the people he or she is studying. And if the wrong problem is being addressed, any "answers" that are found are not likely to be relevant to the actual lives of people. Not surprisingly, these "answers" will be seen all too often (and quite appropriately) as irrelevant by the community.

In turn, however, if community members collaborate in the definition of the problems of development that they are confronting, and if they participate in the research process, then the obtained answers are more likely to be considered significant by the community members. This will increase the likelihood of these answers being used to build community-specific policies and programs. Moreover, community empowerment and capacity building occur by engaging in a collaborative process wherein the community places value and meaning on, and participates in, the research and outreach being conducted within its boundaries (Dryfoos, 1990, 1994; Schorr, 1988, 1997).

Implications for Policies and Programs

In order to be complete, the integrative research promoted by a developmental contextual view of human development must be synthesized with two other foci. Research in human development that is concerned with one or even a few instances of individual and contextual diversity cannot be assumed to be useful for understanding the life course of all people. Similarly, policies and programs derived from such research, or associated with it in the context of a researcher's tests of ideas pertinent to human plasticity, cannot be assumed to be applicable, or equally appropriate and useful, in all contexts or for all individuals. Accordingly, developmental and individual differences-oriented policy development and program (intervention) design and delivery would need to be integrated fully with the new research base for which we are calling (Lerner & Miller, 1993; Lerner et al., 1994).

As emphasized in developmental contextualism, the variation in settings within which people live means that studying development in a standard (e.g., a "controlled") environment does not provide information pertinent to the actual (ecologically valid), developing relations between individually distinct people and their specific contexts (e.g., their particular families, schools, or communities). This point underscores the need to conduct research in real-world settings, and highlights the ideas that (1) policies and programs constitute natural experiments, i.e., planned interventions for people and institutions; and (2) the evalua-

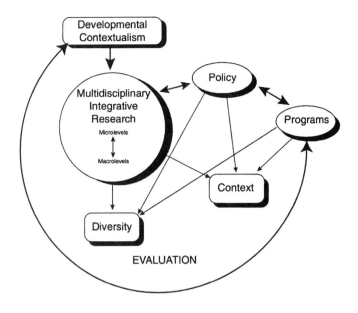

Figure 1. A developmental contextual model of the integration of multilevel, multidisciplinary research, aimed at diversity and context, with policies, programs, and evaluations.

tion of such activities becomes a central focus in the developmental contextual research agenda we have described.

In this view, then, policy and program endeavors do *not* constitute secondary work, or derivative applications, conducted after research evidence has been compiled. Quite to the contrary, policy development and implementation, and program design and delivery, become integral components of this vision for research; the evaluation component of such policy and intervention work provides critical feedback about the adequacy of the conceptual frame from which this research agenda should derive. This conception of the integration of multidisciplinary research endeavors centrally aimed at diversity and context, with policies, programs, and evaluations is illustrated in Figure 1.

In short, developmental research informs and is informed by social policy. It is our contention that policy development, program design and delivery, and developmental research need to be integrated fully to optimally benefit the recipients of social programs.

CONCLUSIONS AND FUTURE DIRECTIONS

Developmental contextualism provides an agenda not only for a developmental, dynamic, and systems approach to interventions with and research about child and family development. As well, such theory allows us to envision the possibility of promoting positive developmental trajectories in youth and families (Lerner, 1995). We, as clinicians, researchers, and policymakers, may actualize this vision if we remain assiduously committed to a developmental systems orientation; if we recognize the "double-edged sword" nature of plasticity that derives from the functioning of this system; and if we therefore create, through policies and programs, a "convoy of social support" (Kahn & Antonucci, 1980) across the life course of children and families. Such a convoy would be a network encompassing the familial, community, institutional, and cultural components of the ecology that impacts a person's behavior and development across his or her life.

The concepts of person, of context, and of the relations between the two found in a developmental contextual perspective are, as a set, quite complex ones. The concepts impose formidable challenges on those who seek to understand the developmental bases of psychopathology and of nonpsychopathologial behavior; to derive feasible research from this perspective; and to use this conception and its associated research for the design and implementation of interventions. As we have argued, this developmental contextual perspective leads to an integrated, multilevel concept of development, one in which the focus of inquiry is the organism–environment dynamic interaction. Furthermore, such an orientation places an emphasis on the potential for intraindividual change in structure and function—for plasticity—across the life span. Moreover, this perspective requires a temporal (historical)/longitudinal and a relational/comparative orientation to intervention and to research.

In sum, the relative plasticity of human development across the life span—a plasticity deriving from the dynamic interactions between organism and context that characterize human functioning—is already well documented (Baltes, 1987; Brim & Kagan, 1980; Featherman, 1983; Hetherington, Lerner, & Perlmutter, 1988; Lerner, 1984; Sørensen, Weinert, & Sherrod, 1986). A future including the sorts of directions we suggest should enrich greatly our understanding of the precise conditions promoting and constraining the development of psychopathology. Given the present literature, and the promise we see for tomorrow, we believe there is reason for great optimism about the future clinical and scientific use of the developmental contextual view of the individual and contextual bases of functional, adaptive behaviors, as well as malfunctional, psychopathological ones.

ACKNOWLEDGMENTS

The preparation of this chapter was supported in part by grants from the W. T. Grant Foundation, the U.S. Department of Education (Fund for the Improvement of Post Secondary Education), and the DeWitt Wallace Reader's Digest Fund.

REFERENCES

Achenbach, T. M. (1990). Conceptualization of developmental psychopathology. In M. Lewis & S. M. Miller (Eds.), *Handbook of developmental psychopathology* (pp. 3–14). New York: Plenum Press.

American Psychiatric Association. (1994). *Diagnostic and statistical manual of mental disorders* (4th ed.). Washington, DC: Author.

Baer, D. M. (1970). An age-irrelevant concept of development. *Merrill Palmer Quarterly of Behavior and Development, 16,* 238–245.

Baer, D. M. (1976). The organism as host. *Human Development, 19,* 87–98.

Baltes, P. B. (1987). Theoretical propositions of life-span developmental psychology: On the dynamics between growth and decline. *Developmental Psychology, 23,* 611–626.

Baltes, P. B., Reese, H. W., & Nesselroade, J. R. (1977). *Life-span developmental psychology: Introduction to research methods.* Monterey, CA: Brooks/Cole.

Barkley, R. A. (1990). Attention deficit disorders: History, definition, and diagnosis. In M. Lewis & S. M. Miller (Eds.), *Handbook of developmental psychopathology* (pp. 3–14). New York: Plenum Press.

Bibace, R., & Walsh, M. (1979). Clinical developmental psychologists in family practice settings. *Professional Psychology, 10,* 441–450.

Bijou, S. W. (1976). *Child development: The basic stage of early childhood.* Englewood Cliffs, NJ: Prentice–Hall.

Bijou, S. W., & Baer, D. M. (Eds.). (1961). *Child development: A systematic and empirical theory.* New York: Appleton–Century–Crofts.

Birkel, R., Lerner, R. M., & Smyer, M. A. (1989). Applied developmental psychology as an implementation of a life-span view of human development. *Journal of Applied Developmental Psychology, 10,* 425–445.

Brabeck, M., Cawthorne, J., Cochran-Smith, M., Gaspard, N., Green, C. H., Kenny, M., Krawczyk, R., Lowery, C., Lykes, M. B., Minuskin, A. D., Mooney, J., Ross, C. J., Savage, J., Soifer, A., Smyer, M., Sparks, E., Tourse, R., Turillo, R. M., Waddock, S., Walsh, M., & Zollers, N. (1998). Changing the culture of the university to engage in outreach scholarship. In R. M. Lerner & L. A. K. Simon (Eds.), *Creating the new outreach university for America's youth and families: Building university–community collaborations for the twenty-first century* (pp. 335–364). New York: Garland.

Brabeck, M., Walsh, M., Kenny, M., & Comilang, K. (1997). Interprofessional collaboration for children and families: Opportunities for counseling psychology in the 21st century. *The Counseling Psychologist, 25*(4), 615–636.

Brim, O. G., Jr., & Kagan, J. (Eds.). (1980). *Constancy and change in human development.* Cambridge, MA: Harvard University Press.

Bronfenbrenner, U. (1979). *The ecology of human development.* Cambridge, MA: Harvard University Press.

Campbell, S. B. (1989). Developmental perspectives. In T. H. Ollendick & M. Herson (Eds.), *Handbook of child psychopathology* (pp. 5–28). New York: Plenum Press.

Carnegie Corporation of New York. (1995). *Great transitions: Preparing adolescents for a new century.* Carnegie Council on Adolescent Development.

Center for the Study of Social Policy. (1995). *Kids count data book.* Washington, DC: Author.

Chess, S., & Thomas, A. (1984). *The origins and evolution of behavior disorders: Infancy to early adult life.* New York: Brunner/Mazel.

Children's Defense Fund. (1996). *The state of America's children yearbook.* Washington, DC: Author.

Cicchetti, D. (1984). The emergence of developmental psychopathology. *Child Development, 55,* 1–7.

Cicchetti, D. (1987). Developmental psychopathology in infancy: Illustration from the study of maltreated youngsters. *Journal of Consulting and Clinical Psychology, 55,* 837–845.

Cicchetti, D., & Garmezy, N. (1993). Prospects and promises in the study of resilience. *Development and Psychopathology, 5,* 497–502.

Cowan, P. A. (1988). Developmental psychopathology: A nine-cell map of the territory. In E. D. Nannis & P. A. Cowan (Eds.), *New Directions for Child Development, No. 39: Developmental psychopathology and its treatment.* San Francisco: Jossey–Bass.

Cowen, E. L. (1984). A general structural model for primary prevention program development in mental health. *Personnel and Guidance Journal, April,* 485–490.

Dryfoos, J. G. (1990). *Adolescents at risk: Prevalence and prevention.* New York: Oxford University Press.

Dryfoos, J. G. (1994). *Full service schools: A revolution in health and social services of children, youth and families.* San Francisco: Jossey–Bass.

Elder, G. H., Jr. (1980). Adolescence in historical perspective. In J. Adelson (Ed.), *Handbooks of adolescent psychology* (pp. 3–46). New York: Wiley.

Elder, G. H., Jr., Modell, J., & Parke, R. D. (Eds.). (1993). *Children in time and place: Developmental and historical insights.* New York: Cambridge University Press.

Featherman, D. L. (1983). Life-span perspectives in social science research. In P. B. Baltes & O. G. Brim, Jr. (Eds.), *Life-span development and behavior* (Vol. 5, pp. 1–57). New York: Academic Press.

Featherman, D. L., & Lerner, R. M. (1985). Ontogenesis and sociogenesis: Problematics for theory about development across the lifespan. *American Sociological Review, 50,* 659–676.

Fisher, C. B., & Lerner, R. M. (Eds.). (1994). *Applied developmental psychology*. New York: McGraw–Hill.

Ford, D. L., & Lerner, R. M. (1992). *Developmental systems theory: An integrative approach*. Newbury Park, CA: Sage.

Freedman, D. G. (1979). *Human sociobiology: A holistic approach*. New York: Free Press.

Grotevant, H. D., & Cooper, C. R. (1986). Individuation in family relationships and the development of identity exploration. *Child Development, 56,* 415–428.

Grotevant, H. D., & Cooper, C. R. (1988). The role of family experience in career exploration: A life-span perspective. In P. B. Baltes, D. L. Featherman, & R. M. Lerner (Eds.), *Life-span development and behavior* (Vol. 7, pp. 231–258). Hillsdale, NJ: Erlbaum.

Hamburg, D. A. (1992). *Today's children: Creating a future for a generation in crisis*. New York: Time Books.

Hartup, W. W. (1978). Perspectives on child and family interaction: Past, present, and future. In R. M. Lerner & G. B. Spanier (Eds.), *Child influences on marital and family interaction: A life-span perspective* (pp. 23–45). New York: Academic Press.

Hetherington, E. M., Lerner, R. M., & Perlmutter, M. (Eds.). (1988). *Child development in life-span perspective*. Hillsdale, NJ: Erlbaum.

Homans, G. C. (1961). *Social behavior: Its elementary forms*. New York: Harcourt, Brace & World.

Huston, A. C. (Ed.). (1991). *Children in poverty: Child development and public policy*. New York: Cambridge University Press.

Huston, A. C., McLoyd, V. C., & García Coll, C. T. (1994). Children and poverty: Issues in contemporary research. *Child Development, 65,* 272–282.

Johnston, L., O'Malley, R. A., & Bachman, J. G. (1996). *National survey results on drug use from the Monitoring the Future Study, 1975–1994. Vol. II: College students and young adults*. Washington, DC: National Institute on Drug Abuse.

Kahn, R. L., & Antonucci, T. C. (1980). Convoys over the life course: Attachment, roles, and social support. In P. B. Baltes & O. G. Brim (Eds.), *Life-span development and behavior* (Vol. 3, pp. 253–286). Hillsdale, NJ: Erlbaum.

Lerner, R. M. (1982). Children and adolescents as producers of their own development. *Developmental Review, 2,* 342–370.

Lerner, R. M. (1984). *On the nature of human plasticity*. New York: Cambridge University Press.

Lerner, R. M. (1986). *Concepts and theories of human development* (2nd ed.). New York: Random House.

Lerner, R. M. (1988). Personality development: A life-span perspective. In E. M. Hetherington, R. M. Lerner, & M. Perlmutter (Eds.), *Child development in life-span perspective* (pp. 21–46). Hillsdale, NJ: Erlbaum.

Lerner, R. M. (1991). Changing organism-context relations as the basic process of development: A developmental-contextual perspective. *Developmental Psychology, 27,* 27–32.

Lerner, R. M. (1993a). Investment in youth: The role of home economics in enhancing the life chances of America's children. *AHEA Monograph Series, 1,* 5–34.

Lerner, R. M. (1993b). Early adolescence: Toward an agenda for the integration of research, policy, and intervention. In R. M. Lerner (Ed.), *Early adolescence: Perspectives on research, policy, and intervention* (pp. 1–13). Hillsdale, NJ: Erlbaum.

Lerner, R. M. (1995). *America's youth in crisis: Challenges and options for programs and policies*. Newbury Park, CA: Sage.

Lerner, R. M. (Ed.). (1998). *Theoretical models of human development*. Volume 1 of the *Handbook of Child Psychology* (5th ed.). Editor-in-Chief: W. Damon. New York: Wiley.

Lerner, R. M. (1996). Relative plasticity, integration, temporality, and diversity in human development: A developmental contextual perspective about theory, process, and method. *Developmental Psychology, 32*(4), 781–786.

Lerner, R. M., & Barton, C. E. (in press). Adolescents as agents in the promotion of their positive development: The role of youth actions in effective programs. In W. Perrig & A. Grob (Eds.), *Control of human behavior, mental processes and consciousness: Essays in honour of the 60th birthday of August Flammer*. New York: Wiley.

Lerner, R. M., & Busch-Rossnagel, N. A. (Eds.). (1981). *Individuals as producers of their development: A life-span perspective*. New York: Academic Press.

Lerner, R. M., & Hood, K. E. (1986). Plasticity in development: Concepts and issues for intervention. *Journal of Applied Developmental Psychology, 7,* 139–152.

Lerner, R. M., & Kauffman, M. B. (1985). The concept of development in contextualism. *Developmental Review, 5,* 309–333.

Lerner, R. M., & Lerner, J. V. (1983). Temperament–intelligence reciprocities in early childhood: A contextual model. In M. Lewis (Ed.), *Origins of intelligence: Infancy and early childhood* (pp. 399–421). New York: Plenum Press.

Lerner, R. M., & Lerner, J. V. (1989). Organismic and social contextual bases of development: The sample case of early adolescence. In W. Damon (Ed.), *Child development today and tomorrow* (pp. 69–85). San Francisco: Jossey–Bass.

Lerner, R. M., & Miller, J. R. (1993). Integrating human development research and intervention for America's children: The Michigan State University model. *Journal of Applied Developmental Psychology, 14,* 347–364.

Lerner, R. M., Miller, J. R., Knott, J. H., Corey, K. E., Bynum, T. S., Hoopfer, L. C., McKinney, M. H., Abrams, L. A., Hula, R. C., & Terry, P. A. (1994). Integrating scholarship and outreach in human development research, policy, and service: A developmental contextual perspective. In D. L. Featherman, R. M. Lerner, & M. Perlmutter (Eds.), *Life-span development and behavior* (Vol. 12, pp. 249–273). Hillsdale, NJ: Erlbaum.

Lerner, R. M., Walsh, M. E., & Howard, K. A. (1998). Developmental-contextual considerations: Person-context relations as the bases for risk and resiliency in child and adolescent development. In T. Ollendick (Ed.), *Comprehensive clinical psychology. Vol. 4. Children and adolescents: Clinical formulation and treatment* (pp. 1–24). New York: Elsevier Science.

Magnusson, D. (1988). *Individual development from an interactional perspective: A longitudinal study.* Hillsdale, NJ: Erlbaum.

Magnusson, D., & Allen, V. L. (Eds.). (1983). *Human development: An interactional perspective.* New York: Academic Press.

Magnusson, D., & Öhman, A. (Eds.). (1987). *Psychopathology: An interactional perspective.* San Diego: Academic Press.

Masten, A. S. (1989). Resilience in development: Implications of the study of successful adaptation for developmental psychopathology. In D. Cicchetti (Ed.), *The emergence of a discipline: Vol. 1. Rochester Symposium on Developmental Psychopathology* (pp. 261–294). Hillsdale, NJ: Erlbaum.

McKinney, M., Abrams, L. A., Terry, P. A., & Lerner, R. M. (1994). Child development research and the poor children of America: A call for a developmental contextual approach to research and outreach. *Family and Consumer Sciences Research Journal, 23,* 26–42.

Öhman, A., & Magnusson, D. (1987). An interactional paradigm for research on psychopathology. In D. Magnusson & A. Öhman (Eds.), *Psychopathology: An interactional perspective* (pp. 3–19). San Diego: Academic Press.

Ollendick, T. H. (Ed.). (1998). *Comprehensive clinical psychology: Vol. 5. Children and adolescents: Clinical formulation and treatment.* New York: Elsevier Science.

Ollendick, T. H., & King, N. J. (1991). Developmental factors in child behavioral assessment. In P. R. Martin (Ed.), *Handbook of behavior therapy and psychological science: An integrative approach* (pp. 57–72). New York: Pergamon Press.

Plomin, R. (1986). *Development, genetics, and psychology.* Hillsdale, NJ: Erlbaum.

Rowe, D. C. (1994). *The limits of family influence: Genes, experience, and behavior.* New York: Guilford Press.

Sameroff, A. J. (1989). Models of developmental regulation: The environtype. In D. Cicchetti (Ed.), *The emergence of a discipline: Vol. 1. Rochester Symposium on Developmental Psychopathology* (pp. 41–68). Hillsdale, NJ: Erlbaum.

Sameroff, A. (1996, Fall). Democratic and republican models of development: Paradigms and perspectives. *Developmental Psychology Newsletter, Fall,* 1–9.

Schneider, S. F. (1996). Random thoughts on leaving the fray. *American Psychologist, 51*(7), 715–721.

Schorr, L. B. (1988). *Within our reach: Breaking the cycle of disadvantage.* New York: Doubleday.

Schorr, L. B. (1997). *Common purpose: Strengthening families and neighborhoods to rebuild America.* New York: Anchor Books.

Skinner, B. F. (1938). *The behavior of organisms.* New York: Appleton.

Sørensen, B., Weinert, E., & Sherrod, L. R. (Eds.). (1986). *Human development and the life course: Multidisciplinary perspectives.* Hillsdale, NJ: Erlbaum.

Sroufe, L. A. (1990). Considering normal and abnormal together: The essence of developmental psychopathology. *Development and Psychopathology, 2,* 335–347.

Sroufe, L. A., & Rutter, M. (1984). The domain of developmental psychopathology. *Child Development, 55,* 17–29.

Super, C. M. (1987). The role of culture in developmental disorder. In C. M. Super (Ed.), *The role of culture in developmental disorder* (pp. 2–7). San Diego: Academic Press.

Super, C. M., & Harkness, S. (1982). The infant's niche in rural Kenya and metropolitan America. In L. L. Adler (Ed.), *Cross-cultural research at issue* (pp. 47–56). New York: Academic Press.

Super, C. M., & Harkness, S. (1986). The developmental niche: A conceptualization at the interface of child and culture. *International Journal of Behavioral Development, 9,* 1–25.

Thomas, A., & Chess, S. (1977). *Temperament and development.* New York: Brunner/Mazel.

Tobach, E. (1981). Evolutionary aspects of the activity of the organism and its development. In R. M. Lerner & N. A. Busch-Rossnagel (Eds.), *Individuals as producers of their development: A life-span perspective* (pp. 37–68). New York: Academic Press.

Tobach, E., & Greenberg, G. (1984). The significance of T. C. Schneirla's contribution to the concept of levels of integration. In G. Greenberg & E. Tobach (Eds.), *Behavioral evolution and integrative levels* (pp. 1–7). Hillsdale, NJ: Erlbaum.

Tobach, E., & Schneirla, T. C. (1968). The biopsychology of social behavior of animals. In R. E. Cooke & S. Levin (Eds.), *Biologic basis of pediatric practice* (pp. 68–82). New York: McGraw-Hill.

United States Department of Health and Human Services. (1996). *Trends in the well-being of America's children and youth: 1996.* Washington, DC: Department of Health and Human Services, Office of the Secretary for Planning and Evaluation.

Valsiner, J. (1998). The development of the concept of development: Historical and epistemological perspectives. In R. M. Lerner (Ed.), *Theoretical models of human development.* Volume 1 of the *Handbook of Child Psychology* (5th ed., pp. 189–232). Editor-in-Chief: W. Damon. New York: Wiley.

Walsh, M. E. (1992). *"Moving to nowhere": Children's stories of homelessness.* Westport, CT: Auburn House.

Walsh, M. E., Brabeck, M. M., & Howard, K. A. (1997, August). A theoretical framework for engaging in interprofessional collaboration. In M. E. Kenny & M. E. Walsh (Chairs), *Opportunities for counseling psychology: Interprofessional collaboration for children and families.* Symposium conducted at the annual meeting of the American Psychological Association, Chicago.

Walsh, M. E., & Buckley, M. A. (1994). Children's experiences of homelessness: Implications for school counselors. *Elementary School Guidance and Counseling, 29*(1), 4–15.

Walsten, D. (1990). Insensitivity of the analysis of variance to heredity–environment interaction. *Behavioral and Brain Sciences, 13,* 109–120.

Wapner, S., & Demick, J. (1988, October 25–27). *Some relations between developmental and environmental psychology: An organismic developmentalorganismicdevelopmental systems perspective.* Paper presented at the "Visions of Development, the Environment, and Aesthetics: The Legacy of Joachim Wohlwill" conference, The Pennsylvania State University, University Park.

Weissbourd, R. (1996). *The vulnerable child: What really hurts America's children and what we can do about it.* Reading, MA: Addison–Wesley.

Werner, E. E. (1990). Protective factors and individual resilience. In S. Meisels & J. Shonkoff (Eds.), *Handbook of early childhood intervention* (pp. 97–116). New York: Cambridge University Press.

Werner, E. E. (1995). Resilience in development. *Current Directions in Psychological Science, 4*(3), 81–85.

Wilson, E. O. (1975). *Sociobiology: The new synthesis.* Cambridge, MA: Harvard University Press.

4

Ethical and Legal Issues in the Treatment of Children and Families

WILLIAM A. RAE and CONSTANCE J. FOURNIER

The ethical and legal treatment of children and families engaged in psychotherapy is the greatest responsibility of any psychotherapist. In many ways, therapy with children and families requires the highest standard of ethical behavior because of the special vulnerabilities of children and the complexities involved with interacting with multiple family members. Ethical guidelines are most often written for adult patients and, as a result, they may be difficult to apply to children and families. Special considerations are needed to understand the child's capacity to make treatment decisions, conflicting legal and ethical standards involved in the treatment of children, differing needs of children and their family members, and the special vulnerabilities of children. In addition, most child and family therapists believe that it is an ethical duty to be an advocate for the child and family. In fact, Koocher (1976) has stated that child therapists are morally bound to serve as an advocate for their child clients. This advocacy also adds complexities to the treatment process, as disagreements can occur between the child, therapist, and/or parent(s) with regard to the best interests of the child or family. The therapist must constantly strive to maintain the highest ethical and legal practices, yet in doing so, will face dilemmas that challenge the therapist's thinking and behavior.

Therapists are often compelled to make decisions about what to do regarding an ethical or legal issue. Regardless of the complexity of the issues, the therapist must eventually make a binary decision that could have ramifications for the long-term well-being of the child and family. In addition, therapists should be aware of

WILLIAM A. RAE • Department of Educational Psychology, Texas A&M University, College Station, Texas 77843-4225.   CONSTANCE J. FOURNIER • Division of Educational Psychology, University of Missouri, St. Louis, Missouri 63110.

Handbook of Psychotherapies with Children and Families, edited by Russ and Ollendick. Kluwer Academic/Plenum Publishers, New York, 1999.

the difference between being unethical and being negligent. Negligence is a legal concept. For a therapist to be negligent, the therapist must commit a wrongful act for which there can be civil action. For instance, a therapist could inappropriately breach confidentiality. To be negligent the therapist must not only commit a breach of ethical and/or professional standards, but also cause damage or injury to the patient. To continue the example, if the breach in confidentiality causes the client to lose his or her job, there may be cause for a malpractice lawsuit against the therapist because of negligence. A therapist can be in violation of ethical principles, but not be negligent (Schaefer & Call, 1994). At the same time, negligence can usually be avoided by therapists if the highest standards of ethical behavior are followed.

There are several general ethical principles that child and family therapists must practice. First, therapists should never practice outside of their areas of competence. Therapy services should only be provided if the therapist has adequate experience and/or training. For example, family therapists who are not trained in psychotherapy with young children should not treat young children even within the context of the family. Second, therapists must adjust their interventions to fit the needs of any special population with whom they work. For example, when engaging in therapy with a young child, the therapist must explain the therapy process differently than the therapist would to an adult. In the same way, the therapist must be sensitive to the gender, ethnic, cultural, economic status, and religious differences of each family that is treated. Third, therapists must always be concerned with the welfare and rights of the child and family. Therapists must treat the child and family with respect and promote their well-being and welfare as a primary concern. Finally, therapists must be honest and straightforward in the way they professionally interact with their patients. Therapists must also be aware of their own values and biases and should communicate these in a straightforward way to the patient and family.

Many professions have written ethical guidelines for their members including general counseling (American Counseling Association, 1995), social work (National Association of Social Workers, 1990), psychiatry (American Psychiatric Association, 1993), marriage and family therapy (American Association for Marriage and Family Therapy, 1991), school counseling (American School Counselor Association, 1992), mental health counseling (American Mental Health Counseling Association, 1987), and psychology (American Psychological Association, 1992). Cottone and Tarvydas (1998) have provided a good summary of many relevant ethical and professional issues of several professions providing mental health services. In addition, overviews of the legal and ethical issues also exist for therapists dealing with children and families (Melton & Ehrenreich, 1992; Rae, Worchel, & Brunnquell, 1995; Schaefer & Call, 1994). The purpose of this chapter is to describe some of the legal and ethical issues that might affect the psychotherapeutic treatment of children and families.

This chapter focuses on common ethical issues during the course of therapy. The reader should recognize that certain ethical issues are not exclusive to any one stage, but actually occur throughout psychotherapy. In the first section, ethical issues common to the initiation of therapy will be discussed. This includes obtaining informed consent, structuring the professional relationship, and dealing with the complexities involving families seen by other mental health professionals. In the second section, ethical issues common to an ongoing therapy process will be discussed. This involves confidentiality and dual relationship issues including sexual intimacy and custody disputes. In the third section, ethical issues common to termination and providing continuity of care will be discussed. In the fourth section, research issues in psychotherapy with children and families are described. In the last section, suggestions are made for enhancing the ethical decision process for the therapist.

ETHICAL ISSUES COMMON TO THERAPY INITIATION

Informed Consent

When treating children and families, the potential risks and benefits of the intervention must be thoroughly explained. This explanation is the basis for obtaining informed consent for treatment. Unfortunately, fully informing children is often difficult as they may lack the cognitive ability to truly make an informed decision. By virtue of their lack of experience and age-related diminished capabilities, children and adolescents have limitations in their ability to understand the process of treatment. In addition, the child or family may be experiencing significant emotional distress and, as a result, they may not be capable of fully comprehending what they are told. Because of these factors, obtaining informed consent from families requires the highest standard of practice. Informed consent with children and families involves four essential elements: (1) participants must be competent to make a decision about treatment, (2) participation in treatment must be voluntary, (3) participants must be knowledgeable about the treatment, and (4) the consent must by appropriately documented.

At the centerpiece of informed consent is the first element, which is the capacity to competently assess treatment. Minors and their families who are involved in treatment must not only be informed about the assessment or treatment, but must also be competent to make a decision about participation. Unfortunately, the assessment of competence is poorly articulated in the law (Melton & Ehrenreich, 1992) and is often not even attempted by child-oriented practitioners (Rae & Worchel, 1991). Therapists should inform children of the proposed interventions in a manner commensurate with their psychological capabilities, seek their assent to those interventions, and consider the child's preferences and best interests.

The evaluation of the child's capacity to consent or assent requires that the therapist assess the child's cognitive development. Each child will then need assistance in understanding the therapeutic process with terminology and examples that are compatible with the child's own life experiences and developmental abilities. Each child should be assessed as to his or her stage of cognitive development. Koocher and Keith-Spiegel (1990) have summarized the abilities at each stage of Piagetian development. At the preoperational stage the child is egocentric in his or her thought; a self-centered point of view with magical thinking permeates this stage. At this stage the child has difficulty making an informed decision because his or her reasoning is significantly influenced by egocentrism. The child with preoperational thinking may believe the problems in the family are his or her fault and, in the same way, the child may believe that his or her thoughts might influence the family problems or therapy outcome. Explaining the therapeutic process in terms of who is responsible for treatment progress might be helpful. At the concrete operational stage the child has developed the capacity for empathy and seeing alternative points of view. At this stage the child can understand the concrete elements of the intervention and may be able to assent to treatment, but the child will not be able to process the more abstract underpinnings involved in the psychotherapy process. The child with concrete operational thinking might benefit from a discussion of the roles and expected behaviors during the therapy process. At the formal operational stage the child or adolescent will be able to engage in hypothetical-deductive reasoning, to understand cause and effect, to generalize, and to abstract. The child or adolescent at the formal operational stage will need the therapeutic process explained in terms of feelings, roles, processes, and other family member's point of view. Weithorn (1982) has stated that when children acquire formal operations (usually between the ages of 11 and 14 years), they are cognitively capable of providing consent. Although adolescents at the formal operational stage are in a good position to make an informed decision, the therapist must be aware that the adolescent is also prone to cognitive distortions that might affect a rational decision (Rae et al., 1995).

The second element states that the treatment must be voluntary by all participants. This is often problematic when a child is brought in for treatment by the parents. There has been a trend over the last three decades to expand children's legal rights (Melton & Ehrenreich, 1992). For children, this might include getting their written assent for treatment. At the same time, according to most state laws only parents have the legal right to consent to treatment for their minor children; minor children cannot legally consent to or refuse treatment. Many children do not see the need for being treated and, as a result, it is difficult to enlist their support in the treatment process. The therapist must develop an atmosphere where coercion is kept to a minimum. Participation must be voluntary if it is to be effective; any coercion from the parents or the therapist could adversely affect treatment. Although obtaining consent is legally required, once the parent has consented to treatment, the child's wishes are legally irrelevant. Regardless, coerced treatment is usually ineffective and should be avoided.

Exceptions exist to the legal rights of parents if parental knowledge of a minor seeking some types of treatment would interfere with that minor's ability to obtain that treatment. For example, in most states minors can obtain psychotherapy independent of parental consent for pregnancy, drug use or addiction, physical or sexual abuse, sexually transmitted diseases, and suicidal or homicidal ideation. In addition, four other exceptions to parental consent for treatment include "emancipated" minors who are legally considered an adult, "mature" minors who can understand the nature and consequences of therapy, minors who are court ordered to obtain therapy, and minors who must receive treatment on an emergency basis (Plotkin, 1981). Psychotherapeutic treatment can be required of minors against their will. Like adults, minors can also be involuntarily hospitalized in a psychiatric facility if they are a danger to themselves, a danger to others, or have diminished capacity to care for themselves. The legal aspects of treatment, the type of treatment, and the minimum age of consent vary from state to state.

The third element dictates that children and their families must be knowledgeable about the treatment being offered. It is the therapist's responsibility to fully explain all elements of the treatment in a way that is understandable, clear, and unambiguous. Making reasonable efforts to answer questions and to avoid apparent misunderstandings is important. Not only must the information be accessible to parents, it must also be understandable and accessible to children and adolescents. Special materials might be developed for children, such as a concrete description of the specific activities in therapy for young children, basic confidentiality information and goal information for school-age children, and a complete description of goals, confidentiality issues, and crisis situation procedures for adolescents. Parents would need to get their own information including therapeutic procedures, financial arrangements, emergency and crisis situation procedures, confidentiality issues, and any specific organizational policies such as appointment cancellation procedures. The parents should also be given a copy of the information that their child or adolescent receives.

The final element states that consent must also be appropriately documented. In practice, many therapists have the parents sign a statement indicating that they give permission to have their child treated. Handelsman and Galvin (1988) have attempted to provide a format to facilitate the informed consent process for adults. It is best practice to have all minors assent to treatment as their voluntary participation would facilitate the treatment process. Fact sheets can be useful in defining the basic relationships between the therapist and the family and appear to have the added bonus of reducing liability claims (see the Informed Written Consent for Treatment Checklist in Cottone & Tarvydas, 1998).

Structuring of the Psychotherapeutic Relationship

Early in the therapeutic relationship, the therapist must structure the relationship and address the issue of the relationships between family members and the therapist. In structuring the relationship, there are two issues to be considered. First, the therapist must develop a therapeutic contract between the therapist and the child and family. Fees, and specific arrangements regarding situations such as cancellations would need to be covered at this time. Confidentiality is also addressed at this time.

The relationships between the therapist and various family members should also be addressed. It is important that the therapist clearly specify the relationship with the identified patient and with the other family members. A common dilemma for therapists working with families in distress and/or conflict is that what may be beneficial to one family member may be countertherapeutic to another. Other dilemmas may occur when the therapy changes format, as when the parents or child are seen separately after being previously seen within the entire family (Gottlieb, 1995). A clear delineation of the therapeutic relationships may avoid this potential problem.

In structuring the psychotherapeutic relationship the therapist must bring up the nature of the intervention and anticipated course of treatment. Special care should be taken in explaining treatment outcome expectations to children and families. It is important that therapists use treatments that are effective and empirically supported. Unfortunately, many therapeutic interventions have not been empirically examined (e.g., dynamic therapies) and/or have not been appropriately disseminated (Task Force on the Promotion and Dissemination of Psychological Procedures, 1995). When the therapist engages in a treatment with less proven validity, the child and family must be fully informed about the nature of the treatment, relative potential risks and benefits, and current understanding of reliability and validity. In the same way, therapists should fully inform children and families about the effect of managed care on the treatment process. For example, if an empirically supported, cognitive–behavioral intervention for the child's problem would require eight sessions of treatment and the family's insurance only covers five sessions of treatment, this situation must be thoroughly discussed with the family.

Although the issues involved in structuring the therapeutic relationship would seem to be fairly straightforward, there are several special considerations for the family and child. Timing is one consideration. Whereas most therapists would usually conduct this discussion in the first interview, there may be exceptions, such as when the family is in a crisis situation (Hare-Mustin, Marecek, Kaplan, & Liss-Levinson, 1995). Whether or not the child should be present during certain phases of the discussion must also be considered. For example, the financial arrangements portion of the discussion may not be appropriate with the child present, who may have feelings such as guilt or confusion about the costs. Another key issue is that although these issues may be discussed in great detail at the appropriate time, the family may be overwhelmed with information and new terminology. Special care must be taken to ensure that children understand the therapeutic contract in terms of their own life experience (LoCicero, 1976). Including this information with the consent/assent material and having additional methods to review the information in general, such as brochures and videos, are helpful to the family.

Another source of structuring the relationship involves the discussion of supervision when the therapist is being supervised. The family must be informed of the nature of the supervision and how it might impact the family directly (Gottlieb, 1995). If there are implications in terms of insurance coverage, these must be addressed as well. In some situations, the supervisor may be meeting the family so as to fulfill agency, policy, or insurance requirements. In this case, the roles of the therapist and the supervisor must be explained to children, as confusion may ensue regarding who is the therapist. In the same way, if the therapist is a trainee, this fact must be clearly explained in the initial session, as many families may not differentiate the level of training of their therapist.

Therapy for Patients Currently under Mental Health Treatment

In working with children and families, the issue of having more than one mental health provider must be assessed carefully. There may be several situations where another mental health service is provided to the family, such as parents receiving individual and/or couples therapy, other siblings in individual therapy, or the child in other therapy at school. Although care must be taken to find out if these situations are occurring, there are times that the child and the family do not recognize school-based interventions as mental health services. In addition, a family might want a second opinion from another mental health practitioner because the family might be angry with the first therapist, a mismatch exists between the first therapist and the family, or the family has a change in insurance carriers. Also, a second opinion may be requested by mandated policy such as is required by the Individuals with Disabilities Education Act (IDEA).

The issue of multiple providers must be discussed with the family, usually in the first session. It may be helpful to discuss procedures that will be utilized regarding confidentiality and information sharing with other therapists, recognizing that clear and specific releases of information must be used for every agency involved. In dealing with school providers, it is helpful to have the family designate a contact person, usually the school psychologist or school counselor. If multiple mental health providers will be serving the family, coordination of treatment is essential. If the therapist is dealing with divorce issues in the family, and the school counselor is addressing study skills, then the situation may be less difficult than if the school counselor has the child in a group for children whose parents are divorcing. Caution and sensitivity are called for, with recognition that the family must be informed about each contact, and the implications of these contacts in regard to therapeutic issues must be addressed. There must be full documentation of the discussion with the family, release of information forms, and documentation of the discussions with other mental health care providers in the client's records. If the family refuses permission to contact other mental health providers, if it is not possible to contact other providers (e.g., the other therapist is not available at the time of the current therapy), or if it is inappropriate to contact another provider (e.g., a parent getting therapy for a specific phobia that is unrelated to the current treatment), this circumstance must also be documented in the record.

ETHICAL ISSUES COMMON TO ONGOING PSYCHOTHERAPY

Confidentiality

Ensuring confidentiality is one of the ethical hallmarks of psychotherapy and it is often the most frequent ethical dilemma for therapists (Pope & Vetter, 1992). In fact, if confidentiality was not practiced, children and families might not seek out treatment for fear that their most private information would be divulged. By keeping information confidential, children and families are encouraged to be open and honest with their therapist. It is recognized that confidentiality issues with children are different from confidentiality issues with adults. Adult clients expect that the therapist will keep all personal information confidential without their express approval. In contrast, young children do not expect the same kind of broad confidentiality as their parents are often knowledgeable about most of the private details of their lives. On the other hand, adolescents require more assurances of confidentiality as they are often suspicious of parental motives and intentions. Adolescents are often compelled by their parents to attend therapy (Rae, 1992). Many therapists make it a condition of treatment with adolescents that confidentially is maintained from parents even though there may not be a legal basis for such an arrangement (Gustafson & McNamara, 1987; Keith-Spiegel & Koocher, 1985).

The limits of confidentiality are often a problem for therapists dealing with the conflicting expectations of family members. Margolin (1995) has stated that family therapists often take one of two approaches with families. In the first, the therapist treats each family member's confidences as though that person were an individual client. In the second, the therapist adopts a policy of not keeping any secrets from other family members. Regardless of the preference, the therapist should attempt to clarify any potential difference in understanding of confidentiality issues early in treatment. Even when this is clarified, family members may have their own idiosyncratic expectations of the limits of privacy both within and without the therapy session. For example, a therapist may receive a telephone call from the mother of a child complaining about her husband's lack of help in management of their behavior-disordered child. Unless it is clarified beforehand, it is unclear if this information is to be only for the therapist or if it is to be shared at the upcoming family session. The therapist has the duty to be sure that all family members explicitly understand the limits to confidentiality so there will be no confusion about what information is conveyed to other family members. In addition, it must be recognized that if the confidentiality expectations change during the course of the treatment, the therapist must clarify his or her role to all family members. For example, if the parents' irreconcilable marital differences lead to a divorce, it is important that the therapist clearly communicate his or her role regarding the potential release of confidential information during divorce proceedings.

A discussion of confidentiality should take place with all family members at the initial contact. In fact, it is recommended that the parents (and possibly the child) sign a statement acknowledging the mutual understanding of confidentiality including the fact that no written or oral information can be communicated to schools, physicians, mental health agencies, insurance providers, and/or others without the written approval of the parents. The child and family in treatment must also understand that at times cases will be discussed within institutions and between colleagues, but the family must be reassured that the therapist has taken precautions to only reveal information necessary to achieve the purposes of the consultation; no information will be revealed that could lead to the identification of the family. The child and family must also be reassured that written permission will always be obtained prior to audio or video recording of the sessions. It is also helpful to delineate some of the limits of confidentiality including those circumstances when confidentiality would be broken either by ethical guidelines (e.g., danger to self or others) or by statute (e.g., child abuse). In addition, it is important that care be taken in explaining these issues to children who may have diminished capacities. Unfortunately, there is often a difference between the therapist's desire to follow ethical principles and the adherence to those principles. In a recent study of pediatric psychologists, 97% of the psychologists reported that it was ethical to assess the pediatric client's understanding of confidentiality, but in practice 13% "never" or "rarely" assessed it (Rae & Worchel, 1991).

There are several instances when confidential information can be disclosed without the consent of the family. First, information can be disclosed in order to provide needed therapeutic services to the child or family. For example, receptionists, clerks, and secretaries are often privy to confidential information incidental to working in the therapist's office. Second, therapists are allowed to obtain appropriate professional consultations as a way of promoting appropriate patient care. During consultation with other professionals, the therapist must take care only to reveal that information that is relevant to obtaining the consultation. Third, the therapist is allowed to reveal information to insurance companies to facilitate payment of services. The therapist should only reveal the most minimal of information to the insurance companies even though insurance companies often demand more detailed information.

Breaking confidentiality to report child abuse is both a legal and an ethical issue. Although reporting suspicion of abuse is legally mandated in all 50 states, the manner and timing of reporting may be influenced by the consideration of the best interest or welfare of the child and family. In fact, therapists do not always report abusive situations even though it is legally mandated (National Research Council, 1993; Rae & Worchel, 1991). From the therapist's point of view of trying to promote the welfare of the child and family, a delay in reporting abuse can help the family institute steps to be protected from further abuse by the perpetrator. In other cases, the abuse must be reported even though the therapist knows that the therapeutic relationship will be broken. In this case, the therapist may have to transfer the case using appropriate ethical guidelines.

Another area of breaking confidentiality without the client's consent involves disclosing information so as to protect the child and/or family from harm to themselves or others. The therapist must assess the potential of danger to self or others and disclose that information only to appropriate professional workers, public authorities, the potential victim, and/or the family of the client. The therapist must use clinical judgment to evaluate the risk of imminent and serious harm being inflicted. Although most therapists would agree that if a patient or family member has threatened and is able to commit suicide or homicide, then confidentiality must be broken. On the other hand, real-life situations are often less clear-cut; the decision to break confidentiality is influenced by the therapist's values and biases. For example, the clinical judgment of "imminent and serious harm" is defined by each therapist. Some therapists might break confidentiality if an adolescent is engaged in reckless and risky behaviors such as using illicit drugs or alcohol. At the same time, other therapists would not break confidentiality because in doing so the therapeutic alliance would be broken, which might precipitate premature termination of treatment. This variation of opinion for breaking confidentiality for risky behaviors has been illustrated in a survey of pediatric psychologists for such diverse topics as alcohol or drug use, sexual behavior, criminal or illegal behavior, suicidal or homicidal intentions, and child abuse (Rae & Worchel, 1991). It is important that the therapist discuss his or her values and biases during the first session with the child and family prior to the beginning of therapy. In addition, the therapist must be familiar with relevant state statutes and always be ready to consult with legal and professional colleagues (Gustafson & McNamara, 1987).

Therapists are responsible for maintaining appropriate confidentiality in the creation, storage, transfer, and disposal of records. This would include written, recorded, or computerized records. The services the therapist performs must be documented with current and accurate information. The records should have sufficient detail to allow for continuity of treatment if the case is transferred to another therapist. Any documentation (e.g., progress notes, reports, or letters) should only include information that is germane to the purposes of that documentation. This situation often creates a dilemma for the therapist who wants to document thoroughly and accurately, but also is sensitive to the potentially harmful effects to the child or family of revealing this information. For example, the therapist may want to write a detailed progress note, but is concerned that the parents might obtain the note as they have the legal rights to all records. More specifically, if a teenager while experimenting with alcohol got drunk and this incident was documented in the therapy progress note, the parents might learn of this incident if they obtained a copy of the record. In the same way, the minor child or adolescent may also obtain copies of the record when they reach legal majority. Both of these situations could result in countertherapeutic treatment effects for the patient. The therapist must address confidentiality in general during the initiation phase, but more specific issues must be addressed during the therapy.

Multiple Relationships

Therapists should try to avoid multiple or dual relationships with patients and their families. Although it might be difficult in certain situations to avoid social or nonprofessional contacts with current or former patients, therapists must always be cognizant of the problems inherent within these multiple relationships. By engaging in social relationships with patients or their families, the therapist's objectivity could be compromised. This lack of objectivity could lead to ineffective and/or inappropriate therapy. Gottlieb (1993) has described three dimensions of a dual relationship. The first dimension refers to the degree of power the therapist has in relationship to the client. Because of the nature of the therapist–client relationship, a clear power differential exists, which could lead to exploitation. A second dimension refers to the duration of the relationship. A brief therapeutic relationship such as a single session assessment would probably have less potential for negative impact than a long-term therapeutic relationship. The third dimension refers to the clarity of termination and the likelihood that there will be continued contact between the therapist and the client. An implicit trust exists in the psychotherapeutic relationship that the therapist will protect the patient and family against any harm. Even behaviors that might seem innocuous, such as bartering or trading for therapy services, have potential for being overtly or covertly exploitive.

Nowhere is the standard regarding dual relationships so clear as in sexual intimacies with patients or their families. Obviously, sexual intimacy with any minor child or adolescent is not only unethical, it is illegal. In addition, under no circumstances are sexual intimacies ever appropriate with any family member of a current patient. Physical touches such as hugs must be carefully considered in light of the child and family situation (e.g., for the family addressing abuse issues). This same care must be taken in dealing with nonphysical contact as well, such as in asking for a sexual history. Any sexual intimacy with former patients or family members is almost always inappropriate. If sexual intimacies are being considered, there must be no exploitation potential in the relationship. It is recognized that situations could occur (e.g., considering an intimate relationship with an adult sibling of a child who was seen for a learning disability evaluation several years ago) that are potentially not exploitive. The best practice is to avoid sexual involvement with any former client or any client's family member at any time.

Therapist Participation during Child Custody Disputes

When therapists work with children and families in emotional distress, the parents might have significant marital disputes that culminate in divorce proceedings. Often therapists are asked to provide expert advice and/or forensic assessments as to the suitability of one parent over the other for custody of the children. Obviously, a request from one parent to provide that kind of assessment would be inappropriate as the original roles agreed on for the intervention made with both parents would be altered in a way that would not respect the rights of the other individuals (parent and children) in therapy. Therapists must be very careful to avoid role conflicts in any forensic matter. In addition, it is also important to assess any adult or child only with their fully informed consent. It is possible for a former therapist to perform a custody evaluation with the fully informed consent of all parties, but the process of the forensic evaluation would destroy any possibility of a future therapeutic relationship. For example, as the therapist would judge one parent versus another, it would be difficult if not impossible to maintain future trust. Substantive issues are involved in custody evaluations such as who is the client, what kind of therapist–patient privilege might be applicable, and the changing nature of the therapeutic contract. In fact, Melton, Petrila, Poythress, and Slobogin (1997) have written that mental health professionals probably have little expertise that is directly relevant to custody disputes and any opinion about custody given by a therapist of one or both parents is probably inappropriate. The dual role for the therapist performing a custody evaluation should be avoided (Stahl, 1994). The issues involved in custody evaluations are beyond the scope of this chapter, but have been well articulated elsewhere (Practice Directorate, 1994). The reader is advised that specific forensic training should be attained before conducting custody evaluations (Bricklin, 1995; Stahl, 1994).

ETHICAL ISSUES COMMON TO PSYCHOTHERAPY TERMINATION

Terminating Psychotherapy

Three issues must be considered when terminating psychotherapy. First, there is the issue of abandonment. Abandonment is thought to occur when the family is left without an appropriate resource if the therapist discontinues treatment without a formal termination and referral. Even when therapy is terminated in the most responsible and ethical manner, the child may feel that there is a significant loss of an important caregiver. The abrupt termination of services should be avoided, but if it does occur, a plan should already be in place as to how the family will be informed and how the transition to other services can be facilitated.

The second issue occurs when the therapist terminates the professional relationship in the best interest of the patient or family because the therapy is no longer beneficial or might even be harmful. Care must be taken that the termination is therapeutically indicated and that the patient and family have been appropriately advised of the issues for the termination. In addition, the therapist must be sure that appropriate referrals are made at the time of termination. In the case of children, there must be adequate explanation in clear and appropriate language about the termination procedures. For younger children, it is helpful to be clear that they are not responsible for a premature termination. For older children and adolescents, it is helpful to discuss the specifics of the termination procedures. It may also be helpful to discuss what will happen to the relationship after the therapy is terminated. There may be situations where the relationship is not totally severed at termination. For example, an adolescent may want to send a graduation announcement to the therapist who was helping with academic skill development. The nature of the relationship during transition should also be considered. For example, what the family should do if a crisis situation arises before they have seen their new therapist should be addressed. As much as possible, these situations should be anticipated and discussed prior to termination.

The final issue involves the transfer of patients and their families. The therapist is responsible for suggesting alternate service providers, and ensuring that the appropriate information is sent to the provider in a timely manner. Although some of these procedures may be covered by a particular agency or organization, care should be given to facilitate as smooth a transition as possible. In some cases, names and telephone numbers may be provided to the family if the therapist has access to this information. In other cases, such as the family moving to another state or country, the therapist should educate the family on how to find another therapist in general, such as contacting licensing boards, asking related providers such as pediatricians and school counselors, and contacting appropriate agencies that might assist the family.

Continuity of Psychotherapy

The therapist must have a prior plan developed in case therapy services are interrupted. Such issues as the therapist's unavailability, the therapist's incapacity, the patient's relocation, or the patient's financial limitations are issues that should be addressed with a plan developed by the therapist. Death and relocation are usually covered through contracts and agency rules. Illness and unavailability are usually addressed by providing other coverage, and having this arrangement disseminated to the family. For the above situations, explanations and plans should be individualized for each client. For example, if the therapist is out ill for the day, rescheduling the appointment within two days may be appropriate for most families, but may not be appropriate for the family in crisis, and as such, other plans are made. If the client relocates, generally a referral is made, along with an explanation of confidentiality and report issues that are pertinent to that family situation.

In terms of financial limitations of the client, the welfare of the client is the primary consideration. This situation may occur as clients change insurance carriers and therapists change insurance panels. If the situation is anticipated, then plans can be made for transition. It is also recognized that through no fault of the client or the therapist, the financial situation can change with little or no warning. In this type of situation, the welfare of the client is paramount, and arrangements must be made that can address the therapeutic needs of the family, with financial reimbursement a secondary consideration.

RESEARCH ISSUES WITH PSYCHOTHERAPY WITH CHILDREN AND FAMILIES

All therapists must evaluate the effectiveness of their therapy. This evaluation of interventions has become even more important with the advent of managed care; insurance companies will not pay for ineffective treatments. In addition, within the scientist-practitioner model it is expected that therapists will conduct research to empirically validate new treatments. In settings with an institutional mandate for research such as in medical schools and universities, formal research is commonplace and may coexist with a therapist's practice.

Although research issues are covered in Part V of this book, a few comments about research ethics are necessary. Informed consent must always be obtained from research participants. In addition, parents of any minor must give full informed consent to participation. A child must have the research explained in a way that is appropriate for his or her developmental level in order to obtain informed assent. Unfortunately, the therapist might be in a position to unduly influence the family's decision to participate, which could be exploitive. In the same way, the therapist turned researcher may be biased in the decision to include a child or family in their research as the researcher's need to conduct the research might overshadow the therapist's desire to promote the welfare of the family. Children can be easily led by well-intentioned adults (including the therapist) into situations where the child might experience distress or harm. Because of the inherent conflict of a dual relationship, a therapist for a child and family should be very cautious about conducting research with a child or family that is in active treatment with that therapist. A case can be made for certain kinds of nonreactive research such as single case studies or unobtrusive group data analysis, but the therapist must always be cognizant of the potential conflicts of interest and dual relationship potential in such situations.

A thorough discussion of risks and benefits of the research should be undertaken for full consent or assent. Unfortunately, young children do not have the intellectual and reasoning capacity to fully understand the ramifications of their decision or to fully weigh the risks versus the benefits. For these reasons we have argued that no child functioning below the concrete operational Piagetian stage should be a subject in research that has even a minimal risk (Rae & Fournier, 1986). At the same time, the potential benefits must be also weighed, but it is rare in psychosocial research that the benefits would warrant even minimal risk to the child. The well-being of the child and family should be the most important consideration for the therapist who is involved in research.

PROCESS FOR MAKING ETHICAL DECISIONS

Ethical principles are guidelines and not absolute laws for therapist behavior; professional judgment and decision making must be undertaken (Tarvydas, 1998). Fine and Ulrich (1995) suggest that merely having a working knowledge of ethical codes and rules is not enough. The practitioner must have a framework in place for ethical decision making. First, a general ethical framework must be established, which is based on major principles. Second, reasoning is applied based on specific principles derived from the ethical framework. The third level of decision making involves developing specific rules or codes derived from the ethical principles. Finally, the practitioner must make judgments regarding the specific actions that can be taken. This deductive approach is but one method of ethical decision making. In another model, Kitchener (1984) has described an intuitive level of decision making that is based on ethical beliefs about what is right or wrong. She contrasted that with a critical-evaluative approach in which the decision-maker considers three hierarchical and exclusive levels of reasoning, including considering ethical rules, ethical principles, and ethical theory. This inductive approach is seen as helpful in several arenas such as in clinical situations or in the classroom (Zygmond & Boorhem, 1989).

Whether the therapist is more comfortable with a deductive or inductive approach, the therapist must do several things before a good decision can be made. First, the therapist should be self-aware as to his or her own values and beliefs. Because any professional judgment could be influenced by bias, therapists must be keenly aware of how their own ethical decision could be biased. Second, the therapist must have knowledge of the ethical principles and applicable laws that might pertain to the treatment of children and families. In addition, therapists should know the laws and policies in their state pertaining to child and family law (e.g., reporting child abuse, consent for treatment of sexually transmitted diseases for minors). Third, the therapist should create liaisons with other professionals to discuss ethical decisions. Ideally these liaisons might include multidisciplinary professionals including attorneys. Familiarity of the ethical guidelines from other mental health practitioners (e.g., psychiatrists, school counselors, psychologists) is helpful especially when coordinated treatment between mental health professionals is necessary. Therapists should also keep up to date on changes in standards by reading professional journals, going to workshops, and attending inservices. Finally, the therapist should set up policies and procedures that incorporate and apply the highest ethical standards in their practice. Prevention of problem situations can eliminate many ethical dilemmas from occurring. For example, if the child and family have been fully informed about the limits of confidentiality, fewer conflicts will occur if the therapist must break confidentiality.

Despite these practices, issues will arise that demand decision making about ethical issues. Although there are several models to assist in decision making (Arambula, DeKraai, & Sales, 1993; Eberlin, 1995; Koocher & Keith-Spiegel, 1990; Schaefer & Call, 1994; Tarvydas, 1998), common elements may be helpful to the practitioner as follows:

- *Identify the issue or dilemma.* This entails identifying the conditions that contributed to the situation, and identifying the possible outcomes of the situation. It is important to identify the important stakeholders in the situation. It is possible that the problem situation may be covered under an already established procedure. If it is not covered, then the following steps should be considered.
- *Analyze the situation.* Pertinent ethical guidelines and laws should be reviewed. In addition, colleagues should be consulted. Several possible actions may be evident, or there may be only one appropriate to the situation. The potential positive and negative consequences of a decision should be reviewed. In addition, the therapist should consider contextual influences (e.g., institutional pressures) and the therapist should also reflect on the impact of competing personal values. In any case, the therapist has the responsibility to select the best ethical course of action under the circumstances.
- *Implement the decision.* Once the decision has been made, it must be implemented with due deliberation. This includes setting a time line for im-

plementation, contacting relevant people, and documenting what has been done. The speed in implementing a time line will depend on the nature of the ethical dilemma. For example, in an imminent danger to others situation, the therapist may have little time for reflection, and may have to act very quickly. Other situations, such as releasing information to a third party, may allow for more thoughtful deliberation. There may be several people involved in the actions surrounding the decision. At times, other parties may facilitate the decision. For example, in reporting suspected abuse by someone outside the family several years earlier, both parents and the child will need information about what will happen and possible consequences, and with assistance, may be part of the initial report to authorities. Whatever the decision is, documentation is essential, and should include the initial situation, rationale for the decision, what was done, how it was done, who was involved, and the time lines that were followed.

- *Evaluate the decision.* Evaluation is a critical step in any ethical decision and a valuable component of any therapist's practice. By reviewing past ethical decisions, the therapist may be able to improve the quality of future decision making. The therapist should consider if it was the best possible decision under the circumstances and discuss with colleagues ways that the decision could have been improved in the future. The review of ethical decisions is especially important in light of the therapist's personal values that may have contributed to the ethical dilemma. The therapist should also consider what other circumstances could have contributed to the ethical dilemma and be prepared to make changes in practice to prevent or minimize ethical dilemmas in the future.

CONCLUSIONS

Therapy with children and families presents unique challenges for the therapist. The therapist has to communicate at various levels of cognitive understanding so as to match parent and child levels of understanding of the meaning of therapy. Within the family, the therapist must recognize the various relationships and often conflicting needs between family members as well as fully recognizing their relationships outside the family. Because most professional ethical standards and many legal standards were not specifically written for families and children, the quest to practice ethically becomes even more complex.

Continuous quality improvement and professional development are not only hallmarks of good therapeutic practice; they represent a necessity for therapists working with children and families. Updating knowledge and thoughtfully planning for the potential of ethical problems at the initiation, maintenance, and termination of therapy is an important part of any therapy practice. Building a network of colleagues for consultation in ethical decision making is also crucial. The therapist must be able to participate in a reflective decision making process along with collegial debate. Despite the therapist's good intentions and thoughtful anticipation of potential ethical problems, ethical dilemmas will always arise when working with children and families.

REFERENCES

American Association for Marriage and Family Therapy. (1991). *AAMFT code of ethics*. Washington, DC: Author.

American Counseling Association. (1995). American Counseling Association code of ethics and standards of practice. *Counseling Today, 37*, 33–40.

American Mental Health Counseling Association. (1987). *AMHCA code of ethics*. Alexandria, VA: Author.

American Psychiatric Association. (1993). *Principles of medical ethics, with annotations especially applicable to psychiatry*. Washington, DC: Author.

American Psychological Association. (1992). Ethical principles of psychologists and code of conduct. *American Psychologist, 47*, 1597–1611.

American School Counselor Association. (1992). *Ethical standards for school counselors*. Alexandria, VA: Author.

Arambula, D., DeKraai, M., & Sales, B. (1993). Law, children, and therapists. In T. R. Kratochwill & R. J. Morris (Eds.), *Handbook of psychotherapy with children and adolescents* (pp. 583–619). Boston: Allyn & Bacon.

Bricklin, B. (1995). *The custody evaluation handbook: Research-based solutions and applications*. New York: Brunner/Mazel.

Cottone, R. R., & Tarvydas, V. M. (1998). *Ethical and professional issues in counseling*. Englewood Cliffs, NJ: Prentice–Hall.

Eberlin, L. (1995). Introducing ethics to beginning psychologists: A problem-solving approach. In D. N. Bersoff (Ed.), *Ethical conflicts in psychology* (pp. 118–125). Washington, DC: American Psychological Association.

Fine, M. A., & Ulrich, L. P. (1995). Integrating psychology and philosophy in teaching a graduate course in ethics. In D. N. Bersoff (Ed.), *Ethical conflicts in psychology* (pp. 116–117). Washington, DC: American Psychological Association.

Gottlieb, M. C. (1993). Avoiding exploitive dual relationships: A decision-making model. *Psychotherapy, 30*, 41–47.

Gottlieb, M. C. (1995). Ethical dilemmas in change of format and live supervision. In R. H. Mikesell, D. Lusterman, & S. H. McDaniel (Eds.), *Integrating family therapy: Handbook of family psychology and systems theory* (pp. 561–569). Washington, DC: American Psychological Association.

Gustafson, K. E., & McNamara, J. R. (1987). Confidentiality with minor clients: Issues and guidelines for therapists. *Professional Psychology: Research and Practice, 18*, 503–508.

Handelsman, M. M., & Galvin, M. D. (1988). Facilitating informed consent for outpatient psychotherapy: A suggested written format. *Professional Psychology: Research and Practice, 19*, 223–225.

Hare-Mustin, R. T., Marecek, J., Kaplan, A. G., & Liss-Levinson, N. (1995) Rights of clients, responsibilities of therapists. In D. N. Bersoff (Ed.), *Ethical conflicts in psychology* (pp. 305–310). Washington, DC: American Psychological Association.

Keith-Spiegel, P., & Koocher, G. P. (1985). *Ethics in psychology: Professional standards and cases*. New York: Random House.

Kitchener, K. S. (1984). Intuition, critical evaluation and ethical principles: The foundation for ethical decisions in counseling psychology. *Counseling Psychologist, 12*, 43–55.

Koocher, G. P. (1976). A bill of rights for children in psychotherapy. In G. P. Koocher (Ed.), *Children's rights and the mental health professions* (pp. 23–32). New York: Wiley.

Koocher, G. P., & Keith-Spiegel, P. C. (1990). *Children, ethics, and the law: Professional issues and cases*. Lincoln: University of Nebraska Press.

LoCicero, A. (1976) The right to know: Telling children the results of clinical evaluations. In G. P. Koocher (Ed.), *Children's rights and the mental health professions* (pp. 13–21). New York: Wiley.

Margolin, G. (1995). Ethical and legal considerations in marital and family therapy. In D. N. Bersoff (Ed.), *Ethical conflicts in psychology* (pp. 326–334). Washington, DC: American Psychological Association.

Melton, G. B., & Ehrenreich, N. S. (1992). Ethical and legal issues in mental health services for children. In C. E. Walker & M. C. Roberts (Eds.), *Handbook of clinical child psychology* (pp. 1035–1055). New York: Wiley.

Melton, G. B., Petrila, J., Poythress, N. G., & Slobogin, C. (1997). *Psychological evaluations for the courts: A handbook for mental health professionals and lawyers*. New York: Guilford Press.

National Association of Social Workers. (1990). *Code of ethics*. Silver Spring, MD: Author.

National Research Council. (1993). *Understanding child abuse and neglect*. Washington, DC: National Academy Press.

Plotkin, R. (1981). When rights collide: Parents, children, and consent to treatment. *Journal of Pediatric Psychology, 6*, 121–130.

Pope, K. S., & Vetter, V. A. (1992). Ethical dilemmas encountered by members of the American Psychological Association: A national survey. *American Psychologist, 47*, 397–411.

Practice Directorate. (1994). Guidelines for child custody evaluations in divorce proceedings. *American Psychologist, 49*, 677–680.

Rae, W. A. (1992). Common adolescent–parent problems. In C. E. Walker & M. C. Roberts (Eds.), *Handbook of clinical child psychology* (pp. 555–564). New York: Wiley.

Rae, W. A., & Fournier, C. J. (1986). Ethical issues in pediatric research: Preserving psychosocial care in scientific inquiry. *Children's Health Care, 14*, 242–248.

Rae, W. A., & Worchel, F. F. (1991). Ethical beliefs and behaviors of pediatric psychologists: A survey. *Journal of Pediatric Psychology, 16*, 727–745.

Rae, W. A., Worchel, F. F., & Brunnquell, D. (1995). Ethical and legal issues in pediatric psychology. In M. C. Roberts (Ed.), *Handbook of pediatric psychology* (pp. 19–36). New York: Guilford Press.

Schaefer, A. B., & Call, J. A. (1994). Legal and ethical issues. In R. A. Olson, L. L. Mullins, J. B. Gillman, & J. M. Chaney (Eds.), *The sourcebook of pediatric psychology* (pp. 405–413). Boston: Allyn & Bacon.

Stahl, P. M. (1994). *Conducting child custody evaluations*. Newbury Park, CA: Sage.

Tarvydas, V. M. (1998). Ethical decision-making process. In R. R. Cottone & V. M. Tarvydas (Eds.), *Ethical and professional issues in counseling* (pp. 144–155). Englewood Cliffs, NJ: Prentice–Hall.

Task Force on the Promotion and Dissemination of Psychological Procedures (1995, Winter). Training in and dissemination of empirically-validated psychological treatments: Report and recommendations. *The Clinical Psychologist, 48*, 3–23.

Weithorn, L. (1982). Developmental factors and competence to make informed treatment decisions. *Child and Youth Services, 5*, 85–100.

Zygmond, M. J., & Boorhem, H. (1989). Ethical decision making in family therapy. *Family Process, 28*, 269–280.

Part II

Basic Theoretical Approaches

5

Psychodynamic Psychotherapy

PETER FONAGY

THEORETICAL BACKGROUND

What Is Psychodynamic Psychotherapy?

Psychodynamic psychotherapy covers a wide range of treatment approaches: from child psychoanalysis (Sandler, Kennedy, & Tyson, 1980), through once-weekly individual therapy (Kernberg, 1995), group implementation (Rose, 1972), family-based implementations (Selvini Palazzoli, Boscolo, Cecchin, & Prata, 1978) and many others. Psychodynamic therapies in themselves differ in terms of the use made of expressive versus supportive techniques (Luborsky, 1984), the emphasis placed on play (Schaefer & Cangelosi, 1993; Simon, 1992), or drama (Johnson, 1982). In addition, there are major theoretical divisions that overlap in part with issues of technique originating from different understandings of the nature of development and psychopathology (King & Steiner, 1991).

Psychodynamic approaches, however, share an understanding of psychological abnormality as being a consequence of conflicting motivational states. Such states are often seen to be unconscious and the conflict created seems to be intrapsychic (e.g., Brenner, 1982). It is not invariably the case that approaches emphasizing interpersonal rather than intrapsychic conflicts have been gaining ground in contemporary psychodynamic theorization (Klerman, Weissman, Ronsaville-Chevron, & Chevrones, 1984). Psychodynamic treatment is considered to be therapeutic by the assisting of individuals to build on their inherent capacities for understanding and emotional responsiveness. This is facilitated by a therapeutic relationship, and in particular by the therapist's communication of her understanding of the patient's conflicting motivations and responses to these conflicts. (For reasons of simplicity, therapists will be referred to generically as

PETER FONAGY • The Anna Freud Centre, London NW3 5SD, England; Sub-Department of Clinical Health Psychology, University College London, London WC1E 6BT, England; and Child and Family Center for Outcomes Research and Effectiveness, Menninger Foundation, Topeka, Kansas 66601.

Handbook of Psychotherapies with Children and Families, edited by Russ and Ollendick. Kluwer Academic/Plenum Publishers, New York, 1999.

"she" and patients as "he.") Via such intervention the patient may be enabled to arrive at more adaptive solutions than the rather limited strategies that brought him to seek psychological help.

Theoretical Frameworks in Psychodynamic Therapy

Psychodynamic approaches to the treatment of children are based on a heterogeneous set of theories. Freud's original developmental formulations (Freud, 1905) suggest that the child is constitutionally predisposed to an inevitably partially successful struggle to adapt his sexual and aggressive instincts to the demands of a civilized society. Freud (1933) paints a picture of the child as an individual in turmoil, in a constant struggle to master biological needs and make these acceptable to the external world, or rather society at large. The drama takes place universally in the development of every human being within the microcosm of the family (Freud, 1930).

Over a period of 45 years of psychoanalytic writing, Freud's thinking gradually moved away from a position where he saw psychological problems as arising out of suppressed emotions gaining expression through symptomatology, to an increasingly complex view, where the counterbalance of psychological forces within the mind was seen as the critical aspect of psychological adaptation. In his last full formulation (the so-called "structural" model) (Freud, 1923), Freud envisioned three psychic agencies: (1) instinctual, principally sexual and aggressive energies located within the *id;* (2) a moral coda encoded within the *superego;* and (3) adaptive mechanisms organized within the *ego.* He elaborated a complex model whereby normal adaptation could be seen as the harmonious functioning of these agencies, whereas psychological abnormality invariably reflected a breakdown of the ego's capacity to respond to the demands of the id, the superego, and the external environment.

U.S. ego psychology, particularly the work of Heinz Hartmann (1939/1958), was highly successful in elaborating the model. Hartmann, and other ego psychologists, were the first to clearly delineate how adverse experiences in early development may jeopardize the development of mental structures essential to adequate adaptation. Ego psychologists were also able to be more specific about how the reactivation of early developmental structures (ego regression) was an important component of most psychopathology (Hartmann, 1955/1964).

Freud's daughter, Anna Freud, was strongly influenced by these psychological ideas of the North American psychoanalytic tradition, although her practice was in London, England. Her major contribution was in linking normal emotional development to diagnosable psychopathology (Freud, 1965). She charted normal development along a series of "developmental lines" and made the powerful suggestion that equilibrium between developmental processes was a key aspect of normal development. A child whose environment selectively compromised some but not other developmental processes was considered at risk of maladjustment and psychopathology. Her vision of the relationship of development and psychopathology lies, conceptually at least, at the heart of the new, integrative discipline of developmental psychopathology (e.g., see Sroufe, 1990).

While Anna Freud elaborated her father's work, particularly in the context of the child's relationship to external reality (e.g., see Goldstein, Freud, & Solnit, 1973), other psychodynamic thinkers focused on the potentially conflictual aspects of intrapersonal development. Margaret Mahler (1968), for example, drew attention to a paradoxical aspect of self development. She pointed out that the achievement of an independent identity, on which Western civilization places such high value, brings with it the sacrifice of a gratifying and intimate relationship with the primary caregiver. She observed that parents varied in their capacity to facilitate the child's achievement of "individuation." She suggested that the failure to develop a separate coherent sense of self may be rooted in the caregiver's reaction to the toddler. Rather than supporting the child's independence, the caregiver shows a tendency to withdraw from the child, as the child manifests early signs of independence (Masterson, 1972; Rinsley, 1977). The ego psychological model was further elaborated by Edith Jacobson (1964) and Joseph Sandler (1987). Both of these theoreticians suggested a move away from the mechanistic psychological model suggested by Freud to a model far more compatible with modern cognitive neuroscience. These models deemphasize the biologically rooted notions of drives and instincts and replace these with constructs such as wishes and the role of representational structures in the child's mind and how these might mediate both reality and its distortion associated with internal conflict.

In the meantime, in the United Kingdom a completely different approach to psychodynamic theory grew out of the work of Melanie Klein (Klein, Heimann, Isaacs, & Riviere, 1946). One of her fundamental postulates was the assumption of two radically different modes of mental functioning. The first, *the paranoid-schizoid position,* described the state of mind (prototypically in the human infant) that was incapable of tolerating simultaneous loving and destructive feelings toward his love object and dealt with the conflict by splitting, that is, creating separate images of the loved and the hated figure. With cognitive development, this inevitably leads to what Klein called *the depressive position,* when the child recognizes that the object he loved and the one he hated are one and the same. Klein's original ideas met with considerable skepticism because of the extravagant assumption she was ready to make about the cognitive capacities of infants which were incompatible with the then state of developmental knowledge. More recently, developmental research has confirmed many of Klein's claims (Gergely, 1992), such as those concerning the perception of causality (Bower, 1989) and causal reasoning (Golinkoff, Hardig, Carlson, & Sexton, 1984). Her ideas rapidly became popular, principally because of the helpfulness of her clinical observations. For example, she proposed the notion of *projective identification* to account for the common experience of therapists that patients can exert significant influence over their state of mind. Working within a Kleinian framework, a number of psychoanalysts have elaborated ideas on how early emotional conflict may impact on the child's developing cognitive capacities (e.g., Bion, 1962; Rosenfeld, 1971/1988). Klein believed that projection was the most basic mechanism available to children to deal with destructiveness. They struggle to rid themselves of their destructive fantasies by placing them onto other persons. It is only through the therapist's interpretive work, particularly of such destructive fantasies, that children are enabled to reclaim disowned aspects of themselves and allow for the development of a less malevolent and more realistic appraisal of others.

Early development was also the focus of another extremely important strand of psychoanalytic thought, namely, that of the British object relations theorists. Foremost among these was Fairbairn (1952) who shifted theoretical emphasis from the satisfaction of biological desires to the individual's need for the other. Working in this tradition, and also influenced by Melanie Klein, Donald Winnicott (1965) proposed a number of fundamental psychodynamic developmental notions such as *primary maternal preoccupation,* the *mirroring* function of the caregiver, and the *transitional space* in development between fusion and separateness within which symbolic thought and play were considered to be rooted. Most recent studies offer support for Winnicott's assertions concerning the traumatic consequences of early maternal failure, particularly maternal depression (e.g., see Cummings & Davies, 1994).

Probably influenced by the work of Winnicott, Heinz Kohut (1977) rekindled the interest of psychoanalysts in North America in the interpersonal aspects of early development. The caregiver's role is seen as one of mirroring and the goal of development is one of achieving a coherent sense of self. If the caregiver is able to become a "selfobject," empathically attuned to the infant's or young child's mental states, the child's sense of personhood will be firmly established. Within a self psychology, drive theory took secondary importance. Kohut (1971) suggested that the dominance of drives were themselves indications of the child's failure to have attained an integrated self structure which would normally adequately regulate drive states. Kohut's formulations concerning narcissistic personality structures have been highly influential and helpful in extending the applicability of psychodynamic approaches from the strictly neurotic to the so-called character disorder spectrum of disorders.

A similar extension of the application of psychodynamic concepts may be attributed to the work of Otto Kernberg (Kernberg, 1976, 1987). Kernberg followed Jacobson and Sandler in seeing the mind as principally a representational organ. He postulated the existence of relationship representations consisting of self, object, and affect which characterize the specific relationship. Kernberg reconceptualized the theory of drives, seeing these as developmental achievements, integrations of multiple *triadic self–object–affect representations.* While in neurotic cases the integration achieved is relatively complete, in personality disorder the self and other representations are only partial and infused with overwhelming and extreme emotional states of both ecstasy and persecutory terror and aggression. Kernberg's ideas have been enormously influential in psychoanalytic thinking and are particularly helpful because they lend themselves relatively well to operationalization and empirical study.

Sharing the virtue of openness to empirical scrutiny is John Bowlby's proposal of attachment theory (Bowlby, 1969,1I973, 1980). Bowlby's ideas placed primary emphasis on the earliest relationship within which safety and predictability must be experienced in order for the child to acquire a capacity for relatively problem-free later interpersonal relationships. Bowlby assumes that representational systems, *internal working models,* evolve based on a template created by the earliest relationship of the infant to the caregiver. If the expectancy of need and distress being met by comforting is encoded into these models, the child will be able to approach relationships in a relatively undefensive way. If this is not the case, if the child's caregivers lacked sensitivity (Ainsworth, Blehar, Waters, & Wall, 1978), the child's representational system will be defensively distorted so as to either minimize or heighten experiences of arousal and dismiss or become entangled in the response of others (Main, Kaplan, & Cassidy, 1985).

Daniel Stern (1985) took a novel approach to the psychoanalytic study of childhood. His description is exceptional in being normative rather than pathomorphic and prospective rather than retrospective. His main concern, as that of Kohut, is the development of a coherent self structure. His psychoanalytic model, however, has much in common with Sandler's representational theory as well as Kernberg's focus on the affective aspect of early relationships.

As this brief overview of current psychoanalytic models should indicate, there is no agreed-upon formulation that is shared by all psychoanalytic schools. In fact, intense controversy, such as that between Melanie Klein and Anna Freud in the 1940s and 1950s (King & Steiner, 1991), often characterizes psychoanalytic theoretical discussion. Nevertheless, more recently there has been considerable cross-fertilization of ideas and an integrated psychodynamic model may not be too far away (e.g., see Pine, 1985). There is also an increased emphasis on behavioral research (Emde & Fonagy, 1997), which, in turn, may facilitate the emergence of a core set of psychodynamic theoretical assumptions well supported by empirical data.

Basic Assumptions in Psychodynamic Therapy

Notwithstanding the theoretical heterogeneity of psychoanalytically based therapeutic approaches, there are probably a core set of assumptions to which all psychodynamic therapists would, to a greater or lesser extent, subscribe. These can be basically summarized as follows.

1. *The notion of psychological causation.* This is not an assumption concerning the psychogenic nature of psychological disturbance, but rather refers to the preferred level of conceptualization for psychodynamic clinicians. Whether psychological problems are genetically or socially determined, psychodynamic therapists assume that the representation of past experience, its interpretation and its meaning, whether conscious or unconscious, determine children's reaction to the external world and their capacity or lack of capacity to adapt to it. This formulation does not imply lack of respect for other levels of analysis of childhood psychological problems, the biological, the sociocultural, or the systemic. Rather, psychological difficulties are conceived of as meaningful organizations of a child's conscious or unconscious beliefs, thoughts, and feelings and therefore they are assumed to be accessible to psychotherapeutic intervention.

2. *The assumption of unconscious mental processes.* Psychodynamic clinicians assume that the explanation of conscious ideation and intentional behavior requires the assumption of complex mental processes functioning outside of awareness. Although psychodynamic clinicians probably no longer think in terms of "an unconscious," in the sense of a physical space where forbidden or repudiated feelings and ideas are stored, they assume that nonconscious fantasies associated with wishes for gratification or safety, profoundly influence children's behavior, their capacity to regulate affect and to adequately handle their social environment.

3. *The assumption of a representational model of the mind.* In common with cognitive scientists, psychodynamic therapists assume that the experience of self with others is internalized, and forms the basis for relatively enduring representational structures of social and interpersonal interactions. These representational structures determine interpersonal expectations and shape the mental representation of the self.

4. *The pathogenic significance of conflict.* Intrapsychic conflict (incompatible wishes, affects, or ideas) is assumed to be ubiquitous in development. It is seen as the cause of displeasure as well as an absence of safety. Adverse environments tend to intensify conflicts as well as undermine the development of capacities that may help the child in dealing with conflictual aspects of ordinary life. For example, the loss of a caregiver or severe neglect or abuse may aggravate a natural predisposition to relate with mixed feelings to the caregiver, as well as reducing the child's competence in resolving such incompatible ideas.

5. *The assumption of psychic defenses.* It is assumed that children rapidly develop an unconscious capacity to modify unacceptable or dangerous ideas, desires, or affects by resorting to a set of mental operations that have in common the function of distorting these mental states in a direction of reducing their capacity to generate anxiety, distress or displeasure. As all mental operations, defenses have a developmental or maturational hierarchy. More complex defenses, such as intellectualization or humor, come into effect relatively late in development or perhaps never. Simpler processes such as projection, denial, or splitting are available to the child from a relatively early stage.

6. *The assumption of complex meanings.* Psychodynamic therapists assume that children's communication within the treatment context has meanings beyond that intended by the child. Likewise, children's symptoms might carry multiple meanings reflecting the nature of the children's internal representations of themselves and others. Within a classical formulation, symptoms express a combination of a wish as well as the children's attempt to erect a defensive, self-protective set of mental operations to protect themselves from that wish. The therapist's task is to make appropriate links between the child's behaviors in different contexts so as to show the child that the behavior that is seemingly bizarre, confusing, frightening, or even self-destructive has a meaningful and even rational facet when looked at from a different perspective or in a different context. Elaborating and clarifying such meaning structures may be seen as the essence of psychodynamic psychotherapy.

7. *The assumption of transference displacement.* It is generally accepted that internalized representations of interpersonal relationships that determine the child's behavior with others in the outside world, also become active in the context of the therapeutic relationship. The displacement of patterns of expectation from important others in the child's life to the therapist serves as a window on the child's internal world. This function becomes all the more important because the relative neutrality and ambiguity of the therapeutic relationship encourages externalizations of repudiated aspects of past relationships (Tyson & Tyson, 1986). The situation becomes more complicated because the child's verbal and nonverbal behavior must naturally have an impact on the therapist's experience. However, modern psychodynamic therapists tend to make extensive use of their subjective reactions to help them understand the roles that they are implicitly asked by the child to play. In this way the therapist is able to gain a view of the child's internal struggles and representations of both themselves and others.

8. *The therapeutic aspect of the relationship.* Psychodynamic therapists assume that, in addition to new understanding and insight that the child might gain through the experience of therapy, aspects of the relationship with a supportive and respectful empathic adult will also have benefits for the child's functioning.

In particular, the therapist's interest in the child's mental states, talk and play, thoughts and feelings, and the therapist's commitment to find meaning even in the disruptive or distressing aspects of the child's behavior provides him with an opportunity to reflect on and reorganize experiences and identify more adaptive solutions to the interpersonal and intrapsychic conflicts he faces.

The Evolution of Psychodynamic Child Psychotherapy

Freud was an acute observer of the behavior of young children. He used his observations to support and elaborate his assumptions about infantile mental processes (e.g., see Freud, 1900, 1909, 1920, 1926). Although these observations were detailed and accurate, he was skeptical about their value in clinical work with psychologically disordered children. It was Hug-Helmuth (1920) who first used the play of children as part of an insight-oriented technique. She saw the child's play in a therapeutic context as providing insight into the child's unconscious sexual fantasies, which could then be interpreted.

The true originators of psychodynamic psychotherapy for children were Anna Freud (1946) and Melanie Klein (1932). They evolved somewhat different, yet in important ways compatible, approaches that enabled psychodynamic clinicians to work with children. Klein's approach was based on the assumption that children's play was essentially the same as the free association of adults. She saw such play as motivated by unconscious fantasies activated principally by specific aspects of the relationship with the therapist. It therefore required interpretation, or at least clarification, if the child's anxiety was to be addressed by the therapist. The principal focus of Klein's therapeutic work was the interpretation of the child's deeply unconscious concerns related to destructive and sadistic impulses. Klein was exclusively concerned with the unconscious aspects of the child's behavior in the therapeutic setting and had minimal interest in other aspects of the child's life, such as the child's relationship with his parents or other adults.

At the heart of the Kleinian psychotherapeutic technique is the notion of projection. Projection is considered by Klein (1946, 1952/1975) as an unconscious fantasy placing part of the child's self into another person and obtaining a degree of relief from experiencing unwanted feelings as no longer belonging to the self. This leads to a form of fragmentation of the self (the paranoid-schizoid position) that, while normal in infancy, may cause significant pathology later in life. The transference is seen by Kleinian therapists as central to interpretive work, as it is the unwanted projected aspects of the child's experience of himself that need to be reintegrated in order to achieve therapeutic benefit.

Kleinian technique with children has changed considerably since the early days. Modern Kleinians (e.g., DeFolch, 1988; O'Shaughnessy, 1988) would not frequently give direct interpretations of deeply unconscious material. Bion (1959) emphasized the importance of "containment," that is, the therapist's capacity to understand and accept the child's projections. This may be critical in normal development (in the caregiver) as well as in the therapist's experience of the countertransference.

Anna Freud's approach was deeply rooted in the developmental context of the child's efforts to achieve a reasonable adaptation to a social and an internal environment. She was reluctant to make assumptions concerning the meaning of the child's play and, in comparison with Melanie Klein, approached the work of interpretation far more gradually. She worked in close collaboration with both parents and teachers. She assumed that changes in the child's environment brought about by communicating to carers an understanding of the child's problems derived from therapy, might have equal if not greater long term benefit for the child's functioning. Her emphasis was on conflicts arising from the child's sexual impulses rather than, as was Klein's, on innate aggression. The essential aspect of her technique was the interpretation of the child's strategies of adapting to conflict, the interpretation of defense, and only through this the anxieties that brought them into play. The therapeutic goal is less the achievement of the integration of a fragmented sense of self and object, but rather the developmental goal of returning the child to a normal path of maturation. Consequently, she was far more accepting of supportive and educational techniques to address the child's poorly developed ego functions (Pine, 1985).

The third important strand in the development of psychodynamic technique originates in the work of Donald Winnicott (1965, 1971). Although influenced by Klein in his model of childhood pathology, his technique, in common with Anna Freud, emphasized the importance of a holding environment as well as the importance of play. Play was seen, not simply as a vehicle for communicating unconscious fantasy, but as an activity that is uniquely generative of human development. A major contribution of Winnicott is his description of a "transitional space" between self and object where the subjective object and the truly objective other could be simultaneously seen (Winnicott, 1971). This duality of representation created an important bridge between psychodynamic thinking and interpersonalist approaches such as that of Sullivan (1953). Within the interpersonal approach the therapist becomes an active and real participant in the therapeutic situation (Altman, 1992, 1994; Warshaw, 1992).

These trends evolved to some degree independently in different parts of the world. Whereas Kleinian thinking dominated the United Kingdom and, to some degree, Latin America, it was the work of Anna Freud that was most readily integrated into psychodynamic ideas in the United States and some parts of Europe. More recently, interpersonal approaches to psychodynamic therapy have taken hold in many treatment centers in the United States motivated partly by self-psychological Kohutian therapeutic orientation as well as the integration of Winnicottian object relations approaches. There has also been considerable cross-fertilization of psychoanalytic psychodynamic techniques, even in the more committed Kleinian (e.g., Alvarez, 1993) and Anna Freudian (e.g., Bleiberg, Fonagy, & Target, 1997) traditions.

CURRENT PSYCHODYNAMIC PSYCHOTHERAPY

The Selection of Clients for Psychodynamic Therapy

Traditionally psychodynamic therapists work with relatively less severely disturbed young people. The criteria of suitability for psychodynamic psychotherapy have been identified by Glenn (1978), Hoffman (1993), Sandler and colleagues (1980), and others as the following:

1. Good verbal skills and psychological mindedness, that is, the ability to conceive of behavior as mediated by mental states (thoughts and feelings). Equally important here is the child's capacity to tolerate awareness of conflicts and anxieties, particularly those previously kept unconscious, without risking substantial disorganization or disintegration of the personality.
2. A supportive environment that is able to sustain the child's involvement in an intense and demanding long-term interpersonal relationship. Particularly important here is the willingness of parents to respect the boundaries of the child's therapy and promote the child's commitment to the treatment.
3. It is assumed that successful treatment depends on internal conflicts being the cause of the child's disturbance.
4. Further, traditionally psychotherapists were reluctant to treat children with major developmental deficits (ego deviations) that were not the result of unconscious conflict and therefore could not be seen as resolvable through insight.
5. As the child's motivation for treatment stems from anxiety, guilt, or other unpleasant affects, these experiences are often seen as essential to ensuring the child's commitment to the treatment as well as a sense of agency (a sense of responsibility for their problems and actions).
6. It is assumed that a capacity to form relationships and develop trust must be present for psychodynamic therapy to operate.

The above description corresponds to what has traditionally been referred to as *neurotic disturbance.* For example, Tyson (1992) describes neurosis as characterized by (1) a predominance of internalized conflicts producing symptoms, (2) a capacity for affect regulation, and (3) a capacity for self-responsibility. Kernberg (1975) has added to this list the predominance of repression as a mechanism of defense. However, *neurosis* is a term largely discredited in modern descriptive psychiatry as lacking in clarity and reliability and probably also overinclusive and based on an outmoded theory of psychological disorder. There is evidently a group of children commonly treated by psychodynamic psychotherapy who do not meet the criteria as described above. We have described this group in our retrospective examination of case records at the Anna Freud Centre (Fonagy & Target, 1996a,c). Other descriptions by Bleiberg (1987, 1994a), Cohen, Towbin, Mayes, and Volkmar (1994), and Towbin, Dykens, Pearson, and Cohen (1993) have arrived at strikingly similar descriptions. This group of children appear to suffer from a variety of deficiencies of psychological capacities, indicated for example by lack of control over affect, lack of stable self and other representations, and diffusion of their sense of identity.

Whereas the two groups may be readily distinguished in terms of descriptive criteria, elsewhere we have tentatively suggested a conceptual framework that may help provide theoretically based psychodynamic distinction (Fonagy, Edgcumbe, Moran, Kennedy, & Target, 1993). In this model we distinguish children whose problems may be seen as a consequence of distortion in *mental representations,* either of others or of themselves. Such distorted representations may arise out of exceptional environmental factors or defensive distortions associated with various forms of intrapsychic conflict. Broadly speaking, these children correspond to what has traditionally been regarded as the neurotic category. By contrast, children with more severe problems who usually present with multiple disorders, low levels of adaptation, and poor personality functioning may be seen as suffering from defensive inhibition or distortion of *mental processes* rather than just the mental representations that such processes generate. Thus, for this group of children a wide variety of situations are likely to bring about maladaptive functioning as the very capacities that may be involved in achieving adaptive functioning are impaired. It is important to note that while biological factors may play an important role in both types of pathology, in both cases the focus on psychological causation is retained. For example, inhibitions on specific ways of thinking occur as attempts at adaptation.

There are important considerations from the point of view of psychotherapeutic technique that arise out of this distinction. Disorders of mental representation are well served by a primarily interpretive therapeutic process that aims at addressing distorted ideas and integrating repudiated or incoherent notions of self and other. The reintegration of split-off (repressed), often infantile but troublesome ideas, into the child's developmentally appropriate mental structures is the therapeutic aim (Abrams, 1988). In the more severely disturbed group of patients, this kind of approach has limited usefulness. There is a need for strengthening or disinhibiting mental processes that may have been disengaged (decoupled) or distorted for defensive or constitutional biological reasons. These patients may, for example, need assistance in labeling and verbalizing affects and ideas. Much of psychodynamic intervention aimed at the so-called neurotic patient may change the organization or the shape of the child's mental representation (Sandler & Rosenblatt, 1962). To regenerate mental processes, an alternative set of psychodynamic techniques, emphasizing a developmental approach, are necessary. Our review of current therapeutic approaches will be based around this distinction.

Therapeutic Approaches Addressing Disorders of Mental Representation

It follows from the assumptions of psychodynamic psychotherapy reviewed above that child therapists using these techniques expect children to be using distorted and/or unconscious mental representations in maladaptive ways. For example, the child may unconsciously represent his father as cruel and rageful, a representation distorted by the child's unconscious aggression. Further, it is anticipated that these distortions have a developmental dimension whereby ideas or feelings are more appropriate to an earlier stage of development and are likely to confuse the child's current perceptions (Abrams, 1988). The separation (repression, denial, displacement) of such early ideas is assumed to be defensive. For example, the perception of a caregiver as cruel and destructive may be based on an infantile perception of that parent. As a consequence of the pain associated with this perception of a loving father, this representation never came to be integrated into the evolving representation of the father in the child's mind. It exists as a separate, yet disturbing idea. The child may react to the presence of such a representation as potentially painful and incompatible with his perception of his parent as loving and affectionate. By displacing this perception onto others whom he then perceives as frightening, he may, for example, exaggerate the subjective likelihood of burglars or other intruders attacking him and his family. Of course, if such ideas are based on the externalization of his own aggressive feelings toward the father, then it is these feelings that have to be addressed in the context of the therapy.

The therapist, using the child's verbalization, nonverbal play, dream reports, or other behaviors, attempts to create a model of the child's conscious and unconscious thoughts and feelings. On the basis of such a model the therapist assists the child to acquire an understanding of his irrational or at times inappropriate feelings and beliefs. This kind of understanding may, under ideal conditions, result in the integration of developmentally earlier modes of thinking into a more mature and age-appropriate framework. The structure of the treatment appears to be relatively unimportant. Some therapists use toys or games, others more readily engage children in a process of self exploration. In most contexts the therapist works to draw attention to possible unconscious determinants of the child's behavior. Therapists tend to use material of the child's fantasy and play in conjunction with other information they have obtained about the child (e.g., parental reports, school reports) to construct a plausible picture of the child's emotional concerns. The most common foci of psychodynamic child therapists tend to be the child's concerns about his body, anxieties about conscious or unconscious destructive or sexual impulses, and concerns about relationships with or between caregivers or siblings or peers.

A range of techniques are standardly used by psychodynamic therapists. These have been systematized on the basis of empirical studies by Paulina Kernberg (1995) who observed a number of somewhat overlapping but reliably distinguishable categories of interventions. These include:

1. *Supportive interventions* aimed at reducing the child's anxiety or increasing his sense of competence and mastery using suggestion, reassurance, empathy, or the provision of information.
2. *Summary statements* or paraphrases of the child's communication to that point that support and develop the therapeutic exchange with the child.
3. *Clarifications* of the child's verbalization or affect. These help prepare the child for interpretation or simply direct his attention to noticeable aspects of his behavior such as a repeated tendency to behave in self-defeating, self-destructive ways.
4. *Interpretations* attempt to identify and spell out representations that the child is likely not to be aware of and therefore is likely to find difficult or totally unacceptable. It is thus expected that the child will show a certain degree of resistance to such verbalizations on the part of the therapist. Interpretations have to be carefully timed to maximize their acceptability to the child. Ideally the therapist would have accumulated considerable evidence to support her conjectures making their acceptance more or less automatic.

In formulating an interpretation, the therapist is well advised to concentrate her attention on the therapeutic situation itself where evidence is most likely to become available. Although the therapist may often be able to identify significant connections between the child's behavior in therapy and what the therapist knows about the child's past experience, interpretations, at least in the early phase of treatment, are best restricted to the child's current conflicts, in the immediate context brought into the therapy. The ultimate aim of the therapist is to provide the child with an emotionally meaningful comprehensive understanding of the connections between past experiences and current methods of coping with conflict.

Kernberg (1995) distinguishes between three kinds of interpretation: (1) interpretations addressing repudiated wishes, (2) interpretations of defense, and (3) reconstructive interpretations. The first of these draws the child's attention to actual exclusion of certain ideas from awareness. This focuses attention on certain contents but also invites the child to consider alternative strategies for coping with or expressing these ideas or feelings. The second kind of interpretation generally aims to explain the child's behavior in terms of a putative nonconscious wish. Most frequently, the need for defense is explained in terms of the presence of an unconscious wish. For example, the therapist might say: "I think you tend to forget your dreams because in these dreams you are able to think about how angry you feel with your father and that you wish to punish him in cruel ways for how he has treated you."

Reconstructive interpretations aim not only to explain a current state of affairs in the child's mind, but also to give an account of how this may have come about. The reconstruction of early experience in this context is somewhat controversial. While psychodynamically oriented psychotherapists frequently assume that the representation that the child constructs of them is powerfully influenced by the child's prior experiences with caregivers, it does not by any means invariably follow that these experiences find direct expression in such representations. For example, a child might see the therapist as a critic who persistently undermines the child's sense of confidence and well-being. He is thus evidently externalizing an internal representational figure who constantly bombards the self with disparagement and criticism. Such a representation may well be the product of defensive maneuvers rather than an indication of the presence of a severely critical adult figure in the child's past. Thus, the therapist might safely interpret that "I think you are worried about my criticizing you because there is a voice inside your head that constantly says that you are such a naughty child that nobody could love you." It would probably be unwise to assume, however, that such a critical figure was actually part of the child's earlier experience. Such an "internal object" is more likely to be a split part of the child's self representation that may indeed be based on the internalization of an actually destructive and aggressive caregiver, or it may be a disowned destructive or aggressive part of the child, separated off precisely because the perceived kindness of the actual parent made such aggressive impulses seem totally unacceptable and intolerable to the child. In either case what needs to be addressed in reconstructive interpretations is how unacceptable a child finds even a small amount of residual aggression and destructiveness that has remained as part of the self structure; for example, the unacceptability of such feelings toward the therapist/father and how the child's anxieties about, say, burglars link to his image of father responding to his angry feelings. Through verbalization of these defensive aspects, the child is gradually able to modify his internal standards for acceptable ideas and feelings and take on board the destructive aggression as part of his self representation leading to greater integration and flexibility in his psychic functioning.

Thus, the therapists' interventions tend mostly to combine a focus on defenses, wishes, and past or current experience. What all such interventions have in common is a focus on the child's emotional experience in relation to these domains. The therapeutic action of psychoanalytic psychotherapy is assumed to be "work in the transference" (Strachey, 1934). The child's interaction with the therapist becomes increasingly invested with affect as the therapy progresses, as internal representations of relationships find expression in the relationship with the therapist. "Working through," helping the child to understand his reactions to the therapist in terms of anxieties, conflicts, and defenses, is regarded as the essence of therapeutic work. The development of the transference is facilitated by (1) the therapist's neutrality, (2) emotional availability (attunement to the child's predicament), (3) encouragement to freely express thoughts and feelings, (4) the regularity and consistency of the therapeutic structure, and (5) the child's underlying perception of the therapist as a benign figure (Chethik, 1989). The transference relationship offers a window on both the nature of the child's relationship with the caregiver, as experienced by the child, and aspects of the child's experience of himself—particularly those aspects that the child experiences as unacceptable and wishes quickly to externalize onto the figure of the therapist. The role in which she finds herself, enables the therapist to learn about the child's internal world. Distorted mental representations are identified, clarified, and understood and ideally reintegrated with the mature aspects of the child's thinking (Abrams, 1988).

For example, shy, frightened, and withdrawn, a boy, aged 8, who was referred because of his depression, developed an exceptionally acrimonious relationship with his therapist. The therapist frequently found herself shamed and ridiculed, endlessly failing in the tasks set by the child, accused of being stupid and so on. The child simultaneously bullied and patronized the therapist. The therapist gently showed the child how he often considered himself not to be good enough and placed himself in situations where this would be all too evident. Gradually the idea was presented that being insignificant and "no good" was preferable (safer) as it avoided the even more unpleasant possibility of observing that the therapist or his parents might be disappointed with him. Eventually, the problem was traced back to his guilt feelings about his sadistic aggressive feelings toward his younger brother whose birth precipitated his depressive episode.

Termination of the treatment is signaled by (1) symptomatic improvement, (2) improved family and peer relationships, (3) the ability to take advantage of normal developmental opportunities, (4) the ability to deal with new environmental stressors, and (5) the ability to use the therapy more effectively (experience the therapy as helpful, allow the therapist's interpretive work to continue, express feelings more readily, show gratitude as well as criticism and anger, show insight, humor, and healthy self-mockery, and so on) (Kernberg, 1995). "Traditional" psychodynamic treatment of this sort is rarely prolonged; much may be achieved in once-weekly meetings over 1 year, although treatment length is generally 18 months to 2 years (Fonagy & Target, 1996c).

Therapeutic Approaches Addressing Disorders of Mental Processes

Not all childhood disorders respond readily to psychotherapeutic intervention. Diagnostically these children are often categorized as narcissistic, borderline or severely conduct disordered and delinquent. Over recent decades the psychodynamic approach has been extended to these children as well (e.g., see Bleiberg, 1987, 1994a,b; Marohn, 1991; Rinsley, 1989). Although from a psychodynamic perspective most children with so-called neurotic disorders may be understood in terms of distortions of mental representations of either self or other (Sandler & Rosenblatt, 1962), the distorted ideas with which more severely disturbed children tend to present cannot be readily addressed solely by interpretive psychotherapeutic work. Ideas that, in less severely disturbed children, appear to be repudiated (aggression or aggressive sexual ideation) are often consciously accessible for such children; insight into these seems of little therapeutic relevance. Defenses, as normally conceived, are often hard to identify. Referring to the child's anxiety, rarely makes the child feel understood, it simply leaves him confused. Psychodynamic understanding of these children is possible if we assume that defensive operations for this group do not simply entail the modification of specific ideas and feelings but rather the mental processes responsible for generating the mental representations (Fonagy et al., 1993). For example, children traumatized by their caregivers find contemplating the caregiver's feelings and ideas intensely painful, because, at least in their eyes, these must involve the caregiver's wish to harm them (Fonagy, 1991). They thus defensively inhibit the psychological functions (mental processes) responsible for generating representations of mental states, at least in the context of attachment relationships (Fonagy et al., 1995).

The therapeutic approaches required to address problems of inhibited mental processes are qualitatively different from those that may be helpful in treating neurotic children. The therapist's task is to make the child feel once again that it is safe to make full use of his mind. It may be assumed that most mental processes are, at least potentially, available and the free exploration of thoughts and ideas serves to disinhibit the child's pervasive defensive stance. Therapeutic approaches with such children have increasingly emphasized the promotion of opportunities for playing with ideas (Fonagy & Target, 1996b). To some degree the therapeutic approach is unchanged. It is the aim of therapy that is modified (Fonagy & Target, 1998). Neither the recovery of repressed memories or feelings, nor arriving at an understanding of unconscious reasons for their avoidance is relevant to therapeutic change. The very process of achieving understanding or the very act of contemplating feelings and ideas may, in and of themselves, assist severely disturbed children in recovering their capacity to regulate, organize, and represent mental states. Some techniques required to achieve this end have been previously systematically excluded from psychodynamic work with neurotic children because of their expected interference with therapeutic neutrality.

Effective interventions are surprisingly simple and include strategies such as (1) the enhancement of reflective processes through observation and verbalization of the child's feelings; (2) the enhancement of impulse control through helping the child identify ways of channeling impulses into socially acceptable forms of behavior; (3) building cognitive self-regulatory strategies through symbolization and metaphor and by the demonstration of the therapist's own capacities for the modulation of experience through reflective thinking and talking; (4) generating interest in the mental states of others often, at least initially, by focusing on the child's perception of the therapist's mental state; (5) developing the child's capacity to play, at first with objects, then with others, and finally with feelings and ideas; and (6) the demonstration to the child of multiple ways of seeing physical reality and so on (Bleiberg et al., 1997). Looked at in this way, psychodynamic therapy is no longer considered a predominantly insight-oriented, conflict-solving psychological treatment, but rather a developmentally based mentalization-enhancing approach. It may link diverse therapeutic orientations such as systemic family therapy and cognitive–behavioral treatments (CBT). For example, both CBT and mental process-oriented psychodynamic psychotherapy aim to enhance the child's capacity to organize and structure experiences. The difference lies in the focus of the cognitive approach on particular mental schemas while the psychodynamic approach aims at promoting a broad set of capacities. We expect that an important component of the effectiveness of both therapeutic orientations may be mediated through the rekindling of the child's confidence in the self-organization of internal states. A more focused approach is likely to be more appropriate to children with less pervasive dysfunction. There is as yet no evidence available to substantiate this kind of distinction.

Research on Psychodynamic Psychotherapy

There is very little research available on the outcome of psychodynamic treatment (Weisz, Weiss, Morton, Granger, & Han, 1992). The most extensive study of intensive psychodynamic treatment was a chart review of more than 700 case records at a psychoanalytic clinic in the United Kingdom (Fonagy & Target, 1994, 1996c; Target & Fonagy, 1994a,b). The observed effects of psychodynamic treatment were relatively impressive, particularly with younger children and those with emotional disorder or those with disruptive disorder whose symptom profile included anxiety. Children with pervasive developmental disorders or mental retardation appeared to respond poorly to psychodynamic treatment. There was some evidence that more intensive treatment was desirable for children with emotional disorders whose symptomatology was extremely severe and pervasive.

Some smaller-scale studies demonstrated that psychodynamic therapy could bring about improvement in aspects of psychological functioning beyond psychiatric symptomatology. Heinicke (1965; Heinicke & Ramsey-Klee, 1986) demonstrated that general academic performance was superior at 1-year follow-up in children who were treated more frequently in psychodynamic psychotherapy. Moran and Fonagy (Fonagy & Moran, 1990; Moran & Fonagy, 1987; Moran, Fonagy, Kurtz, Bolton, & Brook, 1991) demonstrated that children with poorly controlled diabetes could be significantly helped with their metabolic problems by relatively brief intensive psychodynamic psychotherapy. Lush et al. (1991) in a naturalistic study offered preliminary evidence that psychodynamic therapy was helpful for children with a history of severe deprivation who were fostered or adopted. Improvements were only noted in the treated group. Negative findings were, however, reported by Smyrnios and Kirkby (1993). In this study no significant differences were found at follow-up between a time-limited and a time-unlimited psychodynamic therapy group and a minimal contact control group.

All of these studies suffer from severe methodological shortcomings. These include (1) small sample size, (2) nonstandardized unreliable assessment procedures, (3) nonrandom assignment, (4) nonindependent or overnarrow assessments of outcome, (5) lack of full specification of the treatment offered, and (6) the absence of measures of therapist adherence and so on.

Better evidence is available for the success of therapeutic approaches that cannot be considered as direct implementation of psychoanalytic ideas. For example, Kolvin et al. (1981) demonstrated that psychodynamic group therapy had relatively favorable effects when compared with behavior therapy and parent counseling, particularly on long-term follow-up. Similar encouraging results have been reported in a smaller-scale study by Lochman, Coie, Underwood, and Terry (1993). A sobering finding is reported by Szapocznik et al. (1989) treating disruptive adolescents using individual psychodynamic therapy or structural family therapy. Both forms of treatment led to significant gains. But on 1-year follow-up family functioning had deteriorated in the individual therapy group while the child functioning was improved for both groups. Interpersonal psychotherapy, although not a psychodynamic treatment (Klerman et al., 1984), nevertheless incorporates interpersonal psychodynamic principles. In a preliminary implementation of this therapy for depressed adolescents, Mufson, Moreau, Weissman, and Klerman (1993) report promising results.

EVALUATION

Psychodynamic psychotherapy has a well-developed and helpful body of theory that has inspired many generations of clinicians. Psychodynamic ideas are applied in contexts well beyond the treatment of psychiatric disorders: in psychology, other social sciences, literature, the arts, and so on. Psychodynamic psychotherapy is one of the oldest theory-driven forms of psychological treatment of mental disorders (probably antedated only by hypnosis). Nevertheless, in terms of empirical investigations of either its underlying constructs or its therapeutic outcome, it is still in its infancy.

The shortcomings of psychodynamic approaches include (1) the absence of operationalization, (2) the uncritical application of the approach to a wide range of disorders ("one size fits all"), (3) limited sound evidence of efficacy, (4) an overreliance on individual case reports, (5) vagueness of treatment goals, (6) the possibility of unnecessarily prolonged treatments, (7) significant heterogeneity of therapeutic approaches within this category defying integration and rationalization, and (8) an antagonism on the part of many psychodynamic practitioners to the idea of systematic evaluation and scrutiny.

There are many of us, however, who notwithstanding our awareness of the current limitations of the approach remain convinced of its unique value, not just as a methodology for the study of the psychological difficulties of childhood but also as a method of clinical intervention with children whom we find it hard to reach using other methods. Psychodynamic child clinicians are for the most part well aware of the tremendous challenge they face in persuading health care organizations as well as consumers of services of the unique value of their approach. Considerable work remains to be done but a new culture of research is now emerging within the psychoanalytic community (Emde & Fonagy, 1997). It is, we believe, a realistic hope that over the next decade substantial evidence will emerge that will delineate the specific value of the approach for the long-term development of children with psychological disorders. Work is already under way at a number of centers internationally and time will tell if psychodynamic treatment works, and if so, for whom.

REFERENCES

Abrams, S. (1988). The psychoanalytic process in adults and children. *Psychoanalytic Study of the Child, 43,* 245–261.

Ainsworth, M. D. S., Blehar, M. C., Waters, E., & Wall, S. (1978). *Patterns of attachment: A psychological study of the Strange Situation.* Hillsdale, NJ: Erlbaum.

Altman, N. (1992). Relational perspectives on child psychoanalytic psychotherapy. In N. J. Skolnick & S. C. Warshaw (Eds.), *Relational perspectives in psychoanalysis* (pp. 175–194). Hillsdale, NJ: Analytic Press.

Altman, N. (1994). The recognition of relational theory and technique in child treatment. Special Issue: Child analytic work. *Psychoanalytic Psychology, 11,* 383–395.

Alvarez, A. (1993). *Live company.* London: Routledge.

Bion, W. R. (1959). Attacks on linking. *International Journal of Psycho-Analysis, 40,* 308–315.

Bion, W. R. (1962). A theory of thinking. *International Journal of Psycho-Analysis, 43,* 306–310.

Bleiberg, E. (1987). Stages in the treatment of narcissistic children and adolescents. *Bulletin of the Menninger Clinic, 51,* 296–313.

Bleiberg, E. (1994a). Borderline disorders in children and adolescents: The concept, the diagnosis, and the controversies. *Bulletin of the Menninger Clinic, 58,* 169–196.

Bleiberg, E. (1994b). Neurosis and conduct disorders. In J. M. Oldham & M. B. Riba (Eds.), *American Psychiatric Press Review of Psychiatry* (Vol. 13, pp. 493–518). Washington, DC: American Psychiatric Press.

Bleiberg, E., Fonagy, P., & Target, M. (1997). Child psychoanalysis: Critical overview and a proposed reconsideration. *Psychiatric Clinics of North America, 6,* 1–38.

Bower, T. R. (1989). *The rational infant: Learning in infancy.* New York: Freeman.

Bowlby, J. (1969). *Attachment and loss: Vol. 1. Attachment.* London: Hogarth Press and the Institute of Psycho-Analysis.

Bowlby, J. (1973). *Attachment and loss: Vol. 2. Separation: Anxiety and anger.* London: Hogarth Press and the Institute of Psycho-Analysis.

Bowlby, J. (1980). *Attachment and loss: Vol. 3. Loss: Sadness and depression.* London: Hogarth Press and the Institute of Psycho-Analysis.

Brenner, C. (1982). *The mind in conflict.* New York: International Universities Press.

Chethik, M. (1989). *Techniques of child therapy: Psychodynamic strategies.* New York: Guilford Press.

Cohen, D. J., Towbin, K. E., Mayes, L., & Volkmar, F. (1994). Developmental psychopathology of multiplex developmental disorder. In S. L. Friedman & H. C. Haywood (Eds.), *Developmental follow-up: Concepts, domains and methods* (pp. 155–182). New York: Academic Press.

Cummings, E. M., & Davies, P. T. (1994). Maternal depression and child development. *Journal of Child Psychology and Psychiatry, 35,* 73–112.

DeFolch, T. E. (1988). Guilt bearable or unbearable: A problem for the child in analysis. Special Issue: Psychoanalysis of children. *International Review of Psycho-Analysis, 15,* 13–24.

Emde, R. N., & Fonagy, P. (1997). An emerging culture for psychoanalytic research? Editorial. *The International Journal of Psycho-Analysis, 78,* 643–651.

Fairbairn, W. R. D. (1952). *An object-relations theory of the personality.* New York: Basic Books.

Fonagy, P. (1991). Thinking about thinking: Some clinical and theoretical considerations in the treatment of a borderline patient. *International Journal of Psycho-Analysis, 72,* 639–656.

Fonagy, P., Edgcumbe, R., Moran, G. S., Kennedy, H., & Target, M. (1993). The roles of mental representations and mental processes in therapeutic action. *The Psychoanalytic Study of the Child, 48,* 9–48.

Fonagy, P., & Moran, G. S. (1990). Studies on the efficacy of child psychoanalysis. *Journal of Consulting and Clinical Psychology, 58,* 684–695.

Fonagy, P., Steele, M., Steele, H., Leigh, T., Kennedy, R., Mattoon, G., & Target, M. (1995). The predictive validity of Mary Main's Adult Attachment Interview: A psychoanalytic and developmental perspective on the transgenerational transmission of attachment and borderline states. In S. Goldberg, R. Muir, & J. Kerr (Eds.), *Attachment theory: Social, developmental and clinical perspectives* (pp. 233–278). Hillsdale, NJ: Analytic Press.

Fonagy, P., & Target, M. (1994). The efficacy of psychoanalysis for children with disruptive disorders. *Journal of the American Academy of Child and Adolescent Psychiatry, 33,* 45–55.

Fonagy, P., & Target, M. (1996a). A contemporary psychoanalytical perspective: Psychodynamic developmental therapy. In E. Hibbs & P. Jensen (Eds.), *Psychosocial treatments for child and adolescent disorders: Empirically based approaches* (pp. 619–638). Washington, DC: APA and NIH.

Fonagy, P., & Target, M. (1996b). Playing with reality: I. Theory of mind and the normal development of psychic reality. *International Journal of Psycho-Analysis, 77,* 217–233.

Fonagy, P., & Target, M. (1996c). Predictors of outcome in child psychoanalysis: A retrospective study of 763 cases at the Anna Freud Centre. *Journal of the American Psychoanalytic Association, 44,* 27–77.

Fonagy, P., & Target, M. (1998). Mentalization and the changing aims of child psychoanalysis. *Psychoanalytic Dialogues, 8,* 87–115.

Freud, A. (1946). *The psychoanalytic treatment of children.* London: Imago Publishing.

Freud, A. (1965). *Normality and pathology in childhood.* Harmondsworth: Penguin Books.

Freud, S. (1900). The interpretation of dreams. In J. Strachey (Ed.), *The standard edition of the complete psychological works of Sigmund Freud* (Vols. 4, 5, pp. 1–715). London: Hogarth Press.

Freud, S. (1905). Three essays on the theory of sexuality. In J. Strachey (Ed.), *The standard edition of the complete psychological works of Sigmund Freud* (Vol. 7, pp. 123–230). London: Hogarth Press.

Freud, S. (1909). Analysis of a phobia in a five-year-old boy. In J. Strachey (Ed.), *The standard edition of the complete psychological works of Sigmund Freud* (Vol. 10, pp. 1–147). London: Hogarth Press.

Freud, S. (1920). Beyond the pleasure principle. In J. Strachey (Ed.), *The standard edition of the complete psychological works of Sigmund Freud* (Vol. 18, pp. 1–64). London: Hogarth Press.

Freud, S. (1923). The ego and the id. In J. Strachey (Ed.), *The standard edition of the complete psychological works of Sigmund Freud* (Vol. 19, pp. 1–59). London: Hogarth Press.

Freud, S. (1926). The question of lay analysis. In J. Strachey (Ed.), *The standard edition of the complete psychological works of Sigmund Freud* (Vol. 20, pp. 77–172). London: Hogarth Press.

Freud, S. (1930). Civilization and its discontents. In J. Strachey (Ed.), *The standard edition of the complete psychological works of Sigmund Freud* (Vol. 21, pp. 57–146). London: Hogarth Press.

Freud, S. (1933). New introductory lectures on psychoanalysis. In J. Strachey (Ed.), *The standard edition of the complete psychological works of Sigmund Freud* (Vol. 22, pp. 1–182). London: Hogarth Press.

Gergely, G. (1992). Developmental reconstructions: Infancy from the point of view of psychoanalysis and developmental psychology. *Psychoanalysis and Contemporary Thought, 14,* 3–55.

Glenn, J. (1978). *Child analysis and therapy.* Northvale, NJ: Aronson.

Goldstein, J., Freud, A., & Solnit, A. J. (1973). *Beyond the best interests of the child.* New York: Free Press.

Golinkolf, R. M., Hardig, C. B., Carlson, V., & Sexton, M. E. (1984). The infant's perception of causal events: The distinction between animate and inanimate ob1jects. In L. P. Lipsitt & C. Rovee-Collier (Eds.), *Advances in infancy research* (Vol. 3, pp. 145–151). Norwood NJ: Ablex.

Hartmann, H. (1958). *Ego psychology and the problem of adaptation.* New York: International Universities Press. (Original work published 1939)

Hartmann, H. (1964). Notes on the theory of sublimation. *Essays on ego psychology* (pp. 215–240). New York: International Universities Press. (Original work published 1955)

Heinicke, C. M. (1965). Frequency of psychotherapeutic session as a factor affecting the child's developmental status. *The Psychoanalytic Study of the Child, 20,* 42–98.

Heinicke, C. M., & Ramsey-Klee, D. M. (1986). Outcome of child psychotherapy as a function of frequency of sessions. *Journal of the American Academy of Child Psychiatry, 25,* 247–253.

Hoffman, L. (1993). An introduction to child psychoanalysis. *Journal of Clinical Psychoanalysis, 2,* 5–26.

Hug-Helmuth, H. (1920). Child psychology and education. *International Journal of Psycho-Analysis, 1,* 316–323.

Jacobson, E. (1964). *The self and the object world.* New York: International Universities Press.

Johnson, E. (1982). Principles and techniques in drama therapy. *International Journal of Arts and Psychotherapy, 9,* 83–90.

Kernberg, O. F. (1975). *Borderline conditions and pathological narcissism.* Northvale, NJ: Aronson.

Kernberg, O. F. (1976). *Object relations theory and clinical psychoanalysis.* Northvale, NJ: Aronson.

Kernberg, O. F. (1987). An ego psychology–object relations theory approach to the transference. *Psychoanalytic Quarterly, 51,* 197–221.

Kernberg, P. F. (1995). Child psychiatry: Individual psychotherapy. In H. I. Kaplan & B. J. Sadock (Eds.), *Comprehensive textbook of psychiatry* (6 ed., pp. 2399–2412). Baltimore: Williams & Wilkins.

King, P., & Steiner, R. (1991). *The Freud–Klein controversies.* London: Routledge.

Klein, M. (1932). *The psycho-analysis of children.* London: Hogarth Press.

Klein, M. (1946). Notes on some schizoid mechanisms. In M. Klein, P. Heimann, S. Isaacs, & J. Riviere (Eds.), *Developments in psychoanalysis* (pp. 292–320). London: Hogarth Press.

Klein, M. (1975). The origins of transference. *The writings of Melanie Klein* (pp. 48–56). London: Hogarth Press. (Original work published 1952)

Klein, M., Heimann, P., Isaacs, S., & Riviere, J. (Eds.). (1946). *Developments in psychoanalysis.* London: Hogarth Press.

Klerman, G. F., Weissman, M. M., Ronsaville-Chevron, B., & Chevrones, J. (1984). *Interpersonal psychotherapy of depression.* New York: Basic Books.

Kohut, H. (1971). *The analysis of the self.* New York: International Universities Press.

Kohut, H. (1977). *The restoration of the self.* New York: International Universities Press.

Kolvin, I., Garside, R. F., Nicol, A. R., MacMillan, A., Wolstenholme, F., & Leitch, I. M. (1981). *Help starts here: The maladjusted child in the ordinary school.* London: Tavistock.

Lochman, J. E., Coie, J. D., Underwood, M. K., & Terry, R. (1993). Effectiveness of a social relations intervention program for aggressive and nonaggressive, rejected children. *Journal of Consulting and Clinical Psychology, 61,* 1053–1058.

Luborsky, L. (1984). *Principles of psychoanalytic psychotherapy: A manual for supportive-expressive (SE) treatment.* New York: Basic Books.

Lush, D., Boston, M., & Grainger, E. (1991). Evaluation of psychoanalytic psychotherapy with children: Therapists' assessments and predictions. *Psychoanalytic Psychotherapy, 5,* 191–234.

Mahler, M. (1968). *On human symbiosis and the vicissitudes of individuation.* New York: International Universities Press.

Main, M., Kaplan, N., & Cassidy, J. (1985). Security in infancy, childhood and adulthood: A move to the level of representation. In I. Bretherton & E. Waters (Eds.), *Growing points of attachment theory and research. Monographs of the Society for Research in Child Development* (Vol. 50, pp. 66–104). Chicago: University of Chicago Press.

Marohn, R. C. (1991). Psychotherapy of adolescents with behavioral disorders. In M. Slomowitz (Ed.), *Adolescent psychotherapy* (pp. 145–161). Washington, DC: American Psychiatric Press.

Masterson, J. F. (1972). *Treatment of the borderline adolescent: A developmental approach.* New York: Wiley–Interscience.

Moran, G. S., & Fonagy, P. (1987). Psychoanalysis and diabetic control: A single case study. *British Journal of Medical Psychology, 60,* 357–372.

Moran, G., Fonagy, P., Kurtz, A., Bolton, A., & Brook, C. (1991). A controlled study of the psychoanalytic treatment of brittle diabetes. *Journal of the American Academy of Child and Adolescent Psychiatry, 30,* 926–935.

Mufson, L., Moreau, D., Weissman, M. M., & Klerman, G. L. (1993). *Interpersonal psychotherapy for depressed adolescents.* New York: Guilford Press.

O'Shaughnessy, E. (1988). W. R. Bion's theory of thinking and new techniques in child analysis. In E. B. Spillius (Ed.), *Melanie Klein today: Developments in theory and practice. Vol. 2. Mainly practice* (pp. 177–190). London: Routledge.

Pine, F. (1985). *Developmental theory and clinical process.* New Haven, CT: Yale University Press.

Rinsley, D. B. (1977). An object relations view of borderline personality. In P. Hartocollis (Ed.), *Borderline personality disorders: The concept, the syndrome, the patient* (pp. 47–70). New York: International Universities Press.

Rinsley, D. B. (1989). Notes on the developmental pathogenesis of narcissistic personality disorder. *Psychiatric Clinics of North America, 12,* 695–707.

Rose, S. D. (1972). *Treating children in groups.* San Francisco: Jossey–Bass.

Rosenfeld, H. (1988). Contribution to the psychopathology of psychotic states: The importance of projective identification in the ego structure and object relations of the psychotic patient. In E. B. Spillius (Ed.), *Melanie Klein today* (pp. 117–137). London: Routledge. (Original work published 1971)

Sandler, J. (1987). *From safety to the superego: Selected papers of Joseph Sandler.* New York: Guilford Press.

Sandler, J., Kennedy, H., & Tyson, R. (1980). *The technique of child analysis: Discussions with Anna Freud.* London: Hogarth Press.

Sandler, J., & Rosenblatt, B. (1962). The concept of the representational world. *The Psychoanalytic Study of the Child, 17,* 128–145.

Schaefer, C. E., & Cangelosi, D. M. (Eds.). (1993). *Play therapy techniques.* Northvale, NJ: Aronson.

Selvini Palazzoli, M., Boscolo, L., Cecchin, G., & Prata, G. (1978). *Paradox and counter-paradox.* Northvale, NJ: Aronson.

Simon, M. R. (1992). *The symbolism of style: Art as therapy.* London: Routledge.

Smyrnios, K. X., & Kirkby, R. J. (1993). Long-term comparison of brief versus unlimited psychodynamic treatments with children and their parents. *Journal of Consulting and Clinical Psychology, 61,* 1020–1027.

Sroufe, L. A. (1990). An organizational perspective on the self. In D. Cicchetti & M. Beeghly (Eds.), *The self in transition: Infancy to childhood* (pp. 281–307). Chicago: University of Chicago Press.

Stem, D. N. (1985). *The interpersonal world of the infant: A view from psychoanalysis and developmental psychology.* New York: Basic Books.

Strachey, J. (1934). The nature of the therapeutic action of psychoanalysis. *International Journal of Psycho-Analysis, 50,* 275–292.

Sullivan, H. S. (1953). *The interpersonal theory of psychiatry.* New York: Norton.

Szapocznik, J., Rio, A., Murray, E., Cohen, R., Scopetta, M., Kivas-Valquez, A., Hervis, O., Posada, V., & Kurtines, W. (1989). Structural family versus psychodynamic child therapy for problematic Hispanic boys. *Journal of Consulting and Clinical Psychology, 57,* 571–578.

Target, M., & Fonagy, P. (1994a). The efficacy of psychoanalysis for children with emotional disorders. *Journal of the American Academy of Child and Adolescent Psychiatry, 33,* 361–371.

Target, M., & Fonagy, P. (1994b). The efficacy of psychoanalysis for children: Prediction of outcome in a developmental context. *Journal of the American Academy of Child and Adolescent Psychiatry, 33,* 1134–1144.

Towbin, K. E., Dykens, E. M., Pearson, G. S., & Cohen, D. J. (1993). Conceptualising "borderline syndrome of childhood" and "childhood schizophrenia" as a developmental disorder. *Journal of the American Academy of Child and Adolescent Psychiatry, 32,* 775–782.

Tyson, P. (1992, December). *Neurosis in childhood and in psychoanalysis.* Paper presented at the Annual Meeting of the American Psychoanalytic Association.

Tyson, R. L., & Tyson, P. (1986). The concept of transference in child psychoanalysis. *Journal of the American Academy of Child Psychiatry, 25,* 30–39.

Warshaw, S. C. (1992). Mutative factors in child psychoanalysis: A comparison of diverse relational perspectives. In N. J. Skolnick & S. C. Warshaw (Eds.), *Relational perspectives in psychoanalysis* (pp. 141–173). Hillsdale, NJ: Analytic Press.

Weisz, J. R., Weiss, B., Morton, T., Granger, D., & Han, S. (1992). *Meta-analysis of psychotherapy outcome research with children and adolescents.* Unpublished manuscript, University of California, Los Angeles.

Winnicott, D. W. (1965). *The maturational process and the facilitating environment.* London: Hogarth Press.

Winnicott, D. W. (1971). *Playing and reality.* London: Tavistock.

6

Client-Centered Child and Family Therapy

NED L. GAYLIN

THEORETICAL OVERVIEW

Conceived and developed by Carl Rogers, client-centered therapy and its sister philosophy, the person-centered approach, fall basically under the category of self psychology. Their theoretical orientation and methods of therapy derive summarily from respect for the uniqueness of individuals and their life experiences.

During its heyday in the 1950s and 1960s, client-centered therapy's great success enabled its tenets to be disseminated and applied throughout the United States and Europe. Today its major premises are thought to be well understood by mental and allied health practitioners and the lay public alike. Further, virtually every mode of psychotherapy practiced today pays some homage to many of Rogers's contributions, particularly his articulation of the empathic stance of the therapist and the special relationship that exists between the client and therapist. Ironically, today these concepts seem so basic and rudimentary to the practice of psychotherapy that many consider them simplistic and thus unworthy of serious applied, theoretical, or empirical consideration.

Rogers's special genius surrounded his ability to conceptualize therapeutic process in an elegantly lean manner, employing only a few well-defined terms and a parsimony of easy-to-understand postulates. Rogers's theory of therapy is best spelled out in his 1957 paper, "The Necessary and Sufficient Conditions for Therapeutic Personality Change" (Rogers, 1957) in which he delineated six core conditions that are requisite for psychotherapeutic change. Two years later, he produced another seminal work, "A Theory of Therapy, Personality, and Interpersonal Relationships, As Developed in the Client-Centered Framework" (Rogers, 1959), which outlined a

NED L. GAYLIN • Department of Family Studies, University of Maryland, College Park, Maryland 20742.

Handbook of Psychotherapies with Children and Families, edited by Russ and Ollendick. Kluwer Academic/Plenum Publishers, New York, 1999.

client-centered theory of personality. Nonetheless, client-centered theory clearly focuses more on therapeutic process than the structure and organization of personality.

Person-centered philosophy and client-centered therapy draw on elements of, among others, William James's (1890) ideation regarding the self and consciousness and Kurt Goldstein's concept of the organism (1940). Accordingly, all living things, from ameba to sequoia, have one drive or motive—*the actualizing tendency.*

The actualizing tendency is the universal press of all organisms to fulfill their destinies. For humans, the actualizing tendency becomes refined in a manner distinct from all other beings. Children, early on, in interaction with their environment (with significant others, in particular) begin to develop sentience and awareness of themselves as perceptual objects in their experience of the world (Rogers, 1959). This self experience gives rise to a complex *self system* (Gaylin, 1996) from which the uniquely human process of *self-actualization* derives.

The process of self-actualization is focal to all client-centered theory and practice. During this process, each of us, as individuals, acts in a manner that we believe will promote the realization of our potential. Our self-actualizing tendency "may become deeply buried under layer after layer of encrusted psychological defenses; it may be hidden behind facades which deny its existence, but . . . it exists in every individual, and awaits only the proper conditions to be released and expressed" (Rogers, 1961, p. 351). Thus, we all strive to become ever more "fully functioning."

However, there are times when our experience and conceptualization of self are at odds. At these times we feel threatened, vulnerable, and anxious—"incongruent." Incongruence can cause us to lose our sense of integration and wholeness. We all feel incongruent at times. When this incongruence becomes so great that we feel discomfited and debilitated, we may seek relief through psychotherapy.

Thus, the process of psychotherapy is one where, in a climate of trust and warmth, individuals may reexperience their views of self and the world in such a way that the individuals become more congruent and integrated. Such wholeness in turn unencumbers the actualizing tendency heretofore impeded by personal incongruences.

Rogerian theory is, above all, based on the experience of the client. Reality is what individuals experience and perceive. The therapist must understand, be empathic with, and reflect the client's reality to enable the client to reexperience and reintegrate old experiences and thus become more open to new experiences. This is the means by which the client's self-actualizing tendency is empowered, and the client becomes more fully functioning. Although greatly oversimplified, these are the primary elements of client-centered theory.

HISTORY

Carl Rogers began his career in psychotherapy by working with children. Although not widely known for his work with children, his first major published effort in 1939 (written while he was at the Rochester Guidance Center, 1928–1940) dealt with the treatment of the "problem" child (Rogers, 1939). Client-centered therapy had not yet been born. Rogers himself (1974) dated that event at December 11, 1940, in a talk he gave at the University of Minnesota. Although the term *nondirective* therapy was introduced then, its antecedents were clearly in evidence in the earlier 1939 book.

In his initial work, Rogers made clear his discontent with the then highly touted, psychoanalytically oriented, interpretive approach to working with troubled children—an approach proposed by Anna Freud (1928) and Alexander and Healy (1935) among others. Further, Rogers underscored the desirability of helping difficult children by practicing that which he referred to as "relationship" therapy, a concept drawn from the work of Jessie Taft (1933).

Rogers moved to Ohio State University in 1940 where he continued to explicate "nondirective therapy" (1942). In 1945 Rogers moved from Ohio to the University of Chicago to direct its Counseling Center. Here "client-centered therapy" (1951) was born, and an emphasis on empirical research (Rogers & Dymond, 1954) brought client-centered therapy to full flower. During the Chicago period, Rogers's "nondirective" principles stimulated others like Virginia Axline, who published her influential work on play therapy (1947).

Rogers moved from Chicago to the University of Wisconsin in 1957. Here he focused his efforts on applying client-centered principles to his work with severely disturbed, institutionalized clients. Heretofore, virtually all client-centered practice and research had been conducted in nonmedical settings. In 1963 Rogers left Wisconsin for La Jolla, California, where education, group facilitation, and world peace became the focus of his attention. During this final period he coined the term *person-centered*, signaling efforts directed at applying his philosophy and principles beyond the realm of psychotherapy.

ASSESSMENT AND CASE FORMULATION

In the client-centered framework, the concepts of assessment, diagnosis, and case formulation are irrelevant. The entire focus of the therapist in client-centered practice is the phenomenological world of the client. Accordingly the therapist (1) enters the client's inner world, (2) accepts the client's world-view as the client's reality, (3) becomes empathic with that world-view, and (4) nonjudgmentally conveys that empathic acceptance to the client. This process frees the client's own restorative forces.

There is no differential treatment prescription or treatment. Therefore, differential diagnosis is unnecessary. The therapist learns the client's language, rather than vice versa as in other theoretical orientations. Although trying to understand the extent of the client's incongruence might be construed as a form of assessing the state of the client, scrutiny of it and its counterpart, congruence, is more usual in the research arena than in clinical practice.

MECHANISMS OF CHANGE AND INTERVENTION PROCEDURES

Rogers's keystone work (1957) concerned the process of therapy including the (1) necessary and sufficient conditions and (2) mechanisms for change in individual psychotherapy. It would be impossible to improve on the elegance of his original formulation, which to this day stands as a model for client-centered practitioners. Rogers's (1957, p. 96) six conditions are:

1. Two persons are in psychological contact.
2. The first, whom we shall term the *client,* is in a state of incongruence, being vulnerable or anxious.
3. The second person, whom we shall term the *therapist,* is congruent or integrated in the relationship.
4. The therapist experiences unconditional positive regard for the client.
5. The therapist experiences an empathic understanding of the client's frame of reference and endeavors to communicate this experience to the client.
6. The communication to the client of the therapist's empathic understanding and unconditional positive regard is to a minimal degree achieved.

No other conditions are necessary. If these six conditions exist, and continue over a period of time, this is sufficient. The process of constructive personality change will follow.

Empathic reflection of feeling is the only method of intervention practiced by client-centered therapists. Therapists, who are congruent (in touch with an integrated self), relate empathically to the client. If accurate, therapists' expression of their empathic understanding of the client's internal frame of reference conveys to the client a sense of being heard and understood, a sense of acceptance by another. It is this validation of experience that enables self acceptance and mending within the client. It should be noted that although the method appears simple, its execution requires exquisite attention and concentration on the part of therapists.

Working with Children

Client-centered psychotherapy with children requires the same intervention methodology as therapy with adults, despite their apparent procedural differences. Empathic reflection of feeling is the method; entering the internal realm of the client, of whatever age, is the means of realizing empathy. Despite Axline's (1947) having called her paradigmatic work with children "play" therapy, the appellation merely connotes that in working with children, the vehicle is often play. Play, be it imaginary, role-taking, and other forms, may be seen as the child's experiential experimentation. In the therapy session this play often expresses the child's feelings of incongruence and much-hungered-for congruence.

Unfortunately, many professionals and nonprofessionals view psychotherapy with children as a palpably different endeavor from that with adults. Calling psychotherapy with children "play" therapy exacerbates the perceived chasm between the two endeavors. The inference, too often drawn, is that therapy with children requires a special venue or environment, exotic equipment, and an inherently different therapeutic stance and style from those required for work with adults. In actuality, all that therapeutic work with children does require is a comfort with and sensitivity to children, a willingness and ability to engage intimately with a child on the child's terms, and an internal integrity (i.e., congruence) that permits therapists access to recollections of their own experiences during their own growing up years. Indeed, one might easily contend that working with children in a therapeutic context best allows the therapist to develop the form of congruence that characterizes and is required for a therapeutic stance. Therefore, child therapy provides a sound foundation for therapists working with any population.

Children are amazingly resilient, creative, and imaginative by nature. Observant parents are quick to note that children simply "supply" equipment via their imaginations when and if the need arises. Thus, parents who have determined not to allow their children to play with violent toys are often aghast when they see those children playing "cops and robbers" and shooting at each other with erect thumbs and extended forefingers. Therefore, psychotherapy with children does not require special and elaborate equipment like doll houses, family dolls, animal puppets, sandboxes, and running water. An office with interesting nonspecific and attractive objects, e.g., a few simple toys, some modest drawing equipment, and several children's books tenders stimuli sufficient for engaging in psychotherapeutic communication with most children.

By nature, children are usually eager to relate to adults and have their attention. Like the young of most other mammalian species, children need and generally look to adults for guidance and approbation, significant primers of their (our) actualizing tendency. However, when children become troubled, typical functional patterns may break down. Troubled children may withdraw into themselves, act out, or generally behave in antisocial ways. When such behavior is severe enough, they are often brought for psychotherapy. Thus, an attentive, patient, and caring adult may create an interpersonal environment where the child's trust in others, particularly adults, may be established, so that functional developmental interaction may resume.

Work with any client, particularly those who have not yet reached adulthood, makes evident that clients may not use spoken language as the primary vehicle for conveying their inner experiences. Thus, therapists must additionally and actively attend to their younger clients' nonverbal behaviors. Therapists who can grasp the meaning of clients' inner experiences through those nonverbal behaviors should thus be able to reflect their empathic understanding to their young clients. Sometimes those reflections, reciprocally, are offered nonverbally, thereby paralleling the behavior of the child.

Working with children makes therapists aware of the need for keeping the client's agenda primary, allowing the client to lead. Language often acts as an accompaniment to the broader repertoire of doing something. Therapists need to be prepared to engage in the child's repertoire, which often includes, in addition to playing with objects, doing things and role-taking.

The following is an excerpt from a session with an 11-year-old boy, referred because of a mild learning disability and his consequent growing anxiety surrounding school.

Andrew came into the therapist's office smirking broadly and carrying a large paper bag.

    T. Hi Andrew. From the look on your face I would guess you have something very special in that bag.

    C. (Grin broadening). Guess!

T. You want me to figure out what you brought here today.

C. (Nods animatedly)

T. Hmm, it must be something very special—a treasure.

C. Yeah, but what? *Guess!*

T. It's a treasure, but something more . . .

C. (Interrupting excitedly) Something I made.

T. Something you made at school?

C. No, no—at home. (Dumping the contents on the coffee table.) It's origami!

T. (Truly impressed by the amount and complexity of the paper folding) Wow! Look at all those things! Looks like animals, *lots* of animals, and . . .

C. Balls and jumping frogs (demonstrating how to make the frog jump).

T. They really *do* jump like frogs.

C. Want me to show you how to make one?

T. You want to teach me how to make a jumping frog.

C. (Nods) Sure, they're easy . . . (catching the look of skepticism on the therapist's face) . . . it's not that hard—really!

T. You think I could learn, they're easy when you know how to do it, eh?

C. Yeah (hands T. a piece of origami paper from the pile on the table and takes another piece for himself, beginning, almost at once, to fold it). First you fold it in half, like this.

T. (Following instructions, folding the paper as C.) So far so good.

C. (Folding increasingly more rapidly as he gets engrossed in the task) Then like this, then like that, then turn it over and . . . (noticing the therapist is hopelessly lost) . . . here, let me help you (taking the paper from T.).

T. I guess it would be easier to do it yourself rather than teach a dummy like me.

C. You're not a dummy! You just never did origami before, did you?

T. Not really, I think I tried once but didn't have the patience. It's hard to try something new, eh?

C. Yeah, I know (looks wistful). Maybe we could do something simpler, like a boat—they're reaaal easy.

T. We should work up to something complicated like a frog.

C. Yeah. (Smiling, taking another piece of paper for himself and handing one to the therapist).

The foregoing represents role-taking by both client and therapist that facilitates the learning (and perhaps healing) for this learning-disabled client who, in this situation, is in charge of a task at which he is competent and the therapist is not. The role reversal appears satisfying to the child and enables him to display both a sense of mastery as well as empathy with the (sincerely) inept therapist. Led by the client, the therapist's ability to engage and express real feelings of ineptitude, involve the client in a healing process that simply talking about his difficulties with new learning situations probably could not.

Client-Centered Family Therapy

For the client-centered family therapist, work with children and/or adults in a family context follows naturally from client-centered work with individuals. Unlike more widely practiced family systems approaches that profess to treat the family as a unit, client-centered family therapy requires that the therapist respond to family members in a manner that philosophically is identical to, and methodological only minimally different from, the way that they work with individual clients. However, understanding how to provide therapy within the intimate, interpersonal context of the family requires some elaboration of the original core conditions and the therapeutic behaviors they imply (see Gaylin, 1989a).

The Six Conditions

1. *Psychological contact: the relationship*

In individual client-centered psychotherapy, a relationship between client and therapist is virtually a given—little more is said. In client-centered family psychotherapy the relationship between therapist and family members, individually and collectively, becomes far more intricate. The complexity emanates from the often strained and disturbed intrafamilial relationships that prevail and generally have impelled the family to seek help. During the therapy session, the therapist develops a therapeutic relationship with each individual family member in the presence of all of the other of its members. The therapist sustains these relationships in a manner that allows all family members—singly and in concert—to experience trusting contact with the therapist. This first condition—the relationship between therapist and family members—is the foundation on which each of the other five conditions rests.

2. *Incongruence of the client(s): psychological distress*

Incongruence, the discomfiture that an individual feels when the experience of self is at odds with the conceptualization of self, prompts individuals to seek help. With more than one client (family member) present, both intrapersonal as well as interpersonal incongruities embellish and profoundly complicate—even enrich—the therapeutic process. Thus, a family member's feeling of incongruence resulting from experiences and perceptions of self in relationship to any and/or all other members may all become focal therapeutic issues that demand the therapist's attention. Thus, in client-centered family therapy, the therapist and clients may deal with intrapersonal incongruence as well as a complex range of interpersonal incongruences.

3. *The congruence of the therapist in the therapeutic relationship: therapist presence*

The integrity, transparency, and full presence of the client-centered therapist is paramount in both individual and family therapy. Although therapists need not be paragons of psychological well-being, they must be aware of who they are in the client–therapist relationship. They must be abundantly cognizant, as well, of their own self experiences (Gaylin, 1996). It is this integrity and awareness that make the next two conditions both possible and powerful in facilitating clients' healing.

4. *Unconditional positive regard: nonjudgmental prizing*

To hear the client fully, without preconception and prejudice, capacitates the client's expression of those aspects of self that have been previously judged by self or others as somehow deficient, unlikable, or unworthy. Within an accepting atmosphere, enriched by the therapist's genuine concern for the client's sense of self-worth, the client may feel safe enough to disclose those negatively perceived aspects of self. Once aired, these self-perceived disfigurements become available for examination, reexperiencing, assimilation, and potential healing. The power of this healing condition is compounded and enhanced when experienced in the midst of the family. The therapist's fully nonjudgmental acceptance, in turn, of each family member's expression of self, acts as a model for everyone. This acceptance also helps dissipate negatively charged attributions and accusations by family members in both previous and present interactions.

5. *Empathy: seeing the world through the client's eyes*

Empathy, the ability to hear, experientially understand, and not be overwhelmed by the felt experience of another, is the heart of all client-centered therapeutic endeavor. It requires that therapists be in touch with many aspects of themselves and call on previous experiences in order to resonate with experiences of their clients in a recognizably authentic manner. Like unconditional positive regard, this condition is powerfully enhanced when members of the client's family are present. Empathic understanding by the therapist allows those family members who have lost the ability to hear each other and have grown weary from conflict to get in touch with the inner experiences of their loved ones.

6. *The client's perception of being understood and prized: validation*

At some level, clients must feel that they have been heard and their perspectives validated. They must also feel that the therapist cares about them. Although each may not feel the therapist's empathy, minute by minute, most (if not all) of the time the condition must be experienced by all family members. Each must, however, feel the therapists caring all of the time.

Client-Centered Methods in Family Therapy

Once again, empathic reflection of clients' feelings is really the one and only method in client-centered therapy and the person-centered approach. In this process, therapists enter their client's frame of reference, grasp their client's experience as fully as possible, and, as accurately as possible, reflect their understanding of the client's feelings back to the client. Basic empathic behavior of the therapist does not vary in client-centered therapy, be it with children, adults, or families. A perceptual shift occurs, however, in the switch from individual to family therapy. With individuals, the therapist maintains the world-view of only a single client; the client-centered family therapist maintains the world-views of multiple clients simultaneously—all family members, sometimes even absent ones.

Accordingly, when a child reports an experience, the therapist, by evoking his or her own childhood encounters, may perceive as fully as possible what the child has experienced, and then reflect back to the child an empathic understanding of the child's experience. In individual therapy, this reflection would be sufficient. In family therapy, however, the therapist's perception or projection of self as parent is additionally primed, ready to feel the parents' reactions and feelings to their child's report of that same event. Experiencing the multiple views and reactions among respective family members enables the therapist to experience a sense of the ecosystemic interaction of these members. Thus, once having practiced client-centered family therapy, one can never do individual therapy in quite the same manner as before. A therapist, tuned in to the interactional nature of the developing self, is aware of the omnipresence of family members, even in their absence.

Reflection of feelings of individual family members is related to but subtly different from reflection of the interactions of family members, the latter better referred to as *interspace reflection* (Gaylin, 1990). This reflection derives from the therapist's empathic understanding of the observed or reported interactions between or among family members. It serves the same function as a reflection of feelings, but, instead of reflecting the expressions of an individual, it captures the interaction and feelings between and among individuals.

The following is an excerpt from an interview with an 8-year-old boy and his single mother. The mother has brought the child for therapy because of (1) a growing power struggle between her and the boy and (2) his growing stubbornness both at home and at school. The boy is sitting in the back of the room, out of range of the camera. The mother knows that the therapist is recording and that the boy is not in camera range. At the outset of the interview the therapist is unaware of mother's motivation.

Mo. LeRoy, sit over here (motioning to a chair next to hers. L. doesn't move). LeRoy, I told you to sit over here.

L. (Mumbles) I don't wanna, I wanna sit here.

T. Mom, you want LeRoy to sit next to you, but LeRoy you want to sit in the back.

Mo. (Seeming to ignore therapist's interspace reflection) LeRoy, I ain't playin' with you—come sit over here by me. (L. folds his arms in defiance. Mother gets up and physically drags him to the chair and forces him into it. L. gets out of the seat of the chair and half stands, half sits on the arm. Mo. does not react to L.'s continued minor defiance, but seems satisfied with the outcome.)

T. (Recognizing that mother wanted L. in camera range for the videotape) Mom, I guess you just wanted LeRoy to sit where he would be on camera (Mo. nods yes), but LeRoy didn't know that, did you?

L. (Shakes his head "no," and slides down into the seat of the chair. Both seem more relaxed)

T. I guess it's easy to get into a snit when you don't know what's going on sometime.

The foregoing demonstrates that just reflecting the interaction is often sufficient to discharge a potentially escalating misunderstanding, clarifying meaning for the individual members, while offering empathy with both.

Subsumed in empathic reflection are the related phenomena *intergenerational echoing* and *ghosting* (Gaylin, 1993), both of which seem to emanate naturally when family members interact in a therapeutic milieu. The first, intergenerational echoing, often occurs spontaneously when, for example, a father and son are interacting regarding their relationship—in the present—and the father becomes aware of similarities to interactions that occurred between him and his own father in the past. The child, for example, may express his feelings of hurt and anger at the reactions of his father under certain circumstances. The resulting exploration may remind the father that he experienced similar feelings in response to his own father under like circumstances. The recognition and exploration of the parallel are often accompanied by heavy emotionality and a kind of nostalgic discovery that, invariably, have a profound positive impact on all family members.

Ghosting refers to the sensed presence or actual verbal reference to a family member not present in the session, which can lead the therapist to empathically "stand in" for the absent member. Under certain circumstances the therapist may feel empathy with the absent member to the extent that the therapist feels impelled to respond, for example, "Gee, if I were Sally, and had heard all this, I might feel such and such." Family members frequently respond with interest and thoughtfulness on hearing a ghosting response from the therapist. They may even continue the dialogue, responding to the therapist as the absent member. After a session, therapy participants often report approaching the absent member regarding an issue evoked and/or expressed during the session. Resulting interactions are virtually always reported as positive and beneficial to family relationships. Moreover, as a consequence of such interactions, absent member are sometimes induced to join the family in therapy.

EXTENSION OF THE CLIENT-CENTERED APPROACH

Because of the inherent simplicity of the client-centered method, its extensions beyond traditional clinic settings have been rather successful. In one of the most noteworthy efforts, Guerney (1964) focused on training parents to do client-centered play therapy with their children. The parents then conducted play sessions at home and attended weekly group meetings to discuss their home sessions and other issues. Similarly, Stollak (1968) trained college students in client-centered play therapy methods and concluded that they were able to perform effectively as therapists. Gordon (1970) extended the method by running workshops for parents, training them in empathic listening skills.

Perhaps the most dramatic of more recent efforts to apply the client-centered methods are those of Prouty (1994) who works with exceedingly disturbed clients. These clients range from seriously retarded, barely verbal children and adults to severely withdrawn and nonverbal clients, i.e., those diagnosed as schizophrenic and catatonic. His endeavors using client-centered methods have worked where all else has failed with many of these clients.

RESEARCH EVIDENCE

From its inception, client-centered therapy has emphasized and thrived on its pragmatism and its empirical base. Rogers was among the first to introduce electronic recording of the therapy hour, heresy in the 1940s. The contention was that such recording could have only a profound negative impact on the therapy relationship and the course of therapy. Empirical studies conducted at the University of Chicago in the 1950s (Rogers and Dymond, 1954) rejected that contention. The collection and analysis of detailed data from recorded psychotherapy hours profoundly influenced the study of psychotherapy process and outcome, resulting in a paradigm shift in psychotherapy research.

Successful psychotherapy outcome continues to be dogged by difficulties in determining the criteria for success. For some, e.g., medical modelists and behaviorists, the reduction of symptoms is the obvious and summary goal of all therapeutic enterprise. Thus, health is defined as an absence of symptoms. Contrarily, the conceptual foundation of client-centered therapy is humanistic, and health is seen as a state of general well-being and robustness that transcends the absence of pathology (Rogers, 1961). The person-centered view embraces a positive conceptualization of psychological well-being (Gaylin, 1974). Thus, facilitating the individual's growth and development—the actualizing tendency—is the goal of all therapeutic endeavor.

To measure such apparently amorphous qualities as congruence and self-actualization, normative measures, i.e., those comparing the individual with others, are less than satisfactory. As a consequence, efforts to develop a new paradigm for measuring personal attributes were undertaken. The key to this paradigmatic shift was a technique and methodology (Q-Technique) developed by Stephenson (1953) that relied on *ipsative* or self-referent as opposed to normative measures (Gaylin, 1989b). Using Stephenson's methodology, Butler and Haigh (1954) developed a Q-Sort composed of 100 statements (culled from psychotherapy hours) that clients used to describe themselves as they felt themselves to be, and an ideal self, as they would like to be. These sorts were administered before and after therapy. Butler and Haigh demonstrated "an increase in congruence between the self and the self-ideal concepts" following client-centered psychotherapy (p. 73).

Later, Gaylin (1966, 1974) employing the Rorschach, Q-Technique, and outcome ratings of therapists and clients demonstrated an improvement in attributes associated with creativity following brief, time-limited, successful client-centered therapy, thus showing the effect of client-centered therapy on the actualizing tendency.

Innovative process measures have been developed by Rice and Wagstaff (1967) who demonstrated that voice quality assessments in the first two psychotherapy sessions were predictive of client-centered therapy outcome. These vocal styles were stylistic, reflecting intrapersonal and interpersonal qualities of the communication process, and unrelated to the content of the utterances.

In part, because of the difficulty in ascertaining incongruence in children, except inferentially, there is a paucity of empirical evidence of outcome regarding psychotherapy with children. Elaine Dorfman (1951) reports on early efforts to ascertain outcome using client-centered methods in individual and group clinical settings, as well as in school venues. Following time-limited client-centered therapy, improvements in such variables as IQ scores, reading scores, and observers' ratings on adaptation, were shown in populations of physically handicapped, learning disabled, retarded, and emotionally disturbed children. However, Dorfman is quick to point out that most of these studies lacked rigorous empirical design parameters.

Perhaps the most famous and comprehensive of all the case reports of client-centered work with children is Axline's now-classic work, *Dibs: In Search of Self* (1964). This book stands as a model of single case analysis process and outcome. Employing client-centered techniques to train parents, Andronico, Fidler, and Guerney (1967, p. 10) demonstrated "reduction of physical and behavioral symptoms, increased harmony between parents and children, and improved academic performance." Unfortunately, however, there have been few controlled empirical studies conducted in recent years.

UTILIZING CLIENT-CENTERED THERAPY
IN A MANAGED CARE FRAMEWORK

At this time, it is difficult to discern just what managed care is, and what direction it is taking. For the purposes of discussion here, an idealistic definition of managed care is taken to mean the administration of health care delivery in a manner that contains costs while simultaneously delivering quality service equitably.

Under such a definition, psychotherapy with children—particularly in the family context—is aptly suited for dealing with children's emotional difficulties, be they constitutional or functional in nature. Because of the slope of the growth curve there is face validity to the notion that the earlier one comes to grips with a child's problem, the more likely the problem can be treated expeditiously. Second, in the family therapy context, the parent(s) as well as other children are also accessible to the effects of therapy. This maximizes the likelihood that environmental influences will also change positively and be available to accommodate to the change of the troubled family member(s).

SUGGESTIONS FOR FUTURE RESEARCH AND PRACTICE

The person-centered approach holistically addresses the individual. It focuses on enhancing the psychological well-being of the person—facilitating self-actualization. Such a view requires a research model that addresses different outcome measures. Suggestions from previous research in the client-centered tradition need to be employed to develop appropriate measures for ascertaining effectiveness of client-centered therapy with children and families. Thus, ipsative measures, such as Q-sorts for children and families (van der Veen, 1969) or analysis of voice quality process, might well be more vigorously investigated and applied to working with children and families.

With regard to practice applications, perhaps no other form of therapy has demonstrated its ability to adapt itself to efforts outside of clinical settings. Examples from Guerney (1964), Gordon (1970), as well as Rogers (1977, 1980) suggest possibilities for effecting change using client-centered methods in homes, schools, and in the community. Furthermore, these efforts have demonstrated their effectiveness in relatively short (i.e., under 20 sessions) time limits. With growing budgetary constraints, community efforts may well prove worthy of more extensive evaluation and application.

SUMMARY

Perhaps the major misconception regarding client-centered therapy by those looking at it from without—as opposed to those of us who practice it—is its apparent reliance on technique rather than philosophy. The heart of the client-centered process—that which makes it work—is the belief in the actualizing tendency of all organisms to fulfill their biological destinies. For our species, whose special sentience incorporates self-awareness, that actualizing tendency fulminates in the self-actualizing tendency. "Reflection of feeling," "active listening," and "evocative responding" are efforts to describe the client-centered method. The goal of this method is for therapists to convey their understanding of their clients' inner experience. Each therapist's empathic understanding creates an atmosphere of safety and trust that enables clients to reexperience aspects of their lives, thereby freeing and enabling their ability to grow—to actualize themselves. The process is exactly the same for all individuals irrespective of age.

REFERENCES

Alexander, F., & Healy, W. (1935). *Roots of crime: Psychoanalytic studies.* New York: Knopf.

Andronico, M. P., Fidler, J., & Guerney, B. (1967). The combination of didactic and dynamic elements in filial therapy. *International Journal of Group Psychotherapy, 17,* 10–17.

Axline, V. M. (1947). *Play therapy.* Boston: Houghton Mifflin.

Axline, V. M. (1964). *Dibs: In search of self.* New York: Ballantine.

Butler, J. M., & Haigh, G. V. (1954). Changes in the relation between self-concepts and ideal concepts consequent upon client-centered counseling. In C. R. Rogers & R. F. Dymond (Eds.), *Psychotherapy and personality change* (pp. 55–75). Chicago: University of Chicago Press.

Dorfman, E. (1951). Play therapy. In C. R. Rogers, *Client-centered therapy* (pp. 235–277). Boston: Houghton Mifflin.

Freud, A. (1928). *Introduction to the technique of child analysis.* New York: Nervous and Mental Disease Publishing Co.

Gaylin, N. L. (1966). Psychotherapy and psychological health: A Rorschach structure and function analysis. *Journal of Consulting Psychology, 30,* 494–500.

Gaylin, N. L. (1974). On creativeness and a psychology of well-being. In D. Wexler & L. N. Rice (Eds.), *Innovations in client-centered therapy* (pp. 339–366). New York: Wiley.

Gaylin, N. L. (1989a). The necessary and sufficient conditions for change: Individual versus family therapy. *The Person-Centered Review, 4,* 263–279.

Gaylin, N. L. (1989b). Ipsative measures: In search of paradigmatic change and a science of subjectivity. *The Person-Centered Review, 4,* 429–445.

Gaylin, N. L. (1990). Family-centered therapy. In G. Lietaer, J. Rombauts, & R. Van Balen (Eds.), *Client-centered and experiential psychotherapy towards the nineties* (pp. 813–828). Leuven: University of Leuven Press.

Gaylin, N. L. (1993). Person-centered family therapy. In D. Brazier (Ed.), *Beyond Carl Rogers: Towards a psychotherapy for the 21st century* (pp. 181–200). London: Constable.

Gaylin, N. L. (1996). The self, the family, and psychotherapy. *The Person-Centered Journal, 3,* 31–43.

Goldstein, K. (1940). *The organism.* Boston: Beacon Press.

Gordon, T. (1970). *Parent effectiveness training.* New York: Peter H. Wyden.

Guerney, B. (1964). Filial therapy: Description and rationale. *Journal of Consulting Psychology, 4,* 304–310.

James, W. (1890). *The principles of psychology.* New York: Holt.

Prouty, G. (1994). *Theoretical evolutions in person-centered/experiential therapy.* Westport, CT: Praeger.

Rice, L. N., & Wagstaff, A.K. (1967). Client voice quality and expressive style as indexes of productive psychotherapy. *Journal of Consulting Psychology, 31,* 557–563.

Rogers, C. R. (1939). *The clinical treatment of the problem child.* Boston: Houghton Mifflin.

Rogers, C. R. (1942). *Counseling and psychotherapy.* Cambridge, MA: Harvard University Press.

Rogers, C. R. (1951). *Client-centered therapy.* Boston: Houghton Mifflin.

Rogers, C. R. (1957). The necessary and sufficient conditions for psychotherapeutic personality change. *Journal of Consulting Psychology, 21,* 95–103.

Rogers, C. R. (1959). A theory of therapy, personality, and interpersonal relationships, as developed in the client-centered framework. In S. Koch (Ed.), *Psychology: A study of a science: Vol. 3. Formulations of the person and the social context* (pp. 184–256). New York: McGraw–Hill.

Rogers, C. R. (1961). *On becoming a person.* Boston: Houghton Mifflin.

Rogers, C. R. (1974). In retrospect: Forty-six years. *American Psychologist, 29,* 115–123.

Rogers, C. R. (1977). *Carl Rogers on personal power*. New York: Delacourte.

Rogers, C. R. (1980). *A way of being*. Boston: Houghton Mifflin.

Rogers, C. R., & Dymond, R. F. (Eds.). (1954). *Psychotherapy and personality change*. Chicago: University of Chicago Press.

Stephenson, W. (1953). *The study of behavior: Q-Technique and its methodology*. Chicago: University of Chicago Press.

Stollak, G. E. (1968). The experimental effects of training college students as play therapists. *Psychotherapy: Theory, Research, and Practice, 5,* 77–80.

Taft, J. (1933). *The dynamics of therapy in a controlled relationship.* New York: Macmillan.

van der Veen, F. (1969). Family psychotherapy and a person's concept of the family: Some clinical and research formulations. *Institute for Juvenile Research Reports, 6,* 16. Chicago: Institute for Juvenile Research.

7

Cognitive–Behavioral Therapy

AMY L. KRAIN and PHILIP C. KENDALL

THEORETICAL OVERVIEW OF COGNITIVE–BEHAVIORAL THERAPY

The cognitive–behavioral approach to the treatment of children and adolescents integrates cognitive restructuring and problem solving with behavioral techniques such as contingency management and modeling (Kendall, 1991). The primary aim of cognitive–behavioral therapy (CBT) is to modify or improve a child's maladaptive emotional, cognitive, and behavioral responses to his environment. It is fairly structured, and often time-limited. As part of the treatment, the therapist helps the client to better understand the mechanisms by which thoughts and feelings influence and mediate behavior. This perspective is not explained to the clients—they are children—but becomes evident through shared experiences and exposure tasks. The theory is problem-solving oriented, focusing on cognitive information processing, as well as social skills and interactions. Learning to generate alternatives and evaluate outcomes are essential tools for adaptive functioning across the life span. Through use of performance-based procedures, new skills are refined and reinforced by feedback and encouragement. Contingencies help to encourage involvement and stimulate motivation.

The theoretical model that guides CBT is interactional, considering both the internal and external environments surrounding the child (Southam-Gerow, Henin, Chu, Marrs, & Kendall, 1997). External social environments (family, school, peers) play a crucial role in the child's cognitive and affective development. For this reason, each of these contexts must be considered and examined to determine possible influences on the child's difficulties and on improvement. Children and adolescents learn how to identify cues in their social environment that may be influencing their own thoughts and feelings; they can then learn to problem-solve around such issues. In addition, children often do not realize the direct connection between their cognitions and attitudes and their overt behaviors. CBT aims to edu-

AMY L. KRAIN and PHILIP C. KENDALL • Department of Psychology, Temple University, Philadelphia, Pennsylvania 19122.

Handbook of Psychotherapies with Children and Families, edited by Russ and Ollendick. Kluwer Academic/Plenum Publishers, New York, 1999.

cate clients about the relationship between thought processes and affective reactions and behavior (Kendall, 1991).

Within the cognitive–behavioral framework, the therapist assumes the roles of consultant, diagnostician, and educator (Kendall, 1991). As a consultant, the therapist helps the client to arrive at solutions and determine the most suitable option. Instead of providing the answers to a child's problems, the therapist assists in the problem-solving process, helping the client to identify options and choose a solution. The therapeutic relationship is a collaborative one, in which the therapist plays the role of coach, and the child is encouraged to arrive at his own solutions. Being a diagnostician may include use of the DSM, but it involves more—it entails an exploration and integration of data from the client, parents, and other sources, with knowledge of normal development and psychopathology to generate hypotheses concerning the sources of, and influences on, the child's difficulties. Such a process facilitates the therapist's determination of a likely-to-be-effective treatment plan. The therapist also acts as an educator, helping the client to learn new skills. This process also involves assessing the child's strengths and working to help maximize them. As an educator, the therapist must decide on the best strategies for teaching the child methods of behavioral control, cognitive skills, and emotional development.

The cognitive component of the treatment focuses on the ways in which the child thinks about himself and his environment. The child's thoughts may be maladaptive: either distorted or deficient (Kendall, 1985, 1993). Children who experience *distorted* thinking often misinterpret their environment and social interactions. These children and adolescents may present with internalizing disorders such as anxiety and depression because they are erroneously processing the cues in their environment. Children with *deficiencies* in thinking exhibit behavior that results from a lack of forethought—they often act without thinking of the consequences of their actions. Children with externalizing disorders, such as attention-deficit hyperactivity disorder (ADHD), often demonstrate deficient thinking. Aggressive children have been found to exhibit both deficient and distorted thinking (Kendall & MacDonald, 1993; Kendall, Ronan, & Epps, 1991). During cognitive–behavioral treatment, the child learns to identify elements of his distortions or deficient thinking, and practice new ways to think. For example, a child who does not consider the consequences before he strikes out at another child can learn to read social cues and take the time to examine possible outcomes before raising his fist. Distorted processing may also need to be changed. For instance, a child who is depressed may inaccurately attribute negative events to internal, global, and stable causes (e.g., Hilsman & Garber, 1995) and such a child would need to identify these maladaptive attributions and learn to consider alternative ones. During this process, the child is encouraged to problem-solve and arrive at new solutions with some coaching from his therapist.

Within cognitive–behavioral treatment, contingent reinforcement is used to help the child to modify behavior and acquire skills. It is critical, however, that the child learn to reward himself and not rely solely on external rewards. The child learns to congratulate himself for a job well done—helping to attribute gains to personal effort, which can, in turn, help to maintain therapeutic gains. Techniques such as modeling and role-playing encourage the child's participation in the learning process, as well as provide opportunities for the use of newly learned coping strategies to deal with success and failure. The therapist is an active participant in treatment—serving as a coping model and engaging in the role-play activities.

HISTORY OF CBT

The cognitive–behavioral approach to the treatment of children emerged primarily from a bidirectional movement as behaviorists shifted toward cognitive procedures and cognitive therapists adopted behavioral techniques (Kendall & Hollon, 1979). As the inevitable link between cognition and behavior became apparent, therapists developed techniques that would utilize this interface between overt and covert processes to induce change. Cognitive restructuring techniques were aimed at altering maladaptive ways of thinking (e.g., Ellis, 1962) and modifying illogical attributions (e.g., Beck, 1976), which then induce changes in behavior. Behavioral techniques such as modeling (Bandura, 1969) and problem solving (e.g., D'Zurilla & Goldfried, 1971) were reconceptualized as tools for implementing cognitive as well as behavioral changes. Some of the procedures employed in CBT were designed for adult clients and later modified to become developmentally appropriate for youth, whereas other treatments were designed specifically with children in mind.

As the cognitive–behavioral approach emerged, it maintained the emphasis on empirical support that was critical to the behaviorist approach. Cognitive–behavioral theories and interventions are based on research findings supporting the role of cognition in behavior change and the integrative role of both behavior and cognition in affective changes. The use of manualized treatments facilitates cognitive–behavioral outcome research because it minimizes between-therapist and across-site differences. Improvements in treatment procedures can then be instituted based on empirical findings. This inherent tie to empiricism is also apparent in cognitive–behavioral procedures and case formulations —both the therapist and client are encouraged to formulate hypotheses, perform experiments, and evaluate outcomes.

ASSESSMENT AND CASE FORMULATION

To formulate the case, the cognitive–behavioral therapist strives to learn about the child's emotions, thoughts, and behavior within the context/environment in which he lives. The cognitive–behavioral therapist uses a hypothesis-testing approach to assessment and often consults several sources to help construct an accurate picture of the child's difficulties. These sources usually include parents and teachers, as well as other adults who play a significant role in the child's life. Because a child's behavior is rarely entirely consistent across settings, it is critical to learn about the child as he behaves and interacts in several different contexts.

One goal of cognitive–behavioral assessment is to determine the nature of the cognitive *distortions* or *deficiencies* and the related behavioral patterns that are contributing to the child's difficulties. For such assessment, a multimethod approach is often the most useful, as it allows for differences in response styles and permits the therapist to obtain information from a variety of sources. The therapist may utilize a combination of techniques such as semistructured or structured interviews, self-report instruments, or direct observation, to formulate a case. Empirically validated measures are often used in research, as well as in private clinical practice because they yield more reliable results and may not rely as much on individual judgment. This allows for greater consistency in diagnosis across cases and treatment settings. In addition, these measures have been designed for specific populations and do account for developmental levels and a child's ability to report symptoms. Scales that have been designed for use by several sources (e.g., CBCL, TRF, YSR; Achenbach, 1991a,b; Achenbach & Edelbrock, 1989) provide access to cross-situational information while maintaining consistency of scale items. From a variety of sources, the clinician gathers information regarding the child's thinking and behavior in different situations.

Within this cognitive–behavioral approach to assessment, the child's difficulties are placed in a framework where emotions, thoughts, and behavior are causally interrelated. The therapist looks at each of these elements, as well as the impact each has on the others. For example, if a parent brings her child in and states that he is "depressed," the therapist does not diagnose the child as having a depressive disorder and begin treatment; instead, he or she further questions the child and parent about other behavior, as well as cognition and feelings, to better understand the child's emotional state. Perhaps the parents and teachers are expecting too much from the child; or it may be that the child is unhappy or distressed about a part of his life and withdraws as a means of coping.

Assessment procedures must also identify the developmental level of the child, as this helps the therapist tailor and provide developmentally appropriate treatment. Cognitive–behavioral treatments are often manualized and structured although they do allow and encourage a significant level of flexibility (Kendall & Chu, 1999; Kendall, Chu, Gifford, Hayes, & Nauta, 1999). An adolescent, for instance, may identify more with sports figures, whereas a younger child may relate to superheroes or cartoon characters. Manual-guided cognitive–behavioral approaches are available for anger and aggression (e.g., Nelson & Finch, 1996), depression (e.g., Stark & Kendall, 1996), anxiety (e.g., Kendall, Kane, Howard, & Siqueland, 1990), and impulsive behavior (e.g., Kendall & Braswell, 1985). Each of these manual-guided programs has a workbook that the youths use to follow the materials in the treatment program (e.g., *Keeping Your Cool,* Nelson & Finch, 1996; *Taking Action,* Stark & Kendall, 1996; *Coping Cat Workbook,* Kendall, 1990; *Stop and Think Workbook,* Kendall, 1992). Although the manuals provide the specific goals and strategies for treatment, and the workbooks offer hands-on materials that facilitate the learning of the therapy content, a sensitive and flexible treatment application is intended and preferred.

INTERVENTION PROCEDURES AND MECHANISMS OF CHANGE

The cognitive–behavioral treatment of children involves numerous techniques adopted from both cognitive and behavioral theory (see the earlier cited manuals and workbooks for details). The child's difficulties are believed to reflect a complex integration of behavior, affect, and cognition, and therefore it is critical to address each of these elements. Nevertheless, depending on the nature of the disorder, some cognitive–behavioral treatments may use more behavioral techniques whereas others may rely more strongly on cognitive restructuring or emotion management (Kendall, 1993).

Cognitive interventions include identifying self-talk and cognitive appraisals, and learning about more adaptive ways of thinking. The first step toward the cognitive treatment of the child is to develop his awareness of thoughts and feelings in difficult situations. The youthful client is taught strategies of identifying self-talk, problem solving, and attribution retraining. Interestingly, following a pair of randomized clinical trials evaluating the outcomes of a cognitive–behavioral treatment for anxiety disorders (discussed later), Treadwell and Kendall (1996) conducted analyses of changes in the children's self-talk from pretreatment to posttreatment and follow-up. The findings suggest that the positive changes (reduced anxiety disorders) were associated with reduction in negative thinking. That is, the effectively treated participants engaged in significantly less negative self-talk after treatment. It should also be noted that positive self-talk was not associated with successful treatment and did not change from pretreatment to posttreatment. In other words, successful treatment was not linked to changing positive self-talk, but success was tied to the reduction in negative self-talk (the "power of nonnegative thinking," Kendall, 1984).

Youths participate in activities to learn problem-solving skills. This process includes identifying environmental cues (What's the problem?), taking the perspective of others, determining options and their consequences, arriving at a solution, and implementing the plan. The problem-solving sequence is a meaningful portion of the procedures of the intervention. First, the child works to identify and describe the problem(s) and consider any major goals accomplished by the solution. Alternatives are then generated and the consequences of each considered. Finally, the therapist guides the child to act as a "scientist" and test out the options (possibilities). Within this cognitive framework, the child is aiming to construct a coping template (Kendall, 1993). The therapist works with the child to strategize ways to cope with difficult situations. For example, if the child tests out one of his solutions to a problem and it is unsuccessful, he must learn adaptive ways of coping with this outcome.

Behavioral techniques include modeling, role playing, exposure experience, relaxation training, and reinforcement contingencies: Each is aimed at helping the child to identify maladaptive thoughts and feelings (and behaviors) and make changes as needed. For example, to cope with anxiety-provoking situations, the therapist teaches the child how to relax. The child is taught how to relax each muscle group one at a time (King, Hamilton, & Ollendick, 1988). This technique is not used alone; rather, relaxation is combined with other affective and cognitive coping skills.

The process of modeling allows the child to witness and participate in difficult situations, try alternative ideas, and observe the outcomes. There are several different types of modeling: symbolic, live, and participant modeling. Symbolic modeling involves videotapes or audiotapes, such as someone performing a task that the child finds difficult. The child can see how someone else handled the situation. Live modeling requires the therapist or another person to demonstrate coping while the child watches. Participant modeling is encouraged because it allows the child to "tag along" and contribute to the problem-solving process. Role playing is another method that allows the child to rehearse newly learned skills. Role-plays are often the first step toward gaining comfort with the use of these skills and achieving a sense of mastery (Southam-Gerow et al., 1997). The child helps the therapist succeed, and thereby better understands how to problem-solve successfully as well.

Modeling can take different emphases; the therapist may demonstrate mastery modeling, in which a successful outcome is demonstrated, or coping modeling, in which the therapist models taking steps to cope with obstacles that are preventing a successful outcome. Coping modeling is preferred because it allows the child to witness the use of problem-solving skills to cope with difficult situations. It also demonstrates to the child that problems or mistakes will happen but coping with them is an acceptable outcome.

A central, though often final step in cognitive–behavioral treatments is the exposure of the client to stress-producing situations. The exposure tasks allow the child to use the new skills in real life situations and to do so with the support of the therapist. Exposure tasks are usually graduated. The child is first presented with a mildly difficult situation and later with increasingly more stressful scenarios. Avoidance behavior is not permitted; rather, the child is encouraged to engage in the situation and to evaluate behavior and provide self-rewards. One way to have an initial exposure task that is not too distressing is to begin with imaginal exposures; the child imagines the stressful situation, identifying his thoughts and feelings, and describes how the coping skills would be implemented. In later exposures, the child is placed in real (or simulated) situations in which active coping with anxiety is required. Each success increases the child's confidence and acts to empower the child as a reward. The child can then self-define as a successful "coper" and can attempt more difficult exposure tasks. It is critical that this graduated process proceed at a pace that is comfortable for the child and therapist. One wants the task to be emotionally challenging but one does not want the child to be ill-prepared and mistakenly misperceive the situation or feel like a failure.

RESEARCH SUPPORT

There is empirical support for use of CBT with children and adolescents (Kazdin & Weisz, 1998). Studies have shown these treatments to be effective in reducing both internalizing and externalizing disorders. Treatments for children with anxiety or depression may emphasize coping skills and cognitive restructuring, whereas treatments for conduct problems may rely more heavily on contingent reinforcements and social problem solving. Nevertheless, most of these treatments have several similar features and all are manual-guided and time-limited. In this section we will describe the studies addressing the treatment of problems with anxiety, depression, anger, and attention.

With reference to anxiety problems, several studies have investigated the efficacy of CBT to reduce fears and specific phobias in children and adolescents (e.g., Hagopian, Weist, & Ollendick, 1990; Kanfer, Karoly, & Newman, 1975) and medical and dental fears (Heitkemper, Layne, & Sullivan, 1993; Melamed & Siegel, 1975; Peterson & Shigetomi, 1981). Although the results are supportive, several of these studies relied on scores on various dependent measures of anxiety for entry requirements and did not evaluate for presence of anxiety disorders.

For CBT with youths, treatments are designed specifically to address the nature of the disorder. With reference to anxiety disorders, for example, intervention is guided by findings such as anxious children's tendency to focus on social and environmental cues in a distorted manner and their often being preoccupied with concerns about evaluation and the likelihood of negative consequences (Kendall & Chansky, 1991). Anxious children also exhibit excessive nonfunctional coping self-talk (Kendall & Chansky, 1991) and endorse more threat-related self-statements than nonanxious children (Ronan, Kendall, & Rowe, 1993).

With these and other features in mind, Kendall and colleagues (Kendall, 1994; Kendall et al., 1997) have designed (Kendall et al., 1990) and evaluated (e.g., Kendall, 1994; Kendall et al., 1997) a multicomponent cognitive–behavioral treatment for anxious children aged 9–13. The approach (Kendall et al., 1990) places the greatest emphasis on integrating the modification of cognitive information-processing of interpersonal and social contexts with behavioral practice in skill building. The treatment stresses the learning process, including the influence of contingencies in the environment, and the centrality of the individual's mediating information processing style in the remediation of psychological distress (Kendall, 1985). This treatment program (16–20 weeks) combines cognitive strategies and behavioral procedures (e.g., relaxation, cognitive strategies, problem solving, and imaginal and *in vivo* exposure) organized into two segments. The first sessions are the cognitive–educational training segment, during which children learn, among other strategies, to identify anxious processing. The second eight sessions constitute the practice segment during which children use skills acquired in the first eight sessions in specific situations that are anxiety-provoking for the child.

The first randomized clinical trial of this treatment examined 47 youth (ages 9–13) who were diagnosed, according to DSM-III-R, as having either overanxious disorder ($n = 30$), SAD ($n = 8$), or avoidant disorder ($n = 9$). Participants were randomly assigned to either treatment or a wait-list control. Posttreatment evaluation found that participants and their parents reported increased coping skills and decreased anxiety. Behavioral observation data also provided support for the effects of the treatment. With regard to diagnosis, 65% of the children no longer met criteria for their primary anxiety disorder as primary at the end of treatment. These effects were maintained at 1–year follow-up. Long-term follow-up (3.35 years on average) of 36 of these cases found treatment gains to be largely maintained (Kendall & Southam-Gerow, 1996). Maintenance of gains was not significantly related to the amount of time since therapy, further supporting the beneficial effects of this cognitive–behavioral treatment.

Recently, a second randomized clinical trial of 94 youths (ages 9–13) replicated the findings of the previous study (Kendall et al., 1997). At the posttreatment assessment, over 70% of treated children no longer had their primary anxiety diagnosis as primary and over 50% of treated children no longer met diagnosis for their primary anxiety disorder at all. Of those in the wait-list condition, only two children no longer qualified for their primary anxiety diagnosis following the waiting period. As in the earlier study, these gains were largely maintained at 1-year follow-up. In addition, using normative comparisons (Kendall & Grove, 1988), the treated youths were found to have been returned from outside the normal range on several measures to within the normal range. These analyses provide support for the clinical significance of the outcomes.

Children and adolescents with obsessive-compulsive disorder (OCD) have also been found to benefit from cognitive–behavioral treatments. The majority of these studies are case reports of behavioral interventions (e.g., Fisman &Walsh, 1994), single-case designs (for a review, see March, 1995), or multiple-baseline evaluations of cognitive–behavioral treatment (e.g., Henin & Kendall, 1999). March, Mulle, and Herbel (1994) designed a 16-week cognitive–behavioral treatment called "How I Ran OCD Off My Land." This program integrates anxiety management training with behavioral exposure and response prevention techniques. The first step is to externalize the symptoms and to view OCD as an illness. The therapist then helps the child to identify areas where the child has success resisting the behaviors; this allows the client and therapist to develop a hierarchy. The therapist then teaches the child anxiety management techniques such as relaxation and cognitive restructuring. The final step of the treatment is exposure and response prevention; the child is exposed to anxiety-provoking stimuli and encouraged to prevent obsessive or compulsive reactions. In a study of 15 children, 6 of them were asymptomatic posttreatment and 9 were no longer symptomatic at follow-up. Ten of the fifteen showed a reduction of over 50% in self-report scores at follow-up.

Panic disorder in youths has been treated using cognitive–behavioral approaches. For example, Ollendick (1995) reported a multiple-baseline evaluation of four adolescents with panic disorder and agoraphobia. The treatment included relaxation, cognitive coping, and exposure interventions. Three of the four clients exhibited decreased panic attack frequency and agoraphobic avoidance, as well as decreased anxiety and depression. These gains were generally maintained at 6-month follow-up.

Akin to CBT for anxiety disorders, cognitive–behavioral treatments for children and adolescents with major depression or dysthymia target the nature of the disorder. For instance, depression often co-occurs with changes in behavior, affect, and cognition. Depressed children tend to attribute negative events to internal, stable, and global causes and successes to external, transient, and specific causes. They tend to distort experience consistent with their negative view of the world (Curry & Craighead, 1990; Joiner & Wagner, 1995) and often catastrophize the consequences of negative events, attending to the negative features of events (Kendall & MacDonald, 1993; Leitenberg, Yost, & Carroll-Wilson, 1986). Situational factors can act to precipitate and cognition can work to moderate depression (Lewinsohn, Hoberman, Teri, & Hautzinger, 1985). Although the number of studies is limited, research on CBT with depressed youths has found cognitive–behavioral treatment to result in greater gains than traditional counseling (Stark, Rouse, & Livingston, 1991) and relaxation training alone (Wood, Harrington, & Moore, 1996). It should be mentioned that antidepressant medications, such as tricyclics and serotonin-specific reuptake inhibitors (SSRIs), while some data are supportive (Emslie et al., 1977; Emslie, Rush, Weinberg, Kowatch, Camody, & Mayes, 1998), have not consistently been found to be superior to placebo in child and adolescent populations (Sommers-Flanagan & Sommers-Flanagan, 1996). These findings reinforce the value of alternative treatments such as cognitive–behavioral approaches which have received empirical support (see also Brent et al., 1997; Kazdin & Weisz, 1998).

Randomized clinical trials of a 16-session cognitive–behavioral treatment for depression have found encouraging results (Lewinsohn, Clarke, Hops, & Andrews, 1990; Lewinsohn, Clarke, Rohde, Hops, & Seeley, 1996). Lewinsohn et al. (1990) developed a treatment for adolescents based on a program for adults, Coping With Depression (Lewinsohn, Antonuccio, Steinmetz, & Teri, 1984), which had been found to be effective (e.g., Hoberman, Lewinsohn, & Tilson, 1988). Coping With Depression–Adolescent version is a group treatment with two sessions per week for 8 weeks. The group members are taught self-monitoring and self-reinforcement and they are encouraged to increase their participation in pleasant activities. Relaxation techniques may also be used. The program aims to decrease depressogenic cognition by teaching adolescents to identify, challenge, and change their negative thoughts and irrational beliefs. Communication, negotiation, and problem-solving skills help the adolescent to better communicate with those around him, including parents. Two joint parent–child sessions are included as practice sessions for the youths and their parents to practice new communication skills.

Lewinsohn et al. (1990) examined this treatment comparing three groups: group treatment, group treatment with concurrent parent group treatment, and a wait-list control group. Adolescents (N = 59) meeting DSM-III criteria for major depression or intermittent depression were assigned randomly. At posttreatment, 42.9% of the adolescent-only treatment group and 47.6% of the adolescent and parent group, no longer met criteria for a depressive disorder. This is in great contrast to the 5.3% of the wait-list group that no longer continued to meet diagnostic criteria. At 6-month follow-up, 83% of the treated sample no longer met diagnostic criteria.

A second randomized clinical trial found similar results (Lewinsohn et al., 1996). Ninety-six adolescents diagnosed with DSM-III-R major depressive disorder or dysthymia were placed in either a treatment group or a wait-list condition. At posttreatment, 67% of the treated adolescents no longer met criteria for a depressive disorder, as compared with 48% of the wait-list controls. At 12-month follow-up, 81.3% of treated adolescents failed to meet diagnostic criteria and at 24 months, the recovery rate was 97.5%.

Interventions designed to prevent future difficulties with depression in adolescents have used the cognitive–behavioral approach (Clarke et al., 1995). Clarke et al. (1995) developed a Coping with Stress Course to teach at-risk adolescents cognitive techniques to identify and modify negative and irrational thoughts. Adolescents (N = 172) considered at-risk for developing depressive disorders were assigned to either the treatment condition or a usual-care control condition, in which they were free to continue any existing interventions. Those adolescents in the prevention program were found to have an incidence of depression of 14.5% over a 12-month period versus 25.7% for the control condition.

Unlike the internalizing disorders (e.g., anxiety, depression), the externalizing problems (e.g., aggression) have been a more longstanding target for treatment research. Most cognitive–behavioral interventions for aggression focus on social problem-solving skills and interpersonal conflict resolution. Aggressive youths often display distorted as well as deficient cognitive processes. They tend to misread social cues (e.g., Dodge, 1986) and often act without thinking. CBT can help aggressive children to identify social and environmental cues, practice perspective-taking, analyze options, and better consider consequences.

Lochman and colleagues developed the *Anger Coping Program* for aggressive youths; it integrates affective education into a program of social problem-solving skills training and behavioral contingency training (Lochman, Lampron, Gemmer, Harris, & Wyckoff, 1989). Nelson and Finch (1996) created the *Keeping Your Cool* workbook, which helps children to identify physiological and affective cues and environmental precipitants of anger arousal. When anger expression emerges impulsively, a program for impulsive children that presents social problem-solving steps as self-instructions to "Stop and Think" (Kendall, 1992; Kendall & Braswell, 1982, 1985) may be useful.

CBT with aggressive youths has been systematically applied and evaluated. For example, Kazdin and colleagues examined the effectiveness of problem-solving skills training with inpatient children referred for antisocial behaviors (Kazdin, Bass, Siegel, & Thomas, 1989; Kazdin, Esveldt-Dawson, French, & Unis, 1987). Children receiving the skills training treatment were found to display fewer externalizing and aggressive behaviors, more prosocial behavior, and greater overall adjustment, than children in the control condition or children receiving nondirective relationship therapy (Kazdin et al., 1987).

Relative to other applications of CBT, use of CBT with children with ADHD has received less empirical support. Youth with ADHD exhibit several behavioral and cognitive difficulties including limited performance in rule-governed situations, impaired social functioning, and elevated levels of inattention, impulsivity, and activity. Taking these difficulties into account, CBT appears to be a theoretically consistent treatment option, as it addresses both cognitive and behavioral dysfunction. Interventions have been designed to teach self-talk as a means of self-control, to use rewards and response–cost contingencies, model problem-solving strategies, provide affective education and practice in perspective-taking activities (Kendall & Reber, 1987).

Despite the theoretical consistency between the nature of ADHD and CBT, these programs have demonstrated limited success. Such outcomes may be related to high rates of comorbidity with other disorders, both internalizing and externalizing, in children with ADHD (Hinshaw, 1987). In addition, these children often exhibit learning difficulties and have problems that may inhibit their ability to learn and apply problem-solving skills. In one study, CBT was combined with pharmacological treatment (Whalen & Henker, 1991). The medications may help to increase the childrens' attention span and task persistence, allowing them to better acquire the skills taught in cognitive–behavioral interventions. By integrating these two treatments, lower doses of medication may be as effective as higher doses alone, reducing the likelihood of aversive side effects (Horn et al., 1991). Horn et al. (1991) conducted a randomized clinical trial with 96 children with ADHD studying the effects of a combined intervention that included methylphenidate, child-focused CBT (based on Camp & Bash, 1981; Kendall & Braswell, 1982; Meichenbaum, 1977), and a behavioral parent-training program (Barkley, 1981; Forehand & McMahon, 1981; Patterson, 1976). Results showed that lower doses of methylphenidate in combination with the psychosocial treatments were as effective as higher doses of medication alone. However, the combined treatment was not found to be superior to higher medication doses. Further research on these combination treatments may uncover successful pharmacological and psychosocial integration programs.

UTILIZING CBT WITHIN A MANAGED CARE FRAMEWORK

Recent developments in the health care system in the United States have caused great concern for clinical psychologists and other mental health care providers. The primary aim of managed care is to lower costs to the consumer by eliminating "unnecessary" procedures and increasing efficiency (Rodwin, 1995). However, these goals are often in conflict as reducing expenditures may limit the health care available to an individual and may result in necessary procedures not being performed. A major issue is that managed care places unnecessary limits on the services provided to patients. Clearly, the unsupported restriction of sessions can have serious detrimental effects—and is obviously not to be supported. Nevertheless, one feature of the managed care design deserves applause. Managed care systems have tried to close the gap between research and clinical practice by recommending and supporting those treatments that have been empirically supported (Giles, 1991).

Although we do not support all of the managed care movement, it is worth noting that the cognitive–behavioral treatment of children and adolescents fits with the needs of a managed care system; the treatments are time-limited, brief, and problem focused. Assessment procedures are used to determine the nature of the child's difficulty so that a treatment can be outlined that meets the specific needs of the child. Cognitive–behavioral treatments are often manual-driven, therefore reducing the variability in treatment delivery between clinicians. In addition, CBT has been empirically supported (Kazdin & Weisz, 1998) and continues to be applied and evaluated across populations and treatment sites. It is beneficial to the psychological community that people are looking at the evidence for efficacy in making decisions regarding treatment: CBT can provide such evidence. However, this is not to say that cognitive–behavioral therapists support the limits placed on health benefits by some managed care systems; it simply remains that, given the current managed care systems, CBT is one treatment option.

FUTURE RESEARCH AND PRACTICE

Because of the relatively recent emergence of cognitive–behavioral approaches to the treatment of children and adolescents, there is a great amount of research that remains to be done in this field. Despite the growing literature on the efficacy of cognitive–behavioral treatments, there is little research on the specific elements of these treatments and their contribution to therapeutic outcome. By breaking down the treatments and examining the effects of different elements on treatment gains, one can develop a more comprehensive understanding of what each factor of treatment is contributing.

The future of cognitive–behavioral treatments relies on the transportability of these treatments from research centers to practitioners (Kendall & Southam-Gerow, 1995). Research support has been provided for numerous manual-guided treatments; however, replication of these findings in different settings is critical if we are to propose the widespread use of such techniques. For a treatment to be useful to the entire mental health community, it must be shown to be transportable from research clinic to outpatient facility and to private practitioner. Additional studies of the effectiveness of treatment in different ethnic and socioeconomic populations will also allow for more effective use of these treatments in various settings. Although we know that, for example, the CBT for anxiety disorders in youth is effective across gender and ethnicity (Kendall et al., 1997), we still need to continue to examine these issues in more depth.

Treatment research may also be used to learn more about psychopathology. By further examining the moderators and mediators of treatment outcome, we can develop a better understanding of psychological difficulties. This heightened understanding will then allow researchers to develop more effective treatments.

SUMMARY

The cognitive–behavioral approach to the treatment of youths is one that has received a significant amount of empirical support over the past several years. Through use of techniques such as cognitive restructuring, modeling, role playing, and exposure, the child learns to modify cognition as well as behavior to elicit affective change. Developmentally appropriate manuals are used that outline specific techniques in a brief, time-limited format. The use of a manual to guide therapy encourages the transportability of these treatments, although this issue requires additional research. Overall, cognitive–behavioral treatments provide empirically supported theory-based procedures that meet the increasing demands of the modern health care community.

REFERENCES

Achenbach, T. M. (1991a). *Manual for the Child Behavior Checklist/ 4–18 and 1991 Profile*. Burlington: University of Vermont.

Achenbach, T. M. (1991b). *Manual for the Teacher's Report Form and 1991 Profile*. Burlington: University of Vermont.

Achenbach, T. M., & Edelbrock, C. (1989). *Manual for the Youth Self Report*. Burlington, Vermont: Queen City Publishers.

Bandura, A. (1969). *Principles of behavior modification*. New York: Holt, Rinehart & Winston.

Barkley, R. A. (1981). *Hyperactive children: A handbook for diagnosis and treatment*. New York: Guilford Press.

Beck, A. T. (1976). *Cognitive therapy and the emotional disorders*. New York: International Universities Press.

Brent, D. A., Holder, D., Kolko, D., Birmaher, B., Baugher, M., Roth, C., Iyengar, S., & Johnson, B. A. (1997). A clinical psychotherapy trial for adolescent depression comparing cognitive, family, and supportive therapy. *Archives of General Psychiatry, 54,* 877–885.

Camp, B. W., & Bash, M. A. (1981). *Think aloud: Increasing social and cognitive skills—A problem-solving program for children*. Champaign, IL: Research Press.

Clarke, G. N., Hawkins, W., Murphy, M., Sheeber, L. B., Lewinsohn, P. M., & Seeley, J. R. (1995). Targeted prevention of unipolar depressive disorder in an at-risk sample of high school adolescents: A randomized trial of a group cognitive intervention. *Journal of the American Academy of Child and Adolescent Psychiatry, 34,* 312–321.

Curry, J. F., & Craighead, W. E. (1990). Attributional style in clinically depressed and conduct disordered adolescents. *Journal of Consulting and Clinical Psychology, 58,* 109–116.

Dodge, K. A. (1986). A social information processing model of social competence in children. In M. Perlmutter (Ed.). *Minnesota Symposium on Child Psychology* (Vol. 18, pp. 77–125)). Hillsdale, NJ: Erlbaum,

D'Zurilla, T J., & Goldfried, M. R. (1971). Problem solving and behavior modification. *Journal of Abnormal Psychology, 78,* 107–126.

Ellis, A. (1962). *Reason and emotion in psychotherapy.* New York: Stuart.

Emslie, G. J., Rush, A. J., Weinberg, W. A., Kowatch, R. A., Carmody, T., & Mayes, T. L. (1998). Fluoxetine in child and adolescent depression: Acute and maintenance treatment. *Anxiety and Depression, 7,* 32–39.

Emslie, G. J., Rush, A. J., Weinberg, W. A., Kowatch, R. A., Hughes, C. W., Carmody, T., & Rintelmann, J. (1997). A double-blind, randomized, placebo-controlled trial of fluoxetine in children and adolescents with depression. *Archives of General Psychiatry, 54,* 1031–1037.

Fisman, S. N., & Walsh, L. (1994). Obsessive-compulsive disorder and fear of AIDS contamination in childhood. *Journal of the American Academy of Child and Adolescent Psychiatry, 33,* 349–353.

Forehand, R., & McMahon, R. J. (1981). *Helping the non-compliant child: A clinician's guide to parent training.* New York: Guilford Press.

Giles, T. R. (1991). Managed mental health care and effective psychotherapy: A step in the right direction? *Journal of Behavior Therapy and Experimental Psychiatry, 22,* 83–86.

Hagopian, L. P., West, M. D., & Ollendick, T. H. (1990). Cognitive–behavior therapy with an 11-year-old girl fearful of AIDS infection, other diseases, and poisoning: A case study. *Journal of Anxiety Disorders, 4,* 257–265.

Heitkemper, T., Layne, C., & Sullivan, D. M. (1993). Brief treatment of children's dental pain and anxiety. *Perceptual and Motor Skills, 76,* 192–194.

Henin, A., & Kendall, P. C. (1999). Obsessive-compulsive disorder in children: A multiple-baseline evaluation of a cognitive–behavioral therapy. In *Cognitive and behavioral practice.* Submitted for publication.

Hilsman, R., & Garber, J. (1995). A test of the cognitive diathesis-stress model of depression in children: Academic stressors, attributional style, perceived competence, and control. *Journal of Personality and Social Psychology, 69,* 370–380.

Hinshaw, S. P. (1987). On the distinctions between attentional deficits/hyperactivity and conduct problems/aggression in child psychopathology. *Psychological Bulletin, 101,* 443–463.

Hoberman, H. M., Lewinsohn, P. M., & Tilson, M. (1988). Group treatment of depression: Individual predictors of outcome. *Journal of Consulting and Clinical Psychology, 56,* 393–398.

Horn, W. F., Ialongo, N. S., Pascoe, J. M., Greenberg, G., Packard, T., Lopez, M., Wagner, A., & Puttler, L. (1991). Additive effects of psychostimulants, parent training, and self- control therapy with ADHD children. *Journal of the American Academy of Child and Adolescent Psychiatry, 30,* 233–240.

Joiner, T. E., & Wagner, K. D. (1995). Attribution style and depression in children and adolescents: A meta-analytic review. *Clinical Psychological Review, 15,* 777–798.

Kanfer, F., Karoly, P., & Newman, P. (1975). Reduction of children's fear of dark by competence-related and situational threat-related verbal cues. *Journal of Consulting and Clinical Psychology, 43,* 251–258.

Kazdin, A. E., Bass, D., Siegel, T., & Thomas, C. (1989). Cognitive–behavioral therapy and relationship therapy in the treatment of children referred for antisocial behavior. *Journal of Consulting and Clinical Psychology, 57,* 522–535.

Kazdin, A. E., Esveldt-Dawson, K., French, N. H., & Unis, A. S. (1987). Problem-solving skills training and relationship therapy in the treatment of antisocial child behavior. *Journal of Consulting and Clincal Psychology, 55,* 76–85.

Kazdin, A. E., & Weisz, J. R. (1998). Identifying and developing empirically supported child and adolescent treatments. *Journal of Consulting and Clinical Psychology, 66,* 19–36.

Kendall, P. C. (1984). Behavioral assessment and methodology. In G. T. Wilson, C. M. Franks, K. D. Brownell, & P. C. Kendall. *Annual review of behavior therapy: Theory and practice* (Vol. 9, pp. 39–94). New York: Guilford Press.

Kendall, P. C. (1985). Toward a cognitive–behavioral model of child psychopathology and a critique of related interventions. *Journal of Abnormal Child Psychology, 13,* 357–375.

Kendall, P. C. (1990). *Coping cat workbook.* Ardmore, PA: Workbook Publishing.

Kendall, P. C. (1991). Guiding theory for therapy with children and adolescents. In P. C. Kendall (Ed.), *Child and adolescent therapy: Cognitive–behavioral procedures* (pp. 3–22). New York: Guilford Press.

Kendall, P. C. (1992). *Stop and think workbook.* Ardmore, PA: Workbook Publishing.

Kendall, P. C. (1993). Cognitive–behavioral strategies with youth: Guiding theory, current status, and emerging developments. *Journal of Consulting and Clinical Psychology, 61*, 235–247.

Kendall, P. C. (1994). Treating anxiety disorders in children: Results of a randomized clinical trial. *Journal of Consulting and Clinical Psychology, 62*, 100–110.

Kendall, P. C., & Braswell, L. (1982). Cognitive–behavioral self-control therapy for children: A components analysis. *Journal of Consulting and Clinical Psychology, 50*, 672–689.

Kendall, P. C., & Braswell, L. (1985). *Cognitive–behavioral therapy with impulsive children.* New York: Guilford Press.

Kendall, P. C., & Chansky, T. E. (1991). Considering cognition in anxiety-disordered children. *Journal of Anxiety Disorders, 5*, 167–185.

Kendall, P. C., & Chu, B. (1999). Therapist flexibility in a manualized treatment for anxiety-disordered youth. *Journal of Clinical Child Psychology,* in press.

Kendall, P. C., Chu, B., Gifford, A., Hayes, C., & Nauta, M. (1998). Breathing life into a manual. *Cognitive and Behavioral Practice, 5*, 177–198.

Kendall, P. C., Flannery-Schroeder, E., Panichelli-Mindel, S. M., Southam-Gerow, M., Henin, A., & Warman, M. (1997). Therapy for youths with anxiety disorders: A second randomized clinical trial. *Journal of Consulting and Clinical Psychology, 65*, 366–380.

Kendall, P. C., & Grove, W. (1988). Normative comparisons in therapy outcome research. *Behavioral Assessment, 10*, 147–158.

Kendall, P. C., & Hollon, S. D. (1979). *Cognitive–behavioral interventions: Theory, research, and procedures.* New York: Academic Press.

Kendall, P. C., Kane, M., Howard, B., & Siqueland, L. (1990). *Cognitive–behavioral therapy for anxious children: Treatment manual.* Available from the author, Temple University, Department of Psychology, Philadelphia, PA 19122.

Kendall, P. C., & MacDonald, J. P. (1993). Cognition in the psychopathology of youth and implications for treatment. In K. S. Dobson & P. C. Kendall (Eds.), *Psychopathology and cognition* (pp. 387–427). San Diego: Academic Press.

Kendall, P. C., & Reber, M. (1987). Cognitive training in treatment of hyperactivity in children. *Archives of General Psychiatry, 44*, 296.

Kendall, P. C., Ronan, K. R., & Epps, J. (1991). Aggression in children/adolescents: Cognitive-behavioral treatment perspectives. In D. J. Pepler & K. H. Rubin (Eds.), *The development and treatment of childhood aggression* (pp. 341–360). Hillsdale, NJ: Erlbaum.

Kendall, P. C., & Southam-Gerow, M. A. (1995). Issues in transportability of treatment: The case of anxiety disorders in youth. *Journal of Consulting and Clinical Psychology, 63*, 702–708.

Kendall, P. C., & Southam-Gerow, M. A. (1996). Long term follow-up of a cognitive–behavioral therapy for anxious youth. *Journal of Consulting and Clinical Psychology, 64*, 724–730.

King, N. J., Hamilton, D., & Ollendick, T. (1988). *Children's phobias: A behavioral perspective.* New York: Wiley.

Leitenberg, H., Yost, L. W., & Carroll-Wilson, M. (1986). Negative cognitive errors in children: Questionnaire development, normative data, and comparisons between children with and without self-reported symptoms of depression, low self-esteem and evaluation anxiety. *Journal of Consulting and Clinical Psychology, 54*, 528–536.

Lewinsohn, P. M., Antonuccio, D., Steinmetz, J., & Teri, L. (1984). *The coping with depression course: A psychoeducational intervention for unipolar depression.* Eugene, OR: Castalia.

Lewinsohn, P. M., Clarke, G. N., Hops, H., & Andrews, J. (1990). Cognitive–behavioral treatment for depressed adolescents. *Behavior Therapy, 21*, 385–401.

Lewinsohn, P. M., Clarke, G. N., Rohde, P., Hops, H., & Seeley, J. R. (1996). A course in coping: A cognitive–behavioral approach to the treatment of adolescent depression. In E. D. Hibbs & P. S. Jensen (Eds.), *Psychosocial treatments for child and adolescent disorders* (pp. 109–135). Washington, DC: American Psychological Association.

Lewinsohn, P. M., Hoberman, H., Teri, L., & Hautzinger, M. (1985). An integrative theory of depression. In S. Reiss & R. Bootzin (Eds.), *Theoretical issues in behavior therapy* (pp. 331–359). New York: Academic Press.

Lochman, J. E., Lampron, L. B., Gemmer, T. C., Harris, R., & Wyckoff, G. M. (1989). Teacher consultation and cognitive behavioral interventions with aggressive boys. *Psychology in the Schools, 26*, 179–188.

March, J. S. (1995). Cognitive–behavioral psychotherapy for children and adolescents with obsessive-compulsive disorder: A review and recommendations for treatment. *Journal of the American Academy of Child and Adolescent Psychiatry, 34,* 7–18.

March, J. S., Mulle, K., & Herbel, B. (1994). Behavioral psychotherapy for children and adolescents with obsessive-compulsive disorder: An open trial of a new protocol-drive treatment package. *Journal of the American Academy of Child and Adolescent Psychiatry, 33,* 333–341.

Meichenbaum, D. (1977). *Cognitive–behavior modification: An integrative approach.* New York: Plenum Press.

Melamed, B. G., & Siegel, L. J. (1975). Reduction of anxiety in children facing hospitalization and surgery by use of filmed modeling. *Journal of Consulting and Clinical Psychology, 43,* 511–521.

Nelson, W. M., & Finch, A. J. (1996). *"Keeping your cool." The anger management workbook.* Ardmore, PA: Workbook Publishing.

Ollendick, T. H. (1995). Cognitive behavioral treatment of panic disorder with agoraphobia in adolescence: A multiple-baseline design analysis. *Behavior Therapy, 26,* 517–531.

Patterson, G. R. (1976). *Living with children: New methods for parents and teachers.* Champaign, IL: Research Press.

Peterson, L., & Shigetomi, C. (1981). The use of coping techniques to minimize anxiety in hospitalized children. *Behavior Therapy, 12,* 1–14.

Rodwin, M. C. (1995). Conflicts in managed care. *New England Journal of Medicine, 332,* 604–607.

Ronan, K. R., Kendall, P. C., & Rowe, M. (1993). Negative affectivity in children: Development and validation of a self-statement questionnaire. *Cognitive Therapy and Research, 18,* 509–528.

Sommers-Flanagan, J., & Sommers-Flanagan, R. (1996). Efficacy of antidepressant medication with depressed youth: What psychologists should know. *Professional Psychology: Research and Practice, 27,* 145–153.

Southam-Gerow, M. A., Henin, A., Chu, B., Marrs, A., & Kendall, P. C. (1997). Cognitive–behavioral therapy with children and adolescents. *Child and Adolescent Psychiatric Clinics of North America, 6,* 111–136.

Stark, K., & Kendall, P. C. (1996). *Treating depressed children: Therapist manual for "Taking Action."* Ardmore, PA: Workbook Publishing.

Stark, K. D., Rouse, L. W., & Livingston, R. (1991). Treatment of depression during childhood and adolescence: Cognitive–behavioral procedures for the individual and family. In P. C. Kendall (Ed.), *Child and adolescent therapy: Cognitive–behavioral procedures* (pp. 165–206). New York: Guilford Press.

Treadwell, K. R. H., & Kendall, P. C. (1996). Self-talk in youth with anxiety disorders: States of mind, content specificity, and treatment outcome. *Journal of Consulting and Clinical Psychology, 64,* 941–950.

Whalen, C. K., & Henker, B. (1991). Therapies for hyperactive children: Comparisons, combinations, and compromises. *Journal of Consulting and Clinical Psychology, 59,* 126–137.

Wood, A., Harrington, R., & Moore, A. (1996). Controlled trial of a brief cognitive–behavioural intervention in adolescent patients with depressive disorders. *Journal of Child Psychology and Psychiatry and Allied Disciplines, 37,* 737–746.

8

Family Systems Therapy

WILLIAM C. NICHOLS

[Family therapy is] any psychotherapeutic endeavor that explicitly
focuses on altering the interaction between or among family members and seeks to improve the functioning of the family as a unit, or
its subsystems and/or the functioning of individual members of the
family.

Gurman, Kniskern, and Pinsof (1986, p. 565)

THEORETICAL OVERVIEW OF FAMILY THERAPY

Family therapy represents an emphasis on wholeness and focusing on examining
persons and their behaviors in context, in contrast to a reductionist approach that
seeks to reduce the client's problems to personal, individual, and internal conflicts
or deficiencies. Family therapy moves the focus, as one pioneer in the field (Jay
Haley) has put it, from concentrating on what is inside the person's head to what is
between people. Rather than focusing essentially on the individual—e.g., assuming
that a child has a problem, or is a problem—family therapy examines the context
and how the context and the child are interrelated. One looks, as Gregory Bateson
(1979) put it, for "the pattern which connects." Family therapy, as used here, refers
to "an orientation, a perspective, in which issues are seen in the context of family
structure and process; it does not refer to a particular set of techniques or the number of individuals seen in an interview" (Nichols & Everett, 1986, p. 56).

The common feature linking more than a dozen contemporary "schools" of
family therapy is adherence to a theoretical underpinning based on systems theory, specifically on various adaptations of General System Theory following Ludwig von Bertalanffy (1968). He defined a system as a set of elements standing in
interaction. That is, it is something that is put together in such a way that what-

---

WILLIAM C. NICHOLS • The Nichols Group, Inc., Watkinsville, Georgia 30677-4212.

Handbook of Psychotherapies with Children and Families, edited by Russ and Ollendick.
Kluwer Academic/Plenum Publishers, New York, 1999.

ever affects one part affects other parts. Those elements are "organized by the consistent nature of the relationship between the elements" (Steinglass, 1978, p. 305).

Key features of organization include wholeness, boundaries, and hierarchies (Gurman & Kniskern, 1981). Wholeness refers to the fact that family therapists perceive patterns rather than reduce entities to their parts in a reductive fashion (Nichols, 1996). Another aspect of this is captured in the concept of nonsummativity, the idea that the whole is different from the sum of its parts, i.e., a family system cannot be understood simply by summing the characteristics of individual members. Boundaries deal with who is included within a system and the processes of interaction and feedback between the system and other systems. Boundaries may be relatively open or closed. Permeable boundaries permit feedback or interchange between a system and outside entities. The nature of the feedback determines whether the system is affected in positive or negative ways. Hierarchy is concerned with the fact that advanced and complicated living systems are composed of simpler and more basic system levels (i.e., cells, organs, organisms, groups, organizations, societies, and supranational societies, Miller & Miller, 1980). As these concepts are applied to families, the family system contains several important subsystems, specifically the marital or spousal, the parental, the sibling, and the individual subsystems. Change in one of these parts results in alteration in other parts of the system.

Other intriguing and important systems concepts are the notions of equifinality and feedback. Equifinality refers to the fact that the same end point or results can be reached by different means—methods, techniques, or approaches—and by starting from different original points. Systems theory holds that rather than being linear (A leads to B leads to C) as in a mechanistic, reductionist approach, causality is essentially circular. Hence, it is not necessary in a systems approach to move from a specified starting point to a predetermined outcome in a mechanistic manner. Feedback loops enable a system to engage in self-correcting behaviors and thus to maintain a steady-state condition. Practical implications of these concepts include the fact that no single kind of family or parental subsystem is required to produce healthy children, as illustrated by Westley and Epstein's (1970) finding that healthy young adults were reared in families with disturbed parents as well as in families with emotionally healthy parents. For the therapist, of course, there is the implication that several different techniques, methods, interventions, or approaches can be effective in producing desired change (Nichols, 1996).

Although changing the family system is the general goal of family therapists (Nichols & Everett, 1986, p. 2), the family may not be the lone focus of therapeutic intervention. A key issue in dealing with persons and their problems in a systemic fashion is to determine which parts of their multiple contexts should serve as the nub of assessment and intervention. With children this may involve not only assessment of the child and his or her parents but also any sibling relationships and extrafamily settings—especially the neighborhood and school contexts—that are especially relevant.

The case of Johnny and his family provides an illustration. Johnny was referred because of his disruptive behaviors and the fact that he was "a problem" at school. Previously, traditional play therapy had resulted in some changes in the youngster's attitudes toward the therapist and the therapy sessions but had not been accompanied by any alterations in his outside, real world behaviors. Assessment of this 10-year-old boy, his family, and the relevant contexts—home, com-

munity, and school—disclosed that the complaints about Johnny covered his behaviors not only at school but also at home and in the neighborhood in which he
lived. Exploration also revealed serious marital discord and the fact that Johnny
was rejected by both parents because of factors over which he had no control (a
physical resemblance to his father's family toward which his mother felt resentment and identification of Johnny by his father with the father's own despised
brother). Consequently, Johnny was occupying a classical scapegoat role in the
family and responding by rebelling against the unfair treatment. Some family therapists would reframe the boy's "misbehavior" positively as showing strength by
refusing to accept the scapegoat role passively and by fighting back.

Interventions with the family succeeded in bringing to a halt the automatic
cry from his siblings that "Johnny did it" whenever something untoward occurred.
An incident in which the mother discovered that she had falsely accused Johnny
of taking some missing money—which she discovered where she had secreted it
and forgotten about doing so—led to an apology to the youngster and to a command to the other children to stop automatically blaming him for incidents. As the
parents and siblings changed their attitudes and behaviors toward Johnny at
home, in the neighborhood, and at school, two other obvious alterations occurred.
Other neighborhood children and school personnel, who were asked to make certain that Johnny had actually committed a disapproved act before assigning him
responsibility for it, gradually ceased to blame him reflexively, and he ceased to be
any more of a "behavior problem" than his peers. Changing the family system, the
sibling subsystem, and the significant contexts in which Johnny lived was the key
to changes in Johnny.

THE HISTORY OF FAMILY THERAPY

The advent of family therapy represents one of the three great developments
in the mental health field along with the appearance of psychoanalysis and behavior therapy. Psychotherapy, until the appearance of family therapy, essentially
involved the treatment of individuals as individuals in a reductionist approach in
which the focus was on what was wrong inside the person to cause the problem
behavior. Even group therapy brought together individuals who were unrelated.
Family therapy represents perhaps the most radical of all innovations in the history of psychotherapy. With regard to the treatment of children, family therapy
shares with behavior therapy an emphasis on dealing with the social context of
children—the family and, in some instances, the school, as well as on the child
(Estrada & Pinsof, 1995).

Family therapy emerged in the United States in the 1950s out of a lengthy and
complex background. Although it is often claimed that "family therapy came out
of the study of schizophrenia," that is an oversimplified description. What has become the field of marital and family therapy—the fastest growing part of the mental health field by the beginning of this decade (Pinsof, 1990)—developed as a
result of four major streams: the child guidance movement, which developed early
in the twentieth century; classical family life education and marriage counseling,
which emerged following World War I; marital therapy, which was practiced by a
few therapists in the 1920s including some creative psychoanalysts but made its
way into professional literature in the 1930s and subsequently; and the study of

schizophrenia and families, which had its roots in the 1920s and 1930s in the clinical and theoretical work of Harry Stack Sullivan (1927) and J. L. Moreno in the United States and the research of E. Beaglehole (1958) in New Zealand. The story of research into schizophrenia and attempts to cure it during the 1940s and 1950s is too well-known to require repeating here. (For more extensive descriptions of the background and development of family therapy, see Broderick & Schrader, 1981, 1991; Nichols & Everett, 1986, pp. 1–63).

Many clinicians were doing psychotherapy in the United States by the 1950s but, for philosophical and particularly political reasons, avoided use of the term *therapy*. Some proclaimed publicly and occasionally vehemently that they were not performing psychotherapy but counseling. They denied that they were performing therapy because in some instances only physicians were permitted to claim they were therapists and were doing therapy. At the same time, there was a virtual hegemony of psychoanalysis and psychoanalytic influence that regarded only "depth" therapy and uncovering work aimed at past traumata as genuine therapy. Psychoanalytic strictures against seeing more than one person because of concerns over threats to the transference relationship between therapist and client resulted in the attitude among many that real therapy could not occur if multiple parties were physically present in the interview.

One of the services provided by the revolutionary and, at that time, daring efforts of doughty figures such as Lyman Wynne, Murray Bowen, Ivan Boszormenyi-Nagy, James Framo, Gerald Zuk, Carl A. Whitaker, Nathan Ackerman, John Elderkin Bell, Peter A. Martin, Bela Mittelman, C. P. Oberndorf, Bernard L. Greene, and others (Boszormenyi-Nagy & Framo, 1965; Nichols & Everett, 1986) was their establishment of acceptance of work with multiple clients (families and marital couples) as genuine therapy. Such breakthroughs enabled those who were working with families and couples to acknowledge that they were doing therapy and to call their work *therapy*.

Once the barriers were down, the right to perform psychotherapy gained, and the shift from focusing on the individual psyche to family systems established, family therapy was on its way to legitimation. What was founded as the American Association of Marriage Counselors in 1942 was renamed the American Association of Marriage and Family Counselors in 1970 and became the American Association for Marriage and Family Therapy in 1978. Another major organization, the American Family Therapy Association (now the American Family Therapy Academy), emerged in 1977. Two decades ago, marital and family therapy achieved formal recognition as a separate and distinct field of education with its own unique curricula when what is now the Commission on Accreditation for Marriage and Family Therapy Education was recognized by an agency of the U.S. government as the accrediting body for the field (Nichols, 1992). The legitimation of the theory and practice of marital and family therapy has been further established by the enactment of legislation credentialing and regulating practitioners in 40-plus states. The majority of those states require as part of the credentialing process successful passage of an examination sponsored by the Association of Marital and Family Therapy Regulatory Boards and conducted by Professional Examination Service (Lee & Sturkie, 1997). Currently, the practice of marital and family therapy—or family therapy, for short—is engaged in both by professional marital and family therapists and by others whose professional identity rests in other professions.

Family therapy practice and organizations have evolved in other nations around the world. The International Family Therapy Association, which annually conducts an international family therapy congress involving family therapists from across the globe, was established in 1987.

To date, family therapy has been used with a wide range of problems. Clinicians and researchers have described its use with problems and syndromes ranging from agoraphobia to schizophrenia. It is employed with difficulties affecting children such as anxiety, autism, conduct disorders, depression, eating disorders, school phobia, and other forms of psychopathology, as well as with youngsters in adjustment to parental divorce.

Ethnicity and cultural diversity, along with awareness of gender differences and inequities, are major concerns for the field of family therapy today. McGoldrick and colleagues' *Ethnicity and Family Therapy,* probably the best source for information on parent–child relations and child-rearing values and practices in different ethnic groups, is in its second edition (McGoldrick, Giordano, & Pearce, 1996; McGoldrick, Pearce, & Giordano; 1982). The complex interaction between gender and sex, between social and biological factors (Unger & Crawford, 1993), continues to be an issue for family therapists as well as for individually oriented clinicians (Cantor, 1990). Some therapists, however (e.g., Sandra Coleman, 1990), are able to integrate feminist theory and concepts with family therapy.

Like the field of individual psychotherapy, family therapy consists of multiple schools of theory and practice. Among the more prominent are Bowen family therapy, experiential, structural, two forms of strategic (Jay Haley and others), and strategic Mental Research Institute/Paul Watzlawick and others), Milan systemic, behavioral, cognitive behavioral, contextual, psychodynamic, integrative, psychoeducational, and others. While the various schools have some features in common, each has some unique elements. The descriptions that follow will be as general as seems practical, and are not intended to cover the extensive variations found in the various approaches in the field.

ASSESSMENT/INTERVENTION AND CASE FORMULATION

Like many other therapists, family therapists in their initial meeting with clients are concerned with making contact and establishing a working relationship, ascertaining the difficulties presented and the clients' resources for dealing with them, and formulating both short-term and outcome goals.

Clinical assessment, the process by which clinicians secure the understanding that is necessary for making informed decisions (Korchin, 1976), should constitute the primary linkage by which theoretical constructs are translated into practice. Unlike some traditional approaches in which assessment and treatment could be separated into different stages or even into different endeavors in which one professional might meet with clients initially and a therapist be assigned subsequently, assessment and treatment are conducted simultaneously in family therapy from the beginning. Assessment is, of course, an ongoing process in which the therapist makes observations and interventions and subsequently changes his or her assessment and perceptions as feedback flows from the contact and interaction with the client system.

Broadly speaking, assessment may take a standardized route (e.g., families assessed with structured interview guides or formal assessment devices) or a tailored approach (e.g., flexibly covering the factors that seem to be most significant to the family). A significant and growing number of formal assessment devices are available for working with families, couples, and children (L'Abate & Bagarozzi, 1993; Touliatos, Perlmutter, & Straus, 1990). Perhaps the most complete approaches are found in the Family Assessment Device and the companion McMaster Clinical Rating Scale (Miller et al., 1994) and the Beavers Family Systems Model (Beavers & Hampson, 1990).

Rather than use the concept of symptoms, many family therapists refer to pathological reactions. According to Framo (1972), psychopathology (or behavior pathology, as other family therapists term it) does not have to be regarded as an intrapsychic conflict, but as a peculiar or specific kind of relationship between intimately related people. Reactions of anxiety, depression, and others including psychosis, for example, frequently occur when the developmental strivings of the individual encounter opposing pressures from a dysfunctional family (Nichols, 1985; Robinson, 1979). Those family therapists reject the notion of diagnosis, because it is an individually based construct that conflicts with systems understandings of human behavior. Hence, they may not attempt to classify individuals into categories of disease, but they do attempt to determine or estimate the significance or value of what they observe with a family and its members. When they use standard psychiatric nomenclature, they typically are making a practical compromise with the requirements of reimbursement practices, rather than using categories that are consonant with their theory.

Important steps have been taken recently toward providing an alternative to the individual psychopathology classification approach. These efforts to provide for the classification of relationships and their disorders should eventually produce adequate consensus on family classification. The major product of this work is the *Handbook of Relational Diagnosis and Dysfunctional Family Patterns,* edited by Florence W. Kaslow (1996). It includes relational diagnoses focused on children and adolescents, couples, and families covering many of the disorders found in the individual diagnostic categories of the *Diagnostic and Statistical Manual of Mental Disorders* (American Psychiatric Association, 1994). With regard to children and adolescents, the following topics are covered: depression (N. J. Kaslow, Deering, & Ash, 1996); learning disabilities and attention deficit hyperactivity disorders (Culbertson & Silovsky, 1996); oppositional behavior and conduct disorders (Alexander & Pugh, 1996); and life-threatening illnesses: psychological difficulties and interpersonal relationships (Kazak & Simms, 1996).

There is no standard way of conducting the first interviews, although most family therapists probably wish to have the entire nuclear family or at least as many members as possible come to the first session. Some do not include very young children; for example, Bell (1975) excluded children under the age of 9. Bell (1975) and Satir (1964) tended to see the parents without the children for the first session or so. Bell would follow the initial session with the parents with a child-centered phase, and then a parent-centered phase, and finally a family-centered phase. Satir would include the children from the start if the marriage were too dysfunctional to tolerate therapeutic focus at the beginning and the children were needed as a safe focus (Goldenberg & Goldenberg, 1985).

The approaches taken by family therapists range from a relatively spontaneous encounter between the therapist(s) and the family (e.g., "dancing with the family," Whitaker & Bumberry, 1988) to conscious attempts to "join" the family and to alter it from inside (Salvador Minuchin, 1974) to using a precisely planned strategy (Haley, 1976).

One of the best descriptions of a variation of Whitaker's experiential approach is furnished by Napier (1976). An adherent of seeing whole families, Napier describes how therapy begins with the initial telephone contact and how the therapist should attempt to respond to the family's anxiety by manifesting firmness, insight, and sensitivity. Suggesting that the therapist identify with family members who feel most threatened—especially the husband-father who typically is less involved in family life than his spouse—he attempts to reach and involve them first. As part of winning this "battle for structure," the therapist strives to surmount the formidable problem of getting the family to shift the focus from the identified patient to the family as a whole. Although aware of the presence of problems in emotionally charged areas, such as the marriage, the therapist is advised to approach them later in therapy.

Haley's (1976) strategic approach is one in which the therapist takes control of the session and maintains control, whether speaking or listening to and observing the family's interactions. This involves orienting the family to the reason all members have been asked to attend (to get the views of all members), listening carefully to the various members' definition of the problem while involving each of them in the process, noting the disagreements and conflicts among members and redefining the problem from being a problem of one individual to being a problem of other members as well, encouraging them to discuss their various perspectives among themselves, and issuing a directive (i.e., assigns an out-of-session task) that is intended to bring about behavioral change. Similar to the approach described by Napier, the therapist in this approach observes the family's organizational and interactional patterns but makes no immediate comments, reserving the observations as guidelines for future interventions.

There is wide variation among family therapists in deciding whether to secure family history or to focus on current actions and issues. Strategic and structural family therapists, for example, tend to center attention on the present. Conversely, intergenerational and psychodynamic therapists are concerned with cross-generational relationships and family patterns and their transmission through the extended family as well as their appearance and role in the nuclear family. Some, such as Bowen systems therapists, tend to construct a family genogram for the adults in the session (McGoldrick & Gerson, 1985). Change is sought not only in the parent–child relationship but typically also in the patterns between the parent and his or her parent and family of origin so as to break the chain of multigenerational transmission of pathological patterns

Observation of the family as an integrated system and unit and careful scrutiny of the patterns of interaction among its members across time, two basic principles of family assessment (Reiss, 1980), illustrate both the complex nature and processual nature of family assessment. One needs to let a "live history" emerge from the family's interaction, rather than relying solely on verbal data (Ackerman, 1958). As the family interaction unfolds and the therapist asks questions and makes interventions, it is helpful to engage in an internal process of reflecting on such questions as the following: How are the presenting problems and the difficulties manifested in the reactions of the identified individual related to the family system? Does the current family dysfunction reflect an acute situation or a characteristic, long-term pattern of functioning? Why has the family come in at this time, rather than earlier or at some future time? (Nichols & Everett, 1986).

Integrative family therapy, the approach followed by the author (Nichols, 1988, 1996; Nichols & Everett, 1986), does not consist of standardized therapeutic interventions. Rather, treatment is tailored to the client system. Nichols and Everett (1986) have provided a list of questions to be used flexibly in approaching a family (p. 183) and described guidelines for observing process and making interactive inquiries with various family subsystems (pp. 189–204). They also give an example of constructing a family assessment containing a blending of individual, family subsystem, intergenerational, and social network data (pp. 204–215). Their approach includes a summary of the therapist's clinical impression of each member's individual development in terms of ego development, capacity for intimacy and bonding, maturity, and management of anxiety and stress; evaluation of interpersonal dynamics within the parent–child, spousal, and sibling subsystems including patterns of coalitions, parentification, internal and external family boundaries, scapegoating, and triangles; identification of broad family system and transgenerational patterns including myths and secrets; and characterization of the family's social network patterns including living environment, school, work, religious, and other relevant social patterns.

Closely associated with the assessment process is the task of establishing therapeutic goals. Family therapists generally agree that symptom relief without the appearance of new symptoms is an outcome goal (Green & Framo, 1981). Several different methods are used in determining both outcome goals and process goals. A pattern in which the presenting problems/symptoms of various systems levels are assessed and specific treatment goals developed for each level has proven clinically useful: individual: DSM-IV symptoms; marriage: marital problems; parent–child: parent-child problems; family: nuclear family and extended family problems; and community: social and community factors (Nichols, 1996, pp. 119–121).

ADDITIONAL INTERVENTION PROCEDURES AND MECHANISMS OF CHANGE

The form and nature of the therapeutic interventions used by family therapists is essentially shaped by:

- The theoretical orientation, experience, and clinical expertise of the therapist and the kind of therapeutic alliance he or she establishes and maintains with the family and its subsystems
- The problems presented by the family system initially and during the ensuing course of treatment

- The functional abilities and strengths of the family. For therapists concerned with transgenerational issues, this includes the historical elements that affect family functioning.
- The stages of development of the family and its effectiveness or lack of effectiveness in fulfilling the essential developmental tasks of the relevant stages.

(Nichols, 1996, p. 55, adapted).

Depending on such factors, a family therapist may work with the entire family as a unit, with subsystems within the family, or with individual family members in order to help change the family social system. A strategically oriented family therapist such as Haley (1976), for example, who works with the entire family unit would be expected to engage in the following actions during the course of therapy: monitor the family's behaviors; continue to issue directives regarding reframing the problems/symptoms and family rules, and restraining change as indicated; join various family coalitions so as to create imbalance in the family and compel the family to take steps to create a new balance; and meet with the family long enough and adequately to ensure family stabilization and maintenance of a supportive family structure.

A considerable amount of family therapy work aimed at effecting changes in a disturbed or behavior disordered child focuses on the parents and on their marriage. The evidence seems abundantly clear from both clinical observation and empirical research that problems, tensions, and conflicts extruded from the marriage result in problems in the child. Some empirical research, for example, finds that marital discord is associated with inconsistent parenting, use of decreased reasoning and increased punitiveness, fewer rewards for children, and negative perceptions of the child's functioning (Stoneman, Brody, & Burke, 1988). Clinical experience indicates that changing patterns of aggressive behavior in marital interaction often are accompanied by significant drops in conduct disorders in a child or in children in the family. In some rare cases, parents may be seen without the child or children ever coming to the therapist and the complaints about the child resolved.

Consistent with systems theory, one finds that children's problems also may be related to the appearance of problems in the parent (Steinberg, Sayger, & Szykula, 1997).

Sibling subsystem sessions may be used during the course of therapy with intact nuclear families (Nichols, 1996, pp. 209–213). Particularly during marital breakup and family reorganization—the predivorce, divorcing, and postdivorce stages—sibling work is helpful (Nichols, 1985, 1986; Schibuk, 1989). Clinically, it has been found that siblings often have great ability to provide mutual support during times of family transition, especially if they are in the late middle years (approximately age 12) or older. As Schibuk (1989) points out, sibling subsystem therapy provides a focus on the "unit of continuity" as the subsystem that remains intact during family reorganization The major goals in sibling subsystem therapy at the postdivorce stage are (1) immediate: helping the children to cope with the losses that have occurred and to adapt to the changed circumstances of living as best they can, and (2) long range: helping them to get back on track and to resume their normal developmental progress through their life cycles as rapidly and effectively as they can (Nichols, 1986).

In some instances, postdivorce therapy can be conducted in which formerly married persons, and on occasion even a new spouse, are involved in conjoint sessions for the purpose of lessening tensions and improving interaction in the new "family" of the children. Such an approach obviously requires careful preparation and firm control by the therapist as well as the recognition that some ex-spouses care enough about their children and have sufficient maturity to be able to accept the challenge to put aside personal animosities and estrangements and cooperate for the sake of the children.

Most effective therapy probably contains educational components and family therapy for children is no exception. Parenting education appears to be an increasingly important need in complex cultures and rapidly changing societies. Traditional patterns are often ineffective and do not fit in times of widespread and rapid sociocultural change in which parents are dealing with different and more challenging situations than did their own parents. One of the questions that arises is when should parent education be used along with family therapy or instead of family therapy. Ainsworth (1996), for example, suggests that parent education and training is a more effective alternative than family therapy in group care programs with parents of abused children. Others, such as Guerney (1977), go further and would eliminate the term *psychotherapy* altogether and replace the practice with educational endeavors, specifically his "relationship enhancement" programs.

The either therapy or education question appears to be misplaced. Rather, what kind of therapy and what kind of educational endeavors and under what circumstances should each be used appears more appropriate. Skill-training programs have been widely accepted as useful and effective with some couples and families, but are not a good choice for chaotic couples and families, families in crisis, uncooperative couples and families, or couples and families manifesting psychotic, paranoid, and psychosomatic syndromes (L'Abate, 1981). One matter that sometimes is not addressed in parent education is that of sensitivity to transgenerational issues. What kinds of conflicts are engendered in a parent when he or she is expected to do things differently than his or her own parents did? Careful attention to the arousal of loyalty conflicts (Boszormenyi-Nagy & Spark, 1973) is required in such situations. Support of the client parents and sensitive and respectful disqualification of the parents' parents as experts frequently is needed to secure client cooperation and make skill-training effective.

RESEARCH EVIDENCE SUPPORTING THE USE OF FAMILY THERAPY

Researchers and clinicians have described the successful use of family therapy with a wide range of difficulties, including agoraphobia (Hafner, 1986), depression (Coyne, 1986, 1988; Dobson, Jacobson, & Victor, 1988), drug abuse (Kaufman & Kaufmann, 1979), eating disorders (Foster, 1986), and others. In studying divorce, Spanier and Casto (1979) found that the children were the focus of major adjustment problems for the adults in every marriage they studied that had dependent children. Gurman et al. (1986) found, as they had in earlier studies, that family therapy methods produced improvement with marital conflicts.

A sampling of available research findings regarding child and adolescent problems follows.

Specifically, with regard to child and/or adolescent problems, Gurman et al. (1986) concluded that improvement occurred in 71% of cases of behavior problems treated by any of a number of clearly defined family therapy or by eclectic psychotherapy methods. Estrada and Pinsof (1995) found that family interventions have consistently improved functioning in both children and parents in families in which children manifested conduct disorders and autism. Parents and other family members also directly benefit from child-focused interventions, gaining in knowledge, child-management skills, and attitudinal improvements. Estrada and Pinsof (1995) concluded that the most promising therapy for autism and child conduct are strategies that include family members and that "there is a significant body of evidence supporting the efficacy of family therapy in the treatment of childhood psychopathology" (p. 434).

After a comprehensive review of treatment research, Kazdin (1987) concluded that family interventions are the most promising methods for the treatment of child and adolescent conduct disorders. The meta-analysis of results from 163 studies led Shadish et al. (1993) to support that conclusion.

In describing "what we know" from marital and family research (MFT), Pinsof and Wynne (1995) concluded, in part, that for child and adolescent problems:

- MFT works (is significantly and clinically more efficacious than no psychotherapy) for adolescent conduct disorders, anorexia in young adolescent girls, adolescent drug abuse, child conduct disorders, aggression and noncompliance in attention deficit/hyperactivity disorder children, childhood autism, chronic physical illnesses in children (asthma, diabetes, and others), child obesity, and cardiovascular risk factors in children.
- MFT is more efficacious (than standard and/or individual treatments) for adolescent conduct disorders, adolescent drug abuse, anorexia in young adolescent females, childhood autism, and various chronic physical illnesses in adults and young children.
- MFT is not sufficient in itself to treat several severe problems and disorders, but family involvement is a critical and necessary component in the treatment of these problems (e.g., the most effective treatment of childhood autism, severe adolescent conduct disorders, and adolescent drug abuse also involve additional treatment and education components besides MFT).

Estrada and Pinsof (1995) expressed disappointment regarding the lack of research on family interventions for childhood schizophrenia, depression, learning disabilities, and suicide. They did, however, indicate that research on therapy with adults affected by such disorders definitely supports the superiority of treatment involving families and expressed the view that results from studying the family-oriented treatment of children manifesting those disorders would be even more powerful than with the adults.

USING FAMILY THERAPY WITHIN A MANAGED CARE FRAMEWORK

As simple or simplistic as this may sound, the major problem involved in using family therapy within a managed care framework may be the reluctance some family therapists have in applying individual diagnostic labels to clients.

Publications are beginning to appear that offer advice on ways to cooperate with managed care (e.g., Araoz & Carrese, 1996).

Family therapy tends to be a short-term or medium length approach to treatment. Pioneer family therapist John Elderkin Bell (1975) estimates that 8 to 20 sessions is a reasonable expectation for family group treatment. Jay Haley (1976) set a fixed number of family interviews—such as 6 sessions—when he found the family especially doubtful or resistant regarding continuing and provided that more sessions could be scheduled at that time if they decided they were needed. Others estimate that marital therapy typically takes 6 months or so, although it should be noted that the range is quite wide.

Pinsof and Wynne (1995) suggest that marital and family therapies may be more cost effective than individual therapies because MFT treats more clients in a single session and the broader scope of MFT (which includes the health of other family members in addition to the index client) at least theoretically expands MFT's impact.

SUGGESTIONS FOR FUTURE RESEARCH AND PRACTICE

Several specific suggestions can be made regarding future research and practice:

- More research is needed to test the general efficacy of MFT versus alternate treatments. To date, results generally support MFT but there are some negative findings (Chamberlain & Rosicky, 1995).
- MFT researchers should clearly define the disorder/problem being studied and control for its severity (Pinsof & Wynne, 1995).
- MFT researchers should carefully define, verify, and empirically describe MFT treatments (Pinsof & Wynne, 1995).
- MFT researchers should incorporate cost-effectiveness measures (Pinsof & Wynne, 1995).
- MFT clinicians and researchers should develop and test longer term treatments in addition to continuing to test the shorter term treatments that have been tested up to this time (Pinsof & Wynne, 1995).

Family therapists need to devote considerably more attention to issues with at-risk children and commonly used diagnoses. Children labeled Attention Deficit/Hyperactivity Disorder (ADHD and ADD) frequently are given drugs because of their symptoms but receive little or no therapy or attention to family factors. The expressed need for love found in teenagers who become pregnant similarly requires attention that is generally not provided. The most common characteristics of at-risk children such as low-income, low literacy, limited supervision, and poor role models are tied to family issues.

SUMMARY

Family therapy is distinguished by its theoretical orientation, namely, its rootage in family systems theory. It shares many techniques within its current "schools" and with therapists from other fields (Nelson & Trepper, 1993). This chapter has addressed family therapy in a broad sense rather than being devoted to the explication of one of the field's "schools." Sample illustrations of various approaches within the general rubric of family therapy have been provided.

REFERENCES

Ackerman, N. W. (1958). *The psychodynamics of family life*. New York: Basic Books.

Ainsworth, F. (1996). Parent education and training or family therapy: Does it matter which comes first? *Child and Youth Care Forum, 25*(2), 101–110.

Alexander, J. F., & Pugh, C. A. (1996). Oppositional behavior and conduct disorders of children and youth. In F. W. Kaslow (Ed.), *Handbook of relational diagnosis and dysfunctional family patterns* (pp. 210–224). New York: Wiley.

American Psychiatric Association. (1994). *Diagnostic and statistical manual of mental disorders* (4th ed.). Washington, DC: Author.

Araoz, D. L., & Carrese, M. A. (1996). *Solution-focused brief therapy for adjustment disorders: A guide for providers under managed care*. New York: Brunner/Mazel.

Bateson, G. (1979). *Mind and nature: A necessary unity*. New York: Bantam Books.

Beaglehole, E. (1958). *Social change in the South Pacific*. New York: Macmillan.

Beavers, W. R., & Hampson, R. B. (1990). *Successful families: Assessment and intervention*. New York: Norton.

Bell, J. E. (1975). *Family therapy*, Northvale, NJ: Aronson.

Boszormenyi-Nagy, I., & Framo, J. L. (Eds.) (1965). *Intensive family therapy*. New York: Harper & Row (Hoeber).

Boszormenyi-Nagy, I., & Spark, G. M. (1973). *Invisible loyalties*. New York: Harper & Row.

Broderick, C. B., & Schrader, S. S. (1981). The history of professional marriage and family therapy. In A. S. Gurman & D. P. Kniskern (Eds.), *Handbook of family therapy* (pp. 5–35). New York: Brunner/Mazel.

Broderick, C. B., & Schrader, S. (1991). The history of professional marriage and family therapy. In A. S. Gurman & D. P. Kniskern (Eds.), *Handbook of family therapy* (Vol. II, pp. 3–40). New York: Brunner/Mazel.

Cantor, D. (Ed.). (1990). *Women as therapists*. Northvale, NJ: Aronson.

Chamberlain, P., & Rosicky, J. G. (1995). The effectiveness of family therapy in the treatment of adolescents with conduct disorders and delinquency. *Journal of Marital and Family Therapy, 21,* 441–459.

Coleman, S. B. (1990). A family therapist views the case. In D. Cantor (Ed.), *Women as therapists* (pp. 96–112). Northvale, NJ: Aronson.

Coyne, J. C. (1986). Marital therapy for depression. In N. S. Jacobson & A. S. Gurman (Eds.), *Clinical handbook of marital therapy* (pp. 495–511). New York: Guilford Press.

Coyne, J. C. (1988). Strategic therapy. In J. F. Clarkin, G. L. Haas, & I. D. Glick (Eds.), *Affective disorders and the family: Assessment and treatment* (pp. 89–113). New York: Guilford Press.

Culbertson, J. L., & Silovsky, J. F. (1996). Learning disabilities and attention deficit hyperactivity disorders: Their impact on children's significant others. In F. W. Kaslow (Ed.), *Handbook of relational diagnosis and dysfunctional family patterns* (pp. 186–209). New York: Wiley.

Dobson, K. S., Jacobson, N. S., & Victor, J. (1988). Integration of cognitive therapy and behavioral marital therapy. In J. F. Clarkin, G. L. Haas, & I. D. Glick (Eds.), *Affective disorders and the family: Assessment and treatment* (pp. 53–88). New York: Guilford Press.

Estrada, A. U., & Pinsof, W. M. (1995). The effectiveness of family therapies for selected behavioral disorders of childhood. *Journal of Marital and Family Therapy, 21,* 403–440.

Foster, S. W. (1986). Marital treatment of eating disorders. In N. S. Jacobson & A. S. Gurman (Eds.), *Clinical handbook of marital therapy* (pp. 575–593). New York: Guilford Press.

Framo, J. L. (1972). Symptoms from a family transactional viewpoint. In C. J. Sager & H. S. Kaplan (Eds.), *Progress in family and group therapy* (pp. 271–308). New York: Brunner/Mazel.

Goldenberg, H., & Goldenberg, I. (1985). *Family therapy: An overview* (2d ed.). Monterey, CA: Brooks/Cole.

Green, R. J., & Framo, J. L. (1981). *Family therapy: Major contributions*. New York: International Universities Press.

Guerney, B. G. (1977). *Relationship enhancement: Skill-training programs for therapy, problem prevention, and enrichment.* San Francisco: Jossey–Bass.

Gurman, A. S., & Kniskern, D. P. (Eds.). (1981). *Handbook of family therapy.* New York: Brunner/Mazel.

Gurman, A. S., Kniskern, D. P., & Pinsof, W. M. (1986). Research on the process and outcome of family therapy. In S. L. Garfield & A. E. Bergin (Eds.), *Handbook of psychotherapy and behavior change* (3rd ed., pp. 525–623). New York: Wiley.

Hafner, R. J. (1986). Marital therapy for agoraphobia. In N. S. Jacobson & A. S. Gurman (Eds.), *Clinical handbook of marital therapy* (pp. 471–493). New York: Guilford Press.

Haley, J. (1976). *Problem-solving therapy.* San Francisco: Jossey–Bass.

Kaslow, F. W. (Ed.). (1996). *Handbook of relational diagnosis and dysfunctional family patterns.* New York: Wiley.

Kaslow, N. J., Deering, C. G., & Ash, P. (1996). Relational diagnosis of child and adolescent depression. In F. W. Kaslow (Ed.), *Handbook of relational diagnosis and dysfunctional family patterns* (pp. 171–185). New York: Wiley.

Kaufman, E., & Kaufmann, P. N. (Eds.). (1979). *Family therapy of drug and alcohol abuse.* New York: Gardner Press.

Kazak, A. E., & Simms, S. (1996). Children with life-threatening illnesses: Psychological difficulties and interpersonal relationships. In F. W. Kaslow (Ed.), *Handbook of relational diagnosis and dysfunctional family patterns* (pp. 225–238). New York: Wiley.

Kazdin, A. E. (1987). *Conduct disorders in childhood and adolescence.* Newbury Park, CA: Sage.

Korchin, S. K. (1976). *Modern clinical psychology.* New York: Basic Books.

L'Abate, L. (1981). Skill training programs for couples and families. In A. S. Gurman & D. P. Kniskern (Eds.), *Handbook of family therapy* (pp. 631–661). New York: Brunner/Mazel.

L'Abate, L., & Bagarozzi, D. A. (1993). *Sourcebook of marriage and family evaluation.* New York: Brunner/Mazel.

Lee, R. E., & Sturkie, K. (1997). The national marital and family therapy examination program. *Journal of Marital and Family Therapy, 23,* 255–269.

McGoldrick, M., & Gerson, R. (1985). *Genograms in family assessment.* New York: Norton.

McGoldrick, M., Giordano, J., & Pearce, J. K. (Eds.). (1996). *Ethnicity and family therapy* (2nd ed.). New York: Guilford Press.

McGoldrick, M., Pearce, J. K., & Giordano, J. (Eds.). (1982). *Ethnicity and family therapy.* New York: Guilford Press.

Miller, I. W., Kabacoff, R. I., Epstein, N. B., Bishop, D. S., Keitner, G. I., Baldwin, L. M., & van der Spuy, H. I. J. (1994). The development of a clinical rating scale of the McMaster Model of Family Functioning. *Family Process, 33,* 53–69.

Miller, J. G., & Miller, J. L. (1980). The family as a system. In C. K. Hotaling & J. M. Lewis (Eds.), *The family: Evaluation and treatment* (pp. 141–184). New York: Brunner/Mazel.

Minuchin, S. (1974). *Families and family therapy.* Cambridge, MA: Harvard University Press.

Napier, A. Y. (1976). Beginning struggles with families. *Journal of Marriage and Family Counseling, 2,* 3–11.

Nelson, T. S., & Trepper, T. S. (Eds.). (1993). *101 interventions in family therapy.* New York: Haworth Press.

Nichols, W. C. (1985). Family therapy with children of divorce. *Journal of Psychotherapy and the Family, 1*(2), 55–68.

Nichols, W. C. (1986). Sibling subsystem therapy in family system reorganization. *Journal of Divorce, 9*(3), 13–31.

Nichols, W. C. (1988). *Marital therapy: An integrative approach.* New York: Guilford Press.

Nichols, W. C. (1992). *The AAMFT: Fifty years of marital and family therapy.* Washington, DC: American Association for Marriage and Family Therapy.

Nichols, W. C. (1996). *Treating people in families: An integrative framework.* New York: Guilford Press.

Nichols, W. C., & Everett, C. A. (1986). *Systemic family therapy: An integrative approach.* New York: Guilford Press.

Pinsof, W. M. (1990, November). *What's wrong with family therapy?* Paper presented at the annual conference of the American Association for Marriage and Family Therapy, Washington, DC.

Pinsof, W. M., & Wynne, L. C. (1995). The efficacy of marital and family therapy: An empirical overview, conclusions, and recommendations. *Journal of Marital and Family Therapy, 21,* 585–613.

Reiss, D. (1980). Pathways to assessing the family: Some choice points and a sample route. In C. K. Hofling & J. M. Lewis (Eds.), *The family: Evaluation and treatment* (pp. 86–121). New York: Brunner/Mazel.

Robinson, L. J. (1979). Basic concepts in family therapy: A differential comparison with individual treatment. In J. G. Howells (Ed.), *Advances in family psychiatry I* (pp. 428–435). New York: International Universities Press.

Satir, V. (1964). *Conjoint family therapy.* Palo Alto, CA: Science & Behavior Books.

Schibuk, M. (1989). Treating the sibling subsystem: An adjunct of divorce therapy. *American Journal of Orthopsychiatry, 59,* 226–237.

Shadish, W. R., Montgomery, L. J., Wilson, P., Wilson, M. R., Bright, I., & Okwumabua, T. (1993). Effects of family and marital psychotherapies: A meta-analysis. *Journal of Consulting and Clinical Psychology, 61,* 992–1002.

Spanier, G. B., & Casto, R. F. (1979). Adjustment to separation and divorce: A qualitative analysis. In G. Levinger & O. C. Moles (Eds.), *Divorce and separation* (pp. 211–227). New York: Basic Books.

Steinberg, E. B., Sayger, T. V., & Szykula, S. A. (1997). The effects of strategic and behavioral family therapies on child behavior and depression. *Contemporary Family Therapy, 19,* 537–551.

Steinglass, P. (1978). The conceptualization of marriage from a systems theory perspective. In T. J. Paolino & B. S. McCrady (Eds.), *Marriage and marital therapy* (pp. 298–365). New York: Brunner/Mazel.

Stoneman, Z., Brody, C., & Burke, M. (1988). Marital quality, depression, and inconsistent parenting: Relationship with observed mother–child conflict. *American Journal of Orthopsychiatry, 59,* 105–117.

Sullivan, H. S. (1927). The onset of schizophrenia. *American Journal of Psychiatry, 7,* 105–134.

Touliatos, J., Perlmutter, B. F., & Straus, M. A. (Eds.) (1990). *Handbook of family measurement techniques.* Newbury Park, CA: Sage.

Unger, R. K., & Crawford, M. (1993). Commentary: Sex and gender: The troubled relationship between terms and concepts. *Psychological Science, 4,* 122–124.

von Bertalanffy, L. (1968). *General system theory.* New York: Braziller.

Westley, W. A., & Epstein, N. B. (1970). *The silent majority.* San Francisco: Jossey–Bass.

Whitaker, C. A., & Bumberry, W. M. (1988). *Dancing with the family: A symbolic- experiential approach.* New York: Brunner/Mazel.

9

Parent Training

ROBERT J. McMAHON

THEORETICAL OVERVIEW OF PARENT TRAINING

Parent training (PT) can be defined as an approach to treating child behavior problems by using

> procedures in which parents are trained to alter their child's behavior in the home. The parents meet with a therapist or trainer who teaches them to use specific procedures to alter interactions with their child, to promote prosocial behavior, and to decrease deviant behavior. (Kazdin, 1995b, p. 82)

PT has received substantial attention during the past 30 years, and has been applied to a broad array of child problems (see volumes by Briesmeister & Schaefer, 1998, and Dangel & Polster, 1984). These include attention-deficit/hyperactivity disorder, anxiety disorders, enuresis, sleep problems, feeding difficulties, and as an intervention for child-abusing and neglectful parents. PT has also been employed with mentally handicapped and/or autistic children and their families. However, PT has been primarily employed in the treatment of preadolescent (i.e., preschool- to school-age) children who exhibit overt conduct-problem (CP) behaviors such as temper tantrums, aggression, and excessive noncompliance, and it is in this area that PT has the greatest empirical support. In recent reviews of various treatment approaches for child CP, PT has consistently emerged as the most successful intervention to date with these youngsters (e.g., Kazdin, 1995b; McMahon & Wells, 1998). This chapter will focus on PT interventions for preadolescent children who engage in excessive levels of overt CP. These children typically meet DSM-IV (American Psychiatric Association, 1994) criteria for Oppositional Defiant Disorder or Conduct Disorder.

ROBERT J. McMAHON • Department of Psychology, University of Washington, Seattle, Washington 98195-1525.

Handbook of Psychotherapies with Children and Families, edited by Russ and Ollendick. Kluwer Academic/Plenum Publishers, New York, 1999.

The Development of CP in Children

Longitudinal studies have shown that there are multiple developmental pathways that lead to the display of CP in childhood, adolescence, and adulthood (e.g., Moffitt, 1993). The "early starter" (Patterson, Capaldi, & Bank, 1991) pathway is characterized by the onset of CP in the preschool and early school-age years, and by a high degree of continuity throughout childhood and into adolescence and adulthood. It is thought that these children progress from relatively less serious (e.g., noncompliance, temper tantrums) to more serious (e.g., aggression, stealing, substance abuse) CP behaviors over time; that overt behaviors (e.g., defiance, fighting) appear earlier than covert behaviors (e.g., lying, stealing); and that later CP behaviors expand the children's behavioral repertoire rather than replacing earlier behaviors (e.g., Edelbrock, 1985; Patterson, Reid, & Dishion, 1992). Furthermore, there is an expansion of the settings in which the CP behaviors occur over time, from the home to other settings such as the school and the broader community.

On school entry, these children's coercive style of interaction is likely to extend to interactions with teachers and peers, resulting in frequent disciplinary confrontations with school personnel, rejection by peers, and continued coercive interchanges with parents (e.g., Patterson et al., 1992). By age 10 or 11, this recurrent constellation of negative events places the children at increased risk for association with deviant peer groups in middle school and high school (with a likely escalation in CP behaviors). Adolescents who have progressed along the early starter pathway are not only at significant risk for continuing to engage in more serious CP behaviors throughout adolescence and into adulthood; as adults, they are also at increased risk for other psychiatric diagnoses and a variety of negative life outcomes (e.g., lower occupational adjustment and educational attainment, poorer physical health) (e.g., Kratzer & Hodgins, 1997; Moffitt, 1993).

The Special Role of Noncompliance

Noncompliance (i.e., excessive disobedience to adults) appears to be a keystone behavior in the development of CP. It appears early in the progression of CP, and continues to be manifested in subsequent developmental periods (e.g., Chamberlain & Patterson, 1995; Edelbrock, 1985), playing a role in these children's subsequent academic and peer relationship problems as well. Low levels of compliance are also associated with referral for services in children with CP (Dumas, 1996). Furthermore, intervention research has shown that when child noncompliance is targeted, there is often concomitant improvement in other CP behaviors as well (Russo, Cataldo, & Cushing, 1981; Wells, Forehand, & Griest, 1980).

Familial Risk Factors for Early Starting CP

There is a growing body of evidence concerning the many individual, familial, and broader contextual factors that may increase the likelihood of a child's entering and progressing along the early starter pathway (see Kazdin, 1995b, and McMahon & Wells, 1998, for reviews). In this chapter, family-based risk factors will be highlighted.

The critical role of parenting practices in the development and maintenance of CP has been well established (e.g., Chamberlain & Patterson, 1995; Patterson et al., 1992). Types of parenting practices that have been closely associated with the development of child CP include inconsistent discipline, irritable explosive discipline, low supervision and involvement, and inflexible rigid discipline (Chamberlain, Reid, Ray, Capaldi, & Fisher, 1997). The most comprehensive family-based formulation for the early starter pathway has been the coercion model developed by Patterson and his colleagues (Patterson, 1982; Patterson et al., 1992). The model describes a process of "basic training" in CP behaviors occurring in the context of an escalating cycle of coercive parent–child interactions in the home that begins prior to school entry. The proximal cause for entry into the coercive cycle is thought to be ineffective parental management strategies, particularly in regard to child compliance with parental directives during the preschool period. As this process continues over long periods, significant increases in the rate and intensity of these coercive behaviors occur as family members are reinforced by engaging in aggressive behaviors. Furthermore, the child also observes his or her parents engaging in coercive responses, and this provides the opportunity for modeling of aggression to occur (Patterson, 1982).

Various other family risk factors that may have direct or indirect effects on parenting practices have been identified. Parents of children with CP display more maladaptive social cognitions, and they experience more personal (e.g., depression, antisocial behavior) and interparental (e.g., marital problems) distress and greater social isolation (e.g., insularity) than do parents of nonreferred children. Parents of clinic-referred children with CP are more likely to have fewer positive and more negative family-referent cognitions (Sanders & Dadds, 1992), and to perceive CP behaviors as intentional and to attribute them to stable and global causes (Baden & Howe, 1992). Sense of parenting efficacy has been shown to relate negatively to child CP in both clinic-referred and nonreferred samples (e.g., Johnston & Mash, 1989; Roberts, Joe, & Rowe-Hallbert, 1992).

Parental personal adjustment has been implicated in the development of child CP. Maternal depression may adversely affect parenting behavior, and it may also negatively bias maternal perceptions of children with CP (e.g., Dumas & Serketich, 1994). Parental antisocial behavior has received increasing attention as both a direct and an indirect influence on the development and maintenance of CP (see Frick & Loney, in press).

Similarly, parental substance abuse has been associated with child CP, at least partly because of its association with disrupted parenting practices (e.g., Patterson et al., 1992). In families with parental alcohol problems, the parents are less able to engage their children and are less congenial (e.g., Jacob, Krahn, & Leonard, 1991). In addition, children's inappropriate behavior increases parental alcohol consumption (for parents with a positive family history of alcohol problems) and distress (for all parents) (Pelham & Lang, 1993).

Marital distress and conflict have been shown to be associated with child CP, negative parenting behavior, and parental perceptions of child maladjustment (Cummings & Davies, 1994). The most commonly offered hypothesis for the relationship has been that marital distress and conflict interfere with the parents' ability to engage in appropriate parenting practices, which then leads to child CP.[1]

---

[1]However, other explanations are possible (see Rutter, 1994). These include direct modeling of aggressive and coercive behavior, and the cumulative stressful effects of such conflict, including maternal depression.

More narrowly focused constructs that relate directly to parenting, such as disagreement over child-rearing practices, marital conflict in a child's presence, or the strength of the parenting alliance, may demonstrate stronger relationships to CP than may broader constructs such as marital distress (e.g., Jouriles et al., 1991; Porter & O'Leary, 1980).

Parents of children with CP also appear to experience higher frequencies of stressful events, both minor ones (e.g., daily hassles) and those of a more significant nature (e.g., unemployment, major transitions) (e.g., Patterson, 1983). The effects of stress on child CP may be mediated through parenting practices such as disrupted parental discipline (e.g., Forgatch, Patterson, & Skinner, 1988) and maladaptive parental social cognitions (e.g., Johnston, 1996).

Some parents of children with CP may be quite isolated from friends, neighbors, and the community. Wahler and his colleagues have developed a construct called *insularity,* which is defined as a "specific pattern of social contacts within the community that is characterized by a high level of negatively perceived coercive interchanges with relatives and/or helping agency representatives and by a low level of positively perceived supportive interchanges with friends" (Wahler & Dumas, 1984, p. 387). Insularity is positively related to negative parent behavior directed toward children and oppositional child behavior directed toward parents (Dumas & Wahler, 1985). It has also been associated with poor maintenance of PT effects (e.g., Dumas & Wahler, 1983). Thus, when a mother has a large proportion of aversive interactions outside the home, the interactions between the mother and her child in the home are likely to be negative as well.

HISTORY OF PT

The concise definition of PT presented at the beginning of this chapter fails to capture the historical antecedents of PT or the sense of its active, ongoing development into a true "behavioral family therapy" (Griest & Wells, 1983). Since the earliest attempts to teach parents to alter their children's CP behaviors (Williams, 1959), PT has gone through three distinct stages of development (McMahon, 1991).

The first stage, which occurred during the 1960s and early 1970s, was concerned with the development of a "parent training" model of intervention (O'Dell, 1974) and determining whether it was a viable approach to dealing with a wide variety of child behavior problems. Based on Tharp and Wetzel's (1969) triadic model, the PT model employed a therapist (consultant) who worked directly with the parent (mediator) to ultimately alleviate the child's (target) CP behavior. The underlying assumption of this model was that some sort of parenting skills deficit had been at least partly responsible for the development and/or maintenance of the CP behaviors. The PT model came about because of the confluence of several events (Kazdin, 1985): (1) the development of behavior modification techniques, especially reinforcement and punishment procedures based on operant conditioning; (2) the trend toward using paraprofessionals (including parents) to deliver mental health services; and (3) an awareness that utilizing parents as therapists could enhance the effectiveness of child therapy.

With respect to this last point, the PT model presented several advantages over more traditional approaches to child therapy in which the therapist worked one on one with the child in hour-long weekly sessions (Berkowitz & Graziano, 1972). First, because of the importance of familial and broader contextual factors in the development and maintenance of CP behavior, it is unlikely that clinically significant changes can be obtained by treating the child "out of context." Second, even if improvements are achieved in the child's behavior in the treatment setting, these will most likely dissipate when the child is returned to the natural environment that produced the problems in the first place. Finally, parents have the greatest contact with the child and the greatest control over the child's environment and, by virtue of their parenthood, have the major moral, ethical, and legal responsibility to care for the child.

Although much of the research during this first stage of the development of PT was limited to descriptive case studies or single-case designs with data collected in the clinic or laboratory (and less frequently in the home), the available evidence strongly supported the short-term efficacy of this approach in terms of immediate posttreatment improvements in both parent and child behavior. For example, children were shown at posttreatment to be less physically and verbally aggressive, more compliant, and less destructive, while their parents were less directive, controlling, and critical, and more positive toward their children (see O'Dell, 1974, for a review of these early studies).

Although the short-term efficacy of PT in producing changes in both parent and child behaviors has been demonstrated repeatedly, the generalization of those effects has been less consistently documented. This concern about generalization of treatment effects led to the second stage in the development of PT, which occurred from the mid-1970s to the early 1980s. In a seminal paper, Forehand and Atkeson (1977) discussed four major types of generalization relevant to PT interventions with children. *Setting generalization* refers to the transfer of treatment effects to settings in which treatment did not take place (e.g., from the clinic to the home or school), whereas *temporal generalization* pertains to the maintenance of treatment effects following termination. *Sibling generalization* concerns the transfer of the newly acquired parenting skills to untreated siblings in the family, and the siblings' responding in the desired manner. *Behavioral generalization* refers to whether targeted changes in specific CP behaviors are accompanied by improvements in other nontargeted behaviors.

Generalization is important for the success of a PT approach from at least two perspectives (Forehand & Atkeson, 1977). In terms of treatment, generalization results in a more optimal use of therapist time, as the therapist will no longer be required to treat recurrences of previously treated problems, problem behaviors in new settings, all of a child's problem behaviors, or the behavior problems of the child's siblings. In terms of prevention, generalization minimizes repeated professional intervention and should result in a diminution of future behavior problems of the child (and siblings). Assessing generality also allows therapists to monitor the potential occurrence of any negative side effects of PT.

Pertinent to the generalization of effects is the *social validity* of the intervention, which refers to whether therapeutic changes are "clinically or socially important" for the client (Kazdin, 1977, p. 429). PT interventions for the treatment of children with CP have demonstrated their generalizability and social validity to varying degrees—some quite impressively, others to a moderate degree, and others not at all. This emphasis on the generalization and social validity of treatment effects and the increased awareness of the multiple causal and maintaining factors of CP led to the third and current stage of development of PT. Since the early 1980s, clinical researchers have focused on ways to enhance the effectiveness of PT, not only with respect to short-term efficacy but especially with regards to generalization. Enhancement and expansion of the PT model have included strengthening basic parenting skills; adding new parenting skills; an increased focus on parental adjustment factors, expectations, and social stressors; and multisystem approaches that include a focus on the child (peer and school domains) and broad ecological approaches (Miller & Prinz, 1990). One consequence of this approach has been that the PT model has been broadened to what is referred to as "behavioral family therapy" (Griest & Wells, 1983). Although still in its formative stages (Miller & Prinz, 1990; Taylor & Biglan, 1998), the model is an attempt to acknowledge and incorporate into treatment the variety of child, parent, and contextual variables that have been implicated in the development and maintenance of CP.

ASSESSMENT AND CASE FORMULATION

Assessment Methods

As knowledge of the characteristics, causes, and correlates of CP has grown, the scope of assessment has broadened as well. For a thorough description and evaluation of methods employed in the assessment of children with CP, see McMahon and Estes (1997). This chapter will focus on those aspects of assessment most directly related to the parent–child system. To obtain an accurate representation of the referred child's CP behavior in the home, particularly with regard to its interactional aspects, the therapist must rely on multiple assessment methods, including interviews with the parents, behavioral observations in the clinic and home settings, behavioral rating scales, and questionnaires.

The primary purpose of the clinical interview with the parent is to determine the nature of the typical parent–child interactions that are problematic, the antecedent stimulus conditions under which CP behaviors occur, and the consequences that accompany such behaviors. A number of interview formats are available to aid the clinician in structuring the information obtained from the parents (e.g., Forehand & McMahon, 1981; Patterson, Reid, Jones, & Conger, 1975).

Direct behavioral observation has long been a critical component of the assessment of children with CP and their families, both for delineating specific patterns of maladaptive parent–child interaction and for assessing change in those interactions as a function of treatment. Observational data can be compared with data gathered via other methods to assist the clinician in determining whether the focus of treatment should be on the parent–child interaction or on parental perceptual and/or personal adjustment issues.

Three widely used, structured, microanalytic observation procedures available for assessing parent–child interactions in the clinic and the home are the Behavioral Coding System (BCS; Forehand & McMahon, 1981), the Dyadic Parent–Child Interaction Coding System II (DPICS II; Eyberg, Bessmer, Newcomb, Edwards, & Robinson, 1994), and the Interpersonal Process Code (IPC; Rusby, Estes, & Dishion, 1991). As employed in the clinic, both the BCS and DPICS II place the parent–child dyad in standard situations that vary in the degree to which parental control is required, ranging from a free-play situation to one in which the parent directs the child's activity. In each system, a variety of parent and child behaviors are scored, many of which emphasize parental antecedents (e.g., commands) and consequences (e.g., praise, time-out) for child compliance or noncompliance. The IPC has been used in a number of different interactional contexts, such as teaching and free-play situations in the clinic with young school-aged children and their families; problem solving in the clinic with preadolescents and their families; and family therapy process. The IPC consists of three behavioral dimensions: activity (e.g., on-task, off-task), content (i.e., verbal, nonverbal, physical), and affect (e.g., happy, aversive, sad). Psychometric properties of all three coding systems are adequate, and they have been employed as intervention outcome measures.

An alternative to observations by independent observers in the natural setting is to train significant adults in the child's environment to observe and record certain types of child behavior. The most widely used procedure of this type is the Parent Daily Report (PDR; Chamberlain & Reid, 1987), a parent observation measure that is typically administered during brief telephone interviews. Parents are asked whether any of a variety of negative child behaviors have occurred in the past 24 hours. Some versions also record the setting in which the problem behavior is occurring (home, school, community, other) or parental disciplinary practices. There is also a parallel form for children (see Patterson & Bank, 1986). The Daily Telephone Discipline Interview (Webster-Stratton & Spitzer, 1991) was developed as an addendum to the PDR to provide more detailed information about parental interventions subsequent to child misbehavior reported on the PDR. The PDR has been employed on a pretreatment basis to assess the magnitude of behavior problems, to monitor the progress of the family during therapy, and to assess treatment outcome.

Several questionnaires also have been specifically designed to assess parenting practices. These questionnaires may be potentially quite useful as adjuncts to behavioral observations and/or to assess parental behaviors that either occur infrequently or are otherwise difficult to observe (e.g., physical discipline, parental monitoring practices), as screening instruments, and to measure the effects of PT interventions. Examples include the Parenting Scale (Arnold, O'Leary, Wolff, & Acker, 1993) and the Alabama Parenting Questionnaire (Frick, 1991).

Behavioral rating scales completed by parents can be excellent measures of parental perceptions of the child, and as such, have been extensively employed as treatment outcome and social validation measures in treatment studies with children with CP and their families. Although there are many behavioral rating scales, the Child Behavior Checklist (Achenbach, 1991) and the Eyberg Child Behavior Inventory (ECBI; Eyberg, 1992) have been recommended as the most appropriate parent-completed rating scales for clinical and research use with children with CP (McMahon & Estes, 1997). Written, audiotaped, or videotaped vignettes describing various child behaviors or parent–child interactions have also been employed to assess parental perceptions of the child (e.g., Sanders & Dadds, 1992). When examined in the context of behavioral observation data and the clinician's own impressions, these perception measures can be important indicators as to whether the parents may have a perceptual bias in their assessment of the referred child's behavior. Examples of measures that assess aspects of parental self-esteem (e.g., satisfaction, self-efficacy, and locus of control with the parenting role) are the Parenting Sense of Competence Scale (as adapted by Johnston & Mash, 1989) and the Parental Locus of Control Scale (Campis, Lyman, & Prentice-Dunn, 1986).

To assess the extent to which parents' personal and marital adjustment problems may be playing a role in the child's presenting behavior problems, a set of screening procedures that includes brief questions in the initial interviews with the parents and certain parental self-report measures can be utilized. The Beck Depression Inventory (Beck, Rush, Shaw, & Emery, 1979) has been the most frequently employed measure of maternal depression. Parental antisocial behavior can be assessed with structured diagnostic interviews, the MMPI, or the Antisocial Behavior Checklist (Zucker & Fitzgerald, 1992). With respect to substance use, examples of screening instruments that may prove useful in working with parents of children with CP include the short version of the Michigan Alcoholism Screening Test (SMAST; Selzer, Vinokur, & van Rooijen, 1975) and the Drug Abuse Screening Test (DAST; Skinner, 1982).

With respect to marital discord, the Marital Adjustment Test (Locke & Wallace, 1959) and the Dyadic Adjustment Scale (Spanier, 1976) have been the most widely used instruments with parents of children with CP. Two questionnaires are often used to assess general marital conflict: the O'Leary–Porter Scale (OPS; Porter & O'Leary, 1980) and the Conflict Tactics Scale-Partner (CTS-Partner; Straus, 1990). Instruments designed to measure parenting-related conflict have also been developed, such as the Parenting Alliance Inventory (Abidin & Brunner, 1995) and Child Rearing Disagreements (Jouriles et al., 1991).

General measures of stress (e.g., life event scales) and specific measures of parenting-related stress have been employed with parents of children with CP. Examples of the former include the Life Experiences Survey (Sarason, Johnson, & Siegel, 1978) and the Family Events List (Patterson, 1982). Measures specific to parenting-related stress include Parenting Daily Hassles (Crnic & Greenberg, 1990) and the Parenting Stress Index (Abidin, 1995). The Parenting Stress Index has been extensively employed with parents of children with CP (e.g., Kazdin, 1990; Webster-Stratton, 1994). With respect to maternal insularity, the Community Interaction Checklist (CIC; Wahler, Leske, & Rogers, 1979), which is a brief interview usually administered on multiple occasions, has been extensively employed in research with children with CP and their families.

Finally, parental satisfaction with treatment, which is one form of social validity, may be assessed in terms of satisfaction with the outcome of treatment, therapists, treatment procedures, and teaching format (McMahon & Forehand, 1983). The Therapy Attitude Inventory (Eyberg, 1992) and the Parent's Consumer Satisfaction Questionnaire (Forehand & McMahon, 1981; McMahon, Tiedemann, Forehand, & Griest, 1984) are examples of measures designed to evaluate parental satisfaction with PT interventions.

Case Formulation

The ultimate goal of the assessment process is to facilitate selection of the most appropriate intervention strategy or strategies. Primary indicators of the appropriateness of a PT intervention include evidence of significant familial influences on the development or maintenance of the child's CP behavior, and parental recognition of the child's problem and willingness to participate in the intervention (Sanders & Dadds, 1993). Once it has been determined that a PT approach is warranted, then the therapist must be concerned with several treatment selection issues, such as:

> a) when the "standard" parent training approach is beneficial; b) when to intervene in additional areas such as other child disorders, parental personal or marital adjustment difficulties, child or parental perceptual biases, and/or extrafamilial functioning (e.g., insularity); and c) if intervention is to take place in one or more of these areas, should it occur before, after, instead of, or concurrently with a parent training type of intervention? (McMahon, 1987, p. 248)

Algorithms for matching clinic-referred families with PT interventions exist (e.g., Embry, 1984), but they have been quite limited in scope, have not been closely tied to underlying assessment strategies, and have yet to be empirically tested. Sanders and colleagues (Sanders & Dadds, 1993; Sanders & Lawton, 1993) have delineated more clinically oriented strategies for integrating and interpreting information from comprehensive assessments to families, as well as outlined five levels of PT intervention, ranging from brief written instructions to basic PT to more broadly based behavioral family therapy. A comprehensive, empirically based treatment selection model for children with CP is sorely needed.

DESCRIPTION OF INTERVENTION PROCEDURES AND MECHANISMS OF CHANGE

Common Elements

The core elements of PT have been delineated by a number of authors (Dumas, 1989; Kazdin, 1995b; Miller & Prinz, 1990): (1) treatment is conducted primarily with the parents, with relatively less therapist–child contact; (2) there is a refocusing from a preoccupation with CP behavior to an emphasis on prosocial goals; (3) the content of these programs typically includes instruction in the social learning principles underlying the parenting techniques; training in defining, monitoring, and tracking child behavior; training in positive reinforcement procedures, including praise and other forms of positive parent attention, and token or point systems; training in extinction and mild punishment procedures such as ignoring, response cost, and time-out in lieu of physical punishment; training in giving clear instructions or commands; and problem solving; and (4) there is extensive use of didactic instruction, modeling, role-playing, behavioral rehearsal, and structured homework exercises.

PT interventions with children with CP have been successfully utilized in the clinic and home settings, have been implemented with individual families or with groups of parents, and have involved some or all of the instructional techniques listed above. O'Dell (1985) has provided an extensive review of the myriad parametric considerations involved in PT.

Examples of Programs

Three PT programs are presented as examples of family-based interventions for preadolescent children with overt CP. Descriptions of the clinical procedures utilized in these programs are widely available in therapist manuals, and each of the programs has been extensively evaluated.

The first PT program is specifically designed to treat noncompliance in younger children (3–8 years of age). The program was originally developed by Hanf (1969), but has been modified and subsequently evaluated by Forehand and McMahon (1981) and others (e.g., Schuhmann, Foote, Eyberg, Boggs, & Algina, 1998). As described by Forehand and McMahon (1981), the "Helping the Non-compliant Child" program presents a number of discrete parenting skills that are taught to the parent by didactic instruction, modeling, and role-playing. The parent also practices the skills in the clinic with the child while receiving prompting and feedback from the therapist. Finally, the parent employs these newly acquired skills in the home setting.

Sessions are typically conducted with individual families rather than in groups. The treatment program consists of two phases. During the differential-attention phase of treatment (Phase I), the parent learns to break out of the coercive cycle of interaction with the child by increasing the frequency and range of social attention (attending, praise) and by reducing the frequency of competing verbal behavior. The primary goal is to establish a positive, mutually reinforcing relationship between the parent and child. The parent also learns to ignore minor inappropriate behaviors. Homework is assigned in the form of daily 10-minute practice sessions with the child, using the skills taught in the clinic. The parent is also required to develop programs for use outside the clinic to increase at least two child behaviors using the new skills.

Phase II of the treatment program consists of teaching the parent to use appropriate commands, positive attention for compliance, and a time-out procedure to decrease noncompliant behavior exhibited by the child. When the parent is able to administer these procedures successfully in the clinic, he or she is instructed to begin using the procedure for noncompliance at home. Finally, parents are taught to use permanent "Standing Rules" as an occasional supplement to this sequence.

Progression to each new skill in the treatment program is determined by the use of behavioral and temporal (number of sessions) criteria. These criteria ensure that the parent has attained an acceptable degree of competence in a particular skill before being taught additional parenting techniques, and allow for the individualization of the treatment program by allocating training time more efficiently.

A second PT program for young (3- to 8-year-old) children with CP, which includes some components of the Hanf (1969) and Forehand and McMahon (1981) programs, is the videotape modeling/group discussion (BASIC) program developed by Webster-Stratton (1996a). What is unique about this particular intervention is its use of a standard package of 10 videotape programs of modeled parenting skills shown by a therapist to groups of parents. The 250 vignettes (each of which lasts approximately 2 minutes) include examples of parents interacting with their children in both appropriate and inappropriate ways. After each vignette, the therapist leads a discussion of the relevant interactions and solicits parental responses to the vignettes. In this particular program, the children do not attend the therapy sessions, although parents are given homework exercises to practice various parenting skills with their children.

The third PT program, developed by Patterson and colleagues, has been employed with a broader age range of children (age 3 to 12 years). The procedures are delineated in the treatment manual by Patterson et al. (1975). Prior to beginning treatment, parents are given a copy of either *Living with Children* (Patterson, 1976) or *Families* (Patterson, 1975) to provide a conceptual background for the specific skills training in the treatment sessions and to facilitate generalization and maintenance. The next step is to teach the parents to pinpoint the problem behaviors of concern and to track the child's behavior. Then parents are assisted in establishing a positive reinforcement system, using points, backup reinforcers such as privileges or treats, and social reinforcement (i.e., praise). Over time, the tangible reinforcers are faded. After the point system is well established, the parents are taught to use a 5-minute time-out procedure for noncompliance or aggressive behavior. Response cost (e.g., loss of privileges) and work chores are also sometimes used with older children. As treatment progresses, parents become increasingly responsible for designing and implementing behavior management programs for various child behaviors. Parents are also taught to monitor or supervise their children. Problem-solving and negotiation strategies are taught to the parents at this point in treatment.

Processes of Change

There has been significant progress in the attention being paid to the role of engagement in PT interventions for children with CP in the past few years. Of prime importance has been the development of conceptual frameworks for examining the engagement process in general (e.g., Kazdin, Holland, & Crowley, 1997; Prinz & Miller, 1996; Webster-Stratton & Herbert, 1993, 1994) and therapist behavior in particular (e.g., Patterson & Chamberlain, 1994). Prinz and Miller present four domains that they posit affect parental engagement in PT interventions for CP: (1) parents' personal expectations, attributions, and beliefs (e.g., expectations about the nature of the intervention, attributions about the source of the child's problem and/or about their own self-efficacy) (also see Johnston, 1996); (2) situational demands and constraints (e.g., financial and social stressors, marital and personal adjustment, daily hassles, and competing demands of other activities); (3) intervention characteristics (e.g., group versus individual PT, home versus clinic delivery, type of intervention, homework); and (4) relationships with the therapist. Kazdin et al. (1997) present a similar "barriers-to-treatment" model. Their model focuses on (1) stressors and obstacles that compete with intervention, (2) intervention demands and issues, (3) perceived relevance of the intervention, and (4) relationship with the therapist.

The work of Webster-Stratton and her colleagues (e.g., Webster-Stratton & Herbert, 1994; Webster-Stratton & Spitzer, 1996) has been especially innovative, as it has involved the use of qualitative research methods to describe the process of intervention from the perspective of the parents. Participants in the BASIC version of her PT program went through five phases during the course of intervention (Spitzer, Webster-Stratton, & Hollinsworth, 1991): acknowledging the problem, alternating despair and hope, "tempering the dream" (settling for less than total recovery), tailoring the program to their own family situations, and coping effectively. Parents' experiences during a 3–year period following the intervention have also been analyzed (Webster-Stratton & Herbert, 1994; Webster-Stratton & Spitzer, 1996).

The importance of the therapist establishing a collaborative relationship with the parent during PT has been emphasized, and therapist activities in such a relationship have been delineated (Sanders & Dadds, 1993; Webster-Stratton & Herbert, 1993, 1994). For example, Webster-Stratton and Herbert have delineated a number of roles for the therapist in the context of the BASIC PT program (Webster-Stratton, 1996a): building a supportive relationship, empowering parents, active teaching, interpreting, leading (e.g., dealing with resistance), and prophesying (e.g., anticipating problems and setbacks, resistance to change, and positive change/success).

Patterson and Chamberlain (1994) have presented a conceptualization of parental resistance that includes both within-session (refusal, stated inability to perform) and out-of-session (homework) resistance. Initial resistance is thought to be a function of the parent's history of parent–child interaction, preexisting parental psychopathology, and social disadvantage, as well as therapist behavior (Patterson & Chamberlain, 1988). Patterson and Chamberlain (1994) demonstrated that these contextual variables were associated with parental resistance throughout PT. According to their "struggle hypothesis," parental resistance is expected to increase initially, but then eventually decrease as the parent begins to meet with success.

Directive therapist behaviors of "teach" and "confront" increased the likelihood of parental noncooperative behavior within the session, whereas supportive and facilitative therapist behaviors had the opposite effect (Patterson & Forgatch, 1985). This poses an intriguing paradox for therapists: The directive therapist behaviors that seem to be intrinsic to PT would also be those that predict parent noncompliance during treatment. Patterson and Forgatch conclude that two sets of therapist skills are required: "standard" PT skills, and relationship characteristics to deal with parental noncompliance.

RESEARCH EVIDENCE IN SUPPORT OF PT

Generalization and Social Validity

Each of the three programs described earlier in the chapter has documented setting generalization from the clinic to the home for parent and child behavior and for parents' perception of the child's adjustment (e.g., Fleischman, 1981; Peed, Roberts, & Forehand, 1977; Taplin & Reid, 1977; Webster-Stratton, 1984). Temporal generalization of treatment effects has also been demonstrated over follow-up periods of 1 to 3 years (e.g., Baum & Forehand, 1981; Patterson & Fleischman, 1979; Patterson & Forgatch, 1995; Webster-Stratton, 1990b; Webster-Stratton, Hollinsworth, & Kolpacoff, 1989). Maintenance of effects for the Forehand and McMahon (1981) PT program has been demonstrated for up to 4½ years after treatment (Baum & Forehand, 1981), and less rigorous studies done 4½ to 14 years after treatment suggest that the children were functioning well compared with their peer group in terms of parent-, teacher-, and self-reported adjustment (Forehand & Long, 1988; Long, Forehand, Wierson, & Morgan, 1994). Other PT programs with young children with CP have also demonstrated long-term temporal generalization effects of 3 years or more (e.g., Strain, Steele, Ellis, & Timm, 1982).

Several investigators have now assessed setting generalization from the clinic or home to the school. In their meta-analytic study, Serketich and Dumas (1996) reported an effect size of 0.73 for PT when the outcome was based on teacher report. While several investigators have reported evidence of generalization in the form of teacher ratings of child CP behavior (e.g., Webster-Stratton, Kolpacoff, & Hollinsworth, 1988), one study (McNeil, Eyberg, Eisenstadt, Newcomb, & Funderburk, 1991) demonstrated generalization to the classroom using both observational data and teacher ratings of CP behavior (but not of teacher-rated social competence or observed on-task behavior). McNeil et al. also demonstrated that change in home behavior was positively correlated with changes in school behavior (based on parent and teacher ratings, respectively). Evidence of behavioral contrast effects (e.g., Johnson, Bolstad, & Lobitz, 1976) has occasionally been found. Other investigators have failed to find evidence of generalization to the school or a failure of this generalization to maintain (e.g., Breiner & Forehand, 1981; Forehand et al., 1979; Patterson & Forgatch, 1995; Webster-Stratton et al., 1989). Therefore, when a child presents with problems in both the home and school settings, improvement in school functioning should not necessarily be expected to occur as a function of family-based intervention in the home; rather, intervening directly in the school may be required. Furthermore, the therapist should monitor the child's behavior in the school regardless of whether this was an initial referral problem, because of the possibility of a behavioral contrast effect.

Both the Forehand and McMahon (1981) and Patterson et al. (1975) PT programs have demonstrated sibling generalization at the end of treatment (e.g., Arnold, Levine, & Patterson, 1975; Humphreys, Forehand, McMahon, & Roberts, 1978), and this generalization has been maintained for up to 1 year for Patterson's program. However, many of the siblings in the Arnold et al. investigation had been directly involved in the actual treatment program.

Behavioral generalization from the treatment of child noncompliance to other deviant behaviors (e.g., aggression, temper tantrums) has been demonstrated for both the Forehand and McMahon (Wells, Forehand, & Griest, 1980) and Webster-Stratton (1984) PT programs for younger children with CP, as well as by other parent trainers (e.g., Russo et al., 1981). Significant reductions in a composite measure of observed coercive child behaviors and in PDR scores over the course of treatment suggest that Patterson's PT program for preadolescent children with CP also manifests behavioral generality (e.g., Fleischman, 1981; Patterson, 1974), although Patterson and Reid (1973) did not find generalization of treatment effects from targeted to nontargeted observed deviant behaviors.

The social validity of family-based interventions with children with CP has been assessed by parental consumer satisfaction (see McMahon & Forehand, 1983), treatment acceptability (e.g., Cross Calvert & McMahon, 1987), and by determining the clinical significance of posttreatment improvements. All three PT programs have provided strong evidence of consumer satisfaction at posttreatment and/or follow-up periods of a year or more (e.g., Baum & Forehand, 1981; McMahon et al., 1984; Patterson, Chamberlain, & Reid, 1982; Webster-Stratton, 1984, 1989). They have also provided normative comparisons indicating that, by the end of treatment, child and/or parent behavior more closely resembles that in nonreferred families (e.g., Forehand, Wells, & Griest, 1980; Patterson, 1974; Webster-Stratton, 1990b; Webster-Stratton et al., 1989). In their meta-analytic review of PT,

Serketich and Dumas (1996) reported that 17 of 19 intervention groups dropped below the clinical range after treatment on at least one measure, and 14 groups did so on all measures.

Adjunctive Procedures to Enhance Effectiveness and Generalization

It is apparent that evidence for the generalization and social validity of PT interventions with preadolescent children with overt CP is extensive and, for the most part, positive. A number of studies have examined the role of adjunctive treatments in facilitating generalization and/or social validity, over and above that obtained by standard PT programs. Adjunctive treatments focused on parenting skills and adjustment have included components designed to facilitate maternal self-control/self-management (e.g., Sanders & Glynn, 1981; Wells, Griest, & Forehand, 1980); parental knowledge of social learning principles (McMahon, Forehand, & Griest, 1981); generalization of parenting skills to specific settings in the home and community (e.g., Powers & Roberts, 1995; Sanders & Dadds, 1982); marital support, communication, and problem solving (e.g., Dadds, Schwartz, & Sanders, 1987; Webster-Stratton, 1994); discrimination training for mothers ("Synthesis Teaching"; Wahler, Cartor, Fleischman, & Lambert, 1993); and parental social support (Dadds & McHugh, 1992). One of the more comprehensive parenting adjuncts to date is Parent Enhancement Therapy (Griest et al., 1982), which includes components related to parental perceptions of the child's behavior, marital adjustment, parental personal adjustment, and the parents' extrafamilial relationships. Similarly, Prinz and Miller (1994) developed an "enhanced" version of parent training that incorporated supportive discussions with the parent about other issues of concern. Webster-Stratton (1998) demonstrated that the combination of her PT program with an adjunct to promote teachers' classroom management skills and their promotion of parental involvement in school resulted in greater positive parent and child behavior changes in a sample of Head Start families than did the regular Head Start program.

Other adjunctive procedures have focused on the children, with respect to self-control (Baum, Reyna McGlone, & Ollendick, 1986) and social skills training (e.g., Kazdin, Siegel, & Bass, 1992; Webster-Stratton & Hammond, 1997). The combination of PT with child social skills training seems to be more effective than either alone.

The utility of these adjunctive treatments when employed in conjunction with the basic PT programs lends support to the current movement toward a broader behavioral family therapy model of intervention (Griest & Wells, 1983; Miller & Prinz, 1990). (However, it is important to note that not all of these adjunctive procedures have resulted in enhanced generalization or social validity [e.g., Dadds & McHugh, 1992].)

Comparison Studies

Each of the three PT programs described earlier in the chapter has been positively evaluated in comparison with no-treatment and waiting-list control conditions (e.g., Peed et al., 1977; Webster-Stratton, 1984; Wiltz & Patterson, 1974) or an attention-placebo condition (Walter & Gilmore, 1973). Furthermore, comparisons with groups of nonreferred "normal" children and their parents have indicated greater similarity in parent and child behaviors and/or parental perceptions of children after treatment (e.g., Forehand et al., 1980; Patterson, 1974). Other investigators have also reported the superiority of PT over waiting-list control conditions (e.g., Schuhmann et al., 1998; Scott & Stradling, 1987).

As evidence for the efficacy of PT with children with CP has accumulated, increased attention has been focused on the relative efficacy of this intervention compared with other forms of treatment. PT interventions have been compared with family systems therapies (e.g., Patterson & Chamberlain, 1988; Wells & Egan, 1988), the STEP program (Baum et al., 1986), client-centered therapy (Bernal, Klinnert, & Schultz, 1980), and available community mental health services (Patterson et al., 1982; Taylor, Schmidt, Pepler, & Hodgins, 1998). With the exception of the Bernal et al. investigation, which indicated superiority of PT over client-centered therapy on parent report measures at posttreatment but not at 6– and 12–month follow-ups, the other comparative investigations have supported the relative efficacy of PT.

Predictors of Outcome

In this section of the chapter, various predictors of PT outcome will be discussed, not only with respect to positive treatment effects, but also with respect to decreasing dropouts (i.e., increasing parent and child engagement). The review has been divided into child and family characteristics and characteristics of intervention (e.g., client engagement/resistance, therapist characteristics).

Child Characteristics

A myriad of characteristics of the child with CP could conceivably affect outcome in a differential manner. These include the nature of the CP behavior (e.g., subtype, severity, duration); comorbid disorders (e.g., ADHD); the child's age, gender, and race; and variables such as temperament, problem-solving abilities, attributional biases, and so on (McMahon & Wells, 1998). With the few exceptions described here, there has been a dearth of research in this area.

More severe or frequent levels of CP at pretreatment have been associated with dropout and negative outcome at posttreatment and at follow-up for PT interventions (e.g., Dumas, 1984b; Holden, Lavigne, & Cameron, 1990; Patterson & Forgatch, 1995; Webster-Stratton, 1996b). Similar findings have been noted by Kazdin (1990, 1995a; Kazdin, Mazurick, & Bass, 1993) for PT or PT plus child skills training. Other investigators have not found initial severity of child CP behavior to be associated with PT outcome or dropout (e.g., Fleischman, 1981).

Several investigators have found that relatively younger children are more likely to succeed in treatment (Strain et al., 1982; Strain, Young, & Horowitz, 1981) and that their families are less likely to drop out of PT interventions (Dishion & Patterson, 1992; Fleischman, 1981; Scott & Stradling, 1987) than are older children and their families. McMahon, Forehand, and Tiedemann (1985) reported no differential treatment effects for their PT program, either at posttreatment or at a 2-month follow-up, as a function of the children's age (which ranged from 3 to 8 years). However, a meta-analytic study of PT (Serketich & Dumas, 1996) found larger effect sizes for PT conducted with elementary school-aged children than with preschool-aged children.

PT interventions for CP appear equally effective for boys and girls (e.g., Kazdin, 1995a; Kazdin et al., 1993; Strain et al., 1981, 1982; Webster-Stratton, 1996b). The most comprehensive assessment of the effects of child gender on outcome has been presented by Webster-Stratton (1996b). She reported that both boys and girls responded in a similarly favorable fashion to her PT intervention, and that these effects were maintained at 1- and 2-year follow-ups. Predictors of outcome in the school were similar, but in the home, pretreatment level of CP behavior was the best predictor of outcome for boys at follow-up, whereas for girls, maternal negativity and depression and paternal negativity and life stress were the best predictors.

The relative effectiveness of PT interventions for CP with children of different ethnicities has been largely unexplored (Forehand & Kotchick, 1996). Strain et al. (1981, 1982) did not find ethnicity to predict outcome at posttreatment and follow-up after a PT intervention. However, minority status was associated with dropout from another PT program (Holden et al., 1990) and from Kazdin and colleagues' (1993) intervention (PT, child skills training, or the combination).

Family Characteristics

Characteristics that have been investigated include parent behavior, perceptions of the child's adjustment, personal and marital adjustment, insularity, and structural variables such as family composition (single-parent versus two-parent households) and socioeconomic status (SES).

With respect to parental behaviors, maternal aversive and indiscriminate behavior (Dumas, 1984b), higher rates of maternal commands (McMahon, Forehand, Griest, & Wells, 1981), maternal and paternal "negativity" (Webster-Stratton, 1996b), and parental monitoring and problem solving (Patterson & Forgatch, 1995) have been associated with negative outcome or dropout. Parental perceptions of children's adjustment prior to treatment have not been associated with treatment outcome (Dumas, 1984a; Dumas & Albin, 1986) or with dropout (McMahon, Forehand, Griest, & Wells, 1981), although maternal shifts to fewer blaming attributions and indiscriminate reactions and more specific and less global summary descriptions of the children have been shown to be associated with maintenance of treatment effects (e.g., Wahler et al., 1993).

The role of parental personal and marital adjustment in predicting treatment outcome is somewhat unclear. Parenting locus of control did not influence dropout from the Forehand and McMahon (1981) PT program, although parents who completed the program displayed a more internalized parenting locus of control at posttreatment (Roberts et al., 1992). Maternal adult attachment status has been recently demonstrated to moderate the relationship between pretreatment and follow-up (1 to 3½ years) levels of child CP (Routh, Hill, Steele, Elliott, & Dewy, 1995), in that this relationship held only when mothers were insecurely attached. Both maternal and paternal depression and negative life events have been significant predictors of outcome at either posttreatment or at follow-up for PT and of dropout (e.g., Kazdin, 1990, 1995a; Kazdin et al., 1993; McMahon, Forehand, Griest, & Wells, 1981; Webster-Stratton, 1985b, 1996b; Webster-Stratton &

Hammond, 1990). Kazdin et al. (1993) reported that a maternal history of childhood antisocial behavior was also associated with dropout from his interventions (PT, child skills training, or a combination). Dumas and Albin (1986) found maternal report of psychopathological symptoms to account for 17% of the variance in predicting treatment outcome in their sample of 82 families.

For the most part, level of marital satisfaction has not been found to differentially affect treatment outcome and generalization at posttreatment or brief follow-up assessments (e.g., Dadds et al., 1987; Forehand, Griest, Wells, & McMahon, 1982). However, Dadds and colleagues failed to find maintenance of the effects of PT at a 6–month follow-up for maritally distressed families; this suggests that, over longer periods of time, marital distress may ultimately impede temporal generalization. In addition, paternal marital satisfaction was found to be a predictor of posttreatment (but not 1-year follow-up) success for both observed paternal and child behavior (Webster-Stratton & Hammond, 1990).

Although there is evidence that fathers' behavior and/or perceptions regarding their children with CP change as a function of participation in PT interventions (e.g., Taplin & Reid, 1977; Webster-Stratton, 1985a, 1994; Webster-Stratton et al., 1988), whether or not such participation enhances outcome and generalization is unclear. The relatively few studies to address this issue have generally not indicated the necessity of including the father in PT; however, those studies suffer from a number of methodological weaknesses (e.g., small sample size, nonrandom assignment to groups, lack of follow-up data, reliance on self-report data) (Budd & O'Brien, 1982; Coplin & Houts, 1991). Webster-Stratton and Hammond (1990) found that predictors of successful outcome at posttreatment and at a 1-year follow-up were similar for mothers and fathers when parental ratings of child behavior served as the measure of outcome.

Similarly, single-parent status has failed to emerge as a consistent predictor of treatment outcome when examined as an entity. Although a number of investigators have reported single-parent status to be associated with increased risk of dropping out of PT or with a lack of treatment success (e.g., Dumas & Albin, 1986; Kazdin et al., 1993; Strain et al., 1981, 1982; Webster-Stratton, 1985a,b; Webster-Stratton & Hammond, 1990), other investigators have failed to obtain similar results (e.g., Dumas & Wahler, 1983; Fleischman, 1981; Holden et al., 1990; Kazdin, 1995a). In one investigation, single mothers were less likely to drop out than were married mothers (Scott & Stradling, 1987). Serketich and Dumas (1996) did not find either single-parent status or SES to be associated with effect size in their meta-analytic study of PT outcome.

Lower SES has been associated with subsequent dropout in at least one PT program (McMahon, Forehand, Griest, & Wells, 1981), although for mothers who complete that program, SES does not affect treatment outcome (Rogers, Forehand, Griest, Wells, & McMahon, 1981). Similar findings have been reported with respect to dropout from other PT interventions (e.g., Holden et al., 1990; Kazdin, 1990; Kazdin et al., 1993). Dumas and Wahler (1983) found that a composite index of socioeconomic disadvantage and maternal insularity each contributed unique variance to predicting outcome, and together they accounted for 49% of the variance. Noninsular but disadvantaged families (or vice versa) had approximately a 50% chance of having a favorable outcome, whereas those mothers who were insular and disadvantaged were virtually assured of failure at the 1-year follow-up.

Other investigators have reported similar findings with similar indices of socio-economic disadvantage (Routh et al., 1995; Webster-Stratton, 1985b), and with cumulative counts of total risk factors (e.g., Kazdin et al., 1993; Prinz & Miller, 1994).

Characteristics of Intervention

As noted above, there has been increasing attention paid to the role of parental engagement in PT. Prinz and Miller (1994) demonstrated that participation variables (e.g., in-session quality of participation, homework completion) were stronger predictors of dropout than various child and family characteristics. Kazdin et al. (1997) found that these aspects of engagement added additional explanatory variance to predicting dropout from intervention (PT, child skills training, or a combination) over and above that provided by the child, parent, and family factors described above. Furthermore, there was a clear dose–response relationship between the number of barriers experienced by the family and the likelihood of subsequent dropout. High levels of resistance in the first two therapy sessions are associated with subsequent dropout (Chamberlain, Patterson, Reid, Kavanagh, & Forgatch, 1984). Growth-curve analyses of parental resistance over the course of PT have shown a pattern of increasing resistance that peaks at about the midpoint, followed by a gradual decrease in resistance (Stoolmiller, Duncan, Bank, & Patterson, 1993). In addition, Stoolmiller et al. reported that chronic maternal resistance (i.e., failure to work through resistance issues) was associated with child arrest over a 2-year follow-up period. In general, these findings are supportive of the struggle hypothesis proposed by Patterson and Chamberlain (1994).

UTILIZING PT WITHIN A MANAGED CARE NETWORK

There are a number of features of PT that make it a likely candidate for implementation in managed care settings. First, PT has strong empirical support for its effectiveness, generalization, and social validity. It is one of the few interventions for child (as opposed to adult) behavior problems to achieve official recognition as an empirically validated therapy (Chambless et al., 1998). Second, a large number of well-validated PT programs have been manualized, which assists in their dissemination and standardized use (e.g., Forehand & McMahon, 1981; Patterson et al., 1975; Sanders & Dadds, 1993; Webster-Stratton, 1996a).

Third, there are a variety of levels of intervention and delivery systems for PT. With respect to the former, Sanders and Dadds (1993) have described five levels of intensity of PT intervention, including self-administered written instructions (with or without different levels of therapist consultation), "basic" PT, and PT plus various adjunctive procedures. The appropriate level of intervention is selected on the basis of results of an individualized assessment of the child and family. Self-administered PT interventions can be effective with certain families (e.g., Connell, Sanders, & Markie-Dadds, 1997; Webster-Stratton, 1990a), while other families may require more intensive interventions. Sanders (Sanders & Markie-Dadds, 1996) is currently implementing a multilevel PT system of intervention called Triple P (Positive Parenting Program) on a large scale in several states in Australia.

With respect to delivery systems, group-based PT can be a cost-effective alternative to working with individual families in some instances (e.g., Webster-Stratton, 1984), although guidelines for the selection of one form of intervention over the other are needed. Cunningham, Bremner, and Boyle (1995) have recently described a large-group (25–35 participants), community-based PT program that may enhance service utilization among economically disadvantaged and minority families, while at the same time providing cost-beneficial effects.

Fourth, interest in interventions for the *prevention* of CP has burgeoned over the past 10 years, stimulated partly by increased knowledge about the early starter pathway of CP. PT may have significant preventive effects, especially if it is applied during the preschool period (Reid, 1993; Sanders, 1996), or is a component of broader preventive interventions for school-age children at risk for CP (e.g., Conduct Problems Prevention Research Group, 1992; Tremblay et al., 1992). Two of the PT programs described in this chapter (Forehand & McMahon, 1981; Webster-Stratton, 1996a) have been identified as model family interventions for delinquency prevention by the Office of Juvenile Justice and Delinquency Prevention (1996). If PT can play a role in the prevention of CP, then that will have important implications for reducing the need for ongoing interventions throughout the developmental period and adulthood.

Perhaps the most compelling reason for the utilization of PT within a managed care network is its potential cost-effectiveness. The empirical support for PT, the availability of manuals and multiple-level delivery systems, and its potential for preventive effects are all conducive to cost-effectiveness. A recent economic analysis of the costs and benefits of several intervention strategies indicated that PT was more cost-effective in preventing later crime than either home visiting plus day care or supervision of delinquents (Greenwood, Model, Rydell, & Chiesa, 1996).

SUGGESTIONS FOR FUTURE RESEARCH/PRACTICE

Studies of PT interventions with preadolescent children comprise the largest and most sophisticated body of intervention research with children with CP, and present the most promising results (McMahon & Wells, 1998). Not only has immediate treatment outcome been quantified by changes in parents' and children's behavior and in parental perceptions of the children's adjustment in a large number of investigations, but generalization of such effects to the home, over reasonable follow-up periods (3 years posttreatment and longer), to untreated siblings, and to untreated behaviors has been demonstrated for many of these families as well. The social validity of these effects has also been documented by a number of PT programs. Investigators associated with these PT interventions have broadened the basic model to include family-related variables that may enhance outcome and generalization. This has resulted in the development of adjunctive intervention modules to deal with marital conflict, parental distress, and the like, as well as the ongoing development and elaboration of the Behavioral Family Therapy model (Griest & Wells, 1983; Miller & Prinz, 1990).

Despite this very positive evaluation of PT as an intervention for young children with CP, there are a number of areas that warrant increased attention in both research and clinical practice. These include (1) development of treatment selection guidelines; (2) continued emphasis on identification and elaboration of the processes of family engagement and change in PT; (3) examination of how outcome and generalization of effects can be enhanced, especially with respect to underserved groups, such as the economically disadvantaged and various minority groups; (4) the role of PT as a preventive intervention; and (5) greater attention to large-scale dissemination.

As noted above, a comprehensive, empirically based treatment selection model for children with CP is greatly needed. The early starter pathway is a useful starting point for such an endeavor, in that it provides guidance concerning the extent of CP behavior and the contexts in which it is most likely to occur. However, greater attention needs to be given to the processes by which clinicians decide to use a PT intervention, how they select the type and level of PT, and how they decide to incorporate other adjunctive procedures that address other aspects of child or family functioning. Elaboration of these clinical decision-making processes may then serve to stimulate empirical research on treatment selection guidelines.

The development of conceptual models of family engagement in PT intervention (e.g., Kazdin et al., 1997; Prinz & Miller, 1996) has been an important advance in terms of providing a template for future research in this area. Similarly, the rich clinical descriptions of family engagement and resistance in PT as well as requisite therapist behaviors (e.g., Webster-Stratton & Herbert, 1993, 1994), should provide clinicians with useful suggestions for enhancing parental engagement and reducing resistance, and serve a heuristic function as well.

More work is needed to ensure that PT interventions are available to, appropriate for, and effective with as many families as possible. On a more microscopic level, this may involve parametric studies concerning the relative effectiveness or acceptability of various parenting skills employed in PT (e.g., time-out) or complete PT interventions with different family members (e.g., fathers) or family subtypes (e.g., single parents, stepfamilies). At a macrosystem level, more research is needed to ascertain the extent to which the effectiveness of PT interventions is moderated by the cultural background of children with CP (Forehand & Kotchick, 1996). Prinz and Miller (1991) have suggested three levels at which interventions for children with CP can be made more culturally sensitive. First, the interface between the intervention and the cultural group can be enhanced (e.g., by matching the ethnicity of intervention staff to the target population). Second, the content of the intervention can be adapted for a particular ethnic group (e.g., tailoring materials or examples to enhance the relevance of the intervention). Third, an intervention that is specifically developed for a particular ethnic group can be developed. There is a need for these suggestions to be applied systematically to PT interventions.

As noted above, PT has great potential as a preventive intervention for children with CP. There are currently a number of large-scale ongoing prevention trials that employ PT as the primary intervention (e.g., Sanders & Markie-Dadds, 1996) or as a component in a more broadly based intervention (e.g., Conduct Problems Prevention Research Group, 1992). Although preliminary results of these projects are encouraging (e.g., Conduct Problems Prevention Research Group, 1997; Reid, Eddy, Bank, & Fetrow, 1994), it will be several years before the long-term outcome is known.

In order for PT to have the most significant impact on CP, it will be necessary for it to be disseminated in a large-scale and cost-effective manner. With few exceptions (e.g., Sanders & Markie-Dadds, 1996; Taylor & Biglan, 1998), there has been a lack of attention paid to the conceptual, empirical, and pragmatic issues that are involved in such dissemination. The same care and systematic approach to evaluation that has characterized the empirical research on PT described in this chapter must be brought to bear on research concerning the dissemination of PT as well.

SUMMARY

This chapter has described the use of PT as an intervention for CP in young children. Advances in the delineation of the early starter pathway for serious CP have illuminated the significant role that family-related factors play in the development and maintenance of child CP. A multimethod, multi-informant approach to the assessment of children with CP and their families was presented. Descriptions of three well-validated PT interventions were provided, along with research evidence in support of the effectiveness, generalization, and social validity of PT interventions. The chapter concluded with discussions on the potential of PT for use in managed care networks, and several suggestions for future research and practice.

REFERENCES

Abidin, R. R. (1995). *Parenting Stress Index—professional manual* (3rd ed.). Odessa, FL: Psychological Assessment Resources.

Abidin, R. R., & Brunner, J. F. (1995). Development of a parenting alliance inventory. *Journal of Clinical Child Psychology, 24,* 31–40.

Achenbach, T. M. (1991). *Manual for the Child Behavior Checklist/4–18 and 1991 Profile.* Burlington: University of Vermont Department of Psychiatry.

American Psychiatric Association. (1994). *Diagnostic and statistical manual of mental disorders* (4th ed.). Washington, DC: Author.

Arnold, D. S., O'Leary, S. G., Wolff, L. S., & Acker, M. M. (1993). The Parenting Scale: A measure of dysfunctional parenting in discipline situations. *Psychological Assessment, 5,* 137–144.

Arnold, J. E., Levine, A. G., & Patterson, G. R. (1975). Changes in sibling behavior following family intervention. *Journal of Consulting and Clinical Psychology, 43,* 683–688.

Baden, A. D., & Howe, G. W. (1992). Mothers' attributions and expectancies regarding their conduct-disordered children. *Journal of Abnormal Child Psychology, 20,* 467–485.

Baum, C. G., & Forehand, R. (1981). Long-term follow-up assessment of parent training by use of multiple-outcome measures. *Behavior Therapy, 12,* 643–652.

Baum, C. G., Reyna McGlone, C. L., & Ollendick, T. H. (1986, November). *The efficacy of behavioral parent training: Behavioral parent training plus clinical self-control training, and a modified STEP program with children referred for noncompliance.* Paper presented at the meeting of the Association for Advancement of Behavior Therapy, Chicago.

Beck, A. T., Rush, A. J., Shaw, B. F., & Emery, G. (1979). *Cognitive therapy of depression.* New York: Guilford Press.

Berkowitz, B. P., & Graziano, A. M. (1972). Training parents as behavior therapists: A review. *Behaviour Research and Therapy, 10,* 297–317.

Bernal, M. E., Klinnert, M. D., & Schultz, L. A. (1980). Outcome evaluation of behavioral parent training and client-centered parent counseling for children with conduct problems. *Journal of Applied Behavior Analysis, 13,* 677–691.

Breiner, J. L., & Forehand, R. (1981). An assessment of the effects of parent training on clinic-referred children's school behavior. *Behavioral Assessment, 3,* 31–42.

Briesmeister, J. M., & Schaefer, C. E. (Eds.). (1998). *Handbook of parent training: Parents as co-therapists for children's behavior problems* (2nd ed.). New York: Wiley.

Budd, K. S., & O'Brien, T. P. (1982). Father involvement in behavioral parent training: An area in need of research. *The Behavior Therapist, 5,* 85–89.

Campis, L. K., Lyman, R. D., & Prentice-Dunn, S. (1986). The Parental Locus of Control Scale: Development and validation. *Journal of Clinical Child Psychology, 15,* 260–267.

Chamberlain, P., & Patterson, G. R. (1995). Discipline and child compliance in parenting. In M. H. Bornstein (Ed.), *Handbook of parenting: Vol. 4. Applied and practical parenting* (pp. 205–225). Hillsdale, NJ: Erlbaum.

Chamberlain, P., Patterson, G., Reid, J., Kavanagh, K., & Forgatch, M. (1984). Observation of client resistance. *Behavior Therapy, 15,* 144–155.

Chamberlain, P., & Reid, J. B. (1987). Parent observation and report of child symptoms. *Behavioral Assessment, 9,* 97–109.

Chamberlain, P., Reid, J. B., Ray, J., Capaldi, D. M., & Fisher, P. (1997). Parent inadequate discipline. In T. A. Widiger, A. J. Frances, H. A. Pincus, R. Ross, M. B. First, & W. Davis (Eds.), *DSM-IV sourcebook* (Vol. 3, pp. 569–629). Washington, DC: American Psychiatric Association.

Chambless, D. L., Baker, M. J., Baucom, D. H., Beutler, L. E., Calhoun, K. S., Crits-Christoph, P., Daiuto, A., DeRubeis, R., Detweiler, J., Haaga, D. A. F., Johnson, S. B., McCurry, S., Mueser, K. T., Pope, K. S., Sanderson, W. C., Shoham, V., Stickle, T., Williams, D. A., & Woody, S. R. (1998). Update on empirically validated therapies, II. *The Clinical Psychologist, 51,* 3–21.

Conduct Problems Prevention Research Group. (1992). A developmental and clinical model for the prevention of conduct disorders: The FAST Track program. *Development and Psychopathology, 4,* 509–527.

Conduct Problems Prevention Research Group. (1997, August). Testing developmental theory of antisocial behavior with outcomes from the Fast Track prevention project. In G. R. Patterson (Chair), *Randomized prevention trials as a basis for testing developmental theory.* Symposium conducted at the meeting of the American Psychological Association, Chicago.

Connell, S., Sanders, M. R., & Markie-Dadds, C. (1997). Self-directed behavioral family intervention for parents of oppositional children in rural and remote areas. *Behavior Modification, 21,* 379–408.

Coplin, J. W., & Houts, A. C. (1991). Father involvement in parent training for oppositional child behavior: Progress or stagnation? *Child & Family Behavior Therapy, 13,* 29–51.

Crnic, K. A., & Greenberg, M. T. (1990). Minor parenting stresses with young children. *Child Development, 61,* 1628–1637.

Cross Calvert, S., & McMahon, R. J. (1987). The treatment acceptability of a behavioral parent training program and its components. *Behavior Therapy, 18,* 165–179.

Cummings, E. M., & Davies, P. (1994). *Children and marital conflict: The impact of family dispute resolution.* New York: Guilford Press.

Cunningham, C. E., Bremner, R., & Boyle, M. (1995). Large group community-based parenting programs for families of preschoolers at risk for Disruptive Behaviour Disorders: Utilization, cost-effectiveness, and outcome. *Journal of Child Psychiatry and Psychology, 36,* 1141–1149.

Dadds, M. R., & McHugh, T. A. (1992). Social support and treatment outcome in behavioral family therapy for child conduct problems. *Journal of Consulting and Clinical Psychology, 60,* 252–259.

Dadds, M. R., Schwartz, S., & Sanders, M. R. (1987). Marital discord and treatment outcome in behavioral treatment of child conduct disorders. *Journal of Consulting and Clinical Psychology, 55,* 396–403.

Dangel, R. F., & Polster, R. A. (Eds.). (1984). *Parent training: Foundations of research and practice.* New York: Guilford Press.

Dishion, T. J., & Patterson, G. R. (1992). Age effects in parent training outcome. *Behavior Therapy 23,* 719–729.

Dumas, J. E. (1984a). Child, adult-interactional, and socioeconomic setting events as predictors of parent training outcome. *Education and Treatment of Children, 7,* 351–364.

Dumas, J. E. (1984b). Interactional correlates of treatment outcome in behavioral parent training. *Journal of Consulting and Clinical Psychology, 52,* 946–954.

Dumas, J. E. (1989). Treating antisocial behavior in children: Child and family approaches. *Clinical Psychology Review, 9,* 197–222.

Dumas, J. E. (1996). Why was this child referred? Interactional correlates of referral status in families of children with disruptive behavior problems. *Journal of Clinical Child Psychology, 25*, 106–115.

Dumas, J. E., & Albin, J. B. (1986). Parent training outcome: Does active parental involvement matter? *Behaviour Research and Therapy, 24*, 227–230.

Dumas, J. E., & Serketich, W. J. (1994). Maternal depressive symptomatology and child maladjustment: A comparison of three process models. *Behavior Therapy, 25*, 161–181.

Dumas, J. E., & Wahler, R. G. (1983). Predictors of treatment outcome in parent training: Mother insularity and socioeconomic disadvantage. *Behavioral Assessment, 5*, 301–313.

Dumas, J. E., & Wahler, R. G. (1985). Indiscriminate mothering as a contextual factor in aggressive-oppositional child behavior: "Damned if you do and damned if you don't." *Journal of Abnormal Child Psychology, 13*, 1–17.

Edelbrock, C. (1985). *Conduct problems in childhood and adolescence: Developmental patterns and progressions.* Unpublished manuscript.

Embry, L. H. (1984). What to do? Matching client characteristics and intervention techniques through a prescriptive taxonomic key. In R. F. Dangel & R. A. Polster (Eds.), *Parent training: Foundations of research and practice* (pp. 443–473). New York: Guilford Press.

Eyberg, S. (1992). Parent and teacher behavior inventories for the assessment of conduct problem behaviors in children. In L. VandeCreek, S. Knapp, & T. L. Jackson (Eds.), *Innovations in clinical practice: A source book* (Vol. 11, pp. 261–270). Sarasota, FL: Professional Resource Press.

Eyberg, S., Bessmer, J., Newcomb, K., Edwards, D., & Robinson, E. (1994). *Dyadic Parent–Child Interaction Coding System II: A manual.* Unpublished manuscript, University of Florida, Gainesville.

Fleischman, M. J. (1981). A replication of Patterson's "Intervention for boys with conduct problems." *Journal of Consulting and Clinical Psychology, 49*, 342–351.

Forehand, R., & Atkeson, B. M. (1977). Generality of treatment effects with parents as therapists: A review of assessment and implementation procedures. *Behavior Therapy, 8*, 575–593.

Forehand, R., Griest, D. L., Wells, K. C., & McMahon, R. J. (1982). Side effects of parent counseling on marital satisfaction. *Journal of Counseling Psychology, 29*, 104–107.

Forehand, R., & Kotchick, B. A. (1996). Cultural diversity: A wake-up call for parent training. *Behavior Therapy, 27*, 187–206.

Forehand, R., & Long, N. (1988). Outpatient treatment of the acting out child: Procedures, long term follow-up data, and clinical problems. *Advances in Behaviour Research and Therapy, 10*, 129–177.

Forehand, R., & McMahon, R. J. (1981). *Helping the noncompliant child: A clinician's guide to parent training.* New York: Guilford Press.

Forehand, R., Sturgis, E. T., McMahon, R. J., Aguar, D., Green, K., Wells, K., & Breiner, J. (1979). Parent behavioral training to modify child noncompliance: Treatment generalization across time and from home to school. *Behavior Modification, 3*, 3–25.

Forehand, R., Wells, K. C., & Griest, D. L. (1980). An examination of the social validity of a parent training program. *Behavior Therapy, 11*, 488–502.

Forgatch, M. S., Patterson, G. R., & Skinner, M. L. (1988). A mediational model for the effect of divorce on antisocial behavior in boys. In E. M. Hetherington & J. D. Arasteh (Eds.), *Impact of divorce, single parenting, and stepparenting on children* (pp. 135–154). Hillsdale, NJ: Erlbaum.

Frick, P. J. (1991). *The Alabama Parenting Questionnaire.* Unpublished rating scale. University of Alabama.

Frick, P. J., & Loney, B. R. (in press). Understanding the association between parent and child antisocial behavior. In R. J. McMahon & R. DeV. Peters (Eds.), *The effects of parental disorders on children.*

Greenwood, P. W., Model, K. E., Rydell, C. P., & Chiesa, J. (1996). *Diverting children from a life of crime: Measuring costs and benefits.* Santa Monica, CA: RAND.

Griest, D. L., Forehand, R., Rogers, T., Breiner, J. L., Furey, W., & Williams, C. A. (1982). Effects of parent enhancement therapy on the treatment outcome and generalization of a parent training program. *Behaviour Research and Therapy, 20*, 429–436.

Griest, D. L., & Wells, K. C. (1983). Behavioral family therapy with conduct disorders in children. *Behavior Therapy, 14*, 37–53.

Hanf, C. (1969). *A two-stage program for modifying maternal controlling during mother–child (M-C) interaction.* Paper presented at the meeting of the Western Psychological Association, Vancouver, BC.

Holden, G. W., Lavigne, V. V., & Cameron, A. M. (1990). Probing the continuum of effectiveness in parent training: Characteristics of parents and preschoolers. *Journal of Clinical Child Psychology, 19*, 2–8.

Humphreys, L., Forehand, R., McMahon, R., & Roberts, M. (1978). Parent behavioral training to modify child noncompliance: Effects on untreated siblings. *Journal of Behavior Therapy and Experimental Psychiatry, 9,* 235–238.

Jacob, T., Krahn, G. L., & Leonard, K. (1991). Parent–child interactions in families with alcoholic fathers. *Journal of Consulting and Clinical Psychology, 59,* 176–181.

Johnson, S. M., Bolstad, O. D., & Lobitz, G. K. (1976). Generalization and contrast phenomena in behavior modification with children. In L. A. Hamerlynck, L. C. Handy, & E. J. Mash (Eds.), *Behavior modification and families* (pp. 160–188). New York: Brunner/Mazel.

Johnston, C. (1996). Addressing parent cognitions in interventions with families of disruptive children. In K. S. Dobson & K. D. Craig (Eds.), *Advances in cognitive-behavioral therapy* (pp. 193–209). Thousand Oaks, CA: Sage.

Johnston, C., & Mash, E. J. (1989). A measure of parenting satisfaction and efficacy. *Journal of Clinical Child Psychology, 18,* 167–175.

Jouriles, E. N., Murphy, C. M., Farris, A. M., Smith, D. A., Richters, J. E., & Waters, E. (1991). Marital adjustment, parental disagreements about child rearing, and behavior problems in boys: Increasing the specificity of the marital assessment. *Child Development, 62,* 1424–1433.

Kazdin, A. E. (1977). Assessing the clinical or applied importance of behavior change through social validation. *Behavior Modification, 1,* 427–452.

Kazdin, A. E. (1985). *Treatment of antisocial behavior in children and adolescents.* Homewood, IL: Dorsey Press.

Kazdin, A. E. (1990). Premature termination from treatment among children referred for antisocial behavior. *Journal of Child Psychology and Psychiatry, 31,* 415–425.

Kazdin, A. E. (1995a). Child, parent and family dysfunction as predictors of outcome in cognitive-behavioral treatment of antisocial children. *Behaviour Research and Therapy, 33,* 271–281.

Kazdin, A. E. (1995b). *Conduct disorders in childhood and adolescence* (2nd ed.). Thousand Oaks, CA: Sage.

Kazdin, A. E., Holland, L., & Crowley, M. (1997). Family experience of barriers to treatment and premature termination from child therapy. *Journal of Consulting and Clinical Psychology, 65,* 453–463.

Kazdin, A. E., Mazurick, J. L., & Bass, D. (1993). Risk for attrition in treatment of antisocial children and families. *Journal of Clinical Child Psychology, 22,* 2–16.

Kazdin, A. E., Siegel, T. C., & Bass, D. (1992). Cognitive problem-solving skills training and parent management training in the treatment of antisocial behavior in children. *Journal of Consulting and Clinical Psychology, 60,* 733–747.

Kratzer, L., & Hodgins, S. (1997). Adult outcomes of child conduct problems: A cohort study. *Journal of Abnormal Child Psychology, 25,* 65–81.

Locke, H. J., & Wallace, K. M. (1959). Short marital adjustment and prediction tests: Their reliability and validity. *Marriage and Family Living, 21,* 251–255.

Long, P., Forehand, R., Wierson, M., & Morgan, A. (1994). Does parent training with young noncompliant children have long-term effects? *Behaviour Research and Therapy, 32,* 101–107.

McMahon, R. J. (1987). Some current issues in the behavioral assessment of conduct disordered children and their families. *Behavioral Assessment, 9,* 235–252.

McMahon, R. J. (1991). Parent Management Training. In V. E. Caballo (Ed.), *Manual de tecnicas de terapia y modificacion de conducta (Handbook of behavior therapy methods and techniques)* (pp. 445–471). Madrid: Siglo XXI de Espana Editores, S.A.

McMahon, R. J., & Estes, A. M. (1997). Conduct problems. In E. J. Mash & L. G. Terdal (Eds.), *Assessment of childhood disorders* (3rd ed., pp. 130–193). New York: Guilford Press.

McMahon, R. J., & Forehand, R. (1983). Consumer satisfaction in behavioral treatment of children: Types, issues, and recommendations. *Behavior Therapy, 14,* 209–225.

McMahon, R. J., Forehand, R., & Griest, D. L. (1981). Effects of knowledge of social learning principles on enhancing treatment outcome and generalization in a parent training program. *Journal of Consulting and Clinical Psychology, 49,* 526–532.

McMahon, R. J., Forehand, R., Griest, D. L., & Wells, K. C. (1981). Who drops out of treatment during parent behavioral training? *Behavioral Counseling Quarterly, 1,* 79–85.

McMahon, R. J., Forehand, R., & Tiedemann, G. L. (1985, November). *Relative effectiveness of a parent training program with children of different ages.* Paper presented at the meeting of the Association for Advancement of Behavior Therapy, Houston.

McMahon, R. J., Tiedemann, G. L., Forehand, R., & Griest, D. L. (1984). Parental satisfaction with parent training to modify child noncompliance. *Behavior Therapy, 15,* 295–303.

McMahon, R. J., & Wells, K. C. (1998). Conduct problems. In E. J. Mash & R. A Barkley (Eds.), *Treatment of childhood disorders* (pp. 111–207). New York: Guilford Press.

McNeil, C. B., Eyberg, S., Eisenstadt, T. H., Newcomb, K., & Funderburk, B. (1991). Parent–child interaction therapy with behavior problem children: Generalization of treatment effects to the school setting. *Journal of Clinical Child Psychology, 20,* 140–151.

Miller, G. E., & Prinz, R. J. (1990). Enhancement of social learning family interventions for childhood Conduct Disorder. *Psychological Bulletin, 108,* 291–307.

Moffitt, T. E. (1993). "Adolescence-limited" and "life-course-persistent" antisocial behavior: A developmental taxonomy. *Psychological Review, 100,* 674–701.

O'Dell, S. L. (1974). Training parents in behavior modification: A review. *Psychological Bulletin, 81,* 418–433.

O'Dell, S. L. (1985). Progress in parent training. In M. Hersen, R. M. Eisler, & P. M. Miller (Eds.), *Progress in behavior modification* (Vol. 9, pp. 57–108). New York: Academic Press.

Office of Juvenile Justice and Delinquency Prevention. (1996, October). *Second National Training Conference on Strengthening America's Families,* Snowbird, UT.

Patterson, G. R. (1974). Interventions for boys with conduct problems: Multiple settings, treatments, and criteria. *Journal of Consulting and Clinical Psychology, 42,* 471–481.

Patterson, G. R. (1975). *Families: Applications of social learning to family life* (rev. ed.). Champaign, IL: Research Press.

Patterson, G. R. (1976). *Living with children: New methods for parents and teachers* (rev. ed.). Champaign, IL: Research Press.

Patterson, G. R. (1982). *Coercive family process.* Eugene, OR: Castalia.

Patterson, G. R. (1983). Stress: A change agent for family process. In N. Garmezy & M. Rutter (Eds.), *Stress, coping and development in children* (pp. 235–264). New York: McGraw–Hill.

Patterson, G. R., & Bank, L. (1986). Bootstrapping your way in the nomological thicket. *Behavioral Assessment, 8,* 49–73.

Patterson, G. R., Capaldi, D., & Bank, L. (1991). An early starter model for predicting delinquency. In D. J. Pepler & K. H. Rubin (Eds.), *The development and treatment of childhood aggression* (pp. 139–168). Hillsdale, NJ: Erlbaum.

Patterson, G. R., & Chamberlain, P. (1988). Treatment process: A problem at three levels. In L. C. Wynne (Ed.), *The state of the art in family therapy research: Controversies and recommendations* (pp. 189–223). New York: Family Process Press.

Patterson, G. R., & Chamberlain, P. (1994). A functional analysis of resistance during parent training therapy. *Clinical Psychology: Science and Practice, 1,* 53–70.

Patterson, G. R., Chamberlain, P., & Reid, J. B. (1982). A comparative evaluation of a parent training program. *Behavior Therapy, 13,* 638–650.

Patterson, G. R., & Fleischman, M. J. (1979). Maintenance of treatment effects: Some considerations concerning family systems and follow-up data. *Behavior Therapy, 10,* 168–185.

Patterson, G. R., & Forgatch, M. S. (1985). Therapist behavior as a determinant for client noncompliance: A paradox for the behavior modifier. *Journal of Consulting and Clinical Psychology, 53,* 846–851.

Patterson, G. R., & Forgatch, M. S. (1995). Predicting future clinical adjustment from treatment outcome and process variables. *Psychological Assessment, 7,* 275–285.

Patterson, G. R., & Reid, J. B. (1973). Intervention for families of aggressive boys: A replication study. *Behaviour Research and Therapy, 11,* 383–394.

Patterson, G. R., Reid, J. B., & Dishion, T. J. (1992). *Antisocial boys.* Eugene, OR: Castalia.

Patterson, G. R., Reid, J. B., Jones, R. R., & Conger, R. E. (1975). *A social learning approach to family intervention: Vol. 1. Families with aggressive children.* Eugene, OR: Castalia.

Peed, S., Roberts, M., & Forehand, R. (1977). Evaluation of the effectiveness of a standardized parent training program in altering the interaction of mothers and their noncompliant children. *Behavior Modification, 1,* 323–350.

Pelham, W. E., & Lang, A. R. (1993). Parental alcohol consumption and deviant child behavior: Laboratory studies of reciprocal effects. *Clinical Psychology Review, 13,* 763–784.

Porter, B., & O'Leary, K. D. (1980). Marital discord and childhood behavior problems. *Journal of Abnormal Child Psychology, 8,* 287–295.

Powers, S. W., & Roberts, M. W. (1995). Simulation training with parents of oppositional children: Preliminary findings. *Journal of Clinical Child Psychology, 24,* 89–97.

Prinz, R. J., & Miller, G. E. (1991). Issues in understanding and treating childhood conduct problems in disadvantaged populations. *Journal of Clinical Child Psychology, 20,* 379–385.

Prinz, R. J., & Miller, G. E. (1994). Family-based treatment for childhood antisocial behavior: Experimental influences on dropout and engagement. *Journal of Consulting and Clinical Psychology, 62,* 645–650.

Prinz, R. J., & Miller, G. E. (1996). Parental engagement in interventions for children at risk for conduct disorder. In R. D. Peters & R. J. McMahon (Eds.), *Preventing childhood disorders, substance abuse, and delinquency* (pp. 161–183). Thousand Oaks, CA: Sage.

Reid, J. B. (1993). Prevention of conduct disorder before and after school entry: Relating interventions to developmental findings. *Development and Psychopathology, 5,* 243–262.

Reid, J. B., Eddy, J. M., Bank, L., & Fetrow, R. (November 1994). Some preliminary findings from a universal prevention program for Conduct Disorder. Paper presented at the 4th National Institute of Mental Health Conference on Prevention Research, Washington, DC.

Roberts, M. W., Joe, V. C., & Rowe-Hallbert, A. (1992). Oppositional child behavior and parental locus of control. *Journal of Clinical Child Psychology, 21,* 170–177.

Rogers, T. R., Forehand, R., Griest, D. L., Wells, K. C., & McMahon, R. J. (1981). Socioeconomic status: Effects on parent and child behaviors and treatment outcome of parent training. *Journal of Clinical Child Psychology, 10,* 98–101.

Routh, C. P., Hill, J. W., Steele, H., Elliott, C. E., & Dewey, M. E. (1995). Maternal attachment status, psychosocial stressors and problem behaviour: Follow-up after parent training courses for Conduct Disorder. *Journal of Child Psychology and Psychiatry, 36,* 1179–1198.

Rusby, J. C., Estes, A., & Dishion, T. (1991). *The Interpersonal Process Code (IPC).* Unpublished manuscript, Oregon Social Learning Center, Eugene.

Russo, D. C., Cataldo, M. F., & Cushing, P. J. (1981). Compliance training and behavioral covariation in the treatment of multiple behavior problems. *Journal of Applied Behavior Analysis, 14,* 209–222.

Rutter, M. (1994). Family discord and Conduct Disorder: Cause, consequence, or correlate? *Journal of Family Psychology, 8,* 170–186.

Sanders, M. R. (1996). New directions in behavioral family intervention with children. In T. H. Ollendick & R. J. Prinz (Eds.), *Advances in clinical child psychology* (Vol. 18, pp. 283–331). New York: Plenum Press.

Sanders, M. R., & Dadds, M. R. (1982). The effects of planned activities and child management procedures in parent training: An analysis of setting generality. *Behavior Therapy, 13,* 452–461.

Sanders, M. R., & Dadds, M. R. (1992). Children's and parents' cognitions about family interaction: An evaluation of video-mediated recall and thought listing procedures in the assessment of conduct-disordered children. *Journal of Clinical Child Psychology, 21,* 371–379.

Sanders, M. R., & Dadds, M. R. (1993). *Behavioral family intervention.* Boston: Allyn & Bacon.

Sanders, M. R., & Glynn, T. (1981). Training parents in behavioral self management: An analysis of generalization and maintenance. *Journal of Applied Behavior Analysis, 14,* 223–237.

Sanders, M. R., & Lawton, J. M. (1993). Discussing assessment findings with families: A guided participation model of information transfer. *Child & Family Behavior Therapy, 15,* 5–35.

Sanders, M. R., & Markie-Dadds, C. (1996). Triple P: A multilevel family intervention program for children with disruptive behaviour disorders. In P. Cotton & H. Jackson (Eds.), *Early intervention and preventive mental health applications of clinical psychology* (pp. 59–85). Melbourne: Australian Psychological Society.

Sarason, I. G., Johnson, J. H., & Siegel, J. M. (1978). Assessing the impact of life changes: Development of the Life Experiences Survey. *Journal of Consulting and Clinical Psychology, 46,* 932–946.

Schuhmann, E. M., Foote, R. C., Eyberg, S. M., Boggs, S. R., & Algina, J. (1998). Efficacy of parent–child interaction therapy: Interim report of a randomized trial with short-term maintenance. *Journal of Clinical Child Psychology, 27,* 34–45.

Scott, M. J., & Stradling, S. G. (1987). Evaluation of a group programme for parents of problem children. *Behavioural Psychotherapy, 15,* 224–239.

Selzer, M. L., Vinokur, A., & van Rooijen, L. (1975). A self-administered short Michigan Alcoholism Screening Test. *Journal of Studies on Alcohol, 36,* 117–126.

Serketich, W. J., & Dumas, J. E. (1996). The effectiveness of behavioral parent training to modify antisocial behavior in children: A meta-analysis. *Behavior Therapy, 27,* 171–186.

Skinner, H. A. (1982). The Drug Abuse Screening Test. *Addictive Behaviors, 7,* 363–371.

Spanier, G. B. (1976). Measuring dyadic adjustment: New scales for assessing the quality of marriage and similar dyads. *Journal of Marriage and the Family, 38,* 15–28.

Spitzer, A., Webster-Stratton, C., & Hollinsworth, T. (1991). Coping with conduct-problem children: Parents gaining knowledge and control. *Journal of Clinical Child Psychology, 20,* 413–427.

Stoolmiller, M., Duncan, T., Bank, L., & Patterson, G.R. (1993). Some problems and solutions in the study of change: Significant patterns in client resistance. *Journal of Consulting and Clinical Psychology, 61,* 920–928.

Strain, P. S., Steele, P., Ellis, T., & Timm, M. A. (1982). Long-term effects of oppositional child treatment with mothers as therapists and therapist trainers. *Journal of Applied Behavior Analysis, 15,* 163–169.

Strain, P. S., Young, C. C., & Horowitz, J. (1981). Generalized behavior change during oppositional child training: An examination of child and family demographic variables. *Behavior Modification, 5,* 15–26.

Straus, M. A. (1990). The Conflict Tactics Scales and its critics: An evaluation and new data on validity and reliability. In M. A. Straus & R. J. Gelles (Eds.), *Physical violence in American families: Risk factors and adaptations to violence in 8,145 families* (pp. 49–73). New Brunswick, NJ: Transaction Publishers.

Taplin, P. S., & Reid, J. B. (1977). Changes in parent consequences as a function of family intervention. *Journal of Consulting and Clinical Psychology, 45,* 973–981.

Taylor, T. K., & Biglan, A. (1998). Behavioral family interventions for improving child-rearing: A review of the literature for clinicians and policy makers. *Clinical Child and Family Psychology Review, 1,* 41–60.

Taylor, T. K., Schmidt, F., Pepler, D., & Hodgins, C. (1998). A comparison of eclectic treatment with Webster-Stratton's Parents and Children Series in a children's mental health center: A randomized controlled trial. *Behavior Therapy, 29,* 221–240.

Tharp, R. G., & Wetzel, R. J. (1969). *Behavior modification in the natural environment.* New York: Academic Press.

Tremblay, R. E., Vitaro, F., Bertrand, L., LeBlanc, M., Beauchesne, H., Boileau, H., & Lucille, D. (1992). Parent and child training to prevent early onset of delinquency: The Montreal longitudinal experimental study. In J. McCord & R. E. Tremblay (Eds.), *Preventing antisocial behavior: Interventions from birth through adolescence* (pp. 117–138). New York: Guilford Press.

Wahler, R. G., Cartor, P. G., Fleischman, J., & Lambert, W. (1993). The impact of synthesis teaching and parent training with mothers of conduct-disordered children. *Journal of Abnormal Child Psychology, 21,* 425–440.

Wahler, R. G., & Dumas, J. E. (1984). Changing the observational coding styles of insular and noninsular mothers: A step toward maintenance of parent training effects. In R. F. Dangel & R. A. Polster (Eds.), *Parent training: Foundations of research and practice* (pp. 379–416). New York: Guilford Press.

Wahler, R. G., Leske, G., & Rogers, E. S. (1979). The insular family: A deviance support system for oppositional children. In L. A. Hamerlynck (Ed.), *Behavioral systems for the developmentally disabled: Vol. 1. School and family environments* (pp. 102–127). New York: Brunner/Mazel.

Walter, H. I., & Gilmore, S. K. (1973). Placebo versus social learning effects in parent training procedures designed to alter the behavior of aggressive boys. *Behavior Therapy, 4,* 361–377.

Webster-Stratton, C. (1984). Randomized trial of two parent-training programs for families with conduct-disordered children. *Journal of Consulting and Clinical Psychology, 52,* 666–678.

Webster-Stratton, C. (1985a). Predictors of treatment outcome in parent training for conduct disordered children. *Behavior Therapy, 16,* 223–242.

Webster-Stratton, C. (1985b). The effects of father involvement in parent training for conduct problem children. *Journal of Child Psychology and Psychiatry, 26,* 801–810.

Webster-Stratton, C. (1989). Systematic comparison of consumer satisfaction of three cost-effective parent training programs for conduct problem children. *Behavior Therapy, 20,* 103–115.

Webster-Stratton, C. (1990a). Enhancing the effectiveness of self-administered videotape parent training for families with conduct-problem children. *Journal of Abnormal Child Psychology, 18,* 479–492.

Webster-Stratton, C. (1990b). Long-term follow-up of families with young conduct problem children: From preschool to grade school. *Journal of Clinical Child Psychology, 19,* 144–149.

Webster-Stratton, C. (1994). Advancing videotape parent training: A comparison study. *Journal of Consulting and Clinical Psychology, 62*, 583–593.

Webster-Stratton, C. H. (1996a). Early intervention with videotape modeling: Programs for families of children with Oppositional Defiant Disorder or Conduct Disorder. In E. S. Hibbs & P. S. Jensen (Eds.), *Psychosocial treatments for child and adolescent disorders: Empirically-based strategies for clinical practice* (pp. 435–474). Washington, DC: American Psychological Association.

Webster-Stratton, C. (1996b). Early-onset conduct problems: Does gender make a difference? *Journal of Consulting and Clinical Psychology, 64*, 540–551.

Webster-Stratton, C. (1998). Preventing conduct problems in Head Start children: Strengthening parenting competencies. *Journal of Consulting and Clinical Psychology, 66*, 715–730.

Webster-Stratton, C., & Hammond M. (1990). Predictors of treatment outcome in parent training for families with conduct problem children. *Behavior Therapy, 21*, 319–337.

Webster-Stratton, C., & Hammond, M. (1997). Treating children with early-onset conduct problems: A comparison of child and parent training interventions. *Journal of Consulting and Clinical Psychology, 65*, 93–109.

Webster-Stratton, C., & Herbert, M. (1993). "What really happens in parent training?" *Behavior Modification, 17*, 407–456.

Webster-Stratton, C., & Herbert, M. (1994). *Troubled families—Problem children*. New York: Wiley.

Webster-Stratton, C., Hollinsworth, T., & Kolpacoff, M. (1989). The long-term effectiveness and clinical significance of three cost-effective training programs for families with conduct-problem children. *Journal of Consulting and Clinical Psychology, 57*, 550–553.

Webster-Stratton, C., Kolpacoff, M., & Hollinsworth, T. (1988). Self-administered videotape therapy for families with conduct problem children: Comparison to two other cost effective treatments and a control group. *Journal of Consulting and Clinical Psychology, 56*, 558–566.

Webster-Stratton, C., & Spitzer, A. (1991). Development, reliability, and validity of the Daily Telephone Discipline Interview. *Behavioral Assessment, 13*, 221–239.

Webster-Stratton, C., & Spitzer, A. (1996). Parenting a young child with conduct problems: New insights using qualitative methods. In T. H. Ollendick & R. J. Prinz (Eds.), *Advances in clinical child psychology* (Vol. 18, pp. 1–62). New York: Plenum Press.

Wells, K. C., & Egan, J. (1988). Social learning and systems family therapy for childhood oppositional disorder: Comparative treatment outcome. *Comprehensive Psychiatry, 29*, 138–146.

Wells, K. C., Forehand, R., & Griest, D. L. (1980). Generality of treatment effects from treated to untreated behaviors resulting from a parent training program. *Journal of Clinical Child Psychology, 9*, 217–219.

Wells, K. C., Griest, D. L., & Forehand, R. (1980). The use of a self-control package to enhance temporal generality of a parent training program. *Behaviour Research and Therapy, 18*, 347–358.

Williams, C. D. (1959). The elimination of tantrum behaviors by extinction procedures. *Journal of Abnormal and Social Psychology, 59*, 269–270.

Wiltz, N. A., & Patterson, G. R. (1974). An evaluation of parent training procedures designed to alter inappropriate aggressive behavior of boys. *Behavior Therapy, 5*, 215–221.

Zucker, R. A., & Fitzgerald, H. E. (1992). *The Antisocial Behavior Checklist.* Michigan State University Family Study, Department of Psychology, E. Lansing, MI 48824-1117.

10

Behavior Analysis

ALAN HUDSON

THEORETICAL OVERVIEW OF THE APPROACH

The behavior analysis approach to therapy with children and families has its roots in the various learning theories of psychology, particularly the work by Skinner (1938, 1953, 1957, 1969) on operant conditioning. It is important to note that while operant conditioning is seen as the foundation on which behavior analysis procedures are developed, not all behavior is seen as resulting from operant conditioning. A useful conceptualization of the causes of behavior is offered by Ross (1976). He argued that the determinants of a person's behavior are (1) long-term genetic/constitutional factors, (2) past learning history, (3) current physiological state, and (4) current environmental factors. As Ross has indicated, the first three of these are difficult to manipulate so as to alter behavior. However, the individual's current environment can be changed, and it is the manipulation of the environment in accordance with the principles of operant conditioning that is the basis of the behavior analysis approach to therapy.

Within the framework of operant conditioning, behavior is viewed as occurring between two sets of events, those that precede the behavior and those that follow it. The first are referred to as antecedents (or antecedent stimuli), and the second as consequences (or consequent stimuli).

Consequences that follow a behavior are important because they affect the likelihood of the future occurrence of the behavior. The use of a consequence that increases the probability that a behavior will occur again is called reinforcement, whereas the use of a consequence that reduces the probability of a behavior occurring again is called punishment.

Reinforcement can occur in two quite different ways. First, if the consequence of a behavior is that the individual experiences the presentation of a pleasant

ALAN HUDSON • Department of Psychology and Intellectual Disability Studies, Royal Melbourne Institute of Technology, Bundoora 3083, Australia.

Handbook of Psychotherapies with Children and Families, edited by Russ and Ollendick. Kluwer Academic/Plenum Publishers, New York, 1999.

event or stimulus, the process is called positive reinforcement, and the pleasant stimulus a positive reinforcer. However, if the consequence involves the individual experiencing the removal of an unpleasant stimulus, the process is called negative reinforcement, and the unpleasant stimulus a negative reinforcer. A child being given an ice cream as a consequence of behaving well is an example of positive reinforcement, and a child being exempted from household chores as a result of behaving well is an example of negative reinforcement.

Similarly, punishment can occur in two ways. The first involves the presentation of an unpleasant stimulus (a negative reinforcer) as a consequence of a behavior, and the second involves the removal of a pleasant stimulus (a positive reinforcer) as a consequence of a behavior. These two processes could be called *positive* and *negative punishment,* but more often are referred to as *type 1* and *type 2 punishment.* A child being scolded as a consequence of bad behavior is an example of type 1 punishment, and a child having toys removed because of bad behavior is an example of type 2 punishment.

It is important to note that both reinforcers and punishers are defined purely in terms of the effects that they have when they are delivered as a consequence of behavior. If a consequence does not lead to an increase in the probability of the behavior occurring again, it is not a reinforcer. If a consequence does not lead to a decrease in the probability of the behavior occurring again, it is not a punisher. The behavior analysis meaning of the term *punishment* is very different from that in common usage, which involves elements of retribution, and may not necessarily reduce the behavior it has followed.

Another way that the probability of occurrence of a behavior can be changed is by removing all consequences of the behavior. This will have the effect of reducing the rate of the behavior, and the process is called extinction.

In summary, then, the frequency of occurrence of a behavior can be increased by manipulation of the consequences of that behavior. Behavior that is followed by reinforcement (either positive or negative) will increase in frequency, whereas behavior that is followed by punishment or extinction will decrease in frequency.

One facet of reinforcement that has attracted substantial research is the effect of what is called the schedule of reinforcement. A behavior that is reinforced every time it occurs (called a continuous reinforcement schedule) may occur at a different rate if reinforced only after it occurs a number of times (called an intermittent schedule). Intermittent schedules can be of many types. They might involve reinforcement after an exact number of responses (a fixed ratio schedule), or after an average of that number of responses (a variable ratio schedule). Alternatively, they might involve the delivery of reinforcement for the first response after an exact period of time has elapsed (a fixed interval schedule), or for the first response after periods of time that vary (a variable interval schedule).

The antecedents of behavior are also important in behavior analysis theory. They can act as a signal that indicates that a particular behavior will be reinforced if it occurs. For example, a young child knows that asking his mother for some candy will not be reinforced, but when his grandmother is minding him, the same request results in a more favorable outcome. Here the presence of the grandmother is a discriminative stimulus for reinforcement. Sometimes it is important that a behavior is only emitted under particular circumstances. Whereas it may be safe for a young child to pat the friendly dog next door, it could be very dangerous for him to pat any dog in the street. Here the child needs discrimination training so the behavior of patting the dog will occur under some stimulus conditions, but not under others.

Knowledge of the ways in which antecedents and consequences affect behaviors is fundamental to behavior analysis theory. In recent years there has been an interest in studying not only relevant antecedents and consequences that occur immediately before or after a behavior (referred to as proximal), but also those that occur a considerable time before or considerable time after the behavior (referred to as distal).

An important point in relation to the antecedent–behavior–consequence sequence is that a single behavior may be associated with more than one antecedent and/or more than one consequence. Take the child who throws an object in class. The antecedents to this could be the teacher turning his back on the class and the child across the room making a face at the offending child. The consequences could be that the second child throws the object back, a third child complains to the teacher, and other children laugh. A knowledge of the potential multiplicity of antecedents and consequences is important to practitioners developing interventions based on the theory of behavior analysis.

Another important theoretical concept underpinning the theory of behavior analysis is what is called rule-governed behavior. This is not behavior that has been developed by directly reinforcing it. Instead, a person engages in rule-governed behavior because someone has told him that a particular behavior will be reinforced if it occurs. Take, for example, the case of visitors to a new city who are told that if they go to the top of a nearby hill, they will be rewarded with a great view. The visitors climb the hill and enjoy the view. Here the behavior of climbing the hill has never occurred before and could not have been developed by reinforcement. The behavior has been controlled by following an "If you do X, then you will receive Y" type of rule. For rule-governed behavior to work, the people involved must possess the required language skills, and also must have learned from their past history that the following of this general class of rule (i.e., taking advice when traveling) will be helpful to them.

The example given above is what is called an advice rule. It is called this because the person making the statement "If you do X, you will get Y" does not really control the "Y." When the visitors climbed the hill, it might have been foggy and the usual view obscured. Another type of rule is a command rule. This is where the person making the statement does control the "Y." Take the example of a mother saying to her child "I will give you some ice cream if you eat your vegetables." Here the mother is in control of whether the ice cream is given to the child.

HISTORY OF THE APPROACH

Behavior analysis as an approach to therapy is part of the more general set of learning theory-based approaches that developed as a result of dissatisfaction with the psychodynamic approaches that dominated in the early part of this century. Proponents of the learning theory approaches argued that there was a lack of empirical support for the psychodynamic therapies. It was considered that these therapies erred in studying proposed intrapsychic phenomena that could not be reliably measured, and that the direct observation of behavior was more productive. An emphasis on clear specification of behavior and precise measurement has been a hallmark of the behavioral approaches.

As indicated earlier, the behavior analysis approach to therapy has been built primarily on the principles of operant conditioning. The principles of classical conditioning (Hull, 1943; Pavlov, 1927) were also influential in the development of learning theory approaches to therapy. Scholars such as Eysenck (1959) and Wolpe (1958) were eminent in this regard, and contributed significantly to the treatment of anxiety disorders in particular. An important difference between their approach to therapy and the traditional behavior analysis approach is the emphasis on what are termed private events. These are a person's thoughts and feelings, things that cannot be observed by someone else, but rely on self-report for measurement. Although Skinner recognized the existence of private events, he preferred to focus on overt behavior, rather than covert behavior, because it could be measured more reliably.

In recent decades, there have been significant efforts to apply the basic principles of behavior analysis to covert behavior. Theoreticians such as Bandura (1969, 1977), Ellis (1979), Mahoney (1974), and Meichenbaum (1977) developed models of behavior in which cognitive events played a major role. This development is generally referred to as cognitive behavior therapy (CBT). In CBT, cognitions are considered to be affected by antecedents and consequences in the same manner as overt behaviors. Further, cognitions can themselves be the antecedents and consequences that affect other behaviors, both overt and covert. It is beyond the scope of this chapter to describe CBT in detail (see Chapter 7), but many practitioners incorporate cognitive procedures into the basic behavior analysis approach. The rest of this chapter will focus on the applications of behavior analysis to solve problems of overt behaviors (usually referred to as applied behavior analysis [ABA]), but these can be generalized easily to incorporate contemporary CBT.

ASSESSMENT AND CASE FORMULATION

Interested readers can find a very detailed description of behavior analysis procedures in texts such as Cooper, Heron, and Heward (1987), Grant and Evans (1994), Martin and Pear (1996), and Sulzer-Azaroff and Mayer (1991). This chapter will summarize the procedures that are more fully covered in these texts.

There are three steps involved in assessment and case formulation using ABA. These are specification of the behavior, measurement of the behavior, and assessment of the function of the behavior.

Specification of Behavior

The first step in the assessment of any behavior is the specification of that behavior. This involves describing it in very precise terms. General descriptions of behavior are problematic because they can be interpreted in a variety of ways. What does it mean to say "John is aggressive"? Does it mean he yells at other people? Does he hit them? If so, where and how hard? If John's behavior is to be reliably measured, it would need to be specified in precise terms such as "John forcibly hits others in the head with a closed fist."

Measurement of Behavior

Once we have a precise specification of the behavior of interest, we can select a method of measuring it. Exact measurement of behavior is necessary as part of a behavior analysis assessment for two reasons. First, there is a need to determine if any intervention is required at all. Take the case of a teacher who is concerned that one of his students seems excessively shy and does not interact with other children very much. After careful observation it might be found that the child's interaction with other children is within the normal range, and hence no intervention is warranted. The second reason for precise measurement of behavior is that, if intervention is warranted, the initial measurement becomes a baseline against which the success of intervention can be assessed. This means, of course, that measurement of the behavior must be continued once intervention has started.

The most common methods used are frequency counts, duration measures, and permanent product measures. Taking a frequency count simply involves counting the number of times the behavior of interest occurs. This method is most useful for behaviors that occur quickly and often, and for these a frequency count will give a "good picture" of the extent of the behavior. Sometimes the behavior of interest can take a long time to occur, and a frequency count might not give a good picture of its extent. Take the case of a parent who is concerned about the amount of time his son spends watching television. The child arrives home from school, sits down in front of the TV, and stays there until forced by the parent some time later to come to dinner. The frequency of this behavior would be one. He sat down and got up once. A better picture would be given here by measuring the amount of time he spends watching television. Such duration measures can be in minutes or even hours. The final common method of behavioral measurement involves counting the relatively permanent products of the behavior. If a parent wants to assess the amount of his child's mathematics homework, he might count the number of problems completed. Most behavior analysis interventions involve one of these three types of measurement. As mentioned earlier, the one used is selected on the basis that it gives the best picture of the extent of occurrence of the behavior of interest.

Once a behavior has been specified and measured, the decision about whether intervention is warranted has to be made. This is done by considering if it is occurring too much, in which case it is called a behavioral excess, or too little, hence a behavioral deficit. This decision needs to be well considered and take into account matters such as what is usual for a child of that age and culture. Once the need for intervention has been established, the task becomes to strengthen (i.e., increase) the behavioral deficits, and to weaken (i.e., reduce) the behavioral excesses. The behavior that has been selected for strengthening or weakening is now referred to as the target behavior.

Assessment of the Function of Behavior

The third and final step in case formulation is the assessment of the function of the target behavior. This involves the identification of the antecedents and consequences that are functionally related to the target behavior. It is important to distinguish between antecedents and consequences that might happen to occur before and after the behavior (i.e., are temporally related), and those antecedents and consequences that actually have an effect on the target behavior (i.e., are functionally related). This is typically done by collecting information about the target behavior from as broad a range of sources as possible.

Interviews

In the behavior analysis approach to therapy, the gathering of information about target behaviors usually begins with an interview. When working with children, the initial interview is typically conducted with someone who knows the child well. Most often this will be a parent, but could be a teacher or a child care worker. This is a logical starting point as it is usually the adult, not the child, who makes the initial referral.

The purpose of the initial interview is to gather as much information as possible about the target behavior. This begins with a clear specification of the target behavior, or behaviors if there is more than one presenting problem. In addition there will be some estimates of the prevalence of the target behavior, and some speculation about the antecedents and consequences that are functionally related to the behavior. The therapist will also gather information about what is reinforcing for the child in question, as this will be necessary when developing an intervention program. Initial interviews rarely provide all of the information that is required, and the significant other is usually required to systematically collect some more information about the child and the target behaviors. Thus, the interview would include instruction in procedures for collecting baseline data.

The therapist may conduct interviews with other people who know the child, and probably also the child if he has the necessary communication skills. These interviews will cover much the same ground as the initial interview, and will possibly provide the therapist with a different perspective for developing an intervention.

Written Materials

To supplement the information gained in interviews, a range of what are described as written materials can be used. These might include checklists about the child's functioning, such as the Child Behavior Checklist (Achenbach & Edelbrock, 1983). Alternatively, they might be measures of family functioning or parental affective status. Although these written materials provide valuable information for case formulation, they can also be administered after intervention to provide a measure of success.

Direct Observation of the Behavior

An element of information collection that is germane to behavior analysis is the collection of data resulting from the direct observation of the target behavior. In therapy with young children, the direct observation is typically carried out on a daily basis by the significant other in the child's environment (usually a parent). For the purposes of case formulation, the direct observation will include not only the baseline measurement of the target behavior, but also close observation of the antecedents and consequences that appear to be functionally related to the behavior. To ensure that useful data are collected by the significant others, the therapist needs to develop structured sheets that are easy to fill in, and also to provide some practice recording for the observer.

Adolescents who present for therapy might also be involved in measuring their own behavior by direct observation procedures. This will be absolutely necessary for target behaviors that are covert, such as depressive thoughts.

A final source of direct observation data can be provided by an independent observer (such as the therapist). Although independence of the observer can be an advantage in terms of providing unbiased data, this can be offset by the fact that the introduction of a new person into the environment can affect the natural rate of occurrence of the target behavior.

Developing a Hypothesis Regarding the Function of the Behavior

The use of interviews, written materials, and direct observation procedures will provide extensive information about the target behavior. Although the therapist might have some hunches about the antecedents and consequences that are functionally related to the behavior, their precise identity will not be known. The therapist must therefore formulate some hypotheses regarding them, and then test the validity of these by manipulating the antecedents and consequences and observing the behavior. The hypotheses will only by confirmed by a resulting change in the behavior. If the behavior does not change in the desired direction, the therapist will need to reconsider and revise his original opinions. This hypothesis testing element of the behavior analysis approach to therapy is generally not well understood by many, but is essential to the successful use of the approach.

INTERVENTION PROCEDURES AND MECHANISMS OF CHANGE

The intervention developed to change the target behavior of any given individual will be unique for that individual. Not only does the intervention need to result from the identification of the antecedents and consequences that are functionally related to the behavior, it also needs to take into account characteristics of the individual such as skill level and preferred reinforcers. Despite this idiographic approach to the development of interventions, there are some general behavioral procedures that are used to strengthen or weaken behavior.

Procedures for Strengthening Behavior

The most commonly used procedures for strengthening behavior are the systematic use of reinforcement, prompting, shaping, chaining, and modeling.

Systematic Use of Reinforcement

The simplest procedure for strengthening a behavior is to wait until it occurs, and then to reinforce it. This is referred to as contingent reinforcement. Care must be taken to ensure that the consequence chosen is actually reinforcing for the individual concerned, and not just thought to be reinforcing.

There are many types of reinforcers, and theorists like to classify them. One typology breaks them up into social reinforcers (e.g., praise, attention), edible reinforcers (candy, ice cream), activity reinforcers (e.g., watching television, playing with a favorite toy), and token reinforcers (points to be exchanged for other reinforcers, money).

A second way of distinguishing between reinforcers is whether they are primary or secondary reinforcers. A primary reinforcer is one that does not depend on prior learning to develop its reinforcing properties, such as food and drinks. A secondary reinforcer is one that has become reinforcing because some learning has taken place. If a child finds reading books to be a reinforcing activity, he must have previously learned to read.

A final but very important distinction between reinforcers is whether they are naturally occurring or artificial. A naturally occurring reinforcer is one that is usually present in the child's environment and can be readily used to strengthen the target behavior. In most homes, attention from parents or access to television are naturally occurring. However, if expensive chocolate cookies are not usually in the home but are purchased specifically to be used as a reinforcer, they are an example of an artificial reinforcer. Therapists prefer to use naturally occurring reinforcers whenever possible, as the ongoing use of artificial reinforcers may be difficult. The family may not want to continue the purchase of the expensive cookies.

When using reinforcement to strengthen behavior, the basic principles of operant conditioning need to be adhered to. The learning will be quickest if the reinforcement is continuous to begin with. After the behavior has been established, the reinforcement schedule needs to be thinned by moving to an intermittent schedule. This makes the behavior more resistant to extinction.

Prompting

Whereas reinforcement will strengthen a behavior, it can only do so if the behavior has occurred in the first place. If the target behavior is not occurring, there is a need to make it do so by using a prompt. There are various types of prompts. A visual prompt is something that the child sees and this helps him with the response. A child learning colors and asked to pick up the green block may be prompted by the parent pointing to the block. A note on the fridge to remind the child to do something is also a visual prompt. A verbal prompt involves the use of words or sounds to assist with the behavior. If the child learning colors is asked to name the color of a red block, the parent might prompt by saying "It is rrrrrrr. . . . . ." A simple verbal instruction about how to complete a task can also be considered to be a verbal prompt. Finally, a physical prompt is one that involves the adult providing physical assistance to the child to perform the behavior. Parents typically employ physical prompts to help children with tasks such as using a spoon.

Although a prompt may be used to help get a behavior going in the first place, we would not want to have to use it forever. There has to be some systematic plan to fade the prompt as the behavior becomes established. Also, it is important to understand that the purpose of using a prompt is to get the behavior to occur so that it can be reinforced. Learning will occur far more efficiently if all prompted responses are reinforced.

Shaping

Prompting and reinforcing will be adequate procedures for strengthening most behaviors. However, some behaviors are quite complex in structure and the best prompting will not produce them in a complete form. Under these circumstances, the complex behavior is built by prompting and reinforcing successive approximations to it. This procedure is referred to as shaping the behavior.

Chaining

Behaviors can also be complex in that they consist of a number of smaller behaviors that are linked together in a behavioral chain. Chaining is a procedure for strengthening all of the components of the chain to produce the final behavior. Each part of the chain is separately prompted and reinforced as necessary. Forward chaining involves focusing on the first step in the chain, and when it is mastered, moving progressively through the other steps. Backward chaining begins with a focus on the last step first and working back to the first step. The choice of chaining procedure will depend on the nature of the behavior being developed. Total task chaining is used when the child has mastered most but not all of the steps, and only the weaker steps are focused on.

Modeling

Modeling is sometimes referred to as a type of visual prompting, but it is really more complex than that. Used properly, modeling involves demonstrating complex behaviors to the learner, having the learner practice the behavior, and then providing reinforcement and corrective feedback as necessary.

Procedures for Weakening Behavior

Although the term *reinforcement* is usually associated with the strengthening of behavior, the first three weakening procedures to be described also include the term *reinforcement* in their title. This is because they involve weakening the target behavior by strengthening one or more other behaviors. The other weakening procedures to be discussed will be extinction, time-out, overcorrection, and punishment.

Differential Reinforcement of Incompatible Behavior

Differential reinforcement of incompatible behavior (DRI) weakens the target behavior by strengthening a behavior that is topographically incompatible with it. For example, consider the child who incurs his parents' displeasure by writing on the walls of the family home. A DRI procedure for this would involve reinforcing him for writing in his coloring book, the rationale being that he cannot at the same time write in his book and write on the walls.

Differential Reinforcement of Alternative Behavior

Differential reinforcement of alternative behavior (DRA) also involves reinforcing the child for some behavior other than the target behavior. The difference here is that the other behavior is not incompatible with the target behavior. Take the child who annoys his parents by screaming when they are on the telephone. A DRA procedure used to reduce screaming might involve reinforcing him for playing with his train set. He could, of course, still scream while playing with the trains, but it is hoped that he would be so interested in them that he would not scream.

Differential Reinforcement of Other Behavior

Differential reinforcement of other behavior (DRO) also involves reinforcement, but it is conceptually different from DRI and DRA. For both of these, specific behaviors are identified and systematically reinforced. For DRO, however, there is no selection of specific behaviors, but rather any other behavior is reinforced. This is tantamount to reinforcing the absence of the target behavior. In fact, the child receives reinforcement after a set period of time if the target behavior did not occur during that period.

There are many procedural variations to the use of DRO, and interested readers are referred to Vollmer and Iwata (1992) for a discussion of these.

Extinction

The procedure of extinction is based on the basic principle of operant conditioning that a behavior that is never reinforced will be weakened and eventually disappear. This means that the therapist has to identify the reinforcement that is maintaining the target behavior, and make sure that it is stopped. In practice, this can be quite a difficult task for several reasons. First, the reinforcement that is maintaining the behavior may be intrinsic reinforcement and hence impossible to stop. Second, a given target behavior might have several sources of reinforcement and all have to be stopped. Third, it is important to completely stop the reinforcement. If reinforcement is allowed to occur occasionally, the target behavior will be on a thin schedule of reinforcement. This will not only maintain it, but make it very resistant to extinction when the reinforcement is stopped. Finally, it is well documented that immediately after the introduction of extinction there may be a temporary increase in the target behavior, and this extinction burst has to be able to be tolerated.

Time-Out

Time-out literally means time out from reinforcement. In practice, this means that whenever the target behavior occurs, the amount of reinforcement available in the child's environment is reduced for a predetermined short period of time, usually a few minutes. The most common way this is done is by removing the child and placing him alone in a relatively boring environment. This is referred to as exclusionary time-out. Time-out can also be applied without removing the child, and this is referred to as nonexclusionary time-out. An example of this would be leaving the child in the room, but making him sit on a chair in a boring corner of the room.

There are several important elements to the successful use of time-out. First, it is paramount that the time-out area be less reinforcing than the area in which the target behavior has occurred. Occasionally parents will send a child to his bedroom if he breaks a house rule. If the bedroom is full of toys, it might be more reinforcing than the area he has been removed from. Time-out will not work under these circumstances. A second important issue in relation to the use of time-out is the behavior of the child when the predetermined time is up. Let us take the child who is sent to time-out for 3 minutes, and screams and shouts for the entire 3 minutes. If he is let out while still having a tantrum, he may get the idea that the way to get out of time-out is to scream and shout. Under these circumstances, it is usual to require the child to sit quietly for a period of time before being allowed out. Of course this means that a child might be in time-out for a long time before meeting this requirement. In practice, this might happen on one or two occasions, but the child usually learns the rules and will settle quickly. It is important that this aspect of time-out be explained to the child before he is placed there.

Overcorrection

The procedure referred to as overcorrection has two elements, restitution and positive practice. Take the example of a child who enters the house after school and flings his bag across the room knocking over a table bearing a vase of flowers. The restitution component of overcorrection would require the child to replace the table and flowers, and clean up any other resulting mess. The positive practice component would require him to take his bag outside and reenter the room, carefully placing his bag wherever it is supposed to go. The positive practice component might be required to be completed on several occasions.

Punishment

Punishment as a behavior analysis procedure has two forms. The first involves the removal from the child of something that he finds to be reinforcing. A child who rides his bicycle on a forbidden road might be prohibited from riding his bicycle for a week. This is sometimes referred to as response cost.

The other form of punishment involves the delivery of an aversive consequence when the target behavior occurs. This typically would take the form of something such as extra household chores. For children who have exhibited very serious self injurious behavior, aversive consequences such as electric shock have been used. Not unexpectedly, this type of punishment is quite controversial.

Principle of the Least Restrictive Alternative

The procedures for weakening behavior described above have been placed in a particular order. The earlier procedures, the differential reinforcement procedures, achieve their desired effect of weakening the target behavior by strengthening desirable behaviors. The procedures that follow these, extinction through to punishment, increase progressively in what has been called their level of aversiveness. The particular procedure selected by a therapist will depend on many things, but one of these is what is called the principle of the least restrictive alternative (Turnbull, 1981). Put simply, this means that the therapist ought select the least aversive of the procedures that are available.

One issue that has received significant attention in recent years relates to whether it is ever really necessary to use aversive procedures such as punishment. One point of view is that therapists can successfully treat any excess target behavior by using positive means such as the differential reinforcement procedures. Others argue that some behaviors have proven to be resistant to these, and that therapists occasionally need recourse to aversive procedures. A good coverage of all of the issues relevant to this debate is given by Repp and Singh (1990).

Complex Procedures for Changing Behavior

To date, a range of relatively specific procedures for strengthening and weakening behavior have been discussed. The behavior analysis approach to therapy has developed some more complex procedures that are combinations of the more specific procedures. Examples of these are seen in the use of token economies, behavioral contracts, and problem-solving training.

Token Economies

A token economy is a specially constructed system in which tokens are given to reinforce desirable behaviors, or removed to punish undesirable behaviors. Tokens can be tangible objects such a plastic chips, or can be points that are tallied and recorded in places such as on a notice board, or in a notebook. The tokens can, at a later time, be exchanged for "backup" reinforcers. Teachers often use token systems in classrooms. Here tokens might be gained for work completion and exchanged for things such as extra time on classroom computers. Additionally, tokens would be lost for disruptive behavior. The use of money in developed countries is an example of a large-scale token economy.

Extensive planning must go into the development of a token economy. Steps must be taken to ensure that the tokens can only be gained through contingent reinforcement of appropriate behavior, and not be acquired through illicit means such as stealing. Care must be taken to ensure that the backup reinforcers are sufficiently powerful to motivate the children. Finally, the currency must be structured so that the most attractive backup reinforcers are expensive, but are still accessible.

Behavioral Contracts

A behavioral contract is essentially an agreement, usually written, that specifies desirable behavior and the reinforcement that will be delivered contingent on that behavior. The contract may also specify undesirable behavior and the punishment that is contingent on that behavior. Children who are behavior problems at school are often placed on behavioral contracts. The reinforcement for desirable behaviors such as prompt attendance at class and completion of work is specified, along with the punishment for behaviors such as hitting other children.

In establishing a behavioral contract, it is essential to be specific about the behaviors of interest. This is necessary to prevents disputes at a later time about whether or not a particular behavior has occurred. It is also important to ensure that the other party keeps to the contract and delivers the reinforcement (and punishment) as required.

Behavioral contracts can be seen as a means of developing rule governed behavior in children. The effective use of written contracts can lead to the child learning to comply to verbal instructions (a particular form of rule governed behavior) given by the other party to the contract.

Problem-Solving Training

The objective of problem-solving training is to teach a child a general procedure for solving a broad range of presenting problems. It begins with the selection of a particular problem, and then teaching the child to specify the problem precisely, to identify all of the behavioral options that are available, and to select and try out one of these options. After the first problem has been effectively dealt with, the child then tackles other problems, but with the help provided by the trainer being progressively faded out.

Like behavioral contracting, problem solving training is relevant to the development of rule-governed behavior in children, but there is a difference between them. In contracting, the other party is usually in control of the delivery of reinforcement, and hence the rules involved are command rules. In problem-solving training, however, the trainer is unlikely to be in control of the delivery of reinforcement, and hence the rules involved are advice rules.

RESEARCH SUPPORT

One of the defining characteristics of the behavior analysis approach to therapy is its heavy reliance on the direct measurement of behavior. Behavior is measured not only as part of the assessment process in case formulation, but also in intervention as part of the evaluation of treatment outcome.

So important has measurement been to behavior analysis that an evaluation methodology has emerged from it. A series of "$N=1$" or "within subject" research designs have been developed to examine the effects of behavioral interventions. These designs rely on repeated measurements of the target behavior during baseline and intervention phases. Changes in patterns of the data collected in this way are used to draw conclusions about the extent to which the treatment is producing behavior change. Inferences drawn from these changing patterns can be based on either visual analysis or statistical analysis of the data, although the relative emphasis that ought be placed on these types of analysis has been an issue of contention (Crosbie, 1993).

The most common types of $N=1$ designs that are reported in the scientific literature are the ABAB (or reversal) design and multiple-baseline designs (Hersen & Barlow, 1984; Kazdin, 1982). The ABAB design involves a baseline phase, followed by a treatment phase, then a return to baseline, and then another treatment phase. There are various types of multiple-baseline designs, and these are referred to as multiple baseline across behaviors, multiple baseline across subjects, or multiple baseline across settings. The multiple baseline across behaviors measures three target behaviors concurrently during baseline, and then introduces the treatment phase for each of them in a sequential fashion. The multiple baselines across subjects and settings follow similar structures.

Although it is beyond the scope of this chapter to discuss these designs in detail, it is important to note that they meet the usual standards of internal validity required for research designs (Campbell & Stanley, 1963). This means that if a change occurs in the target behavior, the design needs to be good enough for the therapist to have confidence that the change has resulted from the treatment.

Designs such as those described above or more complex derivatives of them have been used extensively to demonstrate that the behavior analysis approach can be used with a wide variety of presenting child problems. These include externalizing disorders such as conduct disorders (Kazdin, 1987) and attention deficit hyperactivity disorder (Barkley, 1990), and internalizing disorders such as anxiety disorders (Siegel & Ridley-Johnson, 1985) and depression (Kazdin, 1990).

Although the success of behavioral approaches has been noted for some time, there initially was concern about what is described as the generalization of the outcomes. If an aggressive child is successfully treated at home, does his behavior also improve at school? And if it does improve, how long does the improvement last? Generalization of outcome is quite a complex issue, and authors such as Drabman, Hammer, and Rosenbaum (1979) and Allen, Tarnowski, Simonian, Elliot, and Drabman (1991) have identified as many as 16 different types of generalization. The important point to make is that a behavioral intervention will not have a problem with generalization if procedures for promoting it are incorporated into the intervention (Stokes & Baer, 1977; Stokes & Osnes, 1989).

Another concept that has become important in the evaluation of behavioral approaches to therapy is what is described as the social validity of the intervention (Kazdin, 1977; Wolf, 1978). Social validity is considered to have three components. The first of these is the social significance of the goals of the intervention, that is, have the right behaviors been selected as targets of change? The second is the social appropriateness of the intervention strategies, that is, are they socially acceptable? The third is the social importance of the outcomes, that is, are the outcomes clinically significant?

UTILIZING THE APPROACH WITHIN A
MANAGED CARE FRAMEWORK

Managed care has caused some concern among many who deliver health services. The behavior analysis appoach to therapy with children should operate well within a managed care system. As has been mentioned earlier, evaluation of outcome is an integral part of behavioral intervention, and success has been demonstrated in the treatment of a wide range of presenting child problems. Indeed, behavioral approaches generally are performing well in contemporary searches to identify empirically validated treatments (American Psychological Association, 1993; Roth & Fonagy, 1996).

In addition to empirical validation, a second feature of behavioral approaches is that treatment is usually brief compared with that developed from other theoretical foundations. Indeed, the extended nature of psychodynamic treatment was one of the factors that provided the impetus for the initial development of behavioral approaches to therapy.

As pointed out by Masia, Anderson, McNeil, and Hawkins (1997), most behavioral therapists probably support some type of managed care system in that they believe in "accountabililty, in setting measurable goals, and in documenting progress."

SUGGESTIONS FOR FUTURE RESEARCH AND PRACTICE

As was indicated earlier, a substantial amount of research has been conducted to demonstrate that procedures derived from behavior analysis theory are successful in the treatment of internalizing and externalizing disorders of children. An interesting distinction between types of reseach into therapeutic outcomes has been made by Hoagwood, Hibbs, Brent, and Jensen (1995). A therapy is considered to have demonstrated efficacy if it has positive outcomes when evaluated using tightly controlled clinical trials. This type of outcome reseach is typically conducted in universities or university-linked hospitals. The question still remains about whether the therapy is successful when applied in more natural settings (e.g., local health clinics), and when administered by practitioners who have a heavy caseload and might not be as highly trained as the therapists in university settings. Hoagwood *et al.* (1995) describe positive outcomes of therapy in these conditions as demonstrations of the effectiveness of the therapy. It is probably not unreasonable to suggest that most of the successful research conducted to date on behavioral approaches to therapy has been efficacy research. Although this is an important first step in empirical validation of therapies, there is need for more research demonstrating the effectiveness of behavioral approaches.

Most of the reseach conducted on behavioral approaches has focused on the treatment of fully developed psychological problems. Caplan (1964) would describe this as tertiary prevention, rather than primary or secondary prevention of mental health problems. Primary prevention is absolute prevention as we know it, secondary prevention is early identification and treatment of problems before they fully develop. Given the success of behavioral approaches with fully developed problems, it would seem sensible to use behavioral principles to construct environments that promote healthy development. The challenge here is not so much in the technology of constructing an environment to systematically deliver reinforcement and punishment so as to foster sound development in children, but rather to convince society that this is a good thing to do. The theories of child development that are prevalent in families and schools typically eschew child-rearing practices that are consistent with the principles of applied behavior analysis.

SUMMARY

Behavior analysis as an approach to therapy has been developed from the principles of operant conditioning. Key facets of the approach are the direct measurement of the behavior of interest, the identification of the antecedents and consequences that are functionally related to that behavior, and the manipulation of those antecedents and consequences to produce behavior change. The empirical evaluation of intervention is also an essential component of the approach.

Behavior analysis has proven to be an effective therapy for a wide range of both internalizing and externalizing clinical problems of children. The challenge for behavior analysts in the future is to use the technology more for prevention of the mental health problems of children.

REFERENCES

Achenbach, T. M., & Edelbrock, C. S. (1983). *Manual for the Child Behavior Checklist and Revised Child Behavior Profile.* Burlington, CT: University Associates in Psychiatry.

Allen, J. S., Tarnowski, J. K., Simonian, S. J., Elliot, D., & Drabman, R. S. (1991). The generalization map revisited: Assessment of generalized treatment effects in child and adolescent behavior therapy. *Behavior Therapy, 22,* 393–405.

American Psychological Association. (1993). *Final report of the Task Force on Promotion and Dissemination of Psychological Procedures.* New York: American Psychological Association. Division of Clinical Psychologists (Division 12).

Bandura, A. (1969). *Principles of behavior modification.* New York: Holt, Rinehart & Winston.

Bandura, A. (1977). *Social learning theory.* Englewood Cliffs, NJ: Prentice–Hall.

Barkley, R. A. (1990). *Attention-deficit hyperactivity disorder: A handbook for diagnosis and treatment.* New York: Guilford Press.

Campbell, D. T., & Stanley, J. C. (1963). *Experimental and quasi-experimental designs for research.* New York. McGraw–Hill.

Caplan, G. (1964). *Principles of preventative psychiatry.* New York: Basic Books.

Cooper, J., Heron, T., & Heward, W. (1987). *Applied behavior analysis.* Columbus, OH: Merrill.

Crosbie, J. (1993). Interrupted time-series analysis with single-subject data. *Journal of Consulting and Clinical Psychology, 61,* 966–974.

Drabman, R. S., Hammer, D. A., & Rosenbaum, M. S. (1979). Assessing generalization in behavior modification with children: The generalization map. *Behavioral Assessment, 1,* 203–219.

Ellis, A. (1979). Rational-emotive therapy as a new theory of personality and therapy. In A. Ellis & J. M. Whitely (Eds.), *Theoretical and empirical foundations of rational-emotive therapy* (pp. 1–61). Monterey, CA: Brooks/Cole.

Eysenck, H. J. (1959). Learning theory and behavior therapy. *Journal of Mental Science, 195,* 61–75.

Grant, L., & Evans, A. (1994). *Principles of behavior analysis.* New York: Harper Collins.

Hersen, M., & Barlow, D. (1984). *Single case experimental designs :Strategies for studying behavior change* (2nd ed.). New York: Pergamon Press.

Hoagwood, K., Hibbs, E., Brent, D., & Jensen, P. (1995). Introduction to the special edition: Efficacy and effectiveness in studies of child and adolescent psychotherapy. *Journal of Consulting and Clinical Psychology, 63,* 683–687.

Hull, C. L. (1943). *Principles of behavior.* New York: Appleton–Century–Crofts.

Kazdin, A. E. (1977). Assessing the clinical or applied importance of behavior change through social validation. *Behavior Modification, 1,* 427–451.

Kazdin, A. E. (1982). *Single-case research designs: Methods for clinical and research settings.* New York: Oxford University Press.

Kazdin, A. E. (1987). *Conduct disorder in children and adolescents.* Newbury Park, CA: Sage.

Kazdin, A. E. (1990). Childhood depression. *Journal of Child Psychology and Psychiatry, 31,* 121–160.

Mahoney, M. J. (1974). *Cognition and behavior modification.* Cambridge, MA: Ballinger.

Martin, G., & Pear, J. (1996). *Behavior modification: What it is and how to do it* (5th ed.). Englewood Cliffs, NJ: Prentice–Hall.

Masia, C. L., Anderson, C. M., McNeil, D. W., & Hawkins, R. P. (1997). Managed care and graduate training: A call for action. *The Behavior Therapist, 20,* 145–148.

Meichenbaum, D. (1977). *Cognitive behavior modification: An integrative approach.* New York: Plenum Press.

Pavlov, I. P. (1927). *Conditioned reflexes.* New York: Oxford University Press.

Repp, A. C., & Singh, N. N. (Eds.) (1990). *Current perspectives on the use of nonaversive and aversive interventions for persons with developmental disabilities .* New York: Sycamore.

Ross, A. O. (1976). *Psychological disorders of children: A behavioral approach.* New York: McGraw–Hill.

Roth, A., & Fonagy, P. (1996). *What works for whom? A critical review of the psychotherapy research.* New York: Guilford Press.

Siegel, L. J., & Ridley-Johnson, R. (1985). Anxiety disorders of childhood and adolescence. In P. H. Bornstein & A. E. Kazdin (Eds.), *Handbook of clinical behavior therapy with children* (pp. 266–308). Homewood, IL: Dorsey Press.

Skinner, B. F. (1938). *The behavior of organisms.* New York: Appleton–Century–Crofts.

Skinner, B. F. (1953). *Science and human behavior.* New York: Macmillan.

Skinner, B. F. (1957). *Verbal behavior.* New York: Macmillan.

Skinner, B. F. (1969). *Contingencies of reinforcement: A theoretical analysis.* New York: Appleton–Century–Crofts.

Stokes, T. F., & Baer, D. M. (1977). An implicit technology of generalization. *Journal of Applied Behavior Analysis, 10,* 349–367.

Stokes, T. F., & Osnes, P. G. (1989). An operant pursuit of generalization. *Behavior Therapy, 20,* 337–355.

Sulzer-Azaroff, B., & Mayer, G. R. (1991). *Behavior analysis for lasting change.* New York: Holt, Rinehart & Winston.

Turnbull, H. R., III (Ed.) (1981). *The least restrictive alternative: Principles and practice.* Washington, DC: American Association on Mental Deficiency.

Vollmer, T. R. , & Iwata, B. A. (1992). Differential reinforcement as treatment for behavior disorders: Procedural and functional variations. *Research in Developmental Disabilities, 13,* 393–417.

Wolf, M. M. (1978). Social validity: The case for subjective measurement or how applied behavior analysis is finding its heart. *Journal of Applied Behavior Analysis, 11,* 203–214.

Wolpe, J. (1958). *Psychotherapy by reciprocal inhibition.* Stanford, CA: Stanford University Press.

11

Psychopharmacological Approaches

CYNTHIA R. ELLIS and NIRBHAY N. SINGH

INTRODUCTION

Although there is a paucity of empirically based studies on the use of psychotropic drugs in the treatment of childhood disorders, medication is often considered an integral part of a treatment plan for children with psychiatric and behavioral disorders (Olfson, Pincus, & Sabshin, 1994). However, it is important to remember that medication is typically used as only one component of a broad therapeutic approach to alleviate psychiatric symptoms in children. For psychiatric problems, such as anxiety or depression, medication provides symptomatic relief, allowing the child to function more fully at school and at home. In general, medication should be used to improve the child's general functioning and quality of life rather than strictly for reducing undesirable behaviors or symptoms (Singh, 1995). Further, although medication may relieve the child's symptoms of psychiatric illness, it does not remove vulnerability to its recurrence because the environmental and constitutional stressors that gave rise to the illness are not affected by the medication.

About 12 to 22% of U.S. children (i.e., up to 14 million children) have a diagnosable mental illness, and it is very likely that many of these children may benefit from medication treatment (Institute of Medicine, 1990). Given the large number of children who receive psychotropic medication, it is important for clinicians and therapists who work with this population to have a basic knowledge of psychopharmacology in order to monitor the child and provide feedback to the prescribing physician. Studies have shown that informed feedback greatly enhances treatment-related decisions (Sprague & Gadow, 1976). Indeed, recent models of the assessment, diagnosis, and treatment of behavioral and psychiatric

CYNTHIA R. ELLIS • Munroe-Meyer Institute for Genetics and Rehabilitation, University of Nebraska Medical Center, Omaha, Nebraska 68198. **NIRBHAY N. SINGH** • Medical College of Virginia of Virginia Commonwealth University, Richmond, Virginia 23298.

Handbook of Psychotherapies with Children and Families, edited by Russ and Ollendick. Kluwer Academic/Plenum Publishers, New York, 1999.

disorders rely heavily on informed feedback from parents, clinicians, teachers, and therapists to enhance clinical decision making in multidisciplinary teams (Singh, Parmelee, Sood, & Katz, 1993). Having a good knowledge of psychopharmacology enables all members of the treatment team to take an active collaborative role in recommending medication and dosing changes to the child's physician.

HISTORY OF PEDIATRIC PSYCHOPHARMACOLOGY

The biological revolution in adult psychiatry in the early 1950s and the explosive growth of psychotherapeutic drugs in that decade changed the nature of U.S. psychiatry. Psychopharmacology became a mainstay of adult psychiatric treatment, especially for individuals with severe mental illness. However, the findings in adult psychopharmacology were merely extrapolated for use in child and adolescent psychiatry, and it was not until the late 1950s and the 1960s that case reports and experimental studies began to appear that reported the effects of medications for the treatment of psychiatric disorders in children and adolescents. Although most of these case reports and studies had serious methodological flaws, they did provide preliminary data on the effects of certain drugs for specific disorders.

The 1970s saw an increase in the scientific evaluation of psychopharmacotherapy for childhood disorders. Several advances were made in this period, including (1) the development of diagnostic criteria for psychiatric disorders (e.g., Research Diagnostic Criteria, DSM) so that the same disorders could be targeted across drug studies; (2) increasingly sophisticated methodologies for drug evaluation studies; (3) development of reliable and valid instruments sensitive to drug effects; (4) increasing knowledge of pharmacokinetics of psychiatric drugs used with both children and adults; and (5) increasing monitoring of intended and adverse effects of drugs, in both the short and long term. Further, children were found to be drug responsive to a number of conditions that had previously not been the focus of pharmacotherapy, including eating disorders, aggressive conduct disorders, separation anxiety disorders (school phobia), bipolar disorders, depressive disorders, and Tourette's syndrome. However, even as late as in the 1970s, few child and adolescent psychiatrists prescribed medication for childhood disorders (Towbin, 1995).

Since the 1980s, there has been an exponential growth in the number of studies published on the effects of medication in childhood disorders reflecting a period of explosive growth in the use of pharmacotherapy. For example, anticonvulsant medications (e.g., carbamazepine, valproate) were found to be effective not only for seizure disorders but also for treating some children with bipolar disorder. The selective serotonin reuptake inhibitors (e.g., fluoxetine, sertraline, paroxetine) and the serotonergic-specific tricyclic drug, clomipramine, were found to be useful for a number of conditions, particularly depression and anxiety disorders, including obsessive-compulsive disorder. Further, dopamine receptor antagonists (e.g., clozapine, risperidone, olanzapine) that have far fewer neurological adverse effects than the traditional neuroleptics (e.g., chlorpromazine, thioridazine), and two new antidepressants (i.e., venlafaxine, nefazodone) were added to our pharmacotherapeutic armamentarium. Indeed, the search for new drugs that are more effective and have a better adverse effects profile than those currently available is now one of the most vigorous and exciting areas of research in child and adolescent psychiatry.

ASSESSMENT AND CLINICAL FORMULATION

Comprehensive Assessment

A comprehensive psychiatric assessment and diagnosis is essential before a child is prescribed medication for a psychiatric or behavioral disorder. An understanding of the child's presenting problems or symptoms within the context of the highest level of diagnostic sophistication can best be reached on the basis of a multidisciplinary assessment, integrating the skills and knowledge of a number of disciplines (e.g., psychiatry, psychology, behavioral pediatrics, social work, education, nursing). There are four levels of diagnostic sophistication: (1) *symptomatic,* which includes isolated symptoms (e.g., auditory hallucinations) that provide an indication of a possible diagnosis (e.g., psychosis, not otherwise specified); (2) *syndromic,* which includes a constellation of signs and symptoms that have been present for a given time, and standardized inclusionary and exclusionary criteria can be used to derive a diagnosis (e.g., depression); (3) *pathophysiologic,* which includes structural or biochemical changes (e.g., elevated thyroid function tests; lowered thyroid-stimulating hormone) that indicate the diagnosis (e.g., hyperthyroidism); and (4) *etiologic,* in which the diagnosis is based on known causative factors (Janicak, Davis, Preskorn, & Ayd, 1993). As we do not currently have a good understanding of the underlying etiologies of many psychiatric disorders in childhood, most of the diagnoses are at the syndromic level of sophistication. Thus, children may be diagnosed with the same syndrome because they have similar presentations but with substantially different underlying mechanisms. This can lead to wide variability in treatment outcome.

Baseline Assessments

The baseline assessment provides the basis for determining the child's psychiatric diagnosis, establishing the specific indications for treatment, identifying the resources that are required for treatment and their availability, and the development of a comprehensive treatment plan. It is multidimensional and multidisciplinary, incorporating assessments of the child's symptoms and functioning across multiple domains, as well as an evaluation of his family history and his physical and cultural environment. The role of the child's family in the assessment process cannot be overstated. Parents know their child best and an understanding of the family's daily routine, their treatment goals, and their anticipated outcome is important when designing a comprehensive treatment plan. Typically, a baseline assessment includes (1) source and the reason for referral, including the target symptoms that may be the focus of treatmen, (2) history of the presenting symptoms, (3) psychiatric history and current mental status, (4) developmental and medical history, (5) physical examination and appropriate laboratory studies, (6) family and education/school history, and (7) cultural context of the family (e.g., determine if there are any specific religious or cultural beliefs of the family that may interact with the child's psychiatric treatment in general, and psychopharmacological treatment in particular). Different mental health professionals may take the lead role in obtaining the baseline assessment data through interviews, behavioral observations, and standardized rating scales. Typically, a working hypothesis regarding the child's diagnosis is developed during these initial assessments. An interdisciplinary treatment team uses these assessments to develop a comprehensive treatment plan, including medication treatments (Singh et al., 1993).

Baseline Assessments Specifically for Psychopharmacological Treatment

If a child is referred specifically for psychopharmacological treatment, medical and psychiatric assessments are administered prior to initiation of medication. The initial baseline assessments can be used to provide the psychiatric diagnosis of the child, the nature and specific components of a comprehensive treatment plan, as well as to aid in the identification of the target symptoms to be treated with pharmacotherapy (Sood & Singh, 1996). A premedication workup typically includes a treatment-focused psychiatric interview in addition to a complete medical history and physical and neurological examinations. Further, if data from initial baseline assessments are unavailable, other data may have to be gathered prior to formulating a medication treatment plan.

Psychiatric Interview

As an adjunct to the referral from the interdisciplinary treatment team, a psychiatric interview with the child, alone and together with his parents, is undertaken to confirm the psychiatric diagnosis or diagnoses for which medication may be indicated. Further, this assessment enables the clinician to more specifically identify the target symptoms for treatment. Although it is often thought that medication is prescribed for a target disorder, such as bipolar disorder, in reality this is not the case. The clinician targets specific symptoms that serve as markers for the underlying psychopathology and the changes in these symptoms over the course of treatment are used to evaluate the effects of medication. Multiple symptoms are used as markers because some may respond to medication before others. For example, a child with bipolar disorder may show improvements in his sleep and appetite disturbances earlier than his mood. Further, the clinician is careful to determine the phase of the child's illness (i.e., acute, relapse, recurrence) because of its importance in clinical decision making with regard to initial treatment as well as the need for, and duration of, maintenance and prophylactic therapy. Information on the temporal patterns of drug response and the phase of a child's illness is critical in the overall pharmacological management of the child (Janicak et al., 1993).

Medical Evaluation

Although typically included as a component of the initial baseline assessment, a comprehensive physical and neurological examination, including the child's temperature, pulse rate, respiratory rate, blood pressure, height, and weight, should be completed, if not previously done. Any laboratory tests and diagnostic procedures that were done during the baseline medical evaluation do not need to be repeated. According to Green (1995, p. 26), standard laboratory tests for a premedication workup may include the following: complete blood cell count, differential, and hematocrit; urinalysis; blood urea nitrogen level; serum electrolyte levels; liver function tests; and serum lead level determination in children under 7 years of age and in older children, when indicated. In addition, other laboratory tests may be indicated prior to using specific psychoactive medications. For example, thyroid function tests are recommended prior to using tricyclic antidepressants and lithium; kidney function tests prior to using lithium carbonate; baseline and periodic electrocardiogram for tricyclic antidepressants and lithium; an electroencephalogram for antipsychotics, tricyclic antidepressants, or lithium for those who "have a history of seizure disorder, who are on an antiepileptic drug for a seizure disorder, or who may be at risk for seizures" (Green, 1995, p. 27). Because drugs may have adverse effects on the developing fetus, girls of childbearing age should be given a pregnancy test.

Behavioral Observations and Rating Scales

Except in emergency situations (e.g., violent, explosive behavior), a child is observed for 7 to 10 days for patterns in her general behavior as well as the target symptoms before initiating pharmacotherapy. In addition to the psychiatrist, clinical psychologists are in the best position to provide valid and reliable observational data on the child's behavior from multiple settings. These observations are useful in determining the stability of the child's problems as well as the need for medication.

Behavioral observations are labor-intensive and often impractical in clinical practice. Fortunately, there are various rating scales that can be used to obtain reliable data on a child across multiple settings and by multiple raters (Sood & Singh, 1996). For example, the Child Behavior Checklist (Achenbach, 1991) is used widely for initial assessment of children and adolescents referred for psychiatric assessment, and the various Conners rating scales are used extensively with children with ADHD (Conners, 1990). Interested readers should consult Aman (1993) and Sood and Singh (1996) for reviews of an extensive array of rating scales that can be used for this purpose.

Periodic Reassessments Specific for Psychopharmacological Response

Once medication treatment is initiated, periodic evaluations of the drug response using repeated assessment measures, such as rating scales and behavioral observations, and monitoring of the side effects are necessary to determine the outcome of the treatment. Standard medication management includes dose titration at periodic intervals based on the data obtained by the monitoring process. In most cases, if a positive response to medication occurs, it will be evident within a dose range that is specific to each medication. Dosing is usually initiated with a low dose and is titrated to higher doses based on clinical effects and the emergence of side effects. A number of assessment instruments have been designed to record the effects of medication in general as well as instruments designed to record specific side effects of medications (Sood & Singh, 1996). A reassessment of the need for continued medication should be undertaken at least once every 30 to 90 days to prevent unnecessarily prolonged treatment. In the rare case where a child is on medication for more than a year, it is important that a drug holiday (i.e., a period of time off the medication) be instituted every year to determine the continued need for the medication.

Clinical Formulation

The diagnostic formulation follows the standard biopsychosocial model, which means that biological, psychological, and social factors are taken into account in developing a comprehensive framework for understanding the child's symptomatic presentation. Once the relevant data are gathered, the clinician synthesizes the information and reaches a working diagnosis. However, before a psychiatric diagnosis is reached, any general medical conditions that may account for the child's problems are ruled out. In addition, it is critical that deviation from the normal range of development is also considered. Further, a child may have symptoms of multiple conditions and all relevant diagnoses need to be considered (e.g., ADHD and learning disorders).

In the diagnostic formulation for psychopharmacological interventions, the clinician pays particular attention to signs and symptoms associated with psychiatric disorders that have a biological basis. These disorders have the potential for being responsive to psychoactive agents. Much of this information is obtained from the clinician's use of a descriptive, phenomenological assessment of the child's feelings, emotions, and behaviors because it provides important insights on the child's disorder(s). Information on the clinical course helps the clinician to place the disorder in a specific context because many pharmacologically responsive disorders have "characteristic beginnings, occur during particular stages of development, or are associated with particular sequelae" (Walkup, 1995, p. 26). For example, attention and concentration difficulties at age 5 or 6 may be related to ADHD, but at age 15 or 16 these symptoms are more likely to be associated with a mood disorder (Walkup, 1995). Detailed family history is also useful in diagnostic formulation for a number of reasons, such as providing additional support for the clinician's working hypothesis. The clinician uses all of this information to formulate a treatment plan that includes pharmacotherapy, as well as some type of educational and psychosocial intervention because pharmacotherapy alone is rarely sufficient for complete recovery.

GENERAL PRINCIPLES OF PHARMACOLOGY

Psychopharmacology is a rapidly evolving area in child and adolescent psychiatry, and it is important for clinicians working with children with psychiatric disorders to remain current with the research literature in this field. Although we do not think that it is critical for nonmedical clinicians to be experts in the pharmacology of psychiatric drugs, it may be helpful for them to have a working knowledge of basic concepts in the field so that their collaboration with physicians can be more meaningful. For example, it may help them to better understand the theoretical bases of the choices made by a psychiatrist in the selection of specific agents for treating single or multiple childhood disorders. We will briefly mention three areas that are important for clinical psychologists as well as other nonmedical clinicians to be familiar with. However, we emphasize that this is a very complex, technical, and specialized field that cannot be adequately covered here, and we suggest that interested readers begin with general overviews before delving deeper into the field (e.g., Clein & Riddle, 1995; Paxton & Dragunow, 1993).

Pharmacokinetics

Pharmacokinetics describes the time course and effects of drugs and their metabolites on the body. Thus, it describes what the body does to a drug. The most important pharmacokinetic factors that affect the time course and the effects of drugs on patients, include (1) *absorption*, which is the process that determines how a drug travels from the site of administration to the site of measurement (e.g., plasma, whole blood); (2) *first-pass effect*, which is the hepatic extraction of orally administered drugs before they reach the systemic circulation; (3) *distribution*, which indicates how much of a drug is distributed to the various organs or sites of action throughout the body; (4) *steady-state concentration*, which indicates the concentration of the drug when the amount administered is equal to the amount eliminated per unit time; (5) *half-life*, which is the time required for the concentration of the drug in plasma or whole blood to fall by one-half; (6) *elimination rate constant*, which is the proportion of the drug in the body that is eliminated per unit time; (7) *clearance*, which provides a measure of elimination of the drug from the body and is calculated by multiplying the amount of drug in the body by the elimination rate constant; (8) *first-order kinetics*, which occurs when the amount of the drug eliminated per unit time is directly proportional to its plasma concentration; and (9) *zero-order kinetics*, which occurs only when a fixed amount of the drug is eliminated per unit time regardless of plasma concentration. Data on these factors can be used to draw a unique kinetic profile of a given drug.

Together with pharmacodynamics, pharmacokinetics provides the bases for understanding the relationship of drug concentrations to clinical effects in children. Over the last four to five decades, pharmacologists have developed the theoretical pharmacokinetic bases for most types of dosage regimens and have identified the therapeutic plasma concentration ranges for a number of psychotropic drugs that are currently used to derive rational dosage regimens (Evans, Schentag, & Jusko, 1986). Indeed, child psychiatrists rely on pharmacokinetic principles to optimize the effects of pharmacotherapy in children (Clein & Riddle, 1995; Greenblatt & Shader, 1987).

Pharmacodynamics

Pharmacodynamics deals with the relationship between drug dosage or concentration in the body and the effects of the drug, both desirable and undesirable. Thus, it deals with the mechanism(s) of drug action and generally describes what a drug does to the body. The most important pharmacodynamic considerations include (1) *receptor mechanism*, which describes how the drug binds at the cellular level and initiates its pharmacodynamic effects; (2) *dose–response curve*, which plots the drug concentration against the effects of the drug and allows comparison of the efficacy and potency of drugs; (c) *therapeutic index*, which provides a relative measure of the toxicity and safety of a drug, and is calculated by dividing the median toxic dose by the median effective dose; (4) *lag time*, which is the time taken for the full therapeutic effects of a given drug to appear, and the reasons for a delay in effects may be pharmacokinetic, pharmacodynamic, or both; and (5) *tolerance*, which refers to the responsiveness of a child to a particular drug as it is administered over time.

Children differ widely in terms of the drug dose that produces a given effect. Thus, clinicians must have a good knowledge of current pharmacodynamic principles to understand a child's response to psychotropic drugs (Dingemanse, Danhof, & Breimer, 1988; Paxton & Dragunow, 1993).

Pharmacogenetics

Pharmacogenetics deals with idiosyncratic or unusual drug responses that have a hereditary basis (Kalow, 1990). Responses to psychotropic and other drugs in children are modulated by their genetic predisposition. This is because "genes encoding enzymes or proteins that play a role in the drug response differ in some respect from one individual to the next" (Nebert & Weber, 1990, p. 469). When all other variables are held constant, the individual's pharmacogenetic response reflects a genetic difference in the metabolic rate relative to that of a control subject. For example, Zhou, Koshakji, Silberstein, Wilkinson, and Wood (1989) compared the physiological effects and the pharmacological disposition of propranolol in a group of Caucasian Americans and a group of Chinese Orientals. They reported that the Chinese subjects were more responsive to the drug, displaying a larger reduction in heart rate and blood pressure, because they metabolized the drug more efficiently than the subjects in the Caucasian group. According to Nebert and Weber (1990, p. 473), idiosyncratic drug responses that may be caused by genetic variation in any of the subcellular steps involved in pharmacokinetics include the following mechanisms: (1) transport (absorption, plasma protein binding), (2) transducer mechanism (receptors, enzyme induction, or inhibition), (3) biotransformation, and (4) excretory mechanisms (renal and biliary transport). Typically, clinical observations, family or twin studies, protein polymorphisms, animal modeling, and DNA polymorphism characterizations are methods used to discover new atypical drug responses that may have a pharmacogenetic basis. The clinical import of pharmacogenetics is that clinicians should be aware of the possibility of differences in drug response and in dose requirements among children from various ethnic and racial groups.

Other Factors Affecting the Outcome of Pharmacotherapy

The effects of psychotropic drugs are seldom determined solely by their pharmacological properties, such as those discussed above. Indeed, psychotropic medication is prescribed and used within a transactional system between the child, his family, physician and other clinicians, as well as others (e.g., teachers, peers) who are significant in the life of the child (Moerman, 1979; Singh & Aman, 1990; Singh, Ellis, & Axtell, 1998). The child's views of the treatment process, the child–physician therapeutic alliance, and the child's attributions of the effects of medication are also important and may be responsible for at least some of the effects of pharmacotherapy (Towbin, 1995). Further, other factors (e.g., compliance, comorbidity, placebo effects, and sociocultural and ecobehavioral factors) are important in treatment outcome. However, the majority of studies in child psychopharmacology have focused on biological variables (e.g., pharmacokinetics, pharmacodynamics, and pharmacogenetics) to the exclusion of virtually all others.

PSYCHOTROPIC MEDICATION IN CHILDHOOD DISORDERS

Drugs can be classified according to their chemical structure, their mechanism of action, their behavioral effects, or their therapeutic usage. The most common classification system is by therapeutic usage, and the drugs that are prescribed for the treatment of a given clinical diagnosis are typically grouped together. However, some individual drugs or drug groups may be used for a number of different indications. For example, selected antiepileptics, such as carbamazepine (Tegretol), are sometimes used for their antiepileptic as well as for their psychotropic properties. The drug groups that are commonly used in children include antipsychotics, antidepressants, stimulants, anxiolytics, antimanics, and antiepileptics. Only general principles and procedures of psychopharmacological therapies will be covered here and readers are referred to in-depth references for further information (e.g., Singh & Ellis, 1998).

Antipsychotics

The antipsychotics have been called *major tranquilizers* because of an early observation that chlorpromazine, the prototypical drug in this class, produced somnolence and relaxation. Antipsychotics have also been called *neuroleptics* because they are noted for producing signs of neurological dysfunction, principally Parkinson's syndrome, and other extrapyramidal reactions. Although the term *neuroleptic* continues to be used interchangeably with *antipsychotic*, the discovery of clozapine, an antipsychotic that is not a neuroleptic, means that this practice may now be inappropriate.

The antipsychotics consist of a group of eight classes of drugs: phenothiazines (e.g., chlorpromazine [Thorazine], fluphenazine [Prolixin], thioridazine [Mellaril]), thioxanthenes (e.g., thiothixene [Navane]), dibenzoxazepines (e.g., loxapine [Loxitane]), dihydroindoles (e.g.,molindone [Moban]), butyrophenones (e.g., haloperidol [Haldol], droperidol [Inapsine]), diphenylbutylpiperidines (e.g., pimozide [Orap]), benzamides (e.g., sulpiride [Dogmatil]), and benzisoxazole (e.g., risperidone [Risperdal]). Pharmacologically, the major classes of antipsychotics are remarkably similar and, when given in equivalent doses, they produce comparable benefits and induce a similar range of adverse effects.

Mechanism of Action

The antipsychotics produce their therapeutic effects by blocking the D_2 subtype of dopamine receptors, although some of them may block the D_1 receptors as well. The blockade of the dopamine receptors is also responsible for most of the neurological and endocrinological adverse effects of antipsychotics. The difference in the adverse effects profiles of the antipsychotics is related to the fact that some of the antipsychotics also block noradrenergic, cholinergic, and histaminergic receptors. When compared with the low-potency antipsychotics (e.g., chlorpromazine, thioridazine), those with high potency (e.g., haloperidol, pimozide) are typically less sedating, produce less hypotension, and they generally have less effect on seizure threshold, fewer anticholinergic effects, less cardiovascular toxicity, less weight gain, and minimal effect on bone marrow and liver. Risperidone, a new antipsychotic medication, has D_2 as well as serotonergic (5-HT2) antagonist properties and lacks the acute extrapyramidal adverse effects of the traditional antipsychotics. Clozapine, an atypical antipsychotic, has weak D_2 antagonist properties but a high affinity for D_4 dopamine receptors, as well as a relatively strong antagonistic interaction with central α_1-adrenergic, cholinergic, histaminic (H1), and serotonergic (5-HT2) receptors (Baldessarini & Frankenburg, 1991; Lieberman, Kane, & Johns, 1989). Like risperidone, clozapine also lacks acute extrapyramidal adverse effects.

Indications

In children, the antipsychotics are used mainly in the treatment of psychotic disorders, typically the positive symptoms, as well as other behavioral symptoms, such as agitation, aggression, tics, and stereotypies (Green, 1995; Kutcher, 1997). The positive symptoms include hallucinations, delusions, thought disorder (i.e., incoherency), and catatonic symptoms (e.g., stupor, negativism, rigidity, excitement, and posturing) or bizarre affect. The negative symptoms, which include affective blunting, poverty of speech and thought, apathy, anhedonia, and poor social functioning, respond well to the atypical antipsychotics (e.g., clozapine, risperidone). Among the antipsychotics, haloperidol and pimozide are the drugs of choice for treating children with Tourette's disorder. The low-potency drugs (e.g., chlorpromazine, thioridazine) are used to treat mania and, as a last resort, to treat aggressive behavior and severe agitation in children. The high-potency drugs (e.g., fluphenazine, perphenazine) are used for severe insomnia and severe self-injury. Clozapine is useful in treating refractory psychosis in adolescence, and risperidone is useful in treating both positive and negative symptoms of psychosis, as well as some symptoms associated with pervasive developmental disorder. Until recently, antipsychotics have been used widely in the treatment of self-injury, aggression, and agitation in children with developmental disorders (Ellis, Singh, & Singh, 1997).

In terms of effects, there are little data to support the use of one antipsychotic drug over another because the action of these drugs is related to their structural similarities (Janicak et al., 1993). Thus, clinicians typically base their choice of one antipsychotic over another with regard to the adverse effects profile of the drugs. For example, because children should maintain a relatively high level of activity for their developmental and psychological well-being, the clinician may choose haloperidol (which has fewer sedative and cardiovascular effects) over chlorpromazine (which has fewer extrapyramidal complications). Further, clinical experience suggests that some children do respond to one antipsychotic but not to another. It may be that this is related to differences between the drugs in terms of absorption, distribution, accumulation at receptor sites, pharmacodynamic actions, metabolism of their derivatives, and adverse cognitive effects (e.g., as a result of sedation). In addition, the drugs may appear to act differentially if their effects are not compared at optimum dosages for the child.

Adverse Effects

The antipsychotics have well-known side effects that range from mild to severe, including drowsiness and sedation, hypotension, weight gain, and anticholinergic side effects (e.g., dry mouth, dry eyes, constipation, urinary retention, blurred vision, and tachycardia). Certain abnormal muscle and movement disorders have also resulted from antipsychotic usage, including acute dystonic reactions (muscle spasms, usually of the face and neck); tardive dyskinesia (involuntary movements of the face, mouth, tongue, trunk, or extremities); and parkinsonian symptoms (such as muscle rigidity, hand tremor, and a masklike facial appearance). It is important to monitor systematically for the possible emergence of tardive dyskinesia. When tardive dyskinesia is suspected, a referral to a neurologist is recommended.

Antidepressants

As the name implies, antidepressants are used to treat depression in children and adults. The serendipitous finding that iproniazid, a drug used to treat tuberculosis, had mood-elevating properties and inhibited the enzyme monoamine oxidase led to the development of a class of antidepressants, namely the monoamine oxidase inhibitors (MAOIs). Some years later, the drug imipramine (Tofranil) was developed, followed by a number of others with a similar structure—the tricyclic antidepressants. Recently, a new generation of antidepressants have become available, with some of them (e.g., fluoxetine) enjoying remarkable clinical success in the treatment of depression.

Mechanisms of Action

The different classes of antidepressants can be categorized according to their structure and/or presumed mechanism of action. For example, Janicak et al. (1993, p. 242) categorized them as follows:

1. Heterocyclics (e.g., imipramine [Tofranil]), which block the neuronal reuptake of norepinephrine and/or serotonin
2. Selective serotonin reuptake inhibitors (SSRIs, e.g., fluoxetine [Prozac]), which modify serotonin neurotransmission by inhibiting the reuptake carrier
3. Monoamine oxidase inhibitors (e.g., isocarboxazid [Marplan]), which increase the concentration of several biogenic amines
4. Aminoketones (e.g., bupropion [Wellbutrin]), whose most potent known effect is neuronal dopamine reuptake blockade, but whose mechanism of action is unknown
5. Triazolopyridines (e.g., trazodone [Desyrel]), which have mixed effects on the serotonin system, with the predominant effect being 5-HT2 receptor blockade
6. 5-HT1A receptor partial agonists (e.g., buspirone [BuSpar]), marketed as anxiolytics, but which also have proven antidepressant properties, especially at higher doses

Although the different classes of antidepressants have specific mechanisms of action, in general, the antidepressants block the reuptake of one or more catecholamines (i.e., norepinephrine, serotonin, and dopamine) thereby decreasing or downregulating the number of postsynaptic receptors. The MAOIs have a different mechanism of action; they increase the availability of catecholamines by blocking the enzyme monoamine oxidase.

Indications

In general, the antidepressants are used with children to treat depression, ADHD, obsessive-compulsive disorder (OCD), enuresis, anxiety, and tic disorders. The tricyclic antidepressants (e.g., imipramine, desipramine, nortriptyline) are used to treat major depressive disorders (MDD), enuresis, ADHD, tic disorders, and anxiety disorders. Clomipramine has been found to be effective with OCD. The SSRIs (e.g., fluoxetine, sertraline, paroxetine, fluvoxamine) are used to treat MDD, OCD, and anxiety disorders. Bupropion is used to treat ADHD and MDD; trazodone is used for MDD, aggression, and insomnia; and venlafaxine is used for MDD, OCD, and anxiety disorders. The MAOIs are now rarely used with children because of potential problems with medication compliance and adverse effects in this population (Viesselman, Yaylayan, Weller, & Weller, 1993).

Adverse Effects

The antidepressants have several side effects similar to those reported for the antipsychotics, including dry mouth, constipation, difficulty with urination, and blurred vision. Tricyclic antidepressants may also cause a decrease in blood pressure, a rapid heart rate, and, occasionally, more serious changes in heart function. Because of the serious nature of the potential changes in cardiac conduction associated with the use of certain tricyclic antidepressants (particularly desipramine in children), appropriate EKG monitoring is mandatory. Indeed, the potential cardiotoxic effects of the tricyclic antidepressants, and particularly the reports of sudden death associated with desipramine therapy (Riddle et al., 1991), have reduced the use of tricyclic antidepressants by some clinicians. The newer SSRIs have less adverse anticholinergic, sedative and cardiovascular effects than the tricyclic antidepressants.

Antimanics

Lithium carbonate is the main antimanic drug used to treat children who have bipolar disorder, with the anticonvulsants carbamazepine (Ballenger & Post, 1980) and valproic acid (McElroy, Keck, & Pope, 1987) being used as alternative antimanic agents.

Mechanism of Action

Little research has been done on the use of these antimanic agents with children, and their therapeutic mechanism(s) is virtually unknown. What we know is that they interact with various neurotransmitters, such as the catecholaminergic, indolaminergic, cholinergic, and γ-aminobutyric acid systems. It is likely that they affect both the pre- and postneuronal receptors as well as the postreceptor activity of these neurotransmitters.

Indications

Lithium is currently indicated for the treatment of bipolar disorder, aggression, impulsivity, and temper tantrums in children (Alessi, Naylor, Ghaziuddin, &

Zubieta, 1994). The drug works reasonably well in children with behavior problems characterized by impulsivity, aggressiveness, rage, or emotional lability (Popper, 1995). However, clinicians are cautioned that most of this understanding comes from clinical experience and not from double-blind, placebo-controlled studies. Carbamazepine and valproic acid are indicated for bipolar disorder and as an adjunct treatment in refractory MDD.

Adverse Effects

The most serious side effect of lithium carbonate is the potential for a CNS confusional state, including sluggishness, tremor, ataxia, coma, and seizures. Kidney abnormalities leading to increased urination and thirst, gastrointestinal distress, fine hand tremor, possible thyroid abnormalities, weight gain, and electrolyte imbalances may also occur.

Anxiolytics

The anxiolytics are used to treat pathological anxiety states. Two general classes of drugs, antidepressants (mainly the tricyclics and the MAOIs) and the antianxiety agents (most notably the benzodiazepines), are used to treat the various anxiety disorders seen in children (e.g., separation anxiety disorder, panic disorder, agoraphobia, school phobia, and generalized anxiety disorder). The benzodiazepines are also known as sedative-hypnotics because they act as hypnotics in high doses, as anxiolytics in moderate doses, and as sedatives in low doses. In general, the sedatives reduce daytime activity, temper excitement, and generally calm the child, and hypnotics produce drowsiness and facilitate the onset and maintenance of sleep. The following benzodiazepine drugs are currently labeled as antianxiety agents for use in the United States: chlordiazepoxide (Librium), clorazepate (Tranxene), diazepam (Valium), lorazepam (Ativan), oxazepam (Serax), prazepam (Centrax), halazepam (Paxipam), and alprazolam (Xanax). Flurazepam (Dalmane) and temazepam (Restoril) are two other benzodiazepine drugs but these are marketed for insomnia. Buspirone, a nonbenzodiazepine anxiolytic, is an azaspirodecanedione that lacks sedative, anticonvulsant, or muscle relaxant properties.

Mechanism of Action

The benzodiazepines are closely associated with γ-aminobutyric acid (GABA), the most prevalent inhibitory neurotransmitter system in the brain (Zorumski & Isenberg, 1991). The recognition sites for GABA are coupled to chloride ion channels, and when GABA binds to its receptors, these channels open, thereby increasing the flow of chloride ions into the neurons. There are two subtypes of CNS benzodiazepine receptors, BZ_1 and BZ_2. The BZ_1 receptors are involved in the mediation of sleep, and the BZ_2 receptors are involved in cognition, memory, and motor control. Theoretically, a benzodiazepine hypnotic can have more affinity for one or the other receptor, thereby producing differential response.

The mechanism of action of buspirone does not involve interaction with a benzodiazepine–GABA receptor. It interacts with presynaptic dopamine receptors and with postsynaptic 5-HT1A (serotonin) receptors, for which it is a partial agonist. However, despite its affinity to dopamine receptors, buspirone is not a neuroleptic and it does not have adverse effects or the risk profile of neuroleptics.

Indications

The high-potency benzodiazepines (e.g., clonazepam [Klonopin], alprazolam [Xanax], lorazepam [Ativan]) are used in the treatment of anxiety disorders, as an adjunct in the treatment of refractory psychosis and mania, severe agitation, Tourette's disorder, severe insomnia, and major depressive disorder with anxiety. The atypical anxiolytic buspirone (BuSpar) is also used for anxiety disorders and as an adjunct in the treatment of refractory OCD. It is also used for treating aggressive behaviors in children with mental retardation and autism.

Adverse Effects

Over the short term, the most frequent side effects involve the sedative actions of the drugs; other short-term effects include headaches, nausea, skin rashes, and impaired sexual performance. Even at low doses, the anxiolytics may induce aggressiveness and irritability. At higher doses, there may be an increase in activity, psychoticlike behavior, and suicidal actions. The long-term side effects include a continuation of some of the short-term effects, along with the potential for physical and psychological dependence with the benzodiazepines.

Stimulants

Stimulants are probably the most widely used psychotropic drugs with children. They are sympathomimetic drugs that are structurally similar to the endogenous catecholamines. The most commonly used stimulants include dextroamphetamine (Dexedrine), methylphenidate (Ritalin), magnesium pemoline (Cylert), and a mixed salts product consisting of dextroamphetamine sulfate, dextroamphetamine saccharate, amphetamine sulfate, and amphetamine aspartate (Adderall).

Mechanism of Action

The stimulants act in the central, as well as in the peripheral, nervous system by blocking the reuptake of catecholamines into the presynaptic nerve endings and by blocking the degradation of the nerve endings by the monoamine oxidase enzyme. It is likely that each of the stimulants has a distinct mode of action and therefore the group have differential clinical effects. Indeed, the precise mechanism of action of these compounds is still poorly understood. At therapeutic doses, the onset of action for these drugs is very rapid, producing a clinical response almost immediately.

Indications

The stimulants are indicated for ADHD, ADHD with comorbid disorders, ADHD in children with developmental disabilities, and as adjunctive therapy for refractory depression. Generally, stimulants are effective in controlling the symptoms of ADHD, especially hyperactivity, impulsivity, distractibility, and inattention (Barkley, DuPaul, & Costello, 1993). Further, they are effective in improving parent–child interactions, peer relationships, academic productivity, and classroom behavior (Barkley, 1990). However, academic achievement is minimally affected by the stimulants, but they do enhance performance on measures of vigilance, impulse control, fine motor coordination, and reaction time.

Adverse Effects

Insomnia, decreased appetite, weight loss, abdominal pain, and headaches are the most frequently reported side effects of the stimulant drugs. Less common side effects are drowsiness, sadness, increased talkativeness, and dizziness. Studies of children with developmental disabilities have shown that those with mental retardation have a higher rate of adverse effects (e.g., tics and social withdrawal) from stimulants than children in the general population (Handen, Feldman, Gosling, Breaux, & McAuliffe, 1991). Because of increased risk of liver toxicity with pemoline, it is generally not considered a first line stimulant medication.

Antiepileptics

There is increasing indication that carbamazepine, clonazepam, and valproic acid are being used alone and in combination with standard psychotropic medications to treat adults with various psychiatric disorders, such as mania, depression, treatment-resistant or atypical panic disorder, and bulimia, among others (Post, 1987). As discussed above, carbamazepine and valproic acid are used as alternative mood-stabilizing antimanic agents in children with bipolar disorders. Case reports and uncontrolled trials suggest that carbamazepine may be useful in treating ADHD, intermittent explosive disorder, aggressive disorders, conduct disorder, and some mood disorders in children (Carpenter & Vining, 1993). However, there are few well-controlled studies attesting to the efficacy of carbamazepine in childhood disorders (Evans, Clay, & Gualtieri, 1987; Remschmidt, 1976), and it has not been approved by the Food and Drug Administration for neuropsychiatric indications in children.

Antiepileptics have a history of use in the developmental disabilities, especially for controlling intractable behavior problems. The primary psychiatric use of antiepileptics in children with developmental disabilities is for affective disorders, such as mania, bipolar disorder, or schizoaffective disorder, particularly if these disturbances have been resistant to standard psychotropic medication. Carbamazepine, valproic acid, and, to a much lesser extent, clonazepam are currently being used for this purpose (Ellis et al., 1997). Much remains to be done with regard to establishing the efficacy of the antiepileptics in childhood psychiatric disorders, their mechanism(s) of action, dosage, and adverse effects.

FUTURE DIRECTIONS FOR RESEARCH AND PRACTICE

Psychopharmacology as a treatment modality for children and adolescents is a relatively young discipline that is based more on the collective experiences of clinicians than on empirical verification of the effects of various classes of psychoactive medications on childhood disorders. This is one of the reasons why, until recently, pharmacological therapy was seen as the treatment of last resort. During the last decade, however, child and adolescent psychopharmacology has achieved the status of a field worthy of scientific study in its own right. In general, nearly every area of psychopharmacology of childhood disorders needs further research. In support of this, the FDA now requires that all drugs intended for use in children be tested with children so that the indications for these drugs, as well as their effects and dosages can be appropriately determined.

In terms of specific areas of future research, there is little known about the pharmacokinetics and pharmacodynamics of most major psychoactive drugs as they pertain to children. Because developmental factors play such an important role in the outcome of pharmacotherapy, we need research that considers the interaction between the child's developmental level, environment, and different classes of drugs. Further, the high prevalence of comorbid psychiatric disorders in children necessitates further research on the use of combined psychotropic drugs for comorbid disorders. Finally, because psychopharmacological treatment is only one component of a comprehensive treatment plan, including psychosocial and educational interventions, more research is needed to assess the individual, combined, and interactive effects of these treatments.

REFERENCES

Achenbach, T. M. (1991). *Manual for the CBCL/4–18 and Profile.* Burlington: Department of Psychiatry, University of Vermont.

Alessi, N., Naylor, M. W., Ghaziuddin, M., & Zubieta, J. K. (1994). Update on lithium carbonate therapy in children and adolescents. *Journal of the American Academy of Child and Adolescent Psychiatry, 33,* 291–304.

Aman, M. G. (1993). Monitoring and measuring drug effects. II. Behavioral, emotional, and cognitive effects. In J. S. Werry & M. G. Aman (Eds.), *Practitioner's guide to psychoactive drugs for children and adolescents* (pp. 99–159). New York: Plenum Press.

Baldessarini, R., & Frankenburg, F. R. (1991). Clozapine: A novel antipsychotic agent. *New England Journal of Medicine, 324,* 746–754.

Ballenger, J. C., & Post, R. M. (1980). Carbamazepine in manic-depressive illness: A new treatment. *American Journal of Psychiatry, 137,* 782–790.

Barkley, R. A. (1990). *Attention deficit hyperactivity disorder: A handbook for diagnosis and treatment.* New York: Guilford Press.

Barkley, R. A., DuPaul, G. J., & Costello, A. (1993). Stimulants. In J. S. Werry & M. G. Aman (Eds.), *Practitioner's guide to psychoactive drugs for children and adolescents* (pp. 205–237). New York: Plenum Press.

Carpenter, R. O., & Vining, E. P. G. (1993). Antiepileptics (anticonvulsants). In J. S. Werry & M. G. Aman (Eds.), *Practitioner's guide to psychoactive drugs for children and adolescents* (pp. 321–346). New York: Plenum Press.

Clein, P. D., & Riddle, M. A. (1995). Pharmacokinetics in children and adolescents. *Child and Adolescent Psychiatric Clinics of North America, 4,* 59–75.

Conners, C. K. (1990). *Conners' Rating Scales Manual, Conners' Teacher Rating Scales, Conners' Parent Rating Scales. Instruments for use with children and adolescents.* North Tonawanda, NY: Multi-Health Systems.

Dingemanse, J., Danhof, M., & Breimer, D. D. (1988). Pharmacokinetic-pharmacodynamic modeling of CNS drug effects: An overview. *Pharmacology and Therapeutics, 38,* 1–52.

Ellis, C. R., Singh, Y. N., & Singh, N. N. (1997). Use of behavior-modifying drugs. In N. N. Singh (Ed.). *Prevention and treatment of severe behavior problems: Models and methods in developmental disabilities* (pp. 149–176). Monterey, CA: Brooks/Cole.

Evans, R. W., Clay, T. H., & Gualtieri, C. T. (1987). Carbamazepine in pediatric psychiatry. *Journal of the American Academy of Child and Adolescent Psychiatry, 26*, 2–8.

Evans, W. E., Schentag, J. J., & Jusko, W. J. (1986). *Applied pharmacokinetic principles of therapeutic drug monitoring* (2nd ed.)San Francisco: Applied Therapeutics.

Green, W. H. (1995). *Child and adolescent clinical psychopharmacology* (2nd ed.). Baltimore: Williams & Wilkins.

Greenblatt, D. J., & Shader, R. I. (1987). Introduction: Pharmacokinetics in clinical psychiatry and psychopharmacology. In H. Y. Meltzer (Ed.), *Psychopharmacology: The third generation of progress* (p. 1339). New York: Raven Press.

Handen, B. L., Feldman, H., Gosling, A., Breaux, A., & McAuliffe, S. (1991). Adverse side effects of Ritalin among mentally retarded children with ADHD. *Journal of the American Academy of Child and Adolescent Psychiatry, 30*, 241–245.

Institute of Medicine (1990). *Research on children and adolescents with mental, behavioral, and developmental disorders.* Bethesda: National Institute of Mental Health.

Janicak, P. G., Davis, J. M., Preskorn, S. H., & Ayd, F. J. (1993). *Principles and practice of psychopharmacology.* Baltimore: Williams & Wilkins.

Kalow, W. (1990). Pharmacogenetics: Past and future. *Life Sciences, 47*, 1385–1397.

Kutcher, S. P. (1997). *Child and adolescent psychopharmacology.* Philadelphia: Saunders.

Lieberman, J. A., Kane, J. M., & Johns, C. A. (1989). Clozapine: Guidelines for clinical management. *Journal of Clinical Psychiatry, 50*, 329–338.

McElroy, S. L., Keck, P., & Pope, H. G. (1987). Sodium valproate: Its use in primary psychiatric disorders. *Journal of Clinical Psychopharmacology, 7*, 16–24.

Moerman, D. E. (1979). Anthropology of symbolic healing. *Currents in Anthropology, 20*, 59–80.

Nebert, D. W., & Weber, W. W. (1990). Pharmacogenetics. In W. B. Pratt & P. Taylor (Eds.), *Principles of drug action* (pp. 469–531). New York: Churchill Livingstone.

Olfson, M., Pincus, H. A., & Sabshin, M. (1994). Pharmacotherapy in outpatient psychiatric practice. *American Journal of Psychiatry, 151*, 580–585.

Paxton, J. W., & Dragunow, M. (1993). Pharmacology. In J. S. Werry & M. G. Aman (Eds.), *Practitioner's guide to psychoactive drugs for children and adolescents* (pp. 23–55). New York: Plenum Press.

Popper, C. W. (1995). Balancing knowledge and judgement: A clinician looks at new developments in child and adolescent psychopharmacology. *Child and Adolescent Psychiatric Clinics of North America, 4*, 483–513.

Post, R. M. (1987). Mechanisms of action of carbamazepine and related anticonvulsants in affective illness. In H. Y. Meltzer (Ed.), *Psychopharmacology: The third generation of progress* (pp. 567–594). New York: Raven Press.

Remschmidt, H. (1976). The psychotropic effects of carbamazepine in non-epileptic patients, with particular reference to problems posed by clinical studies in children with behavioral disorders. In W. Birkmayer (Ed.), *Epileptic seizures, behavior, pain* (pp. 253–258). Bern: Huber.

Riddle, M. A., Nelson, J. C., Kleinman, C. S., Rasmusson., A., Leckman, J. F., King, R. A., & Cohen, D. J. (1991). Sudden death in children receiving Norpramin: A review of three reported cases and commentary. *Journal of the American Academy of Child and Adolescent Psychiatry, 30*, 104–108.

Singh, N. N. (1995). Moving beyond institutional care for individuals with developmental disabilities. *Journal of Child and Family Studies, 4*, 129–145.

Singh, N. N., & Aman, M. G. (1990). Ecobehavioral assessment of pharmacotherapy. In S. Schroeder (Ed.), *Ecobehavioral analysis in developmental disabilities* (pp. 182–200). Berlin: Springer-Verlag.

Singh, N. N., & Ellis, C. R. (1998). Pharmacological therapies. In A. S. Bellack & M. Hersen (Ser. Eds.), T. Ollendick (Vol. Ed.), *Comprehensive clinical psychology: Vol. 4. Children and adolescents: Clinical formulation and treatment* (pp. 267–293). New York: Elsevier Science.

Singh, N. N., Ellis, C. R., & Axtell, P. K. (1998). Psychopharmacology and steady-state behavior. In J. K. Luiselli & M. J. Cameron (Eds.), *Beyond consequences: Antecedent control approaches for the behavioral support of persons with developmental disabilities* (pp. 137–162).Baltimore: Paul H. Brookes.

Singh, N. N., Parmelee, D. X., Sood, A., & Katz, R. C. (1993). Collaboration of disciplines. In J. L. Matson (Ed.), *Handbook of hyperactivity in children* (pp. 305–322). Boston: Allyn & Bacon.

Sood, A., & Singh, N. N. (1996). Diagnostic instruments. In D. X. Parmelee (Ed.), *Child and adolescent psychiatry* (pp. 19–31). St. Louis: Mosby.

Sprague, R. L., & Gadow, K. D. (1976). The role of the teacher in drug treatment. *School Reviews, 85*, 109–140.

Towbin, K. E. (1995). Evaluation, establishing the treatment alliance, and informed consent. *Child and Adolescent Psychiatric Clinics of North America, 4*, 1–14.

Viesselman, J. O, Yaylayan, S., Weller, E. B., & Weller, R. A. (1993). Antidysthymic drugs (antidepressants and antimanics). In J. S. Werry & M. G. Aman (Eds.), *Practitioner's guide to psychoactive drugs for children and adolescents* (pp. 239–268). New York: Plenum Press.

Walkup, J. T. (1995). Clinical decision making in child and adolescent psychopharmacology. *Child and Adolescent Psychiatric Clinics of North America, 4*, 23–40.

Zhou, H. H., Koshakji, R. P., Silberstein, D. J., Wilkinson, G. P., & Wood, A. J. (1989). Racial differences in drug response: Altered sensitivity to and clearance of propranolol in men of Chinese descent as compared with American whites. *New England Journal of Medicine, 320*, 565–570.

Zorumski, C. F., & Isenberg, K. E. (1991). Insights into the structure and function of GABA-benzodiazepine receptors: Ion channels and psychiatry. *American Journal of Psychiatry, 148*, 162–163.

Part III

Empirically Validated Applications of Theoretical Approaches to Specific Problems and Populations

12

Brief Psychodynamic Therapy with Anxious Children

C. SETH WARREN and STANLEY B. MESSER

BASIC APPROACH UTILIZED

Introduction

A great deal of the psychotherapy conducted with children is of relatively brief duration. Children are often available only for brief therapy because of limited financial resources, level of family motivation, or institutional mandate. As early as the 1970s, Parad (1970–1971) noticed the apparent contradiction between the brevity of much child therapy and the simultaneous emphasis on the study of long-term treatment approaches. Numerous studies conducted since then have strongly supported the notion that the modal number of treatment sessions is rather small across a range of treatment settings, diagnoses, age, presenting complaints, and whether the treatment was planned as time-limited or unlimited (Dulcan & Piercy, 1985; Garfield, 1978; Koss, 1979; Langsley, 1975; Phillips, 1985).

It also appears to be the case that much of the psychotherapy conducted with children is either psychodynamic in orientation or substantially influenced by psychoanalytic ideas about psychopathology, development, play therapy, and the mechanisms of therapeutic change. The paucity of clinical research and systematic study of the brief psychodynamic treatment of children is therefore striking given the prevalence of both time limitations and psychodynamic methods in the treatment of children in private and clinic settings (Clark, 1993). One can only conclude that much psychodynamic child treatment is time-limited therapy by default rather than by preference or design.

C. SETH WARREN and STANELY B. MESSER • Graduate School of Applied and Professional Psychology, Rutgers University, Piscataway, New Jersey 08855-0819.

Handbook of Psychotherapies with Children and Families, edited by Russ and Ollendick. Kluwer Academic/Plenum Publishers, New York, 1999.

Brief psychotherapies based on psychoanalytic theory and technique have been influential for more than three decades, as Messer and Warren (1995) have documented in their review of the different models of brief psychodynamic therapy. These approaches have been applied for the most part to adult and older adolescent outpatients, although there has been at least some effort to tailor such techniques to the needs of children and younger adolescents. We will examine the latter approaches in the present chapter.

In addition to practical justifications for use of time-limited models, there are developmental factors supporting it as well. Children manifest greater plasticity than adults, and the important aspects of their character structure have not yet been settled. They are much more in the process of becoming who they will be than their adult counterparts. Thus, we have good reason to count on the force of the developmental process itself to be a potential ally of the treatment process. For many children, usually those with the least severe psychopathology, a brief intervention may suffice to remove an obstacle to development, permitting the resumption of the growth process. That is, an effective psychotherapeutic intervention at the right time may have a disproportionately large effect on the rapidly developing child. Given these reasons, as well as current economic realities regarding the limited availability of psychotherapy, there is a pressing need for the development and application of planned, time-limited psychotherapy, including those models derived from psychoanalytic developmental theory.

In this chapter we will draw on the work of a number of groups that have developed brief psychodynamic child therapy models or techniques. In addition, we believe it is necessary to extrapolate many of the theoretical principles and techniques of brief psychodynamic therapy with adults to clinical work with children.

The Roles of Developmental Theory, Crisis Intervention, and Psychodynamic Theories in Brief Psychodynamic Therapy

Developmental Theory

Psychoanalytic theory alone has not been sufficient to address important questions about child and human life-span development. Other influences have been necessary in the expansion of developmental models, which historically have had a close and fruitful relation to psychodynamic theory, including observation of infants and children in normal and clinical settings (Bowlby, 1969; Mahler, 1968; Spitz, 1945, 1946), child therapy (A. Freud, 1926; Klein, 1932), and experimental developmental research on human capacities and individual differences (see Beebe, 1994, for a review).

The concept of life-span development, with its emphasis on particular stage-specific issues and conflicts that occur during the various phases of life, has provided another way in which to understand human difficulties and their resolution. Most critically for the brief psychodynamic therapist, the developmental approach allows the therapist to understand and treat focal problems in their immediate, here-and-now context rather than requiring sustained exploration of early life, as is the case with more traditional, open-ended psychodynamic approaches.

Developmental concepts form a basis for understanding the predictable or expectable challenges, crises, or transitions an individual is likely to face at various stages of life. In this way the developmental context is a vital part of the clinical assessment process, with problems identified not only in terms of symptoms and longstanding personality structures, but also in terms of a failure to meet developmentally determined challenges. Such a perspective does not supplant psychodynamic theory, but rather adds another dimension to it, enriching the assessment process.

Crisis Intervention Theory

In a crisis intervention model, the patient's problem is defined in terms of an adaptive failure, usually in the face of new demands from the patient's total life situation. These demands may be accidental, such as illness or other losses, or they may result from the developmental process itself, such as beginning school. The natural correlate of a developmental framework is an emphasis on situational factors in psychopathology and emotional crisis, as well as the intrapsychic structure of personality. The latter, usually central to psychoanalytically oriented work, is understood more as a background variable in terms of the person's predispositions and previous efforts at adaptation. A crisis intervention model identifies the disparity between the patient's adaptive resources and the situational demands, with the change process primarily aimed at reducing or eliminating the gap. This may or may not require specific psychodynamic change; other interventions may suffice, such as modifying the environment or simply enabling the patient to better utilize existing psychological resources.

The goal of crisis intervention is to enable the child to attain new and stable adaptive structures, which ideally will result in an improved ability to manage life stresses. At a minimum, the goal is to foster a return to a level of functioning that existed prior to the crisis. Outcome is defined more in terms of the child's adaptive functioning than any particular psychodynamic achievement. Thus, the relevant approach is through developmental theory and a theory of change processes in systemic terms, rather than through a psychodynamic theory of personality per se. In fact, advocates of a crisis-intervention approach to treatment greatly deemphasize the importance of stable and enduring personality characteristics, and instead focus on the qualities of the situation and the interaction between patient and environment (Budman & Gurman, 1984).

Psychodynamic Theory

Time-limited psychodynamic treatment for children utilizes the basic principles of psychoanalytic diagnosis, play therapy, the concepts of transference and resistance, defense mechanisms, and psychoanalytic models of development including the notions of regression, fixation, and developmental breakdown. We emphasize the importance of a developmental perspective, and a practical, contextual approach, but view these as compatible with the theory and practice of psychodynamic psychotherapy. In fact, much of what we are describing as "developmental theory" in the context of this chapter is an outgrowth of psychoanalytic theory and observation. Furthermore, the techniques of psychodynamic psychotherapy are easily and naturally related to the goals and aims of crisis intervention (Bellak & Siegel, 1983; Bellak & Small, 1978).

DESCRIPTION OF THE PROBLEM OR DISORDER

Epidemiological studies suggest that diagnosable anxiety disorders are quite common among children, affecting perhaps 12% of the general population (Costello, 1989). Some studies suggest that the prevalence of these disorders is underestimated as children with emotional disorders may be less likely to be referred for treatment than children with behavioral disorders. (See Target & Fonagy, 1996, for a review of epidemiological studies.)

The category of anxiety disorders is actually quite heterogeneous, including simple childhood phobias, school avoidance, obsessive-compulsive disorders, separation anxiety of various degrees of intensity, overanxious disorders, and posttraumatic disorders. Thus, it appears fruitless to try to generalize about anxiety disorders in terms of natural history, need for treatment, and response to treatment. Nonetheless, research suggests that many of these disorders tend to be persistent over time, indicating a need for intervention (Target & Fonagy, 1996).

There is further evidence that children with anxiety disorders tend to show higher rates of other psychological diagnoses, as well as difficulties in their families, in school, and with peers (Kashani & Orvaschel, 1990), again pointing to the need for effective psychological treatments.

It should be mentioned that psychodynamic approaches tend to emphasize symptoms and character structures such as defense mechanisms and ego functions more than do the more medically inspired categories of the DSM-IV diagnostic system. Thus, while the clinical approach to any particular child will be highly individualized, psychodynamic methods in general do not pursue the specificity of other clinical approaches. Although in the present chapter we are discussing anxious children, much of what we have to say would apply equally well to children suffering from depression or conduct problems.

We would suggest further that children, particularly younger ones, often present with some mixture of emotional and behavioral problems. This is not surprising given that they rely so much more than adults on motor activity and bodily gestures to express feelings and modes of relating. Many anxious children appear to their parents, teachers, or other caretakers to be angry and acting out, depressed, hyperactive, or oppositional. Thus, our conclusion is that psychotherapy can be based on general principles of psychodynamic and developmental theories and the techniques of play therapy, applied with some necessary modifications to a wide range of childhood problems (see Kaduson, Cangelosi, & Schaefer, 1997, for an approach to the prescriptive application of play therapy techniques to specific clinical populations). An obvious difficulty with this view is that it directly contradicts the aims of specifying a relationship among diagnostic populations, treatment procedures, and outcome criteria, making psychodynamic treatment much more difficult to study using traditional empirical methods. Nonetheless, we do not believe such treatments should be discarded because they do not conform to a particular model of scientific progress, based as they are on other forms of validation which are more contextual and configurational, and relying more heavily on clinical experience with clients treated over time, as well as on systematic research.

GENERAL PRINCIPLES OF BRIEF PSYCHODYNAMIC PSYCHOTHERAPY

All brief psychodynamic psychotherapies share a number of organizing principles, which can be adapted to the treatment of children. These include patient selection for suitability of the treatment approach, the use of a time limit (whether made explicit or not), the development of a central focus of the treatment, and particular forms of therapeutic activity that would differentiate brief treatment from long-term approaches. In addition, there are a number of special considerations in the time-limited psychodynamic treatment of children, centering on developmental issues, technical problems, and the centrality of family involvement.

Patient Selection and Suitability

Selection of suitable candidates for time-limited psychotherapy is a well-established tradition in brief therapies for adults. Likewise, it is desirable to identify children who are likely to benefit from brief psychotherapy based on diagnosis or other clinical criteria. Selection criteria for existing models of time-limited psychodynamic child psychotherapy are congruent with the treatment models for adults. Lester (1968) notes that most important is the assessment of the child's movement through successive developmental phases without serious impass or breakdown. Thus, the types of difficulties she views as amenable to brief psychotherapy would be transient regressions, mild exaggerations of otherwise age-appropriate behaviors, acute phobias, and other more circumscribed problems. These are distinguished from difficulties unlikely to be successfully treated briefly, including more long-standing, chronic, characterological difficulties and ego weakness, which she views as the result of early defects in the development of object constancy.

Mackay (1967) similarly emphasizes the absence of chronic, characterological psychopathology as a selection criterion, noting that adaptive responses to crises are most likely to be successfully treated in brief therapy. He adds that flexibility and responsiveness to interpretation is a key indicator of suitability. Like other workers, Mackay highlights the importance of such parental attributes as motivation, flexibility, and the absence of pathogenic attitudes.

Proskauer (1969, 1971) presents a number of criteria for case selection, such as the child's ability to rapidly engage and develop a working relationship with the therapist, the presence of a focal dynamic issue that can be identified, flexible and adequate defenses, and the presence of sufficient basic trust. The qualities of the child's environment must be supportive enough so that treatment efforts will not be undermined. Like Mackay, Proskauer relies on the child's responsiveness to interpretations as an indicator of suitability. Similarly, Sloves and Peterlin (1994) emphasize ability to engage and form a positive relationship, as well as supportive qualities in the family, adding a child's capacity to understand the passage of time.

We offer the following synthesis of suitability criteria: Generally, it appears that children with less severe psychopathology are seen as more responsive to brief psychodynamic therapy than those with chronic, developmental difficulties. The developmental context is critical for this assessment. The more severe the history of object loss, parental deprivation, parental psychopathology, or history of traumatic abuse, the less optimistic one can be about the value of a brief psychotherapy. As with adults, the presence of psychotic symptoms that are not transient contraindicates brief treatment.

We wish to emphasize that identifying a child as being in a particular diagnostic category does not appear to be as helpful in the prediction of treatment process and outcome as the relative presence of the intrapsychic and object relational capacities required by the tasks of brief therapy. Qualities such as basic trust, ego defenses that are functioning adequately and flexibly, and a capacity to rapidly engage in, and then disengage from, a meaningful relationship—all essential ingredients in a useful brief treatment—are not necessarily correlated with diagnostic categories. Thus, just as with adult patients, the assessment is most usefully conducted from an interpersonal and psychodynamic point of view, with consideration of those characteristics that are most closely related to the psychotherapeutic process itself.

Finally, the assessment of a child for brief treatment must address the characteristics of the child's social and familial milieu to a greater extent than in the treatment of adults. Because the child remains powerfully within the force field of family and community, such influences have a disproportionate impact on the likelihood of treatment success. The effect of parents is not primarily as fully internalized objects as would be the case with an adult patient, but in the form of ongoing daily transactions and interactions that powerfully affect the child's functioning and ability to use psychotherapy. Family resources are all the more important as the maintenance of a therapeutic effect will depend to a great extent on the continuing influence of the family; potential therapeutic gains can be so easily undone by family psychopathology.

Use of the Time Limit

As with models of adult treatment, there is some difference of opinion as to the necessity of relying on an explicit time limit. Proskauer (1969), working in the same vein as James Mann (1973), advocates the use of a clear termination date to be set in the first treatment session, though the time limit does not seem quite so fixed as is the case with Mann's model. However, like Mann, Proskauer emphasizes *the impact and meaning* of the time limit. It is understood that termination issues are activated from the beginning of treatment with the statement of a termination date, and the child's ambivalent responses to the issue of loss and separation are utilized throughout the treatment but especially in the termination phase. The theoretical emphasis is on the use of the time limit to enable the child to address unresolved issues of loss, separation, and differentiation, much as is the case with Mann's 12-session approach.

In a similar vein, Turecki (1982) advocates the use of a fixed (and explicit) number of sessions so as to enable meaningful work around the issue of object loss. Like Mann, Turecki suggests that brief therapy "replicates in a condensed form, the evolution of an important object relationship followed by the harsh reality of object loss" (p. 482). Likewise, Peterlin and Sloves (1985) and Sloves and

Peterlin (1986, 1993) describe the use of explicit time limit, emphasizing the developmental issues of separation and loss that are activated by the time limit, sugggesting that "[o]ne way to understand the actual process of time-limited play therapy is to think of the entire treatment as a condensed, intensified rendition of the termination phase of long-term therapy, but without the negative transference" (Sloves & Peterlin, 1993, p. 303).

Others make use of an explicit time limit, but do not emphasize the theoretical centrality of the intertwining of the clinical focus and the time limit. Mackay (1967) suggests the use of an explicit contract for the duration of brief treatment in order to encourage a higher level of engagement and involvement with the therapist. Still others, such as Lester (1968), do not make use of an explicit time limit, but instead emphasize principles of affective engagement, focused work, and the provision of a corrective experience. Time is not made a central issue, but is utilized by the therapist to organize therapeutic activities and aims.

Many authors emphasize the importance of the child's sense of time, particularly those whose work follows Mann's model of time-limited therapy. These authors tend to stress the importance of termination, and the child's capacity to work with the time limit and to resolve the issue of loss of the therapy relationship. It may be that this emphasis is more the result of the adaptation of an adult model of treatment than an actual requirement of child psychotherapy, particularly with younger children. It is an open question as to whether very young children have a sufficiently developed sense of time to make therapeutic use of time limits or interpretations aimed at termination issues in brief treatments (Clark, 1993). Sloves and Peterlin (1993) attempt to bypass this problem by selecting cases on the basis of a child's capacity to understand the passage of time, but this would exclude most children under the age of about 6 to 8.

Contrary to the above, it may be possible to make use of the lack of a sense of time in childhood when exercising therapeutic leverage in a brief contact with a child. If the unconscious is "timeless" and children's functioning is marked by a fluid boundary between reality and fantasy, then perhaps a relationship that is actually limited in time can nevertheless have a lasting impact, as the therapist becomes quickly assimilated to the child's inner world of fantasy (see also Proskauer, 1969). That is, there can be a disproportionate effect of a relatively brief contact because children's fluid boundaries allow them to internalize a therapist rather readily.

Use of the Central Focus

As with adult models of brief psychodynamic treatment, all approaches to working with children articulate the need for an organizing clinical theme to be developed in the early sessions and to form a center of interpretive and therapeutic activity. Such a central theme or focus is a statement of the therapist's understanding of the child's presenting symptoms which are viewed as representing an underlying problem or dynamic conflict. It strives to incorporate as much of the current situation and relevant history as can be rapidly obtained. Some therapists verbalize the focus directly to the child in the form of a working contract and use it to increase the child's motivation and interest in the therapy process. Others do not state the central focus explicitly, but rather employ it as a heuristic device to organize the ongoing flow of clinical information and to guide their interventions.

Proskauer (1969) recommends the use of a mutually agreed-upon focus, whereas in most other approaches the central issue is selected by the therapist (Mackay, 1967; Peterlin & Sloves, 1985; Sloves & Peterlin, 1986; Turecki, 1982). In each case, the central issue is formulated on the basis of the child's presenting symptoms, the developmental history, and the current family situation. It is presented to the child clearly and directly (even in written form, in some cases) so that the child can understand it and can respond in an affective way. Further interventions are related to the central issue, thus providing structure and organization for the therapy.

Because the central issue is presented verbally, it is necessary that the child have sufficient capacity for the use of language. Proskauer (1969) notes that with younger children the focus need not be explicitly stated. Indeed, brief child therapists appear to struggle with a tension between the necessity to organize their therapeutic activities into a formal, verbally representable structure, while at the same time, for younger children at least, relying on the nonverbal treatment modality of play therapy. The challenge is to understand the child's communications in the modality of play, and to translate that understanding into a verbal form that is nonetheless meaningful to the child. We believe that while the use of a stated therapeutic focus may be of great value in the time-limited treatment of older children and young adolescents, younger children may simply not possess the cognitive or verbal skills to use a stated central issue. The use of a focus, however, need not be explicit; the therapist can still be guided by a central formulation of the child's dilemma and make interventions accordingly.

In work with children, the central focus must incorporate aspects of development, psychodynamics, environmental factors, and the immediate crisis that precipitated the need for treatment. Anxiety and other symptoms can be understood in terms of the child's unsuccessful efforts to cope with the experience of being overwhelmed by traumatic or chronic stressors. Psychodynamic concepts addressing personality structure, such as "ego strength," "reality testing," "tolerance for frustration," and so on, are considered in the context of the adequacy of external support. Character structure as an independent variable is deemphasized, while the adaptive fit of child and environment becomes the locus of attention.

Relative to longer-term models of treatment, there is greater clinical emphasis in brief psychodynamic child psychotherapy on familial and other social factors. Because of the brevity of therapeutic contact, there is less stress on restructuring the child's personality, with interventions aimed instead at modifying the existing balance of forces, both internal and external to the child. The formulation of the clinical focus will likely center on some observable, current stressor or life situation, with the hope of alleviating that obstruction, permitting the resumption of adaptive and integrative development in the child. (See Messer & Warren, 1995, for a full discussion of developmental and psychoanalytic aspects of the central focus in child treatment.)

Therapeutic Activity

Therapist activity is the last of the four defining features of brief psychodynamic psychotherapy. The concept of "active technique" (Ferenczi, 1921/1980) derives its meaning from a contrast with the traditionally lesser role of therapist activity in long-term psychoanalytic therapy. It refers to any of a variety of techniques aimed at accelerating the therapeutic process to make it possible to accomplish goals of psychodynamic importance in the more limited time frame of a brief therapy. Historically, psychoanalysts have been wary of intervening in ways that were thought to interfere with the development of the transference, either by offering direct suggestions, by disclosing personal information and feelings, or by directly gratifying transference wishes. On the other hand, brief therapists have long experimented with ways to modify the stance of analytic neutrality to increase therapeutic efficacy (Alexander & French, 1946; Ferenczi, 1921/1980; Rank, 1929/1978). These modifications have typically involved the use of time limits (Mann, 1973; Rank, 1929/1978), direct suggestions (Ferenczi, 1921/1980), the active confrontation and interpretation of defenses (Davanloo, 1980; Sifneos, 1972, 1979), and early and active interpretation of transference (Davanloo, 1980; Malan, 1976).

We have already discussed the issue of the use of time limits to increase motivation and to accelerate the therapeutic process. What other techniques of the brief psychodynamic therapies would be applicable to work with children? It would appear that some methods often used with adults are clearly inappropriate for child treatment, such as persistent confrontation of defenses, or active pursuit of strong affects such as anger, as children do not generally possess sufficient ego strength or affect tolerance to make therapeutic use of them.

Melanie Klein (1932) implemented the use of active and early interpretation of transference, a defining feature of Kleinian analysis, and she believed that this modification enabled access to deep levels of anxiety in child treatment. Her analytic play therapies were briefer in general than contemporary analyses, but could not be considered short-term treatment.

A more recent approach by Sloves and Peterlin (1993) makes use of "structured play," which involves the therapist actively choosing the play materials and structuring the play situation, offering play scenarios and direct participation. "The child is quite free to play out any resistances and any defenses, but the therapist channels the means of expression" (p. 305). Materials that promote regression, such as finger-painting or water play, are avoided. The authors present an extended case example illustrating their method, but a small fragment from an early session gives a flavor of the difference from more usual play therapy:

> [Therapist]: Let me tell you about this kid. He's a . . .
> [Patient]: A boy?
> [T]: Yes, a boy and he's, let's see, he could be how many years old?
> [P]: Eight?
> [T]: That's just about right. How did you know?
> [P]: Don't know, he just looks about eight.
> [T]: Let's see, where was I?
> [P]: [pointing to the play figures] He lives with them.
> [T]: He used to, a long time ago. When he was 2 and 3 and 4 years old they all lived together and it was great and wonderful and everything was wonderful and he was happy to have a whole complete family. You know, a mother and a father. But then one day, something horrible happened.
> [P]: This is a story?
> [T]: Sort of, but are you thinking what I'm thinking? Do you think this is a real story? (p. 314)

This fragment illustrates the use of highly active structuring, a kind of "leading the witness" that, when skillfully applied, results in a joint creation of meaning by patient and therapist. The work goes straight to the heart of the matter for this boy who lost his father, leaving little to slow and spontaneous evolution of the clinical material. The goal, similar to the work of Davanloo (1980), is to avoid regression and negative transference, working actively instead to facilitate a positive alliance and high motivation.

Work with Families and Parents

In addition to the above features, all models of brief dynamic child therapy give parents and family a central role in the treatment process. Not only is the family viewed as an important variable in both selection and outcome, but parents are actively engaged in either separate or conjoint therapy sessions. It is worth noting that there is an avoidance of "splitting the treatment" between a child therapist and a family therapist, relying instead on one therapist to work with both parents and child (Clark, 1993).

Parents are typically involved at the outset of treatment both for information gathering and in the development of a therapeutic contract (Lester, 1968; Mackay, 1967; Proskauer, 1969). Regular contact is suggested, most often without the child present (Mackay, 1967; Proskauer, 1969). Sloves and Peterlin (1993) report using a few family meetings, emphasizing to the child that they do not "lose" any sessions to such meetings, but that they are in addition to the set number of therapy sessions. Mackay notes the importance of helping parents recognize and resolve their own conflicts, taking a parent-educational approach. Turecki (1982) also emphasizes the use of educative interventions with parents, providing them with support, clarification, and direction.

To summarize, it would be ill-advised to conduct a time-limited treatment for a child that did not directly involve the family. As most child therapists, including those who conduct open-ended treatment, arrange contact with parents, this recommendation is not unusual. However, the active participation of parents would seem to be integral to brief treatment in a way not always advocated by psychodynamic clinicians. Because contact with the child is time-limited, the family must be counted on to support and maintain treatment goals and accomplishments, thus necessitating the recruitment of parents as allies in the therapeutic enterprise.

MAJOR MECHANISMS OF CHANGE

The Acquisition of Insight

The most frequently referred-to mechanism of change in the general psychoanalytic literature is the acquisition of insight through therapists' clarifications and interpretations. Such interventions, whether with an adult or child, may refer to: a defense, or to the relations of a drive (or its derivatives: impulse, feeling, wish) to a defense against it (e.g., repression, reaction formation); to feelings toward the therapist, which are transferred from other important figures; or to clients' perception of people or events in their current life as well as figures from the past. Interpretations may also refer to perceived parallels between the client's psychological experience of past or present figures and the way in which the therapist is viewed. The expansion of clients' self-understanding and awareness is said to bring about greater freedom from and control over neurotic conflicts, allowing the process of growth and maturation to proceed apace.

Expressive Play

We believe that there is a tendency among those writing about brief work with children to overestimate the therapeutic effects of interpretation and clarification of children's verbal expression, which is most typically carried out in connection with their play. There is an overreliance on verbal and interpretive modalities of therapist intervention and not enough trust in the therapeutic effects of expressive play in and of itself (Messer & Warren, 1995). Clinical examples of interpretations in the literature (e.g., Peterlin & Sloves, 1985) may seem, from the point of view of a younger child, long-winded and intellectualized.

Direct expression, the hallmark of healthy play in children, may be therapeutic in its own accord (Russ, 1993, 1995). The capacity to play is impaired when the child's development is thwarted; the creation of a "transitional space" (Winnicott, 1971) in which play can take place may permit the resumption of development. In fact, if we rely on Winnicott's conception of the function of play, then the goal of therapy is to encourage and promote in the child the possibility of creative psychic activity that is itself a vehicle of change. Schaefer (1993) has outlined a taxonomy of 14 "therapeutic factors" of play in child therapy (such as mastering fears, overcoming resistance, carthasis, role-play, attachment formation), with associated therapeutic benefits of each (e.g., growth and development, working alliance, emotional release, practice, attachment).

The Therapeutic Relationship: Holding, Support, and the Corrective Experience

Winnicott's (1965) notions of the "holding environment," the maturational environment," and "transitional" phenomena are examples of the important role that relational factors may play in bringing about change. In his view what is curative is the gradual resumption of developmental processes that had been hampered or interfered with by deficient contributions of the primary maternal object. The therapist facilitates such progress to a very great extent through being reliable, available, nonintrusive, and respectful of the child's autonomy and separateness—in short, functioning much in the fashion of an optimal parental figure.

By virtue of children saying what they feared to say and doing what they feared to do in the presence of the therapist, and not being punished, criticized, or harmed, they learn that they can think, talk, and act differently than they have before. Their ego functions are strengthened by the calm, accepting demeanor of the therapist in the face of their "shameful" secrets. This mechanism of change is known as the "corrective emotional experience" (Alexander & French, 1946).

In general, treating children in brief therapy calls for a shift from a more exploratory, interpretive mode to offering therapist support, a curative factor in its own right. This calls for the presence of therapist qualities such as warmth, empathy, emotional accessibility, and other ego-supportive characteristics of a "real relationship." There is less interpretation of defenses and more support for the adaptive function of defenses. In this sense, there is an increased reliance on nonpsychodynamic interventions and mechanisms of bringing about change such as education, counseling, modeling, reframing, and encouragement. Clearly, the nature of change is a multidimensional phenomenon and the therapist must rely on a variety of change factors. Such modes help to bring about a reduction in children's anxiety, resulting in their continued developmental progress.

RESEARCH SUPPORT FOR EFFICACY

There is a notable paucity of empirical studes of brief psychodynamic child therapy, and the studies that have been conducted during the past 25 years or so tend to suffer from a variety of methodological problems (Weisz, Weiss, Alicke, & Klotz, 1987). This makes it difficult to draw firm conclusions about the efficacy of brief psychodynamic treatment with children. In particular, reviewers have noted the absence of appropriate control groups, small sample sizes, insufficiently described therapeutic methods, and inadequate outcome measures (Dulcan, 1984; Smyrnios & Kirby, 1993). Given these methodological weaknesses, conclusions may be drawn only tentatively from the literature.

The results of the studies reviewed (MacLean, Macintosh, Taylor, & Gerber, 1982; Rosenthal & Levine, 1970, 1971; Smyrnios & Kirby, 1993) suggest in general that time-limited psychotherapy with children is effective, and in many cases, as effective as time-unlimited therapy, although methodological problems raise questions about much of the work done thus far. Rosenthal and Levine (1970, 1971), in what they describe as a pilot study, reported the efficacy of brief therapy, although the therapeutic methods applied are not well described. In this study, 33 children were treated with brief psychotherapy (8 hours of therapy contact) and compared with 35 children who were treated with "more traditional long-term psychotherapy." The authors report that 76% of the brief treatment group showed "definite or marked improvement," while 79% of the longer-term comparison group did so, suggesting that the brief treatment was as effective as the longer-term treatment. Absent in this study was a no-treatment or minimal treatment group that controls for nonspecific or presumably peripheral effects of therapy.

Smyrnios and Kirby (1993) reported the results of a carefully conducted study of brief (12 session) versus time-unlimited psychodynamic psychotherapy with children, comparing both groups with a minimal contact group (assessment interviews, a feedback session, and a 12-week follow-up interview only). The authors report significant clinical improvement in both treatment groups at posttreatment and at 4-years follow-up, but also note that the minimal treatment group showed improvement on many of the same measures. MacLean et al. (1982) have described, in a more anecdotal report, successful outcomes using a "brief focal dynamic therapy approach" with a wide range of clinical problems in the context of an outpatient child psychiatry team. The therapies were organized around a "focal hypothesis" and kept to a maximum of eight therapy sessions, emphasizing either individual or family-focused work. The authors do not indicate the number of cases treated, nor do they provide systematic comparisons of their treatment approach.

A serious problem reflected in these and other outcome studies is that relevant comparison groups, namely, wait-list control groups and minimal intervention treatment groups, have tended to exhibit as much improvement as the brief treatment groups. Thus, it is difficult to argue on the basis of existing studies alone that brief treatment is better than no treatment or minimal intervention treatments (Fisher, 1980; Miller, Barrett, Hampe, & Noble, 1972; Rosenthal & Levine, 1970; Smyrnios & Kirby, 1993). Although this lack of treatment effect may reflect factors other than an actual lack of efficacy, such as measurement and statistical problems, or the action of nonspecific curative effects in so-called control groups, it nonetheless points to a clear need for future research to improve on most extant studies.

It has also been reported that time-limited psychotherapy with children is as effective as longer-term psychotherapy (Smyrnios & Kirby, 1993; Wattie, 1973). Again, however, this finding must be considered in the context of the lack of differential outcome for various treatment groups in most other studies, a puzzle that tends to plague psychotherapy outcome research generally (Lambert & Bergin, 1994). Overall, it would appear that considerably more work needs to be done to address, in a meaningful fashion, questions about the process, technique, and efficacy of brief psychodynamic child treatment.

CLINICAL CASE

A clinical case vignette is offered to illustrate some of the themes identified in this chapter.

History

The patient, Kristin, is a 4-year-old girl, brought to the therapist by her mother, Ms. N., to deal with regressive behaviors that included secondary enuresis, difficulties going to bed, and being overweight. Kristin's father moved out of the home when she was 2, and the parents have been separated since, although they have not been legally divorced. The treatment, which is ongoing at the time this is being written, was planned as a time-limited intervention in accordance with the stated wishes of the mother.

An intial session was held with the mother so as to gain an understanding of Kristin's developmental history, the current situation, and the history of the presenting problems. Although Ms. N. did not see her daughter as anxious, Kristin clearly was exhibiting signs of emotional strain and developmental derailment. Her mother did not seem to fully grasp the extent of the strain on Kristin that was posed by her father's leaving, and she also seemed somewhat unclear about the status of the marriage and why divorce had not been finalized.

Ms. N. reported that Kristin's overeating began about the time her father left, although the other symptoms developed only recently. The return to bedwetting and the anxiety at bedtime seemed to arise around the time her father did not appear as promised on Kristin's 4th birthday. There have been other occurrences of unreliability on his part around visitation.

Suitability

Although this patient is quite young, she appeared to be a reasonable candidate for time-limited play therapy. Along with obvious weaknesses in her family environment, there were substantial strengths. Her mother is bright and reasonably well-adjusted, and has substantial support from her own family of origin as well as that of her husband. She is educated, does well in a responsible professional position, and is not under significant financial strain.

From an initial meeting using play materials, it was determined that Kristin was quite well-adjusted and functioning adequately in many areas. Her use of language was age-appropriate, and she was able to enter the new situation of therapy with little anxiety, allowing her mother to leave the room promptly. Her use of play materials, mostly figures and Play-Doh, reflected a capacity to use such materials to express inner reality, articulating through play her fantasy life and areas of conflict. She rapidly formed an alliance with the therapist.

Central Focus

Although the central focus for therapeutic intervention suggested itself based on the previous history alone, the issue of the absent father had to be refined to take account of the recent changes in Kristin's behavior and mood, the evolving family situation, and the "moving target" of Kristin's own developmental process. It appeared that Kristin was experiencing her father's absence in a new way, possibly occasioned by expectable development changes in her cognitive abilities including her sense of time and increased object constancy. Also, changes in the parental relationship had to be considered, as it seemed to Ms. N. that her husband may have begun to date other women, although she had not begun dating men. An interesting complication involved Ms. N.'s continued relationship with her in-laws, who appeared to be angry at their son. Mr. N. was apparently struggling with his family of origin around their anger toward him, and he had been feeling distanced from all sources of emotional support.

Thus, while the formulation was centered on Kristin's emotional crisis and was intended to address her feelings of abandonment and anxiety over the loss of an intact family, it was also understood that interventions would have to be made at the level of the mother–daughter relationship, taking into account the additional extended family forces.

The elements of the focus could be stated as follows: Kristin has become symptomatic in the attempt to manage the strain of losing a close relationship with her father, while her mother was having difficulty providing the sympathetic support Kristin needed in this context because of her own strains and guilt. Kristin's father was unable to respond adequately to her because of immaturity, feelings of guilt, and alienation. The primary function of the central focus in this case was to organize the therapist's perception and activity in relation to both child and family.

The full formulation was not given to either the child or her mother, although both received parts of it. The child was told simply that "her father was too far away" and that made her unhappy. The mother was told that her daughter was under extra strain beyond the usual developmental ones, and needed additional support. She was also told that perhaps she needed to clarify for herself in her own therapy, in which she was already engaged, where the family was headed.

Time Limits

The therapist decided that Kristin was too young to make use of an explicit time limit, although her mother made it clear that she expected to have some idea of the duration of therapy at the outset. While one might easily make a case for an extended psychotherapy for this child, it did not seem likely to be accepted by the mother, and so the arrangement was made for a duration of "some months," with the option to reevaluate this at a later time. The issue of a time limit can be more a factor for the therapist, who cannot help but respond to the awareness of time constraints, than it will be for so young a patient, or even for the parent, who had minimally formed ideas about what therapy for her daughter would be like.

Techniques and Clinical Process

The techniques used were those of psychodynamic play therapy and the play materials were selected with this modality in mind. Included were human figures of different ages and genders, a small house, vehicles, animals, crayons, and paper. The therapist tuned into the play themes initiated by the child, amplifying aspects of the play that were most relevant to the central focus.

Kristin immediately arranged the figures into her own family configuration, with a mother and a daughter constituting the main group. Father was placed quite intentionally at a distance from the others: "Daddy lives here." She made much of travel by moving figures back and forth between two locations. Aggressive themes also appeared early, with an elaborate and rhythmic banging game that involved human figures.

The theme of hunger also appeared early on and with great force. Kristin began with a game of "cooking" Play-Doh food, but the game seemed to overstimulate her feeling of hunger and she lost the "transitional space" of the play and began to nibble on the Play-Doh in actuality. The therapist commented on how very hungry she seemed to be, even while the "game" continued. She often requested food or treats from her mother when the session was just ended.

A significant transference element appeared almost immediately. When told the time was almost up, Kristin half hid herself and began to cry, repeating, "daddy, daddy, daddy" in a mournful and plaintive way. Although the behavior seemed in part forced and attention-seeking, somewhere halfway between real tears and "as if," crocodile ones, her cries were responded to as though they were entirely real, as the therapist commented on her sadness and unhappiness and how much she needed her daddy. It should be noted that the therapist does not simply "become" the daddy, as though playing the role deliberately, but instead is a sympathetic and involved figure (e.g., saying, "poor, sad little girl!") thus allowing for a certain degree of ambiguity. This complex interaction illustrates the nature of transference as a transitional phenomenon, as the therapist both is and is not the child's father, offering the child the opportunity to directly express painful affects and to simultaneously communicate with the therapist: "you see, this is how I feel."

Mother's response to her daughter's striking and affectively charged expressions was "Oh, you faker!" which Kristin would hear as her mother came in to collect her. Although in this way Ms. N. could get her daughter to smile and give up the crying, her response also seemed to contain the theme of denial of Kristin's distress and the latter's need to communicate it to a sympathetic other. In separate sessions with her mother, the therapist posed the question as to why she thought her daughter would "fake" in this particular way with a male therapist who was about her father's age, and at the particular moment when the session was ending. In this way Kristin's enactment of her problem in the transference was used not only to help her express and deal with her loss, but also to inform the concurrent clinical work being done with the mother. This opened up a dialogue between the therapist and Ms. N. about her daughter's current emotional state and special needs.

Therapist activity was thus understood to involve both early and active use of the transference and its interpretation, as well as immediate processing of the clinical interaction with the child's family. Likewise, the brief context informed the entire clinical process by encouraging the therapist to remain focused on the central issue and to draw play expressions back to that focus rather than to allow play to be entirely free-form, regressive, and open-ended.

Discussion of the Case

After about ten individual sessions, mother reported that the bedwetting had stopped, and other forms of acting out had diminished. The therapy appeared to have given validity to the reactions of both daughter and mother to the stresses of the marital separation, and made room especially for Kristin to articulate, in her own developmentally appropriate way, her feelings of anger, sadness, and neediness. The play situation provided a vehicle for her to process more openly and without the defensiveness of the adults in her life what will undoubtedly remain a central loss in her life. Discussions with mother to educate her about the nature of Kristin's reactions and her emotional needs had a positive impact, enabling Kristin's immediate family to become more receptive and responsive to her experience and feelings. While the issue of her being overweight was not given great emphasis, it was suggested to mother that she seemed to be offering Kristin food treats as a way to handle her own sense of guilt and inadequacy in the face of Kristin's needs. It is hoped that the family can continue to provide more of what Kristin may need beyond the termination of the psychotherapy.

CONCLUSION: BRIEF PSYCHOTHERAPY AND MANAGED CARE

It continues to be important to find ways to work with children and their families that are sensitive to practical realities as well as clinical necessities. Valuable work has already been done to articulate models of brief psychodynamic therapy with children, and, to a lesser extent, to evaluate these models systematically. Clinical work and research studies carried out thus far suggest the usefulness of brief psychodynamic therapies with children relative to longer-term work as well as to other treatment approaches, although the results of systematic study do not prove its efficacy compared with minimal treatment. More work is needed to validate particular approaches and techniques and to better specify target populations likely to benefit from such treatment approaches.

Psychodynamic therapists will continue to work briefly with children, and given the time-limited nature of much of this work, it is only reasonable to develop and evaluate clinical methods that are as effective as possible. We would caution, however, against undue limitations on the duration of treatment given the present state of our knowledge about brief psychotherapy process and outcome. Managed care has increased the demands on therapists for brief and effective treatments in the absence of clear indications of the appropriateness of such restrictions. Furthermore, although many of the treatments described in the chapter are quite brief, they would still exceed the number of sessions frequently available within the constraints of managed care, and therefore would remain out of the reach of many families who need such care, let alone those who may require more intensive and time-unlimited treatment.

Brief psychotherapy for children, thoughtfully derived and systematically evaluated, is a necessity, but longer-term treatment is likewise necessary in many instances. We believe it is important not to allow the political and economic concerns of our present-day health-care system to curtail the full range of treatments that are available and appropriate for children and families in need.

REFERENCES

Alexander, F., & French, T. M. (1946). *Psychoanalytic therapy: Principles and application.* New York: Ronald Press.

Beebe, B. (1994). Representation and internalization: Three principles of salience. *Psychoanalytic Psychology, 11,* 127–165.

Bellak, L., & Siegel, H. (1983). *Handbook of intensive brief and emergency psychotherapy (B. E. P.).* Larchmont, NY: C. P. S., Inc.

Bellak, L., & Small, L. (1978). *Emergency psychotherapy and brief psychotherapy* (2nd ed.). New York: Grune & Stratton.

Bowlby, J. (1969). *Attachment and loss: Vol. I. Attachment.* New York: Basic Books.

Budman, S. H., & Gurman, A. S. (1988). *Theory and practice of brief therapy.* New York: Guilford Press.

Clark, B. E. (1993). *Towards an integrated model of time-limited psychodynamic therapy with children* (Doctoral dissertation, Rutgers–The State University, 1992). *Dissertation Abstracts International, 54,* 1659B.

Costello, E. J. (1989). Developments in child psychiatric epidemiology. *Journal of the American Academy of Child and Adolescent Psychiatry, 28,* 836–841.

Davanloo, H. (1980). *Short-term dynamic psychotherapy.* Northvale, NJ: Aronson.

Dulcan, M. K. (1984). Brief psychotherapy with children and their families: The state of the art. *Journal of the American Academy of Child Psychiatry, 23,* 544–551.

Dulcan, M. K. & Piercy, P. (1985). A model for teaching and evaluating brief psychotherapy with children and their families. *Professional Psychology: Research and Practice, 16,* 689–700.

Ferenczi, S. (1980). The further development of an active therapy in psychoanalysis. In J. Suttie (Ed.), *Further contributions to the theory and technique of psycho-analysis* (pp. 189–197). London: Hogarth Press. (Original work published 1921)

Fisher, G. (1980). The use of time-limits in brief psychotherapy: A comparison of six-sessions, twelve-sessions, and unlimited treatment with families. *Family Process, 23,* 101–106.

Freud, A. (1926). *The psychoanalytic treatment of children.* London: Imago.

Garfield, S. L. (1978). Research on client variables in psychotherapy. In S. L. Garfield & A. E. Bergin (Eds.), *Handbook of psychotherapy and behavior change* (3rd ed., pp. 213–256). New York: Wiley.

Kaduson, H. G., Cangelosi, D. M., & Schaefer, C. (Eds.). (1997). *The playing cure: Individualized play therapy for specific child problems*. Northvale, NJ: Aronson.

Kashani, J. H., & Orvaschel, H. (1990). A community study of anxiety in children and adolescents. *American Journal of Psychiatry, 147,* 313–318.

Klein, M. (1932). *The psycho-analysis of children*. London: Hogarth Press.

Koss, M. P. (1979). Length of psychotherapy for clients seen in private practice. *Journal of Consulting and Clinical Psychology, 47,* 210–212.

Lambert, M. J., & Bergin, A. E. (1994). The effectiveness of psychotherapy. In A. E. Bergin & S. L. Garfield (Eds.), *Handbook of psychotherapy and behavior change* (4th ed., pp. 143–189). New York: Wiley.

Langsley, D. G. (1975). Comparing clinic and private practice of psychiatry. *American Journal of Psychiatry, 135,* 702–706.

Lester, E. (1968). Brief psychotherapy in child psychiatry. *Canadian Psychiatric Association Journal, 13,* 301–309.

Mackay, J. (1967). The use of brief psychotherapy with children. *Canadian Journal of Psychiatry, 12,* 269–278.

MacLean, G., Macintosh, B., Taylor, E., & Gerber, M. (1982). A clinical approach to brief dynamic psychotherapies in child psychiatry. *Canadian Journal of Psychiatry, 27,* 113–118.

Mahler, M. S. (1968). *On human symbiosis and the vicissitudes of individuation*. New York: International Universities Press.

Malan, D. (1976). *The frontier of brief psychotherapy*. New York: Plenum Press.

Mann, J. (1973). *Time-limited psychotherapy*. Cambridge, MA: Harvard University Press.

Messer, S. B., & Warren, C. S. (1995). *Models of brief psychodynamic therapy: A comparative approach*. New York: Guilford Press

Miller, L. C., Barrett, C. L., Hampe, E., & Noble, H. (1972). Comparison of reciprocal inhibition, psychotherapy, and waiting list control for phobic children. *Journal of Abnormal Psychology, 79,* 269–279.

Parad, L. G. (1970–1971). Short-term treatment: An overview of historical trends, issues, and potentials. *Smith College Studies in Social Work, 41,* 119–146.

Peterlin, K., & Sloves, R. (1985). Time-limited psychotherapy with children: Central theme and time as major tools. *Journal of the American Academy of Child and Adolescent Psychiatry, 24,* 785–792.

Phillips, E. L. (1985). *Psychotherapy revised: New frontiers in research and practice*. Hillsdale, NJ: Erlbaum.

Proskauer, S. (1969). Some technical issues in time-limited psychotherapy with children. *Journal of the American Academy of Child and Adolescent Psychiatry, 8,* 154–169.

Proskauer, S. (1971). Focused time-limited psychotherapy with children. *Journal of the American Academy of Child and Adolescent Psychiatry, 10,* 619–639.

Rank, O. (1978). *Will therapy*. New York: Norton. (Original work published 1929)

Rosenthal, A. J., & Levine, S. V. (1970). Brief psychotherapy with children: A preliminary report. *American Journal of Psychiatry, 127,* 106–111.

Rosenthal, A. J., & Levine, S. V. (1971). Brief psychotherapy with children: Process of therapy. *American Journal of Psychiatry, 128,* 33–38.

Russ, S. W. (1993). *Affect and creativity: The role of affect and play in the creative process*. Hillsdale, NJ: Erlbaum.

Russ, S. W. (1995). Play psychotherapy research. In T. H. Ollendick & R. J. Prinz (Eds.), *Advances in clinical child psychology* (pp. 365–391). New York: Plenum Press.

Schaefer, C. E. (1993). *The therapeutic powers of play*. Northvale, NJ: Aronson.

Sifneos, P. E. (1972). *Short-term psychotherapy and emotional crisis*. Cambridge, MA: Harvard University Press.

Sifneos, P. E. (1979). *Short-term dynamic psychotherapy*. New York: Plenum Press.

Sloves, R., & Peterlin, K. (1986). The process of time-limited psychotherapy with latency-aged children. *Journal of the American Academy of Child and Adolescent Psychiatry, 25,* 1341–1347.

Sloves, R., & Peterlin, K. B. (1993). Where in the world is . . . my father? A time-limited play therapy. In C. E. Schaefer & T. Koffman (Eds.), *Play therapy in action: A casebook for practitioners* (pp. 301–346). Northvale, NJ: Aronson.

Smyrnios, K. X., & Kirby, R. J. (1993). Long-term comparison of brief versus unlimited psychodynamic treatments with children and their families. *Journal of Consulting and Clinical Psychology, 61,* 1020–1027.

Spitz, R. A. (1945). Hospitalism: An inquiry into the genesis of psychiatric conditions in early childhood. *Psychoanalytic Study of the Child, 2*, 53–73.

Spitz, R. A. (1946). Anaclitic depression: An inquiry into the genesis of psychiatric conditions in early
childhood, II. *Psychoanalytic Study of the Child, 2*, 313–342.

Target, M., & Fonagy, P. (1996). The psychological treatment of child and adolescent psychiatric disorders. In A. Roth & P. Fonagy (Eds.), *What works for whom? A critical review of psychotherapy research* (pp. 263–320). New York: Guilford Press.

Turecki, S. (1982). Elective brief psychotherapy with children. *American Journal of Psychiatry, 36*,
479–488.

Wattie, B. (1973). Evaluating short-term casework in a family agency. *Social Casework*, December,
609–616.

Weisz, J. R., Weiss, B., Alicke, M. C., & Klotz, M. L. (1987). Effectiveness of psychotherapy with children and adolescents: A meta-analysis for clinicians. *Journal of Consulting and Clinical Psychology, 55*, 542–549.

Winnicott, D. W. (1965). *The maturational process and the facilitating environment.* New York: International Universities Press.

Winnicott, D. W. (1971). *Playing and reality.* London: Tavistock.

13

Interpersonal Psychotherapy for Depressed Adolescents (IPT-A)

LAURA MUFSON and DONNA MOREAU

The purpose of this chapter is to review the nature of depression in adolescents and to discuss the empirical validation of a psychosocial treatment for the disorder. Interpersonal psychotherapy for depressed adolescents (IPT-A) is the treatment of focus. The empirical work to be discussed includes epidemiological research on rates of depression in children and adolescents, and results from an open and randomized controlled clinical trial of IPT-A. An overview of the principles and techniques of IPT-A is provided and the work is viewed in the context of changing practices in the delivery of mental health care today.

BASIC APPROACH

To date, very little research has been conducted on the efficacy of treatments for depressed adolescents. Individual clinicians' experiences tell of some success in treating adolescents with antidepressants; however, the psychopharmacological trials on the use of tricyclic antidepressants with depressed adolescents have not been able to demonstrate efficacy over the use of placebo (Kramer& Feiguine, 1981; Ryan, et al., 1986; Ryan, Meyer, Cahille, Mazzie, & Puig-Antich, 1988; Strober, Freeman, & Rigali, 1990). More rigorously designed research protocols with greater numbers of adolescents and improved methodologies are needed to better evaluate the role of medication in the treatment of adolescent depression.

LAURA MUFSON and DONNA MOREAU • New York State Psychiatric Institute, New York, New York 10032.

Handbook of Psychotherapies with Children and Families, edited by Russ and Ollendick. Kluwer Academic/Plenum Publishers, New York, 1999.

Adolescent patients are regularly treated with psychotherapy, although there have been few published controlled clinical trials of individual psychotherapy with adolescents diagnosed with a major depression. Several studies have been conducted with a more heterogeneous sample of depressed adolescents (Lewinsohn, Clarke, Hops, & Andrews, 1990; Reynolds & Coats, 1980; Robbins, Alessi, & Colfer, 1989; Wood, Harrington, & Moore, 1996). Wilkes, Belsher, Rush, and Frank (1996) have published a treatment manual for using cognitive therapy with depressed adolescents based on their experience treating depressed adolescents in an open clinical trial. The need for empirical testing of psychotherapy modalities has increased given the equivocal findings of the adolescent pharmacotherapy studies and the reports of persistent psychosocial impairment in recovered depressed adolescents.

IPT seemed appropriate for use with adolescents for two reasons: (1) adolescents would be attracted to the time-limited quality and (2) the focus on interpersonal issues is in keeping with an adolescent developmental focus. The fact that adolescent symptomatology is very similar to that of adult depressed individuals engendered a hopefulness that it might be as efficacious with adolescents as it is with adults. The impact of a brief effective treatment could be significant for preventing associated impairments in adolescent development and social functioning that often accompany the depression and that persist after recovery.

DESCRIPTION OF PROBLEM/DISORDER

Major Depression

Studies that have compared depressed adolescents with depressed adults conclude that, despite minor variations attributable to developmental stages, the symptom profile is the same (Carlson & Strober, 1979; Friedman, Hurt, Clarkin, Corn, & Aronoff, 1983; Inamadar, Siomopoulous, Osborn, & Bianchi, 1979). Both can have chronic or recurrent symptoms and/or episodes, significant psychosocial impairment, negative self-cognitions, problems with sleep and appetite, depressed mood, tearfulness, difficulty concentrating, and suicidal ideation (Kashani, Rosenberg, & Reigh, 1989; Ryan et al., 1987). They tend to differ in that adolescents often do not report the pervasive anhedonia that is characteristic of adult depressed patients and they appear to respond differently to tricyclic antidepressants (Carlson & Strober, 1979; Mitchel, McCauley, Burke, & Moss, 1988). Minor variations include adolescent reports of more hypersomnia, less terminal insomnia, and hyperphagia. The adolescents exhibit a more fluctuating course characterized by more interpersonal problems (Simeon, 1989), and also make more suicide attempts than depressed adults (Shaffer et al., 1996).

The effects of developmental changes in cognition and emotional expression on the presentation of depression over time have yet to be fully delineated. From childhood to adolescence there appears to be a transition from predominantly vegetative and behavioral symptoms to more inner psychological or cognitive ones. Adolescents, in comparison with children, begin to resemble adults in their depth of despair, sense of hopelessness, propensity for suicide, and accompanying anxiety and agitation (Bemporad & Lee, 1988). Ryan et al. (1987) conclude from their review of studies that developmental changes across childhood and adolescence have only mild to moderate effects on the expression of a limited number of affective symptoms in children with major depression.

Studies using semistructured interviews and applying more rigorous diagnostic criteria to reported symptoms have yielded reduced but significant rates of depressive disorders in adolescents. There are six reported studies on the prevalence rates of depressive disorders in adolescents, and four other studies on children and adolescents (Fleming & Offord, 1990). The prevalence rates for current major depression range from 0.4 to 5.7%, and 8.3% for lifetime rate of major depression (Fleming & Offord, 1990).

Dysthymic Disorder

Dysthymic disorder is distinguished from a major depressive episode in that it requires a longer duration but milder constellation of depressive symptoms. Dysthymia has an earlier age of onset than MDD (Kovacs, Feinberg, Crouse-Novac, Paulauskas, & Finkelstein, 1984) and is frequently comorbid with major depression. Kovacs et al. (1984) followed children aged 8–13 years for approximately 5 years and found that 93% of the children diagnosed with dysthymia had other concurrently diagnosed conditions, the most common being MDD (57%) and anxiety (36%). For each year that the child had the disorder, the probability for remission decreased.

Course of Adolescent Depression

Clinical experience suggests that the course of adolescent depression may differ from that of adult depression. Some adolescents tend to have more episodically intense periods of depression interspersed with periods of improved functioning (Angst, Merikangas, Scheidegger, & Wicki, 1990). The few follow-up studies that exist have indicated a generally poor prognosis with a high risk for future episodes of affective illness and chronic psychosocial problems (Garber, Kriss, Koch, & Lindholm, 1988; Keller, Beardslee, Lavori, & Wunder, 1988; McCaulay et al., 1993). Kandel and Davies (1986) found in their 9 year follow-up of a high school sample that depressive symptoms in adolescence were the most significant predictive factor for depressive symptoms in adulthood. Studies of recurrence rates of depression in adolescence include both community and clinic-referred samples. Factors associated with earlier recurrence included prior suicidal ideation and attempt, and later age at first onset of disorder (Lewinsohn et al., 1990).

Research (Harrington, Fudge, Rutter, Pickles, & Hill, 1990; Keller et al., 1988; Kovacs et al., 1984) strongly suggests that children and adolescents with a major depression are at significant risk for future episodes of depression both in late adolescence and in young adulthood. The studies conclude that chronic and significant psychosocial impairment and interpersonal difficulties are associated with adolescent depression, and these difficulties persist into adulthood.

INTERVENTION PROCEDURES

IPT-A is a 12-week, once-a-week psychotherapy treatment. The therapist's goals are to identify one or two problem areas to be the focus of treatment and to emphasize the current interpersonal aspects of the problem in the patient's significant relationships. The overall goals and problem areas previously defined for IPT for adults also apply to IPT for adolescents. A major change is the addition of a fifth problem area, single-parent families, to the original four areas (grief, role disputes, role transitions, interpersonal deficits). The treatment also has been adapted to address common adolescent developmental issues such as separation from parents, initial experience with death, peer pressure, and exploring one's individuality and independence from parents and authority figures. Guidelines have been added to address such problems as school refusal, suicidality, physical and sexual abuse, aggression, and protective service agency involvement. The modifications and general strategies have been organized and are presented in a treatment manual specifically for depressed adolescents (Mufson, Moreau, Weissman, & Klerman, 1993). The treatment has been conceptualized into three phases: the initial phase, the middle phase, and the termination phase.

Initial Phase

The initial phase is comprised of the first four therapy sessions. There are several tasks to be accomplished by the conclusion of the fourth session: (1) a complete diagnostic assessment is conducted and the nature of depression, its symptoms, and treatment options are reviewed with the patient and parent; (2) an interpersonal inventory is conducted providing an assessment of the patient's significant familial and nonfamilial relationships; (3) a specific problem area is identified; (4) the goals and strategies of the treatment are explained to the patient along with clarification of his or her role in the treatment; and (5) a treatment contract is set with the patient outlining the identified problem area and the rules and guidelines for the therapeutic relationship.

The therapist is able to identify a problem area with the patient after conducting an interpersonal inventory during which patient and therapist discuss in detail the patient's current and past relationships. The discussion includes mutual expectations for the relationship, perceptions of others' expectations for the relationship, positive and negative aspects of the relationships, changes desired in the relationships, and the association between these interpersonal problems and the depressive episode. A parent, typically the mother, also is involved in the initial sessions. The parent is similarly educated about depression in adolescents, treatment options, and the therapeutic process.

In making the therapeutic contract with the therapist, the adolescent is encouraged to think of him- or herself as being in treatment and is formally given the limited sick role. That is, the adolescent is told that he or she has a mental health problem that affects everyday functioning, but the adolescent should do as many normal activities as possible because it will help him or her to feel better. The adolescent also is told to keep doing them even if he or she can't do them as well as before the depression began. The adolescent is encouraged to maintain the usual social roles in the family, at school, and with friends. Similarly the parent is advised to be supportive of the child's efforts to maintain the normal activities even if the quality of the performance is worse than usual. The assignment of the sick role is meant to help break the negative critical cycle that parents and their children often engage in particularly when the adolescent is depressed and feeling negative already. The contract specifies which of the five problem areas will be the focus of treatment, the limits of confidentiality, session frequency, parental involvement in treatment, and patient's responsibilities in treatment. The therapist often utilizes the telephone to maintain contact and flexibility in scheduling due to adolescent activities. In addition, with adolescent and familial consent, the therapist generally establishes a relationship with the school to keep abreast of the adolescent's functioning and to advise the school. Once the treatment contract is set, the middle phase of treatment begins.

Middle Phase

It is at this time that patient and therapist begin to work directly on the identified problem area. The goals of the middle phase are clarification of the problem area, identification of effective strategies to address the problem, and application of the interventions to the problem (Mufson et al., 1993). The long-term goals are to alleviate the depressive symptomatology and improve the adolescent's interpersonal functioning. The therapist encourages the patient to become more active in the sessions bringing in feelings and events that occur in between sessions that are related to the identified problem area. The therapist also continues to monitor the depressive symptoms and the family's support of the treatment. Specific techniques vary according to the problem area but some commonly used techniques include exploratory questioning, encouragement of affect, clarification of conflicts, communication analysis, and linkage of feelings with interpersonal events. The connection between the depressive symptoms and the interpersonal problems is stressed. There is continuous feedback regarding the adolescent's use of the strategies, application to problems in between sessions, and observed changes in the patient's conduct of his or her relationships. The feedback is designed to improve the patient's self-esteem and give a sense of social competence.

Another powerful tool of IPT-A is the therapist–patient relationship. The therapist and patient work together in the treatment as a team. Together, they assess the formulation of the problem, the need for any revisions or shift in focus, and possible solutions to the problem. Interpersonal communication styles that appear in the session between patient and therapist also may be discussed as they relate to interactions that occur in other relationships. Family members are involved in the middle phase as needed to help negotiate solutions to particular problems and in accordance with the desires of the adolescent. A brief discussion of the strategies and goals for each problem area follows below. For a detailed discussion of the individual problem areas, see Mufson et al. (1993).

Problem Areas

Grief

Grief is considered to be a problematic response to a death when it is prolonged or becomes abnormal in that it is a distorted, delayed, or chronic reaction. As such, it can lead to depression either immediately or at a later date when the patient is reminded of the loss (Raphael, 1983). During adolescence, loss of a parent engenders premature separation and individuation in addition to the usual tasks of mourning. Common signs of a grief reaction include withdrawal, depressed feelings, overidentification with the deceased, feelings of abandonment, and/or regression to an earlier developmental stage (Raphael, 1983). The adolescent may manifest his or her difficulties in behavior problems rather than changes in affect. Therefore, the therapist must be alerted to problems of substance abuse, sexual promiscuity, and/or truancy (Raphael, 1983).

The therapist's goals are to help the adolescent discuss the impact of the loss on his or her life and to identify and express the accompanying feelings. The therapist must consider the adolescent's role in the family system, the nature of the relationship lost, the remaining social support network, and the adolescent's psychological maturity so as to fully address the impact of the loss for the adolescent. As the loss becomes better understood and accepted, the symptoms will likely dissipate enabling the adolescent to establish new relationships.

While the main goal of IPT-A is to help the adolescent with an abnormal grief reaction, the therapist also is able to help an adolescent cope with normal grief as a preventive measure to avert an abnormal grief reaction. For adolescents who fall in the latter category, IPT-A helps the adolescent accept the loss and negotiate the separation from the deceased. For the adolescent who has an abnormal grief reaction, IPT-A addresses the depression that is a result of failure to go through the phases of the normal grieving process.

Interpersonal Role Disputes

An interpersonal role dispute is defined as a situation in which the individual and at least one significant other person have nonreciprocal expectations about their relationship (Klerman, Weissman, Rounsaville, & Chevron, 1984). Common adolescent disputes with parents occur over issues of sexuality, authority, money, and life values. Different values can lead to conflicting expectations for the adolescent's behavior that result in frequent misunderstandings. This often can be seen when the adolescent attempts to separate from the family by rebelling and disagreeing with everything the parents say or want to happen. The strategies for treating disputes include identifying details of the dispute, making choices about negotiations, reassessing expectations for the relationship, clarifying role changes, and/or modifying communication patterns to assist in resolution of the dispute. The therapist must explain to the adolescent and the parent how the role dispute contributes to the adolescent's depressive symptoms and how better communication can make them both feel better. The therapist can facilitate parental understanding by actually bringing in the appropriate family member into the session with the therapist. Desired improvements include a change in the expectations and behavior of the person, or dissolution of the relationship. IPT-A tries to discourage the latter unless absolutely necessary for the child's well-being. Generally, the goal is to help the adolescent find strategies for coping with the problematic situation.

Role Transitions

Role transitions are defined as changes that occur as a result of progression from one social role to another. Problems can arise when the adolescent has difficulties coping with the changes associated with the transition, if it has occurred too rapidly, or if it is experienced as a loss. There are normal and unexpected role transitions. Normal role transitions are expected and are typically handled successfully (Miller, 1974). They include passage to puberty, initiation of sexual relationships, separation from parents and family, or changes in work, college, career planning. Some problems that can arise include the parents' resistance to accepting the concomitant changes to the adolescent's transition or the adolescent's inability to cope with the changes. Unexpected or imposed transitions include parenthood, change in family role resulting from divorce, death, or impairment in parental functioning, or separation from parent. These unexpected changes can result in a loss of self-esteem, a sense of failing to meet others' expectations, increasing pressures and responsibilities, and inability to separate from family because of either family or adolescent resistance.

If the adolescent transition is problematic within the family context, the therapist is likely to include the parents in several sessions. The goal of their inclusion would be to teach them how to support the adolescent's transition and/or help the family adjust to the transition. The parent's own role transition difficulty can exacerbate the child's and must be dealt with simultaneously either by the IPT-A therapist or by the parent's own therapist.

Interpersonal Deficits

Interpersonal deficits are identified when an individual appears to lack the requisite social skills to establish and maintain appropriate relationships within and outside the family. This can adversely affect the adolescent's ability to make same-age friends, participate in activities with peers, and learn to make choices about relations, career, and sexuality (Hersen & Van Hasselt, 1987). The adolescent can become socially isolated, which can lead to feelings of depression. This in turn exacerbates the social withdrawal and can engender a lag in acquiring interpersonal skills. This impairment in development persists even after the depression resolves.

Strategies for treating such adolescents include focusing on those deficits that are more a result of the depression rather than longstanding personality traits. Once those deficits are identified, then the therapist must examine them in the context of past significant relationships, exploring for repetitive patterns or similar problems. The second step is to identify and discuss new strategies and to apply them to current relationships. The therapist may also use role-playing to foster practice and application of the new strategies and communication skills. The in-session practice gives the adolescent the confidence to try these strategies outside of the therapeutic relationship and can result in a sense of increased social competence.

Single-Parent Families

Single-parent family structure has many etiologies including divorce, separation, incarceration, death, and the increase in crime or drug abuse. Each of these situations can create unique conflicts between parents and children which can result in depression. The nature of the depressive reaction is related to the degree of finality to the structure, its abruptness in occurrence, and the frequency with which the comings and goings of the parent occur. The child's relationship with both the absent parent and the custodial parent are also significant factors. Common reactions to a recent departure of a parent include depressed mood, increased behavior problems, and increased conflicts with the custodial parent about issues such as discipline and independence.

The therapist has several tasks for the treatment of these adolescents. First, the therapist must help the adolescent acknowledge that there has been a significant disruption in his or her life and express the feelings of loss, abandonment, and/or punishment that have been engendered. The therapist must also clarify the expectations for the relationship with the absent parent and the parameters of the relationship with the remaining custodial parent. They must also negotiate some sort of acceptance of the state of the current situation. While negotiating the terms of the relationship with the custodial parent, it is often helpful to have that parent participate in the sessions to help put the event in perspective and correct any misconceptions the adolescent may have about the parents. If necessary, the therapist may also meet separately with the parent to review parenting issues such as appropriate methods of discipline and reasonable limits for an adolescent.

Termination

Termination occurs approximately during sessions 9 through 12. However, it should have been addressed at the beginning of treatment and should be discussed periodically during the course of therapy. The two goals of termination are to help the adolescent establish a sense of independence from the therapist and a sense of competence to cope with future interpersonal problems. It is not unusual for patients to have feelings of apprehension, anger, or sadness on termination and may in fact have a slight recurrence of symptomatology. This does not necessarily mean that the depression has returned, but rather should be observed to see whether it is just a temporary sadness associated with the termination. To foster the adolescent's sense of competence, the therapist should emphasize the patient's newly acquired skills and identified sources of external support.

Termination sessions are conducted with the adolescent alone and then with the family members who have been involved in the treatment. The therapist should try to elicit a discussion of feelings engendered by the termination, review the newly acquired interpersonal strategies and communication skills, review events of interpersonal success and competence, and problem-solve in anticipation of any upcoming events. These tasks for individual termination should occur with the family members as well. In addition, any changes that occurred in the family as a result of the treatment should be discussed. The therapist needs to review with everyone the possible warning signs of a recurrence and appropriate management of recurrent episodes.

At times, the therapist and family can decide there is a need for further treatment. Reasons for further treatment include (1) the depression has not fully remitted, (2) there are other issues that the adolescent may need to work on now that the depression has lifted, and (3) the therapy is a necessary stabilizing force in the adolescent's life. The decision to continue in treatment can be made immediately or the adolescent may take a few weeks and see how he or she feels and then reassess the need. Long-term treatment may be indicated for patients with longstanding personality problems, chronic or recurrent depression, histories of abuse, and nonresponders.

MAJOR MECHANISMS OF CHANGE

The underlying principle of IPT-A is that regardless of the biological or environmental etiology of the depression, it occurs in an interpersonal context that can significantly influence its course. If one can identify and improve problem-solving strategies in the person's interpersonal relationships, it is likely that the depression will be alleviated. The therapy focuses on current interpersonal problems that appear to be associated with the depression. The therapist and patient work together to choose one or two of five problem areas: grief, interpersonal role disputes, role transitions, interpersonal deficits, and single-parent families. The focus during the middle phase is on learning new interpersonal skills that will facilitate resolution of interpersonal conflict, improve communication within the patient's significant relationships, and improve the patient's expression of feelings and emotional needs. The primary mechanism of change is believed to be improved communication. This is achieved through a variety of strategies such as functional communication analysis of interpersonal conflict, role-playing, and therapist modeling of effective communication of feelings and needs. Functional communication analysis refers to the technique of analysis of discrete examples of conversations between the patient and significant other person that led to or was associated with feelings of depression. The interpersonal event is analyzed according to every statement said. The therapist periodically stops the patient and asks such questions as: How did that make you feel? What could you have said differently? How would that have felt for you or the other person? How do you think that made him/her feel? Was that your goal? What else could you have said? Could you have said it in a different way? What would have been the impact? The goal is to get the patient to start thinking and practicing other more adaptive ways of communicating in relationships. Often it is not always what the patient is saying, but how he or she is saying it that creates the problems. The communication or interpersonal events are constantly linked back to the patient's feelings to increase awareness of the association between interpersonal events and feelings of depression.

Significant interpersonal issues also are addressed through (1) use of role-playing conversations, (2) encouraging appropriate expression of affect, (3) clarification of feelings about a situation or person, (4) feedback from therapist regarding the impact of how one expresses feelings on others within the actual therapeutic session, and (5) learning to see another person's perspective on a situation so one can learn to negotiate and/or compromise for a solution. The most therapeutic aspects of treatment for a patient can be (1) conceptualization of different roles in the family and how they conflict with each other or how the patient is making a transition from one role to another and (2) learning to communicate his or her feelings and clarifying them within the significant relationships. The work on mechanisms of change occurs during the middle phase of treatment but continues to be reinforced, encouraged, and emphasized during the termination phase.

RESEARCH SUPPORT

The efficacy of IPT for adult depressed outpatients has been established in five controlled clinical trials for acute (Elkins et al., 1989; Sloane, Stapes, & Schneider, 1985; Weissman et al., 1979) and maintenance treatment (Klerman, DiMascio, Weissman, Prusoff, & Paykel, 1974; Kupfer, Frank, & Perel, 1989). IPT has been modified and tested in patients with depressive symptoms (not disorders) coming to primary care practice (Klerman et al., 1987), in a conjoint format for depressed patients with marital disputes (Foley, Rounsaville, Weissman, Sholomskas, & Chevron, 1989), in the elderly depressed patient (Reynolds & Imber, 1988), and in opiate addicts (Rounsaville, Glazer, Wilber, Weissman, & Kleber, 1983). See Klerman and Weissman (1993) for a description of all of the current adaptations of IPT.

A major review of child and adolescent psychotherapy research (Barnett, Docherty, & Frommelt, 1991) demonstrated that there has been very little research in adolescent individual psychotherapy that adheres to the contemporary methodological standards established in the adult clinical trial literature. Robbins et al. (1989), in a pilot treatment strategy for 38 adolescents hospitalized with major depression, conducted an open trial of psychotherapy that they described as similar to IPT. They noted that 47% of the patients responded with a reduction of symptoms when treated with the psychotherapy alone. The nonresponders were then treated with a combined tricyclic antidepressant and psychotherapy, and 92% responded. Results of this study are confounded by the fact that there appears to be a 50% placebo response rate in depressed adolescents regardless of type of treatment (i.e., medication or nonspecific psychotherapeutic intervention alone). Also, it is not possible to know whether responders in the second stage of the study improved because of medication, psychotherapy, or combined treatment.

Robbins et al. (1989) conducted this study without modifying the manual specifically for depressed adolescents; thus, the procedures for the treatment are not defined. Since this study was conducted, Mufson et al. (1993) have written a treatment manual of IPT-A that is the basis of a completed open clinical trial of IPT-A and a recently completed randomized controlled clinical trial of IPT-A. Fourteen depressed adolescents were treated in an open clinical trial of IPT-A using the standardized treatment manual (Mufson et al., 1994). In general, results demonstrated the feasibility and acceptability of the treatment and suggested a potential for efficacy (Mufson et al., 1994). The patients reported a significant decrease in depressive symptomatology and symptoms of psychological and physical distress as well as significant improvement in functioning. These 14 patients were contacted 1 year later and 10 participated in a follow-up evaluation. Only 1 of the 9 patients who returned for the follow-up evaluation reported symptoms meeting criteria for a depression diagnosis. She was a patient who had dropped out of treatment following the third session and had not been compliant with any other treatment since then. The remaining 9 patients still reported being in remission and also reported improved interpersonal functioning (Mufson & Fairbanks, 1996). There were no reported hospitalizations, pregnancies, or suicide attempts since completion of the treatment and all were attending school regularly.

A randomized controlled clinical trial of IPT-A versus clinical management has just been completed. Forty-eight depressed adolescents who met criteria for major depression were randomized to receive either 12 weeks of IPT-A or clinical management treatment. Twenty-four patients were treated in each group. IPT-A patients were seen once a week for 12 weeks with an option for a second visit during the week if having a crisis. The control patients had a once-a-month therapy session with an option for a second if feeling worse, and the ability to call the therapist when needed. Patients in both treatments were seen every 2 weeks by an independent evaluator to assess their depressive symptoms and global functioning and to confirm that it was alright for the patient to remain in the protocol. The evaluator was blind to treatment group. Therefore, the patients in the control treatment were actually seen 3 out of 4 weeks of the month and during the 1 week with no visit, they received a phone call from their therapist. At the end of the 12 weeks, patients were referred for further treatment as needed. Preliminary data analyses suggest that IPT-A is an acceptable treatment for depressed adolescents. They demonstrated higher rates of treatment compliance and a more significant decrease in depressive symptoms than for adolescents in the clinical management condition according to clinician and self-report measures. In addition, the IPT-A patients in comparison with control condition patients showed greater improvements in global functioning, and significantly greater improvement in social problem-solving skills. There was significantly greater attrition in the control treatment as a result of increased suicidality and noncompliance. Data analyses are still under way examining clinical status at 3- and 9-month follow-up and risk factors for poor treatment outcome. Because this was a relatively small sample, further studies are needed to replicate these results with a more diverse socioeconomic sample and to address issues of parent psychopathology and maintenance treatment.

CASE EXAMPLE

The following is a case example of an adolescent with an identified problem area of role transitions.

Sally is a 13-year-old girl who was referred to the clinic by her school guidance counselor because she appeared depressed in school and her grades had declined. On initial evaluation, she reported the following symptoms: irritable mood, sad feelings nearly every day, loss of interest in her friends, sports, and schoolwork, decline in grades, difficulty concentrating, initial insomnia, loss of appetite though no apparent weight loss, feelings of low self-esteem, and increasing tearfulness. She denied suicidal or homicidal ideation.

Sally had been living alone with her father for the past 5 years. Her parents had divorced when she was 4 years old and she initially lived with her mother. When her mother moved to Puerto Rico, a decision was made for Sally to stay in the United States with her father. Sally spent the summers in Puerto Rico with her mother. Six months prior to her presentation, Sally's father had married his girlfriend with whom he had already had a child, Sally's half-brother. They had been previously living apart. Sally was excited to have a little brother, but unhappy about the stepmother. The presence of the stepmother had increased the tension in the household and negatively impacted on her relationship with her father. She had become much more irritable with him and they were having increased conflicts.

The problem area was defined as role transitions. Sally was having difficulty making the transition to having another woman in the household and sharing her father. Her father also was having difficulties finding the right role for his new wife to have regarding discipline for his daughter. Sally did not like her step-mother telling her what to do around the house, which she had been previously maintaining with her father, and telling her father how to discipline her. Sally felt caught between the two of them and unable to talk to her father because she did not want to have him know how much she disliked his new wife. Apparently, they had gotten along much better when she lived in her own apartment so the conflict came as a surprise to everyone.

During the course of treatment, the therapist met with Sally alone as well as together with her father. Sally was encouraged to express her feelings about the situation to her father and to try to negotiate a situation that would feel comfortable for both of them. The therapist discussed with both of them the difficulties inherent in becoming a new family and assuming new roles within the family, particularly that of stepdaughter. The therapist was able to facilitate communication between Sally and her father and the father worked out a comfortable solution with his daughter that he was able to communicate to his new wife at home. By the end of treatment, Sally reported no depressive symptoms and reported feeling more comfortable with her new family constellation. She also felt more able to discuss with her father the times when she did not feel comfortable or had some difficulty with a family member or a peer.

FUTURE RESEARCH WITH ATTENTION TO MANAGED CARE

IPT is a treatment that fits the managed care framework for delivery of health care services for several reasons: (1) it is a brief, time-limited treatment; (2) it is standardized in a manual; (3) there are empirical data supporting its efficacy with a variety of populations; and (4) it may be cost effective to deliver. Moreover, there is even a version to be administered by nurse practitioners in a primary care setting (Klerman et al., 1987). IPT-A may easily fit the managed care company's needs for a short-term treatment, while also providing an effective therapy for the patient. It would be important, however, to have managed care recognize the importance and health care value of the maintenance treatment as well as the acute treatment. Studies have shown a significant decrease in recurrent episodes following once-a-month maintenance sessions (Frank, Kupfer, Perel, et al., 1990). This is cost effective as well because maintenance treatment costs are probably significantly less than the cost of treating an acute episode of a severe major depression which might even require hospitalization. In the coming years it will be very important to continue producing efficacy data that will support the use of psychotherapy or psychotherapy in conjunction with medication so patients will have the opportunity to receive both treatments. Therapy is needed to address the psychosocial aspects of the illness that can continue to affect the patients' functioning long after the depressive symptoms have remitted. The zeitgeist in health care delivery is to support evidence-based treatments, that is, those that have empirically demonstrated efficacy. In addition, there is a movement to assess whether the treatments that have been tested can look equally efficacious when delivered in a community setting. Therefore, the ideal next step would be to assess whether these treatments can be easily learned by general clinicians and whether delivered in the managed care setting or community setting, it is truly more effective than the eclectic therapy that usually characterizes treatment as usual.

SUMMARY

The goal in adapting IPT-A and conducting efficacy studies is that we will add to the small body of research available on psychosocial treatments for depressed adolescents and develop an effective intervention to treat a serious mental illness in adolescents. The psychopharmacological literature is equivocal, which makes psychosocial treatment development all the more important. However, one needs to keep in mind that even if in time there are efficacious medications for the treatment of depression in adolescents, there are always patients for whom medication may not be an option for other medical reasons. Therefore, it is necessary to develop a variety of efficacious treatment modalities where possible so that there are always nonmedication alternatives. Based on our current experiences, both in an open and in a controlled clinical trial, more studies using IPT-A are warranted to replicate the current findings and to better inform the clinicians about treatment efficacy and patient characteristics. IPT- A does not create new therapeutic techniques, but rather seeks to organize them in an effective brief treatment package. As such, while more efficacy data are awaited, it is likely that therapists will find many of the strategies beneficial to the treatment of depressed adolescents in clinical practice.

REFERENCES

Angst, J., Merikangas, K., Scheidegger, P., & Wicki, W. (1990). Recurrent brief depression: A new subtype of affective disorder. *Journal of Affective Disorders, 19,* 87–98.

Barnett, R. J., Docherty, J. P., & Frommelt, G. M. (1991). A review of child psychotherapy research since 1963. *Journal of the American Academy of Child and Adolescent Psychiatry, 30,* 1–14.

Bemporad, J., & Lee, K. W. (1988). Affective disorders. In C. Kestenbaum & D. Williams (Eds.), *Handbook of clinical assessment of children and adolescents* (Vol. II, pp. 626–650). New York: New York University Press.

Carlson, G., & Strober, M. (1979). Affective disorders in adolescence. *Psychiatric Clinics of North America, 2,* 511–526.

Elkin, I., Shea, M. T., Watkins, J. T., Imber, S. D., Sotsky, S. M. , Collins, J. F., Glass, D. R., Pilkones, P. A., Leber, W. R., Docherty, J. P., Feister, S. F., & Parloff, M.B. (1989). National Institute of Mental Health treatment of depression collaborative research program: General effectiveness of treatments. *Archives of General Psychiatry, 46,* 971–982.

Fleming, J. E., & Offord, D. R. (1990). Epidemiology of childhood depressive disorder: A critical review. *Journal of American Academic Child Adolescent Psychiatry, 29*(4), 571–580.

Foley, S. H., Rounsaville, B. J., Weissman, M. M., Sholomskas, D., & Chevron E. (1989). Individual versus conjoint interpersonal psychotherapy for depressed patients with marital disputes. *International Journal of Family Psychiatry, 10,* 1–2.

Frank, E., Kupfer, D. J., Perel, J. M., Cornes, C., Jarrett, D. B., Mallinger, A. G., Thase, M. E., McEachran, A. B., & Grochocinski, V. J. (1990). Three year outcomes for maintenance therapies in recurrent depression. *Archives of General Psychiatry, 47*(12), 1093–1099.

Friedman, R. C., Hurt, S. W., Clarkin, J. F., Corn, R., & Aronoff, M. S. (1983). Symptoms of depression among adolescents and young adults. *Journal of Affective Disorders, 5,* 37–43.

Garber, J., Kriss, M. R., Koch, M., & Lindholm, L. (1988). Recurrent depression in adolescents: A follow-up study. *Journal of the American Academy of Child and Adolescent Psychiatry, 27* (1), 49–54.

Harrington, R. C., Fudge, H., Rutter, M., Pickles, A., & Hill, J. (1990). Adult outcomes of childhood and adolescent depression. *Archives of General Psychiatry, 47,* 465–473.

Hersen, M., & Van Hasselt, V. B. (1987). *Behavior therapy with children and adolescents: A clinical approach.* New York: Wiley.

Inamdar, S. C., Siomopoulos, G., Osborn, M., & Bianchi, E. (1979). Phenomenology associated with depressed moods in adolescents. *American Journal of Psychiatry, 136*(2), 156–159.

Kandel, D. B., & Davies, M. (1986). Adult sequelae of adolescent depressive symptoms. *Archives of General Psychiatry, 43,* 255–262.

Kashani, J. H., Rosenberg, T. K., & Reigh, N. C. (1989). Developmental perspectives in child and adolescent depressive symptoms in a community sample. *American Journal of Psychiatry, 146,* 871–875.

Keller, M. B., Beardslee, W. R., Lavori, P. W., & Wunder, J. (1988). Course of major depression in nonreferred adolescents: A retrospective study. *Journal of Affective Disorders, 15,* 235–243.

Klerman, G. L., Budman, S., Berwick, D., Weissman, M. M., Damico-White, J., Demby, A., & Feldstein, M. (1987). Efficacy of a brief psychosocial intervention for symptoms of stress and distress among patients in primary care. *Medical Care, 25,* 1078–1088.

Klerman, G. L., DiMascio, A., Weissman, M. M., Prusoff, B., & Paykel, E. S. (1974). Treatment of depression by drugs and psychotherapy. *American Journal of Psychiatry, 131,* 186–194.

Klerman, G. L., & Weissman, M. M. (1993). *New applications of interpersonal psychotherapy.* Washington DC: American Psychiatric Press.

Klerman, G. L., Weissman, M. M., Rounsaville, B. M., & Chevron, E. S. (1984). *Interpersonal psychotherapy of depression.* New York: Basic Books.

Kovacs, M., Feinberg, T. L., Crouse-Novac, M. A., Paulauskas, S. L., & Finkelstein, R. (1984). Depressive disorders in childhood I. A longitudinal prospective study of characteristics and recovery. *Archives of General Psychiatry, 41,* 229–237.

Kramer, A. D., & Feiguine, R. J. (1981). Clinical effects of amitryptiline in adolescent depression: A pilot study. *Journal of the American Academy of Child and Adolescent Psychiatry, 20,* 636–644.

Kupfer, D. J., Frank, E., & Perel, J. M. (1989). The advantage of early treatment intervention in recurrent depression. *Archives of General Psychiatry, 46,* 771–775.

Lewinsohn, P. M., Clarke, G. N., Hops, H., & Andrews, J. (1990). Cognitive–behavioral treatment for depressed adolescents. *Behavioral Therapy, 21,* 385–401.

McCaulay, E., Myers, K., Mitchell, J., Calderone, R., Schlorek, K., & Treder, R. (1993). Depression in young people. *Journal of the American Academy of Child and Adolescent Psychiatry, 32,* 714–722.

Miller, D. (1974). *Adolescence: Psychology, psychopathology, psychotherapy.* Northvale, NJ: Aronson.

Mitchell, J., McCauley, E., Burke, P. M., & Moss, S. J. (1988). Phenomenology of depression in children and adolescents. *Journal of the American Academy of Child and Adolescent Psychiatry, 27*(1),12–20.

Mufson, L., & Fairbanks, J. (1996). Interpersonal psychotherapy for depressed adolescents: A 1-year naturalistic follow up study. *Journal of the American Academy of Child and Adolescent Psychiatry, 35,* 1145–1155.

Mufson, L., Moreau., D., Weissman, M. M., & Klerman, G. L. (1993). *Interpersonal psychotherapy for depressed adolescents.* New York: Guilford Press.

Mufson, L., Moreau, D., Weissman, M. M., Wickramaratne , P., Martin, J., & Samoilov, A. (1994). The modification of interpersonal psychotherapy with depressed adolescents (ITP-A): Phase I and phase II studies. *Journal of the American Academy of Child and Adolescent Psychiatry, 33,* 695–705.

Raphael B. (1983). *Anatomy of bereavement* (pp. 139–177). New York: Basic Books.

Reynolds, C. & Imber, S. (1988) *Maintenance therapies in late-life depression* (MH#43832). Washington, DC: National Institute of Mental Health.

Reynolds, W. M., & Coats, K. I. (1980). A comparison of cognitive–behavioral therapy and relaxation training for the treatment of depression in adolescents. *Journal of Consulting and Clinical Psychology, 44,* 653–660.

Robbins, D. R., Alessi, N. E., & Colfer, M. V. (1989). Treatment of adolescents with major depression: Implication of the DST and the melancholic clinical subtype. *Journal of Affective Disorders, 17,* 99–104.

Rounsaville, B. J., Glazer, W., Wilber, C. H., Weissman, M. M., & Kleber, H. D. (1983). Short-term interpersonal psychotherapy in methadone-maintained opiate addicts. *Archives of General Psychiatry, 40,* 629–636.

Ryan, N. D., Meyer, V., Cahille, S., Mazzie, D., & Puig-Antich, J. (1988). Lithium antidepressant augmentation in TCA refractory depression in adolescents. *Journal of the American Academy of Child and Adolescent Psychiatry, 27,* 755–758.

Ryan, N. D., Puig-Antich, J., Ambrosini, P., Rabinovich, H., Robinson, D., Nelson, B., Iyengar, S. & Twomey, J. (1987). The clinical picture of major depression in children and adolescent. *Archives of General Psychiatry, 44,* 854–861.

Ryan, N. D., Puig-Antich, J., Cooper, T., Ambrosini, P., Rabinovich, H., Robinson, D., Nelson, B., Iyengar, S., & Twomey, J. (1986). Impramine in adolescent major depression in children and adolescents. *Archives of General Psychiatry, 44,* 854–861.

Shaffer, D., Gould, M. S., Fisher, P., Trauman, P., Moreau, D., Kleiman, M., & Flory, M. (1996). Psychiatric diagnosis in child and adolescent suicide. *Archives of General Psychiatry, 53,* 339–348.

Simeon, J. G. (1989). Depressive disorders in children and adolescents. *Psychiatry Journal of the University of Ottawa, 14*(2), 356–361.

Sloane, R. B., Stapes, F. R., & Schneider, L. S. (1985). Interpersonal therapy versus nortriptyline for depression in the elderly. In G. D. Burrows, T. R. Norman, & L. Dennerstein (Eds.), *Clinical and pharmacological studies in psychiatric disorders* (pp. 344–346). London: John Libbey.

Strober, M., Freeman, R., & Rigali, J. (1990). The pharmacotherapy of depressive illness in adolescence: I. An open label trial of imipramine. *Psychopharmacology Bulletin, 26*(1), 80–84.

Weissman, M. M., Prusoff, B. A., DiMascio, A., Neu, C., Goklaney, M., & Klerman, G. L. (1979). The efficacy of the drugs and psychotherapy in the treatment of acute depressive episodes. *American Journal of Psychiatry, 136,* 555–558.

Wilkes, T. C. R., Belsher, G., Rush, A. J., & Frank, E. (1996). *Cognitive therapy for depressed adolescents.* New York: Guilford Press.

Wood, A., Harrington, R. C., & Moore, A. (1996). Controlled trial of a brief cognitive–behavioral intervention in adolescent patients with depressive disorders. *Journal of Child Psychology and Psychiatry & Allied Disciplines, 37*(6), 737–746.

14

Cognitive–Behavioral Interventions with Socially Phobic Children

ANNE MARIE ALBANO, MICHAEL F. DETWEILER, and SUSAN LOGSDON-CONRADSEN

INTRODUCTION

Social anxiety is a universal phenomenon that any individual can recall having experienced at repeated times during his or her life. If asked, most individuals can easily remember their most embarrassing moment, along with more minor social faux pas occurring more often than not. For many persons the physical and emotional discomfort experienced during such events are transitory and soon forgotten or later recalled with sidesplitting laughter. Unfortunately, a significant proportion of children and adolescents tend to experience social anxiety at extreme levels, on a continuous basis, with or without having any objective experience with an embarrassing event. For such individuals, everyday experiences such as attending school and interacting with peers are approached with painful anticipation of rejection, humiliation, embarrassment, and failure.

In this chapter we describe the phenomenology and cognitive–behavioral treatment of social phobia in youth. Although once a neglected disorder, social phobia is receiving increased attention by investigators within the broad fields of clinical psychology, psychiatry, and developmental psychopathology. Most relevant to this chapter is the work of clinical scientists who are actively involved in

ANNE MARIE ALBANO • Child Study Center, NYU School of Medicine, New York, New York 10016.   MICHAEL F. DETWEILER • Department of Psychology, West Virginia University, Morgantown, West Virginia 26506.   SUSAN LOGSDON-CONRADSEN • Department of Psychiatry, School of Medicine, Emory University, Atlanta, Georgia 30322.

Handbook of Psychotherapies with Children and Families, edited by Russ and Ollendick. Kluwer Academic/Plenum Publishers, New York, 1999.

developing empirically valid treatment approaches for children and adolescents with social phobia and related disorders. This chapter describes recent developments in the cognitive–behavioral treatment of social phobia in youth. In particular, we highlight two protocols that hold much promise in alleviating this common and serious anxiety disorder of youth. Social Effectiveness Therapy for Children (SET-C; Beidel, Turner, & Morris, 1996) is a protocol geared toward preadolescent children (ages 8 through 12), while Cognitive–Behavioral Group Treatment (CBGT-A; Albano, DiBartolo, Heimberg, & Barlow, 1995; Albano, Marten, Holt, Heimberg, & Barlow, 1995) is focused on adolescents with the disorder (ages 13–17). Both protocols are based on very similar cognitive–behavioral principles, and each gives unique attention to the cognitive–developmental level of the intended participants.

BASIC APPROACH

The prevailing psychosocial approach to understanding the etiology of social phobia (and anxiety disorders in general) is a combination of genetic and environmental variables, i.e., a diathesis–stress model of psychopathology (Rapee, 1997; Rosenbaum, Biederman, Hirshfeld, Bolduc, & Chaloff, 1991). The psychosocial model incorporates empirical findings from the extant literature, suggesting that behavioral inhibition in early childhood is a diathesis for social phobia and other anxiety disorders. This model further recognizes that the expression of anxiety symptoms is dependent on other factors including environmental variables (see Albano, Chorpita, & Barlow, 1996; Beidel & Turner, 1998) and selective attention to threat-related stimuli (see Kendall, 1992).

Behavioral theory provides a framework for addressing the environmental variables, or the "stress" component of the diathesis–stress hypothesis. Behavioral theory states that anxiety is acquired through learning processes including operant conditioning and modeling. Operant conditioning is the development of behavior as a result of reinforcement experiences. Of particular importance to anxiety disorders is the acquisition of a learned response to avoid anxiety-provoking situations. Consider the child who is fearful of speaking aloud in class. When the teacher asks a question, children who are not fearful and perhaps are sure of the correct response will raise their hands and wave in hopes of being called on to respond. The child with high levels of anxiety, and especially the child with social phobia, will avoid eye contact with the teacher and otherwise may try to appear "busy" or invisible. The teacher may then call on a more assertive student, and the socially anxious child succeeds in avoiding the spotlight. By avoiding this situation (answering aloud) the child or adolescent experiences a reduction in anxiety which is reinforcing. The child then learns to prevent a feared situation from occurring by continuing to avoid feared situations (e.g., continue to look away from the teacher; never raising a hand). Such behavioral responses are very persistent and resistant to change.

Another behavioral mechanism of transmission for anxiety is modeling, or observational learning. Research suggests that anxious behaviors can be learned in childhood by observing others behaving in a fearful way (Kendall, 1992). For example, in a study of adults with social phobia, Öst and Hughdahl (1981) found that 13% of their sample reported vicarious conditioning (modeling effects) as contributing to the onset of the disorder. Similarly, many of the adolescents with social phobia treated in our clinical programs deny having direct experience with being teased or humiliated in a social context. However, they vividly describe the blushing, tears, and trembling of peers who falter during social and evaluative situations, and report the fear that "this could happen to me!"

Several investigations have focused on the familial transmission of anxiety through the mechanism of observational learning and modeling. As compared with agoraphobic patients and control subjects, adult patients with social phobia recall their parents as more socially anxious, less sociable, and more overly concerned with the opinions of others (Bruch, 1989; Bruch & Heimberg, 1994; Bruch, Heimberg, Berger, & Collins, 1989). These findings were supported in a prospective study of 2708 children and adolescents (Caster, Bukowski, Inderbitzen, & Walters, 1996). Children identified with higher levels of social anxiety reported their parents as being overly concerned with the opinions of others and less sociable than did children with lower levels of social anxiety. Moreover, the children with high social anxiety thought their parents were socially isolating them and were ashamed of their poor performance and shyness. These studies indicate that the parents of socially anxious children may somehow be modeling or reinforcing anxious behavior.

Cognitive theories of anxiety focus on the schemas of anxious individuals. Schemas are defined as organized networks of information, developed through observational learning and personal experience, that are used to judge current situations. In essence, a schema is a "mental template of the world" that filters how information is processed (Kendall, 1992). Anxious individuals are believed to have a bias toward interpreting threat (a "threat schema") that causes a person to be overly sensitive to perceptions of danger or harm in an ambiguous situation. Indeed, anxiety is associated with self-focused preoccupation (e.g., "I can't do this," "I'm going to mess up") and misperception of environmental demands (interpreting ambiguous situations as threatening) (Kendall, 1992, 1993).

Interesting and innovative research suggests that a selective bias for threat may be modeled and/or reinforced by the parents of anxious children. Using a family behavioral test paradigm, Barrett, Rapee, Dadds, and Ryan (1994) demonstrated that family interactions influence a child's solution to an ambiguous problem. In their study, families with anxious, oppositional, and nonreferred children were presented with ambiguous situations and asked to agree on a solution. Initially, the children were presented with the situation independent of their parents and asked to give their solution; then the family met to discuss the situation and generate solutions; and finally, the children were again asked for a final solution after the parents had left the room. The results of this study clearly demonstrated that although the percentage of avoidant and aggressive responses decreased following family discussion in the nonclinic families, the converse was evident in the anxious and aggressive groups. That is, following family discussion, anxious children generated a greater percentage of avoidant responses, while aggressive children generated a greater percentage of aggressive solutions. Barrett and colleagues termed this phenomenon the family enhancement of anxious and aggressive responding (FEAR) effect. Additional research has supported these findings with clinically anxious youth (Chorpita, Albano, & Barlow, 1996).

This family behavioral test paradigm has been adapted to directly test the FEAR effect with social phobic youth (see Albano & Barlow, 1996; Albano, DiBartolo et al., 1995). As part of a larger treatment outcome study, adolescents receiving a principal diagnosis of social phobia were presented with ambiguous situations (see Box 1), asked to report how anxious they would be in each situation, and provide a plan for managing the situation. Parents were then invited into the room and left for 10 minutes to discuss with their adolescent ways to manage the situation. After the discussion, the adolescents were again asked for their anxiety rating and plan. Microanalyses of these family discussions are being conducted using the *Coding System for Parent–Child Interactions* (Logsdon-Conradsen, Jones, & Albano, 1996), a manual developed to analyze family interactions on an utterance by utterance basis. Preliminary results with a subsample of 23 families with social phobic adolescents lend support to the FEAR effect (Logsdon-Conradsen, 1998). Family interactions were characterized by frequent parental verbalizations and relatively less frequent adolescent verbalizations, suggesting a tendency for parents to control verbal interactions. Moreover, discussions were characterized by fewer problem solving statements than non problem solving statements. When suggestions were offered for how to manage the problem, these statements were predominantly unconstructive (e.g., focused on avoidance, questioning the problem, or questioning the adolescent's abilities in a neutral or negative manner). For the most part, despite being given the task of devising a solution for two different situations, the families of these social phobic youth spent more time discussing off-task issues than discussing problem-focused solutions. Overall, the family discussions did not diminish the adolescents' anxiety nor did they result in any significant change in postdiscussion plans. Thus, these results suggest that family interactions may have contributed to the maintenance of the level of the adolescents' subjective anxiety and avoidant plan of action.

Results of these family behavioral test studies are bringing to focus the manner in which anxiety is maintained in the family system. This research does not implicate parents as the cause of a child's social phobia. In fact, it is hypothesized that after years of watching a shy or socially anxious child struggle with fears of rejection and humiliation, the parents may have learned to reinforce avoidance so that the child is protected from further anxiety. The child's anxiety may be influencing the parents' natural tendency to protect and comfort the child, and so an unproductive and unhealthy interaction pattern evolves that serves to reinforce and maintain anxious avoidance and responding.

Box 1. Ambiguous Situations to Test the FEAR Effect in Social Phobic Youth

Situation 1: The Cafeteria Scene
You are in the school cafeteria with a group of kids. Some of them are popular, and you don't know them well. They are all making plans for getting together over the weekend. What would you do? How anxious would you feel?

Situation 2: An Oral Report
Your teacher has assigned an oral report. This is one of your most difficult subjects and the report will count heavily toward your final grade in the class. There are many popular kids in the class, and you don't know any of them well. The report can be on any subject that you want, but you don't know what to talk about. What would you do? How anxious would you feel?

To understand the current integrated cognitive–behavioral model of social phobia, one should consider the broad conceptualization of anxiety in general. Recognizing the interaction between biological, cognitive, and learning factors, Barlow (1991) proposed an integrated theory of emotion. This model considers depression and anxiety simultaneously, which is essential when investigating the etiology of anxiety because of the high co-occurrence (comorbidity) between the two disorders and the existence of a broad unitary construct of negative affect (Albano, Chorpita, & Barlow, 1996; Chorpita, Albano, & Barlow, 1998). Barlow's (1991) model of emotional disorders integrates the theoretical knowledge of depression and anxiety and provides a conceptualization of anxiety as a fusion of affective and cognitive components. These components are characterized by the individual's perception of uncontrollability, self-focused attention, and high negative affect (Barlow, 1991). According to this model, anxiety is differentiated from depression based on the degree of uncontrollability on the cognitive dimension; anxious individuals experience a feeling of limited control whereas depressed individuals experience a sense of no control. Generally, an anxious individual will attempt to establish control and if they are unsuccessful the anxiety may develop into depression.

Barlow's (1991) model adheres to the diathesis–stress theory of psychopathology. This model postulates an interaction between temperament (the diathesis) and stressful life circumstances that in turn influence a diffuse stress response. Consequently, the individual may obtain the sense that he or she has little control over his or her stress response, which generates a psychological vulnerability for the development of anxiety. Secondary factors, such as social support or coping strategies, then interact with this vulnerability by either diminishing or intensifying the vulnerability. On the other hand, if the individual perceives him- or herself as having control over environmental stressors, then anxiety symptoms will likely not develop. In essence, the proclivity for perceived stress to activate anxiety is dependent on the degree of control the individual experiences over these stressors (Chorpita & Barlow, 1995).

To summarize the cognitive–behavioral perspective, an individual's biological and psychological vulnerabilities to develop anxiety, interacting with direct and vicarious learning experiences with stressful and/or ambiguous social-evaluative situations, may result in the development of heightened social anxiety and social phobia. A vicious cycle of self-focused attention (negative, self-deprecatory statements) and increasing physiological arousal may interfere with appropriate coping and adequate functioning to contribute to social performance deficits (cf. Albano & Barlow, 1996). Avoidance of social situations becomes a learned response serving in the short term to decrease anxiety and arousal. Unfortunately, over the long term this style of responding results in missed opportunities for acquiring realistic information about perceived threats and the individual's ability to adapt and develop adequate coping skills. Through the active avoidance of perceived threatening situations, a child or adolescent will never learn to tolerate normal, appropriate levels of anxious arousal, nor will the child develop a realistic sense of the probability of experiencing a truly negative event (cf. Albano & Barlow, 1996). Thus, the vicious interaction of anxious arousal, negative thoughts, and active behavioral avoidance sets the child up for the development of long-term problems with social phobia.

Cognitive–behavioral therapy involves assisting an individual with accessing corrective information regarding threatening situations and stimuli, such that new and appropriate coping skills and strategies may be employed when confronting novel or potentially challenging situations. As such, cognitive–behavioral programs for the range of anxiety disorders are focused on intervening within each of the three components of anxiety, the cognitive, somatic, and behavioral components. Through psychoeducation, the child learns corrective information about the nature of his or her social phobia and the mechanisms by which it is maintained. Cognitive restructuring allows the older child and adolescent to identify and challenge anxious and unrealistic thoughts, and replace these thoughts with coping, proactive reasoning. Exposure is the key to effective treatments of anxiety disorders, and this is especially true with social phobia. Systematic within-session and *in vivo* homework exposure situations are constructed to address each child's fears. Also, specific skills deficits such as conversational and basic social skills, problem solving, and assertiveness skills are taught and reinforced through the exposure process. Finally, relapse prevention methods are utilized to assist the child with maintaining and consolidating treatment gains. Overall, cognitive–behavioral programs allow the child or adolescent to access new and adaptive behaviors for managing anxiety and daily challenges.

DESCRIPTION OF THE DISORDER

The fourth edition of the *Diagnostic and Statistical Manual of Mental Disorders* (DSM-IV; American Psychiatric Association, 1994) defines social phobia as "a marked and persistent fear of one or more social or performance situations in which the person is exposed to unfamiliar people or to possible scrutiny by others (and) the individual fears that he or she will act in a way that will be humiliating or embarrassing" (p. 416). When the individual is exposed to the feared situation, he or she becomes anxious and the feared situation is either avoided or endured under extreme distress or anxiety. Children may react with crying, tantrums, or by freezing with fear. In addition, children and adolescents with the disorder may shrink from contact with unfamiliar persons, thus interfering with the establishment of new friendships and social relations. Other diagnostic criteria are that the individual recognizes that the fear is excessive, and that the fear and avoidance causes significant interference in the person's life. Recognition of the excessive nature of this fear is not necessary to make the diagnosis in youth. When compared with individuals with other anxiety disorders (e.g., generalized anxiety disorder or panic disorder), persons with social phobia are more concerned about social failure and negative evaluation. This fear of negative evaluation is the distinguishing diagnostic characteristic of social phobia (Chambless & Gillis, 1993).

Social phobia is particularly underresearched in children and adolescents, and has only recently begun to be empirically investigated (Albano, 1995; Albano, Chorpita, & Barlow, 1996; Francis, Last, & Strauss, 1992; Last, Perrin, Hersen, & Kazdin, 1992; Strauss & Last, 1993). As such, social phobia is one of the more common principal diagnoses in children who present for treatment (Albano, Chorpita, & Barlow, 1996; Chapman, Mannuza, & Fyer, 1995; Last et al., 1992; Vasey, 1995). Further, it is believed that social phobia may be underreported and undertreated in children because, like many of the internalizing disorders, the symptoms may not be easily recognized as evidence of a psychological disorder (Albano, DiBartolo, et

al., 1995). This disorder has an onset in early adolescence (11.3 years), rarely re-
mits, and is represented equally in males and females (Davidson, Hughes, George,
& Blazer, 1993; Last et al., 1992; Vasey, 1995). The finding that social phobia is more
common in adolescence corresponds to the developmental age related social fears
in nonclinical child populations. It is in adolescence that anxieties about school
and social activities increase (King, 1995; Strauss & Last, 1993).

Social phobia causes impairment in the individual's social, academic, and occupational functioning (Rapee, 1995). For instance, children and adolescents with
this disorder may avoid taking classes or joining extracurricular activities that require public speaking or interacting with strangers; they also avoid social gatherings,
which prevents them from making friends. In children and adolescents, the social
avoidance also prevents the person from dating, making friends, participating in
sports, speaking up in class, and joining social or academic groups. Consequently,
adolescents with social phobia meet age-specific developmental challenges such as
employment and dating later than peers (Albano, Chorpita, & Barlow, 1996). Moreover, individuals with social phobia are generally submissive in relationships and
are viewed by their peers as being likely targets of ridicule, isolation, and aggression
(Davidson et al., 1993; Walters, Cohn, & Inderbitzen, 1996).

During feared situations, youth with social phobia are excessively concerned
about being rejected or negatively evaluated and their thoughts are characterized
by negative self-depreciation and physiological symptoms (Albano, DiBartolo, et
al., 1995; Albano, Marten, et al., 1995). Often anticipatory anxiety occurs well before the feared social event creating negative cognitions and expectations, which
can in turn negatively affect the individual's performance in the social situation.
The negative performance (either perceived or real) thus reinforces the individual's fear of negative evaluation and enhances anxiety, creating a vicious cycle (Albano & Barlow, 1996; American Psychiatric Association, 1994).

There are other negative associated features of social phobia. Such individuals often have low self-esteem, are hypersensitive to criticism and rejection, feel
inferior, and are nonassertive. They tend to have poor social networks, under-
achieve in school and work, and have poor social skills (Albano, Chorpita, & Barlow, 1996; Rapee, 1995). Social phobia is also associated with increased suicide
attempts, poor medical health, lack of social support, poor occupational performance, and antisocial behavior (Davidson et al., 1993; Rapee, 1995). Moreover, social phobia in adults is often accompanied by other disorders including
generalized anxiety disorder, mood disorders, simple phobia, substance abuse,
body dysmorphic disorder, avoidant personality disorder, schizophrenia/schizo-
phreniform disorder, and obsessive-compulsive personality disorder (Davidson et
al., 1993; Nordman, Herbert, Kadish, & Kopyt, 1996; Sanderson, DiNardo, Rapee,
& Barlow, 1990; Schneier, Johnson, Hornig, Liebowitz, & Weissman, 1992; Turner,
Beidel, Borden, Stanley, & Jacob, 1991).

Research with children and adolescents has also found high rates of comorbidity among social phobia and other DSM-III-R anxiety disorders (Brady &
Kendall, 1992; Last et al., 1992; Last, Strauss, & Francis, 1987; Perrin & Last, 1995).
Albano, Chorpita, DiBartolo, and Barlow (1996) investigated comorbidity using
DSM-III-R criteria in 174 children and adolescents (aged 7 to 17) referred to an anxiety disorders clinic. Diagnostic categories with fewer than 10 subjects were omitted, resulting in a sample of 138 subjects. The results of this study indicated

extensive comorbidity: 31% of the subjects met criteria for two diagnoses, 20% met criteria for three diagnoses, 15% met criteria for four or more diagnoses, while 34% only met criteria for one diagnosis. Of the sample of 138 subjects, 30% received a principal diagnosis of social phobia. Of the children diagnosed with social phobia, 29% received no additional diagnosis, 26% received one additional diagnosis, 26% received two additional diagnoses, and 19% received three or more diagnoses. The most frequent comorbid diagnoses with the social phobic sample were overanxious disorder (43%), simple phobia (26%), and mood disorder (19%).

In addition, social phobia often precedes the development of several psychological disorders including panic disorder, mood disorders, substance-related disorders, somatization disorder, and agoraphobia (American Psychiatric Association, 1994). In particular, research indicates that children with social phobia are at a high risk for developing major depression (Last et al., 1992) and substance abuse disorders (Kessler et al., 1994). As such, social phobia tends to have a chronic course and individuals rarely recover (Davidson et al., 1993). Thus, when left untreated the potential consequences of social phobia are broad, impacting the emotional, occupational, and social functioning of the individual over the long term. Consequently, social phobia in children and adolescents is an area in need of much research.

DESCRIPTION OF THE PROCEDURES TO BE USED

Behavioral assessment is the cornerstone of behavior therapy (Barrios & Hartmann, 1988), and as such any treatment program begins with a comprehensive assessment of the child's functioning. Assessment is critical for the accurate identification of behaviors or symptoms to target for change, and for devising ideographic plans for each child. Although the prevailing thought is to adhere to a prescriptive treatment approach, which essentially means to prescribe the appropriate empirically supported treatment to fit the diagnostic picture, clinicians must also pay careful attention to each child's individual needs and unique clinical presentation. A behavioral diagnostic assessment will provide a true diagnostic picture, an evaluation of the child's behavioral excesses and deficits, strengths and weaknesses, along with giving the clinician quantifiable data from which to track treatment progress and evaluate outcome.

Assessment Methods

Establishing pretreatment markers of functioning and behavioral limits permits a thorough evaluation of the three components of anxiety, and allows the clinician and children to identify patterns of responding to anxiety-provoking situations. Periodic follow-up assessments provide information on the child's functioning in the long term, along with tests of the efficacy of the treatment program. A summary of suggested assessment methods follows.

Diagnostic Interview

The Anxiety Disorders Interview Schedule for DSM-IV, Child and Parent Versions (ADIS-IV; Silverman & Albano, 1996a,b) allows for the accurate differential diagnosis among the anxiety disorders, affective disorders, and externalizing disorders in youth aged 6 to 17, while also screening for additional problems such as learning and developmental disorders, substance abuse, psychotic symptomatology, eating disorders, and somatoform disorders. Diagnoses are derived separately for the child interview, parent interview, and then combined based on specific guidelines to form the composite diagnosis (Albano & Silverman, 1996). The ADIS-IV allows for the identification of the principal diagnosis (most severe/disabling condition), along with any comorbid conditions. Each diagnosis is assigned a Clinician Severity Rating (CSR) based on a nine-point scale (range 0–8). Diagnoses assigned a CSR of 4 or above are considered clinically significant and warrant intervention. Reliability estimates and psychometric properties of the DSM-III-R version of the ADIS for children are reported in Albano and Silverman (1996). Research is under way evaluating the present DSM-IV version of the interview.

Self-Report Measures

Only two self-report measures have been developed specifically for assessing social anxiety in youth. The *Social Phobia and Anxiety Inventory for Children* (SPAI-C; Beidel et al., 1995) is a 26-item inventory most appropriate for children aged 8 through 14, and assesses anxiety in a variety of social settings. Separate items measure the cognitive, somatic, and behavioral components of social anxiety, thus providing the clinician with an excellent empirically derived measure of the broad construct of social phobia. Items are scored on a three-point Likert scale, with total scores above 18 indicating a need for a detailed diagnostic evaluation. Beidel and Turner (1998) report excellent psychometric support for the scale, and a parent version of the measure is presently under development.

The Social Anxiety Scale for Children–Revised (SASC-R; LaGreca, 1998; LaGreca & Stone, 1993) is composed of 22 items assessing three specific factors: fear of negative evaluation, social avoidance and distress in new situations, and social avoidance and distress in general. The SASC-R is available in both child and adolescent versions. Three- and five-point rating formats are available, although LaGreca (1988) recommends the latter because of better reliability estimates based on this scaling method. The SASC-R has excellent internal consistency and test–retest reliability. Ginsburg, LaGreca, and Silverman (1997a,b) evaluated the scale with a sample of children diagnosed with anxiety disorders. Results suggest the SASC-R is a promising instrument for screening children and adolescents to identify socially based anxiety disorders, and to evaluate social impairment in youngsters in general. Parent versions are also available for both child and adolescent versions.

Behavioral Test (BAT)

Standardized individual behavioral tests can be utilized to assess the behavioral limits of youth with social phobia, and provide an observable index of clinical change. These tasks can be devised on an individual basis, using the child's fear and avoidance hierarchy items, or standardized for comparison across groups. Two standardized behavioral tests were developed for a controlled clinical trial investigating social phobia in adolescents (see Albano & Barlow, 1996; Albano,

DiBartolo, et al., 1995), a brief oral presentation and an interpersonal interaction with a same-gender confederate. During each BAT, the adolescent reports a subjective units of distress (SUDS) rating (on a 0 to 100) scale at 1-minute intervals. At the conclusion of the task the adolescent is asked to list up to six thoughts that he or she recalls having during the task and rate his or her overall performance. Heart rate or other physiological measures can also be taken during the BAT. Such measures provide an index of change within the specific anxiety response domains.

Treatment Measures. In addition to the pretreatment assessment battery, several specific indices of change may be taken throughout the treatment process.

Self-Monitoring

Children and adolescents can be assigned a continuous self-monitoring diary, where they track social situations encountered in their everyday lives and their response to such situations across the three components of anxiety (see Beidel & Turner, 1998). Diary forms can be open ended or structured, depending on the developmental level of the child. Research demonstrates that children as young as 8 can use a continuous self-monitoring task, such as the diary, if the task is structured according to the child's developmental level (Beidel, Neal, & Lederer, 1991). The diary provides a method of direct and immediate feedback about treatment effectiveness, in addition to identifying problem situations that can then be addressed in session.

Fear and Avoidance Hierarchies

An ideographic fear and avoidance hierarchy (FAH) can also be devised for each child, and administered on a weekly basis. The FAH operationally defines the "top ten" social phobic situations for the child or adolescent, which serves as a measure of treatment progress and provides specific targets for behavioral exposures. Each item is rated separately for level of fear and degree of avoidance on a 0 (not at all) to 8 (extreme) scale. The FAH provides an ecologically valid method of defining the behavioral limits of the child's social phobia. In addition, parents can also complete the FAH, providing further data and a more comprehensive overview of the child's functioning.

Treatment Procedures

Cognitive–behavioral treatment of social phobia in youth incorporates education, skill building, cognitive restructuring, and both within- and between-session exposure to anxiety-provoking social situations. In addition, SET-C involves peer-pairing, a method by which nonphobic youth interact with and assist the children in therapy. Brief descriptions of the individual treatment components for SET-C and CBGT-A are presented below.

Education

Accurate information about the nature of anxiety and its three components (cognitive, physiological, behavioral) is presented to increase awareness and understanding about the initiation and maintenance of anxiety. Self-monitoring, in the form of a daily diary and additional specific homework assignments, are assigned to facilitate the identification of social anxiety cues, specific thoughts, and avoidance behavior.

Skill Building

Cognitive Restructuring. In CBGT-A, adolescents are taught to identify cognitive distortions ("errors in thinking") that perpetuate the vicious cycle of anxiety. A process of evaluating these negative thoughts through the use of dispute handles and rationale responding is then presented. Thus, adolescents are taught to devise rational thoughts for anxiety-provoking situations based on a realistic appraisal of the social situation. Therapists rely on modeling, role-playing, and systematic exposure exercises to train the youth in acquiring this skill. Although cognitive restructuring is not a fixed component of SET-C, Beidel and Turner (1998) advise the therapist to flexibly apply these methods where indicated. Children with less developed cognitive abilities (e.g., those in the concrete operational stage) may not necessarily profit from this procedure. However, Kendall's Coping Cat program (1994) provides an age-appropriate format for leading younger children through cognitive restructuring steps. These procedures are easily incorporated into the SET-C protocol.

Social Skills. Social skills training is incorporated into SET-C and CBGT-A as a fixed component. It is hypothesized that some social phobic youth present with deficient social skills because of lack of practice and/or insufficient opportunity to acquire and practice the skill stemming from behavioral avoidance (Albano, 1995; Beidel & Turner, 1998). Following a careful assessment of the individual's skill level, social skills training may be applied for interpersonal interactions, maintenance of relationships, and assertiveness through modeling, role-playing, and peer-pairing methods (see below).

Problem Solving. CBGT-A also provides a component geared toward teaching a "coping template" to identify general problem situations and develop realistic ways to manage such situations. It is again hypothesized that phobic youth may have limited experience in dealing with difficult situations through the use of proactive plans. Problems such as being teased, time pressures, conflict with siblings or parents, and the like can be addressed through this component of treatment.

Exposure

Both SET-C and CBGT-A incorporate systematic exposure procedures to facilitate treatment progress. Indeed, exposure may be the hallmark of behavioral treatments for phobic disorders. In both SET-C and CBGT-A, exposures directly target the cognitive component and behavioral avoidance of anxiety, while demonstrating to the children that the sensations of anxiety will dissipate through habituation. Maintenance and generalization are promoted through the assignment of between-session homework exposures or programmed practice. SET-C also makes use of imaginal exposure to social anxiety provoking cues. In using imaginal exposure, Beidel and Turner (1998) caution that the individual child's "core fear" must be identified and is the crucial element of success for this procedure.

Parent Involvement

At present, parents are actively involved in selected treatment sessions in the CBGT-A protocol, although we are evaluating the relative impact of their involvement in our continuing research. Parental involvement is minimal and focused on providing education about the disorder and encouraging the parents to coach their adolescents in applying their skills between sessions and after termination. SET-C relies on parental involvement mostly through homework assignments, where parents facilitate the design and implementation of these structured interaction tasks. Given the support for the FEAR effect in families of anxious children, the goal of including parents is to break any maladaptive communication styles and teach more healthy, independent means of functioning to the youth and their parents.

Overall Program Structure

SET-C involves 24 treatment sessions held over a 12-week period. Each child participates in one group social skills training session and one individual exposure session each week. Structured homework assignments provide an extension of the within-session experience to the child's real life. The SET-C program relies on parent involvement as needed for assistance with conducting the homework assignments. Peer helpers are recruited to participate in the program on a regular basis. Following each social skills training session, the child with social phobia and a nonanxious peer are sent on an outing lasting 90 minutes. Outings occur at various age-appropriate social settings, such as pizza parlors, skating rinks, and the beach. These peer-assisted outings provide the social phobic child with a direct opportunity to practice using the skills learned in group with a nonanxious peer. Nonanxious peers are usually matched for age with the social phobic child, and are instructed in confidentiality issues. Otherwise, these youth are given minimal training and instructions and are simply told to talk with the child who is "shy," include the child in the arranged activity, and to help the child have fun (Beidel & Turner, 1998).

CBGT-A involves 16 sessions, each 90 minutes in length, administered by two trained cotherapists. Groups are usually coed and have four to six adolescents in attendance. Sessions are tapered in frequency, such that Sessions 1 through 4 occur over the first 2 weeks, Sessions 5 through 11 occur weekly, and Sessions 12 through 16 are held every other week. Phase I involves eight sessions of skills training and psychoeducation, whereas Phase II is comprised of eight exposure sessions. Participants are provided with structured experience during these within-session exposures to practice their skills and confront difficult social situations. Homework assignments are utilized as a mechanism to foster generalization and maintenance of treatment gains.

MAJOR MECHANISMS OF CHANGE

In one word, *exposure* is the key to successful treatment of social phobia. Empirical studies of adults with social phobia point to the overall significance and effectiveness of exposure-based methods for prompting and maintaining clinical change. Support for this statement may be found in summary chapters of relevant reviews and meta-analytic studies in Beidel and Turner (1998) and Heimberg, Leibowitz, Hope, and Schneier (1995). Exposure alone has been found superior to cognitive–behavioral packages or control conditions (Feske & Chambless, 1995) in adults. To date, no systematic study of the relative contribution of treatment components found in SET-C or CBGT-A has been conducted. However, the available literature attests to the effectiveness of behavioral treatment strategies involving imaginal, assisted, simulated, and *in vivo* exposure for the range of phobic disorders in youth (see Barrios & O'Dell, 1989, for a review).

RESEARCH SUPPORT FOR EFFICACY

The SET-C and CBGT-A programs for treatment of social phobia in youth were originally developed based on empirical support for the cognitive–behavioral treatment of shyness in youth and social phobia in adults. SET-C is a developmentally sensitive protocol based on the original adult version of Social Effectiveness Therapy (SET; Turner, Beidel, & Cooley, 1994). Beidel and Turner (1998) report on the preliminary effectiveness of the SET-C program with 16 social phobic children. Self-reported social anxiety, as measured by the SPAI-C, showed a significant decrease following the 12-week program. These results were supported by a significant decrease in parent ratings of their children on the internalizing scale of the Child Behavior Checklist. Furthermore, behavioral test data indicated a significant improvement in the children's social interaction skills and oral reading skills, along with a concurrent reduction from pretreatment in subjective anxiety ratings. The SET-C program is currently being evaluated in a controlled clinical trial.

Cognitive–behavioral group treatment for social phobia in adolescents (CBGT-A) has at its empirical roots the successful treatment of adult social phobia (Heimberg, Salzman, Holt, & Blendell, 1993). The multicomponent CBGT protocol developed by Heimberg and colleagues consists of cognitive restructuring, exposure to simulated phobic events, and systematic homework assignments involving the application of techniques taught in group. This treatment program has been demonstrated to result in significant improvement on various cognitive, behavioral, and self-report measures in adults (see Hope & Heimberg, 1993, for a review). Gains are typically maintained throughout long-term follow-up (Heimberg, Dodge, Hope, Kennedy, & Zollo, 1990; Heimberg et al., 1993). Taking into consideration the developmental differences between adolescents and adults, Albano and colleagues adopted the CBGT program for application with youth. Specifically, a significant literature attests to the effectiveness of behavioral social skills training for shy adolescents (Christoff, Scott, Kelley, Baer, & Kelly, 1985; Franco, Christoff, Crimmins, & Kelley, 1983). It is hypothesized that social phobic adolescents are deficient in specific skills necessary for negotiating social situations and more general problematic situations (Albano, 1995). Thus, social skills and problem-solving skills training were incorporated into CBGT-A.

Albano, Marten, et al. (1995) report on a pilot investigation of the CBGT-A protocol with five adolescents. At 3 months posttreatment, social phobia had remitted to subclinical levels for four of the five adolescents. One-year follow-up indicated that four adolescents were completely remitted of the social phobia, with the fifth adolescent reporting only subclinical symptoms. Behavioral test data indicated that despite continued physiological arousal (heart rate), the adolescents reported lower subjective ratings of anxiety during two behavioral tasks. Their reports of negative cognitions during these tasks decreased significantly across the follow-up period, whereas neutral (task oriented or nonnegative) thoughts increased. Currently, the CBGT-A program is undergoing empirical study in several controlled clinical trials.

CASE EXAMPLES

Description

"These are the worst times of my life."

Kathy, a 15-year-old Caucasian female who attended a private all-girls school, was referred to our program for anxious youth by her school counselor. Although she had attended this school for both ninth and tenth grades, Kathy was observed by the teachers to be "a loner," often off by herself, and extremely quiet and shy. Her written classwork and homework were always rated as excellent, but Kathy consistently was penalized on her semester grades by a failure to volunteer answers or otherwise participate in class discussions and presentations. Also, the school staff noticed that Kathy often secluded herself during lunch period, and she at times looked as though she had been crying. Attempts by her teachers to speak with her were met with visible signs of anxiety (e.g., trembling, looking away) and denial of any problems.

Diagnosis and Assessment

As part of our standard intake procedure, Kathy and her parents were administered the ADIS-IV (Silverman & Albano, 1996a,b). The ADIS-IV provides separate, semistructured interviews for the child and parent, with decision rules for combining information from these sources to form a composite diagnostic picture. Kathy had difficulty with discussing her concerns openly with the interviewer, although the task was made easier by use of the "feelings thermometer," a pictorial representation of increasing levels of "mercury" (Albano & Silverman, 1996). This thermometer measures the degree of a feeling, symptom, or perceived distress and interference on a 0 to 8 scale. For socially anxious children and adolescents, the thermometer provides a means of reporting emotions that are otherwise difficult to express. During the interview, Kathy reported significant levels of fear in most social situations, along with a corresponding strategy of avoiding these situations as often as possible. Thus, on inquiry, Kathy admitted to eating her lunch in a bathroom stall to avoid the highly socially charged atmosphere of the cafeteria. She had never attended any extracurricular activity. Most troubling during the school day were any unstructured situations where someone might try to speak with her (e.g., hanging out by her locker, walking through the halls, waiting for class to begin), formal speaking situations such as oral reports, and her fear of embarrassing herself in front of others. With her eyes downcast and on the verge of tears, Kathy reported to the interviewer that "these are the worst times" of her life.

Kathy's parents provided further information about the extent of her social phobia. For instance, they reported that Kathy never answers the telephone, does not like to eat in public and often will not order for herself in restaurants, and that she retreats to her bedroom when visitors come to the home. They described Kathy as "a very good kid, always shy, but very bright and polite to others." Interestingly, Kathy's parents were becoming increasingly concerned about her, because they had expected her to begin dating and wanting to learn to drive, just like her older sister had done at this age. Moreover, despite being offered a part-time position in her uncle's grocery store, Kathy refused the job. Her parents had suspected that she was too shy to interact with customers, and also may be fearful of running the register. Based on this information, Kathy was diagnosed with social phobia at a clinical severity level of 8 (on a 0 to 8 scale), indicating severe disability/distress and interference in functioning.

Following the diagnostic interview, Kathy and the therapist devised an individual fear and avoidance hierarchy (FAH) of her ten most troubling social situations (Table 1). The FAH situations were rated from 0 to 8 for degree of distress and degree of attempted avoidance. These situations became the focus of Kathy's behavioral exposures, and her ratings provided information about treatment progress and outcome. Kathy's parents gave independent ratings of these situations at both pre- and posttreatment. As part of our standard assessment package for social phobic youth, Kathy also participated in an individual behavioral test (BAT). Kathy was given the instruction to "carry on a conversation on any topic or topics" with a female graduate student assistant. During the 8-minute interaction, Kathy was asked to report her subjective rating of anxiety (0–8 SUDS scale) at 60-second intervals. Following the BAT, Kathy was asked to list up to six thoughts that occurred to her during the interaction (Table 2), while the confederate and two independent observers (viewing from behind a one-way mirror) rated Kathy's social skills on a variety of dimensions. At the conclusion of treatment Kathy participated in this same BAT, but with a novel confederate.

Treatment Progress

Kathy participated in 16 sessions of CBGT-A, following the protocol with parent participation as described in the procedures section of this chapter. The first phase of treatment (Sessions 1 through 8, skill building modules) was particularly

Table 1. Kathy's Fear and Avoidance Hierarchy (FAH)

Situation	Pre		Post	
	Fear	Avoid	Fear	Avoid
1. Answering the telephone	4	8	3	1
2. Ordering food in a restaurant	5	7	2	1
3. Eating in the cafeteria at lunchtime, but not necessarily speaking to anyone	7	8	2	2
4. Smiling and saying hello to a classmate	7	7	1	1
5. Asking a classmate for the homework assignments	7	8	2	3
6. Eating in the cafeteria, and saying hello to the girls at the table (and speaking to them if they address me)	8	8	4	2
7. Volunteering to answer a question in class	8	8	4	4
8. Giving an oral report	8	8	4	4
9. Calling up a classmate just to talk	8	8	3	4
10. Asking a classmate to get together just for fun	8	8	4	4

SUDS ratings: 0–8 for pre- and posttreatment.

Table 2. Self-Reported Cognitions for Kathy during the Pre- and Posttreatment Behavioral Test

Pretreatment thought listing	Posttreatment thought listing
I don't know what to say.	I've never met this girl before.
My mind was just blank.	I wonder if she works here.
I feel like a jerk.	This wasn't as bad as the first time.
This is just like at school.	She seems nice.
I hate this.	What does she think of me?
I want to go home.	I can't really know what she thinks unless she tells me.

Note: Task involves listing up to six thoughts that occurred during the behavioral task of having to speak with a female confederate.

difficult and challenging for Kathy. She reported to her parents feeling very self-conscious sitting in a room with other kids, some of whom were boys, and was afraid of being called on to discuss her fears and feelings. Kathy complained of stomachaches and made attempts to avoid group, although her parents succeeded in talking her through her anxieties and agreeing each week to attend group. The therapists described Kathy as "avoiding eye contact, sitting with her hair hanging down in front of her face, and speaking only in a whisper when called upon." Thus, the therapists decided to shape Kathy's behavior with less direct methods, such as by having one of the cotherapists sit next to her, and engaging her in minimal conversation at the start or end of each group. As the other group members began to discuss their social fears and corresponding avoidance behaviors, Kathy displayed overt evidence of her interest in the group. She would smile and shake her head ever so slightly in agreement of a peer's report. Gradually, Kathy began looking at whichever individual was speaking in group, and stopped turning her eyes away from the gaze of others. Kathy's participation in the short, structured tasks of these early sessions, along with the less formal tasks of the scheduled snack time (break), appeared to become less difficult for her over the course of this first phase of treatment. That is, she began to look at the therapists during group, stopped turning away when an activity was at hand, and she spoke out spontaneously to answer questions toward the sixth session of the protocol. Moreover, although Kathy did not complete any assigned homework during the first three sessions, she turned in complete homework beginning in Session 4, and was offering to discuss her work by Session 6. Each of these behaviors was taken as a sign of her increased participation and growing comfort with this group program.

During Phase II, Kathy participated in six behavioral exposures as the "identified" target, and eight additional exposures as a role player or "extra." Her behavioral goals for each exposure are summarized in Table 3. As noted there, goals are specified as observable by others and quantifiable. Exposures were arranged to be increasingly challenging to test and refine Kathy's skills. For example, during the initial exposures for oral reading the group members were instructed to pay attention and smile at Kathy. After gaining experience with giving an oral report, Kathy's exposure was "heated up" by having the group members giggle, look away, and leave the room during her talk. Also, a question and answer period was added to the exposure, where she had to field questions from her audience. These exposures more realistically simulated the classroom experience that she had come to

Table 3. Behavioral Goals for Kathy's Simulated Exposures

For conversation exposures
   Introduce myself and say hello
   Ask the person three questions
   Keep eye contact for most of the time
   Keep my hair out of my face
   Smile when appropriate
   Speak louder than my usual voice
For the telephone exposure
   Say hello, and identify myself
   Speak clearly and into the phone
   Answer all the questions asked of me, in sentences if possible
For the oral report exposure
   Keep my hair out of my face
   Look up at the audience at least three times
   Speak clearly
   Do not rush through the report
   Speak loudly
More advanced oral report exposure
   When finished, pause, look at the audience, and wait for a question
   Look at the person who is asking a question
   Answer in a loud voice

fear and avoid. However, by engaging in the exposure situation, Kathy was able to utilize her cognitive restructuring skills and focus her attention on the task, thus decreasing her subjective anxiety. The goal of such heated exposures is to demonstrate that despite what others do, an individual can have control over her or his own behavior and emotions, and as such one can manage less than desirable situations. Immediately posttreatment, Kathy's FAH ratings had dropped significantly for the majority of situations. An independent diagnostic assessment revealed the diagnosis to be in partial remission (CSR=4). Of note, Kathy had accepted the position in her uncle's store, and had joined a school service club at our suggestion. These activities were suggested to provide Kathy with a wider breadth of experience in social and evaluative situations. At 6 months posttreatment, Kathy and her parents reported continued improvement in all areas of functioning. She no longer avoided the cafeteria, and had begun to invite several peers to accompany her on age-appropriate outings (e.g., movies, mall). Although in direct evaluative situations (e.g., oral reports, volunteering an answer) Kathy reports continued anxiety, she no longer feels the need to avoid such situations, and has taken to writing in her diary about the actual outcomes of these experiences. The diary was initiated by Kathy as a reminder of her continuing growth and progress. Kathy also reported feeling more optimistic about both her immediate and distant future to her former therapists.

Description

"No one likes me now, and no one ever will."

Michael, a Caucasian male, was referred to our clinic by his high school counselor. Fifteen years old, he was enrolled in the ninth grade of a local public school, and was considered an overachiever by all school reports. However, since the sixth grade Michael had experienced significant problems with peers, and disliked attending school because of "certain kids' attitudes." Specifically, Michael was referred to our clinic as a result of a 4-year history of worry and anxiety centering primarily on social situations and academic competencies. It was reported that Michael had significant problems managing school and peer-related stress since the fifth grade. Despite being an honor roll student, Michael reported severe social anxiety accompanied by a strive for perfectionism. By his own report, these anxieties interfered with his ability to get along with the other students, such as on cooperative class projects. Moreover, despite having excellent grades, less than "perfect" performance on tests caused Michael considerable distress and feelings of failure.

Diagnosis and Assessment

During the ADIS-IV interview, Michael reported severe levels of social anxiety in situations where he may be noticed or teased. Talking in front of the class, group situations at school, and social functions such as dances caused him considerable anxiety and fear. These fears were reinforced when Michael was the target of teasing by certain other peers. He further reported being oversensitive to anticipated rejection by others, such that he often cried in middle school, and hence became an easy target by the school bullies. Michael avoided most school situations, especially those that may have exposed him to peer pressure and scrutiny. In addition to his social phobic concerns, Michael reported several pervasive and uncontrollable worries that were accompanied by physiological symptoms and distress (stomachaches, muscle aches, irritability, sleep disturbance). His worries spanned a number of areas including the future, his health, his friends' problems, and fears of death and dying.

The report of Michael's parents was largely consistent with his self-report. According to his parents, Michael has two friends whom he occasionally sees outside of school, and these boys were themselves the object of teasing by others. Their main concern for Michael was his oversensitivity to rejection, and his strive to be perfect in every aspect of social and academic functioning. Based on the ADIS-IV, Michael received co-principal diagnoses of social phobia and generalized anxiety disorder, with equal clinician severity ratings of 7 (very severe).

Michael's FAH outlined his ten most troubling social and performance situations (Table 4). As seen, these situations centered on social and performance situations, and excluded his concerns with perfectionism. It was decided to first treat Michael for his social phobia with CBGT-A, and then follow this treatment with an individualized program for generalized anxiety disorder.

Treatment Progress

Michael participated in all 16 CBGT-A group sessions, and his parents likewise attended all parent sessions of the program. From the onset of the program, Michael was overly involved, very talkative, and domineering of conversations. His solicited and unsolicited comments (which were made significantly more often than not) were often negative and discouraging to others. It became obvious very early in the program that social skills deficits were predominant in Michael's behavior, and probably a contributing factor to his ongoing problems with peers.

Table 4. Michael's Fear and Avoidance Hierarchy (FAH)

Situation	Pre		Post	
	Fear	Avoid	Fear	Avoid
1. Hanging out by the lockers or in the hallway	6	8	4	6
2. Being assigned to work with a group of kids in class	6	2	4	0
3. Giving an oral report and making a mistake	8	3	6	0
4. Being in the same room or the cafeteria with the guys who tease people	8	8	6	4
5. Sitting at a table in the cafeteria, in the middle of the room	8	8	3	3
6. Saying no to someone who wants to borrow my papers or homework	8	4	4	2
7. Attending an after-school pep rally alone	8	8	3	2
8. Riding the school bus home	8	8	3	0
9. Calling up a classmate for homework	8	8	2	2
10. Changing in the locker room for gym class	8	8	4	2

SUDS ratings: 0–8 for pre- and posttreatment.

Also, Michael approached the world with a very discouraged and negative outlook. Thus, even neutral topics (such as current television shows, music, the weather) were discussed in a very negative and depressing way. In essence, Michael was not projecting an open and friendly manner to the group members, and to his peers at large.

Considerable effort was expended in modifying Michael's behavior through the use of differential reinforcement, direct feedback, skills training, and behavioral practice. A typical exposure involved having Michael engage in a conversation with a peer, with the instructions to not speak a negative word or phrase. These response prevention procedures proved valuable to Michael, in that he was forced to focus on more positive or neutral topics and statements. Additionally, the group members began to challenge him by bringing up more charged topics of conversation (e.g., local sports rivalries). With clear instructions and rehearsal of social skills during the exposure phase of treatment, Michael was able to be more socially appropriate during group. Assisting Michael with managing teasing was accomplished by having a confederate (graduate student) tease him at the intensity and with the same content used by his schoolmates. We opted to use a confederate, rather than have any group member engage in such negative behavior. Michael was taught to ignore the insults, look briefly into the bully's eyes, and turn away with a bored look. This is our typical advice for teasing, to effect an extinction paradigm on the offenders. However, we did instruct Michael and the other group members to report any situation where they feel physically threatened, or situations where sexual harassment or intense teasing occurs. However, the nature of Michael's teasing was largely typical of adolescents, and not considered truly vindictive by his parents or school personnel. Michael was successful in using these procedures (ignoring) in school and related settings, and reported satisfaction with his progress in this area.

Based on the reports by Michael and his parents, he benefited somewhat by the treatment program. As noted in Table 4, Michael reported decreased fear and avoidance of a number of social and evaluative situations. At treatment end, Michael's social phobia was assessed at a lesser level (CSR=4), although his generalized anxiety disorder remained at a higher level of severity (CSR=7). His pervasive worry and accompanying somatic symptoms most likely interfered with his ability to apply the coping skills learned in group to a wider area of his functioning. Because of his continued symptoms, individual treatment for generalized anxiety disorder was initiated. Michael's case illustrates the potential problem of treatment success as a result of issues of comorbidity and pervasive worry. At present, Michael participates in an individualized cognitive–behavioral therapy program for his pervasive anxiety concerns.

TREATMENT OF SOCIAL PHOBIA IN THE ERA OF MANAGED CARE

What is obvious to anyone who has been involved in the health care field within the past 10 years is that the United States is ushering in a new era of reform via managed health care. Changes in the health care system have been publicized mainly by the Health Security Act proposed by President Clinton in 1993 (S. 1757/H.R. 3600, 1993). Public demands to ensure each and every American receive adequate health care coverage have resulted in enormous political pressures to both decrease the cost of health care and increase the effectiveness of the care provided. Indeed, statistics tell us that the United States spends in excess of 12% of its gross domestic product on health care costs, and the cost continues to rise (Hirschfeld, 1995). General practitioners are witnessing firsthand the effects of such federal and state reform. What still remains to be determined, however, is the role that the mental health care field will play in this new era of managed health care.

One of the primary worries of those in the mental health care field is that crucial reform decisions will be based somewhat on biased or erroneous assumptions about the field. This concern is based partially on the fact that mental health professionals are often left out of the executive processes that precipitate health care reform. There are numerous examples of erroneous assumptions impeding a smooth transition of mental health care into the managed health care arena. Among the most blatant assumptions leading the system reform are the reluctance to view psychologists as primary care professionals and the notion that mental health care professionals are wedded to the "solo fee-for-service" medical model (Hersch, 1995). Related is the belief that persistent mind–body dualism prevents mental health professionals from functioning effectively as primary health care providers (Belar, 1995). In addition, the preference for pharmacology as the official primary choice of intervention despite the empirically proven benefits of psychotherapy or even psychotherapy combined with pharmacology (Barlow, 1994) continues to hamper progress in this arena. And, perhaps worst of all is the trivialization of certain psychological disorders (Hirschfeld, 1995).

Taking social phobia as an example, specific issues arise concerning managed health care integration. First, let us consider the trepidation that many mental health care providers have concerning the tendency of some primary care providers to trivialize or downplay certain psychological disorders that do not require an immediate medical intervention. Nowhere is this issue more relevant than for social phobia. Epidemiological studies indicate that people suffering from social phobia seek general outpatient treatment twice as often as those with no mental disorder, yet seek psychiatric treatment (either inpatient or outpatient) at a rate that is lower than those without a mental disorder (Hirschfeld, 1995). Also, subjects were found to be more likely to report phobic symptomatology to GPs when a comorbid depression was present than when suffering from social phobia alone (Weiller, Bisserbe, Boyer, Lepine, & Lecrubier, 1996). This would indicate that either primary care physicians are not identifying social phobia with the brevity it deserves, or that socially phobic individuals encounter other obstacles in receiving the appropriate treatment. Paramount in health care reform is the need to increase practitioners' awareness and diagnostic discrimination of social phobia and other internalizing disorders, as well as the need to facilitate treatment for individuals suffering from psychological disorders in the absence of comorbid medical complications. This issue becomes especially relevant, considering that social phobia may be the third most common mental disorder in adults (Kessler et al., 1994). Social phobia can also often be a precursor to alcohol and substance abuse, suicidal ideation, and functional impairment in the workplace (Hirschfeld, 1995), which can lead to an increased need for health care, which in turn inflates health care costs. To dismiss the symptoms of social phobia as a form of shyness not only does a disservice to our patients, but provides for the mismanagement of crucial health care dollars that could have otherwise been applied to swift and effective treatments.

Issues also arise concerning the debate between the use of pharmacology versus psychotherapy in the treatment of social phobia, as they do with other anxiety disorders. One large misconception of those involved in evaluating the cost-effectiveness of treatments in the new era of managed health care is that cost is primarily a function of the amount of time invested by the professional who applies it. What follows is the notion that treatment through medication is cheaper than any other form of intervention, including psychotherapy (Marks, 1995). What seems to have been overlooked are the treatment outcome studies that evaluate the cost-effectiveness of treatment in the long term. In fact, several cognitive–behavioral group treatments of social phobia are currently available that seem to fit within the primary goals of managed health care. Most have demonstrated adequate maintenance of treatment gains at follow-up, require lower amounts of therapist time investment (when one considers both the length of the treatment and the number of patients in the group compared with the number of therapists required to run the groups), and are even available in standardized, manualized formats (see Albano, Marten, et al., 1995; Beidel & Turner, 1998; Hope & Heimberg, 1993). Our mention of these examples in no way is intended to imply that the treatment of social phobia with medication should be abandoned entirely in favor of psychotherapy, but simply that the benefits of brief, empirically validated forms of psychotherapy, either alone or in combination with pharmacotherapy, should not be overlooked from a cost-effectiveness standpoint.

A final issue concerning the integration of mental health care into a managed health care system concerns the employment of non-doctoral-level individuals (e.g., psychiatric nurses, social workers) because they are generally cheaper and more readily available than doctoral-level psychologists. As warned by Barlow (1994), the notion that any college-educated professional experienced in establishing a relationship with people can effectively perform psychotherapy is not necessarily supported by the treatment outcome data of some disorders. Likewise, noting a study by Berman and Norton (1985) in which highly trained therapists were shown to be more effective in applying short-term therapy than other therapists, Belar (1995) stresses the impact of such findings on our integration into the managed health care system in which the quicker the better seems to be the rule of thumb with accepted therapy protocols. What will remain a challenge for mental health therapists in the future will be to find a way to balance the marketability of a treatment protocol with the amount of prerequisite training required to administer it. Although future emphasis may be placed on the ease with which a particular protocol gets distributed, we continue to have a responsibility as scientist-practitioners to ensure the proper employment of those protocols, for the safety of both our patients as well as ourselves. In the make-it-or-break-it atmosphere of managed health care, the program evaluation of treatments will undoubtedly focus on the training and quality of the therapist providing the treatment, so that effective treatment interventions do not get wrongly dismissed for lacking efficacy. Given the prevalence of comorbid mood disorders with social phobia, having therapists trained in the various psychological processes that may come into play could provide a treatment advantage which could serve to boost the effectiveness of many treatment protocols.

In summary, a number of issues exist regarding the future directions of the treatment of social phobia in an age of managed health care. Program evaluations should focus on long-term treatment effectiveness rather than just short-term findings. Similarly, cost-effectiveness must be considered from a variety of perspectives, and should also focus on the long-term cost-effectiveness of a chosen intervention. In short, factors other than client variables need to be more carefully scrutinized in future evaluations of both the treatment and assessment of social phobia.

FUTURE RESEARCH DIRECTIONS

Cognitive–behavioral protocols for the treatment of social phobia hold much promise for attenuating this serious and disabling condition in youth. As illustrated, the two existing programs developed specifically to meet the needs of social phobic children and adolescents are well grounded in empirical methods spanning a wide literature base of effective adult and child treatment research. Preliminary support for the SET-C and CBGT-A protocols is promising, and further research is currently being conducted in a number of settings. Attention must be paid to the specific needs of youth, such as the inclusion of parents into the active treatment protocols, the relative effectiveness of peer-pairing methods, and the long-term maintenance of gains through times of developmental challenge and transition. As illustrated in the case of Michael, the impact of comorbid conditions on the immediate and long-term effectiveness of treatment for a principal disorder remains a seriously understudied area. At present, only preliminary hypotheses can be offered, based on case studies and small-N designs, suggesting that comorbidity is a serious risk factor for relapse. Research is also necessary to develop and test methods for identifying youth at risk for developing social phobia, and initiating efforts toward the primary prevention of this serious disorder. Along these lines, research is under way in several settings focused on the development of a school-based prevention program for high school students at risk for social phobia and its sequelae (Merikangas, Dierker, & Albano, 1998). At a more global level, ongoing education is needed for primary care physicians, school personnel, and the general public, to alert these individuals to the significance of this disorder. Moreover, lobbyists and others in the position of impacting health care policy must become accustomed to considering the empirical evidence supporting cognitive–behavioral treatments either alone or in appropriate combination with psychopharmacology and appropriate ancillary therapies (e.g., those addressing comorbidity). At present, the field is open to investigators in clinical research settings, services research and primary care settings, and public health programs to turn serious attention to understanding the impact and course of social phobia in children and adolescents.

REFERENCES

Albano, A. M. (1995). Treatment of social anxiety in adolescents. *Cognitive and Behavioral Practice, 2,* 271–298.

Albano, A. M., & Barlow, D. H. (1996). Breaking the vicious cycle: Cognitive behavioral group treatment for socially anxious youth. In E. D. Hibbs & P. S. Jensen (Eds.), *Psychosocial treatments for child and adolescent disorders: Empirically based strategies for clinical practice* (pp. 43–62). Washington, DC: American Psychological Association.

Albano, A. M., Chorpita, B. F., & Barlow, D. H. (1996). Childhood anxiety disorders. In E. J. Mash & R. A. Barkley (Eds.), *Child psychopathology* (pp. 196–241). New York: Guilford Press.

Albano, A. M., Chorpita, B. F., DiBartolo, P. M., & Barlow, D. H. (1996). *Comorbidity in a clinical sample of children and adolescents with anxiety disorders: Characteristics and developmental considerations.* Unpublished manuscript, State University of New York at Albany.

Albano, A. M., DiBartolo, P. M., Heimberg, R. G., & Barlow, D. H. (1995). Children and adolescents: Assessment and treatment. In R. G. Heimberg, M. R. Liebowitz, D. A. Hope, & F. R. Schneier (Eds.), *Social phobia: Diagnosis, assessment and treatment* (pp. 387–425). New York: Guilford Press.

Albano, A. M., Marten, P. A., Holt, C. S., Heimberg, R. G., & Barlow, D. H. (1995). Cognitive-behavioral group treatment for adolescent social phobia: A preliminary study. *Journal of Nervous and Mental Disease, 183,* 649–656.

Albano, A. M., & Silverman, W. K. (1996). *Therapist's guide to the use of the Anxiety Disorders Interview Schedule for DSM-IV—child and parent versions.* San Antonio, TX: Graywind Publications, a Division of The Psychological Corporation.

American Psychiatric Association (1994). *Diagnostic and statistical manual of mental disorders* (4th ed.). Washington, DC: Author.

Barlow, D. H. (1991). Disorders of emotion. *Psychological Inquiry, 2,* 58–71.

Barlow, D. H. (1994). Psychological interventions in the era of managed competition. *Clinical Psychology: Science and Practice, 1,* 109–122.

Barrett, P. M., Rapee, R. M., Dadds, M. M., & Ryan, S. M. (1994). Family enhancement of cognitive style in anxious and aggressive children: Threat bias and the FEAR effect. *Journal of Abnormal Child Psychology, 22.*

Barrios, B. A., & Hartmann, D. P. (1988). Fears and anxieties. In E. J. Mash & L. G. Terdal (Eds.), *Behavioral assessment of childhood disorders* (pp. 196–262). New York: Guilford Press.

Barrios, B., & O'Dell, S. (1989). Fear and anxieties. In E. J. Mash & R. A. Barkley (Eds.), *Treatment of childhood disorders* (pp. 167–221). New York: Guilford Press.

Beidel, D. C., Neal, A. M., & Lederer, A. S. (1991). The feasibility and validity of a daily diary for the assessment of anxiety in children. *Behavior Therapy, 22,* 505–517.

Beidel, D. C., & Turner, S. M. (1998). *Shy children, phobic adults: Nature and treatment of social phobia.* Washington, DC: American Psychological Association.

Beidel, D. C., Turner, S. M., & Morris, T. L. (1995). A new inventory to assess childhood social anxiety and phobia: The Social Phobia and Anxiety Inventory for Children. *Psychological Assessment, 7,* 73–79.

Beidel, D. C., Turner, S. M., & Morris, T. L. (1996). *Social effectiveness training for children: A treatment manual.* Unpublished manuscript, Medical University of Charleston, South Carolina.

Belar, C. D. (1995). Collaboration in capitated care: Challenges for psychology. *Professional Psychology: Research and Practice, 26,* 139–146.

Berman, J. S., & Norton, N. C. (1985). Does professional training make a therapist more effective? *Psychological Bulletin, 98,* 401–407.

Brady, E. U., & Kendall, P. C. (1992). Comorbidity of anxiety and depression in children and adolescents. *Psychological Bulletin, 111,* 244–255.

Bruch, M. A. (1989). Familial and developmental antecedents of social phobia: Issues and findings. *Clinical Psychology Review, 9,* 37–47.

Bruch, M. A., & Heimberg, R. G. (1994). Differences in perceptions of parental and personal characteristics between generalized and nongeneralized social phobics. *Journal of Anxiety Disorders, 8,* 155–168.

Bruch, M. A., Heimberg, R. G., Berger, P., & Collins, T. M. (1989). Social phobia and perceptions of early parental and personal characteristics. *Anxiety Research, 2,* 57–65.

Caster, J. B., Bukowski, A. L., Inderbitzen, H. M., & Walters, K. S. (1996). *Relationship between youth perceptions of family environment and social anxiety.* Poster presented at the Annual Meeting of the Association for Advancement of Behavior Therapy, New York, NY.

Chambless, D. L., & Gillis, M. M. (1993). Cognitive therapy of anxiety disorders. *Journal of Consulting and Clinical Psychology, 61*(2), 248–260.

Chapman, T. F., Mannuza, S., & Fyer, A. J. (1995). Epidemiology and family studies of social phobia. In R. G. Heimberg, M. R. Liebowitz, D. A. Hope, & F. R. Schneier (Eds.), *Social phobia: Diagnosis, assessment, and treatment* (pp. 21–40). New York: Guilford Press.

Chorpita, B. F., Albano, A. M., & Barlow, D. H. (1996). Cognitive processing in children: Relation to anxiety and family influences. *Journal of Clinical Child Psychology, 25,* 170–176.

Chorpita, B. F., Albano, A. M., & Barlow, D. H. (1998). The structure of negative emotions in a clinical sample of children and adolescents. *Journal of Abnormal Psychology, 197,* 74–85.

Chorpita, B. F., & Barlow, D. H. (1995). *Control in the early environment: Implications for psychosocial models of childhood anxiety.* Unpublished manuscript, State University of New York at Albany.

Christoff, K. A., Scott, W. O. N., Kelley, M. L., Baer, G., & Kelly, J. A. (1985). Social skills and social problem-solving training for shy young adolescents. *Behavior Therapy, 16,* 468–477.

Davidson, J. R., Hughes, D. L., George, L. K., & Blazer, D. G. (1993). The epidemiology of social phobia: Findings from the Duke Epidemiological Catchment Area Study. *Psychological Medicine, 23,* 709–718.

Feske, U., & Chambless, D. L. (1995). Cognitive-behavioral versus exposure treatment for social phobia: A meta analysis. *Behavior Therapy, 26,* 695–720.

Francis, G., Last, C. G., & Strauss, C. C. (1992). Avoidant disorder and social phobia in children and adolescents. *Journal of the American Academy of Child and Adolescent Psychiatry, 31,* 1086–1089.

Franco, D. P., Christoff, K. A., Crimmins, D. E., & Kelley, J. A. (1983). Social skills training for an extremely shy young adolescent: An empirical case study. *Behaviour Therapy, 14,* 568–575.

Ginsburg, G., LaGreca, A. M., & Silverman, W. K. (1997a, November). *Social anxiety among children with anxiety disorders: Relation with social functioning.* Association for the Advancement of Behavior Therapy, Miami Beach, FL.

Ginsburg, G., LaGreca, A. M., & Silverman, W. K. (1997b, November). *The Social Anxiety Scale for Adolescents (SAS-A): Utility for youth with anxiety disorders.* Association for the Advancement of Behavior Therapy, Miami Beach, FL.

Heimberg, R. G., Dodge, C. S., Hope, D. A., Kennedy, C. R., & Zollo, L. J. (1990). Cognitive behavioral group treatment for social phobia: Comparison with a credible placebo control. *Cognitive Therapy and Research, 14,* 1–23.

Heimberg, R. G., Liebowitz, M. R., Hope, D. A., & Schneier, F. R. (Eds.). (1995). *Social phobia: Diagnosis, assessment and treatment.* New York: Guilford Press.

Heimberg, R. G., Salaman, D. G., Holt, C. S., & Blendell, K. A. (1993). Cognitive-behavioral group treatment for social phobia: Effectiveness at five-year follow-up. *Cognitive Therapy and Research, 17,* 325–339.

Hersch, L. (1995). Adapting to health care reform and managed care: Three strategies for survival and growth. *Professional Psychology: Research and Practice, 26,* 16–26.

Hirschfeld, R. M. A. (1995). The impact of health care reform on social phobia. *The Journal of Clinical Psychiatry, 56,* 13–17.

Hope, D. A., & Heimberg, R. G. (1993). Social phobia and social anxiety. In D. H. Barlow (Ed.), *Clinical handbook of psychological disorders: A step-by-step treatment manual* (pp. 99–136). New York: Guilford Press.

Kendall, P. C. (1992). Childhood coping: Avoiding a lifetime of anxiety. *Behavioural Change, 9,* 1–8.

Kendall, P. C. (1993). Cognitive-behavioral therapies with youth: Guiding theory, current status, and emerging developments. *Journal of Consulting and Clinical Psychology, 61,* 235–247.

Kendall, P. C. (1994). Treating anxiety disorders in children: Results of a randomized clinical trial. *Journal of Consulting and Clinical Psychology, 62,* 100–110.

Kessler, R. C., McGonagle, K., Zhao, S., Nelson, C. B., Hughes, M., Eshleman, S., Wittchen, H.-U., & Kendler, K. (1994). Lifetime and 12-month prevalence of DSM-III-R psychiatric disorders in the United States: Results from the national comorbidity survey. *Archives of General Psychiatry, 51,* 8–19.

King, N. J. (1995). Simple and social phobias. In T. H. Ollendick & R. J. Prinz (Eds.), *Advances in clinical child psychology* (Vol. 15, pp. 305–341). New York: Plenum Press.

LaGreca, A. M. (1998). *Social Anxiety Scales for Children and Adolescents: Manual and instructions for the SASC, SASC-R, SAS-A and parent versions of the scales.* Unpublished manuscript available from the author. University of Miami, Coral Gables, FL.

LaGreca, A. M., & Stone, W. L. (1993). Social Anxiety Scale for Children–Revised: Factor structure and concurrent validity. *Journal of Clinical Child Psychology, 22,* 17–27.

Last, C. G., Perrin, S., Hersen, M., & Kazdin, A. E. (1992). DSM-III-R anxiety disorders in children: Sociodemographic and clinical characteristics. *Journal of American Child & Adolescent Psychiatry, 31,* 1070–1076.

Last, C. G., Strauss, C. C., & Francis, G. (1987). Comorbidity among childhood anxiety disorders. *The Journal of Nervous and Mental Disease, 176,* 726–730.

Logsdon-Conradsen, S. (1998). *Family interaction patterns in adolescents with social phobia.* Unpublished doctoral dissertation, University of Louisville.

Logsdon-Conradsen, S., Jones, A. L., & Albano, A. M. (1996). *Coding system for parent–child interactions.* Unpublished manuscript, University of Louisville.

Marks, I. M. (1995). Advances in behavioral-cognitive therapy of social phobia. *Journal of Clinical Psychiatry, 56,* 25–31.

Merikangas, K., Dierker, L., & Albano, A. M. (1998). *Implications of familial and genetic risk factors for prevention and treatment of emotional and behavioral problems in youth.* Workshop presented at the Banff Conference on Behavioral Therapy, Banff, Alberta, Canada.

Nordman, J. E., Herbert, J. D., Kadish, D. A., & Kopyt, D. M. (1996). *Body dysmorphic disorder in social phobia.* Poster presented at the annual convention of the Association for Advancement of Behavior Therapy, New York, NY.

Öst, L. G., & Hughdahl, K. (1981). Acquisition of phobias and anxiety response patterns in clinical patients. *Behaviour Research and Therapy, 16,* 439–447.

Perrin, S., & Last, C. G. (1995). Dealing with comorbidity. In A. E. Eisen, C. A. Kearney, & C. Shaeffer (Eds.), *Clinical handbook of anxiety disorders in children and adolescents* (pp. 412–435). Northvale: NJ: Aronson.

Rapee, R. M. (1995). Descriptive symptomatology of social phobia. In R. G. Heimberg, M. R. Liebowitz, D. A. Hope, & F. R. Schneier (Eds.), *Social phobia: Diagnosis, assessment and treatment* (pp. 41–68). New York: Guilford Press.

Rapee, R. M. (1997). The potential role of childrearing practices in the development of anxiety and depression. *Clinical Psychology Review, 17,* 47–67.

Rosenbaum, J. F., Biederman, J., Hirshfeld, D. R., Bolduc, E. A., & Chaloff, J. (1991). Behavioral inhibition in children: A possible precursor to panic disorder or social phobia. *Journal of Clinical Psychiatry, 52,* 5–9.

S. 1757/H.R. 3600, 103d Cong., 1st Sess. (1993).

Sanderson, W. C., DiNardo, P. A., Rapee, R. M., & Barlow, D. H. (1990). Syndrome comorbidity in patients diagnosed with a DSM-III-Revised anxiety disorder. *Journal of Abnormal Psychology, 99,* 308–312.

Schneier, F. R., Johnson, J., Hornig, C. D., Liebowitz, M. R., & Weissman, M. M. (1992). Social phobia: Comorbidity and morbidity in an epidemiologic sample. *Archives of General Psychiatry, 49,* 282–288.

Silverman, W. K., & Albano, A. M. (1996a). *The Anxiety Disorders Interview Schedule for DSM-IV: Child Interview Schedule.* San Antonio, TX: Graywind Publications, a Division of The Psychological Corporation.

Silverman, W. K., & Albano, A. M. (1996b). *The Anxiety Disorders Interview Schedule for DSM-IV: Parent Interview Schedule.* San Antonio, TX: Graywind Publications, a Division of The Psychological Corporation.

Strauss, C. C., & Last, C. G. (1993). Social and simple phobias in children. *Journal of Anxiety Disorders, 7,* 141–152.

Turner, S. M., Beidel, D. C., Borden, J. W., Stanley, M. A., & Jacob, R. G. (1991). Social phobia: Axis I and II correlates. *Journal of Abnormal Psychology, 100,* 102–106.

Turner, S. M., Beidel, D. C., & Cooley, M. R. (1994). *Social effectiveness therapy: A program for overcoming social anxiety and social phobia.* Mt. Pleasant, SC: Turndel.

Vasey, M. W. (1995). Social anxiety disorders. In A. R. Eisen, C. A. Kearney, & C. A. Schaefer (Eds.), *Clinical handbook of anxiety disorders in children and adolescents* (pp. 131–168). Northvale, NJ: Aronson.

Walters, K. S., Cohn, L. G., & Inderbitzen, H. M. (1996). *Social anxiety and peer relations among adolescents: Testing a psychobiological model.* Poster presented at the annual convention of the Association for Advancement of Behavior Therapy, New York, NY.

Weiller, E., Bisserbe, J. C., Boyer, P., Lepine, J. P., & Lecrubier, Y. (1996). Social phobia in general health care. *British Journal of Psychiatry, 168,* 169–174.

15

Treating Aggressive Children with Rational-Emotive Behavior Therapy

RAYMOND DiGIUSEPPE and CINDY ELLEN LI

DESCRIPTION OF THE PROBLEM OF AGGRESSION

Aggressive behaviors remain stable from early childhood through adulthood and are one of the most invariable of human traits. Aggressive children are likely to be aggressive as adults and to engage in physical abuse and criminal behavior (Huesmann, Eron, Lefkowitz, & Walder, 1984; Loeber & Dishion, 1983). To change the trajectory aggressive children all too often follow, professionals need effective early interventions. This chapter addresses the treatment of aggressive children with Rational-Emotive Behavior Therapy (REBT).

Professionals often confuse anger and aggression (DiGiuseppe, Tafrate & Eckhardt, 1994) probably because they often occur together. Distinguishing aggression from anger is important. Anger is an emotion, whereas aggression entails engaging in a physical or verbal action (Bernard & Joyce, 1984). One can be angry without exhibiting aggression, and one can behave aggressively without feeling angry. Aggression involves an external act, whereas angry emotions are private events. The distinction between aggression and anger results in a clinically relevant differentiation between emotionally reactive versus instrumental or predatory aggression. Emotionally reactive aggression occurs when strong emotions of anger that are elicited by some perceived threat to self drive the behavior. Here anger and aggression coexist. Predatory aggression need not arise from any emotion, however. These aggressors simply take things by force that belong to others or coerce others to maintain a sense of power. Individuals engaging in predatory

RAYMOND DiGIUSEPPE and CINDY ELLEN LI • Psychology Department, St. John's University, Jamaica, New York 11439.

Handbook of Psychotherapies with Children and Families, edited by Russ and Ollendick. Kluwer Academic/Plenum Publishers, New York, 1999.

aggression may be categorized as psychopathic or as having antisocial personality disorder.

Often children who are aggressive are classified as having either Oppositional Defiant Disorder (ODD) or Conduct Disorder (CD) (American Psychiatric Association, 1994). Children who are verbally aggressive and exhibit a pattern of hostile behavior particularly toward authority figures may be categorized as having ODD. It is also possible, however, for children who are not aggressive to manifest signs of ODD. CD is a more severe problem occurring when the child violates major societal norms. Most of the CD criteria involve aggressive behavior toward people, animals, or property. CD is categorized further into subtypes of either childhood or adolescent onset. Children with CD who have childhood onset type, where one criterion of CD is present before the age of 10, are more likely to be aggressive than those who manifest signs of CD in adolescence. Because childhood-onset CD is more likely than adolescent-onset CD to develop into Antisocial Personality Disorder (American Psychiatric Association, 1994), we presume that children with childhood-onset CD are more likely than children with adolescent-onset CD to display predatory aggression.

BASIC APPROACH

REBT can provide an effective model for treating aggressive children. As the name implies, REBT is an integrative therapy that allows for many interventions to accomplish its goals (Walen, DiGiuseppe, & Dryden, 1992). Research suggests that disruptive and aggressive behaviors are often best treated by changes in parental or school contingencies. Based on our anecdotal experience, we have found that children with predatory aggression do not respond well to cognitive treatments. As a result, with these individuals, we recommend that one use only concrete behavioral strategies. Nevertheless, because REBT is a cognitive–behavioral approach to treatment, one may question the utility of cognitive interventions with this population. However, these will often be directed at the adults who need to implement the behavioral strategies.

REBT involves strategies for learning to control dysfunctional emotions. REBT can be used to treat aggressive children in two ways: by teaching children to control the underlying angry emotions that lead to aggression, and by teaching parents to control their disruptive emotions that interfere with good parenting skills and thus inhibit their ability to effectively manage their children's aggression.

The trademark of REBT is its emphasis on teaching people to learn the "ABCs" of emotional disturbance, identifying the Activating events, their Beliefs about those events, and the resulting Consequences. REBT teaches that disturbed emotional and behavioral Consequences result from irrational Beliefs individuals hold rather than from Activating events. REBT works to alleviate emotional disturbance by helping people to (1) identify their irrational beliefs, (2) recognize that the irrational beliefs are maladaptive, and (3) replace those dysfunctional cognitions with more adaptive, rational beliefs. Rational cognitions express preferential, flexible desires, whereas irrational cognitions express absolutistic, rigid needs. Rational thinking leads to happiness, and enables individuals to attain goals and strive toward their potential; irrational thinking causes people to be extremely *disturbable,* and thwarts individuals' ability to attain their goals, leading to unhappiness.

REBT also distinguishes between disturbed, dysfunctional emotions and normal, motivating, albeit negative emotions. Negative emotions do not reflect psychopathology. If an activating event occurs (A) and one thinks irrationally (B), one will experience a disturbed emotion such as anger or anxiety (C). If one then challenges one's irrational belief and replaces it with a rational belief (a new B), one will still experience a negative, nondisturbed, motivating emotion. Most psychotherapists understand therapeutic improvement as a quantitative shift in the emotion. However, Ellis (1994; Ellis & DiGiuseppe, 1993) proposed that when people think rational thoughts, they experience a qualitatively different emotion rather than less intensity of the disturbed emotion. The emotions generated by rational thoughts will be in the same family of emotions as the disturbed emotion, but they differ in many aspects. Ellis posits that although irrational thinking leads to anxiety, depression, or anger, rational thinking will lead to concern, sadness, and annoyance, respectively. These emotions are not necessarily less intense but they may lead to qualitatively different phenomenological experiences, and they will elicit different behavioral reactions.

INTERVENTION PROCEDURES BASED ON EMPIRICAL RESEARCH

Several meta-analyses examining the effectiveness of psychotherapy with children and adolescents have concluded that behavioral and cognitive therapies are more effective than nonbehavioral or traditional therapies (Casey & Berman, 1985; Weisz, Weiss, Alicke, & Klotz, 1987; Weisz, Weiss, Han, Granger, & Morton, 1995). However, these reviews failed to address which behavioral and cognitive treatments were most effective with which types of children. We have uncovered more than 30 cognitive and behavioral interventions used with children. Knowing that such interventions are generally more effective than nonbehavioral interventions, still leaves the practitioners with the task of choosing from a variety of therapies. The results of two recent meta-analyses concerning which cognitive and behavioral interventions work best with aggressive children can provide an initial basis for treatment planning.

Wellen (1997) conducted a meta-analysis of 20 single-subject studies of cognitive and behavioral treatments with aggressive children. Studies of children presenting with aggression as the primary problem, and with no other major clinical syndromes such as psychoses or developmental disabilities, were selected from a comprehensive search of the research literature. The subjects in the studies ranged in age from 3 to 17 and exhibited verbal or physical aggression, or both. Wellen coded the dependent variables as measures of prosocial behavior or antisocial behavior. The treatment variables (see below) that made the greatest impact on increasing prosocial behaviors sometimes had small effect on reducing antisocial behaviors. Similarly, the treatments that had the largest effect sizes for reducing antisocial behaviors sometimes had minimal effect for increasing prosocial behaviors. Overall, treatments involving rehearsal (e.g., role-play, modeling, and social skills training) were the most effective.

Kendall's (1993) cognitive distortion and cognitive deficit model can explain Wellen's results. This model suggests that the cognitive processes of aggression involve both cognitive distortions and deficiencies. Aggressive children often engage in dysfunctional thinking and lack the skills to use environmental cues and process information accurately, especially information regarding others' actions. Kendall suggested that practice involving techniques such as modeling and role-play leads to the development of more appropriate coping skills and social skills that are absent in the child's repertoire. In Wellen's meta-analysis, none of the studies used rehearsal alone. Researchers combined rehearsal of new skills with other techniques. The combined treatments with the highest effect sizes were those that paired rehearsal with some form of contingency management such as contingent reinforcement, reprimands, response cost, and time-out.

The type of contingency intervention had differential effects on the types of dependent variables. Positive behavioral interventions (positive rewards and praise) increased prosocial behaviors but did not reduce antisocial behavior. Those studies employing negative interventions (response costs, reprimands, and time-out) had larger effect sizes for reducing antisocial behavior but a much lesser effect on increasing prosocial behavior. In total, negative contingency management procedures yielded a larger effect size than the use of positive interventions.

DiGiuseppe et al. (1996) recently performed a meta-analysis on 20 between-groups outcome studies using cognitive and behavioral treatments for children and adolescents classified primarily as aggressive.[1] The findings suggested that the treatment components of modeling and behavior rehearsal (role-play) were most effective. This supports Wellen's (1997) finding with single-case studies indicating that treatments involving rehearsal were most effective. As in Wellen's (1997) meta-analysis, use of negative contingency management techniques alone was more effective than use of positive treatments alone. Despite the popularity of positive reinforcement, negative consequences might be more effective in reducing aggression. Positive and negative techniques combined were superior to either treatment used alone.

Again similar to Wellen's (1997) findings, positive techniques were most effective at increasing prosocial behaviors, whereas negative techniques were most effective in reducing undesirable behaviors. This suggests that therapists should choose different treatments depending on the types of behaviors targeted for change.

DiGiuseppe et al. (1996) found that the combination of cognitive and behavioral therapies worked better than either one alone. Cognitive treatments included problem solving, coping self-statements, and anger-management training, whereas behavioral components included positive and negative techniques, relaxation training, and rehearsal techniques. Researchers often fail to operationalize their definitions of aggressive children and fail to distinguish between angry/emotionally reactive aggression and predatory aggressive behavior. We believe that this distinction between types of aggression is important, as these different types might respond to different interventions. Cognitive interventions may be more effective with children whose aggression is of the emotional type and less effective with the predatory type. The cognitive skills may help the child learn to calm anger and, by that, limit impulsive aggression. Our clinical experience suggests that children

---

[1]This meta-analysis is part of a larger ongoing meta-analysis of over 260 outcome studies involving a broader population of children with externalized disorders.

with predatory aggression, despite being more resistant to treatment overall, may respond better to contingency management.

Wellen's (1997) meta-analysis of the cognitive interventions consisted only of problem-solving strategies. However, the cognitive components of REBT involve more complex skills that require more motivation than problem-solving techniques alone. We recommend that instead of beginning with both behavioral and cognitive techniques, one first focus on behavioral techniques and then add the cognitive component as needed. At times, it may be necessary to first use negative strategies with the child so that the child's behavior can become more manageable. This approach may subsequently help the child to become more invested and motivated in treatment. At this point we would recommend adding the cognitive component while continuing the behavioral treatments. Also, at this time one might include positive behavioral techniques with rehearsal. For instance, one might introduce a prosocial behavior one would like the child to increase. Besides positively reinforcing this behavior, the research indicates that giving the child an opportunity to practice the behavior, through role-play or modeling, for example, is beneficial.

Results of these meta-analytic reviews suggest that therapists need to develop interventions that model and rehearse new cognitive and behavioral responses to emotionally laden eliciting stimuli. The effectiveness of these rehearsal interventions may be augmented by changes in the contingencies for aggressive behavior. Negative contingencies, such as response cost and time out, may be more effective than positive reinforcement. Also the negative interventions appear to eliminate antisocial behavior and positive contingencies help build new prosocial responses. However, the elimination of antisocial responses appears more important when treating aggressive children. Finally, adding more interventions to the treatment does not lead to more effective treatment, and in fact may reduce effectiveness. This presents a problem for clinicians treating angry children. Treatment usually entails teaching children to evaluate anger-provoking situations differently and to respond in new ways. Parents and teachers learn to control their own anger at the child, to consequate antisocial responses negatively without being punitive, and to reinforce new prosocial responses positively. This is a lot to cover in treatment. Strategies need to be developed that allow these new skills to be developed.

MAJOR MECHANISMS OF CHANGE

REBT theory posits four types of irrational thinking that lead to emotional disturbance: demandingness, awfulizing, global condemnation of human worth, and frustration intolerance. Two of these, demandingness and frustration intolerance, are most likely to be core schemas of children with emotionally reactive aggression.

Demandingness. Demandingness is represented in English by the words *must, should, ought,* and *have to.* These words reflect a demand on how the self, others, or the world must be. REBT makes the distinction between preferences and demands. People's preferences do not cause disturbance. However, when people demand that their preferences be reality, they become disturbed. Demandingness can be thought of as schema assimilation rather than schema accommodation.

When disturbed persons encounter a situation that is inconsistent with their desires, they assimilate and still construct the world as consistent with their desires. Failing to distinguish between the situation as it is and one's desire leads to poor coping. When adjusted people encounter a similar situation, they accommodate and restructure their schema to include the discrepancy between the way the world is and what they want. This construction of the situation as inconsistent with one's desires is more likely to lead to more adaptive coping responses. For example, an adolescent woman might tell herself, "My parents must let me do what I want." Not only does she want her parents to allow her to do as she desires, but she believes that because she wants it, they will comply. She may be shocked when they punish her for transgressions of their rules, and she may continue to behave against their rules despite all of the feedback that they disapprove of the behavior and will initiate consequences for it. A different young woman, who recognizes that her parents will not behave as she wishes just because she wishes it, may try to win them over to her view or pursue other avenues of gratification.

Frustration Intolerance. Frustration intolerance beliefs imply that an individual cannot stand something she finds frustrating or that the individual does not have the endurance to survive in its presence. For example, someone who is addicted to caffeine might say, "I cannot stand feeling the slightest bit tired when I have all this work to do; I must have some coffee." Or, the adolescent mentioned above may say to herself, "I cannot stand it if my parents do not let me do what I want." These types of beliefs are illogical as well, because, short of dying, one is tolerating whatever one claims one cannot stand.

Individual Psychotherapy with Children and Adolescents

Aggressive children often experience disfavor from many sources, including parents and teachers, as well as peers. An important facet of aggressive behavior is that, like many externalized disorders, it is viewed as a problem primarily based on when and how others view it as a problem. In fact, those engaging in aggression are unlikely to view their behavior as a problem. As a result, most children attend therapy against their will. Aggressive children can be particularly difficult to treat because they are often not motivated to change their behaviors. Thus, when therapists encounter aggressive children, the initial goal of therapy is to motivate them for behavior change, that is, to ensure there is agreement on the goals and tasks of therapy.

Discussing the goals and tasks of therapy may be more critical to the establishment of a therapeutic alliance with children than with adults. Prochaska and DiClemente's (1981) constructs of stages of change and processes of change are particularly helpful in designing interventions for those unmotivated to change. They proposed that people pass through a series of stages of attitudes about change. These include the precontemplative stage (the person does not wish to change), the contemplative stage (the person is thinking he might change), the action stage (the person tries to change), and the maintenance stage (the person consolidates his gains and attempts to keep the new behaviors). Prochaska and DiClemente proposed that the type of therapy needs to match the client's stage of change. REBT is an action-oriented therapy, designed for people in the action stage of change. Because most children and adolescents arrive in the precontemplative stage, the therapists must establish agreement on the goals and tasks of therapy to build the therapeutic alliance, before using such an active approach.

DiGiuseppe and colleagues (DiGiuseppe, 1995; DiGiuseppe & Bernard, 1983; DiGiuseppe & Jilton, 1996; Walen et al., 1992) presented a cognitive–behavioral approach to establish the therapeutic alliance in children and adolescents who arrive in therapy in the precontemplative stage. A technique called *motivational syllogism* (Table 1) may be used to help agree on the goals of therapy. The elements of this motivational syllogism are as follows:

1. My present emotion is dysfunctional (for aggressive children the dysfunctional emotion is primarily their anger).
2. An alternative acceptable emotional script exists for this type of activating event (e.g., annoyance).
3. Giving up the dysfunctional emotion and work toward feeling the alternative one is better for me.
4. My beliefs cause my emotions; therefore, I will work at changing my beliefs to change my emotions.

This model proscribes that the therapist asks clients in a Socratic fashion to assess the consequences of their emotional and behavioral responses. This helps them identify the negative consequences for their emotional disturbance and behavior. Next, the therapist presents alternative emotional reactions that are culturally acceptable to each client. Because people learn emotional scripts from their families, and learn that some emotional scripts are acceptable to our cultural group, it is possible that the disturbed child or adolescent has not changed because she cannot conceptualize an acceptable emotional script to experience in place of the disturbed emotion. REBT has adopted the script theories of emotions (DiGiuseppe, 1995) and proposes that clients need to learn adaptive emotional scripts, not just change the intensity of their feelings. As a result, therapists are very careful in the words they use to describe emotions and to help clients choose which emotions they will use to replace their disturbed emotions. They help clients formulate a vocabulary to describe adaptive, albeit negative, affective states

Table 1. The Steps of the Motivational Syllogism to Establish Agreement on the Goals and Tasks of Therapy

---

Prerequisite beliefs to disputing irrational beliefs

1. Insight 1: My present emotion is dysfunctional. *Technique:* Through Socratic questions, get the client to see how the present emotional reaction is dysfunctional for him.
2. Insight 2: There is an alternative acceptable emotional goal. *Technique:* Through teaching and reviewing acceptable models, help them see that there are alternative emotional scripts that are more adaptive.
3. Insight 3: It is better for me to give up my dysfunctional emotion and replace it with the alternative emotional script. *Technique:* Socratically get the client to imagine feeling the new emotional script and review what the consequences for his life are if he experiences the new emotion. *This should accomplish agreement on the goals of therapy.*
4. Insight 4: My beliefs influence my emotions, therefore, it is appropriate to examine and change my thinking. *Technique:* Teach the B—>C connection. *This should accomplish agreement on the tasks of therapy.*

---

that they could experience instead of the disturbed emotions. Therapists need to explore with the clients alternative emotional reactions that are culturally acceptable and adaptive. Next, therapists help clients connect the alternative script with an advantageous outcome.

Therapists then focus on helping the clients to change their dysfunctional cognitions and emotions. As already mentioned, with aggressive children and adolescents, the disturbed thoughts usually are centered around the irrational beliefs of frustration intolerance or demandingness, and the disturbed emotion is that of excessive anger. Therapists explain and demonstrate how thoughts can cause emotions, and that certain thoughts, namely, irrational beliefs (IBs), produce disturbed emotions, whereas other thoughts (RBs) lead to nondisturbed emotions. Some children may have difficulty distinguishing between disturbed and nondisturbed emotions, and therefore, the therapist may need to teach them to identify and label various emotions, and then to be able to distinguish between those that are helpful and those that are hurtful. Further, the therapist teaches that thoughts can be changed to produce nondisturbed emotions. The therapist helps the child practice distinguishing between disturbed and nondisturbed cognitions and emotions. Additionally, the child practices disputing irrational beliefs and replacing them with more rational thoughts. Specific techniques used to help the client practice these skills include modeling, role-playing, and imagery, and homework involving the parents. Other REBT techniques used with children include bibliotherapy and written homework assignments.

Children who have not yet reached the concrete operational phase (those less than 8 years old) will have difficulty with the logic of disputing and with thinking about their thinking. For these children, therapists are recommended to use treatments that focus on concrete skills, such as problem solving (Spivack, Platt, & Shure, 1976; Spivack & Shure, 1974) and rehearsing rational coping statements (DiGiuseppe, 1975; Meichenbaum, 1971).

Adolescents are concerned with forming their own identities. They are often oppositional and refuse to heed the advice of people from a different generation. Therefore, with adolescents it is particularly important to ensure that the therapist has agreement on the goals and tasks of therapy, and to explain to the client how the tasks will improve their current situation. We recommend therapists go through the steps of the motivational syllogism before the discussion of each new problem and before the use of any intervention.

Establishing these four beliefs will help motivate a child or adolescent to engage in the REBT process. This model facilitates agreement on the goals of therapy and moves clients to the action stage of change. Therapists need to assess each child's and adolescent's stage of change and agreement on the goals of therapy before proceeding with any interventions aimed at the goals of treatment. If the child or adolescent has not reached the action stage and does not want to change, techniques outlined by DiGiuseppe and Jilton or other similar techniques like motivational interviewing (Miller & Rollnick, 1991) could be used to accomplish this task.

Parental Involvement in Treatment

In whatever context children are being treated, having the parents involved in the treatment is crucial so that behavioral changes can generalize to the home setting. The problem is that although parents desperately want to see their children's behavior change, they often have difficulty carrying out behavioral interventions with their children. Research has shown that parents' emotional disturbance is the primary reason adults fail to engage in correct parenting practices (Dix, 1991) and fail to benefit from behavioral parent training programs (Dadds & McHugh, 1992). Although behavioral parent training may be the most successful intervention with children with externalized disorders (Kazdin, 1994), parents are unlikely to follow therapists' recommendations if they are emotionally disturbed about their child's behavior. The failure to address parents' emotional reactions to parenting may be the largest void in the extensive parent behavior training literature (Dix, 1991). We believe that the failure to find combined interventions as more effective than singular interventions in our meta-analytic review may occur because parents are too upset while interacting with their children to follow the behavioral interventions taught to them.

DiGiuseppe (1988, 1999) devised a sequential family therapy model for treatment of families with externalized disordered children. In this model changing the parents' irrational cognitions and emotional disturbance is done to get the parents to adopt more effective parenting skills. This is necessary to accomplish the primary goal of changing the child's symptomatic behavior. The parents' disturbance is a crucial target of the interventions. Both the parents' and the child's disturbances are treated with REBT. It is helpful to have the parents involved in treatment from the outset for another reason, so that the therapy does not reinforce what the child is likely to feel at home—that he is the problem child and the cause of the family's problems. This REBT family therapy model focuses on the following steps: (1) a thorough assessment of the child's difficulties, a behavioral analysis of the eliciting stimuli and reinforcers, consequences, and family functioning; (2) forming a therapeutic alliance with the parents; (3) choosing a target behavior and consequences collaboratively with the parents; (4) assessing parents' ability to carry out the interventions, including their emotional reactions and irrational beliefs; (5) changing parents' irrational beliefs and emotions that would interfere with performing the new parenting strategies; (6) have parents predict what resistance they expect to occur to their new parenting strategies from the identified patient or other family members, and generate solutions to confront these attempts at resistance; (7) assess the parents' ability to follow the strategies they choose to handle the resistance, again focusing on their emotions and irrational beliefs; (8) intervening with parents again at changing the irrational beliefs and schema that would prevent them from handling the resistance; (9) continuing to assess the children's progress and the parents' compliance with the behavioral skills, and modify the behavior treatment plan as needed; (10) start individual therapy with the child to internalize gains made by the behavioral intervention. These steps are presented in Table 2.

Even when the child is treated individually, parents can still play a role in treatment. When individual therapy is employed, parents are often unaware of the issues discussed by the therapist and child. Parents often want to be involved in their children's therapy because of their natural concern for their children's well being. If the child agrees, if the problem does not necessarily involve a family matter the child would feel inhibited to discuss in front of the parents, and if the parents are willing, parents can play a helpful role in the child's individual therapy.

Table 2. Sequence of Family Therapy for Treatment of Externalized Disorders

---

Stage 1: *Assessment.* Assess (1) the nature of the psychopathology, (2) the developmental level of functioning, and the discriminative stimulus that elicits the problems and its reinforcers, (3) the structure of the family, (4) the roles of the individual members, (5) who will resist?, (6) the emotions, skills, and cognitions of each member.

Stage 2: *Engaging parents in the therapeutic alliance.* If one parent is resistant to change, use motivational interviewing or problem solving with the motivated parent to engage the resistant parent.

Stage 3: *Behavioral intervention.* Choosing a target behavior and consequences.

Stage 4: *Assessing parents' ability to carry out agreed intervention.* Assess the parents' emotions, and the cognitions that will stop them from carrying out the agreed upon intervention. Some possible parental interfering emotions: guilt, anger, anxiety, and discomfort anxiety. Assess the parents' irrational beliefs. Some possible irrational beliefs: demandingness, catastrophizing, frustration intolerance, self-downing, projected frustration intolerance, condemnation of the child.

Stage 5: *Therapy on the parents.* Cognitive restructuring of the parents' irrational beliefs. Use all of the techniques that one would in adult REBT to focus on the emotions and the cognitions identified in the previous stage.

Stage 6: *Predict resistance.* Determine what the parents believe the child or others will do to sabotage their efforts. Problem-solve how they can respond to those attempts at sabotage. This will help them continue to deal with sabotage on their own after termination.

Stage 7: *Assessment of the parents' ability to follow intervention.* Ask the parents to imagine themselves following through. What emotions and beliefs will they have about this new action? What do they believe their emotional reactions will be to these? Assess the emotions and the cognitions that will get in their way of following through on the intervention chosen to counteract the sabotage.

Stage 8: *Intervention with parents.* Dispute the irrational beliefs that they will experience that could encourage them to give in to the resistance.

Stage 9: *How does child respond to new action?* (1) Repeat the assessment, (2) redesign the interventions through collaborative problem solving, (3) continue to assess the parents' ability to carry out the new interventions, (4) continue to use cognitive restructuring to help them follow through on the planned interventions.

Stage 10: *Individual therapy for the child or adolescent.* At the beginning of each session, assess the progress the child and the parents have made. If parents have followed their interventions, remain in this stage. If they have not, return to Stage 8, use motivational syllogism to help the child internalize the desirability of change and cooperation with the therapist. Use all REBT and CBT methods to reduce the undesirable target behaviors and support the desired positive changes.

Bernard and DiGiuseppe (1990) recommend four different ways that parents can become involved to improve the effectiveness of individual therapy. First, children can be assigned the homework of describing important points of a session to their parents, such as the beliefs–consequences connection or the disputes to irrational beliefs or the rational coping statements they will use when they become upset. This technique gives children opportunities to rehearse the principles therapists want to teach, and allows the parents to feel involved in their children's treatment.

Second, parents can join the therapy session. When problematic activating events or emotional upset occurs between sessions, parents usually attempt to help their children and provide advice. Sometimes parents' comments are inconsistent with the therapists' goals, or they reinforce their children's irrational thinking or sometimes they are just not helpful. If parents have been present during the sessions, they can remind their children of the rational coping statements provided in the session or they can use the principles of REBT that they learned in session to guide their responses to their child when the child experiences problems. Again, parents who participate in this way feel good about being part of the solution and report learning how to talk to their children in ways that are helpful. Some parents even report that it has helped them with their own emotional problems.

Third, parents can provide information that children often forget. Weekly therapy sessions were designed for adults. Children often fail to remember significant events that happen between sessions, thus denying therapists important information on problems they have had between sessions. When parents are present, they often remind the children of successful coping experiences that they have had that therapists can reinforce. The parents also report important activating events that children do not handle well that could be the focus of the session.

Fourth, therapists can often design homework assignments that include the parents. For example, children who react angrily when they are teased need to learn new rational coping statements to verbal attacks by peers. Often therapists can role-play the verbal attacks in the session and the children learn to rehearse their disputes and coping statements. Therapists can enlist the parents to role-play their children's tormentors between sessions. The parent can call out a barb to the child and the child will rehearse his or her new cognitions and new social skills. Here the parent prompts the rehearsal of a new response, and can coach the child because of what he or she has learned in the session. Whenever and however possible, REBT involves parents in the child's treatment.

Case Study

Jamie, a 9-year-old girl, was referred for therapy by her mother, because her parents could not control her behavior and were concerned that soon her behavior would be entirely out of their control. Her parents' primary complaint was that Jamie did not follow their directions. When she did not get what she wanted, she became verbally and physically aggressive. Her parents explained that when they ask Jamie to do something (such as helping them set the table for dinner, or letting her father watch sports events on TV) she often ignores them. At first she pretends she does not hear them and when they persist, she says that she does not want to do whatever it is they have asked of her and that she should not have to do it. Further, several times, when Jamie asks something of her parents (such as if she can have a friend over), if her parents say no to her, she whines and then becomes verbally aggressive, saying things such as "I hate you" or "You do not love me." If she still does not get what she wants, she will, at times, begin to push and hit her parents. Jamie's parents reported that nothing they do helps. Socially, Jamie has few same-aged peers. Her friends are primarily younger children who let her control them. When they do not do what Jamie wants, she uses various verbal threats to scare them and when that does not work she will occasionally hit them. Academically, Jamie gets average grades and can be managed fairly easily in her classroom.

We can conceptualize this case from REBT, and behavioral and systemic perspectives. Because Jamie's parents had never established a pattern of firm limit setting with her, she learned that she could control the interactions with her parents and, therefore, became used to getting her way. Her parents' attempts to enforce limits elicited IBs in Jamie that she must (i.e., demandingness) have her way and that she cannot stand (i.e., frustration intolerance) failing to get what she wants. Feelings of extreme frustration and anger accompanied these IBs, which led Jamie to try even harder to get what she wanted, often by acting aggressively. Her parents' tendency to react to her by eventually giving in only served to reinforce the oppositional and aggressive behavior they wished to extinguish.

The first step in dealing with this case was to teach Jamie's parents to use more effective discipline techniques. Before this could be accomplished, however, it was necessary to identify the core beliefs that were interfering with Jamie's parents' attempts at disciplining their daughter. In working with her parents it was discovered that they felt guilty about punishing Jamie because they thought "It is awful if we cannot give her what she wants because then she might not love us. It must mean that we are not good parents if we make her upset." For Jamie's parents to be able to use behavioral techniques effectively, they first needed to work on challenging their IBs and replacing them with more rational beliefs. This helped them to change their dysfunctional guilt feelings to more helpful feelings of concern.

Then, Jamie's parents were ready to choose a target behavior for Jamie. They chose not hitting her peers or parents. The therapist started with teaching her parents behavioral strategies of employing negative techniques with rehearsal using strategies of time-out and punishment where natural consequences were established. In the therapy room they role-played scenarios where Jamie pretended to hit her parents and her parents set consequences for her. They practiced this, with the therapist providing feedback about how they could better carry out the techniques.

Once the initial negative behavioral strategies were in place, the next step was to begin having individual sessions with Jamie. Working on motivating her to want to change was crucial and therefore we wanted to ensure that she agreed on the goals and tasks of therapy. This was accomplished through Socratic dialogue and the motivational syllogism. Jamie realized that becoming angry when things do not go her way is not helpful for her for various reasons. She said she did not like feeling so upset and seeing her parents get so upset. She recognized that sometimes her anger caused her to say or do things to others that she would rather not do. Further, Jamie began to realize that her anger and the aggressive behaviors she exhibited made it difficult for her to form and maintain friendships. Jamie was taught that she could feel other ways that would be more helpful to her. She worked on learning this new emotional script. Next, she was taught how her beliefs influence her behavior. At this point she was more motivated to change her behavior and specifically to think about what kind of beliefs she has that influence her behavior. As she approached the action stage of change she was willing to use rational self-statements and start challenging her own IBs, saying things to herself such as "I guess I do not have to have my parents do what I ask . . . though I prefer they do what I want. This way I won't feel so angry when they do not do what I want. Instead, I would feel a little mad and not really angry." At this point Jamie's parents were encouraged to begin using positive techniques with rehearsal in the therapy setting and at home. For example, one of Jamie's target behaviors was setting the table. The family, with the therapist, devised a reward system contingent on Jamie's behavior. Jamie's parents continued to use negative strategies once they had successfully implemented the positive techniques.

RESEARCH SUPPORT OF REBT

DiGiuseppe, Goodman, and Nevas (1997) discovered 14 reviews of REBT (DiGiuseppe, Miller, & Trexler, 1977; Engels, Garnefski, & Diekstra, 1993; Gossette & O'Brien, 1992, 1993; Haaga & Davison, 1989; Hajzler & Bernard, 1990; Jorm, 1989; Lyons & Woods, 1991; Mahoney, 1974; McGovern & Silverman, 1984; Silverman, McCarthy, & McGovern, 1992; Zettle & Hayes, 1980). Most of these are narrative reviews. Three have been meta-analyses (i.e., Engels et al., 1993; Lyons & Woods, 1991; Polder, 1986). Most have included studies of adults and children. Others have focused only on adults (Gossette & O'Brien, 1992; Zettle & Hayes, 1980) and two have focused only on research with children and adolescents (Gossette & O'Brien, 1993; Hajzler & Bernard, 1990). Most have been favorable, although some others have been critical. Table 3 lists the reviews alphabetically by author, the year published, the range of years of the studies included, the populations reviewed, and their general conclusions.

Each review employed a different selection criterion. More than 280 outcome studies are mentioned in these 14 reviews. However, the reviews rarely included the same studies. Only 13 studies appeared in 5 reviews, and only 3 studies were included in 6 reviews. No study appeared in 7 or more of the reviews. One hundred and twenty-four studies were mentioned in only 1 review. DiGiuseppe et al. (1997) point out that the reviews had very low agreement on which studies to include. Each of the 14 reviews ignored, excluded, or failed to uncover many studies from the period from which they selected articles. The most comprehensive reviews were those by Silverman and colleagues (McGovern & Silverman, 1984; Silverman et al., 1992).

DiGiuseppe et al. (1997) found more than 70 REBT outcome studies not included in the reviews. More than 350 REBT outcome studies have been found. Many studies exist that compare REBT with no treatment, waiting lists, or placebo controls, and support the efficacy of REBT across a wide range of problems including: social, testing, math, performance, and public speaking anxiety, agoraphobia, neuroticism, stress, depression, anger, teacher burnout, personality disorder, obsessive-compulsive disorder, marriage and relationship problems, alcohol abuse, poor dating skills, overweight/obesity, school discipline problems, unassertiveness, type A behavior, parenting problems, emotional reactions to learning disabilities, school underachievement, sexual fears and dysfunction, bulimia, and anger. Few studies have specifically focused on the treatment of aggression, but the outcome studies conducted on REBT with children who exhibited aggressive behavior displayed successful results (Block, 1978; Morris, 1993).

Despite the large number of investigations of REBT, research has failed to advance our knowledge. The overwhelming majority of studies compared REBT with a no contact, waiting list, or placebo condition. Few studies compare REBT with a viable, alternative treatment. REBT is better than no treatment or placebo treatments for a wide variety of problems. However, no evidence exists that it is more efficacious than alternative treatments or that there is one condition for which it is the treatment of choice.

Also, the research has done little to advance our knowledge concerning the best way to practice REBT. Does the inclusion of imagery, written homework

Table 3. Reviews of the REBT Outcome Literature, Year Published, Years Spanned, Focus, and Conclusions

Authors	Year published	Range of years of studies	Number of studies	Focus of the review	Conclusions
DiGiuseppe, Miller, & Trexler	1977	1970–1977	26	Published and unpublished studies of children and adults	Support for RET "appear(s) generally positive and promising, but far from conclusive" (p. 70)
Engels, Garnefski, & Diekstra	1993	1970–1988	32	Published and unpublished studies of children and adults	"RET on the whole was effective, compared with placebo and no treatment. Its effects were maintained over time, and it produced a delayed treatment effect with regard to behavioral outcome criteria." (p. 1088)
Gossette & O'Brien	1992	1970–1990	85	Published and unpublished studies of children and adults	"RET was effective in 25% of comparisons" (p. 9). RET results in "a decreased score on scales of irrationality. . . . a parallel decrease in self reported emotional distress. Other measures, noticeably behavior, were insensitive to RET. . . . RET has little or no practical benefit." (p. 20)
Gossette & O'Brien	1993	1974–1992	36	Published and unpublished studies of children and adolescents	RET has little or no practical benefit. "The most distinctive outcome of RET is a decrease in the endorsement of irrational beliefs" (p. 21). "We can conclude that continued use of RET in the classroom is unjustified, in fact, contraindicated" (p. 23)
Haaga & Davison	1989	1970–1987	69	Published and unpublished studies of children and adults	
Hajzler & Bernard	1990	1970–1982	45	Published and unpublished studies of children and adolescents	"support for the notion that changes in irrationality and changes in other dimension of psychological functioning"; "changes have been maintained at follow up periods" (p. 31)
Jorm	1989	1971–1986	16	Studies of any type of theory that included a measure of trait anxiety or neuroticism	"While RET and related therapies proved superior in the present meta-analysis (to other therapies), this conclusion is limited by the breadth of studies available" (p. 25)

Author	Year	Years	N	Studies	Conclusions
Lyons & Woods	1991	1970–1988	70	Published and unpublished studies of children and adults	"The results demonstrated that RET is an effective form of therapy. The efficacy was most clearly demonstrated when RET was compared to base-line or other forms of controls. Effect sizes were largest for dependent measures low in reactivity (i.e. low reactivity = behavioral or physiological measures; high reactivity = measures of irrational thinking)" (p. 368)
Mahoney 182)	1974	1963–1974	10	Published and unpublished studies of cognitive restructuring and RET	RET "has yet to be adequately demonstrated" and "may be viewed as tentatively promising" (p.
McGovern & Silverman	1984	1977–1982	47	Published and unpublished studies of children and adults	"there were 31 studies favoring RET. In the re-maining studies, the RET treatment groups all showed improvement and in no study was an-other treatment method significantly better than RET" (p. 16)
Oei, Hansen, & Miller	1993	1982–1988	9	Studies designed to assess whether irrational beliefs mediate change in other psychological constructs	"This review demonstrates that while RET has been demonstrated to be an effective therapeutic intervention for a variety of target problems, there is no evidence to show that improvement in RET is due to changing irrational beliefs to rational beliefs" (p. 199)
Polder	1986	1975–1985	14	Published and unpublished studies of college students and adults	REBT yielded higher effect sizes than other forms of CBT
Silverman, McCarthy, & McGovern	1992	1982–1989	89	Published and unpublished studies of children, adolescents, and adults	"49 studies resulted in positive findings for RET." When compared with other treatments, "no other treatments were found to be significantly better than RET" (p. 166)
Zettel & Hayes	1980	1957–1979	20	Published and unpublished studies of college students and adults	"the clinical efficacy has yet to be adequately demonstrated" (p. 161)

forms, bibliotherapy, or the style of disputation make a difference in the outcome? How many sessions of REBT are necessary for clinical improvement? Researchers have failed to examine the critical components of REBT. No studies have addressed the issue of whether the positive effects of REBT are obtained by changing clients' irrational beliefs before change occurs in other dependent measures (Oei et al., 1993). Lyons and Woods's (1991) meta-analysis suggested that more therapy sessions produced greater effect sizes and that more experienced therapists produced larger effect sizes than less experienced therapists. They concluded that dependent measures low in reactivity produced higher effect sizes than measures high in reactivity. These findings are the opposite of those reported by Gossette and O'Brien (1992, 1993). Several reviews indicated that no alternative treatment was more efficacious than REBT.

Generally, psychotherapy research with children and adolescents has lagged behind research with adults (Kazdin, 1994). This has also been true of research in REBT. Sixty-nine studies mentioned in the 14 reviews of REBT treated children or adolescents. However, most of these studies could be considered analogue studies or tests of REBT as a preventive intervention because they focused on using REBT with normal children in groups or in classrooms. Studies of clinically diagnosed children and adolescents are lacking, and fewer studies exist for externalizing disorders of children. No outcome study yet exists to test the sequential REBT approach to family therapy advocated here. Research on modifying parents' IBs has found REBT to be successful in improving parents' emotional reactions to their children (Joyce, 1988). Greaves (1997) expanded on Joyce's program and showed that the program could reduce stress and improve parenting skills in parents of Down's syndrome children. Although more research is needed, these studies suggest that psychologists may find REBT useful with children and parents.

Meta-analytic reviews of psychotherapy with children and adolescents have demonstrated that behavioral and cognitive therapies produce more change than nonbehavioral or traditional nondirective, or play therapies (Weisz et al., 1987; see Kazdin, 1994, for a review). As REBT shares many similarities with other behavioral and cognitive therapies, research on REBT with children and adolescents will continue to support its effectiveness.

A series of recent studies, not mentioned by any of the reviews, suggests that REBT can be useful for practitioners working in clinics or school settings. Sapp used an REBT program with African-American children to improve their academic performance (Sapp, 1994, 1996; Sapp & Farrell, 1994; Sapp, Farrell, & Durand, 1995).

FUTURE RESEARCH

Researchers have failed to distinguish between instrumental or predatory aggression, and emotionally reactive/anger provoked aggression. We believe that such a distinction may be helpful in designing effective treatments. The relationship between anger and aggression is unclear for adults and unstudied with children (DiGiuseppe, Tafrate, & Eckhardt, 1994). Anger-provoked, or emotionally reactive aggression interventions may respond more to REBT or other individual cognitive interventions. Instrumental or predatory aggression probably will not. Children with predatory aggression may need more time spent on interventions that reflect strategies such as the motivational syllogism. However, most of the efforts of this intervention would be focused on the negative consequences of their aggressive behavior. Children with angry/emotionally reactive aggression require a focus on alternative emotional reactions.

Further, many questions remain unanswered concerning the effectiveness of REBT with aggressive children and their parents. This is especially important in light of managed care demands. Is REBT more efficacious than other CBT or behavioral interventions? Addressing the effectiveness of specific techniques in REBT with children and adolescents is important for research. Do all children benefit from logical disputing, or rehearsing rational coping skills without disputing being as effective? Although some evidence indicates that children can benefit from REBT written homework forms (Miller & Kassinove, 1978), do all children benefit from the bibliotherapy and written homework sheets frequently used in REBT?

More research is needed to examine the effects of modifying parents' irrational beliefs. Specifically, will this help to increase the parents' ability to benefit from parent training and will this directly be related to a decrease in their children's aggressive behavior? Further, research is needed to test the sequential REBT approach to family therapy. These are just a few of the multitude of research questions that need to begin to be addressed for us to develop effective treatment for aggressive children.

SUMMARY

In children with reactive aggression, feelings of anger drive their aggressive behavior. To treat these children most effectively, utilizing both behavioral and cognitive techniques is necessary. REBT is particularly well-suited for this purpose. The use of negative strategies with rehearsal techniques, and positive strategies combined with rehearsal, are critical in decreasing inappropriate behaviors and increasing prosocial behaviors, respectively. One of the most important and challenging aspects of treating aggressive children is stimulating them to become motivated for treatment and helping them progress from the precontemplative to the action stage of change. The use of the motivational syllogism and obtaining agreement on the goals and tasks of therapy are critical to achieving this end. Further, helping the children to dispute and replace their IBs with RBs enables them to substitute feelings of anger with the less disturbing feeling of annoyance. Besides working directly with the children, involving the parents in the treatment as much as possible is crucial. It is often necessary to work with the parents in disputing and replacing their IBs before they can discipline their children effectively.

REBT focuses on the role of irrational, dogmatic, and rigid thinking in causing psychopathology (Ellis, 1994). IBs are tacit, pervasive, rigid schematic representations of the way the world is and ought to be. These beliefs are both factual and evaluative in nature. Beliefs are irrational when they are rigidly held in the face of evidence that shows they are logically inconsistent, antiempirical, and self-defeating. The theory discriminates between adaptive and maladaptive emotions. Its goal is not to eliminate negative emotions, but to replace maladaptive negative emotions with more adaptive negative emotions, and to help the individuals better their lives when they are free of emotional disturbance.

The primary techniques of REBT involve challenging and replacing dysfunctional IBs. Many logical, empirical, and functional strategies to challenging beliefs are recommended. In addition, REBT employs a wide range of behavioral, imaginal, and emotive exercises to cause change. The theory stresses the importance of rehearsal of new ways of thinking, and almost any technique that accomplishes this is appropriate.

Although REBT was originally designed for neurotic adults, it has been used with children and adolescents for more than 25 years. It follows a psychoeducational model that allows it to be used in groups, workshops, and classrooms as a preventive procedure. Because of its psychoeducational format, REBT can easily be integrated into educational settings. It can be used in an educational format to teach students, parents, and teachers how to reduce their emotional disturbance and improve their productivity. REBT provides a model for school mental health services including direct service and consultation.

REBT can be integrated with family systems notions to work with parents. The theory helps identify clients' thinking that reinforces dysfunctional family homeostasis. The use of REBT techniques can eliminate parents' emotional disturbance so they are free to explore and follow more productive models of relating and parenting. Because REBT shares many similarities with other behavioral and cognitive therapies, there is reason to suspect that research in REBT with children and adolescents will continue to support its effectiveness.

There is a substantial body of research supporting the efficacy of REBT. However, this research has employed too few designs and has been limited to comparing REBT with no contact or placebo controls. Future research could focus on identifying the crucial techniques of REBT, the problems and populations for which it is best suited, and identifying more efficient ways of changing clients.

REFERENCES

American Psychiatric Association. (1994). *Diagnostic and statistical manual of mental disorders* (4th ed.). Washington, DC: Author.

Bernard, M. (1990). *Taking the stress out of teaching*. North Blackburn, Victoria, Australia: Collins/Dove.

Bernard, M. E., & DiGiuseppe, R. (1990). Rational emotive therapy and school psychology. *School Psychology Review, 19*(3), 267.

Bernard, M., & Joyce, M. (1984). *Rational emotive therapy with children and adolescents*. New York: Wiley.

Block, J. (1978). Effects of a rational-emotive mental health program on poorly achieving, disruptive high school students. *Journal of Counseling Psychology, 25*, 61–65.

Casey, R. J., & Berman, J. S. (1985). The outcome of psychotherapy with children. *Psychological Bulletin, 98*, 388–400.

Dadds, M. R., & McHugh, T. A. (1992). Social support and treatment outcome in behavioral family therapy for child conduct problems. *Journal of Consulting and Clinical Psychology, 60*, 252–259.

DiGiuseppe, R. (1975). Using behavior modification to teach rational self-statements to children. *Rational Living*, Spring. Reprinted in: A. Ellis & R. Grieger (Eds.) (1977), *Rational emotive psychotherapy: A handbook of theory and practice* (pp. 276–289). New York: Springer.

DiGiuseppe, R. (1988). A cognitive behavioral approach to the treatment of conduct disorder children and adolescents. In N. Epstein, S. Schlesinger, & W. Dryden (Eds.), *Cognitive behavioral therapy with families* (pp. 183–214). New York: Brunner/Mazel.

DiGiuseppe, R. (1995). Developing the therapeutic alliance with angry clients. In H. Kassinove (Ed.), *Anger disorders* (pp. 131–150). London: Taylor & Francis.

DiGiuseppe, R. (1999). Rational emotive behavior therapy. In H. T. Prout & D. T. Brown (Eds.), *Counseling and psychotherapy with children and adolescents* (pp. 252–301). New York: Wiley.

DiGiuseppe, R., & Bernard, M. E. (1983). Principles of assessment and methods of treatment with children: Special considerations. In A. Ellis & M. E. Bernard (Eds.), *Rational emotive approaches to the problems of childhood* (pp. 45–88). New York: Plenum Press.

DiGiuseppe, R., Goodman, R., & Nevas, S. (1996) Selective abstraction errors in reviewing the REBT outcome literature. Manuscript in preparation St. John's University.

DiGiuseppe, R., & Jilton, R. (1996). The therapeutic alliance in adolescent psychotherapy. *Applied and Preventive Psychology, 5*, 85–100.

DiGiuseppe, R. A., Miller, N. J., & Trexler, L. D. (1977). A review of rational-emotive psychotherapy outcome studies. *The Counseling Psychologist, 7*, 64–72.

DiGiuseppe, R., Tafrate, R., & Eckhardt, C. (1994). Critical issues in the treatment of anger. *Cognitive and Behavioral Practice, 1*, 111–132.

DiGiuseppe, R., Turchiano, T., Li, C., Wellen, D., Anderson, T., & Jones, D. (1996, November). Childhood anger and aggression: A meta-analysis of behavioral and cognitive treatments. In E. Feindler (Chair), *Anger in the schools: Diagnosis, assessment, treatment, and the costs to learning.* Symposium conducted at the meeting of the Association for Advancement of Behavior Therapy, Manhattan.

Dix, T. (1991). The affective organization of parenting: Adaptive and maladaptive processes. *Psychological Bulletin, 110*(1), 3–25.

Ellis, A. (1994). *Reason and emotion in psychotherapy: A comprehensive method of treating human disturbance—Revised and updated.* New York: Birch Lane Press.

Ellis, A., & DiGiuseppe, R. (1993). Appropriate and inappropriate emotions in rational emotive therapy: A response to Craemer & Fong. *Cognitive Therapy and Research, 17*(5), 471–477.

Engels, G. I., Garnefski, N., & Diekstra, R. F. W. (1993). Efficacy of rational-emotive therapy: A quantitative analysis. *Journal of Consulting and Clinical Psychology, 61*, 1083–1090.

Gossette, R. L., & O'Brien, R. M. (1993). Efficacy of rational emotive therapy with children: A critical reappraisal. *Journal of Behavior Therapy & Experimental Psychiatry, 24*, 15–25.

Gossette, R. L., & O'Brien, R. M. (1992). The efficacy of rational emotive therapy in adults: Clinical fact or psychometric artifact. *Journal of Behavior Therapy & Experimental Psychiatry, 23*, 9–24.

Greaves, D. (1997). The effect of rational-emotive parent education on the stress of mothers of young children with Down syndrome. *Journal of Rational-Emotive and Cognitive Behavioral Therapy, 15*(4), 249–267.

Haaga, D. A., & Davison, G. C. (1989). Outcome studies of rational-emotive therapy. In Bernard, M. E. & DiGiuseppe, R. (Eds.), *Inside rational-emotive therapy. A critical appraisal of the theory and therapy of Albert Ellis* (pp. 155–197). San Diego, CA: Academic Press, Inc.

Hajzler, D. J., & Bernard M. E. (1990). A review of rational emotive education outcome studies. *School Psychology Quarterly, 6*, 27–49.

Huesmann, L. R., Eron, L. D., Lefkowitz, M. M., & Walder, L. O. (1984). Stability of aggression over time and generations. *Developmental Psychology, 20*, 1120–1134.

Jorm, A. F. (1989). Modifiability of trait anxiety and neuroticism: A meta-analysis of the literature. *Australian and New Zealand Journal of Psychiatry, 23*, 21–29.

Joyce, M. R. (1988). *An evaluation of the effectiveness of a rational emotive parent education program.* Unpublished doctoral dissertation, University of Melbourne, Melbourne.

Kazdin, A. (1994). Psychotherapy for children and adolescents. In A. E. Bergin & S. L. Garfield (Eds.), *Handbook of psychotherapy and behavior change* (4th ed., pp. 543–594). New York: Wiley.

Kendall, P. C. (1993). Cognitive-behavioral therapies with youth: Guiding theory, current status and emerging developments. *Journal of Consulting and Clinical Psychology, 61*(2), 235–247.

Loeber, R., & Dishion, T. J. (1983). Early predictors of male delinquency: A review. *Psychological Bulletin, 94*, 68–99.

Lyons, L. D., & Woods, P. J. (1991). The efficacy of rational-emotive therapy: A quantitative review of the outcome research. *Clinical Psychology Review, 11*, 357–369.

McGovern, T. E., & Silverman, M. S. (1984). A review of outcome studies of rational-emotive therapy from 1977 to 1982. *Journal of Rational Emotive Therapy, 2*(1), 7–18.

Meichenbaum, D. (1971). *Cognitive-behavior modification.* New York: Plenum Press.

Miller, N. J., & Kassinove, H. (1978). Effects of lecture, rehearsal, written homework, and the IQ on the efficacy of a rational-emotive school mental health program. *Journal of Community Psychology, 6*, 366–373.

Miller, W. R., & Rollnick, S. (1991). *Motivational interviewing: Preparing people to change addictive behavior.* New York: Guilford Press.

Morris, G. B. (1993). A rational-emotive treatment program with conduct disorder and attention-deficit hyperactivity disorder adolescents. *Journal of Rational-Emotive and Cognitive Behavior Therapy, 11*(3), 123–134.

Prochaska, J., & DiClemente, C. (1988). *The transtheoretical approach to therapy.* Chicago: Dorsey Press.

Sapp, M. (1994). Cognitive behavioral counseling: Applications for African American middle school students who are academically at risk. *Journal of Instructional Psychology, 21*(2), 161–171.

Sapp, M. (1996). Irrational beliefs that can lead to academic failure for African American middle school students who are at-risk. *Journal of Rational Emotive and Cognitive Behavior Therapy, 14*(2), 123–134.

Sapp, M., & Farrell, W. (1994). Cognitive behavioral interventions: Applications for academically at risk special education students. *Preventing School Failure, 38*(2), 19–24.

Sapp, M., Farrell, W., & Durand, H. (1995). Cognitive behavior therapy: Applications for African American middle school at risk students. *Journal of Instructional Psychology, 22*(2), 169–177.

Silverman, M. S., McCarthy, M., & McGovern, T. (1992). A review of outcome studies of rational-emotive therapy from 1982–1989. *Journal of Rational-Emotive & Cognitive-Behavior Therapy, 10,* 111–175.

Spivack, G., Platt, J., & Shure, M. (1976). *The social problem-solving approach to adjustment.* San Francisco: Jossey–Bass.

Spivack, G., & Shure, M. (1974). *Social adjustment of young children: A cognitive approach to solving real-life problems.* San Francisco: Jossey–Bass.

Walen, S., DiGiuseppe, R., & Dryden, W. (1992). *A practitioners' guide to rational emotive therapy* (2nd ed.). New York: Oxford University Press.

Weisz, J. R., Weiss, B., Alicke, M. D., & Klotz, M. L. (1987). Effectiveness of psychotherapy with children and adolescents: Meta-analytic findings for clinicians. *Journal of Consulting and Clinical Psychology, 55,* 542–549.

Weisz, J. R., Weiss, B., Han, S. S., Granger, D. A., & Morton, T. (1995). Effects of psychotherapy with children and adolescents revisited: A meta-analysis of treatment outcome studies. *Psychological Bulletin, 117*(3), 450–468.

Wellen, D. (1997). *A meta-analysis of single subject studies of therapies for children and adolescents with aggression.* Unpublished doctoral dissertation, St. John's University, Jamaica, NY.

Zettle, R., & Hayes, S. (1980). Conceptual and empirical status of rational emotive therapy. *Progress in Behavior Modification, 9,* 125–166.

16

Family Therapy with Eating-Disordered Adolescents

ARTHUR L. ROBIN and PATRICIA T. SIEGEL

Eating disorders represent potentially life-threatening conditions that impede physical, emotional, and behavioral growth and development. The prognosis is positive if an adolescent's eating disorder is treated soon after its onset; otherwise, the disorder may become a chronic condition by adulthood, with devastating and sometimes irreversible medical, behavioral, and emotional consequences (Lask & Bryant-Waugh, 1993).

Family therapy is an essential component in the effective treatment of eating disorders in adolescents for a number of reasons (Dare & Eisler, 1997; Robin, Gilroy, & Dennis, 1998): (1) the major developmental task of adolescence is individuation from the family, and individuation-related issues often contribute to the development and maintenance of anorexia nervosa (AN) or bulimia nervosa (BN) during the second decade of life; (2) the starvation associated with AN clouds the adolescent's ability to think clearly, making it very difficult for her to initiate or sustain refeeding without the persistent and persuasive direction and structuring of her parents; (3) the denial intrinsic to eating disorders renders the adolescent incapable of objectively appreciating the life-threatening nature of her condition to willingly reach out for treatment, necessitating that parents make sure the adolescent receives adequate treatment; and (4) in this era of managed care, it is very difficult to obtain authorization for the length of inpatient stays often needed to initiate refeeding; instead, the treatment team must creatively help parents manage very low weight adolescents with AN in the home environment.

ARTHUR L. ROBIN and PATRICIA T. SIEGEL • Department of Psychiatry and Behavioral Neurosciences, Wayne State University, Detroit, Michigan 48202.

Handbook of Psychotherapies with Children and Families, edited by Russ and Ollendick. Kluwer Academic/Plenum Publishers, New York, 1999.

DESCRIPTION OF THE PROBLEMS/DISORDER

Eating disorders in adolescents include AN, BN, and various combinations of anorectic and bulimic symptoms that are clinically meaningful but may not meet the full criteria for AN or BN. There is no single cause for AN or BN; rather, they are generally considered to be multidetermined disorders, caused by a combination of biological, cultural, personality, and family factors (Hsu, 1990; Lask & Bryant-Waugh, 1993). The DSM-IV (American Psychiatric Association, 1994) diagnostic criteria for AN include (1) body weight less than 85% of that expected, or failure to grow resulting in maintaining body weight less than 85%, (2) fear of gaining weight, (3) body weight disturbance or denial of the seriousness of low body weight, and (4) absence of three consecutive menstrual cycles in postmonarchal females.

The DSM-IV (American Psychiatric Association, 1994) criteria for BN include (1) recurrent episodes of binge eating, (2) recurrent compensatory behaviors such as vomiting, use of laxatives or diuretics, fasting, or exercise, (3) criteria 1 and 2 occur at least twice a week for 3 months, (4) self-evaluation unduly influenced by body shape and weight, and (5) these disturbances do not exclusively occur in the presence of AN, e.g., the individual does not have to be underweight.

These criteria are not developmentally sensitive to the special factors inherent in adolescent eating disorders. Practitioners should familiarize themselves with the differences between adult and adolescent eating disorders (Fisher et al., 1995). Strict application of the DSM-IV criteria will often result in committing false-negative errors in diagnosis, e.g., overlooking disordered eating and related attitudes that could lead to health impairment. Such youngsters in need of intervention who fail to meet the DSM-IV criteria will formally often fall within the DSM-IV category, Eating Disorder Not Otherwise Specified. This category is defined as a partial or subclinical AN or BN.

The recent publication of the Diagnostic and Statistical Manual for Primary Care (DSM-PC) Child and Adolescent Version (American Academy of Pediatrics, 1996) represents a helpful diagnostic development for practitioners who typically see milder, subclinical behavioral and emotional problems such as eating disorders. Starting with a presenting cluster of symptoms, the DSM-PC provides detailed examples of common developmental presentations during infancy, early childhood, middle childhood, and adolescence at three levels of severity: (1) normal developmental variation, (2) problem, and (3) DSM-IV disorder. In addition, information regarding differential diagnosis from general medical conditions, substance-induced conditions, and other psychiatric disorders is provided, along with a detailed scheme for the classification of common environmental situations and stressors. Clusters were written for Dieting/Body Image Problems, and Purging/Binge Eating. In the Dieting/Body Image Cluster, for example, the normal range of developmental variation for dieting is defined as (1) voluntary dieting and food intake restriction that results in maintaining weight within 95% of that expected for age and height, (2) decreases in food intake and curtailing but not totally eliminating selected foods such as sweets, (3) a mildly distorted body image or mild concern about being too fat, and (4) the individual can stop dieting. In contrast, the problem range is defined as (1) dieting and voluntary food restriction leading to weight loss or failure to gain weight, with weight maintained between 86 and 94% of normal, (2) becoming obsessed with the pursuit of thinness and developing systematic fears of gaining weight, and (3) development of a more significant body image disturbance and denial that weight loss is a problem. The DSM-PC Child and Adolescent Version permits the practitioner not only to code the adolescent's emerging difficulties with dieting, body/image, or binge eating, but also permits the coding of environmental situations that may be contributing to these difficulties.

In this chapter, we will focus primarily on the treatment of AN in both its clinical and subclinical forms, using a comprehensive behavioral family systems therapy approach (BFST). We will not focus on BN because our version of BFST has been tested primarily with AN. We will not be able to provide the practitioner with detailed guidelines for assessment and differential diagnosis of eating. Readers interested in more information about how to conduct such an evaluation in children and adolescents should consult Fisher et al. (1995) and Lask & Bryant-Waugh (1993).

DESCRIPTION OF THE PROCEDURES

BFST for AN must take place within a multidisciplinary context involving a medical and a dietary component in addition to the family therapy (Kreipe et al., 1995). The mental health professional conducting the family therapy may work in the same setting as the pediatrician and dietician, or may regularly communicate with them across settings, but the treatment of adolescents with eating disorders should not be undertaken without having such a team available. The pediatrician's role is to establish the adolescent's target weight and ideal rate of weight gain, decide how much exercise and athletic activity is safe, monitor her medical condition, and hospitalize her as needed. The dietician's role is to outline a nutritionally balanced food plan sufficient to gain weight and to adjust the total daily caloric allotment, assist the family in planning meals that adhere to this food plan, and periodically adjust the total daily caloric allotment to permit the adolescent to achieve the desired rate of weight gain.

The family therapist should be working closely with a pediatrician and a dietician to accomplish five overall goals (Robin, Siegel, Bedway, & Gilroy, 1996). First, the adolescent's health must be restored by refeeding her until she reaches an appropriate body weight for her height and age. In cases of severe starvation resulting in weight loss greater than 25% of original body weight and/or medical complications, the pediatrician may decide to hospitalize the adolescent until she reaches a level of nutrition and medical stability that is safe for resumption of life in the community. Second, the adolescent's eating habits and attitudes must be changed. Instead of eating a highly restrictive diet typically consisting of vegetables, fruits, and selected other low-calorie foods, the adolescent needs to learn to eat a balanced diet including proteins and fats, in sufficient quantities determined by the dietician to at first gain weight and later maintain it. Before eating normally, the adolescent must change her often distorted beliefs about the impact of certain foods on the body and health. Third, she needs to overcome her distorted views of her body and her fear of getting fat, two of the cognitive underpinnings of AN. Fourth, the adolescent needs to deal with a host of psychological and personality factors that have often been summarized under the broad term *weak ego strength*

(Goodsitt, 1997). This includes feelings of personal ineffectiveness, limited ability to experience natural inner affective states, interpersonal distrust, fears of growing up, and generally poor self-esteem. Obsessional, perfectionistic personality styles need to be redirected away from relentless dieting and toward more productive goals. Fifth, maladaptive family interaction patterns that may be impeding appropriate achievement of the developmental goal of adolescent individuation need to be changed. Such patterns often include conflict avoidance, overprotectiveness, enmeshment, and inappropriate involvement of the adolescent in the parents' latent marital problems (Minuchin, Rosman, & Baker, 1978).

The BFST therapist starts with the premise that families do not cause anorexia, and that no one is to blame for the adolescent's plight. However, it is useful to combine behavioral, cognitive, and family systems components to understand how AN is maintained and provide a context for effective treatment (Robin et al., 1996). From the family structure perspective, the appropriate hierarchy of parent-in-charge-of-child is reversed in the area of food and eating (Minuchin et al., 1978). The adolescent is eating or not eating as she wishes, and her parents have very little influence over her eating behavior; in fact, feeling helpless, many parents make extraordinary efforts to appease their adolescents in the hopes of getting them to eat, going to extreme lengths such as obtaining unusual foods. Clearly, an effective therapy must restore the appropriate parent–child hierarchy using strategic–structural family therapy techniques. The physical effects of starvation, compounded by compulsive personality styles and cognitive distortions, render the adolescent helpless to change her eating behavior and attitudes without external intervention. Thus, the BFST therapist must place the parents clearly in charge of the adolescent's eating in order to reestablish the hierarchy and restart the adolescent eating properly, overcoming the momentum of starvation. Parents need specific, reliable routines to follow as they take control. Behavior modification has provided powerful tools for refeeding, gaining weight, and eating habits (Touyz & Beumont, 1997), and the BFST therapist uses behavioral techniques to give parents the reliable routines they need to prompt and consequate their adolescent's eating behavior during the weight gain.

As the adolescent begins to eat, gain weight, and emerge from starvation, all of the cognitive distortions and ego strength/personality issues need to be dealt with (Garner, Vitousek, & Pike, 1997). The BFST therapist relies heavily on cognitive therapy techniques to deal with these issues at the individual and family levels. When the adolescent reaches her target weight, parental control over eating is gradually shifted back to the more normal state of the adolescent being in control of her own eating. At this time, the now healthier and stronger adolescent is typically ready to engage in age-appropriate adolescent individuation behaviors such as increased peer contacts, dating, and even rebelliousness and age-appropriate noncompliance to parental requests. The BFST therapist relies on problem-solving communication training approaches (Robin & Foster, 1989) to help the family adjust to such independence-related conflicts.

The general procedures outlined above are accomplished in four phases: (1) assessment, (2) control rationale, (3) weight gain, and (4) weight maintenance. In the first three phases, the adolescent and her parents are seen together for virtually all of the sessions. In the fourth phase, the adolescent and the parents are generally seen together, with an occasional exception to this rule. Siblings are invited to attend family sessions as needed. Family therapy sessions typically last 60 to 75 minutes and are held weekly during the first three phases of treatment, and twice a month during the fourth phase. The length of treatment typically ranges from 10 to 24 months, with a mean of 16 months in our clinical research study.

Assessment

During the assessment phase, which typically lasts three sessions, the therapist establishes rapport with the family and explains BFST to them; collects information concerning weight, dieting, eating, individual, and family problems, establishing weekly routines for weighing the adolescent and recording in writing all of the food that she eats; and enlists the assistance of the pediatrician to determine the adolescent's medical conditions and determine the need for an inpatient refeeding hospitalization. In addition, the therapist tries to (1) remove blame by emphasizing that through no fault of her own or her parents, the adolescent has slipped into a self-perpetuating cycle of starvation in which she has lost control of her eating, and (2) reframe individual problems within a family context by emphasizing how an eating disorder challenges the entire family, and the adolescent needs her family to work as a team to help her overcome this life-threatening disease.

Clinical experience has taught us families are best engaged in treatment when the adolescent and the parents are seen separately in the first session, then brought together for the remaining sessions. With the adolescent, the therapist attempts to establish trust through reflective listening, open-ended questioning, and careful explanations. The therapist also noncritically lets the adolescent tell her story of dieting and weight loss, fears and body dissatisfactions, family relationships, school, peers, hobbies, and interests. These adolescents often have so much control over their parents that unless the therapist quickly engages the adolescent, they often convince their parents not to enroll them in therapy because they claim to be able to gain weight on their own. The therapist ends the interview by weighing the adolescent, either in street clothes without shoes on, or if the therapist is working near a medical clinic, by having the adolescent change into a hospital gown; the therapist explains that the weight taken at the sessions will serve as the official weight for the record.

With the parents, the therapist takes a history of the onset and course of the dieting and weight loss, previous attempts to treat it, as well as general medical and developmental histories. The therapist arranges for a physical examination by the pediatrician, an initial consultation with the dietician, and asks the parents to begin recording all of the adolescent's food using specially designed food records. The parents are asked to keep the food diary based primarily on their own observations, rather than the adolescent's reports. This request often provokes some controversy because the parents are accustomed to appeasing their daughter around food and may not wish to risk her disapproval by even taking charge of recording her food. The therapist assures the parents that an accurate record is needed for medical and dietary purposes, that their daughter's starvation distorts her thinking, and through no fault of her own, she may inaccurately report her foods; therefore, they need to take this responsibility. In essence, this task introduces at a relatively nonthreatening level the notion of parental control, which will be built on later.

The battery of self-report measures described later under the research discussion are also assigned as homework following the first session.

In the second assessment session, the therapist carefully observes family interaction and interviews the family about their approaches to handling eating, dieting, and non-food-related parent–adolescent issues. At the beginning of the second session, the therapist reviews the homework assignment, collecting the self-report measures and examining the food records, not only for information about eating but more importantly, to learn about family interactions based on how the family reacted to the task. Did the parents work as a team? What difficulties arose? How resistant was the teenager? Did she try to engage one parent in a coalition to sabotage the task? What other problems in family structure arose, such as triangulation or other coalitional patterns? If the task was partially done or not done at all, how does the family explain their actions? As these questions arise, the therapist uses the review of the homework as a springboard to broaden the frame of reference to other situations involving family interaction regarding eating and noneating issues, beginning to build a mental picture of family process. If time permits, the therapist also assesses the parents' families of origin and the parents' and adolescent's interactions with the grandparents. The therapist ends the session by reassigning the task of recording all of the adolescent's food intake.

By the third session, the pediatrician has examined the adolescent and established a target weight, a desirable rate of weight gain per week (usually 1 lb per week), and a weight below which the adolescent will have to be hospitalized. The dietician has met with the family and outlined a balanced food plan starting with a relatively low number of calories (typically 1200 to 1500) and increasing in calories at regular intervals. The therapist reviews the reactions of the adolescent and the parents to the target weight and the food plan and uses these reactions as the basis for building commitment to a behavioral family systems approach and preparing the family for the presentation of the control rationale. Typically, the teenagers are very angry and distraught over the pediatrician's and the dietician's recommendations, and they often vow never to eat that way or reach the specified target weight, and to take extreme actions such as running away from home rather than go into the hospital. The parents are often surprised by the intensity of the previously compliant daughter's reactions, and typically feel even more helpless in the face of these strong negative reactions. The therapist empathizes strongly with the adolescent's plight, but also clearly conveys to the parents how their daughter's strong emotional reaction is one more example of the impact of starvation in clouding her thinking, and that it is going to take a strong commitment from the parents to help the adolescent overcome these reactions and take the steps that are necessary to return to health. The therapist makes sure that the parents support the recommendations of the dietician and the pediatrician, and extracts from the parents a strong verbal commitment to do whatever it takes to help their daughter return to health. Throughout this discussion, the adolescent typically challenges the weight and eating recommendations, alternating between tears and anger; the therapist continues to empathize with the adolescent, express that her plight is not her fault, but nonetheless reject the logic of her challenges, attributing them to a mind tragically clouded by the physical effects of starvation. The therapist urges the parents to take the same caring, nonblaming, but authoritative stance about the need to eat and gain weight. The therapist repeatedly reassures the parents that their daughter's extreme reactions are expected and normal in these circumstances, that the therapist has dealt extensively with such reactions in the past, and that the family is right on target in being ready to begin the weight gain phase at the next session. The therapist must sound confident and hopeful when reassuring the parents; they need a great deal of support and hope to prepare them to make the difficult efforts that lie ahead in refeeding their daughter.

Control Rationale

At the beginning of this phase, the therapist strategically presents a control rationale to the family (Robin et al., 1996). The therapist asks the parents to work as a team, take charge of the hierarchy, and creatively devise a behavioral weight gain program so that their adolescent can be refed according to the specifications outlined by the pediatrician and the dietician. The effects of starvation and the teen's poor record eating are reviewed and related to her currently impaired functioning, noting how she is completely out of control of her own eating, although no one is to blame. The therapist likens food to a medicine used to treat a disease, and illustrates how the nature of her disease makes it very difficult for her to "take her medicine," e.g., her fears of fatness and body image distortions interfere with eating. The therapist points out that when a child is unable to take her medicine for any other disease, the physician asks the parents, who love the child, to see to it that the medicine is taken as prescribed. Similarly, in the case of anorexia, the parents need to ensure that their adolescent consumes the food that is her "medicine."

Therefore, the parents will need to temporarily assume complete responsibility and control over their daughter's eating, until she reaches her target weight, emerges from starvation, can think clearly, and can resume taking her own "medicine." The therapist specifies the parental responsibility to include (1) planning the daily menu, (2) purchasing the necessary groceries, (3) measuring, weighing, and preparing the food for each meal, (4) sitting at the table with their daughter and making sure she eats all of the designated food, (5) writing on food record sheets what was eaten, and (6) staying with their daughter for 45 minutes after each meal to make sure she does not attempt to vomit or exercise. Parents are asked to make arrangements for appropriate monitoring of eating behavior at school or in any other settings where the adolescent will be away from home. Restricting exercise and athletic activities is also defined as part of the parents' responsibilities.

Empathetically acknowledging how difficult it will be for the parents to work as a team in getting the adolescent to eat, the therapist offers to be there at every step to coach and guide the parents. Examples are given of how each meal can be broken down into its components, how the therapist will help the parents plan the menus, keep the adolescent at the table, use positive and negative consequences to encourage the adolescent to eat, and overcome the variety of sources of resistance that the adolescent might display. It is extremely important for the therapist to project an air of complete confidence during this discussion, citing creative approaches to the behavioral weight gain program used by other families in the past. It is also important for the therapist to have already established a reasonably strong alliance with the parents before this session.

Naturally, the control rationale provokes a strong reaction from the family. The adolescent angrily objects that she is not out of control and does not need parental control. Previously quiescent adolescents may have major temper outbursts in the session. The parents express skepticism, despair, helplessness, and even open defiance to carrying out the control rationale, sometimes challenging the therapist's competence. Family members sometimes form a coalition against the therapist.

In the next few sessions, the therapist must stand firm and not become defensive. This is undoubtedly the most difficult point of treatment for the therapist, especially novice therapists, who often need strong support from their colleagues to refrain from caving in to pressure from the family. Angry adolescent objections are empathetically acknowledged, but not debated; the therapist reinforces the temporary nature of the parental controls as well as the previously mentioned impression of how the adolescent's current and past behavior clearly indicate her inability to control her own eating, and adds that it is not her fault, but regrettably these steps need to be taken to prevent her from killing herself from starvation. Parental objections are met nondefensively and openly with understanding, information, paradoxical restraint, and requests for further clarification of the parents' position; we go with the resistance, not against it, as a strategy for overcoming it (Anderson & Stewart, 1983).

If the therapist confidently perseveres in nondefensively listening to everyone's objections and patiently reiterating the need for parental control to restart eating, the majority of parents eventually come to agree. Some more immediately embrace the behavioral weight gain program and experience initial successes with it, strongly reinforcing their commitment to it and their confidence in the therapist. Others cave in to pressure from their daughters and give them "one more chance" to prove they can "do it on their own." Most commonly, the adolescents are unable to eat the required calories and gain weight on their own for any length of time, and the parents come to realize that parental control is necessary. In those rare cases where the adolescent does successfully eat and gain weight, the therapist congratulates everyone, and urges them to continue their efforts, increasing the calories as specified by the dietician.

The therapist coaches the parents to establish a behavioral weight gain program, discussing exhaustively with the family the following issues: (1) continuing to keep written logs of everything the adolescent eats; (2) when will the specific meals be planned; (3) how will responsibility for preparing, monitoring, and recording the meals be divided between the mother and father; (4) how will lunch at school be handled; (5) what will be the positive incentives for completing eating each meal, and how will they be scheduled; (6) what longer-term contracts can be written for gaining 25%, 50%, 75%, and so forth, of the required weight; (7) what will be the consequences for failing to complete a meal; (8) how will calories be preserved, e.g., activity limited, if meals are not eaten; (9) how will they interact with their daughter during mealtime; (10) what will be the rules governing exercise, athletics, dance, or other activities that involve high expenditures of calories. The behavioral weight gain program may be implemented in a step-by-step fashion, often at first for one meal, and gradually extended to cover all of the adolescent's meals and snacks.

As a coach, the therapist raises these issues for the couple to consider, but does not tell the family exactly how to handle them. The couple is guided to creatively generate solutions to each problem, with the therapist helping in suggesting how other families have dealt with the issues, but trying to take a Socratic approach. It is important for the parents to feel that they developed the specific plan, and that it is tailored to their idiosyncratic situation; this increases their commitment to implementing it effectively. As the parents begin to experience success with the behavioral weight gain program and express their commitment to it, the control rationale phase of treatment has been completed.

Weight Gain

The primary goals of the weight gain phase of BFST are to (1) "fine tune" the behavioral weight gain program, closing off any loopholes and continuing the program until the adolescent reaches her target weight, and (2) begin to explore other issues, including cognitive distortions, ego-related issues, and family structure problems.

In the early sessions of this phase, the focus is on "fine tuning" the behavioral weight gain program. At the beginning of each session, the therapist weighs the adolescent and graphs the weight on a chart. Then, the therapist gives the teenager a few minutes to ventilate about any issues of concern to her or bring up any issues that she wants to discuss; we have found that it is very important during this phase of therapy when the adolescent does not have a great deal of choice about the eating program to provide a brief forum for empathetically listening to her concerns at the start of each session. Next, the therapist collects the food logs that the parents have continued to keep, and reviews the food logs in light of whether the adolescent gained weight or lost weight.

If the adolescent has gained weight and eaten most of the required food, the therapist praises her, makes sure her parents gave out any agreed-upon rewards, and asks what it was like to gain weight, acknowledging how upsetting it can be, and reassuring the teen that she will not be permitted to gain too much weight too fast. If she evidences any distorted cognitions about the weight gain, the therapist helps her challenge them. For example, some adolescents believe that eating one cookie will put on 5 pounds, or that all fats are unhealthy. The therapist may provide corrective nutritional information and/or go through a Socratic discussion challenging the logic of such distortions, helping the adolescent develop more accurate cognitions about the impacts of specific foods. The therapist also praises the parents for working effectively as a team, urges them to continue, and prompts them to anticipate and plan to overcome any difficulties that may arise during the next week.

If the adolescent has lost weight or stayed the same, the therapist analyzes with the family which of the following factors may have been operative: (1) she ate an insufficient number of calories, even if the written records suggest otherwise; (2) she dumped or hid some of her food; (3) she exercised secretly; (4) she skipped snacks or lunch at school; (5) she did not eat all that was served and the parents did not notice it or do anything about it; (6) she ate too many low-calorie foods; (7) she took laxatives or vomited; (8) the written records were inaccurate or altered by the teenager; (9) parental teamwork is breaking down, or the adolescent has secretly convinced one parent to back off; (10) there is interference from other family issues, such as marital conflict or sibling issues; (11) the consequences for failing to eat were not enforced. The remainder of the session is devoted to coaching the parents to work on an approach to overcoming the "loopholes" that were identified.

Only if none of these factors sufficiently explains the lack of weight gain does the therapist consult with the dietician about increasing daily caloric intake, usually in increments of 200 calories.

In the later sessions of this phase of BFST, when the adolescent is regularly gaining weight, the therapist begins to shift the focus to non-food-related issues. The therapist gives the parents a "crash course" in adolescent development, emphasizing the importance of autonomy seeking, and helps the family distinguish between autonomy-seeking behaviors and rebellious behaviors, a distinction that enmeshed families find difficult to make (Robin & Foster, 1989). Such "discrimination training" may take the form of asking the family to brainstorm a list of all of the "independent" adolescent behaviors they can, then differentiating the items into "rebellious" versus "autonomous" categories. Such a task usually leads to a cognitive restructuring discussion about the nature of autonomy versus rebellion.

It is also at this point in therapy, as the adolescent is emerging from starvation, that the therapist can more accurately assess the presence of comorbid psychiatric conditions that may have been previously masked by the adolescent's starvation (Hsu, 1990). For example, mood disorders and obsessive/compulsive disorders are difficult to distinguish from the secondary effects of starvation, but by the time the adolescent has moved at least halfway toward her target weight, such distinctions can be made, and appropriate additional interventions can be planned as needed.

When the adolescent reaches her target weight, the emphasis shifts to weight maintenance, the last phase of BFST.

Weight Maintenance

During the weight maintenance phase of BFST, the therapist meets with the adolescent and the family every other week, and works to accomplish the following goals: (1) gradually return control over eating to the adolescent; (2) adjust caloric intake for weight maintenance; (3) teach the teenager healthy strategies to maintain weight within the target range; (4) continue to reduce distorted cognitions and misperceptions; (5) teach the family to openly face problems and conflicts, and resolve them through mutual problem solving; (6) foster adolescent self-efficacy and autonomy; (7) further strengthen the marital dyad, removing the adolescent from any marital issues; and (8) continue to directly target any comorbid psychiatric conditions. Initial efforts to work on goals 4–8 may have already begun during the later sessions of the weight gain phase.

Family therapy sessions are scheduled every other week instead of weekly. The dietician is consulted to suggest a reduction in the number of calories appropriate for maintaining weight instead of gaining weight. The therapist praises the adolescent for attaining target weight despite many obstacles, fears, and anxieties, comments on the teen's regained health, and notes any comments or behaviors by the teen that reflect maturity and good judgment. Now that the teen has demonstrated that she can be trusted about eating, it is time to use behavioral contracting and shaping to gradually return control over eating to the teenager. The therapist assures the parents that they can be as cautious as they feel is necessary in returning control over eating to their daughter.

A "comfort zone" of 3–5 pounds around the target weight is defined. The therapist prompts the family to agree that as the teenager regains responsibility for her eating, weight fluctuations within the comfort zone are treated as "random noise" related to experimentation; however, weight variations above or below the comfort zone become sources of serious concern, necessitating some resumption of parental controls.

The therapist coaches the family to come up with a behavioral contract involving a series of small steps that give the adolescent more decision making control over her eating. At first, such steps might include (1) giving the adolescent responsibility for planning one meal, (2) permitting the adolescent to measure/record food and/or eat without supervision, (3) permitting the adolescent to eat one meal without supervision, and (4) permitting the adolescent to write down her own foods for one meal. The therapist asks the family to carry out the contract over several weeks, and if successful, to extend it to give the adolescent responsibility for two and then three meals in each area. Maintenance of weight within the comfort zone and reports of the adolescent's eating are used to judge the "success" of this contract.

The parents often express "ruinous" beliefs about the negative impact of too much freedom too soon. It is very important for the therapist to gently challenge these ruinous beliefs by emphasizing the built-in safeguards of the comfort zone of weight and reminding the parents that they can always revert to stricter external control if needed. It is also important for the therapist to understand that even though the overt issue is giving the adolescent increased control for her eating, in many such enmeshed families, the covert agenda is the entire individuation process. Success at regaining control over eating will greatly facilitate the parents' generally permitting their daughter to individuate in non-food-related areas.

Inevitably, the family experiences some difficulties returning control over eating to the adolescent. Parents often want to overreact by restoring all external control, spurring increased rebellion by their adolescents. The therapist uses cognitive restructuring to guide families to react appropriately, restoring parental control in stages, not overreacting in an absolutistic manner. Such steps continue to prepare the family for dealing with later adolescent rebellion in non-food-related areas.

The adolescent is helped to adjust her cognitions to foster healthy methods of weight maintenance (Garner et al., 1997). Through an inquiry into the adolescent's perceptions of her foods and her appearance now that she has reached target weight, the therapist identifies any remaining distortions that need to be addressed. Often, for instance, the teenagers continue to fear eating sweets or fats. Reluctance to eat such "forbidden foods" may be dealt with by asking the teen to experiment with eating a small amount of the forbidden food, and carefully evaluating her feelings and weight afterward. The adolescent is encouraged to use exercise appropriately as a method for maintaining weight, and she is encouraged to resume athletic activities. The therapist coaches her to determine how many calories she may need to add to her food plan to maintain weight while exercising as much as she desires.

The therapist builds on the discrimination training conducted earlier on the differences between rebellion and autonomy to develop assignments for the adolescent to become more autonomous. The adolescent is strongly encouraged to spend more time with peers and less time with parents, while the parents are encouraged to do more as a couple. For example, the adolescent may be asked to spend the night with a friend while the parents go out together. It is important to urge the couple to spend more time together, so that they can fill the void left as the adolescent spends less time with her parents.

The therapist legitimizes the adolescent's efforts at individuation, empathizes with her about how difficult it is to define her identity in a world of huge variations in values, and helps her define where she fits in her peer group (Goodsitt, 1997). It is at this stage of therapy that some adolescents benefit from an individual session, to discuss issues of sexuality and dating, for example. It is also at this stage that a female therapist can use her own experiences to help the adolescent deal with the many conflicting roles that our society thrusts on contemporary women. The therapist strongly advocates for the adolescent's right to privacy in the home and independence outside the home. The therapist further assesses rigid, perfectionistic beliefs about school achievement and family life, and encourages more flexible thinking.

Usually, the adolescent begins to engage in age-appropriate rebellious behaviors, spurring normal parent–adolescent conflict. The therapist teaches the family the steps of problems solving (define the problem, brainstorm alternative solutions, evaluate the solutions and reach a compromise, plan the details for implementations) as a means of resolving such conflicts (Robin & Foster, 1989).

The therapist also continues to address comorbid conditions. For example, in the case of a girl with obsessive-compulsive disorder, the therapist would arrange for a psychiatrist to prescribe an appropriate medication and might begin a regimen of behavioral therapy. In the case of a learning disability, the therapist might conduct psychological testing and make recommendations to the school for educational interventions. If the parents manifest significant marital conflict, they might be referred for marital therapy. Such marital conflict often surfaces as the parents are no longer preoccupied with refeeding their daughter and finally have time to deal with each other.

When the adolescent has maintained her weight for 3 months, termination is planned. The interval between sessions is lengthened to 1 month. The therapist coordinates termination with the pediatrician, who has been conducting periodic medical follow-ups. The therapist discusses methods of coping with possible relapses with the family, role-playing crisis situations. In the last session, the changes that have occurred are reviewed, and the family is left with the framework that coping with AN may be a lifelong process, and that they could return for more therapy at any time in the future.

MAJOR MECHANISMS OF CHANGE

We can draw a distinction between the factors that *predispose* an adolescent to develop AN (genetics, body type, personality, culture, family interactions), the factors that *precipitate* the onset of the illness (onset of puberty, peers dieting, major life stresses, an illness causing weight loss), and the factors that *perpetuate or maintain* an existing AN (effects of starvation, isolation and withdrawal, rewarding value of control from weight loss, family conflicts over food). We believe that BFST operates primarily on the perpetuating or maintaining factors, and to a certain extent on the precipitating factors. In other words, BFST is an approach to change, not a model for the etiology of AN.

At the time of intake, the adolescent and her family are stuck in a downward spiral of starvation fueling continued cognitive distortions and refusal to eat, which in turn fuels family conflict and leads the parents to feel helpless and overwhelmed. Asking parents to work as a team to take charge of their adolescent's eating is considered the single most important mechanism of change in BFST; this breaks the downward spiral, gives the parents a renewed sense of control and efficacy in their parenting, and begins to reverse the devastating effects of physical starvation on the adolescent. The use of cognitive restructuring is a second mechanism of change. Providing the family with nonblaming attributions to understand the strange behaviors of the adolescent in starvation and the helpless feelings of the parents is essential; without such a benign cognitive set, parents might not be able to call forth the tremendous effort needed to take charge of their daughter's eating. Cognitive restructuring approaches to correcting a distorted body image, distorted food perceptions, and absolutistic thinking are also essential for helping the adolescent overcome the fears of weight gain and facilitating individuation from the family.

Behavior modification is a third mechanism of change. The use of rewards, punishments, contracts, and shaping provides the parents with the tools for carrying out the mandate to take charge of their daughter's eating, and later return control over eating to their daughter. Without such a detailed plan of action, weight gain and refeeding could not be sustained.

Finally, we also consider strategic/structural interventions to be a fourth active ingredient of BFST. The therapist must employ such interventions repeatedly to encourage the parents to work as a team, to separate marital from adolescent problems, and in the later stages of therapy, to encourage adolescent individuation.

After successful treatment of AN using BFST, interestingly, many of the predisposing factors remain present but no longer lead to the disease. The girls typically have a thin-normal body type for life, and rarely become obese. They may continue to have some unusual eating preferences, e.g., eat very few proteins, but they manage to take in sufficient nutrition to maintain health. They continue to have hard-driving, perfectionistic personalities, but their efforts are directed toward productive outcomes rather than toward relentless dieting. They continue to be subject to the many cultural pressures on women to be thin, but we have helped them individuate and become comfortable with their identity and appearance. They are able to draw appropriate boundaries between their parents and themselves, but often continue later in life to have close relationships with their families. Their parents often continue to have marital and/or other problems, but the adolescents are no longer stuck regulating their parents' poor marriages or hiding family secrets. The successful BFST therapist uses behavioral strategies, cognitive change techniques, and strategic/structural maneuvers to "reengineer" the family system, freeing the adolescents to move ahead with their normal developmental trajectories.

RESEARCH SUPPORT FOR EFFICACY

The effectiveness of BFST for treating adolescents with AN has been assessed in an outcome study comparing it to Ego Oriented Individual Therapy (EOIT) (Robin, 1997; Robin, Siegel, Koepke, Moye, & Tice, 1994; Robin, Siegel, & Moye, 1995). We hypothesized that both therapies would be effective, but that each therapy would prove superior to the other on those domains in which each therapy focused. Specifically, we predicted that (1) BFST would produce greater change than EOIT in weight, eating attitudes, and family relations; but that (2) EOIT would produce greater change than BFST on ego functioning, maturity fears, perfectionism, depression, and internalizing behavior problems.

Methods

Thirty-seven Caucasian girls (aged 11–19) meeting the DSM-III-R criteria for AN were randomly assigned to either BFST or EOIT and to a therapist nested within each condition. The BFST group consisted of 19 girls (mean age = 14.9), and the EOIT group consisted of 18 girls (mean age = 13.4). Thirty-four of the adolescents resided in two-parent and three lived in single-mother households. Five senior female therapists were nested within treatment conditions such that two conducted BFST and three conducted EOIT. Four were doctoral-level psychologists; one was a master's-level social worker.

Each adolescent and her parents attended a preassessment, an average of 15.9 months of therapy, a postassessment, and a 12-month follow-up assessment. Therapists were given a range of 12–18 months per case, rather than a fixed time limit, based on pilot data indicating this flexibility optimized outcomes. Treatment sessions occurred weekly for the first half of therapy, and bimonthly afterward.

The patients underwent a common medical and dietary regimen. The project pediatrician determined an appropriate target weight for height, and the dietician prescribed a balanced diet based on the diabetic exchange diet, starting with approximately 1200 calories per day; the number of calories was periodically adjusted upward, to permit approximately 1 lb of weight gain per week. The pediatrician conducted follow-up medical evaluations. Sixteen patients (11 BFST and 5 EOIT) who were judged to be in acute medical danger because they were below 75% of their ideal weight and/or had significant cardiac or neurological problems were hospitalized for 1–4 weeks on an adolescent medicine unit, where the nursing staff implemented a structured refeeding program based on a written contract consisting of regularly scheduled meals, dietary counseling, and medical management. No psychoactive medications were prescribed. Patients received their assigned therapy in addition to the refeeding program.

BFST was conducted as described earlier in this chapter. In EOIT, the therapist conducted weekly individual therapy sessions with the adolescent, and bimonthly collateral sessions with the parents. Individual sessions focused primarily on the adolescent's ego strength, coping skills, individuation from the nuclear family, confusion about her identity, and other interpersonal issues regarding physical, social, and emotional growth, and the relationship of these issues to eating, weight expectations, and body image. The therapist communicated a nurturant–authoritative stance, e.g., the therapist is strong and available to help a weak adolescent; the therapist respects the adolescent's autonomy and understands her struggle to individuate from a highly dysfunctional family; and the therapist will not coerce the adolescent to gain weight or change her attitudes, but will help her understand how she can choose to be healthy, coping with her dysfunctional family and inner fears without starvation. As the adolescent overcame initial defensiveness, the therapist served as a "tension regulator," helping the adolescent identify problems in daily living, understand their link to eating and cognitions about body image/thinness, and collaborate on constructive solutions that promote physical and emotional health.

Through interpretation, support, reflection, and the power of transference, the therapist set the conditions for the adolescent to realize that she can accept herself as the therapist accepts her; with self-acceptance and a stronger ego, the sense of ineffectiveness, interpersonal distrust, and poor identity formation that made the pursuit of thinness an appealing alternative to the pursuit of individuation dissipated, permitting a resumption of normal eating and appropriate weight gain.

In the collateral sessions, the therapist educated the parents about normal adolescent development, provided support while asking them to refrain from direct involvement in their daughter's eating, and prepared them emotionally to cope with a more assertive, demanding, angrier adolescent.

Dependent variables included (1) Quetelet's Body Mass Index (BMI) = weight (kilograms) divided by the square of height (meters), (2) achievement of target weight, (3) resumption of menstruation, (4) the Eating Attitudes Test (adolescents rating themselves, and their mothers and fathers independently rating their adolescents), (5) five scales of the Eating Disorders Inventory (Interoceptive Awareness, Ineffectiveness, Interpersonal Distrust, Maturity Fears, Perfectionism) as measures of ego functioning, (6) the Beck Depression Inventory and the Internalizing Behavior Problems scores from the Youth Self-Report Scale and maternal and paternal Child Behavior Checklist, and (7) two family interaction measures.

Self-reported family conflict was assessed through the Parent Adolescent Relationship Questionnaire (PARQ), a multidimensional measure with true/false items tapping overt conflict, belief systems, and family structure. Parents and adolescents independently completed the PARQ. Two scores were used for each family member: (1) General Conflict—a factorially based linear composite of 45 items tapping Communication (e.g., "My mom puts me down"), Problem Solving ("We think of many good ideas to solve our problems"), and Warmth/Hostility scales ("Quite honestly, I hate my dad"); and (2) Conflict Over Eating—14 items assessing overt conflict and hostility concerning eating, mealtimes, and food ("I dread mealtimes with my daughter"; "We argue often about food and eating").

Observed family conflict was assessed through the use of two 10-minute videotaped interactions coded with the Interaction Behavior Code, a global inferential coding system that yields positive and negative communication scores for each family member. The general conflict discussion focused on a non-food-related issue, while the eating conflict discussion focused on the eating and weight problems. Two graduate students coded all of the discussions, and the mean of their ratings served as the dependent measure. Correlational reliability ranged from 0.89 to 0.96 (mean = 0.93) for adolescents' scores, from 0.91 to 0.99 (mean = 0.95) for mothers' scores, and from 0.94 to 0.98 (mean = 0.96) for fathers' scores.

All of the measures except the videotaped interactions were obtained at three points in time: before treatment, after treatment, and a 1-year follow-up. The videotaped interactions were only obtained at the pre- and postassessments.

Results

Results for each dependent measure were analyzed using a repeated measures analysis of variance with time as the repeated measures factor and type of therapy as the between-subjects factor. Separate analyses were done for the pre/post data

Table 1. Significant Results from Pre/Post Analysis

Variable	Group	N	Pre	Post	Effects	F (d.f.)	p
BMI	BFST	19	15.2 (1.8)	19.9 (1.9)	Time	113.9 (1,34)	0.001
					Time × Treat	12.6 (1,34)	0.001
	EOIT	17	16.6 (2.1)	18.9 (1.9)			
EAT							
Teen	BFST	19	32.6 (15.6)	11.2 (13.6)	Time	47.3 (1,33)	0.001
					Time × Treat	3.0 (1,33)	0.09
	EOIT	16	20.6 (15.6)	7.9 (9.6)			
Mom	BFST	19	40.5 (12.8)	10.1 (12.2)	Time	85.3 (1,34)	0.001
	EOIT	17	35.9 (14.4)	13.1 (11.8)			
Dad	BFST	19	36.1 (14.0)	14.7 (16.2)	Time	41.3 (1,32)	0.001
	EOIT	15	35.5 (14.3)	16.1 (12.7)			
Interoceptive							
Awareness EDI	BFST	18	7.4 (5.8)	3.7 (6.1)	Time	5.4 (1,32)	0.03
	EOIT	16	4.0 (4.8)	2.8 (5.5)			
Beck Depression							
Inventory	BFST	19	19.4 (12.3)	8.5 (8.4)	Time	15.5 (1,33)	0.001
	EOIT	16	11.3 (10.5)	5.4 (9.0)			
Internalizing CBC							
Teen	BFST	19	56.1 (13.3)	51.8 (13.4)	Time	11.8 (1,32)	0.003
	EOIT	15	52.0 (11.9)	39.8 (14.0)			
Mom	BFST	19	64.1 (11.1)	52.4 (12.8)	Time	13.6 (1,33)	0.001
	EOIT	16	63.5 (18.2)	56.3 (13.7)			
Dad	BFST	18	61.1 (10.6)	52.9 (14.2)	Time	21.7 (1,31)	0.001
	EOIT	15	60.5 (15.2)	46.6 (18.3)			
Eating conflicts							
Teen PARQ	BFST	15	77.7 (19.4)	55.0 (16.3)	Time	12.9 (1,26)	0.001
	EOIT	13	72.3 (16.0)	59.2 (20.7)			
Mom PARQ	BFST	15	89.9 (15.1)	55.3 (18.1)	Time	58.7 (1,26)	0.001
	EOIT	13	92.9 (14.2)	55.2 (17.8)			
Dad PARQ	BFST	15	75.9 (16.6)	50.8 (18.2)	Time	59.6 (1,26)	0.001
	EOIT	13	86.3 (18.5)	50.8 (16.3)			

Note. Standard deviations are in parentheses after each mean. BFST, Behavioral Family Systems Therapy; EOIT, Ego Oriented Individual Therapy; BMI, body mass index; EAT, Eating Attitudes Test; EDI, Eating Disorders Inventory (Ineffectiveness, Interoceptive Awareness, Interpersonal Distrust); CBC, Child Behavior Checklist (Internalizing); PARQ, Parent Adolescent Relationship Questionnaire (eating-related conflict).

and the pre/post/follow-up data because of a reduced sample size at the 1-year follow-up. Table 1 highlights a representative sample of the results.

There were significant main effects of Time, indicating improvement from before to after treatment by both the BFST and EOIT groups, on the following measures: (1) BMI; (2) eating attitudes as rated by adolescents, mothers, and fathers; (3) Beck Depression Inventory and the Internalizing Behavior Problems score of the Child Behavior Checklist (mothers and fathers) and the Youth Self-Report Scale; (4) Interoceptive Awareness scale of the EDI; (5) eating-related conflict on the PARQ (adolescents, mothers, fathers); and (6) 10 out of 12 negative and positive communication scores for the general and eating-related discussions on the IBC. There were no improvements for either group on the other EDI scales of ego functioning and the general conflict scale of the PARQ, where very little conflict was reported at preassessment.

There was only a single significant differential treatment effect (Time by Treatment interaction) on BMI. The BFST group improved more on BMI (4.7) than the EOIT group (2.3). There was also a trend toward greater improvement on adolescent EAT scores for the BFST over the EOIT group.

At postassessment, 66.7% of the BFST group and 68.8% of the EOIT group had attained their target weights, whereas by the 1-year follow-up, the percentages were 80% for BFST and 68.8% for EOIT. There were no significant differences between groups at either time. At postassessment, 94% of the BFST girls had resumed and/or started menstruation, compared with 64.4% of the EOIT girls; this difference was significant, using a chi-square test ($p < 0.03$). By follow-up, 80% of the EOIT girls were menstruating, compared with 92.9% of the BFST girls; the difference was no longer significant.

The follow-up analyses indicated that all of the significant improvements from pre- to postassessment were maintained at the 1-year follow-up interval. In addition, there were significant improvements from preassessment to follow-up on Ineffectiveness, Maturity Fears, and Perfectionism, measures of ego functioning, which had not changed from pre- to postassessment.

These results indicated that BFST and EOIT were both associated with improvements in BMI, eating attitudes, depression and internalizing behavior problems, and eating-related family conflict on self-report and observational measures. These changes were maintained or extended during a 1-year follow-up interval. Interestingly, the changes on measures of ego functioning were much more variable, and in some cases, took longer to occur. BFST did result in greater weight gain and a trend toward greater improvement in eating attitudes, but surprisingly did not result in greater improvement in family relations. These results strongly support the effectiveness of BFST for treating adolescents with restricting AN, although the absence of a control group and the small number of differences between treatments make it difficult to determine the contribution of the specific components of BFST to the overall outcomes.

CASE EXAMPLE

Nicole, 17 years old, was referred to our Eating Disorders Program by a family friend, following a 6-month history of dieting and a weight loss of 50 pounds. At age 16, Nicole had weighed 135 pounds, her highest weight. By the time of referral, she weighed 84 pounds, was 5'4" in height, had amenorrhea for at least 5 months, and restricted her food intake to approximately 750 calories a day (fruits, vegetables, rice cakes, water but no protein or fats). Nicole started dieting because she was self-conscious about her "chubby" appearance and not fitting into size 2 jeans. She routinely skipped lunch at school because she ate slowly and cut her food into tiny pieces causing her friends to "stare." She denied binging or purging but exercised daily in addition to playing soccer and roller blading.

She was given her sister's horse when her sister left for college and recently decided to follow in her sister's footsteps and become a competitive equestrian. Significant stressors at the time of referral included Nicole's transition from junior high to high school, her older sister "running away from home," increased peer pressure to be thin, and a desire to maintain the family's status as having a "star" equestrian. Nicole said that while she had always enjoyed riding for fun, she never had much interest in competitive riding until the past spring. This decision "thrilled" her father because riding was the traditional sport in his family of origin, but concerned her mother who was worried about the potential dangers and pressures of the sport.

Nicole presented as a depressed, emaciated but beautiful teenager who acknowledged several symptoms associated with anorexia. Her longtime best friend had recently moved and her other friends "had changed" and she no longer felt comfortable around them. She admitted to having very high expectations and not being satisfied unless she received all A's in school and being "the best" in sports. She was worried that she did not "have what it takes to be a star equestrian." She admitted to being "obsessed with being thin" and said she felt fine and had no intention of eating more or of gaining any weight. She did not want to be in any kind of a treatment program and stated she planned to leave home when she turned 18 so she could be as thin as she wished.

Developmental and Family History

Nicole is the second daughter of highly educated parents. She was born following a full-term uncomplicated pregnancy and delivery. Developmental milestones were within normal limits and Nicole was described as a "will-o'-the-wisp" child who was everyone's darling and eager to please. She was always very concerned about her grades and perfectionistic about almost everything in her life. Throughout childhood she had lots of friends and was involved in several school activities. Until recently, Nicole had not required much in the way of discipline, although recently had been caught smoking in the restroom at school. Both parents were working at the time of the referral, although the mother had been a stay-at-home mom for most of the daughter's formative years. Father admittedly had very high expectations of his daughters and was perfectionistic and rigid. Mother was a concerned parent but very passive, emotionally private, and somewhat disengaged.

Nicole's father had polio as a young boy, precluding any participation in competitive sports throughout childhood. His intense involvement in his daughters' competitive riding stemmed from his own sense of loss in not being able to ride as a child like his own siblings. Nicole's mother had a chronic history of severe migraine headaches, which often prevented her from attending the girls' sporting events. A 20-year-old maternal niece had a history of anorexia beginning at age 12 and was currently being treated for depression and OCD. Marital problems, substance abuse, and other family psychiatric history were denied. Problems with Nicole's older sister were readily revealed. Mother admitted their relationship was severely strained during the teen years although she did not understand why her daughter was so angry. Family counseling was not successful and discontinued after a few sessions. Buying her a horse and getting her involved in riding was identified as what "saved" her from becoming a "burnout." The family was both distraught and bewildered that this same daughter ran away from home to attend an out-of-state college and live with a good friend. At the time of the referral, she had recently moved back but was not living at home, had not enrolled in any college program, and was teaching riding to young children. Nicole said her sister may also have an "eating problem."

Assessment and Treatment Planning

Over the course of the first two sessions, Nicole was evaluated medically and nutritionally, and psychological/family data were obtained through interviews with Nicole and her parents, separately and together. The treatment team determined that Nicole met the diagnostic criteria for Anorexia Nervosa, Restrictive type, but did not feel her current medical status required immediate hospitalization. The physician established two, nonnegotiable weights: one below which hospitalization was mandatory (80 lb) and a target weight (115 lb) to be reached over time and estimated as needed for full medical recovery, i.e., return of menses. The dietician established a daily caloric intake of 1500 calories for initial weight gain, and provided the family with sample meals and snacks, taking into account Nicole's premorbid food preferences. The therapist presented to the family the nonnegotiable weights, arranged for Nicole to be weighed weekly under standard conditions, and explained that her daily caloric intake would increase gradually over time so that she could gain 1 lb a week.

During the next session, the therapist focused on diagnostic feedback and treatment planning. The family was reassured that although Nicole did meet criteria for AN, she was not currently in a life-threatening situation and therefore could be treated on an outpatient basis. The therapist stressed that a combination of the following factors had probably set the stage for the onset of her AN: (1) there seemed to be a biological vulnerability (niece) for eating disorders in the family, (2) the family had recently been stressed severely (sister running away), (3) peer pressure intensified for Nicole at an already difficult time, and (4) the parents had little prior need to closely manage/monitor Nicole's behaviors. The therapist was careful to remove blame, pointing out that no one was at fault for Nicole's eating disorder; it was the result of a confluence of factors. Moreover, this family had a history of caring and commitment to their children, which was a positive prognostic sign suggesting that, with the proper help, Nicole would fully recover. Furthermore, the therapist had been successful with many similar cases over the past two decades. The therapist promised Nicole that she would not be permitted to gain weight too fast, and that she would be taught how to maintain her weight near the target weight.

The rationale for a family therapy approach to AN was presented. Nicole and her parents voiced strong and immediate objections to family therapy. Both parents did not want to attend every session, and Nicole wanted to talk to the therapist without her parents present. They demanded individual therapy for Nicole instead. Their resistance was empathically accepted, but the therapist did not give into it. The therapist explained that her personal experience and recent scientific research clearly indicated that family therapy was the treatment of choice for restoration of health in cases like Nicole's. It was explained that individual therapy would be used during the last phase of the treatment program, after Nicole reached her target weight. The therapist also acknowledged that the program was very demanding, especially for working parents, and that it was not possible for some families to participate. The parents were offered different scheduling options utilized by other parents with demanding schedules as well as provided with a list of several other programs available in the community as possible treatment alternatives if they found this program unacceptable.

Aside from a review of the nonnegotiable medical weights and weekly weigh-in requirement, no other specific components of the treatment program were mentioned at the feedback/treatment planning session. The parents were instructed to decide together over the next 3 days what they would like to do. The father called 2 days later stating the family had decided to enroll in the program and could attend as designated. Over the course of the next 16 months, both parents attended all but four of the regularly scheduled family sessions.

During the next few sessions, information regarding the parents' reactions to Nicole's dieting, the parents' families of origin, their marital relationship, Nicole's early child development, and her parents' child-rearing practices was collected. The parents were instructed to record in writing everything that they observed Nicole eat, but were told not to try to make her eat. They were reassured that as long as Nicole did not lose more weight, she was not in medical danger. If her weight did reach the "danger" level (< 80), she would be swiftly hospitalized.

Control Rationale

The control rationale was given to the family at the fourth family session. The reaction was fast and furious. Nicole threatened in a loud, menacing voice to run away from home, never eat anything again, and commit suicide; e.g., "I would rather die than gain weight in this dumb program, and it will be your fault [parents] when I die." Her parents were taken aback at her strong, angry reaction; she never had been so adamant about anything before. The therapist was tempted to point out the irony of Nicole's wish to kill herself, in light of her starvation, but that is of course better left unsaid. Instead, the therapist first reassured the shaken parents that Nicole's reaction was "right on target" for girls with AN when the control rationale is given, and that her reaction was another example of how starvation has clouded her mind. The therapist then calmly suggested that the parents develop a plan to address Nicole's threats, in case she tried to act them out. The therapist helped the family design a suicide watch for the next 24 hours. The father agreed to phone all of Nicole's friends' houses where she might go if she ran away and instruct them to contact him if Nicole arrived there; he also agreed to call the police if Nicole became uncontrollable. The mother agreed to phone the insurance company and obtain the necessary authorization for hospitalization.

A special emergency session was scheduled for the next day to give the family support and, if possible, begin discussing how to develop an eating program specifically for Nicole. The family arrived the next day and reported that all of the emergency plans were in place, and that Nicole, although silent and sullen, had not carried out any of her threats. The parents were congratulated for their teamwork. Nicole was praised for her bravery in "making healthy choices." She smirked sarcastically at the therapist.

Weight Gain Phase

Next, the therapist coached the parents in designing the behavioral weight gain program. The family generated and wrote a list of all of the decisions about eating that needed to be made, and how they were going to be shared between the parents, i.e., who prepares the menus, who shops, who prepares the meals, and so on. We find that if these details are not specified in writing, there is a danger that one parent will end up shouldering most of the responsibility. The metaphor of "food as medicine" was explained, and the parents were asked to address the issue of how they were going to motivate Nicole to eat. Activities related to horse-back riding were selected as potential reinforcers. The parents decided that if Nicole ate all her meals and snacks on any given day, she could go to the barn and see her horse. After she reached 95 lb, she could ride her horse for 30 minutes a day; the amount of riding time increased with achievement of later weight goals.

The therapist explained to Nicole that her primary responsibility was to restart eating, but that she did have the choice not to eat. If she chose not to eat, the therapist instructed her parents not to nag, coax, or in any way interfere with her decision. Instead, they were to state in a neutral tone that they regretted that it was too difficult for her to eat that day, and hoped it would get easier tomorrow. However, given that she did not take her "medicine," she would have to rest until the next meal.

On the first day the parents initiated the program (Saturday by design), Nicole refused to eat any meal or snacks. When it was time for the father to go to the barn to groom and run the horse, Nicole was waiting in the car to go with him. The father firmly but gently told her she had not taken her "medicine" and would have to go back into the house and rest. She did not move. The father calmly got out of his car and made it clear he would carry her into the house if she did not go on her own. Nicole stomped into the house. Later that evening, she ate her snack. This moment of truth was a "pivot point" in the weight gain phase; afterwards, Nicole ate more steadily. She needed to see that her parents were seriously committed to restoring her health, and that they would follow through with the consequences that they specified.

Nicole's weight gain phase continued in spurts over the next 8 months. As she gained weight, however, she became increasingly distraught about the change in her appearance. She cringed when people complimented her on her appearance, distorting their compliments to mean she must be fat. The therapist used the cognitive strategies of *reframing* and *relabeling* to help Nicole cope with her distorted cognitions (Robin & Foster, 1989). Nicole was taught to reframe weight gain as "making a difficult but positive decision" and to relabel looking fatter to looking healthier.

Concrete behavioral assignments were also employed to help shift her cognitions. For example, the family was asked to bring in pictures of Nicole before she began to diet and at different points throughout her illness. Nicole identified four people she trusted. They were each asked to review the pictures and select the one that represented the "healthiest" appearance for her. This task was designed to help see herself as others see her. Three of four raters chose the picture in which Nicole had been very close to her ultimate target weight as the "healthiest" and most attractive. Nicole was genuinely surprised; this gave her cause for serious reevaluation of her self-perceptions of her appearance.

A second task involved measuring body parts. Nicole took a baseline measurement of her hips, thighs, and arms. Then, after she had gained several pounds, she remeasured them and compared the two sets of measurements. There was very little change in the measurements. She was then able to reassure herself that although she "felt fatter," the objective data indicated that these body parts were not getting larger. The therapist emphasized the difference between feeling fat and objectively being fat; Nicole may not be able to help how she feels, but at least she could come to objectively understand that she is not fat.

A large positive incentive was planned for achieving the 100 lb mark because a weight in the "three" digits felt "the worst" to Nicole. When she weighed 100 lb, her parents took her to Chicago for the weekend and let her go on a shopping spree.

Weight Maintenance Phase

Ten months after therapy began, Nicole reached her target weight, and when she had maintained it for 1 month, the therapist introduced the idea of a gradual return of control over eating to Nicole. The parents found it easy to let Nicole resume control of her eating. Nicole was much more relaxed, more emotionally expressive, and less obsessed with weight and eating. She said she felt like "her old self again" and was ready "to get on with life." By then she was riding her horse regularly and was also able to tell her father she did not want to be a competitive rider like her sister, but wanted, instead, to ride for fun, enjoy her friends, get good grades in high school, and join the soccer team. Although her relationship with her mother remained "cool," she began to ask her mother more directly what she wanted. For example, it was important that her mother initiate interactions with her as Nicole always felt that her mother avoided being with her or somehow did not really like her. She knew she was loved, but didn't feel "liked." Once this was articulated to the mother, she was able to plan things with Nicole, and mother and daughter were beginning to form a more positive relationship. The father had a very difficult time giving up having a daughter involved in riding competition and several sessions were directed to this issue. It proved to be an opportunity for the mother to be supportive and nurturing of the father as the couple began to plan new ways to spend the weekends together now that the father was not busy at the barn.

As the time to terminate treatment approached, Nicole was seen for several sessions of individual therapy in preparation for leaving for college. She decided to go to a school out of state to "learn who I am and what I want to do." She indicated that she still sometimes felt fat but reassured herself by looking in the mirror and knowing that she is not. She continued to desire that her family become closer but no longer felt an obligation to make this happen. She indicated confidence in her ability to make good decisions for herself and was hopeful for her future. She indicated that she now had more important goals than "being the thinnest girl at school."

Comment

Nicole's AN was diagnosed and treated within 1 year of its onset, and although her family had a variety of problems, we did not uncover any severe parental individual psychopathology or personality disorders. In addition, aside from some mild depression probably secondary to her physical starvation, Nicole did not display any comorbid psychiatric conditions. These factors enabled us to have a more successful outcome, despite some resistance. In cases where the course of the AN is more chronic, the adolescent has comorbid psychiatric conditions, and/or the parents have severe pathology of their own, we use the same treatment approach, but the outcomes are not always as positive.

FUTURE RESEARCH AND SUMMARY

The BFST approach described in this chapter is one of a number of similar family therapies developed for the treatment of children and adolescents with AN (Dare & Eisler, 1997; Robin et al., 1998). At least one other group has carefully researched a similar family therapy involving parents taking control of their daughters' eating. Russell, Szmukler, Dare, and Eisler (1987) refed a group of patients with AN in the hospital until they reached 89.5% of their body weight, then discharged them and randomly assigned them either to a family therapy condition involving parental control over eating or to a supportive individual therapy without any parental control over eating. They found that family therapy had a more favorable outcome than individual therapy for young patients with an early onset and short duration of AN, but that individual therapy was marginally superior to family therapy for an older late-onset, chronic patient group. The positive changes were maintained at a 5-year follow-up (Dare & Eisler, 1997). In a follow-up component analysis with the younger, early onset cases of AN, le Grange, Eisler, Dare, and Russell (1992) studied conjoint family therapy, in which the family is seen together in the treatment sessions, versus family counseling, in which the parents are seen without their daughter present and given the same advice regarding the best way to take charge of their daughter's eating as is given in the conjoint family therapy; the teenager is also seen individually for supportive sessions. Both groups improved equally and maintained these changes at a 2-year follow-up (Dare & Eisler, 1997), suggesting that as long as parents are asked to take control of their adolescent's eating, it may not matter whether the family is seen conjointly.

Taken together with the research reported in this chapter, that of Russell et al. (1987) clearly indicates that family therapy is an effective intervention for treating adolescents with AN. In this chapter we have given the practitioner detailed guidelines for intervening with a conjoint BFST. le Grange et al. (1992) suggest that counseling the parents separately from the adolescent may be equally effective to seeing the entire family together, as long as the parents are instructed to take charge of their daughter's eating. Our results showing slower weight gain when parents were seen separately but told to refrain from taking charge of their daughter's eating are consistent with the findings of le Grange et al. (1992).

Many questions remain to be answered by future research. A study of BFST versus a control condition is necessary, but may need to be done with milder cases of AN because of the ethical issues involved in assigning such cases to a no-treatment or an inert treatment condition. Component analyses are needed to establish the relative contributions of parental control, cognitive restructuring, and strategic/structural interventions to the overall treatment package. Such analyses might also clarify to what extent many of the changes seen in our study and clinical experiences are truly secondary to remission of starvation or a direct result of BFST techniques. Studies are also needed to better understand the role of psychiatric comorbidity in influencing the outcomes of BFST. Better measures of ego functioning and the use of semistructured interviews such as the Eating Disorder Examination (Fairburn & Cooper, 1993) would help us learn more about the extent to which BFST impacts intrapsychic variables as the adolescent emerges from starvation.

Also, our clinical experience and Russell's research suggest that asking parents to take control of their adolescent's eating works best with the younger adolescents; more research is needed to determine at what age the therapist should change to a different strategy, and what strategy should be employed.

Finally, very little research exists about the application of BFST and related family therapies to adolescents with BN. Clinically, we have treated a number of adolescents with BN, asking parents to take charge of their daughter's eating and preventing vomiting, with mixed success. Dodge, Hodes, Eisler, and Dare (1995) treated eight adolescents with BN using a variant of Russell's family therapy; one achieved a good outcome, five had an intermediate outcome, and two had a poor outcome, using Morgan and Russell ratings. Controlled studies of family therapies with adolescents suffering from BN are sorely needed.

Despite the large gaps in the empirical literature, the clinician at least now has available in BFST a carefully manualized approach to treating the adolescent with AN that has proven effective in at least one large outcome study, and that is very similar to other approaches proven effective in additional outcome studies. In closing, the authors would remind the clinician that when successful, BFST has always been applied within the context of a multidisciplinary team environment, where the mental health practitioner is working closely with a physician and a dietician.

ACKNOWLEDGMENT

This chapter was prepared with the partial support of NIMH Grant R01MH41773.

REFERENCES

American Academy of Pediatrics. (1996). *The classification of child and adolescent mental conditions in primary care: Diagnostic and Statistical Manual for Primary Care (DSM-PC) Child and Adolescent Version.* Chicago: Author.

American Psychiatric Association. (1994). *Diagnostic and statistical manual of mental disorders* (4th ed.). Washington, DC: Author.

Anderson, C.M., & Stewart, S. (1983). *Mastering resistance: A practical guide to family therapy.* New York: Guilford Press.

Dare, C., & Eisler, I. (1997). Family therapy for anorexia nervosa. In D. M. Garner & P. E. Garfinkel (Eds.), *Handbook of treatment for eating disorders* (2nd ed., pp. 307–324). New York: Guilford Press.

Dodge, E., Hodes, M., Eisler, I., & Dare, C. (1995). Family therapy for bulimia nervosa in adolescents: An exploratory study. *Journal of Family Therapy, 17,* 59–77.

Fairburn, C. G., & Cooper, Z. (1993). The eating disorder examination (12th ed.). In C. G. Fairburn & G. T. Wilson (Eds.), *Binge eating: Nature, assessment, and treatment* (pp. 317–360). New York: Guilford Press.

Fisher, M., Golden, N. H., Katzman, D. K., Kreipe, R. E., Rees, J., Schebendach, J., Sigman, G., Ammerman, S., & Hoberman, H. M. (1995). Eating disorders in adolescents: A background paper. *Journal of Adolescent Health, 16,* 420–437.

Garner, D. M., Vitousek, K. M., & Pike, K. M. (1997). Cognitive-behavioral therapy for anorexia nervosa. In D. M. Garner & P. E. Garfinkel (Eds.), *Handbook of treatment for eating disorders* (2nd ed., pp. 94–144). New York: Guilford Press.

Goodsitt, A. (1997). Eating disorders: A self-psychology perspective. In D. M. Garner & P. E. Garfinkel (Eds.), *Handbook of treatment for eating disorders* (2nd ed., pp. 205–228). New York: Guilford Press.

Hsu, L. K. G. (1990). *Eating disorders.* New York: Guilford Press.

Kreipe, R. E., Golden, N. H., Katzman, D. K., Fisher, M., Rees, J., Tonkin, R. S., Silber, M., Sigman, G., Schebendach, J., Ammerman, S., & Hoberman, M. M. (1995). Eating disorders in adolescents: A position paper of the Society for Adolescent Medicine. *Journal of Adolescent Health, 16,* 476–480.

Lask, B., & Bryant-Waugh, R. (Eds.). (1993). *Childhood onset anorexia and related eating disorders.* Hillsdale, NJ: Erlbaum.

Le Grange, D., Eisler, I., Dare, C., & Russell, G. F. M. (1992). Evaluation of family treatments in adolescent anorexia nervosa: A pilot study. *International Journal of Eating Disorders, 12,* 347–357.

Minuchin, S., Rosman, B. L., & Baker, L. (1978). *Psychosomatic families.* Cambridge, MA: Harvard University Press.

Robin, A. L. (1997). *Final progress report: Family therapy for anorexia—A controlled study-R01MH 41773.* Unpublished grant report submitted to the National Institute of Mental Health. Detroit: Wayne State University.

Robin, A. L., & Foster, S. L. (1989). *Negotiating parent–adolescent conflict: A behavioral family systems approach.* New York: Guilford Press.

Robin, A. L., Gilroy, M., & Dennis, A. B. (1998). Treatment of eating disorders in children and adolescents. *Clinical Psychology Review, 18,* 421–446.

Robin, A. L., Siegel, P., Bedway, M., & Gilroy, M. (1996). Therapy for adolescent anorexia nervosa: Addressing cognitions, feelings, and the family's role. In E. D. Hibbs & P. S. Jensen (Eds.), *Psychosocial treatments for child and adolescent disorders: Empirically based strategies for clinical practice* (pp. 239–259). Washington, DC: American Psychological Association.

Robin, A. L., Siegel, P. T., Koepke, T., Moye, A. W., & Tice, S. (1994). Family therapy versus individual therapy for adolescent females with anorexia nervosa. *Journal of Developmental and Behavioral Pediatrics, 15,* 111–116.

Robin, A. L., Siegel, P. T., & Moye, A. (1995). Family versus individual therapy for anorexia: Impact on family conflict. *International Journal of Eating Disorders, 17,* 313–322.

Russell, G. F. M., Szmukler, G. I., Dare, C., & Eisler, I. (1987). An evaluation of family therapy in anorexia nervosa and bulimia nervosa. *Archives of General Psychiatry, 44,* 1047–1056.

Touyz, S. W., & Beumont, P. J. V. (1997). Behavioral treatment to promote weight gain in anorexia nervosa. In D. M. Garner & P. E. Garfinkel (Eds.), *Handbook of treatment for eating disorders* (2nd ed., pp. 361–371). New York: Guilford Press.

17

Parent–Child Interaction Therapy with Oppositional Children

Review and Clinical Strategies

ARISTA RAYFIELD, LINDA MONACO, and SHEILA M. EYBERG

BASIC APPROACH UTILIZED

Behavioral parent training, or parent management training (PMT), refers to procedures in which parents are taught to alter their child's behavior at home (Kazdin, 1996). The recognition that parents can become effective agents of therapeutic change in their children has resulted in the development and empirical evaluation of numerous parent training programs. Extensive research indicates that PMT is the single most effective treatment approach for reducing conduct-disordered behavior (Azar & Wolfe, 1989; Brestan & Eyberg, 1998; Kazdin, 1996), and PMT is gaining recognition as an important adjunct to the treatment of child internalizing problems as well (Kendall & Treadwell, 1996; Lewinsohn, Clarke, Rohde, Hops, & Seeley, 1996).

In this chapter we review Parent–Child Interaction Therapy (PCIT), a specific type of PMT for preschool-age children and their parents that targets change in the parent–child relationship as the vehicle through which individual behavior change occurs. The goals of PCIT are to teach parents to establish a secure, nurturant relationship with their child, to teach their child prosocial behaviors, and to decrease their child's inappropriate behaviors (Eyberg & Boggs, 1998). PCIT is based on the

ARISTA RAYFIELD • Department of Pediatrics, University of Kansas Medical Center, Kansas City, Kansas 66160.   LINDA MONACO and SHEILA M. EYBERG • Department of Clinical and Health Psychology, University of Florida, Gainesville, Florida 32610.

Handbook of Psychotherapies with Children and Families, edited by Russ and Ollendick. Kluwer Academic/Plenum Publishers, New York, 1999.

operant, two-stage model of parent training for noncompliant children developed by Hanf (1969). In the first treatment stage of the Hanf model, parents were taught to follow their child's play using differential social attention. Specifically, parents were to reward positive behavior with attention and to extinguish negative behavior with ignoring. In Hanf's second stage, parents were taught to direct their child's play, using praise to reinforce compliance and time-out to punish noncompliance.

Features of the Hanf model, including direct coaching of parents during parent–child play interactions and the training in differential attention and time-out, were retained. PCIT is distinct from the Hanf model in its emphasis on the more traditional play therapy techniques incorporated into the first phase of treatment and its focus on problem-solving skills in the second phase of treatment.

With its special emphasis on changing parent–child interaction patterns and improving the quality of the parent–child relationship, PCIT is informed by developmental psychology (Eyberg, Schuhmann, & Rey, 1998) and draws on both attachment and social learning theories. The model assumes that children's behavior is influenced both by constitutional factors, such as temperament or neurological deficits, and by parent–child interactional patterns (Eyberg & Boggs, 1998) which are influenced as well by specific parent characteristics and the nature of the home environment (Bearss & Eyberg, 1998; Loeber & Dishion, 1983).

DESCRIPTION OF THE PROBLEM

To date, PCIT has been evaluated empirically only for the treatment of conduct-disordered behavior. Conduct problems include a range of acting out behaviors, from minor oppositional behaviors such as arguing and whining to major antisocial and aggressive acts. Estimates of the incidence of conduct-disordered behavior range from 2 to 10% of the general population (McMahon & Estes, 1997) and comprise from one-third to one-half of the mental health referrals for children (McMahon & Estes, 1997; Schuhmann, Durning, Eyberg, & Boggs, 1996).

The importance of early intervention is underscored by increasing evidence of the seriousness and persistence of conduct problems that begin during the preschool years (Hinshaw, Lahey, & Hart, 1993). Epidemiological research suggests that preschool conduct problems may be part of a common pathway for a wide range of adolescent and adult disorders of both an externalizing and internalizing nature (Fisher, Rolf, Hasazi, & Cummings, 1984; Lerner, Inui, Trupin, & Douglas, 1985). In adulthood, children with conduct-disordered behavior are more likely to engage in criminal offenses including elevated rates of violence against women (Fagot, Loeber, & Reid, 1988), and to have increased risk of psychiatric impairment including a higher suicide rate (Loeber, 1982).

DESCRIPTION OF THE PROCEDURES USED

Assessment

PCIT begins with a thorough assessment of child behavior problems and parental concerns because the particular emphases of treatment and individual components are tailored to meet the special needs of each family. The initial assessment data also provide a baseline of child behavior and parenting skills against which the therapist can judge the family's progress in treatment. This is particularly important given the current emphasis of managed care on documented effectiveness.

Interview

The assessment for PCIT begins with a semistructured interview. During this interview, information is collected on the child's developmental history, family stressors, parent concerns, and parental motivation for involvement in their child's treatment. In addition, parents are asked to describe previous discipline techniques so that the clinician may conduct a functional analysis of the child's presenting problems. The initial interview is also an opportunity to discuss the interactive partnership between parents and therapist that is integral to PCIT. As the beginning of a collaborative therapeutic endeavor, the interview may be viewed as an experience that builds therapeutic rapport (Calzada, Amiry, & Eyberg, 1998).

Rating Scales

A second part of the initial assessment is administration of parent- and teacher-report measures such as the Eyberg Child Behavior Inventory (ECBI; Eyberg & Pincus, 1999) and Sutter–Eyberg Student Behavior Inventory-Revised (SESBI-R; Eyberg & Pincus, 1999), to establish the intensity and generality of conduct problem behavior. The ECBI is a brief parent-report measure of externalizing behavior for use in screening and in measuring treatment outcome (Colvin, Eyberg, & Adams, 1998). The 36-item measure has strong interrater and test–retest reliability, and discriminative and concurrent validity (Eyberg, 1992). Numerous studies have demonstrated its sensitivity to treatment effects (e.g., Eisenstadt, Eyberg, McNeil, Newcomb, & Funderburk, 1993; Webster-Stratton, 1984). The ECBI provides an intensity score and a problem score. Similar to other parent rating scales, the intensity score provides an estimate of how frequently the child displays each problem behavior. The problem score allows parents to rate whether they perceive the behavior to be problematic for them, and is a measure of tolerance.

The SESBI-R is a teacher-report measure similar in format to the ECBI, but appropriate for the preschool, kindergarten, or school setting. This measure also has strong internal consistency, test–retest reliability, discriminative validity, and concurrent validity with other rating scales and with behavioral observations in the classroom (Rayfield, 1997; Rayfield, Eyberg, & Foote, 1998). The SESBI-R is useful for assessing generalization of treatment effects outside the home.

Behavioral Observation

Behavioral observations of the parent–child interaction are central to PCIT. In addition to informal observations in the interview, the therapist codes the child's interactions with each parent using the clinic version of the Dyadic Parent–Child Interaction Coding System-II (Eyberg, Bessmer, Newcomb, Edwards, & Robinson, 1994). The DPICS observation system allows the therapist to assess the current level of parenting skills, child responsiveness to the parent, and qualitative aspects of their interaction in three 5-minute standardized situations. These three situations are child-directed interaction (CDI), parent-directed interaction (PDI), and cleanup, and they vary in the amount of parental control required. The therapist conducts these brief, standardized observations throughout treatment to guide and monitor progress in parenting skills. It is also useful to videotape the pretreatment observations for future comparison to posttreatment observations.

Program Overview

PCIT is conducted in weekly 1-hour therapy sessions. Although not time-limited, the average length of treatment is 12 sessions. Most sessions are conducted with both the child and parents present. At the beginning of treatment, parents are introduced to the two-stage model of PCIT. Each phase of therapy begins with one teaching session in which the specific techniques are explained, modeled for the parents, and role-played with them. During the teaching sessions ("CDI Teach" and "PDI Teach" sessions) the parents are asked not to bring the child so that they can both pay full attention to the instruction. Handouts summarizing the techniques used in each phase are given to parents for later review. In subsequent therapy sessions ("Coach" sessions), the therapist briefly reviews home progress and observes each parent for 5 minutes in the play situation with the child before coaching. While observing, the therapist counts ("codes") the frequencies of certain skills the parent is learning so that the therapist and parent can determine which skills need work and when skills are mastered. Most of the session consists of coaching the parent in the skills they are learning. The therapist typically coaches the parent through an electronic "bug-in-ear" device from an observation room, although coaching from within the playroom is effective if an observation room is not available.

MAJOR MECHANISMS OF CHANGE

Child-Directed Interaction

CDI focuses on improving the quality of the parent–child relationship and strengthening the parent–child bond. In this phase, parents are taught nondirective interaction skills similar to the techniques used by traditional play therapists. The therapist explains that parents are often very effective "play therapists" with their child because they can practice and use the skills on a daily basis.

CDI is the first phase of PCIT for several reasons. First, children's behavior often improves substantially with CDI alone (Eisenstadt et al., 1993). The reduced anger and tension in the parent–child interaction that results from CDI provide a foundation to help parents deal calmly with discipline situations. In addition, we believe that children (and parents) more easily accept the discipline stage of treatment in the context of a warm relationship.

The basic rule for the parents' play during CDI is to follow the child's lead. Parents are initially taught several "do and don't" rules (see Table 1). We teach parents specifically how to attend to the child by describing and imitating the child's play, by answering the child's questions, by reflecting the child's statements, and by praising the child. Eyberg (1988) describes the rationales for these

Table 1. Child-Directed Interaction Handout

Rule	Reasons	Examples
1. Describe appropriate behavior	Allows child to lead Shows child you're interested Teaches concepts Models speech Holds child's attention Organizes child's thoughts about play	That's a red block. You're making a tower. You drew a smiling face. You're putting on two more pieces.
2. Imitate appropriate play	Lets child lead Approves of child's choice of play Shows child you are involved Teaches child how to play with others Tends to increase child's imitation of what you do	Child: I'm putting baby to bed. Parent: I'll put sister to bed too. Child: I'm making a sun in the sky. Parent: I'm putting a sun in my picture too.
3. Reflect appropriate talk	Doesn't control the conversation Shows child you're really listening Demonstrates acceptance and understanding of child Improves child's speech Increases verbal communication	Child: I made a star. Parent: Yes, you made a star. Child: The camel got bumps on top. Parent: It has two humps on its back. Child: I like to play with this castle. Parent: This is a fun castle to play with.
4. Praise appropriate behavior	Causes the behavior to increase Lets the child know what you like Increases child self-esteem Adds warmth to the relationship Makes *both* parent and child feel good	That's terrific counting. I like the way you are playing so quietly. You have wonderful ideas for this picture. I'm proud of you for being polite. You did a nice job on that building. Your design is pretty. Thank you for showing the colors to me.
5. Ignore inappropriate behavior (unless it is dangerous or behavior destructive)	Avoids increasing inappropriate behavior Decreases some behaviors Helps child notice differences between your responses to inappropriate and appropriate behavior	Child: (sasses parent and picks up toy) Parent: (ignores sass; praises picking up toy) Child: (hits parent) Parent: (GAME STOPS. This cannot be ignored.)
6. Don't give commands	Doesn't allow child to lead Can cause unpleasantness Child obedience will be taught later	*Indirect* Will you hand me that paper? Could you tell me the alphabet? *Direct* Look at this. Please tie your shoe. Come here.

(*continued*)

Table 1. (*Continued*)

Rule	Reasons	Examples
7. Don't ask questions	Leads the conversation instead of following Many are commands or require an answer May seem like you aren't listening or disagree with child	That's a blue one, right? What color is this? Are you having fun? You want to play with the wastebasket?
8. Don't criticize	Doesn't work to decrease inappropriate behaviors Often increases the criticized behavior May lower the child's self-esteem Creates an unpleasant interaction	You're being naughty. I don't like it when you talk back. Don't scribble on your paper. No honey, that's not right. That design is ugly.

techniques in detail. Interpersonal factors such as parental warmth, attention, and praise serve as the incentives that assist the child in developing self-control.

The therapist teaches each of the "dos and don'ts" of CDI one at a time, along with demonstration of the skill in isolation. Therapists continue to build rapport and a sense of commitment during the CDI Teach session by referring to skills that the parents have already mastered (as observed and counted during the assessment session), by encouraging parents to offer their own rationales for the dos and don'ts whenever possible, and by using humor and enthusiasm while teaching. The therapist describes the mnemonic "PRIDE" (Praise, Reflect, Imitate, Describe, with Enthusiasm) and demonstrates the CDI skills all together, before role-playing with the parent. It is important that the therapist point out to the parents that the therapist's skills come so easily because of practice and that the parents will also become adept at the skills through daily use. The therapist allays parents' apprehension about early practice with their child by describing children's typical reactions to CDI; children enjoy the positive attention and rarely misbehave during CDI. However, parents are instructed to ignore inappropriate behavior and avoid criticizing the child. Should potentially harmful or destructive behavior occur during CDI, parents are instructed to end the game.

Another important discussion concerns how parents will choose the toys that they use for CDI. Parents need to have a set of toys that is always available for CDI. Constructional toys without preset rules are best in this situation. These toys encourage creativity and provide developmentally appropriate opportunities for prosocial behavior. Moreover, they tend to elicit calm and appropriate behavior from the child. Toys that are suitable for CDI include Legos, Tinker Toys, Lincoln Logs, Magna Doodles, Potato Head, and building blocks. By contrast, parents should avoid toys that are conducive to rough or aggressive play, such as Ninja Turtles, Power Rangers, and guns. Preschoolers with conduct-disordered behavior are often overstimulated by these toys and require parental limit setting. Similarly, parents should avoid toys that are messy, such as paint, sand, or bubbles, because they are conducive to parent–child conflict in the treatment families. Also, board games do not work well in CDI because the child may have trouble taking turns, following the rules, or losing in the game. Parents of these children may have difficulty ignoring "cheating" and following the child's "rules." It is important to foster parent–child bonding and not competition during CDI.

Problem solving about when to practice CDI is an important part of the CDI Teach session. Parents with busy schedules often report finding it difficult to set aside 5 minutes for special playtime with their child. This issue should be addressed early, and the therapist should encourage parents to select a regular time for CDI before the first session ends. Common times for CDI are immediately after school, before bed, or after dinner. Parents are instructed to practice CDI daily for at least 5 minutes per day. This is long enough to have a therapeutic effect but not so long as to strain heavy schedules. Parents may practice CDI for longer than 5 minutes, although it is more important to practice daily than for longer periods.

Parent-Directed Interaction

After the parent has mastered or made significant progress with the CDI skills, the therapist moves to the second phase of PCIT, namely, PDI. This transition usually occurs after three or four CDI sessions. PDI is the discipline phase of PCIT. In the PDI Teach session, the parents are instructed to "lead" the game. To increase the chances of the child's compliance, the parent is taught to make positive, age-appropriate, direct commands during play. These skills are first taught through discussion of their rationale and verbal exercises with the therapist. Parents are then taught to follow their commands with contingent consequences. (Figure 1 diagrams the complete procedure.) Briefly, parents are to follow commands with either a labeled praise for compliance or a time-out warning for noncompliance. If a warning is not obeyed, the child goes to a time-out chair for 3 minutes. Parents are instructed to ignore inappropriate behavior in time-out such as yelling, crying, and cursing. However, the parent cannot ignore the child's getting out of the time-out chair. Parents are therefore taught a backup procedure for use if children get off the chair without permission, which helps the child learn to stay on the time-out chair for the required 3 minutes. Several backup methods have been proposed in the literature, and a review of the efficacy, practicality, advantages, and disadvantages of each are available elsewhere (Day & Roberts, 1983; Hembree-Kigin & McNeil,1995).

Parents are taught the exact words to use in the PDI situation and are asked to memorize the words on the training diagram before the next session. Because it is important that PDI be successful on first use, parents must wait until the first PDI Coach session, 1 week later, to begin PDI with their child. This way the therapist is able to coach the parent and ensure that the parent implements all of the procedures correctly. Moreover, many parents need a great deal of support and encouragement to follow through with time-out.

The first PDI Coach session is one of the most important sessions of treatment. At the beginning of the session, the therapist explains and demonstrates the PDI procedure for the child at an age-appropriate level, so that the child has an opportunity to learn about the new consequences for compliance and noncompliance. The first direct commands given by the parent should be simple and related to the child's current play activity (e.g., "Jimmy, please put the blue block here"), to increase the likelihood of compliance and to provide parents with many learning opportunities for the use of contingent labeled praise in this situation. As the ses-

Example: "Please put the block in the box."

"If you don't _____ you will have to sit on the chair."

Stay calm. Take the child immediately to the chair as you say: "You didn't do what I told you to do, so you have to sit on the chair. Stay on the chair until I tell you you can get off." (3 min + 5 sec. quiet)

Take the child directly back to chair while saying: "You got off the chair before I told you you could. If you get off the chair again before I tell you to I will (*). Stay on the chair until I tell you you can get off." (This time-out warning occurs only once.)

Take child directly to the chair while saying: "You got off the chair before I told you you could, so I am going to (*). Stay on the chair until I tell you you can get off."

Take the child to the chair while saying: "You got off the chair before I told you you could, so I am going to (*)." Then bring the child back to the chair and say: "Stay on the chair until I tell you you can get off."

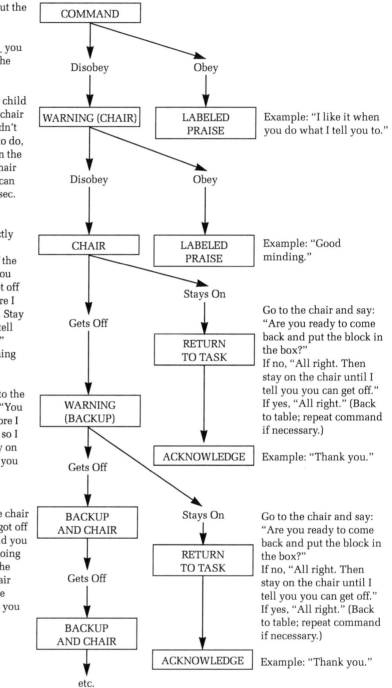

Example: "I like it when you do what I tell you to."

Example: "Good minding."

Go to the chair and say: "Are you ready to come back and put the block in the box?" If no, "All right. Then stay on the chair until I tell you you can get off." If yes, "All right." (Back to table; repeat command if necessary.)

Example: "Thank you."

Go to the chair and say: "Are you ready to come back and put the block in the box?" If no, "All right. Then stay on the chair until I tell you you can get off." If yes, "All right." (Back to table; repeat command if necessary.)

Example: "Thank you."

*Families are given diagrams with A, B, or C filled in. A—spank you (two swats with fingers); B—put you in time-out room (1 minute + 5 seconds quiet); C—hold you in the holding chair (1 minute + 5 seconds quiet).

Figure 1. PDI diagram.

sion progresses, the commands may be made more difficult by being less related to the child's immediate play activity and more natural (e.g., telling a child to pick up the block dropped on the floor or to put away a toy). Approximately 35% of children experience time-out during the first PDI Coach session. It is important to instruct the parent to follow a time-out experience quickly with another command that is very small and easy for the child to obey, so that the child can again experience the positive parental responses that follow compliance to first commands (i.e., enthusiastic labeled praises).

Subsequent PDI coaching sessions are not usually stressful sessions for parents, or children, because they know what to expect. Also, children who require time-out in the first session learn quickly to sit quietly on the time-out chair and to avoid the chair altogether by minding. Parents are coached to refine their skills, and to move easily into CDI following each command–obey–praise sequence. Commonly by the fourth PDI coaching session, the number of time-out warnings needed in home practice has been decreased to less than 20% of commands given, and the child has learned to obey direct commands easily.

Coaching PCIT

The coaching in CDI and PDI skills is a distinctive feature of PCIT that makes this approach suitable for parents with limited cognitive abilities and children with severe behavior problems. Coaching also makes possible a high degree of individualization of the treatment based on the unique needs of the family. Parents take turns being coached during play situations with their child while the other parent observes with the therapist and learns vicariously. At the beginning of CDI it is important for the therapist to provide numerous positive comments to the parent through coaching (e.g., "Nice labeled praise"). Many parents are anxious about the skills they have learned and are sensitive to criticism. The therapist may also provide positive observations ("Amanda really smiled when you helped her with her drawing"). Therapists are highly active during coaching and avoid long silences, which tend to increase anxiety.

When the therapist provides a coaching comment after every parent verbalization, the parent learns quickly. It is helpful for some parents to have exact phrases provided (e.g., "Good job of playing gently with the toys"). As the sessions progress and the parents' skills and confidence improve, corrective feedback can be given, if necessary ("Oops! A question"). We have found it is useful to emphasize one or two skills per session. Parents generally are most comfortable with describing and imitating play. Next the parents may begin to decrease questions and increase reflective statements. Labeled praises are usually the last skill that parents master. If a parent has difficulty with a particular skill, the therapist can initiate an "experiment" with the parent: The therapist might suggest that the parent try to say nothing but labeled praises for 2 minutes, to see whether they increase. The therapist would also continue to coach and count the praises enthusiastically during the experiment, and at the end could point out how the parent was able to master the skill. During CDI, parents learn to respond quickly to therapist coaching, which is useful for the early PDI coaching sessions.

During the first PDI Coach session, the therapist should be prepared to coach rapidly and be able to "feed the lines" to the parent. The first PDI session may be fast paced. Good coaching often requires the therapist to direct most of the activity in the room. Over the "bug," the therapist will not only give the exact words to be used to the parent, but also will track parents' tone of voice, eye contact with the child, manner of escorting the child to the chair, use of ignoring the child on the chair, and a myriad of unanticipated behaviors that may occur during the first use of time-out. The therapist also must monitor the emotional reactions of both parents. The observing parent will have reactions to PDI that may require separate attention. Often, though, the supportive comments provided during coaching can address both parents ("I know it is difficult for both you and your wife when Johnny cries on the chair, but it is important that he learn to mind you . . . you're doing a nice of job of ignoring . . . this is a good time to take a few deep breaths"). Also of note, the therapist and parents should set aside 2 hours for the first PDI Coach session so that there will be sufficient time to follow through with the time-out and to end the session with a positive CDI interaction. The additional time is rarely needed, but is important "just in case." Some children have ingrained the notion that if they refuse to obey for long enough, they will win the battle of wills. Further, it is always important to point out to parents how quickly their child has "recovered" from distress on the time-out chair and has resumed full, cheerful attention to playing with the parent. Coaching in subsequent PDI coaching sessions focuses increasingly on highlighting choice points and supporting parent choices, commenting on the parent's close attention to the child and positive parenting style, noting the child's positive demeanor, new developmental and social skills, and other observations that serve to reinforce the parent's confidence in parenting and pride in their child.

House Rules

Once the child and parent have mastered compliance to the running commands (what-TO-do commands) of PDI, compliance often, but not always, generalizes to standing commands (what-NOT-to-do commands) that are called house rules. If this generalization has not occurred, the therapist will teach the house rules procedure. An example is "No strangling the cat." House rules are always in force. This command would not likely be given unless the cat were being or about to be strangled, when it might serve to reinforce cat strangling. Only a few behavior problems are suitable for house rules. First, the problem should be one that has persisted when incompatible behaviors have been repeatedly praised. Second, it should be a problem that cannot be ignored because of potential harm. Third, the problem should occur unpredictably, and before an incompatible running command could be given.

When a behavior problem is appropriate for the house rules procedure, the therapist helps the parents to define the parameters of the problem very specifically (e.g., is squeezing the cat's tail an instance of strangling?) and to choose words to describe the behavior that the child understands (e.g., "hurting the cat"). If necessary, the parent teaches the child the words before the house rule goes into effect by labeling the behavior each time it occurs during 3 or 4 days (e.g., saying, "That's hurting the cat," on each occurrence). Before implementing the house rule, it is important to explain it to the child at a neutral time. ("You didn't hurt the cat this morning and I like that. But sometimes you forget and hurt the cat. To help you remember, we have a new house rule that's 'No hurting the cat.' From now on, if you forget, and you hurt the cat, you will have to go to time-out. But if you don't hurt the cat, you won't have to go to time-out.")

Unlike PDI, time-out is not preceded by a warning if a child breaks the house rule. Each time the child breaks the house rule, the parent states calmly but firmly, "You hurt the cat, so you have to go to time-out." No other discussion or explanation is given. The child then goes directly to time-out for 3 minutes plus 5 seconds of silence. The child is told when the time-out is over, but there is no discussion of the house rule or procedure until a neutral time. House rules remain in effect until the problem behavior no longer occurs. At that point, the house rule becomes "inactive," and a new rule may be added if necessary. If the child breaks an earlier house rule, however, a time-out is given.

Public Behavior Rules

During PDI, parents and children practice PDI first in play sessions and gradually in situations throughout the day when it is important that children obey. Parents often generalize PDI to public places naturally, but public places present some unique challenges. If children continue to present difficulty in public after PDI has been mastered at home, a specific session is set aside to address public behavior. Because parents have mastered all of the basic PDI principles, the session provides an opportunity to specify concretely the steps of problem solving and to encourage the parents to apply the steps aloud to public behavior (what are the specific problems in public; what are possible solutions; what are the advantages and disadvantages of each solution; which solution seems best). In the second half of the session, the therapist accompanies the parents and child on a trial run in a public area of our facility (e.g., waiting room, office hallway, cafeteria, parking lot) and coaches the PDI skills directly while they try out their plan. The parents then evaluate and modify their solutions, and their homework for the following week includes two to four trips to the public place(s) of concern (e.g., grocery store, mall) with their child to practice. The common problems that are addressed in problem solving often include what can be used for a "chair" (stadium cushion, newspaper, scarf), where can time-out be located to avoid embarrassment or disruption (bench outside the store), and ways to deal with bystander reactions.

Posttreatment Assessment

Termination of PCIT is by mutual agreement between parents and therapist that all or most of the presenting problems have resolved. In addition, the parents should feel comfortable in their ability to address any new behavior problems. It is a good idea to give an objective measure of the behavior before the end of treatment to assess the parents' perceptions more objectively. The final sessions can then focus on any remaining concerns, and on training for maintenance.

We reserve the last regular PCIT session for feedback on treatment progress. The same assessment measures that were used in the pretreatment assessment are repeated in the final session. In this way, a direct comparison to the baseline scores can be made. During this session, the therapist reinforces the parents for their changes and emphasizes the link between their parenting skills and their child's behavior. Changes in the parents' scores on measures of parenting stress and locus of control will show dramatic and clinically significant changes almost certainly, and we believe it is useful to interpret these changes for parents as an added incentive to continue daily "practice" of their new parenting skills. Highlighting the last session is a video presentation of clips from the family's pretreatment and posttreatment parent–child interactions. Through this presentation, parents are able to observe directly the improvement in their skills and their child's behavior as well as the emotional tone of the interactions. We give children a blue ribbon for good behavior at this session.

Follow-Up

At the end of treatment, the therapist describes to families the need to continue to use their PCIT skills as long as the skills are developmentally appropriate for their child. Follow-up or booster sessions are important for helping families maintain their skills and, therefore, their treatment gains (Eyberg, Edwards, Boggs, & Foote, 1998). The booster sessions typically last 90 minutes. They begin with a brief assessment of child behavior problems at home via the ECBI, the brief DPICS observations to assess parenting skills maintenance, and a discussion of the child's progress since the last visit. The session is then spent coaching the parents on their CDI and PDI skills and/or helping them use problem solving with any new problems that have arisen, depending on results from the assessment. At the end of the session, "behavioral prescriptions" can be given to parents to remind them of plans they wish to implement to improve or maintain progress. Booster sessions are typically scheduled at 1, 3, 6, and 12 months during the year following treatment, although individual needs and circumstances may indicate a different schedule for some families.

Research Support for Efficacy

PCIT outcome studies have demonstrated both statistically and clinically significant improvements in child conduct problems and noncompliance (Eisenstadt et al., 1993; Eyberg & Matarazzo, 1980; Eyberg & Robinson, 1982; Schuhmann, Foote, Eyberg, Boggs, & Algina, 1998) as well as child mood and self-esteem (Eisenstadt et al., 1993). These studies have documented change in the interactional style of mothers and fathers in play situations with the child as evidenced by increases in parental reflective listening and number of praises, closer physical proximity between parent and child, and decreases in sarcasm and criticism. Although parent training skills are taught in a controlled clinic setting, treatment effects have been shown to generalize to the home setting (Zangwill, 1983). PCIT has also been compared with parent group didactic training and found to be more effective (Eyberg & Matarazzo, 1980). Recent studies have demonstrated clinically significant improvements that have been maintained at 1- and 2-year follow-up evaluations (Newcomb, Eyberg, Funderburk, Eisenstadt, & McNeil, 1989).

In addition to child behavior change, PCIT has been shown to improve other aspects of family functioning. Eyberg and Robinson (1982) demonstrated decreases in parent MMPI profile scores and marital distress following PCIT. Parenting stress levels have been shown to decrease following PCIT (Eisenstadt et al., 1993), and increased confidence in parenting skills has been demonstrated (Schuhmann et al., 1998). Studies have also found generalization to untreated siblings (Brestan, Eyberg, Boggs, & Algina, 1997; Eyberg & Robinson, 1982). Finally, parents who have participated in PCIT have shown high levels of satisfaction with the treatment (Brestan, Jacobs, Rayfield, & Eyberg, 1999; Eyberg & Matarazzo, 1980).

Changes in conduct problems following PCIT have been shown to generalize to day-care, preschool, and early elementary classrooms (McNeil, Eyberg, Eisenstadt, Newcomb, & Funderburk, 1991). In a small group of ten children referred for problems at home and school, McNeil et al. (1991) demonstrated clinically significant improvements in behavior both by teacher rating and by direct observation after PCIT without additional intervention for school problems. Specific problem behaviors that improved included disobeying teacher directions, talking back, hitting, yelling, and breaking school rules. There were not, however, significant improvements in classroom hyperactivity and inattention. The improvements in conduct were maintained at the 1-year follow-up, and to a significant but lesser extent at the 18-month follow-up (Funderburk, Eyberg, Newcomb, McNeil, & Eisenstadt, 1998). In summary, PCIT is an evidence-based treatment for young, conduct-disordered children and their parents.

CASE EXAMPLE

Melanie S. is 5-year-old girl who was referred for evaluation and treatment by her mother, Ms. S. Ms. S. had divorced 8 months prior to the evaluation and reported that her ex-husband was physically abusive toward her in the past. During the interview, Ms.S. stated that Melanie had violent, destructive temper tantrums and frequently fought with her brother. Melanie obtained an ECBI problem score of 27 and an intensity score of 191, as rated by Ms. S. At the time of the evaluation, Melanie met criteria for Oppositional Defiant Disorder (ODD).

At the CDI Teach session, Ms. S. was receptive to the skills and learned them quickly. When problem solving about practice times, Ms. S. indicated that she may use toys in the bathtub during bath time. Ms. S. was praised for her creativity. At the next meeting, Ms. S. stated that she practiced 5 out of 7 days. She had made excellent progress in her CDI skills, increasing both behavioral descriptions and reflections. In the second CDI Coach session, Melanie was very bossy and did not want her mother to be included in the play. Ms. S. effectively ignored Melanie's inappropriate behavior, and continued to play alongside Melanie with similar toys. Although Ms. S.'s CDI skills continued to improve, she acknowledged her difficulty praising Melanie. She selected labeled praise as her primary homework focus during daily practice sessions. At the third CDI Coach session, Ms. S.'s skills were near mastery criteria. She completed an ECBI during this session, and Melanie obtained an ECBI problem score of 24 and an intensity score of 164, which were still well within the conduct problems range. PDI Teach was scheduled for the next session.

Ms. S. learned PDI quickly, judged by her role-play. The therapists decided to introduce the time-out room as a backup to the time-out chair because of the history of domestic violence in the S. family. At the first PDI Coach session, Ms. S. was initially nervous about the procedure, but became more comfortable and confident as the session progressed. Melanie went to the time-out chair once during this session and to the backup time-out room twice for getting off the chair. Once Melanie stayed on the chair and refused to get off and obey when given permission. Ms. S. remained calm and continued to ignore Melanie's behavior while on the time-out chair. After three refusals, Melanie obeyed the command on the fourth opportunity and subsequently obeyed several small commands before the session ended on a positive note with CDI. Ms. S. was instructed to practice PDI commands during brief play sessions after CDI each day.

At the second PDI Coach session, Ms. S. reported that Melanie went to the time-out chair once each day. The first day she got off the chair without permission and was taken to the time-out room each time. On subsequent days, Melanie remained on the time-out chair until permitted off. In the session, Melanie went to time-out once, but remained on the time-out chair. Ms. S. was told to continue practicing CDI and to practice PDI commands during play and in two or three other situations during the day. At the next PDI Coach session, Ms. S. reported that Melanie went to the chair three times during the week and remained on the time-out chair. Melanie did not go to the time-out chair during this session.

During the fourth PDI Coach session, Ms. S. again completed the ECBI. Melanie obtained a problem score of 10 and an intensity score of 148. House rules were taught and the house rule of "No whining" was established. At the fifth PDI Coach session, Ms. S. reported that Melanie did not go to time-out all week either for a PDI command or for breaking the house rule. A second house rule, "No yelling," was introduced. At the next PDI session, "Public Behavior Rules" were taught. Ms. S. continued to practice CDI and PDI daily. At the seventh PDI Coach session, Ms. S. reported that she had seen significant improvement in Melanie's behavior and that she felt confident about being able to with handle new problems that might arise in the future. In addition, her skills for PDI and CDI met termination criteria.

At the posttreatment assessment, Melanie obtained an ECBI problem score of 0 and an intensity score of 85. Ms. S.'s score on the Therapy Attitude Inventory (TAI), a brief measure of consumer satisfaction, was 49 out of 50. In addition, Melanie no longer met the diagnostic criteria for ODD. Ms. S. and Melanie returned 4 months later for a follow-up assessment. Melanie's ECBI scores remained within the normal range, with an intensity score of 103 and a problem score of 0. The TAI score remained at 49, and Melanie did not meet the criteria for ODD.

FUTURE RESEARCH

Treatment efficacy and maintenance of treatment gains is a principal concern for clinicians and third-party reimbursers. Although PCIT is clearly effective in changing the behaviors of conduct-disordered preschoolers and their families, evidence for long-term maintenance of change is limited and preliminary. Further study investigating long-term maintenance is crucial.

One area for additional study is child and family characteristics that affect maintenance of treatment gains. Comorbidity is one such variable that may affect long-term outcome. Comorbidity is typically defined as the presence of more than one disorder within the child (e.g., ODD and ADHD) but it can also be considered as a dyadic phenomenon between child behavior problems and parent problems, such as substance abuse, depression, or personality disorder (Foote, Eyberg, & Schuhmann, 1988). The influence of process variables during the course of treatment on maintenance of treatment gains is another potentially important research topic. Examination of these and other variables that affect maintenance will help address the issue of whether adjunctive treatments should be offered with parent training. In addition, various posttreatment maintenance strategies must be investigated (Eyberg, Edwards, Boggs, et al., 1998). Specifically, the various levels of posttreatment contact (notecards, phone calls, clinic visits), as well as the content and timing of posttreatment contact may differentially impact maintenance of behavior change.

SUMMARY

In summary, a review of research suggests that PCIT is an effective intervention for many parents and young children with conduct problems. Within PCIT, emphasis is placed on improving family communication, strengthening the parent–child relationship, and increasing prosocial behavior and child compliance. Through direct coaching, parents are taught to carry out therapy skills in the home setting. Ongoing assessment to guide treatment and evaluate outcome is an important component of the treatment program. We predict that collection of treatment progress data will prove to be quite helpful given current trends in third-party reimbursement.

REFERENCES

Azar, S. T., & Wolfe, D. A. (1989). Child abuse and neglect. In E. J. Mash & R. A. Barkley (Eds.), *Treatment of childhood disorder* (pp. 451–489). New York: Guilford Press.

Bearss, K., & Eyberg, S. M. (1998). A test of the parenting alliance theory. *Early Education and Development, 9,* 179–185.

Brestan, E., & Eyberg, S. M. (1998). Effective psychosocial treatments for children and adolescents with disruptive behavior disorders: 29 years, 82 studies, and 5275 kids. *Journal of Clinical Child Psychology, 27,* 179–188.

Brestan, E., Eyberg, S., Boggs, S., & Algina, J. (1997). Parent–child interaction therapy: Parent perceptions of untreated siblings. *Child and Family Behavior Therapy, 19,* 13–28.

Brestan, E., Jacobs, J., Rayfield, A., & Eyberg, S. (1999). A consumer satisfaction measure for parent–child treatments and its relationship to measures of child behavior change. *Behavior Therapy, 30,* 17–30.

Calzada, E., Amiry, A., & Eyberg, S. M. (1998). Principles of psychotherapy with behavior problem children. In G. P. Koocher, J. C. Norcross, & S. S. Hill (Eds.), *Psychologist's desk reference.* New York: Oxford University Press.

Colvin, A., Eyberg, S. M., & Adams, C. (1999). Restandardization of the Eyberg Child Behavior Inventory. Under revision.

Day, D. E., & Roberts, M. W. (1983). An analysis of the physical punishment component of a parent training program. *Journal of Abnormal Child Psychology, 11,* 141–152.

Eisenstadt, T. H., Eyberg, S. M., McNeil, C. B., Newcomb, K., & Funderburk, B. (1993). Parent–child interaction therapy with behavior problem children: Relative effectiveness of two stages and overall treatment outcome. *Journal of Clinical Child Psychology, 22,* 42–51.

Eyberg, S. M. (1988). Parent–child interaction therapy: Integration of traditional and behavioral concerns. *Child and Family Behavior Therapy, 10,* 33–46.

Eyberg, S. M. (1992). Parent and teacher behavior inventories for the assessment of conduct problem behaviors in children. In L. VandeCreek, S. Knaapp, & T. L. Jackson (Eds.), *Innovations in clinical practice: A sourcebook* (Vol. 11, pp. 261–270). Sarasota, FL: Professional Resource Press.

Eyberg, S. M., Bessmer, J., Newcomb, K., Edwards, D., & Robinson, E. (1994). Manual for the Dyadic Parent–Child Interaction Coding System-II. Social and Behavioral Sciences Documents (Ms. No. 2897). (Available from Select Press, P.O. Box 9838, San Rafael, CA 94912.)

Eyberg, S. M., & Boggs, S. R. (1998). Parent–child interaction therapy for oppositional preschoolers. In C. Schaefer & J. Briemeister (Eds.), *Handbook of parent training: Parents as co-therapists for children's behavior problems* (2nd ed., pp. 61–97). New York: Wiley.

Eyberg, S. M., Edwards, D., Boggs, S., & Foote, R. (1998). Maintaining the treatment effects of parent training: The role of booster sessions and other maintenance strategies. *Clinical Psychology: Science and Practice, 5,* 544–554.

Eyberg, S. M., & Matarazzo, R. G. (1980). Training parents as therapists: A comparison between individual parent–child interaction training and parent group didactic training. *Journal of Clinical Psychology, 36,* 492–499.

Eyberg, S. M., & Pincus, D. (1999). *Eyberg Child Behavior Inventory and Sutter–Eyberg Student Behavior Inventory: Professional manual.* Odessa, FL: Psychological Assessment Resources.

Eyberg, S. M., & Robinson, E. A. (1982). Parent–child interaction therapy: Integration of traditional and behavioral concerns. *Child and Family Behavior Therapy, 10,* 33–46.

Eyberg, S. M., Schuhmann, E., & Rey, J. (1998). Psychosocial treatment research with children and adolescents: Developmental issues. *Journal of Abnormal Child Psychology, 26,* 71–82.

Fagot, B. I., Loeber, R., & Reid, J. B. (1988). Developmental determinants of male-to-female aggression. In G. W. Russell (Ed.), *Violence in intimate relationships* (pp. 91–105). New York: PMA Publishing.

Fischer, M., Rolf, J. E., Hasazi, J. E., & Cummings, L. (1984). Follow-up of a preschool epidemiological sample: Cross age continuities and predictions of later adjustment with internalizing and externalizing dimensions of behavior. *Child Development, 55,* 137–150.

Foote, B., Eyberg, S., & Schuhmann, E. M. (1998). Parent–child interaction approaches to the treatment of child behavior problems. In R. Ollendick & R. Prinz (Eds.), *Advances in clinical child psychology* (pp. 125–151). New York: Plenum Press.

Funderburk, B. W., Eyberg, S. M., Newcomb, K., McNeil, C. B., & Eisenstadt (Hembree-Kigin), T. (1998). Parent–child interaction therapy: Maintenance of generalization to the school setting. *Child and Family Behavior Therapy, 20,* 17–38.

Hanf, C. (1969). *A two-stage program for modifying maternal controlling during mother child (M-C) interaction.* Paper presented at the meeting of the Western Psychological Association, Vancouver, B.C.

Hembree-Kigin, T. L., & McNeil, C. B. (1995). *Parent child interaction therapy.* New York: Plenum Press.

Hinshaw, S. P., Lahey, B. B., & Hart, E. L. (1993). Issues of taxonomy and comorbidity in the development of conduct disorders. *Development and Psychopathology, 5,* 31–49.

Kazdin, A. E. (1996). Problem solving and parent management in treating aggressive and antisocial behavior. In E. D. Hibbs & P. S. Jensen (Eds.), *Psychosocial treatments for child and adolescent disorders: Empirically based strategies for clinical practice* (pp. 386–387). Washington, DC: American Psychological Association.

Kendall, P. C., & Treadwell, K. R. (1996). Cognitive-behavioral treatment for childhood anxiety disorders. In E. D. Hibbs & P. S. Jensen (Eds.), *Psychosocial treatments for child and adolescent disorders: Empirically based strategies for clinical practice* (pp. 23–41). Washington, DC: American Psychological Association.

Lerner, J. A., Inui, T. S., Trupin, E. W., & Douglas, E. (1985). Preschool behavior can predict future psychiatric disorders. *Journal of the American Academy of Child Psychiatry, 24,* 42–48.

Lewinsohn, P. M., Clarke, G. N., Rohde, P., Hops, H., & Seeley, J. R. (1996). A course in coping: A cognitive-behavioral approach to the treatment of adolescent depression. In E. D. Hibbs & P. S. Jensen (Eds.), *Psychosocial treatments for child and adolescent disorders: Empirically based strategies for clinical practice* (pp. 109–135). Washington, DC: American Psychological Association.

Loeber, R. (1982). The stability of antisocial and delinquent child behavior: A review. *Child Development, 53,* 1431–1446.

Loeber, R., & Dishion, T. J. (1983). Early predictors of male delinquency: A review. *Psychological Bulletin, 94,* 68–99.

McMahon, R. J., & Estes, A. M. (1997). Conduct problems. In E. J. Mash & L. G. Terdal (Eds.), *Assessment of childhood disorders* (3rd ed., pp. 130–193). New York: Guilford Press.

McNeil, C. B., Eyberg, S. M., Eisenstadt, T. H., Newcomb, K., & Funderburk, B. (1991). Parent–child interaction therapy: Generalization of treatment effects to the school setting. *Journal of Clinical Child Psychology, 20,* 140–151.

Newcomb, K., Eyberg, S. M., Funderburk, B., Eisenstadt, T. & McNeil, C. (1989, August). SESBI and classroom behavioral observations. Paper presented at the annual meeting of the American Psychological Association, New Orleans.

Rayfield, A. (1997). *Concurrent validity of the Sutter–Eyberg Student Behavior Inventory with grade school children.* Unpublished dissertation, University of Florida, Gainesville.

Rayfield, A., Eyberg, S., & Foote, R. (1998). Teacher rating of conduct problem behavior: The Sutter–Eyberg Student Behavior Inventory Revised. *Educational and Psychological Measurement, 58,* 88–98.

Schuhmann, E. M., Durning, P. E., Eyberg, S. M., & Boggs, S. R. (1996). Screening for conduct problem behavior in pediatric settings using the Eyberg Child Behavior Inventory. *Ambulatory Child Health, 2,* 35–41.

Schuhmann, E. M., Foote, R., Eyberg, S. M., Boggs, S., & Algina, J. (1998). Parent–child interaction therapy: Interim report of a randomized trial with short-term maintenance. *Journal of Clinical Child Psychology, 27,* 34–45.

Webster-Stratton, C. (1984). Randomized trial of two parent-training programs for families with conduct-disordered children. *Journal of Consulting and Clinical Psychology, 49,* 633–640.

Zangwill, W. M. (1983). An evaluation of a parent training program. *Child and Family Behavior Therapy, 5,* 1–16.

18

Pharmacotherapy of Pediatric Anxiety Disorders

CHRIS KRATOCHVIL, STAN KUTCHER, SHARON REITER, and JOHN S. MARCH

Epidemiological studies have repeatedly suggested anxiety disorders to be among the more prevalent of the child and adolescent psychopathologies (Costello & Angold, 1995). With advances in the identification of child- and adolescent-onset anxiety (March & Albano, 1996) has come a concomitant increase in the application of pharmacological treatments borrowed in part from successful strategies applied in adult populations with similar disorders (Allen, Leonard, & Swedo, 1995). Conversely, although psychopharmacological interventions are increasingly recognized as an essential part of the treatment armamentarium for anxious youth (Bernstein, Borchardt, & Perwien, 1996), the exact place of medication strategies alone and in combination with psychosocial interventions is as yet unclear for all of the anxiety disorders save OCD (AACAP, 1997; Popper, 1993). Outside of OCD (March, Leonard, & Swedo, 1995b), few empirical studies of the efficacy, much less safety, of specific medications have been conducted (Klein & Slomkowski, 1993), with the use of many compounds in the pediatric population supported solely by clinical lore (Kutcher, Reiter, & Gardner, 1995). Surprisingly, most of the reported investigations either have been open trials or have been conducted in patient populations that are not well characterized (Jensen, Vitiello, Leonard, & Laughren, 1994; Kazdin & Weisz, 1998), making it difficult to interpret the results as standardized baseline diagnostic procedures and objective outcome measures should be precisely defined

CHRIS KRATOCHVIL • Department of Psychiatry, Creighton University, Lincoln, Nebraska 68178. STAN KUTCHER • Department of Psychiatry, Dallhousie University, Halifax, Nova Scotia B3H 3J5, Canada. SHARON REITER • Department of Psychiatry, University of Toronto, Sunnybrook Hospital, Toronto, Ontario M4N 3M5, Canada. JOHN S. MARCH • Departments of Psychiatry and Psychology, Duke University Medical Center, Durham, North Carolina 27710.

Handbook of Psychotherapies with Children and Families, edited by Russ and Ollendick. Kluwer Academic/Plenum Publishers, New York, 1999.

Table 1. Principles and Procedures for Using Anxiolytics

1. Baseline evaluation, including rating scales and laboratory measures if indicated
2. Careful consideration of differential therapeutics to identify potential targets for medication treatment as distinct from psychosocial treatments where possible
3. Establish risk/benefit ratio and obtain informed consent. In general, begin with least complicated and risky drug strategies
4. Determine separate outcome domains to track potential benefits and side effects
5. Insofar as possible, use only one medication at a time to minimize confusion with respect to tracking outcome
6. Consider dose–response and time–response characteristics of patient's condition and medication when adjusting medications
7. Using a stages of treatment model, establish a defined endpoint where a decision is made about whether the expectable benefit has occurred and whether additional treatment(s) must be implemented

Table 2. Most Commonly Used Pharmacotherapeutic Agents

Psychotropic class	Drug	Brand name	Therapeutic applications	Comments
Tricyclic antidepressants	Imipramine Nortriptyline Desipramine	Tofranil Pamelor Norpramin	All anxiety disorders except OCD and specific phobias	Second-line drugs after the SSRIs. Require EKG and laboratory monitoring. Not effective in depression
Serotonin reuptake inhibitors	Clomipramine	Anafranil	Only TCA used for OCD	Use after two or three failed SSRI trials
	Citalopram Fluoxetine Fluvoxamine Paroxetine Sertraline	Cipramil Prozac Luvox Paxil Zoloft	SRIs may be useful in all anxiety disorders except specific phobias	SSRIs are first-line compounds, with broad-spectrum activity in many mood and anxiety disorders and unique activity in OCD. Well tolerated compared with TCAs
Benzodiazepines	Alprazolam Clonazepam Lorazepam	Xanax Klonopin Ativan	Situation and anticipatory anxiety across all anxiety disorders	Best for short-term use while waiting for an SSRI to "kick in." Disinhibition and physiological dependence may be problematic
Other drugs	Buspirone Propranolol	Buspar Inderal	GAD Social phobia	Buspirone is broadly anxiolytic; it is not effective in phobic disorder with agoraphobia (PDAG) or OCD. May be useful in place of a benzodiazepine when substance abuse is an issue. Propranolol, or other β-blockers, are useful primarily in acute performance anxiety

and specific for the disorders under investigation (Conners, Wells, March, & Fiore, 1994; March & Albano, 1998).

With these caveats in mind, this chapter presents a clinically oriented review of the literature on pharmacological management of anxiety disorders in children and adolescents. Table 1 presents an overview of the diagnostic and treatment strategy used in the psychopharmacology of pediatric anxiety disorders. Table 2 lists the drugs typically used in this population. We begin with an overview of assessment and other issues before proceeding to a discussion of classes of compounds often used as anxiolytics in pediatric psychiatry. Readers interested in assessment (March & Albano, 1996, 1998), epidemiology (Costello & Angold, 1995), etiopathogenesis (Marks & Nesse, 1994; Sallee & Greenawald, 1995), psychosocial treatments (Albano & Chorpita, 1995; Kendall et al., 1997), family treatment (Barrett, Dadds, & Rapee, 1996) or medication management (Allen et al., 1995; Kutcher et al., 1995), and combined treatment (Bernstein et al., 1996) are referred to more in depth treatments of these and other topics (March, 1995).

CONTEXT FOR MEDICATION MANAGEMENT

Overview of Assessment

A comprehensive diagnostic assessment, including a clinical interview and a multimethod and multi-informant empirical evaluation, is essential for generating a comprehensive treatment plan that includes psychopharmacological interventions (March & Albano, 1996, 1998). To speed up and concentrate the evaluation process, it is often useful to gather sizable amounts of data prior to the patient's initial visit. In addition to requesting psychiatric/psychological, neuropsychological, hospitalization, and school records, it is helpful to ask patients and family members to complete a packet of materials designed to assess important domains of psychopathology in the context of the patients' presenting concerns. By gathering data in advance of seeing the patient, it is possible to adjust the "prior probabilities" that one or more of the major domains of anxiety are problematic and to estimate the likelihood of complicating comorbidities. By focusing on the primary diagnosis and "rule-outs" or differential diagnosis, the treating clinician then can instantiate a "disease management model" in which psychiatric illness is framed as the object of treatment usually with a combination of psychopharmacological and cognitive–behavioral interventions (Sackett, Richardson, Rosenberg, & Haynes, 1997).

The treatment of pediatric patients entails other complexities that are not present with most adults. For example, children less commonly seek treatment themselves. Alternatively, parents are sometimes "cornered into treatment" by pressure from school or social service agencies. Children commonly fear being labeled a "mental patient" by peers or extended family so that exploring the meaning of the medication to the child is important. Very often, prescribing medication in a medical context, namely, for an illness that is bothering the child and from which he or she wants relief, increases compliance. The form and taste of a medication as well as route of administration influence compliance, especially in younger children. If the cost of the drug is prohibitive, or it is not available locally, treatment may be interrupted. Although there are many methods of assessing compliance, such as direct monitoring, questionnaires, pill counts, and checking levels in body fluids, none are completely reliable. A good therapeutic alliance; careful explanation of benefits and risks coupled to written informed consent; combining medication with targeted psychosocial therapies; and thoughtful monitoring are the factors most likely to result in a positive outcome. Friendly and collegial communication with pediatricians, family physicians, and other professionals involved in the child's care also enhances compliance.

Finally, coexisting medical/psychiatric conditions (and their treatments) potentially complicate child psychopharmacology, and every child should have a complete physical examination, including a brief neurodevelopmental assessment, prior to starting most if not all medications. Routine monitoring of growth parameters, pulse, and blood pressure are rapidly becoming a fixture of good medical practice; some might even say that the sphygmomanometer is replacing the playroom as the hallmark of modern child psychiatry. However, routine laboratory evaluation is not generally warranted, although specific indications for pretreatment testing and ongoing monitoring can be defined. For example, liver function tests are necessary if there is potential for hepatic insult.

The Initial Visit

At the initial visit, each patient should optimally receive an extensive evaluation that includes a clinical interview of the child and his or her parents covering Axis I through V of DSM-IV; careful consideration of the rating scale data, a developmental questionnaire, school records, and previous mental health treatment records; a formal mental status examination; and in some cases, a specialized neurodevelopmental evaluation. Ideally, a structured interview, such as the Anxiety Disorders Interview Schedule for Children (ADIS) (Silverman & Eisen, 1992), also should be part of every diagnostic assessment. For specific disorders, such as OCD, additional specialized scales are necessary. For example, patients with OCD are usually evaluated using the symptom checklist from the Yale–Brown Obsessive Compulsive Scale (YBOCS) (Goodman et al., 1989), and are assigned a baseline score on the YBOCS and the NIMH Global Obsessive-Compulsive Scales. At the end of the initial interview, the child's presenting problems can be summarized in terms of DSM-IV diagnoses, which are then linked to a neurodevelopmental model of anxiety and to reinforcing environmental contingencies. The overall goal is to move in a developmentally sensitive fashion from the present complaint through DSM-IV five-axis diagnosis to an ideographic portrayal of the problems besetting the child patient.

Following a careful discussion of the diagnostic impression with the patient and his or her parents, it is then necessary to make recommendations in each of the following categories: (1) additional assessment procedures, when required; (2) cognitive–behavioral psychotherapies; (3) pharmacotherapies; and (4) behavioral and/or pedagogic academic interventions, when necessary. Unlike less formal evaluations that concentrate solely on story elements (Keith, 1995), this framework for understanding differential therapeutics attempts to implement interventions that present a logically consistent and compelling relationship between the disorder, the treatment, and the specified outcome. In particular, it is critically important to keep the various treatment targets ("the nails") distinct with respect to the various treatment interventions ("the hammers") so that aspects of the symptom picture that are likely to require or respond to a psychosocial as distinct from a psychopharmacological intervention are kept clear insofar as is possible. This method also permits the treating clinician to review in detail the indications, risks, and benefits of proposed and alternative treatments, after which parents and patient generally choose a treatment protocol consisting of CBT alone or CBT in combination with an appropriate medication intervention.

Other Considerations

Once a medication approach is chosen, it is imperative to fully describe and document the indications, risks, and benefits, including the options of no or other nondrug treatments, of the specific drug proposed for a medication trial (Leonard et al., 1996). A careful review of side effects is particularly important as the anxiety disorders are characterized by somatic symptoms, such as headaches, nausea, gastrointestinal distress, diarrhea, and various aches and pains, that are often similar to those that can be induced by medications. Potentially overlapping symptoms must be identified prior to starting treatment with medications to help identify "true" side effects that emerge as a result of treatment.

For each patient, the dosage pattern and the relationship between expected side effects and dosage changes must necessarily be individualized, which requires a careful understanding of both pharmacokinetics and pharmacodynamics of the chosen drug, patient factors, such as a history of genetically determined "slow drug metabolism," and the typical drug-response of the disorder to be treated. Pharmacokinetics addresses what the body does to a medication; pharmacodynamics addresses what the medication does to the body. Less is known about the pharmacokinetics of psychotropic medications in children than in adults (Preskorn, 1993); however, variations in the ways psychotropic medications are absorbed, distributed, and eliminated in children and adolescents do in some instances give rise to meaningful clinical implications (Popper, 1993). (The interested reader is referred to Paxton & Dragunow, 1993, and Greenblatt, 1993, for an overview of basic pharmacokinetic principles.) In this regard, the ability to construct a dose–response curve (the intensity dimension) and to analyze time–action effects (the time to response dimension) is critical, as dose can only be evaluated in the context of the expected time–action profile, including the possibility of delayed responses. Many patients conceptualize the treatment course of any medication on the time–action model of pain relief with analgesics, so it is important to describe the expected course of symptomatic improvement. A patient or family expecting immediate symptom resolution may prematurely wish to stop a potentially effective medication or to prematurely increase the dose in the mistaken belief that "it is not working" when the correct response is to simply wait until the expected response emerges.

Similarly, the treating child psychiatrist, pediatrician, or family physician must be equally clear when describing the anticipated benefits of medication use. Expected degrees of symptomatic improvement should be identified prior to initiating medication treatment and unrealistic expectations openly identified and discussed. For example, a decrement of 70 to 80% in panic attack frequency may often be accepted as maximal improvement with medications (Albano & Chorpita, 1995), while in many cases a 50% decrease in compulsive behaviors may identify the limit of medication effect in OCD (March & Leonard, 1996). Although this degree of symptomatic change does not constitute symptom resolution, it may lead to vastly improved social and academic functioning and, according to clinical lore, may improve the success rate of cognitive–behavioral interventions in some patients. Similarly, patients and their families must be informed that not all medicines help everyone and that a period of medication trial and error may be necessary to find the medication that is most helpful.

Potential drug–drug interactions with other medications (including over-the-counter compounds) should be identified (Nemeroff, DeVane, & Pollock, 1996; Preskorn, 1993). Because illicit drugs or alcohol can render treatment ineffective or confuse the clinical picture in such a way as to make it impossible to evaluate the efficacy of medications, patients must be advised to refrain from using these compounds. As this often may be an issue with adolescents, some of whom may self-medicate in response to symptom-based distress, information about substance abuse must be presented in an accurate, concise manner, with the risks clearly described but not exaggerated.

Because brief crises are usually the result of environmental triggers, and indicate the need to adjust psychosocial treatments, we advise parents that we rarely change medications in the middle of a "crisis." The clinician who chases each crisis by changing medications may do well in the short run simply from manipulating the placebo effect, but the long-term outcome will surely be poorer, especially with unthinking polypharmacy. A better strategy is to reevaluate the effectiveness of medications at preplanned intervals and to monitor carefully for possible side effects. Normal development and/or the natural history of the psychopathological syndrome under treatment may eliminate the need for medication, and periodic discontinuation trials are usually warranted. In this context, a point during treatment should be identified at which the patient's symptoms and functioning will be comprehensively reevaluated and further decisions about the treatment process made. It is necessary that this assessment point be chosen to allow enough time for the maximum expected symptom improvement (as distinct from sufficient improvement to evaluate whether a dose increase is needed) to occur, e.g., for the dose–response curve to show no further change. In some cases, such as the use of the benzodiazepine clonazepam for panic disorder, 4 weeks from treatment initiation may be sufficient at reasonable doses. For other cases, for example, the use of clomipramine for OCD, 8 or 10 weeks is more appropriate. In this regard, the timing of assessments must match the time–response characteristics of the chosen treatments. Different outcome domains sometimes change at different rates (e.g., see Cox et al., 1988); careful matching of independent to the dependent variable(s) over time is imperative in complex multicomorbid patients with multiple treatments having different time–action and dose–response profiles (Brown, Antony, & Barlow, 1995). With anxious patients, tracking improvement and side effects, using anxiety-specific ratings scales, such as the Multidimensional Anxiety Scale for Children (MASC) (March, 1998; March, Parker, Sullivan, Stallings, & Conners, 1997), also makes it much easier to ascertain when the patient has moved into the normal range across the relevant domains of outcome being treated.

TRICYCLIC ANTIDEPRESSANTS

The potential use of various antidepressants in treating anxiety disorders arises from the hypothesized role of specific neurotransmitters, particularly noradrenaline and serotonin, in the pathogenesis of anxiety states (Klein, 1996). Dysregulated central nervous system (CNS) noradrenergic and serotonergic functioning have been described in adults with anxiety disorders (Marks, 1987). Although the evidence for serotonin system dysfunction is perhaps best known for OCD (March, Leonard, & Swedo, 1990), dysregulation of other neurotransmitters, such as norepinephrine or dopamine, may play a role in the anxiety disorders (Rogeness, Javors, & Pliszka, 1992).

Treatment studies of tricyclic antidepressants (TCA), such as imipramine, desipramine, nortriptyline, and clomipramine, have been reported in a variety of child and adolescent anxiety disorders, including separation anxiety disorder and OCD (Allen et al., 1995; Popper, 1993). Several of these compounds have also been evaluated in clinical populations of children and adolescents in whom a high prevalence of anxiety states is found (e.g., school refusers) (Bernstein, Garfinkel, & Borchardt, 1990). Gittelman-Klein (Gittelman-Klein & Klein, 1980) reported a higher rate of return to school and diminished subjective anxiety in a double-blind placebo-controlled trial of imipramine in 35 children and young adolescents diagnosed as school refusers. However, Berney failed to demonstrate similar efficacy in a trial of clomipramine in 46 school refusers, although doses used were subtherapeutic (Berney et al., 1981). Bernstein et al. (1990) studied imipramine versus the benzodiazepine alprazolam combined with an extensive psychosocial treatment (school reentry program) in both open (n = 17) and double-blind placebo-controlled (n = 24) studies of school refusers. Although results tended to favor the medication-treated group, particularly in the open trial, nonsignificant differences between medication and nonmedication groups were found in the double-blind placebo study. Two important factors limit the findings of this study, namely, the small numbers studied and the addition of a medication to what was possibly by itself an effective psychosocial treatment. Although again limited by a small sample size, a more recent study by Klein and colleagues was unable to demonstrate a significant imipramine treatment effect in 20 children and young adolescents diagnosed with separation anxiety disorder (Klein, Koplewicz, & Kanner, 1992). Studies in adult populations have identified the efficacy of TCAs in treating panic disorder (Klerman, 1992); however, no studies have yet been conducted in children and adolescents with panic disorder.

Taken together, these few studies of the TCAs suggest very limited benefit (if that) for a subgroup of children and adolescents with anxiety-driven school refusal or separation/panic anxiety symptoms. More importantly, TCAs have not been shown to be effective in pediatric major depression (Birmaher et al., 1996; Conners, Wells, March, & Fiore, 1994) and many if not most anxious children are comorbid for depressive symptomatology if not major depression itself (Costello & Angold, 1995) plus the TCAs can cause potentially serious cardiovascular side effects (Elliott & Popper, 1991; Wilens et al., 1996). Hence, these drugs have been supplanted by other compounds as first-line agents for the treatment of children and adolescents with anxiety disorders other than OCD.

In contrast to other anxiety disorders, the treatment of pediatric OCD with the TCA clomipramine (CMI) is well supported empirically (March, Leonard, &

Swedo, 1995a). CMI differs from other tertiary amine tricyclics, such as imipramine, in structure only by the addition of a chloro-substituent to the fused-ring system. This change markedly increases the potency of serotonin reuptake inhibition, which presumably accounts for its unique activity in patients with OCD (March, Gutzman, Jefferson, & Greist, 1989). In an initial double-blind placebo-controlled crossover study, CMI proved significantly better than placebo (Flament, Rapoport, & Kilts, 1985). However, fewer than 50% of the subjects reported a minimum of 50% symptom improvement from baseline, and only 10% experienced total symptomatic relief. The specificity of the antiobsessive response to the more serotonergic TCAs was suggested by a similar study of CMI versus desipramine (DMI) in the treatment of child and adolescent OCD (Leonard, Lenane, Swedo, Rettew, & Rapoport, 1991). Using a crossover design, the study demonstrated not only that CMI was significantly better than DMI in reducing obsessive symptoms in the short term, but also that the majority of those patients initially treated with CMI relapsed when blindly switched to DMI illustrating that most OCD patients treated with medication alone (in contrast to CBT) relapse when medication is discontinued (March & Leonard, 1996). Finally, DeVeaugh-Geiss described an 8-week double-blind trial of CMI and placebo in 60 patients with OCD, in which 37% of the CMI group compared with 8% of the placebo group demonstrated a positive treatment response (DeVeaugh-Geiss et al., 1992). The CMI/OCD findings taken together suggest that while some patients experience significant symptomatic improvement with CMI, many retain some degree of symptom severity, although their social functioning and psychological distress may be somewhat improved. Taken together, these studies indicate that CMI is the tricyclic of choice in treating OCD. However, OCD appears to be a relatively refractory disorder, even with pharmacotherapy with CMI. Additionally, the disorder is chronic and tends to wax and wane, perhaps in association with environmental factors (Leonard et al., 1993). These issues need to be discussed with patients and their families before starting CMI treatment in order to keep the expected treatment response in perspective (March et al., 1995b).

Although a variety of studies are now available describing the potential use of TCAs in child and adolescent anxiety disorders, much yet remains unknown about the optimal dosing of these compounds. For example, absent dose finding studies to establish a therapeutic range, treatment remains largely a function of flexible upward dose titration. As well, the clinical relevance of tricyclic plasma levels in anxiety disorders remains unclear—to both therapeutic response and toxicity (Wilens et al., 1996). Cardiovascular side effects may occur more frequently in children and adolescents than in adults, and clinically significant conduction abnormalities may be related to preexisting cardiogram abnormalities (Leonard et al., 1995; Wilens et al., 1996). Prior to initiating tricyclic treatment in children or adolescents, the clinician must complete a full clinical examination including sitting and standing blood pressures and a baseline EKG (Schroeder et al., 1989). Common adverse reactions at therapeutic doses include dry mouth, constipation, nausea, dizziness, sedation, insomnia, and weight changes. The value of routine EKG monitoring is not known, but the EKG should probably be repeated at 3- to 6-month intervals. When withdrawing TCAs, a gradual dosage decrement over 2 to 3 weeks is a useful strategy to avoid tricyclic withdrawal side effects. Rapid tricyclic withdrawal may be associated with a variety of symptoms, including nausea, sweating, restlessness, insomnia, irritability, and vivid dreams, as well as other symptoms suggestive of cholinergic overdrive. Particular importance must be paid to avoiding TCA overdose, either accidental or deliberate. All tricyclics if taken in sufficient quantity can lead to cardiotoxic events, reduced seizure threshold, and CNS toxicity (Preskorn & Fast, 1992; Wilens et al., 1996). As suicide attempts are known to be associated with both anxiety and depressive disorders (Beautrais, Joyce, & Mulder, 1998) (though this relationship with panic is controversial; Andrews & Lewinsohn, 1992), practitioners electing to use TCAs in these patients must carefully weigh the risks and benefits in each particular patient (Brent, 1997).

SELECTIVE SEROTONIN REUPTAKE INHIBITORS (SSRIs)

Serotonergic neurotransmission has been implicated in a wide variety of CNS functions, including sleep, mood, impulse control, aggression, and social reciprocity (Feighner & Boyer, 1991). At the synaptic level, serotonin is released by the presynaptic neuron, diffuses across the synaptic cleft, and causes the postsynaptic neuron to depolarize via binding to the postsynaptic serotonin receptor (Goodwin, 1996). This "on" switch mechanism logically requires an "off" switch. The "off" mechanism operates via (1) diffusion backward and degradation by mitochondrial monoamine oxidase (MAO); (2) binding to the presynaptic 5-HT1A autoreceptor, which in turn decreases presynaptic serotonin release via negative feedback; and (3) recycling serotonin through a reuptake and repackaging mechanism that begins with serotonin binding at the presynaptic transporter. It is this latter step that is competitively inhibited by the nonselective SRI, CMI, and the so-called SSRIs. With increased synaptic concentrations of serotonin come immediate effects (often side effects) and, operating through second-messenger systems eliciting DNA transcription and messenger RNA translation, delayed effects resulting hopefully in desirable or therapeutic effects.

In this context, it is generally acknowledged that the SSRIs have transformed the pharmacological face of child and adolescent psychiatry (DeVane & Sallee, 1996a). Unlike the SRI, CMI, which is a nonselective tricyclic compound, the SSRIs, which now include citalopram, fluoxetine, fluvoxamine, paroxetine, and sertraline, are potent and specific inhibitors of the presynaptic serotonin transporter alone (Feighner & Boyer, 1991; Goodwin, 1996). Despite little empirical supporting data for indications other than OCD, clinical wisdom supports efficacy for the SRIs across a variety of indications as well as unique efficacy for OCD. Additionally, the SRIs show minimal effects on the cardiovascular system, do not require blood tests, and have a very favorable side effect profile (Leonard, March, Rickler, & Allen, 1997). Taken together, these considerations have made the SSRIs the most widely prescribed compounds for the pediatric anxiety disorders (AACAP, 1997). Table 3 presents important prescribing parameters for the SSRIs.

A growing literature supports the effectiveness of the SSRIs in adult anxiety disorders (e.g., see Greist, Jefferson, Kobak, Katzelnick, et al., 1995; Sheehan & Harnett-Sheehan, 1996); relatively less information is currently available to support the use of the SSRIs in the child and adolescent population (DeVane & Sallee, 1996b). Birmaher conducted an open-label study in 21 children and adolescents

Table 3. Selective Serotonin Reuptake Inhibitors

Drug	Brand name	Dosage range (mg)	Average daily dose (mg)	Dosing strategy
Citalopram	Cipramil	10–60	10–30	Push to maximum dose in
Fluvoxamine	Luvox	25–300	100–150	6–8 weeks from the start of
Fluoxetine	Prozac	5–80	10–30	treatment. Depending on
Sertraline	Zoloft	12.5–225	25–100	condition, 6–12 weeks is an
Paroxetine	Paxil	10–60	20–40	adequate trial

with either overanxious disorder, social phobia, or separation anxiety disorder, which suggested fluoxetine may be an effective treatment for pan-anxious youth (Birmaher et al., 1994). Fairbanks similarly described improvements in 16 children and adolescents with mixed anxiety disorders in an open-label pilot study of fluoxetine, with initial data suggesting efficacy in separation anxiety disorder and social phobia (Fairbanks et al., 1997). Black and Uhde (1994) examined the use of fluoxetine in 15 children with elective mutism in a double-blind placebo-controlled trial. Although parents' global ratings as well as ratings of the elective mutism showed more improvement with fluoxetine, teacher and clinician ratings did not show significant group differences. A recent long-term study of open citalopram treatment of school phobia and panic attacks suggested that it too may be helpful in selected patients (Lepola, Leinonen, & Koponen, 1996), though clearly controlled trials are indicated.

Medication trials clearly demonstrate efficacy for SSRIs fluoxetine, fluvoxamine, paroxetine, and sertraline in adults with OCD (Greist, Jefferson, Kobak, Katzelnick, et al., 1995). A recent meta-analysis of data from the adult multicenter registration trials suggested that the SSRIs are perhaps not as effective as CMI (Greist, Jefferson, Kobak, Katzelnick, et al., 1995). However, this conclusion is undermined by findings from recent head comparisons of CMI versus fluvoxamine (Freeman, Trimble, Deakin, Stokes, & Ashford, 1994) and of fluvoxamine, paroxetine, and citalopram (Mundo, Bianchi, & Bellodi, 1997) in which these drugs showed equivalent efficacy. Thus, it would seem that the SRIs as a group are all first-line treatments for OCD, with no clear indication for superiority of a particular compound (March, Frances, Kahn, & Carpenter, 1997). Among the SSRIs, only fluvoxamine (ages 8–18) and sertraline (ages 6–18) have secured FDA approval for the treatment of pediatric OCD, although controlled studies now support the efficacy of all but citalopram and paroxetine in the short-term treatment of pediatric OCD. Fluoxetine was first reported to be safe and effective in an open trial (Riddle, Hardin, King, Scahill, & Woolston, 1990). Using a double-blind placebo-controlled crossover design, they subsequently reported that 20 mg of fluoxetine per day was superior to placebo on the Clinical Global Impressions Scale with a trend toward improvement on the YBOCS (Riddle et al., 1992). Parenthetically, fluoxetine seems to improve OCD symptoms in patients with tic disorders with little effects on tics per se (Scahill et al., 1997). Open trials of fluvoxamine (Apter et al., 1994) and sertraline (Cook, Charak, Trapani, & Zelko, 1994) eventually gave way to industry-funded multicenter registration trials supporting the short-term efficacy of both fluvoxamine (Riddle et al., 1996) and sertraline (March, Biederman, Wolkow,

Safferman, & Group, 1997). Echoing the earlier CMI multicenter registration trial (DeVeaugh-Geiss et al., 1992), these studies showed (1) little or no placebo effect, (2) a 30–40 % reduction in OCD symptoms as measured on the YBOCS, and (3) clinical effects beginning at 3 weeks and plateauing at 10 weeks. Only limited clinical data currently support the use of citalopram or paroxetine (March et al., 1995b; Thomsen, 1997). However, a large multicenter paroxetine trial is now under way, and it is likely that both also are effective treatments for OCD in youth. Hence, given results from the fixed-dose studies of fluoxetine (Tollefson et al., 1994) and sertraline (Greist, Jefferson, Kobak, Chouinard, et al., 1995), which show little or no advantage of high doses, and recent expert recommendations (March, Frances, et al., 1997), clinicians would be well advised to begin with the equivalent of 50 mg of sertraline or fluvoxamine, to wait at least 3 weeks before increasing the dose, and moving to maximum doses by 6–8 weeks in non- or partial responders for an adequate acute trial duration of 10–12 weeks.

In comparison with TCAs, the SSRIs as a group are characterized by increased rates of gastrointestinal side effects. Other bothersome SSRI side effects include headache, rash, and overstimulation in particular (Leonard et al., 1997). Fluoxetine may be the most stimulating; paroxetine the most sedating; fluvoxamine and sertraline the most prone to gastrointestinal side effects. Importantly, "side effects" may be particularly common in the first week of treatment when the treatment itself may cause jitteriness or other anxiety symptoms (Ballenger, 1993). Hematological abnormalities, including increased bleeding times and serum sickness, have been reported but rarely. All SRIs are associated with weight gain, perhaps through a mechanism involving delayed satiety, and with sexual side effects, particularly delayed ejaculation and anorgasmia in women. Sexual side effects are particularly important to ask about with respect to medication compliance in adolescents, who may look oppositional but in reality are having aversive sexual side effects they have been unable or unwilling to mention. The SSRIs show potential for rare extrapyramidal side effects (EPSEs), including acute dystonias, with EPSEs much more likely when these drugs are combined with neuroleptics. Despite these cautions, the absence of typical tricyclic side effects, including cardiac toxicity, gives the SSRIs a significant advantage over CMI, which experts recommend only after two or three failed SSRI trials (March, Frances, et al., 1997). Finally, combining SSRIs with other drugs that potentiate serotonergic neurotransmission—other SRIs, MAOIs, tryptophan, buspirone, for example—may produce the "serotonergic syndrome" characterized by severe gastrointestinal symptoms, autonomic instability, and neuropsychiatric side effects, including delirium (Leonard et al., 1997).

BENZODIAZEPINES

The anxiolytic activity of the benzodiazepines has been related to their ability to enhance CNS inhibition by activating the benzodiazepine/γ-aminobutyric acid (GABA) receptor complex (Coffey, 1990). GABA is the major ubiquitous CNS inhibitory neurotransmitter. In addition to their anxiolytic effects, benzodiazepines suppress Stage IV sleep and possess sedative, hypnotic, anticonvulsant, and muscle relaxant properties that may or may not be related to their anxiolytic activity.

Although the efficacy of benzodiazepines in a variety of anxiety disorders in adults is well established (Jonas & Cohon, 1993), studies of these compounds are to date quite limited with respect to both open and controlled data supporting their utility in treating pediatric anxiety syndromes. Chlordiazepoxide (Librium) has been the most frequently studied benzodiazepine in children followed closely by diazepam (Valium). Several studies have in fact described improvement in anxiety-related symptoms, but the heterogeneity of subjects within studies, lack of specific anxiety symptom measurement, and methodological limitations, do not allow for conclusions regarding use in child or adolescent anxiety disorders (see Coffey, 1990, for review of the early literature).

More recent studies of high-potency benzodiazepines generally show some degree of methodological superiority over these early studies of low-potency drugs. For example, Simeon found alprazolam to be significantly superior to placebo on some but not all measures in 12 patients (aged 8–16) with overanxious or avoidant disorder (Simeon & Ferguson, 1987). In a follow-up study, Simeon et al. (1992) applied a double-blind placebo-controlled design to treat 30 patients with DSM-III-R overanxious disorder ($n = 21$) and avoidant disorder ($n = 9$). The CGI scores showed a treatment-positive trend for alprazolam compared with placebo (Simeon et al., 1992). Klein (personal communication) treated 18 subjects (aged 6–17) with DSM-III-R diagnosed separation anxiety disorder in an open trial of alprazolam (0.5 to 6.0 mg daily). Ratings of anxiety and overall functioning as completed by physicians and mothers showed improvements from baseline of 89 and 82%, respectively. Teacher and child self-reports, although comparatively less marked (64 and 65%, respectively), showed a similar pattern of response. Another high-potency benzodiazepine, clonazepam, has been studied in children and adolescents with panic attacks. Several investigators have described diminished panic symptoms when children and adolescents are treated with clonazepam (Biederman, 1987; Kutcher & MacKenzie, 1988). In a more recent report using a double-blind placebo-controlled treatment design, clonazepam at a dose of up to 2.0 mg per day was found to be significantly better than placebo in decreasing panic attack frequency and daily anxiety ratings in 12 adolescents with DSM-III-R diagnosed panic disorder (Kutcher, Reiter, Gardner, & Klein, 1992). Similarly, in an extension of this study population, this same group found statistically significant reductions in Hamilton Anxiety Ratings Scale scores and significant improvements in school and social functioning in 17 teenagers treated with clonazepam (Reiter, Kutcher, & Gardner, 1992b).

During treatment, the side effects of benzodiazepines tend to be dose related and may include daytime drowsiness, ataxia, slurred speech, diplopia, and tremor. Unusual or paradoxical reactions including irritability, verbal or physical assaultiveness, and temper outbursts have been associated with benzodiazepine use (Allen et al., 1995). The exact incidence of paradoxical or dyscontrol reactions such as disinhibition or aggression with benzodiazepine use in children and adolescents is not known but is thought to be more common than that found in adults (Graae, Milner, Rizzotto, & Klein, 1994). For example, adolescents with a variety of clinical diagnoses have been reported to exhibit severe paradoxical reactions to therapeutic doses of clonazepam (Reiter, Kutcher, & Gardner, 1992a). Although rarely reported in the child and adolescent literature on anxiety disorders, withdrawal phenomenon, including recrudescent anxiety, and, rarely, seizures are a potential hazard when benzodiazepines are discontinued abruptly (Coffey, 1990). When withdrawing benzodiazepines, the clinician must differentiate among withdrawal symptoms (emergence of previously unreported symptoms presumed to have arisen secondary to the medication's CNS effect), rebound (amplification of original symptoms), and relapse (recurrence of initial symptomatology). Treatment of these states differs: Withdrawal and rebound respond to more gradual medication tapering; relapse requires reinstitution of therapy. Benzodiazepines are relatively safe in overdose. However, they do increase the sedative effects of other CNS depressants including alcohol, neuroleptics, antidepressants, narcotic analgesics, and antihistamines. This cross-reactivity is a potential problem, particularly with adolescents who use alcohol recreationally. Accordingly, care and time must be taken to provide the necessary education about potential medication/ alcohol interactions. Counseling to help the anxious teen deal with the peer pressures of drinking is often required. Finally, benzodiazepines with a rapid onset of action, such as diazepam and triazolam, may be more likely to create transient euphoric effects, which may be associated with increased abuse potential (AACAP, 1997; Popper, 1993). Thus, these medications must be used with caution, especially in those patients with premorbid substance abuse or a family history of substance abuse who may be at greater risk for benzodiazepine abuse.

Despite little more than rudimentary empirical evidence supporting the clinical use of benzodiazepines in anxious youths, some patients particularly with panic disorder do seem to respond positively to treatment with a high-potency benzodiazepine at least at the level of clinical utility in the individual patient. In the absence of studies of the entire gamut of possible anxiety disorders and with the lack of dose-finding studies, however, benzodiazepine treatment guidelines must remain tentative and conservative. Patients treated with high-potency benzodiazepines should be started on a low dose that is gradually increased. Doses should be increased every 3–4 days until the maximally effective therapeutic dose level is reached. The patient should then remain on this dose for a minimum of 1 week to determine its anxiolytic potential. If therapeutic effect is not achieved after this time and side effects are tolerable, the dose can again be gradually increased on a weekly basis. Once a good treatment response has been obtained, the dose should be maintained for 4–6 months unless concomitant pharmacotherapy with an SSRI and/or CBT permits earlier withdrawal of the benzodiazepine.

OTHER DRUGS SOMETIMES USED IN PEDIATRIC ANXIETY DISORDERS

5-HT1A Agonists

A variety of azapirone partial agonists at the serotonin (5-hydroxytryptamine, 5-HT) 5-HT1A receptor have been shown in studies of adults to have both anxiolytic (Feighner, 1987) and antidepressant properties (Robinson et al., 1990). At present, buspirone (Buspar, Bristol-Myers Squibb) is the only 5-HT1A agonist currently marketed in the United States, where it is approved for the treatment of generalized anxiety disorder in adults. While tablet buspirone has so far not been studied in controlled trials for any pediatric indication, it is widely used in children and adolescents for indications as diverse as oppositional behavior, anxiety, and depression in part because it is remarkably free of side effects (Kutcher et al., 1995). Other compounds, which are active at pre- and postsynaptic 5-HT1 receptors, also are under development (Dubovsky, 1993; Mosconi, Chiamulera, & Recchia, 1993), and promise similar efficacy and side effect profiles. Among these, flesinoxan (Rodgers, Cole, & Davies, 1994), gepirone (McGrath et al., 1994), ipsapirone (Cutler, Hesselink, & Sramek, 1994), and tandospirone (Evans, Troisi, & Griffiths, 1994) have shown promise in as yet unpublished controlled trials in adults; unfortunately, pediatric experience to date with these newer compounds is negligible.

Controlled trials have shown that buspirone is an effective treatment for major depression (Rickels, Amsterdam, Clary, Puzzuoli, & Schweizer, 1991; Robinson et al., 1990); mixed anxiety and depression (Gammans et al., 1992); and is as effective as the benzodiazepines in generalized anxiety disorder (Ansseau et al., 1990; Enkelmann, 1991). Unlike gepirone (Pecknold, Luthe, Scott-Fleury, & Jenkins, 1993), buspirone does not appear to be an effective treatment for panic disorder (Sheehan et al., 1993) or for OCD as a primary agent (Pato et al., 1991) or as an augmentor (McDougle et al., 1993). Side effects in the adult trials uniformly have been mild: lightheadedness, stomach upset, dizziness, sedation, asthenia, or headaches. Furthermore, the 5-HT1A agonists as a group show no evidence of withdrawal symptoms even after prolonged administration (Rakel, 1990) or of addictive potential (Murphy, Owen, & Tyrer, 1989), making them ideally suited for patients evidencing problems with benzodiazepine abuse.

There are as yet no pharmacokinetic, dose-finding, or controlled studies of tablet buspirone or any other 5-HT1A agonist in mentally ill children or adolescents (Hughes & Preskorn, 1994; Kutcher et al., 1995). In an open trial, Simeon and colleagues (1994) treated 15 patients (aged 6–14) having DSM-III-R anxiety disorders with buspirone for 4 weeks (18.6 mg mean maximum daily dose). Statistically significant improvement occurred after 2 weeks in anxiety, behavior, and hyperactivity, as measured by parents, teachers, and subjects' ratings. Adverse events were infrequent and mild. Case reports also suggest benefit in overanxious disorder (Kranzler, 1988), depression and OCD (Alessi & Bos, 1991), and social phobia (Zwier & Rao, 1994). An interesting literature also has grown up around the use of buspirone in aggressive children (Gross, 1995; Mandoki, 1994; Stanislav, Fabre, Crismon, & Childs, 1994), where speculation has it that benefit may accrue from dopamine antagonist properties seen at high doses as well as from modulation of serotonergic activity. Additionally, buspirone is often used in autistic children (Realmuto, August, & Garfinkel, 1989), where anxiety, impulse control, and hyperactivity have reportedly improved in some patients.

Interestingly, although benzodiazepines are generally well-tolerated and effective in child patients with anxiety disorders other than OCD (Popper, 1993), benzodiazepines, unlike the 5-HT1A agonists, may interfere with short-term memory and learning (Barbee, Black, & Todorov, 1992) and also may lead to paradoxical disinhibition (Graae et al., 1994). Thus, many clinicians prefer to use buspirone because of its more favorable side effect profile, though its lack of efficacy for panic-level anxiety, whatever the diagnostic appellation, leaves a significant gap in buspirone's pharmacotherapeutic indication profile.

Given the seemingly advantageous pharmacological properties of buspirone, the lack of studies in the child and adolescent population is surprising. Kranzler

(1988) reported the successful treatment of a young adolescent with overanxious disorder using 10 mg of buspirone daily. In our clinics, adolescents with generalized anxiety disorder/overanxious disorder without panic attacks have been successfully treated using buspirone at doses ranging from 30 to 90 mg daily. Simeon et al. (1992) reported an open trial of buspirone in 15 children aged 6 to 14 with a mixture of various anxiety disorders. Buspirone treatment over 4 weeks at a mean dose of 18.6 mg daily was associated with significant improvement in a variety of scales measuring anxiety and depressive symptoms. Side effects were mild; the most commonly reported were sleep difficulties and fatigue.

Dosage requirements for the anxiolytic effects of buspirone in pediatric anxiety disorders have not been established; hence, the following suggestions must be regarded as tentative. The average daily dose for teens should be about 30 mg given in divided doses, three times a day (t.i.d.). Maximum doses should probably not exceed the recommended upper adult daily limit of 60 mg, although exceptional cases may benefit from higher amounts (higher doses may be associated with dysphoria and gastrointestinal distress). Adolescents may be started on 10 mg per day and raised to 10 mg t.i.d. over 2 to 3 days. In younger children (aged 5–12), dosage should be started at 5 mg daily and raised to 5 mg t.i.d. over 2 to 3 days. It is important to note that buspirone has a later onset of anxiolytic action than the benzodiazepines: 2–4 weeks is the typical time–response profile at any given dose. Thus, a particular dose during titration should be maintained for a minimum of 2 weeks and further increments made thereafter according to therapeutic response. A maximal daily dosage has not been identified in this age group, but should be dictated by clinical response and side effects. Pharmacological treatment should be continued for at least 4 to 6 months following symptomatic resolution prior to determining the need for ongoing pharmacological interventions. Long-term effects of buspirone in the child and adolescent population are presently unknown.

Minor Drugs

Except for situational social phobia, the efficacy of propranolol, a beta-blocker, as a primary pharmacological treatment for the anxiety disorders is questionable (Jefferson, 1995; Popper, 1993). Further, its side effect profile—sedation, bradycardia, faintness, dizziness—and its bronchoconstrictor qualities do not support its routine first-line use in childhood anxiety disorders.

Although low-potency neuroleptics, such as thioridizine or chlorpromazine, have long been used as anxiolytics, their potential serious side effects allow no indication for the primary use of these or high-potency neuroleptics in the treatment of anxiety disorders in children and adolescents (Kutcher et al., 1995). Conversely, when patients have other disorders for which a neuroleptic is indicated, the adjunctive use of these compounds may also yield anxiolytic effects (Coplan, Tiffon, & Gorman, 1993). Under these circumstances, most pediatric psychopharmacologists would choose one of the newer atypical neuroleptics, such as risperidone or olanzepine, because of their more favorable side effect profile (Stein, Bouwer, Hawkridge, & Emsley, 1997).

Although antihistamines may occasionally be prescribed for the treatment of various child behavioral disorders, there is no clear indication from the literature for their use in treating child and adolescent anxiety disorders (Coffey, 1990; Popper, 1993). Although they may have some minor anxiolytic effect in this population, their sedative properties and other side effects limit their use.

CONCLUSION

Absent empirical data to guide the ordering of treatments, most clinicians treating anxious children and adolescents should begin with CBT, which has considerably more empirical support than pharmacotherapy (Albano & Chorpita, 1995; March, 1995), and advance to a pharmacological intervention only if the patient is not rapidly responsive. Factors leading to early medication intervention might include unavailability of CBT, patient preference, and severe or multiply comorbid illness or suicidality. For many patients with moderately severe to severe symptoms, the combination of CBT and medication may be most likely to lead to durable symptom remission, although empirical evidence for this assertion is largely lacking (March, Frances, et al., 1997). When patients do not respond or only partially respond to initial treatment, it is important to reassess whether treatment targets have been appropriately identified and treatments appropriately implemented. Conversely, increasing the intensity of the treatment—for example, by adding behavioral family therapy or increasing the dose of medication or changing medication—may be necessary (March, Frances, et al., 1997). Rarely, patients will benefit from combination medication regimes (Wilens, Spencer, Biederman, Wozniak, & Connor, 1995), for example with a neuroleptic, such as risperidone, when comorbid schizotypal personality disorder or a tic-spectrum disorder is present in the patient with a primary diagnosis of OCD (March et al., 1995b). In many cases, partial improvement is all that can be expected; distinguishing between improvement and residual impairment in the context of the natural history of the disorder is an important part of differential therapeutics and of the psychoeducational process.

To date, the available data suggest that high-potency benzodiazepines may be appropriate short-term treatments for a broad range of anticipatory and situation-related anxiety symptoms. While empirical data are more limited outside of OCD, where they are robust, the SSRIs are probably the agents of choice when long-term treatment is anticipated. Buspirone is a potentially useful agent in generalized anxiety disorder and its relatively benign side effects profile and low abuse potential make it an attractive choice particularly in an adolescent population at risk for substance abuse. Targeted propranolol may be useful to treat performance anxiety in patients with specific social phobia. TCAs and neuroleptics should be avoided when possible because of their lack of demonstrated efficacy and high potential for serious side effects. Other agents have a smaller role, if any, to play; combinations of various compounds may be useful in treatment-resistant cases. In every patient, careful attention to dose–response relationships (the intensity dimension) and time–action effects (the temporal dimension) is critical to maximize benefit and minimize side effects. Given the limited availability of empirical data on the safety and efficacy of anxiolytic medications for pediatric indications, further systematic investigation should be a priority in treatment research in the anxiety disorders of children and adolescents.

ACKNOWLEDGMENTS

This work was supported in part by NIMH Grants 5R21-MH-52828-03 and MH-55121-02 to J.S.M. and by a generous contribution from the Robert and Sarah Gorrell family and the John and Kelly Hartman Foundation.

REFERENCES

AACAP. (1997). Practice parameters for the assessment and treatment of children and adolescents with anxiety disorders. American Academy of Child and Adolescent Psychiatry. *Journal of the American Academy of Child & Adolescent Psychiatry, 36*(10 Suppl.), 69S–84S.

Albano, A. M., & Chorpita, B. F. (1995). Treatment of anxiety disorders of childhood. *Psychiatric Clinics of North America, 18*(4), 767–784.

Alessi, N., & Bos, T. (1991). Buspirone augmentation of fluoxetine in a depressed child with obsessive-compulsive disorder [letter; comment]. *American Journal of Psychiatry, 148*(11), 1605–1606.

Allen, A. J., Leonard, H., & Swedo, S. E. (1995). Current knowledge of medications for the treatment of childhood anxiety disorders. *Journal of the American Academy of Child & Adolescent Psychiatry, 34*(8), 976–986.

Andrews, J. A., & Lewinsohn, P. M. (1992). Suicidal attempts among older adolescents: Prevalence and co-occurrence with psychiatric disorders. *Journal of the American Academy of Child & Adolescent Psychiatry, 31*(4), 655–662.

Ansseau, M., Papart, P., Gerard, M.-A., & von Frenckell, R. (1990). Controlled comparison of buspirone and oxazepam in generalized anxiety. *Neuropsychobiology, 24*(2), 74–78.

Apter, A., Ratzoni, G., King, R. A., Weizman, A., Iancu, I., Binder, M., & Riddler, M. A. (1994). Fluvoxamine open-label treatment of adolescent inpatients with obsessive-compulsive disorder or depression. *Journal of the American Academy of Child & Adolescent Psychiatry, 33*(3), 342–348.

Ballenger, J. C. (1993). Panic disorder: Efficacy of current treatments. *Psychopharmacology Bulletin, 29*(4), 477–486.

Barbee, J. G., Black, F. W., & Todorov, A. A. (1992). Differential effects of alprazolam and buspirone upon acquisition, retention, and retrieval processes in memory. *Journal of Neuropsychiatry and Clinical Neuroscience, 4*(3), 308–314.

Barrett, P. M., Dadds, M. R., & Rapee, R. M. (1996). Family treatment of childhood anxiety: A controlled trial. *Journal of Consulting & Clinical Psychology, 64*(2), 333–342.

Beautrais, A. L., Joyce, P. R., & Mulder, R. T. (1998). Psychiatric illness in a New Zealand sample of young people making serious suicide attempts. *New Zealand Medical Journal, 111*(1060), 44–48.

Berney, T., Kolvin, I., Bhate, S., Garside, R., Jeans, J., Kay, B., & Scarth, L. (1981). School phobia: A therapeutic trial with clomipramine and short-term outcome. *British Journal of Psychiatry, 138*, 110–118.

Bernstein, G. A., Borchardt, C. M., & Perwien, A. R. (1996). Anxiety disorders in children and adolescents: A review of the past 10 years. *Journal of the American Academy of Child & Adolescent Psychiatry, 35*(9), 1110–1119.

Bernstein, G., Garfinkel, B., & Borchardt, C. (1990). Comparative studies of pharmacotherapy for school refusal. *Journal of the American Academy of Child & Adolescent Psychiatry, 29*(5), 773–781.

Biederman, J. (1987). Clonazepam in the treatment of prepubertal children with panic-like symptoms. Clinical Psychopharmacology Unit of Massachusetts General Hospital Symposium: New uses for clonazepam in psychiatry (1987, Boston, Massachusetts). *Journal of Clinical Psychiatry, 48*(Suppl.), 38–41.

Birmaher, B., Ryan, N. D., Williamson, D. E., Brent, D. A., Kaufman, J., Dahl, R. E., Perel, J., & Nelson, B. (1996). Childhood and adolescent depression: A review of the past 10 years. Part I. *Journal of the American Academy of Child & Adolescent Psychiatry, 35*(11), 1427–1439.

Birmaher, B., Waterman, G. S., Ryan, N., Cully, M., Balach, L., Ingram, J., & Brodsky, M. (1994). Fluoxetine for childhood anxiety disorders. *Journal of the American Academy of Child & Adolescent Psychiatry, 33*(7), 993–999.

Black, B., & Uhde, T. W. (1994). Treatment of elective mutism with fluoxetine: A double-blind, placebo-controlled study [see comments]. *Journal of the American Academy of Child & Adolescent Psychiatry, 33*(7), 1000–1006.

Brent, D. A. (1997). The aftercare of adolescents with deliberate self-harm. *Journal of Child Psychology & Psychiatry & Allied Disciplines, 38*(3), 277–286.

Brown, T. A., Antony, M. M., & Barlow, D. H. (1995). Diagnostic comorbidity in panic disorder: Effect on treatment outcome and course of comorbid diagnoses following treatment. *Journal of Consulting and Clinical Psychology, 63*(3), 408–418.

Coffey, B. J. (1990). Anxiolytics for children and adolescents: Traditional and new drugs. Special Issue: The safe and effective use of psychotropic medications in adolescents and children. *Journal of Child & Adolescent Psychopharmacology, 1*(1), 57–83.

Conners, C., Wells, K., March, J., & Fiore, C. (1994). Methodological issues in the multimodal treatment of the disruptive behavior disorders. In L. Greenhill (Ed.), *Psychiatric Clinics of North America: Disruptive behavior disorders* (pp. 361–378). Philadelphia: Saunders.

Cook, E., Charak, D., Trapani, C., & Zelko, F. (1994). Sertraline treatment of obsessive-compulsive disorder in children and adolescents: Preliminary findings. *Scientific Proceeding of the AACAP Annual Meeting, New York*, pp. 57–58.

Coplan, J. D., Tiffon, L., & Gorman, J. M. (1993). Therapeutic strategies for the patient with treatment-resistant anxiety. *Journal of Clinical Psychiatry, 54*(Suppl.), 69–74.

Costello, E. J., & Angold, A. (1995). Epidemiology. In J. March (Ed.), *Anxiety disorders in children and adolescents* (pp. 109–124). New York: Guilford Press.

Cox, D. J., Ballenger, J. C., Laraia, M., Hobbs, W. R., Peterson, G. A., & Hucek, A. (1988). Different rates of improvement of different symptoms in combined pharmacological and behavioral treatment of agoraphobia. *Journal of Behavioral Therapy and Experimental Psychiatry, 19*(2), 119–126.

Cutler, N. R., Hesselink, J. M., & Sramek, J. J. (1994). A phase II multicenter dose-finding, efficacy and safety trial of ipsapirone in outpatients with generalized anxiety disorder. *Progress in Neuropsychopharmacology and Biological Psychiatry, 18*(3), 447–463.

DeVane, C. L., & Sallee, F. R. (1996). Serotonin selective reuptake inhibitors in child and adolescent psychopharmacology: A review of published experience. *Journal of Clinical Psychiatry, 57*(2), 55–66.

DeVeaugh-Geiss, J., Moroz, G., Biederman, J., Cantwell, D., Fontaine, R., Greist, J. H., Reichler, R., Katz, R., & Landau, P. (1992). Clomipramine hydrochloride in childhood and adolescent obsessive-compulsive disorder—a multicenter trial. *Journal of the American Academy of Child & Adolescent Psychiatry, 31*(1), 45–49.

Dubovsky, S. L. (1993). Approaches to developing new anxiolytics and antidepressants. *Journal of Clinical Psychiatry, 54*(Suppl.), 75–83.

Elliott, G., & Popper, C. (1991). Tricyclic antidepressants: The QT interval and other cardiovascular parameters. *Journal of Child and Adolescent Psychopharmacology, 1*, 187–191.

Enkelmann, R. (1991). Alprazolam versus buspirone in the treatment of outpatients with generalized anxiety disorder. *Psychopharmacology, 105*(3), 428–432.

Evans, S. M., Troisi, J. R., 2nd, & Griffiths, R. R. (1994). Tandospirone and alprazolam: Comparison of behavioral effects and abuse liability in humans. *Journal of Pharmacological Experimental Therapy, 271*(2), 683–694.

Fairbanks, J. M., Pine, D. S., Tancer, N. K., Dummit, E. S., 3rd, Kentgen, L. M., Martin, J., Asche, B. K., & Klein, R. G. (1997). Open fluoxetine treatment of mixed anxiety disorders in children and adolescents. *Journal of Child and Adolescent Psychopharmacology, 7*(1), 17–29.

Feighner, J. P. (1987). Buspirone in the long-term treatment of generalized anxiety disorder. *Journal of Clinical Psychiatry, 48*(Suppl.), 3–6.

Feighner, J., & Boyer, W. (1991). *Selective serotonin reuptake inhibitors.* New York: Wiley.

Flament, M. F., Rapoport, J. L., & Kilts, C. (1985). A controlled trial of clomipramine in childhood obsessive compulsive disorder. *Psychopharmacology Bulletin, 21*(1), 150–152.

Freeman, C. P., Trimble, M. R., Deakin, J. F., Stokes, T. M., & Ashford, J. J. (1994). Fluvoxamine versus clomipramine in the treatment of obsessive compulsive disorder: A multicenter, randomized, double-blind, parallel group comparison. *Journal of Clinical Psychiatry, 55*(7), 301–305.

Gammans, R. E., Stringfellow, J. C., Hvizdos, A. J., Seidehamel, R. J., Cohn, J. B., Wilcox, C. S., Fabre, L. F., Pecknold, J. C., Smith, W. T., & Rickels, K. (1992). Use of buspirone in patients with generalized anxiety disorder and coexisting depressive symptoms. A meta-analysis of eight randomized, controlled studies. *Neuropsychobiology, 25*(4), 193–201.

Gittelman-Klein, R., & Klein, D. (1980). Separation anxiety in school refusal and its treatment with drugs. In L. Hersov & I. Berg (Eds.), *Out of school* (pp. 321–341). New York: Wiley.

Goodman, W. K., Price, L. H., Rasmussen, S. A., Mazure, C., Delgado, P., Heninger, G. R., & Charney, D. S. (1989). The Yale–Brown Obsessive Compulsive Scale. II. Validity. *Archives of General Psychiatry, 46*(11), 1012–1016.

Goodwin, G. M. (1996). How do antidepressants affect serotonin receptors? The role of serotonin receptors in the therapeutic and side effect profile of the SSRIs. *Journal of Clinical Psychiatry, 57*(Suppl. 4), 9–13.

Graae, F., Milner, J., Rizzotto, L., & Klein, R. G. (1994). Clonazepam in childhood anxiety disorders. *Journal of the American Academy of Child & Adolescent Psychiatry, 33*(3), 372–376.

Greenblatt, D. (1993). Basic pharmacokinetic principles and their application to psychotropic drugs. *Journal of Clinical Psychiatry, 54*(9 Suppl.), 8–13.

Greist, J. H., Chouinard, G., DuBoff, E., Halaris, A., Kim, S. W., Koran, L., Liebowitz, M., Lydiard, R. B., Rasmussen, S., & Whole, K. (1995). Double-blind parallel comparison of three dosages of sertraline and placebo in outpatients with obsesesive-compulsive disorder. *Archives of General Psychiatry, 52*(1), 53–60.

Greist, J. H., Jefferson, J. W., Kobak, K. A., Katzelnick, D. J., & Serlin, R. C. (1995). Efficacy and tolerability of serotonin transport inhibitors in obsessive-compulsive disorder: A meta-analysis. *Archives of General Psychiatry, 52*(1), 53–60.

Gross, M. D. (1995). Buspirone in ADHD with ODD [letter]. *Journal of the American Academy of Child & Adolescent Psychiatry, 34*(10), 1260.

Hughes, C. W., & Preskorn, S. H. (1994). Pharmacokinetics in child/adolescent psychiatric disorders. *Psychiatric Annals, 24*(2), 76–82.

Jefferson, J. W. (1995). Social phobia: A pharmacologic treatment overview. *Journal of Clinical Psychiatry, 56*(Suppl. 5), 18–24.

Jensen, P. S., Vitiello, B., Leonard, H., & Laughren, T. P. (1994). Design and methodology issues for clinical treatment trials in children and adolescents. Child and adolescent psychopharmacology: Expanding the research base. *Psychopharmacology Bulletin, 30*(1), 3–8.

Jonas, J. M., & Cohon, M. S. (1993). A comparison of the safety and efficacy of alprazolam versus other agents in the treatment of anxiety, panic, and depression: A review of the literature. *Journal of Clinical Psychiatry, 54*(Suppl.), 25–45; discussion 46–48.

Kazdin, A. E., & Weisz, J. R. (1998). Identifying and developing empirically supported child and adolescent treatments. *Journal of Consulting and Clinical Psychology, 66*(1), 19–36.

Keith, C. (1995). Psychodynamic psychotherapy. In J. March (Ed.), *Anxiety disorders in children and adolescents* (pp. 386–400). New York: Guilford Press.

Kendall, P. C., Flannery-Schroeder, E., Panichelli-Mindel, S. M., Southam-Gerow, M., Henin, A., & Warman, M. (1997). Therapy for youths with anxiety disorders: A second randomized clinical trial. *Journal of Consulting & Clinical Psychology, 65*(3), 366–380.

Klein, D. F. (1996). Panic disorder and agoraphobia: Hypothesis hothouse. *Journal of Clinical Psychiatry, 57*(Suppl. 6), 21–27.

Klein, R. G., Koplewicz, H. S., & Kanner, A. (1992). Imipramine treatment of children with separation anxiety disorder. Special Section: New developments in pediatric psychopharmacology. *Journal of the American Academy of Child & Adolescent Psychiatry, 31*(1), 21–28.

Klein, R. G., & Slomkowski, C. (1993). Treatment of psychiatric disorders in children and adolescents. *Psychopharmacology Bulletin, 29*(4), 525–535.

Klerman, G. L. (1992). Treatments for panic disorder. *Journal of Clinical Psychiatry, 53*(Suppl.), 14–19.

Kranzler, H. R. (1988). Use of buspirone in an adolescent with overanxious disorder. *Journal of the American Academy of Child & Adolescent Psychiatry, 27*(6), 789–790.

Kutcher, S. P., & MacKenzie, S. (1988). Successful clonazepam treatment of adolescents with panic disorder. *Journal of Clinical Psychopharmacology, 8*(4), 299–301.

Kutcher, S., Reiter, S., & Gardner, D. (1995). Pharmacotherapy: Approaches and applications. In J. March (Ed.), *Anxiety disorders in children and adolescents* (pp. 341–385). New York: Guilford Press.

Kutcher, S. P., Reiter, S., Gardner, D. M., & Klein, R. G. (1992). The pharmacotherapy of anxiety disorders in children and adolescents. *Psychiatric Clinics of North America, 15*(1), 41–67.

Leonard, H., Jensen, P., Vitiello, B., Laughren, T., Ryan, N., March, J., Riddle, M., & Biederman, J. (1996). Ethical issues in psychopharmacological treatment research with children and adolescents. In K. Hoagwood, P. Jensen, & C. Fisher (Eds.), *Issues in mental health research with children and adolescents* (pp. 73–88). Hillsdale, NJ: Erlbaum.

Leonard, H. L., Lenane, M. C., Swedo, S. E., Rettew, D. C., & Rapoport, J. L. (1991). A double-blind comparison of clomipramine and desipramine treatment of severe onychophagia (nail biting). *Archives of General Psychiatry, 48*(9), 821–827.

Leonard, H. L., March, J., Rickler, K. C., & Allen, A. J. (1997). Pharmacology of the selective serotonin reuptake inhibitors in children and adolescents. *Journal of the American Academy of Child & Adolescent Psychiatry, 36*(6), 725–736.

Leonard, H. L., Meyer, M. C., Swedo, S. E., Richter, D., Hamburger, S. D., Allen, A. J., Rapoport, J. L., & Tucker, E. (1995). Electrocardiographic changes during desipramine and clomipramine treatment in children and adolescents [see comments]. *Journal of the American Academy of Child & Adolescent Psychiatry, 34*(11), 1460–1468.

Leonard, H. L., Swedo, S. E., Lenane, M. C., Rettew, D. C., Hamburger, S. D., Bartko, J. J., & Rapoport, J. L. (1993). A 2- to 7-year follow-up study of 54 obsessive-compulsive children and adolescents. *Archives of General Psychiatry, 50*(6), 429–439.

Lepola, U., Leinonen, E., & Koponen, H. (1996). Citalopram in the treatment of early-onset panic disorder and school phobia. *Pharmacopsychiatry, 29*(1), 30–32.

Mandoki, M. (1994). Buspirone treatment of traumatic brain injury in a child who is highly sensitive to adverse effects of psychotropic medications. *Journal of Child & Adolescent Psychopharmacology, 4*(2), 129–139.

March, J. (1995). *Anxiety disorders in children and adolescents.* New York: Guilford Press.

March, J. (1998). *Manual for the Multidimensional Anxiety Scale for Children (MASC).* Toronto: Multi-Health Systems.

March, J., & Albano, A. (1996). Assessment of anxiety in children and adolescents. In L. Dickstein, M. Riba, & M. Oldham (Eds.), *Review of psychiatry XV* (Vol. XV, pp. 405–427). Washington, DC: American Psychiatric Press.

March, J., & Albano, A. (1998). New developments in assessing pediatric anxiety disorders. In T. Ollendick (Ed.), *Advances in clinical child psychology* (pp. 213–241). Washington, DC: American Psychological Press.

March, J., Biederman, J., Wolkow, R., Safferman, A., & Group, S. S. (1997). *Sertraline in children and adolescents with obsessive compulsive disorder: A multicenter double-blind placebo-controlled study.* Paper presented at the Annual Meeting of the American Psychiatric Association, San Diego, CA.

March, J., Frances, A., Kahn, D., & Carpenter, D. (1997). Expert consensus guidelines: Treatment of obsessive-compulsive disorder. *Journal of Clinical Psychiatry, 58*(Suppl. 4), 1–72.

March, J. S., Gutzman, L. D., Jefferson, J. W., & Greist, J. H. (1989). Serotonin and treatment in obsessive-compulsive disorder. *Psychiatric Developments, 7*(1), 1–18.

March, J. S., & Leonard, H. L. (1996). Obsessive-compulsive disorder in children and adolescents: A review of the past 10 years. *Journal of the American Academy of Child & Adolescent Psychiatry, 35*(10), 1265–1273.

March, J., Leonard, H., & Swedo, S. (1995a). Pharmacotherapy of obsessive-compulsive disorder. In M. Riddle (Ed.), *Child psychiatric clinics of North America: Pharmacotherapy* (pp. 217–236). New York: Saunders.

March, J. S., Leonard, H. L., & Swedo, S. E. (1995b). Pharmacotherapy of obsessive-compulsive disorder. *Child & Adolescent Psychiatric Clinics of North America, 4*(1), 217–236.

March, J., Leonard, H., & Swedo, S. (1998). Neuropsychiatry of pediatric obsessive compulsive disorder. In E. Coffey & R. Brumback (Eds.), *Textbook of pediatric neuropsychiatry* (pp. 546–562). Washington, DC: American Psychological Press.

March, J., Parker, J., Sullivan, K., Stallings, P., & Conners, C. (1997). The Multidimensional Anxiety Scale for Children (MASC): Factor structure, reliability and validity. *Journal of the American Academy of Child & Adolescent Psychiatry, 36*(4), 554–565.

Marks, I. (1987). *Fears, phobias, and rituals.* London: Oxford Unversity Press.

Marks, I. M., & Nesse, R. M. (1994). Fear and fitness: An evolutionary analysis of anxiety disorders. Special Issue: Mental disorders in an evolutionary context. *Ethology & Sociobiology, 15*(5–6), 247–261.

McDougle, C. J., Goodman, W. K., Leckman, J. F., Holzer, J. C., Barr, L. C., McCance-Katz, E., Heninger, G. R., & Price, L. H. (1993). Limited therapeutic effect of addition of buspirone in fluvoxamine-refractory obsessive-compulsive disorder. *American Journal of Psychiatry, 150*(4), 647–649.

McGrath, P. J., Stewart, J. W., Quitkin, F. M., Wager, S., Jenkins, S. W., Archibald, D. G., Stringfellow, J. C., & Robinson, D. S. (1994). Gepirone treatment of atypical depression: Preliminary evidence of serotonergic involvement. *Journal of Clinical Psychopharmacology, 14*(5), 347–352.

Mosconi, M., Chiamulera, C., & Recchia, G. (1993). New anxiolytics in development. *International Journal of Clinical Pharmacological Research, 13*(6), 331–344.

Mundo, E., Bianchi, L., & Bellodi, L. (1997). Efficacy of fluvoxamine, paroxetine, and citalopram in the treatment of obsessive-compulsive disorder: A single-blind study. *Journal of Clinical Psychopharmacology, 17*(4), 267–271.

Murphy, S. M., Owen, R., & Tyrer, P. (1989). Comparative assessment of efficacy and withdrawal symptoms after 6 and 12 weeks' treatment with diazepam or buspirone [see comments]. *British Journal of Psychiatry, 154*, 529–534.

Nemeroff, C. B., DeVane, C. L., & Pollock, B. G. (1996). Newer antidepressants and the cytochrome P450 system. *American Journal of Psychiatry, 153*(3), 311–320.

Pato, M. T., Pigott, T. A., Hill, J. L., Grover, G. N., Bernstein, S., & Murphy, D. L. (1991). Controlled comparison of buspirone and clomipramine in obsessive-compulsive disorder. *American Journal of Psychiatry, 148*(1), 127–129.

Paxton, J., & Dragunow, M. (1993). Pharmacology. In J. Werry & M. Aman (Eds.), *Practitioner's guide to psychoactive drugs for children and adolescents* (pp. 34–46). New York: Plenum Press.

Pecknold, J. C., Luthe, L., Scott-Fleury, M. H., & Jenkins, S. (1993). Gepirone and the treatment of panic disorder: An open study. *Journal of Clinical Psychopharmacology, 13*(2), 145–149.

Popper, C. W. (1993). Psychopharmacologic treatment of anxiety disorders in adolescents and children. *Journal of Clinical Psychiatry, 54*(Suppl.), 52–63.

Preskorn, S. (1993). Pharmacokinetics of antidepressants: Why and how they are relevant to treatment. *Journal of Clinical Psychiatry, 54*(9 Suppl.), 14–34.

Preskorn, S. H., & Fast, G. A. (1992). Tricyclic antidepressant-induced seizures and plasma drug concentration [see comments]. *Journal of Clinical Psychiatry, 53*(5), 160–162.

Rakel, R. E. (1990). Long-term buspirone therapy for chronic anxiety: A multicenter international study to determine safety. *Southern Medical Journal, 83*(2), 194–198.

Realmuto, G. M., August, G. J., & Garfinkel, B. D. (1989). Clinical effect of buspirone in autistic children. *Journal of Clinical Psychopharmacology, 9*(2), 122–125.

Reiter, S., Kutcher, S., & Gardner, D. (1992). Anxiety disorders in children and adolescents: Clinical and related issues in pharmacological treatment. *Canadian Journal of Psychiatry, 37*(6), 432–438.

Rickels, K., Amsterdam, J. D., Clary, C., Puzzuoli, G., & Schweizer, E. (1991). Buspirone in major depression: A controlled study. *Journal of Clinical Psychiatry, 52*(1), 34–38.

Riddle, M., Claghorn, J., Gaffney, G., Greist, J., Holland, D., Landbloom, R., McConville, B., Pigott, T., Pravetz, M., Walkup, J., Yaryura-Tobias, J., & Houser, V. (1996). *A controlled trial of fluvoxamine for OCD in children and adolescents.* Paper presented at the NCDEU, Boca Raton, FL.

Riddle, M. A., Hardin, M. T., King, R., Scahill, L., & Woolston, J. L. (1990). Fluoxetine treatment of children and adolescents with Tourette's and obsessive compulsive disorders: Preliminary clinical experience. *Journal of the American Academy of Child & Adolescent Psychiatry, 29*(1), 45–48.

Riddle, M. A., Scahill, L., King, R. A., Hardin, M. T., Anderson, G. M., Ort, S. I., Smith, J. C., Leckman, J. F., & Cohen, D. J. (1992). Double-blind, crossover trial of fluoxetine and placebo in children and adolescents with obsessive-compulsive disorder. *Journal of the American Academy of Child & Adolescent Psychiatry, 31*(6), 1062–1069.

Robinson, D. S., Rickels, K., Feighner, J., Fabre, L. F., Jr., Gammans, R. E., Shrotriya, R. C., Alms, D. R., Andary, J. J., & Messina, M. E. (1990). Clinical effects of the 5-HT1A partial agonists in depression: A composite analysis of buspirone in the treatment of depression. *Journal of Clinical Psychopharmacology, 10*(3 Suppl.), 67S–76S.

Rodgers, R. J., Cole, J. C., & Davies, A. (1994). Antianxiety and behavioral suppressant actions of the novel 5-HT1A receptor agonist, flesinoxan. *Pharmacological Biochemical Behavior, 48*(4), 959–963.

Rogeness, G., Javors, M., & Pliszka, S. (1992). Neurochemistry and child and adolescent psychiatry. *Journal of the American Academy of Child and Adolescent Psychiatry, 31*(5), 765–781.

Sackett, D., Richardson, W., Rosenberg, W., & Haynes, B. (1997). *Evidence-based medicine.* London: Churchill Livingstone.

Sallee, R., & Greenawald, J. (1995). Neurobiology. In J. March (Ed.), *Anxiety disorders in children and adolescents* (pp. 3–34). New York: Guilford Press.

Scahill, L., Riddle, M. A., King, R. A., Hardin, M. T., Rasmusson, A., Makuch, R. W., & Leckman, J. F. (1997). Fluoxetine has no marked effect on tic symptoms in patients with Tourette's syndrome: A double-blind placebo-controlled study [In Process Citation]. *Journal of Child & Adolescent Psychopharmacology, 7*(2), 75–85.

Schroeder, J. S., Mullin, A. V., Elliott, G. R., & Steiner, H. (1989). Cardiovascular effects of desipramine in children. *Journal of the American Academy of Child and Adolescent Psychiatry, 28*(3), 376–379.

Sheehan, D. V., & Harnett-Sheehan, K. (1996). The role of SSRIs in panic disorder. *Journal of Clinical Psychiatry, 57*(Suppl. 10), 51–58; discussion 59–60.

Sheehan, D. V., Raj, A. B., Harnett-Sheehan, K., Soto, S., & Knapp, E. (1993). The relative efficacy of high-dose buspirone and alprazolam in the treatment of panic disorder: A double-blind placebo-controlled study. *Acta Psychiatrica Scandinavica, 88*(1), 1–11.

Silverman, W. K., & Eisen, A. R. (1992). Age differences in the reliability of parent and child reports of child anxious symptomatology using a structured interview. *Journal of the American Academy of Child & Adolescent Psychiatry, 31*(1), 117–124.

Simeon, J., & Ferguson, H. (1987). Alprazolam effects in children with anxiety. *Canadian Journal of Psychiatry, 32*, 570–574.

Simeon, J. G., Ferguson, H. B., Knott, V., Roberts, N., Gauthier, B., Dubois, C., & Wiggins, D. (1992). Clinical, cognitive, and neurophysiological effects of alprazolam in children and adolescents with overanxious and avoidant disorders. *Journal of the American Academy of Child & Adolescent Psychiatry, 31*(1), 29–33.

Simeon, J. G., Knott, V. J., Dubois, C., & Wiggins, D. (1994). Buspirone therapy of mixed anxiety disorders in childhood and adolescence: A pilot study. *Journal of Child & Adolescent Psychopharmacology, 4*(3), 159–170.

Stanislav, S. W., Fabre, T., Crismon, M. L., & Childs, A. (1994). Buspirone's efficacy in organic-induced aggression. *Journal of Clinical Psychopharmacology, 14*(2), 126–130.

Stein, D. J., Bouwer, C., Hawkridge, S., & Emsley, R. A. (1997). Risperidone augmentation of serotonin reuptake inhibitors in obsessive-compulsive and related disorders. *Journal of Clinical Psychiatry, 58*(3), 119–122.

Thomsen, P. H. (1997). Child and adolescent obsessive-compulsive disorder treated with citalopram: Findings from an open trial of 23 cases. *Journal of Child & Adolescent Psychopharmacology, 7*(3), 157–166.

Tollefson, G. D., Rampey, A. H., Potvin, J. H., Jenike, M. A., Rush, A. J., Keminguez, R. A., Koran, L. M., Shear, M. K., Goodman, W., & Genduson, L. A. (1994). "A multicenter investigation of fixed-dose fluoxetine in the treatment of obsessive-compulsive disorder": Correction. *Archives of General Psychiatry, 51*(11).

Wilens, T. E., Biederman, J., Baldessarini, R. J., Geller, B., Schleifer, D., Spencer, T. J., Birmaher, B., & Goldblatt, A. (1996). Cardiovascular effects of therapeutic doses of tricyclic antidepressants in children and adolescents. *Journal of the American Academy of Child & Adolescent Psychiatry, 35*(11), 1491–1501.

Wilens, T. E., Spencer, T., Biederman, J., Wozniak, J., & Connor, D. (1995). Combined pharmacotherapy: An emerging trend in pediatric psychopharmacology [see comments]. *Journal of the American Academy of Child & Adolescent Psychiatry, 34*(1), 110–112.

Zwier, K. J., & Rao, U. (1994). Buspirone use in an adolescent with social phobia and mixed personality disorder (cluster A type). *Journal of the American Academy of Child & Adolescent Psychiatry, 33*(7), 1007–1011.

Part IV

Integrative Approaches

19

Integrated Child Psychotherapy
Treatment Ingredients in Search of a Recipe

STEPHEN R. SHIRK

Integrated treatments are not new to child therapy; in fact, surveys have long indicated that child practitioners utilize techniques and procedures from a variety of theoretical sources in their clinical work with children (Koocher & Pedulla, 1977; Tuma & Pratt, 1982). Unfortunately, few of these integrated treatments have been evaluated, and many probably have not been replicated (Kazdin, 1996). This is not to say that integrated treatments are not useful. Instead, it points to the fact that child practitioners have typically been forced to construct integrated treatments based on the pragmatics of specific cases, rather than on the basis of empirical evidence supporting the effectiveness of particular treatment combinations. In this chapter, issues pertaining to psychotherapy integration with children will be placed in an empirical context. Given the paucity of research on combined treatments for children (Kazdin, 1996), it would be premature to advance an empirically based model of integrated child psychotherapy. However, the main aim of this chapter is to highlight what we do know from the empirical literature, and to clarify what we need to learn, in order to construct a framework for integrative child psychotherapy.

THE GAP BETWEEN RESEARCH AND PRACTICE

Although surveys of child clinicians have revealed that eclectic orientations and integrated treatments prevail in practice, most surveys have not examined specific treatment combinations. A survey by Snow and Paternite (1986) indicated that child clinicians who advocate a "mixed approach" that integrates both child and family interventions constitute a majority of practitioners, and that they differ

STEPHEN R. SHIRK • Department of Psychology, University of Denver, Denver, Colorado 80208.

Handbook of Psychotherapies with Children and Families, edited by Russ and Ollendick.
Kluwer Academic/Plenum Publishers, New York, 1999.

in the frequency of their use of specific techniques relative to "individual child-oriented" and "family-oriented" practitioners (p. 243). However, this survey, like the ones before it, provided little insight into typical treatment combinations that are used for individual cases. Integration is examined at a molar level, for example, combination of family and individual child interventions, and the use of specific techniques is summed *across* cases. The absence of information on *within* case treatment combinations, at anything but the global level, precludes the identification of frequently practiced forms of integrated child therapy.

It is likely that many child practitioners who advocate a "mixed approach" to child treatment individually tailor interventions to fit the perceived needs of specific cases. Here procedures or components from different treatment approaches are combined into "customized interventions." Whether such interventions are truly integrated, that is, organized into a coherent intervention sequence, is another question. Nevertheless, it is not surprising that many practitioners resort to customizing unique treatment combinations to meet their clients' needs. After all, many clinic-referred children present with multiple problems at different levels of analysis. For example, it is not uncommon to encounter a child who has problems with self-regulation in school, peer relational difficulties, a parent who is depressed or overwhelmed by life stresses, and a family that is entangled in intergenerational conflicts. Similarly, clinic-referred children often meet diagnostic criteria for more than one disorder (Kazdin, 1996), therefore increasing the likelihood that practitioners will face unique combinations of presenting problems rather than well-defined and delimited disorders. Treatments that are singular in mode or method are likely to be perceived as inadequate to address the complexity of many clinic-referred cases.

The use of individually tailored treatment combinations for clinic-referred children with multiple problems stands in sharp contrast to the prevailing approach to child psychotherapy research. Here well-defined treatments are targeted for children with homogeneous problems, typically defined in terms of a shared diagnosis (Shirk & Russell, 1996). Treatment precision and replication are emphasized, and manualization of intervention sequences is increasingly utilized. This is not to say that treatment packages do not contain multiple types of interventions. At the level of specific techniques, treatment packages often contain a variety of interventions, e.g., modeling self-instructions and coaching relaxation strategies, but these multiprocedure treatments typically draw on techniques from a single theoretical source, e.g., cognitive–behavioral, or from closely related sources, e.g., within the "family" of behavior therapies.

Consequently, one finds a significant gap between the use of eclectic, individually tailored treatments in clinical practice and well-defined, highly specified treatments in clinical research. Furthermore, there is growing concern that these two markedly different approaches to child treatment may yield very different results (Weisz, Donenberg, Han, & Weiss, 1995; Weisz, Weiss, & Donenberg, 1992). Weisz and his colleagues have observed that research therapies, involving recruited youngsters with relatively homogeneous problems who are treated with well-defined interventions, produce moderate to large treatment effects. In contrast, results from a limited sample of clinic-based therapies, involving clinic-referred children with mixed problems who receive flexible, eclectic treatments, are far less promising. In fact, research on child treatments as typically delivered in clinical practice has been hard pressed to find even modest treatment effects (Weisz, Donenberg, Han, & Weiss, 1995). In their analysis of factors that might contribute to this gap, Weisz, Donenberg, Han, and Kauneckis (1995) concluded that clinic-based and research-based treatments differ along a number of important dimensions. Most notably, research treatments tend to be behaviorally oriented with focused methods that are highly structured, whereas clinic-based treatments tend to rely on nonbehavioral methods that are broad in scope and highly flexible in application. Of particular relevance to the question of integrated child therapy is variation in the effectiveness of treatments that can be attributed to the degree of focus and specificity in treatment methods. As Weisz, Donenberg, Han, and Kauneckis (1995) concluded, "the overall picture of what might be needed [to improve clinic-based therapy] is analogous to what the gardener does to water a particular distant, difficult-to-reach spot—i.e., shifting the hose from 'spray' to the 'stream' setting" (p. 103). In other words, it is possible that children treated in clinics or private practices may attain greater benefits if practitioners moved away from eclectic treatments that are broad in scope and utilized focused treatments that are specific in form. With this perspective as backdrop, it seems that the first question that must be addressed is whether one can justify the use of integrated therapies that combine multiple treatment methods. To extend the gardening analogy, such treatments tend to be set on the "spray" setting, and therefore may lack the necessary focus and structure to be optimally beneficial.

Outcome Research on Combined Treatments

Treatment combinations come in a variety of forms. Many treatment packages having a single name, such as cognitive therapy, actually involve the integration of multiple methods at the level of specific techniques or procedures. For example, in the cognitive treatment of childhood depression it is not unusual to find interventions that include procedures for altering children's coping strategies through modeling, modifying maladaptive beliefs through structured self-monitoring, and improving social problem solving through role-playing (Rehm & Sharp, 1996). As Durlak, Fuhrman, and Lampman (1991) have observed, cognitive–behavioral therapy is "an umbrella term for a nonstandardized package of different treatment techniques that can be offered in many sequences and permutations" (p. 211). Thus, even within treatments that draw on a unified theory, at the level of specific techniques, a variety of procedures are commonly integrated.

Alternatively, other combined treatments draw on methods and models of change from multiple theoretical sources. One of the most prominent combinations in the research literature involves the integration of behavioral methods and psychopharmacology in the treatment of attention-deficit hyperactivity disorder (Hinshaw, 1994). Here biological and psychosocial interventions are combined, often in an effort to tackle different sets of co-occurring symptoms. Among psychosocial interventions, one also finds cross-theoretical combinations. Some represent pairings of "cousins" from an "extended family" of interventions, for example, the combination of operant-based parent management training and cognitive-based social problem-solving training in the treatment of antisocial youth (Kazdin, Siegel, & Bass, 1992). Others, however, involve the combination, and often the simultaneous application, of theoretically distinct forms of treatment.

For example, in the treatment of eating disorders the combination of individual psychotherapy—either cognitive–behavioral or psychodynamic—and systemic or structural family therapy has been recommended (Bowers & Andersen, 1994). In such a case, the adolescent participates in treatments of distinctly different theoretical origins, involving markedly different methods and targets of change.

Finally, a third form of treatment combination involves the construction of new treatment techniques derived from different theoretical sources. This form of treatment combination represents a version of "theoretical integration" (Stricker & Gold, 1996) in which original techniques are synthesized from two or more theoretical approaches (Wachtel, 1991). Thus, rather than combining sets of procedures from different theoretical approaches into a single-treatment package, as is typical of technical eclecticism (Norcross & Newman, 1992), interventions are integrated at the level of specific techniques. For example, Knell and Moore (1990) drew on cognitive–behavioral and play therapy principles to construct a play therapy technique that integrates behavioral interventions such as shaping and exposure through the medium of problem-focused play. In this case, symbolic play and exposure are not separate components of a treatment package, but are integrated into a single-treatment technique.

As these examples suggest, treatment combinations can be conceptualized at different levels of analysis—at the level of treatment packages that involve multiple, theoretically consistent procedures or techniques, at the level of multicomponent treatment packages that entail sets of interventions that may or may not be derived from the same theoretical source, and at the level of specific integrated techniques that involve a synthesis of principles from different theoretical sources. In turn, it is possible to identify examples of outcome research for each of these types of treatment combinations, although such a review must be viewed as illustrative rather than comprehensive.

The Evaluation of Multiprocedural Treatment Packages

The vast majority of child treatment outcome studies has evaluated the efficacy of brand-name treatments (Shirk & Russell, 1996). Brand-name treatments, such as cognitive–behavioral or psychodynamic therapy, are typically composed of multiple therapeutic procedures that are implemented in various combinations and doses. Cognitive–behavioral therapy (CBT) provides an illustrative example. In their meta-analysis of the effectiveness of CBT, Durlak et al. (1991) identified eight separate treatment procedures often found in CBT, including social problem-solving training, self-instructional training, and attributional retraining. Analysis of 64 treatment outcome studies revealed that the majority of treatments involved a combination of two or more procedures; in fact, only 16 treatments (25%) utilized a single-treatment procedure. Thus, most outcome studies of CBT (conducted prior to 1987) actually represent evaluations of combined treatments in the sense that they involve multiple-treatment procedures.

Overall, results from these analyses are quite promising. In general, CBT produced medium treatment effects, and large effects for children at the highest level of cognitive development. Analyses of studies with clinical populations also revealed that CBT moved treated children within parameters of normative functioning on cognitive and personality variables (Durlak et al., 1991). Unfortunately,

Durlak and his colleagues did not compare the effectiveness of single-procedure versus multiprocedure treatments. However, given that there were 42 unique combinations of cognitive–behavioral treatment in the sample (Durlak et al., 1991), and that treatments were delivered to children of different ages with varied problems, it is not clear that such a comparison would have shed much light on the relative efficacy of single- versus multiprocedure treatments. Although results of this meta-analysis suggest that multiprocedure treatments derived from a unified theoretical source yield beneficial effects (given that most studies involved multiple procedures), it is possible that single-procedure treatments that were highly focused inflated overall effect sizes. Obviously, resolution of this issue would be addressed most directly by comparisons of single- and multiprocedure treatments for children with similar problems. However, because the child therapy outcome literature has focused on the evaluation of treatment packages, the assessment of the relative contribution of specific procedures or techniques, or variations in their dosage, to treatment outcome has been relatively neglected (Shirk & Russell, 1996).

It is not clear if a similar pattern of results would be obtained for other brand-name therapies. However, many behavioral and psychodynamic treatments involve multiple procedures. For example, behavioral treatments of school avoidance often involve both reinforcement and exposure procedures, and dynamic treatments often involve both expressive (play, discourse) and supportive techniques. Thus, many existing outcome studies actually assess multiprocedure interventions when viewed at the level of specific change processes. Given consistent evidence from multiple meta-analyses for the efficacy of child therapy, it would appear that treatments that combine multiple, theoretically consistent techniques or components can be beneficial. That is, it does not appear that child interventions need to focus on the delivery of a single-treatment procedure in order to yield beneficial effects, although such highly focused interventions have produced positive outcomes (see Dush, Hirt, & Schroeder, 1989).

The Evaluation of Multicomponent Treatment Packages

At the next level of analysis are treatment packages that involve sets of interventions that may or may not be derived from the same theoretical source. Typically, these types of interventions are blocked into distinct components. For example, in clinical practice child treatment can involve a "preparatory phase" that centers around relationship building and the provision of emotional support, followed by a "work phase" that involves collaboration on specific therapeutic tasks such as self-instructional or social skills training. In this example, the initial phase of treatment draws on principles and techniques from the dynamic or play therapy tradition, whereas the second phase is informed by cognitive or behavioral skills training. Combinations of this sort also can draw on separate interventions from a single conceptual approach, e.g., the combined use of token reinforcements and social skills training. This type of treatment combination involves the integration of two or more sets of interventions, each of which could be (or has been) delivered as a "stand alone" treatment (Kazdin, 1996, p. 70).

There are a number of illustrative examples of the utility of multicomponent treatment packages. One of the best examples, in which a multicomponent package was compared with its individual constituents, was reported by Kazdin et al.

(1992) for the treatment of antisocial children. Using a constructive design strategy, Kazdin et al. (1992) compared the relative efficacy of two component treatments—parent management training and problem-solving skills training—with a treatment composed of both sets of interventions. It was hypothesized that all three treatments would provide beneficial effects, but that the combined treatment would result in more "marked, pervasive, and durable" changes in child *and* parent functioning (Kazdin et al., 1992, p. 733). Parent-focused treatment was seen as potentially augmenting cognitive changes produced in individual problem-solving therapy, and as adding to the effectiveness of treatment by addressing problematic parent–child interactions that are often unaltered by child-centered interventions. In addition, it was expected that the combined treatment would not only alter the child's dysfunctional and prosocial behavior, but would reduce parental stress and maternal depression as well. As expected, all three treatments produced beneficial effects, particularly in the area of child functioning. Of central interest, the combined treatment yielded greater beneficial effects in child functioning than either of the component treatments alone, and more systematic effects in parental functioning than the other treatments as well. In addition, there was evidence that the combined treatment moved a greater percentage of children into the nonclinical range of behavior problems than either of the separate treatments, particularly by 1-year follow-up.

As this example illustrates, a combined treatment derived from complementary and theoretically consistent approaches yielded beneficial effects for a difficult-to-treat population. Moreover, this multicomponent treatment, with its multiple treatment foci, was more potent than single-component treatments with a singular focus. These results suggest that it is possible to broaden the scope of treatment without diluting its effectiveness. On the contrary, the combined treatment that targeted both intraindividual processes and interactional processes produced better results than the more narrowly focused treatments. It should be noted that these results could be attributed to the fact that individuals in the combined treatment received more sessions than individuals in the separate treatments. As Kazdin (1996) has noted, it could be the case that either of the separate treatments would have produced comparable results if they had been delivered in equivalent strength. Parametric variations, that is, differences in amount or duration of treatment, represent one of the most likely confounds in the evaluation of combined treatments.

A second prominent example of a treatment that combines two sets of interventions, but in this case, from rather different theoretical sources, is Parent–Child Interaction Therapy (PCIT; Eyberg, 1988). Conducted in the context of dyadic play situations, PCIT combines teaching parents traditional play therapy skills for relationship enhancement and problem-solving skills for the management of emerging problem behaviors. In essence, techniques from two rather disparate conceptual models, play therapy (Axline, 1969) and behavior therapy, are combined in a two-stage treatment. In the first stage, child-directed interaction, parents are taught basic play therapy skills such as following the child's lead, verbal reflection of the child's play, and containing criticism or the use of commands. The major goal of this component of treatment is to build or strengthen a positive relationship between parent and child. In the second stage, parent-directed therapy, parents are taught to direct their child's activity through use of clear and direct commands and through use of consistent, appropriate consequences for behavior. The major goal of this component is to diminish problematic, noncompliant behavior while increasing cooperative behavior. Common to both stages of treatment is the use of coaching, that is, parents are coached by the therapist during ongoing parent–child interactions.

PCIT was developed for preschool and early school-aged children who presented with disruptive behavior problems, especially noncompliance. Evaluations of the efficacy of PCIT have revealed statistically and clinically significant changes in child disruptive behavior and noncompliance (Eyberg & Robinson, 1982). Generalization of positive treatment effects to home (Boggs, 1990) and to school (McNeil, Eyberg, Eisenstadt, Newcomb, & Funderburk, 1991) have been reported. More recently, Eisenstadt, Eyberg, McNeil, Newcomb, and Funderburk (1993) examined the relative effectiveness of the two stages of treatment and their overall effect with a group of young children with disruptive behavior disorders. Rather than comparing each component with the combined treatment, Eisenstadt et al. (1993) varied the order of presentation of each stage and evaluated the two interventions at the midpoint of treatment. Although this approach controls for parametric variation for each of the component interventions, the combined treatment differs from each in duration and number of sessions. The two approaches were expected to differentially affect different sets of outcomes at midtreatment, e.g., it was expected that the child-directed interaction component would enhance the emotional bond between parent and child to a greater degree than the parent-directed component, but results indicated that the parent-directed component yielded greater reductions in disruptiveness and noncompliance than the child-directed component. When delivered separately, the child-directed component showed no significant advantages over the parent-directed component at midtreatment. Furthermore, families who received the parent-directed component first, showed greater improvement in conduct problems than families who received the child-directed component first. Consistent with previous research, both orderings of the combined treatment moved children's behavior problem scores to within normal limits. Although the authors note that the results indicate that it may be advisable to present the parent management stage prior to the play therapy stage for some groups of clinic-referred children, the study raises a serious question about the contribution of the child-directed component to treatment outcome. Many of the indices of relationship quality that were targeted by the child-directed intervention did not change when only that module was delivered. Thus, it may be the case that beneficial effects could be attained without the child-directed component. To address the question of whether the combined treatment is more efficacious, or results in broader benefits, than either of the component treatments, a direct comparison of the combined treatment and parametrically comparable versions of the component treatments should be conducted. Nevertheless, current results from multiple studies indicate that this multicomponent treatment produces significant change in early disruptive behavior problems.

These examples of multicomponent treatments suggest that treatment integrations that combine sets of interventions from either similar or disparate conceptual models can produce beneficial effects. Obviously this is not equivalent to saying all treatment combinations are likely to be beneficial. For example, one of the most commonly practiced treatment combinations derived from the child guidance model—individual child therapy combined with collateral parent therapy—has not produced convincing results. Meta-analytic comparisons of child-only treatments with those that involved both child and parent (in the majority of cases) did not show significantly greater benefits for the group of treatments that included combined therapies (Casey & Berman, 1985). Moreover, the fact that treatment combinations can produce beneficial effects does not necessarily mean that combined treatments are more potent than single-modality treatments, such as parent management training, when such treatments are delivered at similar dosages. Both foregoing examples leave the latter question unanswered. What these examples do suggest is that treatments that combine sets of interventions do not necessarily undermine their effectiveness by broadening the scope of treatment. Given concerns about the potential limitations of broadband treatments, what do these examples tell us about successful treatment combinations?

First, it is noteworthy that the two examples differ in the degree to which combined sets of interventions are drawn from conceptually similar models. As these examples suggest, combined treatments that draw on similar or disparate conceptual models can yield beneficial treatment effects. Therefore, it seems possible to successfully combine treatments of different theoretical origins. However, in the illustrative case of PCIT, where nondirective play therapy techniques are combined with directive behavioral techniques, two factors seem to make this unlikely combination viable. First, interventions are directed at the same target, in this case, the quality of parent–child interaction. However, parent–child interaction is not a unitary process, but instead involves a set of complex behaviors and parenting skills that are complementary. Therefore, the combined intervention is directed at complementary components of a complex process, in this case, mutuality and reciprocity in a relationship. Similarly, in the combined treatment of problem-solving skills training and parent management training, interventions are directed at complementary foci that jointly contribute to maladjustment. In PCIT, a multifaceted process within a single level of intervention—the dyadic relationship—is targeted, whereas in combined problem-solving skills training and parent management training, complementary processes at different levels of intervention—child cognitive processes and parent management skills—are combined. It is noteworthy that the former relies on "stages" of intervention, whereas the latter can be offered simultaneously. It is possible that the simultaneous combination of directive and nondirective interventions in PCIT could dilute or negate the impact of component interventions. Consequently, sequential staging may be essential for effective treatment combinations when working at a single level of intervention. Finally, it should be noted that the successful combination of interventions from disparate conceptual models, as in PCIT, may hinge on the use of a unifying therapeutic procedure. In the case of PCIT, coaching represents the common denominator across disparate sets of interventions. In summary, these two examples of efficacious treatment combination point to some basic parameters for treatment integration that deserve systematic investigation.

The Evaluation of Integrated Treatment Techniques

In contrast to combining sets of procedures into a single intervention, or sets of interventions into a single-treatment package, integrated treatment techniques represent specific treatment processes that are derived from different theoretical sources. Although such techniques may be the quintessential form of treatment integration, relatively few examples have been evaluated in the child treatment literature.

One of the best illustrations of integration at the level of specific technique has been presented by Knell and Moore (1990) in their treatment of encopresis. In their approach, cognitive and behavioral processes are integrated with symbolic play processes. Unlike traditional play therapy in which play process tends to be open-ended, relatively unstructured, and in the service of affect expression, cognitive–behavioral play techniques involve greater focus, structure, and the vehicle for shaping, exposure, reinforcement, and the identification of irrational beliefs. In the treatment of an encopretic 5-year-old, Knell and Moore used the child's spontaneous play about a bear's struggles with toileting as the medium for integrating basic cognitive and behavioral techniques. For example, when the child played with the bear near a toilet, the therapist attempted to shape the child by modeling gradual approach to the toilet with the bear. Although traditional play therapists might be inclined to allow the child to "play out" his or her conflicts around toileting in a nondirective manner, this integrated play technique extended the child's play and utilized a symbolic medium for shaping. In their evaluation of cognitive–behavioral play therapy with a single-case design, Knell and Moore (1990) found that soiling diminished sharply across 15 sessions, and the complete elimination of soiling after the 14th session was maintained at 8- and 45-month follow-ups. However, as the authors note, the use of a collateral reinforcement program makes it difficult to attribute change to the integrated play technique. It is possible that improvement was a function of a different type of treatment combination, namely, the combination of a reinforcement intervention with a play intervention, or that the reinforcement program was sufficient to produce change. Nevertheless, this approach to treatment represents one of the best examples of integration at the level of specific techniques.

In related work, Milos and Reiss (1982) evaluated variations in play techniques with a group of young children presenting with separation anxiety. Although thematic play was the common element across three variations, in one condition children were engaged in thematically relevant (nursery school related) free play, in the second, play was directed in that the parameters of play content were defined (the child was introduced to a scene in which a mother brought her child to school), and in the third, the therapist controlled the behavior of the dolls and modeled positive responses to separation. Both the directive and modeling condition appear to represent departures from traditional play therapy, and clearly the modeling condition represents the integration of play process and modeling techniques. The three variations were compared with a nonthematic play condition in which the children played with blocks, puzzles, and various toys. All three thematic play conditions produced lower posttreatment anxiety scores compared with the nonthematic group, but the three thematic play groups did not differ from each other. Although this study may represent one of the only comparisons of integrated techniques with traditional techniques, the combination of modeling and symbolic play did not produce greater benefits than traditional nondirective play technique. It should be noted, however, that treatment strength was very low across all conditions, three 10-minute sessions, and outcome was measured at only one point in time. Consequently, it is possible that treatments involving integrated techniques offered at higher doses could yield more pronounced or durable effects than traditional techniques.

As these two examples illustrate, there is substantial work to be done in the area of integrated techniques. Few evaluations have been published, which undoubtedly reflects the prevailing research emphasis on the evaluation of treatment packages. It is possible that many other integrated techniques could be found in clinical practice, especially given the remarkable number of published forms of child therapy (Kazdin, 1988). One promising area that is beginning to receive some attention involves the use of narratives or storytelling techniques. For example, Russell and van den Broek (1988) advanced a storytelling approach that integrates psychodynamic and cognitive–developmental principles. Similarly, Buchsbaum, Toth, Clyman, Cicchetti, and Emde (1992) have proposed that narrative story stems could be used to expedite therapy process by tapping core issues through the use of increased structure. Both approaches represent variations on a basic technique in child therapy, the elicitation of narratives. However, specific alterations in technique involving, for example, the provision of narrative frames or changes in therapist response such as telling a rival narrative (Russell & van den Broek, 1988), represent new integrations in treatment process. Research by Malgady, Rogler, and Costantino (1990) has shown that storytelling techniques can be integrated with modeling procedures to produce beneficial effects in the treatment of emotional distress in young school-aged children. In this treatment, labeled cuento therapy, characters in folk tales were posed as therapeutic peer models. According to Malgady et al. (1990), the integration of storytelling and modeling, especially the use of culturally relevant stories, uniquely increases attention to and identification with the characters. Relative to traditional play therapy, this integrated approach produced greater improvement in social judgment and symptoms of anxiety.

Summary

Although research is far from systematic, illustrative examples of different types of treatment combinations are promising. In defining the boundary condition for effective child therapy, it does not appear that treatments need to be restricted to the consistent application of single procedures. Clearly, many brand-name treatments represent a form of treatment combination in that multiple procedures are integrated in a single treatment. Combinations derived from an "extended family" of procedures, as is typical in CBT, have been shown to produce positive effects. Furthermore, there is emerging evidence that multicomponent treatment packages can be beneficial. Here "stand-alone" sets of interventions are combined either sequentially or simultaneously. However, what is not clear, at this point, is whether such combinations are more effective than single-component treatments of similar strength (Kazdin, 1996). Finally, evidence is only beginning to emerge regarding the effectiveness of integrated techniques. Progress in this area may hinge on a paradigmatic shift in child therapy research; that is, the evaluation of treatment packages will need to be replaced, or at least supplemented, with research linking specific processes to treatment outcomes.

It is important to note that most of the combined treatments, either multiprocedural or multicomponent, have been implemented in research contexts. It is likely that the application of these treatments has been highly structured, for example, with specified sequences of interventions, and some have been manualized. In contrast, practitioners often utilize a flexible approach to treatment that involves customizing interventions to the perceived needs of individual child clients. Given that Weisz and his colleagues have proposed that differences in structure may account for differences in the effectiveness of clinic therapies versus research therapies, one must ask: Is there evidence for the effectiveness of "individually tailored" combined treatments that typify clinical practice with children?

To the degree that results from existing studies of clinic-based child psychotherapy reflect typical outcomes (Weisz, Donenberg, Han, & Weiss, 1995), the answer would appear to be "no." Admittedly, there are relatively few studies of clinic-based child therapy, and most treatments have been poorly described so that it is difficult to know what types of treatment combinations are being used, if any. Furthermore, clinic-based studies are relatively difficult to execute with high levels of methodological rigor, and methodological quality does account for variation in treatment effects (Shirk & Russell, 1992). Consequently, definitive conclusions about the usefulness of individually tailored treatment combinations found in clinical practice may be premature. What is clear, however, is that the current literature provides virtually no empirical support for such combinations. This raises the question of whether there is any evidence for the effectiveness of individually tailored treatment combinations.

Perhaps the best evidence for individually tailored combined treatments comes from the work of Henggeler and his colleagues (Henggeler & Borduin, 1990; Henggeler, Melton, & Smith, 1992; Henggeler, Schoenwald, & Pickrel, 1995) on multisystemic therapy (MST). MST was developed as a treatment alternative for very antisocial youth, and is based on a social-ecological model of behavior that acknowledges both multiple pathways to specific disorders and the mutual interplay of multiple causal factors. Thus, MST is broad in scope and targets child and family problems within and across multiple systems, e.g., school, peer group, and neighborhood. Moreover, youths and their families can receive multiple forms of treatment, including family therapy, parent training, problem-solving therapy, and peer-focused interventions. Treatment is individually tailored based on the existing risks and strengths of the various systems involved (individual, family, school, peer environment). Although basic principles are provided to guide the treatment process, treatments are not fixed in character, and the therapist must integrate treatments with their comprehensive assessment. Thus, MST is a clear example of a combined treatment that is individually tailored to the needs of specific cases.

Clinical trials of MST, one conducted in a university context and another through a mental health center, have been extremely encouraging. In the university-based evaluation, MST not only was more effective than individual therapy in improving family correlates of antisocial behavior, it also was more effective in preventing future criminal behavior (Borduin et al., 1995). In the clinic-based trial (Henggeler et al., 1992), family and peer relations were improved to a greater degree in youths treated with MST than youngsters who received usual community services. Moreover, follow-up results indicated that MST significantly reduced the percentage of youths who were rearrested compared with those who received usual services. These findings demonstrate that a treatment that is broad in scope, integrated in character, and individually tailored can produce significant positive outcomes. A major question, then, is what are the factors that contribute to successful child treatment integrations.

PRINCIPLES OF CHILD TREATMENT INTEGRATION

Although there is insufficient evidence to advance an empirically based model of integrated child therapy, existing research does point toward an emerging set of principles for child treatment integration. It is possible that a generic set of principles will only serve as a starting point for conceptualizing treatment integration, and that such principles will ultimately give way to specific guidelines corresponding to different child disorders. Nevertheless, based on the foregoing review, a number of points are worth highlighting, and may represent the beginnings of a recipe for integrating treatment ingredients.

Active Treatment Ingredients

First, treatment combinations are likely to be beneficial when the constituent procedures or interventions have been shown to be effective. A good example of this principle comes from the well-known Fort Bragg study (Bickman, 1996). In this project, a comprehensive child treatment approach that involved the integration of an array of services was compared with treatment as usually provided. Results indicated that the coordinated, and presumably integrated, treatment did not enhance outcomes. As Weisz, Han, and Valeri (1997) observed, one possible reason why integration produced so little payoff is that the individual services that were integrated were not necessarily effective. Although a treatment package is not necessarily equivalent to the sum of the parts, the combination of several inert ingredients is not likely to yield beneficial effects. In contrast, the positive effects of MST appear to be linked, in part, to the use of interventions such as structural family therapy and parent training that have been shown to be effective in other contexts.

One obstacle to identifying potentially useful components or procedures that might be fruitfully integrated is the prevailing approach to child therapy outcome research. Here there appear to be two problems. First, most studies have focused on the efficacy of treatment packages rather than on the impact of specific treatment components or techniques (Shirk & Russell, 1996). For example, research on the efficacy of cognitive therapy with adults has shown that this brand-name treatment yields positive results for depressed individuals. It has been assumed that one of the core active ingredients in this form of therapy is cognitive restructuring. However, recent process-outcome research has shown that this procedure may play less of a central role in producing change than other "noncognitive" processes such as emotion expression and the quality of the therapeutic alliance (Castonquay, Goldfried, Wiser, Rave, & Hayes, 1996). If we are to construct integrated treatments from components or procedures that contribute to change, then we must shift the focus of our research to the level of specific processes in order to begin to identify the active ingredients of treatment.

Second, most studies of child treatment outcome have focused on symptom reduction as the primary index of efficacy (Shirk & Russell, 1996). Treatment components or procedures, in isolation, may be insufficient to produce substantial change in a cluster of symptoms, although each may be involved in altering processes that contribute to the disorder. Two classes of outcome measures need to be included in treatment research. In addition to symptoms of the disorder, mechanisms or pathogenic processes that purportedly contribute to the disorder should be measured, and changes in these mechanisms should be related to specific treatment procedures and to treatment outcome (Kazdin, 1996; Shirk & Russell, 1996). Again, this approach would significantly advance the identification of effective procedures for specific pathogenic mechanisms. Given that cases typically represent configurations of pathogenic mechanisms (Shirk & Russell, 1996), the identification of procedures that are useful in altering specific mechanisms would provide the basis for combining sets of interventions.

Treatment Coherence

Treatments can be combined but unintegrated. One can imagine combinations intended to enhance the effects of a single method of intervention that, in fact, have the unintended consequence of negating the impact of both. For example, it is not clear how one integrates certain forms of family therapy with individual therapy. Reframing a problem from an individual to a family level seems contradictory with continued involvement of the identified patient in individual therapy, even when different sets of therapists are involved. Similarly, a therapist may want to facilitate emotion expression in an angry child client, but recognize that limits and consequences are essential to prevent the child from "acting out." Can a single therapist combine the provision of a permissive environment for emotion expression with contingency contracting without undermining the usefulness of each intervention? In the latter case, it may be necessary to delegate these functions to clinicians in different roles. The main point here is that *more treatment is not necessarily better treatment,* and that some combinations may dilute or negate the effects of constituent interventions.

Based on examples in this review, effective treatment combinations are coherent in the sense that they address complementary processes that contribute to child maladjustment. At the heart of this issue is the notion that combined treatments are likely to be coherent when they are based on models of developmental psychopathology that specify multiple causal factors contributing to a specific disorder. MST represents a clear example. Based on developmental research indicating multiple contributors to antisocial behavior, MST targets different putative causal factors with different sets of interventions (Henggeler et al., 1995). As this example indicates, integrated child therapy will be advanced by the recognition that one-to-one correspondence between manifest disorder and pathogenic process is the exception rather than the rule (Shirk & Russell, 1996), and that different sets of interventions may be needed for different pathogenic processes. A major challenge in this area is whether a single clinician can deliver multiple forms of intervention for a single case without diluting or negating the impact of component interventions.

Treatment Selection

A related issue involves guidelines for the selection of component interventions. Kazdin (1996) has noted that one of the major challenges involves unclear or inexplicit decision-making rules for combining treatments. It has been proposed, given the paucity of sound evidence for combined treatments, that clinicians consider use of the most effective single-modality treatment before attempting to combine treatments (Kazdin, 1996). Such an approach follows the principle of moving from a relatively narrow focus to a broader focus, and has the virtue of serving as a type of extended assessment. Youngsters who respond to a single-modality treatment need not receive a combined treatment that is likely to involve greater cost, time, and energy. The potential liability of such an approach is that many clinic-referred cases involve multiple problems and multiple pathogenic processes. A narrow-band intervention may not be strong enough to produce change, and as a result, families may become demoralized and at risk for dropping out of treatment before a more intensive intervention is implemented.

If a combined treatment is indicated, on what basis does a clinician select from the vast array of methods and modalities? Selection of effective treatment combination clearly depends on the systematic assessment of mechanisms that contribute to a particular pattern of presenting problems, and an evaluation of assets (child, family, and community) that could potentially offset dysfunction. As Kazdin (1996) has suggested, what is needed is a profile of the many factors that contribute to child's current functioning. Such a profile goes far beyond the assessment of symptom covariation, typical of current diagnostic procedures. Instead, integrated child therapies require a case formulation that specifies sets of pathogenic processes contributing to manifest presenting problems. Treatment selection without a case formulation is essentially improvisational therapy that has little chance of replication or evaluation (Shirk & Russell, 1996).

A major question is whether case formulations, which could serve as the basis for specific treatment combinations, can be made reliably. Although some would argue that such judgments are essentially idiographic, a growing body of evidence has shown reasonable interclinician reliability when clinicians are trained within a specific model (Luborsky & Crits-Christoph, 1990; Perry, Augusto, & Cooper, 1989). Furthermore, Shirk and Russell (1996) have proposed a model of child case formulation that identifies sets of basic-level pathogenic processes that could be operative across diverse presenting problems. It is likely that advances in developmental psychopathology will lead to the differentiation and refinement of sets of case formulations for specific disorders.

CONCLUSIONS

At a time when there is growing recognition of multiple pathways and causal contributors to specific disorders, integrated treatments seem to be on firm conceptual ground. However, most treatment combinations have not been evaluated, and there is concern that the practice of combining treatments may run counter to emerging evidence about the efficacy of child therapy. In the research domain, treatments that are focused and highly structured appear to produce beneficial effects. Clinic-based treatments that are broad-band and individually tailored have often produced disappointing results. This disparity raises serious questions about the use of integrated treatments with children.

Existing research reveals that treatment combinations can take a variety of forms at different levels of analysis, ranging from integrated techniques to multicomponent treatment packages. Illustrative studies from each level of analysis indicate that treatment combinations can produce beneficial effects, although comparisons with single-modality treatments of similar strength are scarce. On the basis of this review, it seems reasonable to conclude that narrow-band, highly focused interventions that are offered in a fixed format do not define the boundary conditions of effective child therapy. In fact, there is some evidence to support the use of broad-band, integrated treatments and treatments that are individually tailored. Such a conclusion is offered cautiously. The possibility of effectiveness should not be equated with the probability of effectiveness. Based on the studies reviewed here, effectiveness may be restricted to combined treatments that are selected on the basis of a comprehensive assessment, that make use of constituent interventions that have been shown to be effective, and that are conceptually coherent.

REFERENCES

Axline, V. (1969). *Play therapy.* New York: Ballantine Books.

Bickman, L. (1996). A continuum of care: More is not always better. *American Psychologist, 51,* 689–701.

Boggs, S. (1990, August). *Generalization to the home setting: Direct observation analysis.* Paper presented at meetings of the American Psychological Association, Washington, DC.

Borduin, C., Mann, B., Cone, L., Henggeler, S., Fucci, B., Blaske, D., & Williams, R. (1995). Multisystemic treatment of serious juvenile offenders: Long-term prevention of criminality and violence. *Journal of Consulting and Clinical Psychology, 63,* 569–578.

Bowers, W., & Andersen, A. (1994). Inpatient treatment of anorexia nervosa: Reviews and recommendations. *Harvard Review of Psychiatry, 2,* 193–203.

Buchsbaum, H., Toth, S., Clyman, R., Cicchetti, D., & Emde, R. (1992). The use of narrative story-stem technique with maltreated children: Implications for theory and practice. *Development and Psychopathology, 4,* 603–625.

Casey, R., & Berman, J. (1985). The outcome of psychotherapy with children. *Psychological Bulletin, 98,* 388–400.

Castonquay, L., Goldfried, M., Wiser, S., Rave, P., & Hayes, A. (1996). Predicting the effects of cognitive therapy for depression: A study of unique and common factors. *Journal of Consulting and Clinical Psychology, 64,* 497–504.

Durlak, J., Fuhrman, T., & Lampman, C. (1991). Effectiveness of cognitive-behavioral therapy for maladapting children: A meta-analysis. *Psychological Bulletin, 110,* 204–214.

Dush, D., Hirt, M., & Schroeder, H. (1989). Self-statement modification in the treatment of child behavior disorders: A meta-analysis. *Psychological Bulletin, 106,* 97–106.

Eisenstadt, T., Eyberg, S., McNeil, C., Newcomb, K., & Funderburk, B. (1993). Parent–child interaction therapy with behavior problem children: Relative effectiveness of two stages and overall treatment outcomes. *Journal of Clinical Child Psychology, 22,* 42–51.

Eyberg, S. (1988). Parent–child interactional therapy: Integration of traditional and behavioral concerns. *Child and Family Behavior Therapy, 10,* 33–46.

Eyberg, S., & Robinson, E. (1982). Parent–child interaction therapy: Effects on family functioning. *Journal of Clinical Child Psychology, 11,* 130–137.

Henggeler, S., & Borduin, C. (1990). *Family therapy and beyond: A multisystemic approach to treating the behavior problems of children and adolescents.* Pacific Grove, CA: Brooks/Cole.

Henggeler, S., Melton, G., & Smith, L. (1992). Family preservation using multisystemic therapy: An effective alternative to incarcerating serious juvenile offenders. *Journal of Consulting and Clinical Psychology, 60,* 953–961.

Henggeler, S., Schoenwald, S., & Pickrel, S. (1995). Multisystemic therapy: Bridging the gap between university- and community-based treatment. *Journal of Consulting and Clinical Psychology, 63,* 709–717.

Hinshaw, S. (1994). *Attention deficits and hyperactivity in children.* Newbury Park, CA: Sage.

Kazdin, A. (1988). *Child psychotherapy: Developing and identifying effective treatments.* New York: Pergamon Press.

Kazdin, A. (1996). Combined and multimodal treatments in child and adolescent psychotherapy: Issues, challenges, and research directions. *Clinical Psychology: Science and Practice, 3,* 69–100.

Kazdin, A., Siegel, T., & Bass, D. (1992). Cognitive problem-solving skills training and parent management training in the treatment of antisocial behavior in children. *Journal of Consulting and Clinical Psychology, 60,* 733–747.

Knell, S., & Moore, D. (1990). Cognitive-behavioral play therapy in the treatment of encopresis. *Journal of Clinical Child Psychology, 19,* 55–60.

Koocher, G., & Pedulla, B. (1977). Current practices in child psychotherapy. *Professional Psychology, 8,* 275–287.

Luborsky, L., & Crits-Christoph, P. (1990). *Understanding transference: The core conflictual relationship theme method.* New York: Basic Books.

Malgady, R., Rogler, L., & Costantino, G. (1990). Culturally sensitive psychotherapy for Puerto Rican children and adolescents: A program of treatment outcome research. *Journal of Consulting and Clinical Psychology, 58,* 704–712.

McNeil, C., Eyberg, S., Eisenstadt, T., Newcomb, K., & Funderburk, B. (1991). Parent–child interaction therapy with behavior problem children: Generalization of treatment effects to the school setting. *Journal of Clinical Child Psychology, 20,* 140–151.

Milos, M., & Reiss, S. (1982). Effects of three play therapy conditions on separation anxiety in children. *Journal of Consulting and Clinical Psychology, 50,* 389–395.

Norcross, J., & Newman, C. (1992). Psychotherapy integration: Setting the context. In J. Norcross & M. Goldfried (Eds.), *Handbook of psychotherapy integration* (pp. 3–46). New York: Basic Books.

Perry, J., Augusto, F., & Cooper, S. (1989). Assessing psychodynamic conflicts: Reliability of the idiographic conflict formulation method. *Psychiatry, 52,* 289–301.

Rehm, L., & Sharp, R. (1996). Strategies for childhood depression. In M. Reinecke, F. Dattilio, & A. Freeman (Eds.), *Cognitive therapy with children and adolescents* (pp. 103–123). New York: Guilford Press.

Russell, R., & van den Broek, P. (1988). A cognitive-developmental account of storytelling in child psychotherapy. In S. Shirk (Ed.), *Cognitive development and child psychotherapy* (pp. 19–52). New York: Plenum Press.

Shirk, S., & Russell, R. (1992). A re-evaluation of child therapy effectiveness. *Journal of the American Academy of Child and Adolescent Psychiatry, 31,* 703–709.

Shirk, S., & Russell, R. (1996). *Change processes in child psychotherapy: Revitalizing treatment and research.* New York: Guilford Press.

Snow, J., & Paternite, C. (1986). Individual and family therapy in the treatment of children. *Professional Psychology: Research and Practice, 17,* 242–250.

Stricker, G., & Gold, J. (1996). Psychotherapy integration: An assimilative, psychodynamic approach. *Clinical Psychology: Science and Practice, 3,* 47–58.

Tuma, J., & Pratt, J. (1982). Clinical child psychology practice and training: A survey. *Journal of Clinical Child Psychology, 11,* 27–34.

Wachtel, P. (1991). From eclecticism to synthesis: Toward a more serious psychotherapeutic integration. *Journal of Psychotherapy Integration, 1,* 43–54.

Weisz, J., Donenberg, G., Han, S., & Kauneckis, D. (1995). Child and adolescent psychotherapy outcomes in experiments versus clinics: Why the disparity? *Journal of Abnormal Child Psychology, 23,* 83–106.

Weisz, J., Donenberg, G., Han, S., & Weiss, B. (1995). Bridging the gap between laboratory and clinic in child and adolescent psychotherapy. *Journal of Consulting and Clinical Psychology, 63,* 688–701.

Weisz, J., Han, S., & Valeri, S. (1997). More of what? Issues raised by the Fort Bragg Study. *American Psychologist, 52,* 541–545.

Weisz, J., Weiss, B., & Donnenberg, G. (1992). The lab versus the clinic: Effects of child and adolescent psychotherapy. *American Psychologist, 47,* 1578–1585.

20

Cognitive–Behavioral
Play Therapy

SUSAN M. KNELL

INTRODUCTION

Cognitive–behavioral play therapy (CBPT) is based on cognitive and behavioral theories of emotional development and psychopathology, and on interventions derived from these theories. In addition to the cognitive–behavioral framework, CBPT is developmentally sensitive. It incorporates cognitive and behavioral interventions within a play therapy paradigm.

THEORETICAL OVERVIEW OF CBPT

Cognitive Model of Psychopathology

Cognitive therapy is based on the cognitive model of emotional disorders, which involves the interplay among cognition, emotion, behavior, and physiology (Beck & Emery, 1985). This model contends that behavior is mediated through verbal processes, and that people's behavior and affect are determined in large measure by the way they construe the world (Beck, 1967, 1972, 1976). It is the perception of events—not the events themselves—that determines how a person understands life situations. These cognitions can be in many forms (e.g.,verbal statements, visual images), and are based on schemas (e.g., attitudes, assumptions) developed from earlier life experiences. Cognitive theory contends that these cognitions will determine the individual's emotional experiences.

According to the cognitive model, an individual's emotional reactions can be predicted based on an understanding of the meaning that person attaches to par-

SUSAN M. KNELL • Meridia Behavioral Medicine, Cleveland, Ohio 44124.

Handbook of Psychotherapies with Children and Families, edited by Russ and Ollendick. Kluwer Academic/Plenum Publishers, New York, 1999.

ticular situations. Although the range of cognitive distortions is infinite, certain types of errors in thinking seem to occur with some regularity. For example, there is a great deal of literature on the automatic, negative view of past, present, and future experiences as perceived by depressed individuals (Beck, 1976).

Disturbances in emotions and behavior are considered to be expressions of irrational thinking. There are three major premises of cognitive therapy: (1) Thoughts influence the individual's emotions and behaviors in response to events, (2) perceptions and interpretations of events are shaped by the individual's beliefs and assumptions, and (3) errors in logic or cognitive distortions are prevalent in those who experience psychological difficulties (Beck, 1976). These cognitions are often unrecognized assumptions made by an individual, and as such are often unspoken. Cognitive distortions are considered to be the basis of human behavior and thought, particularly as it relates to psychopathological development.

The thinking of young children is often considered to be maladaptive, rather than irrational. This distinction is important, because the thought processes of young children (preschool and early school age) are considered to be illogical, egocentric, and concrete (Piaget, 1926, 1928, 1930). The label "cognitive distortion" is problematic with young children, as it masks the fact that such cognitions are normal at this developmental stage.

Basic Concepts of Cognitive Therapy

As originally conceptualized, cognitive–behavioral interventions were insight oriented and used introspective techniques to change overt personality (Beck, 1967; Ellis, 1962). These early cognitive therapies focused on the changing of cognitive schemas (controlling beliefs) as well as behavioral symptoms.

Since its inception, Beck and others have adapted cognitive therapy to a diverse set of psychiatric disorders and populations. These adaptations have changed the focus, interventions utilized, and length of treatment, but have not altered the theoretical assumptions on which cognitive therapy is based (J. Beck, 1995). Distorted thinking is common in all psychological difficulties; the modification of such thinking produces an improvement in mood and behavior. Maintenance of such improvements is the result of modification of the individual's underlying dysfunctional beliefs.

Cognitive therapy consists of a set of treatment techniques that aim to relieve symptoms of psychological distress through the "direct modification of the dysfunctional ideation that accompanies them" (Bedrosian & Beck, 1980, p. 128). The cognitive therapist uses a phenomenological approach, using the patient's report as basic data, rather than considering the psychoanalytic view of the patient's experiences as a "screen" behind which more significant unconscious meaning resides. In attempting to understand the patient's phenomenological field, the therapist tries to understand the individual's thoughts.

A primary goal of cognitive therapy is identifying and modifying maladaptive thoughts associated with the patient's symptoms (Bedrosian & Beck, 1980). Maladaptive thoughts are ideations that interfere with the individual's ability to cope with experiences. Such thoughts may disrupt the patient's ability to deal with difficult situations, and may produce emotional reactions that are inappropriate or excessive. The cognitive therapist seeks not only to produce symptom reduction, but also to modify attitudes, beliefs, and expectations.

Developmental Issues

Preschool and early school-age children present some unique challenges in psychotherapy, challenges that are compounded by the demands of cognitive therapy. Among the most critical issues related to working with young children are the cognitive abilities and limitations with which they present. Cognitive issues in child therapy are often obscured by play, which may lead the therapist to focus more on nonverbal rather than verbal communications (Shirk, 1988). Theoretical bases of therapy may influence the significance given to cognitive issues. For example, if abreaction or emotional release is considered to be the basis of change, then cognitive differences may be ignored as play takes the place of words. However, if increased understanding or insight is the treatment goal, then all treatments, even those relying on play, would involve cognitive activities (Shirk, 1988). Shirk argues that these cognitive components may be less sophisticated with young children, but they exist nonetheless.

Piagetian thinking has influenced much of our perceptions of children's cognitive abilities. During the preoperational stage of development (approximately 2–7 years old), thinking is defined as concrete, illogical, and egocentric. To a great degree these categorizations are true, and capture the young child's thinking. However, recent theorists have focused more on the preoperational child's abilities, rather than limitations (e.g., Gelman & Baillargeon, 1983). Nonetheless, the preoperational child presents with striking limitations in thinking, limitations that are thought to interfere with the child's ability to benefit from more verbally focused psychotherapies.

Cognitive therapy with adults assumes that the individual has the capacity to differentiate between rational and irrational and logical and illogical thinking. Although the adult may need some guidance in identifying and labeling irrational, illogical thoughts, once identified, the individual can understand the inconsistencies. Young children, on the other hand, may not be able to distinguish between irrational, illogical thinking and more rational, logical thought. In fact, even when pointed out to them, most young children are unable to see the errors in their logic.

It is these differences in children's thinking that make the application of cognitive therapies with this young population problematic. There has been a significant increase in the literature on cognitive therapies with youngsters (e.g., Kendall, 1991; Wilkes, Belsher, Rush, & Frank, 1994; Zarb, 1992). However, most of the literature deals with school-age children and adolescents, with little attention paid to preschool and early school-age children.

There is much evidence to suggest that preschoolers' ability to understand complex problems can be enhanced by specific approaches. In an important article on developmentally appropriate interviewing, Bierman (1983) recommends providing concrete examples and using less open-ended questions, as two examples of interviewing techniques that may elicit optimal responses from young children. Recent work by Knell and her associates (Knell, 1993a,b, 1994, 1997; Knell & Moore, 1990; Knell & Ruma, 1996) has begun to describe the use of cognitive behavior therapy with very young children. Knell argues that cognitive therapy can be used with young children, although the treatment must be communicated in indirect ways, such as through play. Further, the therapist's ability to be flexible, decrease expectations for verbalizations, and increase reliance on more experiential approaches can contribute significantly to the success of cognitive behavior therapy at this age.

CBPT

CBPT is a developmentally sensitive adaptation of cognitive and behavior therapies. For children to benefit from CBPT, interventions must be presented in a format that is accessible. The most common method is modeling, learning that occurs as a function of observing the behavior of others and the consequences of that behavior (Bandura, 1969). Research shows that modeling is an effective way to acquire, strengthen, and weaken behaviors (Bandura, 1977). Through use of play, therapy is communicated indirectly to children. The therapist may use puppets or stuffed animals to model cognitive change strategies. Many of the published cases of CBPT provide examples of the modeling of cognitive change strategies. For example, in the case of a selective mute 6-year-old (Knell, 1993a,b), the therapist used puppets to identify maladaptive beliefs, counter these beliefs, and provide positive self statements for a puppet who refused to speak.

Research has shown that the efficacy of modeling is improved by use of coping models, in which the model gradually acquires new skills (Bandura & Menlove, 1968; Meichenbaum, 1971). Other methods are role-playing, in which a person or object (e.g., puppet) practices tasks and receives feedback from the therapist. Through role-playing the child may practice skills and receive ongoing feedback regarding progress. For very young children, a combination of modeling and role-playing can be utilized, where the puppets complete the role-play, and the child observes and learns from watching the models practice skills.

The principles of cognitive therapy for adults (Beck & Emery, 1985) can be applied with some modifications to children. CBPT is based on the cognitive model of emotional disorders and is brief, time-limited, structured, directive, and problem oriented. It also relies on a sound therapeutic relationship, and is psychoeducational in nature. The therapeutic process is collaborative, but the nature of therapist–patient collaboration differs with children as compared with adults. Both the inductive method and Socratic methods are important, but play a different role in work with children (see Knell, 1993a, for a more detailed description of the adaptation of these principles to work with children).

CBPT is similar to other types of play therapy in its reliance on a positive therapeutic relationship, use of play as a means of communication between therapist and child, and the effort to communicate to the child that therapy is a safe place. However, it differs from other play therapies in its philosophy about the establishment of goals, selection of play materials and activities, use of play as a means to educate, and acceptance of praise of the child. It also differs from more nondirective, or client-centered play therapies in its use of interpretations or connections between emotions, feelings, and behaviors (see Knell, 1993a, for more detail regarding similarities and differences among various types of play therapies).

DESCRIPTION OF INTERVENTION PROCEDURES AND
MECHANISMS OF CHANGE

According to Beck, cognitive therapy produces a "quieting down of the hyperactive organization" (Rachman, 1968). The patient is then given the opportunity to experience and test the reality of verbal or pictorial cognitions that are causally connected to their affect. In treatment, patients are trained to discriminate between rational and irrational ideas, and between objective reality and the "internal embroidery" they have woven (Beck, 1970, p. 196). Through this process, the patient comes to realize that his or her ideas are irrational and counterproductive. Beck (1970) conceptualized one of the critical mechanisms of cognitive therapy as the modification or shift of the individual's ideational system. He contended that psychopathology lessened as irrational concepts were deactivated. CBPT emphasizes the child's involvement in treatment, and addresses issues of control, mastery, and responsibility for one's own behavior change. Participation in CBPT may provide the child with a structured setting in which to learn self-control and self-management. As part of CBPT, the child observes and interacts with play materials that may be engaged in specific, and individualized dialogues related to his or her own life experiences. The child may gather from this that the therapist understands and accepts the child's situation. In addition to a sense of understanding and acceptance, the therapist can model problem-solving skills for the child.

Freedheim and Russ (1983, 1992) identified six mechanisms of change that occur in individual child psychotherapy. They note that different types of child therapy emphasize different mechanisms of change. These mechanisms of change are: (1) catharsis and labeling of feelings, (2) corrective emotional experience, (3) insight and working through, (4) learning alternative problem-solving and coping strategies, (5) development of internal structure, and (6) a variety of nonspecific variables. Freedheim and Russ (1992) contend that all six mechanisms of change occur in individual psychodynamic and client-centered play therapy. In CBPT, it would seem that all six mechanisms are also part of the change process, although some, such as learning alternative problem-solving and coping strategies, are likely more critical mechanisms of change than others. Although their terminology tends to come from a more psychodynamic perspective (e.g., catharsis), the cognitive behavior therapist also tries to help the child label feelings, and work through various emotions.

Chethik (1989) uses the term *focal therapy* to describe treatment that is of short duration and focuses on a specific problem. Chethik's work is psychodynamic, but the idea of focused treatment is important. Because many of the documented successful cases with CBPT could be described as focal therapy, change may, in part, be attributed to the specific, focused nature of the intervention. However, CBPT also incorporates some aspects of more traditionally oriented, nondirective therapy. In this respect, the nature of play as providing more corrective emotional experiences, and helping the child work through conflicts is incorporated into treatment.

In CBPT, the process of change is considered to take place in both the structured and unstructured components of the sessions. In the unstructured, spontaneously generated material brought to the session by the child, the therapist can gain a sense of the child's own thoughts and perceptions. Alternatively, the structured, goal-directed activities provide the opportunity for the therapist to work with the child on problem solving and the teaching of more adaptive behaviors.

Stages of CBPT

Introductory/Orientation Stage

Preparation for CBPT is important. It is best if the therapist meets with the parents alone, without the child present, at the first appointment, and uses this time to gather history and background information. At this time, it is also important to talk with the parents about their efforts to prepare the child for CBPT. Often, the parents have not told the child anything about seeing a therapist, and are relying on the therapist to help guide them in what to say to the child. It is important for the parents to be honest with the child, and in a simple, noncritical manner, to talk with the child about their concerns and their efforts to seek help. It is often sufficient to have the parents make a statement such as, "We have been concerned about how you have been feeling. We went to talk to a talking doctor about it. Next time we go, you will go with us, and talk to her about what you think about it. She helps kids by talking and playing with them." It is often helpful to the child to hear something about the therapist (e.g., "She seems like a very nice person") and about the office (e.g., "She has lots of toys").

Assessment Stage

The beginning stages of CBPT, beyond the initial parent interview, involve the assessment of the child. This time should be used for both verbal and nonverbal play evaluation, with the therapist aiming to conceptualize a sense of the child's perceptions of his or her situation from the information gathered. This may involve more structured assessment tools (e.g., the puppet sentence completion task, Knell, 1993a), as well as unstructured observations. Additionally, parent report measures (e.g., Child Behavior Checklist, Achenbach, 1991; Social Competence and Behavior Evaluation: Preschool Edition, LaFreniere & Dumas, 1995) can often provide invaluable information.

In addition to the focus on assessment in the early sessions of CBPT, assessment must be viewed as an ongoing process. Throughout therapy, the therapist is continuing to obtain more information about the child, and incorporate this newly gained knowledge into the case conceptualization.

Middle Stages

As therapy progresses into the middle stages, the therapist has a clearer idea of the child's self-perceptions, and the parents' concerns regarding the child's emotional and behavioral status. Treatment is turning to a focus on increasing self-control, a sense of accomplishment, and learning more adaptive responses to deal with specific situations.

There are a wide array of behavioral and cognitive interventions available for use in play therapy. Common behavioral techniques include forms of contingency management, or techniques that modify a behavior by controlling its consequences. Techniques such as positive reinforcement, shaping, and extinction are all forms of contingency management. Behavioral methods utilized in CBPT usually involve an alteration in activity or behavior, whereas cognitive methods deal with changes in cognition.

Cognitive interventions include cognitive change strategies such as identifying and changing beliefs. These strategies aim to help the individual change faulty or maladaptive cognitions. Cognitive change strategies as used with adults often help the individual test hypotheses that are interfering with the person's functioning. Because such hypothesis testing is beyond the realm of most young children, the "scientific testing" of thoughts, beliefs, and assumptions is typically carried out through the therapist's modeling of this process through puppets and dolls.

As the child makes gains, the therapist will focus on these successes, as well as on generalization and relapse prevention. Generalization of adaptive behaviors to the natural environment is a critical component of CBPT. Studies suggest that even after successful treatment, many children fail to generalize their newfound behaviors, and even when such generalization occurs, their gains are not maintained after treatment is terminated (Braswell & Kendall, 1988).

In order for the child to generalize from one setting or caregiver to another, the therapist must build in specific training that helps the child with such connections. Interventions that address self-control, and teach the child new behaviors are important. Interventions should directly address the generalization issues and resemble real-life situations. For example, therapy should include play scenarios in settings that parallel the child's real-life situations. Reinforcement of skills learned in therapy should come from the child's natural environment, as well as from the therapist. Thus, parents and significant others should be aware of adaptive skills that are being learned and should be appropriately positive with the child when such behaviors are observed. Finally, learned adaptive responses should be reinforced and emphasized beyond their initial acquisition so as to strengthen and support their continuation.

In addition to generalization, the middle stages of CBPT focus on relapse prevention. In an effort for the child, and family, to be prepared for setbacks, the therapist tries to prepare the family to handle future stressors and life situations. High-risk situations are identified, and the child is prepared for ways of handling such situations should they arise.

Termination

Ideally, preparation for therapy termination is a gradual process, which takes place over several sessions. Preparation should deal with the concrete reality, as well as the feelings that may accompany the end of treatment. Very young children often benefit from concrete representations of the reality of the end of treatment. For example, a construction paper chain, depicting the number of sessions remaining, can be made with the child. Each link in the chain can be labeled, and removed at the end of the session that it represents. In this way, the child can visually see the number of sessions remaining, and can use this concrete reminder as a springboard for discussing feelings associated with termination.

Feelings regarding termination can be addressed by the therapist either directly (e.g., "I think you may be feeling rather sad to think about not coming here anymore") or indirectly (e.g., "some kids tell me that they feel sad when they think about not coming here anymore"). For some children, it is helpful for the therapist to convey his or her own sense of loss at termination (e.g., "I will miss seeing you, but I will feel good about knowing that you are doing so well").

SPECIFIC PROBLEMS AND POPULATIONS

Published case studies show that CBPT has been used successfully with a wide range of populations. To date, CBPT has been used to treat children presenting with diagnoses such as selective mutism (Knell, 1993a,b), encopresis (Knell, 1993; Knell & Moore, 1990), phobias (Knell, 1993a), and separation anxiety (Knell, 1998). It has also been used to treat children who have experienced traumatic life events, such as sexual abuse (Knell & Ruma, 1996; Ruma, 1993) and divorce (Knell, 1993a).

The preschool years are a time when children are learning about cause–effect relationships and how they can gain control over certain aspects of their environment. In general, CBPT may be an appropriate approach for children who are experiencing difficulties with issues of control (e.g., control over toileting). It may also be appropriate for anxious, depressed, and fearful children, and children who have been maltreated, or otherwise traumatized. Children who need to learn more adaptive coping skills would probably benefit from CBPT. Similarly, when parent-implemented interventions may not be sufficient, CBPT may be helpful for children whose involvement in treatment is considered important.

Children presenting with separation anxiety disorder often experience issues of control and lack of adequate coping skills. In most cases of separation anxiety, children have difficulty separating from their mother, may feel in control of themselves only in the parent's presence, and may lack skills that would facilitate healthy functioning when separated from the parent. CBPT lends itself to these concerns, by helping the child gain control over the environment in an adaptive way. Later in this chapter, a case example of a preschool-age child with separation anxiety will illustrate the approach.

RESEARCH SUPPORT

CBPT is a developmentally based and integrated model of psychotherapy. It utilizes proven techniques, such as modeling, a technique almost always contained in CBPT (Knell, 1994). Modeling has been shown to be an effective way to acquire, strengthen, or weaken behaviors; thus, learning through modeling is an efficient and effective way for children to acquire behaviors and skills (Bandura, 1977). Many other well-documented interventions can be incorporated within CBPT. Another technique, systematic desensitization, can be used to reduce anxiety or fear and replace it with an adaptive response (Wolpe, 1958, 1982). Case studies document the use of systematic desensitization in CBPT with sexually abused children (Knell & Ruma, 1996; Ruma, 1993).

In addition to empirically supported techniques, CBPT also builds on the overall principles of cognitive behavior therapy. Cognitive behavior therapy, as used with adults presenting with specific diagnoses (e.g., anxiety, depression), has been empirically validated. In recently delineated lists of data-based psychological interventions, APA's task force on the promotion and dissemination of psychological procedures lists cognitive behavior therapy as a well-established treatment (Chambless et al., 1996). Such claims cannot yet be made for the adaptations of cognitive therapy for use with young children. Thus, as an integrated model of psychotherapy, CBPT with young children has yet to be subjected to such rigorous, empirical study.

CASE EXAMPLE

Background Information

Cara was a $4\frac{3}{4}$-year-old girl who was brought to treatment because of her difficulties separating from her mother. When left at preschool, Cara would cry and sob for hours. At birthday parties and family gatherings, Cara would cling to her mother and refuse to talk or eat. In general, she preferred to be with adults. Her explanation, when asked by her parents, was "My heart hurts." She was unable to explain any more about her separation concerns. Cara had two separate preschool experiences: She was removed from the first preschool at age $3^3/_4$, after 3 months, because she cried daily, and couldn't be consoled. In the second preschool program, which she entered at age $4^1/_3$, Cara was able to attend, at times, without crying, but most of the time was tearful and sad at being away from her mother. Her parents were unaware of any significant traumas or stressors in her life. She lived in an intact family, with her biological parents and two younger siblings. A pretreatment CBCL, completed by the mother, yielded a nonclinical profile, with elevations on the Anxious/Depressed and Social Problems scales (see Figure 1).

Case Conceptualization

At the time of referral, Cara presented with a classic case of separation anxiety. Her anxiety related to separation from her mother was excessive and developmentally inappropriate. Although it did not appear that Cara had suffered from any traumas or negative life events, it became clearer during the course of treatment that she had been admonished and treated poorly by a previous preschool teacher for her crying and difficulties in adjusting to school.

Cara's fears of separation, and of harm befalling her parents, particularly her mother, are diagnostic of children who present with separation anxiety. The therapist's perception was that Cara's prognosis was good. Given Cara's age, excellent play skills, and developmentally advanced use of language, play therapy was chosen as the primary treatment modality. Her mother was involved in treatment in an effort to help her deal more appropriately with Cara's maladaptive, clingy, separation-avoidant behavior. Further, work with the mother was geared toward helping her facilitate more adaptive behaviors on Cara's part. Specific play activities were chosen based on Cara's lead, her ability to communicate through play, and the usefulness of the activity in meeting treatment goals. The primary treatment goal was to provide Cara with adaptive coping skills that would allow her to separate from her mother, and engage with others in a more developmentally appropriate way, without fear.

Description of Treatment

During play therapy, Cara was encouraged to express her feelings about separation fears through pictures, stories, and puppet play. The therapist guided the child through a series of discussions regarding a bear puppet's fears of being left at school. The therapist and child generated a list of the puppet's fears and lists of positive coping statements that the bear could use to alleviate his anxiety. Through the "voice" of the puppet, the therapist modeled adaptive coping skills for the child. As therapy progressed, the child began to incorporate these skills into her stories, puppet play, and gradually into her own coping behavior at school.

Course of Treatment

At each of the sessions, the mother was seen briefly, and then Cara was seen in CBPT. The following is a summary of the nine sessions.

```
                Internalizing                 CBCL Profile - Girls 4-11              Externalizing        T Score
 C  -|              17        27      |        21    |   24      39    |- ID#No ID
 1  -|      17              26      |   15   13      |   23      37    |- IN:TmpPkScr.tmp
 i  -|            16             |        20    |           |-95 Girl AGE: 4
 n  -|      16      15      25      |   14   12   19   |   21      35    |-   DATE FILLED:
 i  -|      15             24      |   13   11   18   |   20      34    |-
 c  -|            14      23      |   12   10   17   |   19      33    |-90 BY: Missing
 a  -|      14      13      22      |        21    |   18      32    |-   CARDS 02.03
 1  -|                  21      |        16    |   16      31    |-   AGENCY
    -|      13      12      |   11   9    |        30    |-85
 R  -|            11      20      |        15   |   14      29    |-
 a  -|      12             |   10   8   14   |   13      27    |-   # ITEMS    12
 n  -|            10      18      |        |   12      |-80 TOTSCORE   21
 g  -|      11      9      |   9   7   13   |   10      25    |-   TOT T     51
 e  -|      10             16      |   8   6   12   |   9      24    |-   INTERNAL  11
    -|            8      |        11   |        23    |-75 INT T     59
VILE-|      9      7      15      |   7   5    |   7      22    |-   EXTERNAL  2
    -|                  14      |        10   |   6      21    |-   EXT T     40
 98 -|- - -8- - - - - 6 - - - -13- - | - - - -6- - -   4 - - - 9 - - -|- - - -5- - - - 20- - - |-70 ++ Clinical
    -|_ _ 7_ _ _ _ _ 5 _ _ _11 _ _ | _ _ _ _ _ _ _ _ 3_ _ _ _ 8_ _ _|_4_ _ _ _ _17_ _ _|- + Borderline
    -|     6             10      |   5    |   7    |        |-
 93 -|                  |        2    |        16   |-65  OTHER PRCBS
    -|      5      4      ###      |        6   |   15      |-   0  5.ActOppSex$
    -|      4      3      7      |   ###   |   5    |   3   13      |-   0  6.BM Out
 84 -|                  |        |        |-60  0 15.CruelAnim
    -|            2      6      |   3        1    |   4   11      |-   0 18.HarmSelf
    -|     ###             5      |        |        10   |-   0 24.NotEat
 69 -|                  |        |        ###   9    |-55  0 28.EatNonFood
    -|      2      1      4      |        3   |        8   |-   2 29.Fears
    -|            3      |   2    |   2    |   1   7    |-   0 30.FearSchool
 50 -|____0-1____     ###___0-2___|__0-1__   ###___###__|____0___    ###_|-50  0 36.Accidents
          I         II        III        IV        V        VI        VII        VIII         0 44.BiteNail
      WITHDRAWN   SOMATIC   ANXIOUS/   SOCIAL    THOUGHT  ATTENTION DELINQUENT AGGRESSIVE       0 47.Nightmares
                 COMPLAINTS DEPRESSED  PROBLEMS  PROBLEMS  PROBLEMS  BEHAVIOR   BEHAVIOR        0 49.Constipate
```

I WITHDRAWN	II SOMATIC COMPLAINTS	III ANXIOUS/ DEPRESSED	IV SOCIAL PROBLEMS	V THOUGHT PROBLEMS	VI ATTENTION PROBLEMS	VII DELINQUENT BEHAVIOR	VIII AGGRESSIVE BEHAVIOR	
1 42.Rather BeAlone	0 51. Dizzy	0 12.Lonely	0 1. Acts Young	0 9. Mind Off	0 1. Acts Young	0 26.NoGuilt	0 3. Argues	0 53.Overeat
0 65.Won't Talk	0 54. Tired	2 14.Cries	2 11.Clings	0 40.Hears Things	0 8. Concen-trate	0 39.BadCompan	0 7. Brags	- 56h.OtherPhys
0 69.Secret-ive	0 56a.Aches	0 31.FearDoBad	2 25.NotGet Along	0 66.Repeats	0 10.Sit Still	2 63.PrefOlder	0 16.Mean	0 58.PickSkin
1 75.Shy	0 56b.Head-aches	2 32.Perfect	0 38.Teased	0 70.Sees	0 13.Confuse	0 67.RunAway	0 19.DemAttn	0 59.SexPrtsP$
0 80.Stares	0 56c.Nausea	0 33.Unloved	0 48.Not Liked	0 80.Stares*	0 17.Day-dream	0 72.SetFires	0 20.DestOwn	0 60.SexPrtsM$
0 88.Sulks	0 56d.Eye	0 35.Worthless	2 55.Over-Weight*	0 84.Strange Behav	0 41.Impulsv	0 81.StealHome	0 21.DestOthr	0 73.SexProbs$
0 102.Under-active	0 56e.Skin	0 45.Nervous	0 62.Clumsy	0 85.Strange Ideas	0 45.Nervous	0 82.StealOut	0 22.DisbHome*	0 76.SleepLess
0 103.Sad	0 56f.Stomach	2 50.Fearful	0 64.Prefers	0 61.Poor	0 90.Swears	0 23.DisbSchl	0 77.SleepMore
1 111.With-drawn	0 56g.Vomit	0 52.Guilty	Young	School	0 96.ThnkSex*$	0 27.Jealous	0 78.SmearBM
	0 TOTAL	0 71.SelfConsc	2 112.Worries	4 TOTAL	0 62.Clumsy	0 101.Truant	0 37.Fights	0 79.SpeechProc
3 TOTAL	50 T SCORE	0 89.Suspic		50 T SCORE	0 80.Stares	0 105.AlcDrugs	0 68.Screams	0 83.Stores*$
57 T SCORE	40 CLIN T	1 103.Sad	62 T SCORE	40 CLIN T	0 TOTAL	0 106.Vandal*	0 74.ShowOff	0 91.TalkSuicid
42 CLIN T		8 TOTAL	44 CLIN T		50 T SCORE	2 TOTAL	0 86.Stubborn	0 92.SleepWalk
		63 T SCORE			30 CLIN T	57 T SCORE	0 87.MoodChng	0 98.ThumbSuck
		46 CLIN T				44 CLIN T	0 93.TalkMuch	0 99.TooNeat
				Not in Total Problem Score 0 2.Allergy 0 4.Asthma			0 94.Teases	0 100.SleepProb
							0 95.Temper	0 107.WetsSelf
*Items not on Cross-Informant Construct							0 97.Threaten	2 109.Whining
							0 104.Loud	0 110.WshOpSex$
								- 113.OtherPrc:

```
                                                                        IX
                                                                  SEX PROBLEMS .
                                                                  0 TOTAL SCORE   50 T SCORE
Profile Type:  WTHDR  SOMAT  SOCIAL  DEL-AGG   Delinq                 50 T SCORE      28 CLIN T
    ICC:  No ICCs calculated if Total Problem Score is < 30         $=Item on Sex
                                                                   Probs Syndrome
Copyright 1993 T. Achenbach
```

Figure 1. Pretreatment Child Behavior Checklist (CBCL). (Copyright by T. M. Achenbach. Reproduced with permission.)

Session 1

Parent Treatment. Cara's mother was interviewed at the first appointment in order to gather intake information. When the therapist approached the idea of interviewing Cara's mother without her present, Cara burst into tears. Within a few minutes, she was easily calmed by her mother, and she stayed with a secretary in the waiting area. During this time, the secretary reported that Cara was friendly and interactive, and did not express or exhibit any discomfort at separation from her mother.

CBPT. Cara expressed immediate concern about leaving her mother, and then quickly separated without difficulty. Once in the office, she was friendly, engaging, and articulate. She talked enthusiastically about school, although she related that it sometimes "gets a little scary." She was unable to describe what scared her. In talking about other activities, Cara often focused on aspects of the situations or events that frightened her. For example, she talked about the "scary part" of *The Little Engine that Could,* stating that it was frightening when the train could not make it up the hill. The therapist acknowledged Cara's fear, but also described another aspect of the book, namely, the idea that the little engine kept saying "I think I can, I think I can," and eventually found a way. The therapist explained that the engine learned that if it really wanted to do something, it could do it. In a developmentally appropriate way, the therapist described the use of the book as a metaphor for the expression, "where there's a will there's a way." Throughout the discussion, Cara listened intently.

Session 2

Parent Treatment. Mother described that Cara had several good days at school, but was still upset and crying most of the time. She had also been to a birthday party, in which she cried and clung to her mother.

CBPT. Cara began the session by telling the therapist that she hadn't cried at school; that she had started to, but then stopped. She spontaneously offered that when upset, she remembered the little engine that could. The therapist read her the story again, reinforced the theme of the book with her, and praised her for her efforts. During the course of her play, Cara drew a picture of herself "not crying," and dictated a story about herself not crying at school ("Me not crying and I'm so proud of myself. One day I went to school, and I didn't even cry. At one point I started crying and then the teachers told me it's no problem to cry, and then I didn't not cry anymore (sic). The end").

Session 3

Parent Treatment. Mother reported that Cara was doing better at school, and was not crying, although she was still not participating. She had also gone to another birthday party, but would not interact with the other children. Mom was asked to take home *The Little Engine that Could* book and read it to Cara for her bedtime story. She also started to keep a calendar for Cara with smiley faces for her "good days" at school.

CBPT. Cara began to dictate and illustrate a book about school, "Cara's book about school" (see Figure 2). She also played with a stuffed turtle that the therapist had hide in its shell when it was scared. Cara showed how the turtle could pop out of its shell when it wasn't afraid, and hide when it was.

Session 4

Parent Treatment. Mother reported that Cara had received five smiley faces for five good days at school. Cara had shown a marked improvement, and was even raising her hand and participating in class.

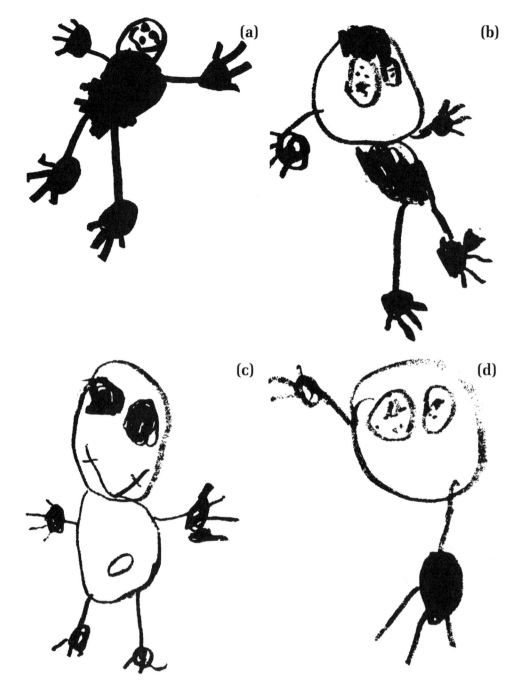

Figure 2. (a) Cara's book about school. (b) One day I didn't even cry at school. I didn't cry 2 days. (c) I didn't even cry at school 10 days. (d) Once when I was painting at school I didn't cry. It was time for story hour. They held up letters and I told them the letter. (This is a picture of my hand raised to answer a question.) (e) I think about the choo choo train that could. (My brain is thinking about the Little Engine that could.) (f) And I picture things in my mind. (I picture someone swinging a bat, and playing baseball.) (g) The next day, I went to school and tried to stop myself from crying. (These are my tears.)

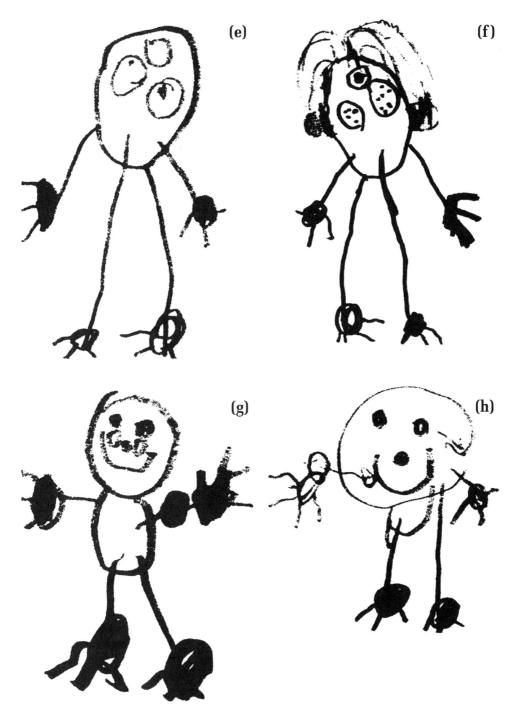

Figure 2. (*continued*) (h) A long, long time ago, I didn't cry at school, and then I had a vacation off. (i) I think about coloring and that makes all my tears go away. Sometimes I worry about if my Mom is OK. I remind myself, "She's OK." One day, I saw a little boy crying and he was worried about his mom picking him up. I told him not to worry. His mom will pick him up because young children are very special. My mom always picks me up. I don't need to worry (no illustration).

CBPT. Cara continued to play with the puppets, and watched as the therapist modeled positive coping statements made by a stuffed bear. She also continued to dictate her school book.

Session 5

Parent Treatment. Mother reported that Cara was actively participating in school, not crying, and volunteering by raising her hand to take a turn. Because of past incidents of regression after vacation time, Mother expressed concern that an upcoming vacation from school might interfere with Cara's progress.

CBPT. Cara did not want to work on her book, but continued to play with the puppets. She was particularly focused on helping a bear puppet who seemed to "worry too much." Together with the therapist, she generated a list of things that would help the bear, entitled, "Mr. Bear's list" (see Box 1). Cara did not want to talk about her concerns at parties when the therapist asked Cara about it. At the end of the session, Cara asked for a train sticker, so that she could wear it and say to herself, "I think I can" if she got worried.

Session 6

Parent Treatment. Mother reported that reentry to school (after vacation) went well. She was concerned that Cara was avoiding playing outside because of a fear of bugs.

CBPT. Cara continued with puppet play and dictated a story about her fear of bugs (see Box 2). She also made up a song about not being afraid (see Box 3), and readily agreed to sing it to a group of staff members who were sitting in the staff lounge.

Session 7

Parent Treatment. Mother reported that Cara was doing well at school, was more interactive socially, and seemed to be taking more age-appropriate risks (e.g., at the playground). Mother felt that Cara was more comfortable at parties, but was not yet ready to leave mom's sight. She was encouraged to make her movements

Box 1. "Mr. Bear's list

Think of something happy
Mom's coming back
Play with toys and have fun
Play with other friends
We did it, and the other children were having fun
I think I can, I think I can
I think I can, don't worry

Box 2. Cara's book about bugs

One day, I looked at a bug and it scared me. Then it flew away, but it didn't bother me.

The next day, I went outside. I walked past the bug. It saw me, but it flew by me, and didn't hurt me. It kept flying by me.

One day, I went outside and I walked past a bug with a stinger. It watched me go by, and then it stinged me. It really hurt. Daddy took the stinger out. He carried me into the house, put a band-aid on, and fixed me up.

Sometimes bugs can hurt, but it's ok, I don't need to be too afraid.

Box 3. "Don't be afraid" song

Stick up to your fears
Don't be worried
This is something I know
When I get a little used to it
I won't be afraid no more
No, No Siree
Then I won't be afraid

away from Cara in a slow, gradual way (e.g., going into another room to get a cup of coffee with Cara's knowledge).

CBPT. Cara continued to work on her bug book, and spontaneously generated many coping statements (e.g., "You don't need to be afraid, it won't sting you"). She was able to describe an incident of being stung that had taken place several years earlier, and use the experience to relate that being stung didn't hurt that much. When the therapist asked her about parties, she said that she was more comfortable, but when asked about being able to leave her mother, Cara stated, "I'm not at that stage yet!" The therapist offered support, and reassurance, telling her that, "As you get older you may feel more ready."

Session 8

Parent Treatment. Mother reported that Cara was going outside, and not showing any fear of bugs. Peer interactions were increasing.

CBPT. In CBPT, Cara had no interest in working on either her bug or school books, but talked at length about her ability to leave mom and take swimming lessons (she was actually taking lessons, but would not leave mom's side).

Session 9

Since Cara was doing well, the ninth session was postponed for 2 months. It took place the day after Cara's first day at kindergarten.

Parent Treatment. Mother reported that Cara got on the school bus by herself, but cried during the ride. She stayed at school without incident, and when she expressed some concern at school, a "roving school counselor" spoke with her briefly, and she was fine.

CBPT. Cara was very positive about school and acknowledged that she carried a "worry stone" around her neck, and touched it when she got scared. She felt that it helped her. She interacted with the therapist and bear puppet around the puppet's concerns about going to school, and tried to help the puppet understand that he would be OK. She made up a song for the puppet, called, "I love going to school," which she sang to him (see Box 4).

Termination and Follow-Up

At termination, Cara's mother reported that her daughter was adjusting without difficulty to school. She noted remarkable progress in Cara's ability to be separated from her. Cara's mother also completed a posttreatment CBCL at the last session, which confirmed her verbal reports of Cara's progress (see Figure 3). In comparing this profile with her pretreatment CBCL, elevations on the Withdrawn, Social Problems, and Delinquent Behavior scales had all dropped to zero. The only elevation on the posttreatment CBCL, although still within the nonclinical range, was on the Anxious/Depressed scale. However, this scale had dropped from the pretreatment CBCL score, thus reflecting that Cara still had some anxieties.

Follow-up was obtained from the mother approximately 4 months after termination of treatment. At that time, Cara had been in kindergarten for 4 months, and was doing "beautifully" according to her mother. She was going to school happily, and without incident. No other problems were reported.

Summary of Treatment

This case provides an example of the successful use of CBPT with a child afraid to separate from her mother. Following the child's lead, the play was goal-directed and geared toward alleviating her separation fears and behaviors. Among

Box 4. "I love going to school" song

I like to ride in a bus
Because it is so fun
We get to talk to new friends
We get to meet new friends
We get to do fun things on the bus
Sometimes it's a little scary
When it gets scary, you pop (sic) your head and get your worry stone
Until you're done worrying for the whole day
We don't want to worry

CBCL Profile - Girls 4-11

Internalizing | Externalizing | T Score

Top-of-chart header information:

```
- ID#No ID
- IN:TmpPkScr.tmp
-95 Girl AGE: 5
-    DATE FILLED:
-90 BY: Missing
-    CARDS 02,03
-    AGENCY
-85
# ITEMS      8
-80 TOTSCORE  11
     TOT T    43
     INTERNAL  7
-75 INT T     54
     EXTERNAL  7
     EXT T     32
-70 ++ Clinical
     + Borderline
-65 OTHER PROBS
     0 5.ActOppSexS
     0 6.BM Out
-60 0 15.CruelAnim
     0 18.HarmSelf
     0 24.NotEat
-55 0 28.EatNonFood
     2 29.Fears
     2 30.FearSchool
-50 0 36.Accidents
     0 44.BiteNail
     0 47.Nightmares
     0 49.Constipate
     0 53.Overeat
     0 56h.OtherPhys
     0 58.PickSkin
     0 59.SexPrts P$
     0 60.SexPrts M$
     0 76.SleepLess
     0 77.SleepMore
     0 78.SmearBM
     0 79.SpeechProb
     0 83.StoresUp
     0 91.TalkSuicid
     0 92.SleepWalk
     0 98.ThumbSuck
     0 99.TooNeat
     0 100.SleepProb
     0 107.WetsSelf
     0 108.WetsBed
     0 109.Whining
     0 110.WshOpSexS
     - 113.OtherProb
```

I WITHDRAWN	II SOMATIC COMPLAINTS	III ANXIOUS/ DEPRESSED	IV SOCIAL PROBLEMS	V THOUGHT PROBLEMS	VI ATTENTION PROBLEMS	VII DELINQUENT BEHAVIOR	VIII AGGRESSIVE BEHAVIOR
0 42.Rather BeAlone	0 51. Dizzy	0 12.Lonely	0 1. Acts Young	0 9. Mind Off	0 1. Acts Young	0 26.NoGuilt	0 3. Argues
0 65.Won't Talk	0 54. Tired	0 14.Cries	0 11.Clings	0 40.Hears Things	0 8. Concentrate	0 39.BadCompan	0 7. Brags
0 69.Secretive	0 56a.Aches	1 31.FearDoBad	0 25.NotGet Along	0 66.Repeats Acts	0 10.Sit Still	0 43.LieCheat	0 16.Mean
0 75.Shy	0 56b.Headaches	2 32.Perfect	0 38.Teased	0 70.Sees Things	0 13.Confuse	0 63.PrefOlder	0 19.DemAttn
0 80.Stares	0 56c.Nausea	0 33.Unloved	0 48.Not Liked	0 80.Stares*	0 17.Day-dream	0 67.RunAway	0 20.DestOwn
0 88.Sulks	0 56d.Eye	0 34.OutToGet	0 55.Over-Weight*	0 84.Strange Behav	0 41.Impulsv	0 72.SetFires	0 21.DestOthr
0 102.Underactive	0 56e.Skin	0 35.Worthless	0 62.Clumsy	0 85.Strange Ideas	0 45.Nervous	0 81.StealHome	0 22.DisbHome*
0 103.Sad	0 56f.Stomach	0 45.Nervous	0 64.Prefers Young	0 TOTAL	0 46.Twitch*	0 82.StealOut	0 23.DisbSchl
1 111.Withdrawn	0 56g.Vomit	1 50.Fearful	1 TOTAL	50 T SCORE	0 61.Poor School	0 90.Swears	0 27.Jealous
1 TOTAL	0 TOTAL	0 52.Guilty	50 T SCORE	40 CLIN T	0 62.Clumsy	0 96.ThnkSex*$	0 37.Fights
50 T SCORE	50 T SCORE	0 71.SelfConsc	33 CLIN T		0 80.Stares	0 101.Truant	0 57.Attacks
36 CLIN T	40 CLIN T	0 89.Suspic			0 TOTAL	0 105.AlcDrugs	0 68.Screams
		0 103.Sad			50 T SCORE	0 106.Vandal*	0 74.ShowOff
		2 112.Worries			30 CLIN T	0 TOTAL	0 86.Stubborn
		6 TOTAL				50 T SCORE	0 87.MoodChng
		59 T SCORE				37 CLIN T	0 93.TalkMuch
		42 CLIN T					0 94.Teases
							0 95.Temper
							0 97.Threaten
							0 104.Loud
							0 TOTAL
							50 T SCORE
							28 CLIN T

Not in Total Problem Score

*Items not on Cross-Informant Construct - 2.Allergy 0 4.Asthma

```
IX
SEX PROBLEMS
0 TOTAL SCORE
50 T SCORE
28 CLIN T
$=Item on Sex
Probs Syndrome!
```

Profile Type: WTHDR SOMAT SOCIAL DEL-AGG Delinq
ICC: No ICCs calculated if Total Problem Score is < 30

Figure 3. Posttreatment Child Behavior Checklist (CBCL). (Copyright by T. M. Achenbach. Reproduced with permission.)

the specific techniques used were behavioral (e.g., modeling, praise) and cognitive (e.g., bibliotherapy, cognitive change strategies, countering irrational beliefs) interventions. Throughout treatment there were examples of the child's verbalizations that she was doing better than her behavior suggested (e.g., telling the therapist that she was separating from her mom at swimming lessons). This information was conceptualized as the child's fantasy about how she wished things could be. As such, they were used to help her continue to strive toward the goal of separation from her mother.

FUTURE RESEARCH

Despite more recent, renewed interest in child psychotherapy outcome studies, there has been little attention to play therapy. It is interesting to note that play is frequently a part of child psychotherapy, yet is rarely the focus of psychotherapy outcome studies (Russ, 1995). Phillips (1985) reviewed play therapy research, and contended that a systematic program of research was needed. He argued that child psychotherapy research often does not include play therapies, and when it does, play interventions are not distinguished from other approaches and/or are given minimal attention. Further, most child psychotherapy research is focused on school-age children, with little attention paid to treatment of preschoolers. This lack of attention is striking, given the increasing clinical interest in play therapy.

CBPT is in its infancy, and as such is yet to be subjected to empirical study. It has a solid foundation from the perspective of data-based psychological interventions, as delineated by APA's recent task force on the promotion and dissemination of psychological procedures (Chambless et al., 1996). Cognitive behavior therapy for a number of specific populations (e.g., anxiety, depression) is one of the well-established treatments on the list. Of course, the fact that cognitive behavior therapies for adults have been empirically validated does not mean the same holds true for children.

Establishing the efficacy of CBPT is an important and critical next step in the development of this therapy. Kazdin (1997) proposes a model to guide psychotherapy research aimed at increasing the likelihood of developing more effective and useful clinical interventions for child psychotherapy. The field is now beyond the question, "Does psychotherapy work?" Instead, research should begin to focus more on questions related to the conceptualization and specification of treatment, as well as conditions that influence treatment outcomes. According to Kazdin, questions such as, "How does this treatment achieve change?" should become more critical foci for child psychotherapy research. The next step for CBPT is to be subjected to this kind of critical research.

SUMMARY

CBPT is a relatively new adaptation of cognitive therapy for young children. It is based on cognitive and behavioral theories of emotional development and psychopathology, and incorporates interventions based on these theories in a developmentally sensitive way. In order to be developmentally appropriate, CBPT interventions are presented through play, and particularly through use of modeling. Although CBPT is directive and psychoeducational, it also incorporates aspects of more traditionally oriented, nondirective therapy. Change is considered to take place through both the goal-directed, structured component of CBPT, as well as the unstructured, spontaneously generated material brought to treatment by the child.

CBPT has been used with a wide range of populations. A case example of an almost 5-year-old girl, presenting with separation anxiety, is described to highlight the successful use of CBPT with a young child. Despite renewed interest in play therapy research, the efficacy of CBPT is yet to be determined. It is a critical next step in the development of CBPT, and one that will be welcomed.

REFERENCES

Achenbach, T. M. (1991). *Manual for the Child Behavior Checklist/4–18 and 1991 Profile.* Burlington, VT: University of Vermont, Department of Psychiatry.

Bandura, A. (1969). *Principles of behavior modification.* New York: Holt, Rinehart & Winston.

Bandura, A. (1977). *Social learning theory.* Englewood Cliffs, NJ: Prentice–Hall.

Bandura, A., & Menlove, F. L. (1968). Factors determining vicarious extinction of avoidance behavior through symbolic modeling. *Journal of Personality and Social Psychology, 8,* 99–108.

Beck, A. T. (1967). *Depression: Clinical, experimental, and theoretical aspects.* New York: Harper & Row.

Beck, A. T. (1970). Cognitive therapy: Nature and relation to behavior therapy. *Behavior Therapy, 1,* 184–200.

Beck, A. T. (1972). *Depression: Causes and treatment.* Philadelphia: University of Pennsylvania Press.

Beck, A. T. (1976). *Cognitive therapy and the emotional disorders.* New York: International Universities Press.

Beck, A. T., & Emery, G. (1985). *Anxiety disorders and phobias: A cognitive perspective.* New York: Basic Books.

Beck, J. (1995). *Cognitive therapy: Basics and beyond.* New York: Guilford Press.

Bedrosian, R., & Beck, A. T. (1980). Principles of cognitive therapy. In M. J. Mahoney (Ed.), *Psychotherapy process: Current issues and future directions* (pp. 127–152). New York: Plenum Press.

Bierman, K. L. (1983). Cognitive development and clinical interviews with children. In B. B. Lahey & A. Kazdin (Eds.). *Advances in clinical child psychology* (Vol. 6, pp, 217–250). New York: Plenum Press.

Braswell, L., & Kendall, P. C. (1988) Cognitive-behavioral methods with children. In K. S. Dobson (Ed.), *Handbook of cognitive behavior therapy* (pp. 167–213). New York: Guilford Press.

Chambless, D. L., Sanderson, W. C., Shoham, V., Johnson, S. B., Pope, K. S., Crits-Christoph, P., Baker, M., Johnson, B., Woody, S. R., Sue, S., Beutler, L., Williams, D. A., & McCurry, S. (1996). An update on empirically validated therapies. *The Clinical Psychologist, 49,* 5–18.

Chethik, M. (1989). *Techniques of child therapy: Psychodynamic strategies.* New York: Guilford Press.

Ellis, A. (1962). *Reason and emotion in psychotherapy.* Secaucus, NJ: Citadel Press.

Freedheim, D. K., & Russ, S. W. (1983). Psychotherapy with children. In C. E. Walker & M. Roberts (Eds.), *Handbook of clinical child psychology* (pp. 978–994). New York: Wiley.

Freedheim, D. K., & Russ, S. W. (1992). Psychotherapy with children. In C. E. Walker & M. Roberts (Eds.), *Handbook of clinical child psychology* (2nd ed., pp. 765–780). New York: Wiley.

Gelman, R., & Baillargeon, R. (1983). A review of some Piagetian concepts. In J. H. Flavell & E. M. Markman (Eds.), P. Mussen (Ser. Ed.), *Handbook of child psychology: Vol. III. Cognitive development* (pp. 167–230). New York: Wiley.

Kazdin, A. (1997). A model for developing effective treatments: Progression and interplay of theory, research, and practice. *Journal of Clinical Child Psychology, 26,* 114–129.

Kendall, P. C. (1991). *Child and adolescent therapy.* New York: Guilford Press.

Knell, S. M. (1993a). *Cognitive–behavioral play therapy.* Northvale, NJ: Aronson.

Knell, S. M. (1993b). To show and not tell: Cognitive–behavioral play therapy. In T. Kottman & C. Schaefer (Eds.), *Play therapy in action* (pp. 169–208). Northvale, NJ: Aronson.

Knell, S. M. (1994). Cognitive–behavioral play therapy. In K. J. O'Connor & C. E. Schaefer (Eds.), *Handbook of play therapy: Vol. Two. Advances and innovations* (pp. 111–142). New York: Wiley.

Knell, S. M. (1997) Cognitive–behavioral play therapy. In K. J. O'Connor & L. M. Braverman (Eds.), *Play therapy: Theory and practice* (pp. 79–99). New York: Wiley.

Knell, S. M. (1998). Cognitive–behavioral play therapy. *Journal of Clinical Child Psychology, 27,* 28–33.

Knell, S. M., & Moore, D. J. (1990). Cognitive–behavioral play therapy in the treatment of encopresis. *Journal of Clinical Child Psychology, 19,* 55–60.

Knell, S. M., & Ruma, C. D. (1996). Play therapy with a sexually abused child. In M. Reinecke, F. M. Dattilio, & A. Freeman (Eds.), *Cognitive therapy with children and adolescents: A casebook for clinical practice* (pp. 367–393). New York: Guilford Press.

LaFreniere, P. J., & Dumas, J. E. (1995). *Social Competence and Behavior Evaluation: Preschool Edition.* Los Angeles: Western Psychological Services.

Meichenbaum, D. (1971). Examination of model characteristics in reducing avoidance behavior. *Journal of Personality and Social Psychology, 17,* 298–307.

Phillips, R. D. (1985). Whistling in the dark: A review of play therapy research. *Psychotherapy, 22,* 752–760.

Piaget, J. (1926). *The language and thought of the child.* London: Routledge & Kegan Paul.

Piaget, J. (1928). *Judgment and reasoning in the child.* London: Routledge & Kegan Paul.

Piaget, J. (1930). *The child's conception of physical causality.* New York: Harcourt, Brace & World.

Rachman, S. (1968). The role of muscular relaxation in desensitization therapy. *Behaviour Research and Therapy, 6,* 159–166.

Ruma, C. D. (1993). Cognitive–behavioral play therapy with sexually abused children. In S. M. Knell, *Cognitive–behavioral play therapy* (pp. 193–230). Northvale, NJ: Aronson.

Russ, S. W. (1995). Play psychotherapy research. In T. H. Ollendick & R. J. Prinz (Eds.), *Advances in clinical child psychology* (Vol. 17, pp. 365–391). New York: Plenum Press.

Shirk, S. R. (1988). Introduction: A cognitive–developmental perspective on child psychotherapy. In S. R. Shirk (Ed.), *Cognitive development and child psychotherapy* (pp. 1–16). New York: Plenum Press.

Wilkes, T. C. R., Belsher, G., Rush, A. J., & Frank, E. (1994). *Cognitive therapy for depressed adolescents.* New York: Guilford Press.

Wolpe, J. (1958). *Psychotherapy by reciprocal inhibition.* Stanford, CA: Stanford University Press.

Wolpe, J. (1982). *The practice of behavior therapy* (3rd ed.). New York: Pergamon Press.

Zarb, J. (1992). *Cognitive–behavioral assessment and therapy with adolescents.* New York: Brunner/Mazel.

21

Multisystemic Therapy
Changing the Social Ecologies of Youths Presenting Serious Clinical Problems and Their Families

JEFF RANDALL and SCOTT W. HENGGELER

THEORETICAL OVERVIEW

Bronfenbrenner's (1979) theory of social ecology provides the underlying theoretical rationale of multisystemic therapy (MST). A key assumption of the theory of social ecology is that behavior is multidetermined from the interplay of individual characteristics and the multiple, interrelated systems in which individuals are embedded. For children and adolescents, these systems include the family, peers, school, neighborhood, community (including social support network), and the larger macrosystem (e.g., the organizational culture, political climate). A second assumption is that interpersonal behavior is reciprocal and bidirectional. That is, individuals and systems influence each other in an ongoing and recursive fashion.

The assumptions underlying the theory of social ecology have important clinical implications—implications that are critical to the central thrusts of MST. For example, the first assumption suggests that to understand the determinants of identified problems, assessment must consider the possible roles of factors within the child as well as characteristics of the family, peer, school, and community systems that involve the child. Moreover, the second assumption suggests that multiple vantage points must be considered when determining the "fit" of problems to their systemic context.

JEFF RANDALL and SCOTT W. HENGGELER • Family Services Research Center, Department of Psychiatry and Behavioral Sciences, Medical University of South Carolina, Charleston, South Carolina 29425-0742.

Handbook of Psychotherapies with Children and Families, edited by Russ and Ollendick. Kluwer Academic/Plenum Publishers, New York, 1999.

With regard to the design of interventions, the implications of the assumptions are straightforward, though contrasting with much of current mental health services for children. Clearly, if behavior problems are multidetermined, interventions that seek to optimize the probability of achieving favorable outcomes must have the capacity to address identified difficulties across a broad range of individual, family, peer, school, and neighborhood factors. Moreover, interventions must focus on those interpersonal transactions that are linked with the identified problems—either contributing to the problems or as protective factors. Such a "multisystemic" view contrasts with most mental health treatment models that focus mainly on the individual child (e.g., cognitive–behavioral therapy, psychodynamic approaches) or family system (parent training, family therapy).

Importantly, the social-ecological model is strongly supported by findings in the fields of child psychopathology and mental health services research. For example, multiple well-designed causal modeling studies of delinquency (e.g., Thornberry, Huizinga, & Loeber, 1995) have shown that criminal activity in youths is linked directly or indirectly with adolescent characteristics (e.g., cognitive variables), family functioning (e.g., discipline, affect, parental characteristics), peer relations (e.g., association with deviant peers), school performance (e.g., low commitment, academic difficulties), and neighborhood factors (e.g., criminal subculture). Likewise, causal modeling studies in the area of adolescent substance use and abuse have uniformly shown that drug use is linked with similar sets of factors within children and throughout their social ecologies (Henggeler, 1997). Moreover, and as discussed later in this chapter, support for the clinical implications of the theory of social ecology is provided from the favorable outcomes of MST. Thus, strong empirical support is evident for the assumptions that problem behavior is reciprocal and multidetermined as well as for the clinical implications derived from these assumptions.

MECHANISMS OF CHANGE, DESCRIPTION OF INTERVENTION PROCEDURE, AND MODEL OF SERVICE DELIVERY

Mechanisms of Change

MST interventions are designed to attenuate those factors across the family's social ecology that are contributing to identified problems (i.e., risk factors) while simultaneously identifying and building youth and family strengths (i.e., protective factors) on an individualized basis. To build protective factors, MST interventions focus on the individual youth and his or her family relations, peer context, school/vocational performance, and neighborhood/community supports. For example, family interventions often seek to build family structure by improving parents' capacity to monitor and discipline their children. The MST therapist identifies barriers to effective parental discipline (e.g., parental drug abuse, psychiatric conditions, and low social support) and intervenes accordingly. Similarly, a common goal of MST when addressing serious antisocial behavior involves removal of the adolescent from deviant peer groups, while facilitating his or her involvement with prosocial peers. School interventions seek to improve the youth's academic performance, and neighborhood/community interventions aim to increase the family's indigenous social support network by developing prosocial linkages with neighbors, extended family, friends, and community organizations such as the church.

Thus, the overarching goal of MST is to empower families to create healthy social ecologies by building protective factors and attenuating risk factors (Henggeler, Schoenwald, & Pickrel, 1995). Critically, MST assumes that long-term outcomes rest on the success of families in changing their own ecologies in ways that place their children on more adaptive trajectories. As such, the role of the therapist as "change agent" is minimized, while the roles of the clinician as consultant, advisor, coach, and advocate are emphasized.

Description of Intervention

In essence, MST has integrated the best of the empirically based intervention techniques into a social-ecological model. For example, MST interventions incorporate cognitive–behavioral approaches (Kendall & Braswell, 1985), social learning interventions (Munger, 1993), and the pragmatic family therapies (e.g., Haley, 1976; Minuchin, 1974). Thus, MST does not present new treatment techniques, per se. Rather, the contribution of MST is the integration of existing techniques into an ecological model, with corresponding emphases on removing barriers to service access and developing strong mechanisms for quality control, accountability, and training.

In light of the complexity of MST, step-by-step, session-by-session treatment manuals are inappropriate. Hence, MST is operationalized by adherence to nine treatment principles (Henggeler, Schoenwald, Borduin, Rowland, & Cunningham, 1998). Importantly, adherence to these principles (i.e., treatment fidelity) has been linked with favorable long-term outcomes for youths presenting serious antisocial behavior and their families (Henggeler, Melton, Brondino, Scherer, & Hanley, 1997).

Principle 1: The primary purpose of assessment is to understand the "fit" between the identified problems and their broader systemic context. The goal of assessment is to determine how a youth's behavior problems "make sense" given his or her natural ecology. The MST therapist evaluates characteristics of the youth (e.g., verbal skills, psychiatric symptomatology, value system, social skills, attitudinal system), family, peer group, school, neighborhood, and social support network to identify factors that contribute directly or indirectly to behavior problems. Additionally, the MST therapist examines transactions between the youth and other systems (e.g., family, peer, school, neighborhood) as well as transactions between systems, such as the family–school interface and family–peer interactions. Multiple methods and multiple perspectives are used to assess problem behaviors. For example, if one identified problem is the youth's antisocial behavior in the presence of peers, the youth, siblings, parents, teachers, and even peers may be asked to report on the youth's peer relations. The MST therapist then synthesizes information from these various sources and develops "testable" hypotheses regarding the factors contributing to association with deviant peers (i.e., the "fit"). These hypotheses are then tested by subsequent interventions and revisions in the hypotheses are made accordingly (i.e., hypotheses that lead to successful outcomes are assumed correct, while those leading to unsuccessful outcomes are reconsidered).

Principle 2: Therapeutic contacts should emphasize the positive and should use systemic strength as levers for change. Emphasizing the positive has several clinical advantages. Such an emphasis facilitates cooperation and collaboration between the MST therapist and the family, helps the therapist to identify protective factors, decreases therapist and family frustration by emphasizing problem solving, and bolsters the family's confidence. To develop a strength focus, the MST therapist identifies and labels those aspects of the family that are favorable and that reflect hope for the future. For example, although the father is addicted to cocaine, he still loves and cares about his children. Similarly, although the adolescent was expelled from school for the third time, she worked hard in two of her classes and had a good relationship with one of her teachers. Therapists might also reframe interactions to emphasize family strengths. For example, children who view their parents' discipline style as too strict may be encouraged to view discipline as an indication of parental love and concern for the children's future.

Principle 3: Interventions should be designed to promote responsible behavior and to decrease irresponsible behavior among family members. Responsible children comply with family and social rules, attend school, assist around the house, and refrain from harming others. The MST therapist assists parents in developing increased family structure that might include contingency schedules and systematic reinforcement and discipline to promote responsible behavior and decrease irresponsible behavior in youth. Social learning theorists offer excellent guidelines on how to make life enjoyable for youths who display responsible behaviors and unpleasant for youths who engage in irresponsible behavior (e.g., Munger, 1993). Likewise, responsible parents provide their children with nurturance and guidance and meet their children's physical needs. Thus, the MST therapist also addresses barriers that prevent parents from fulfilling parental responsibilities (e.g., substance abuse, stress, social isolation, marital discord, laziness). For example, when parental competence is impeded by a psychiatric condition, the MST therapist may provide treatment directly or assist the parent in obtaining appropriate mental health services. Throughout treatment, the MST therapist targets increasing responsible parenting because such is almost always associated with positive changes in children's behavior.

Principle 4: Interventions should be present-focused and action-oriented, targeting specific and well-defined problems. Present-focused interventions attempt to change the family's current circumstances as opposed to devoting excessive attention to the youth's or family's past. Action oriented interventions focus on activating the youth and the family to make changes in their social ecology. Targeting specific and well-defined problems highlights the importance of clear, objective, observable, measurable, and jargon-free treatment goals. For example, improvement of a 15-year-old boy's self-esteem through reexperiencing early childhood trauma would not follow this MST principle. Rather, developing specific parental strategies to get the boy to school on time and to facilitate his involvement with after-school activities might be appropriate for the specific problems of tardiness and lack of prosocial peer relations. Several present-focused and action-oriented interventions that the MST therapist may use include strategic family therapy (Haley, 1976), structural family therapy (Minuchin, 1974), behavioral parent training (Munger, 1993), and cognitive–behavioral therapy (Kendall & Braswell, 1993).

Principle 5: Interventions should target sequences of behavior within or between multiple systems that maintain the identified problems. Consistent with the social–ecological model and reciprocal nature of behavior, MST interventions devote primary attention to transactions within, between, and among systems that are linked with identified problems. Hence, interventions target interpersonal transactions (e.g., the parent–teacher interface, parent–child interactions around affect and discipline) as the main vehicle of changing problems, in contrast to, for example, gaining insight or developing cognitive strategies. Although the development of cognitive strategies may facilitate changes in interpersonal transactions, adherence to Principle 5 ensures that the MST therapist not lose sight of the ultimate goal of MST—changing interpersonal transactions across the youth's social ecology in ways that promote healthy adaptation.

Principle 6: Interventions should be developmentally appropriate and fit the developmental needs of the youth. MST interventions will vary depending on youths' development levels and their caregivers' stage of development. Interventions with children and young adolescents, for example, may focus on increasing parental control, whereas interventions with older adolescents might emphasize preparation for entry into the adult world by increasing social maturity or developing strategies to overcome financial and logistic barriers to independent living. Because of their own developmental stage and possible medical problems, grandparents who are thrust into the role of primary caregivers may not have the physical energy or emotional strength that traditional parents have to address the needs of youth presenting serious clinical problems. Here, the MST therapist may assist grandparents in enlisting the aid of friends, church members, and extended family members to assist with child rearing.

Principle 7: Interventions should be designed to require daily or weekly effort by family members. Interventions requiring daily and weekly effort enable the MST therapist to identify and address problems in the implementation of interventions (e.g., backsliding, nonadherence to treatment protocols, barriers to treatment goals) quickly. Likewise, identifying strong family efforts and favorable progress quickly can enable the MST therapist and other individuals in the ecology to provide positive feedback as family members move toward goals—which support family members' motivation and maintenance of therapeutic gains. Examples of interventions that require daily effort and feedback are those that focus on responsible behavior at home (e.g., completing chores) and in school (e.g., attendance, behavior).

Principle 8: Intervention efficacy is evaluated continuously from multiple perspectives with providers assuming accountability for overcoming barriers to successful outcomes. Continuous evaluations from multiple informants (e.g., parents, the youth, siblings, teachers, peers, classmates, neighbors, and other professionals) enable the MST therapist to receive ongoing and accurate feedback of treatment progress. Using a multiple-method approach to assessing outcomes provides confirmation on the attainment, or lack of attainment, of treatment goals. Importantly, the MST therapist and treatment team are responsible for identifying any barriers to favorable outcome that are encountered and for designing and implementing interventions to overcome those barriers.

Principle 9: Interventions should be designed to promote treatment generalization and long-term maintenance of therapeutic change by empowering caregivers to address family members' needs across multiple systemic contexts. Stokes and Baer (1977) defined generalization as the occurrence of relevant behavior under different, nontraining conditions across subjects, settings, people, behaviors, and time. A central thrust of MST is generalization of treatment gains, and, as such, the MST therapist helps to develop skills in family members and an indigenous support system that will enable family members to successfully address current and future problems. Although the MST therapist plays an important supportive and consultative role, MST interventions should be delivered primarily by the child's caregivers and others (e.g., grandparents, teachers) in the natural ecology.

Model of Service Delivery

MST programs have typically focused on children and adolescents with serious clinical problems and their families. As many of these youths are at imminent risk for out-of-home placements, an intense clinical response that removes barriers to service access is required. Consequently, the majority of MST programs are delivered using a home-based or family preservation model of service delivery. MST delivered via a home-based model has several distinct features. First, MST therapists carry low caseloads of three to six families per full-time therapist. Second, services are provided in the family's natural environments, such as home, school, and neighborhood settings. Third, treatment is time-limited with services lasting an average of 3–5 months. Fourth, the MST therapist or another member of the treatment team is available 24 hours/day and 7 days/week. Fifth, appointments are scheduled at times convenient to families such as evening hours and weekends. Sixth, daily contact can occur with families either face to face or by phone. Moreover, MST delivered via a home-based model provides several other advantages, including a more valid assessment process and facilitation of family engagement and therapeutic alliances through seeing the family on their own turf. A final advantage of the home-based model of service delivery is that the MST therapist can monitor treatment progress more readily and implement midcourse corrections quickly and reliably. Although the intensity of MST may seem costly at first glance, MST can produce substantial cost savings when families truly at imminent risk of out-of-home placement are targeted (Henggeler, Melton, et al., 1997; Henggeler, Melton, & Smith, 1992; Henggeler, Rowland, Pickrel, et al., 1997; Schoenwald, Ward, Henggeler, Pickrel, & Patel, 1996).

SPECIFIC PROBLEMS AND POPULATIONS AND RESEARCH
SUPPORT FOR EFFECTIVENESS

Early MST Trials

Although lacking follow-up data, early trials of MST yielded promising results. In a quasi-experimental design (Henggeler et al., 1986), delinquent youths who received MST treatment were compared with a matched group of delinquent youths who were selected from case files of a diversion program. MST was more effective than the diversion program in reducing youth problem behaviors, increasing favorable aspects of family relations (e.g., communication and positive affect), and decreasing hostile family interactions. Brunk, Henggeler, and Whelan (1987) carried out the first randomized trial of MST, which remains one of the few controlled evaluations of a family-based treatment for child abuse and neglect.

Maltreating families were randomly assigned to MST or clinic-based behavior parent training. At posttest, parent–child dyads in the MST condition demonstrated less risk for maltreatment than counterparts in the behavior parent training condition. Parents who received MST exhibited more control over and greater responsiveness to their children's behavior, and children in the MST condition displayed less passive compliance to parental requests.

Violent and Chronic Juvenile Offenders

The strongest validation of the effectiveness of MST pertains to the treatment of violent and chronic juvenile offenders and their families. Three randomized trials with follow-ups support the capacity of MST to reduce criminal behavior in this population. Such reductions, however, are linked with clinicians' adherence to the MST treatment protocol.

In an investigation conducted by Henggeler et al. (1992) through a community mental health center, violent and chronic juvenile offenders who were at imminent risk for out-of-home placement because of serious criminal activity were assigned randomly to receive MST or usual services provided by the South Carolina Department of Juvenile Justice (SCDJJ). At posttreatment, adolescents in the MST condition reported a significantly greater reduction in criminal activity and family members reported increased family cohesion and reduced adolescent aggression with peers than counterparts in the usual services condition. These outcomes were neither moderated by demographic characteristics, such as race, age, social class, gender, arrest, and incarceration history, nor mediated by psychosocial variables, such as family relations, peer relations, social competence, behavior problems, and parental symptomatology. Moreover, at a 59-week postreferral follow-up, juvenile offenders in the MST condition had significantly fewer rearrests ($M = 0.87$ versus 1.52) and weeks of incarceration ($M = 5.8$ versus 16.2) than youths in the usual services condition. At a 2.4-year follow-up, findings for rearrest continued to significantly favor MST (Henggeler, Melton, Smith, Schoenwald, & Hanley, 1993).

In a university-based study, Borduin et al. (1995) randomly assigned 200 chronic juvenile offenders to individual therapy provided on an outpatient basis versus MST. At posttreatment, youths in the MST condition had significantly decreased psychiatric symptomatology and families in the MST condition evidenced improved cohesion, adaptability, and communication in comparison with counterparts who received individual therapy. Importantly, 4-year follow-up data indicated that MST participants had a significantly lower recidivism rate (22%) than individual therapy participants (72%). MST treatment effects pertained to violent crime, other criminal activity, and the seriousness of the criminal offenses for those youths in the MST condition who did recidivate.

The third randomized trial of MST with violent and chronic juvenile offenders and their families was also conducted through community mental health centers. One of the purposes of this study was to determine key features of the MST training protocol that are critical to its success (Henggeler, 1997). In a randomized design, MST was compared with usual juvenile justice services to determine whether outcomes were influenced if a key quality assurance mechanism of MST was eliminated from the MST program (i.e., weekly consultations with an MST expert used to ensure treatment adherence were omitted from the supervisory and training protocol). Although MST improved adolescent symptomatology at post-treatment and decreased incarceration at a 1.7-year follow-up, the 26% reduction in rearrest was not significant and considerably below that produced by the afore-mentioned studies. Analyses of treatment adherence, however, indicated that therapists' adherence to the MST treatment principles was an important predictor of key outcomes. High levels of adherence were associated with long-term reductions in criminal activity and incarceration.

Substance Use and Abuse

Drug use and abuse are forms of antisocial behavior that share the same risk factors as adolescent criminal activity (Henggeler, 1993, 1997; Thornberry et al., 1995). In the studies by Henggeler et al. (1992) and Borduin et al. (1995), addi-tional analyses were conducted to determine the impact of MST on youths' drug use and abuse (Henggeler et al., 1991). MST significantly reduced drug use in the former project and significantly decreased the number of arrests related to drug use in the latter study. These encouraging findings prompted a randomized clini-cal trial to examine the effectiveness of MST with substance-abusing and sub-stance dependent juvenile offenders (Henggeler, Pickrel, & Brondino, in press).

In this study, 118 substance-abusing and substance-dependent juvenile of-fenders were assigned randomly to receive MST or usual services provided by the SCDJJ. Results indicated that MST youths reported significantly less drug use at posttreatment than did usual services youths and that MST reduced days in out-of-home placement by 50% and rearrest by 26% (nonsignificant) at approximately 12 months postreferral. Examination of the treatment adherence measures sug-gested that the modest results of MST were related, at least in part, to difficulty transporting this complex treatment model. Finally, a cost analysis indicated that costs associated with MST were almost completely offset by savings achieved from reducing days in out-of-home placement (Schoenwald et al., 1996).

Adolescent Sexual Offenders

In the first controlled outcome evaluation with adolescent sexual offenders to appear in the literature, MST was compared with individual counseling. Adoles-cents who received MST had a significantly lower recidivism for sexual crimes (12.5% versus 75%) than adolescents who received individual counseling at a 3-year follow-up (Borduin, Henggeler, Blaske, & Stein, 1990). Further, for nonsex-ual crimes, the mean frequency of rearrest was lower for adolescents who received MST (0.62) than for adolescents who received individual counseling (2.25). The small sample size ($N = 16$) in this study, however, clearly limits the generalizabil-ity of the findings.

Psychiatric Emergencies

Inpatient psychiatric hospitalizations and other out-of-home placements ac-count for 70% of the nation's mental health dollars for children and, yet, have no established effectiveness (Sondheimer, Schoenwald, & Rowland, 1994) and may do more harm than good (Weithorn, 1988). These circumstances coupled with findings from the adult area indicating that outpatient treatment is equally and usually more effective than inpatient treatment (Kiesler, 1982) highlight the critical need for family- and community-based alternatives to restrictive and expensive out-of-home placements such as psychiatric hospitalization.

A randomized clinical trial examining MST as an alternative to inpatient hospitalization for youths presenting psychiatric emergencies is currently in its fourth year (Henggeler, Rowland, Pickrel, et al., 1997). This study represents the first in the field of children's mental health to have psychiatric hospitalization as a treatment condition. Approximately 200 children and adolescents will serve as participants by the time the project is completed. In adapting MST to the needs of children presenting serious emotional disturbance and in psychiatric crisis, key revisions to the MST protocol have been made to address safety issues and intensive clinical needs (internalizing disorders, suicidal and homicidal ideation). Such revisions included reducing MST therapists' caseloads, adding a crisis caseworker, and increasing psychiatric consultation and clinical supervisory time. Preliminary results indicate that MST is at least as effective, and in some cases more effective, as inpatient care in addressing the clinical crises and psychosocial needs of this challenging sample (Henggeler, Rowland, Randall, Ward, & Santos, 1997).

Summary of Outcomes

The capacity of MST to address the mental health needs and to reduce the criminal activity of serious juvenile offenders is relatively strong. With the success of these clinical trials, current studies are examining the effectiveness of MST with other challenging populations including drug-abusing and -dependent juvenile offenders and youths presenting psychiatric emergencies. In addition, trials of MST in the treatment of child abuse and with adolescent sexual offenders are in the planning stages.

Case Example

Alice was a 15-year-old Caucasian female who resided with her grandparents. The grandparents had custody because of domestic violence and substance abuse in Alice's parents' home. Identified problems from the perspective of the grandparents, school, and juvenile justice authorities included failing classes, truancy, hanging out with deviant peers, and repeated shoplifting. Her shoplifting resulted in Alice being placed in a juvenile detention center, and she was referred for MST treatment following her release from the center.

The first objective of the MST therapist was to determine the "fit" or to understand how Alice's problem behaviors made sense within her social ecology. To understand the "fit," the MST therapist examined strengths and weaknesses across individual, caregiver, peer, school, neighborhood, and social support systems. The grandparents, who were in their late 60s, had medical problems that curtailed their mobility, lacked basic parenting skills, and felt frustrated and overwhelmed by Alice's behavior. Because of ongoing conflicts with Alice, the grandparents were on the verge of having Alice placed outside their home. Alice's current group of friends was heavily involved in antisocial behavior, including drug use and petty criminal activity. Alice professed little interest in school, performed poorly academically, and skipped classes. Although the grandparents had a supportive social network of friends and church members, they valued self-reliance highly and rarely took advantage of this network. The MST therapist also noted strengths in several systems. Alice's grandparents loved her and wanted her to stay out of trouble and finish her education. Her grandparents had friends in the neighborhood and extended family members who lived only a short distance away. The neighborhood was predominantly middle class with several churches and outreach programs. Alice's grandparents had a good relationship with her school officials. Finally, Alice had above-average intellectual abilities, which indicated that her potential was underutilized.

Alice's antisocial behavior clearly fit her social-ecological context. Although her grandparents were caring, they were overwhelmed and were unable to provide the monitoring and natural consequences that Alice needed to change her antisocial behavior and peer group. Consequently, Alice behaved as she pleased, with no consistent consequences for engaging in antisocial behavior. Moreover, as she essentially had free reign of the household and the neighborhood, Alice was invested in maintaining the status quo.

A primary assumption of MST is that the probability of favorable long-term outcome is determined primarily by the caregivers' strengths and competence (Henggeler et al., 1995). The MST therapist initially focused on removing barriers that prevented Alice's grandparents from parenting effectively. The MST therapist assisted Alice's grandparents in making the cognitive changes (e.g., viewing "saving Alice" as more important than self-reliance, and deciding to reciprocate the help that members of the support system were to provide) needed to begin accessing their indigenous support system through church, extended family, and neighbors. As the grandparents engaged the help of their support network, the MST therapist assisted the grandparents in implementing explicit monitoring and discipline strategies, such as establishing a curfew and providing consequences for Alice's noncompliance. Importantly, explicit guidelines were developed for calling in neighbors and so forth to help in this implementation.

With assistance from the MST therapist, Alice's grandparents also collaborated with school personnel to improve Alice's school performance. A protocol for ensuring that Alice traveled to school each day was set with concomitant privileges and sanctions. In addition, the teachers provided daily feedback (on a brief checklist) regarding the extent of Alice's academic efforts and the appropriateness of her behavior. Again, consequences at home were based on her daily performance, with backup from the grandparents' support network. With improved behavior and efforts, and with the support of her current school, Alice was encouraged to enroll in a more academically oriented school that had greater structure, academic challenges, and accountability than her previous school. Moreover, this new school provided the opportunity for Alice to more easily disengage from her deviant friends and develop relations with more prosocial peers.

During the course of treatment, a central therapeutic task was to assist the grandparents in identifying and overcoming barriers to therapeutic objectives. One such barrier was the hospitalization of the grandfather. To maintain continuity in monitoring and disciplining Alice, the grandparents enlisted the aid of their friends and extended family members. The grandparents provided their friends and extended family with clear guidance and expectations, thereby maintaining accountability and ultimate responsibility for rearing Alice during the medical crisis.

Throughout therapy, the MST therapist evaluated treatment gains from multiple perspectives. For example, the therapist determined from the grandparents' reports that Alice was complying with curfew during the week and was completing her homework. On one occasion when Alice violated curfew to hang out with deviant peers, her grandparents drove to where she and her friends were, brought her home, and grounded her. Prior to MST interventions, when Alice would plead to hang out with deviant peers, the grandparents would "fuss" with her and eventually give in to her demands. Daily teachers' reports sent to her grandparents indicated that she was completing her schoolwork and not skipping classes, and Alice's grades improved. Finally, Alice participated in an academic/social summer program offered by her new school where she met and made prosocial friends. The grandparents reinforced the new friendships by allowing Alice to spend time at her friends' homes and allowing her friends to visit in their home.

As shown in this case example, the ultimate goal of MST is to empower families to build ecologies that promote effective family functioning. Although the level of progress achieved in Alice's case may not be representative of all MST cases, even minimal progress toward MST objectives can improve the lives of families and their community in many cases (Henggeler et al., 1995).

FUTURE RESEARCH WITH ATTENTION TO MANAGED CARE

Managed care refers to a diverse set of practices that have at least one broad aim in common (Cuffel, Snowden, Masland, & Piccagli, 1996), namely, to "manage" the allocation of mental health resources in ways that are cost effective. Ideally, managed care attempts to produce cost savings while achieving favorable outcomes for recipients. Thus, with regard to children's mental health services, managed care typically provides clinical oversight to reduce hospitalization days and use less restrictive placements. Although managed care initiatives within the private sector have often attempted to exclude the types of "deep end" youths who are referred for MST because of the complex (and costly) nature of their clinical problems, theorists and policymakers are predicting that such youths will increasingly come under the rubric of managed care as accountability for outcome becomes a higher priority of funders.

MST has a documented capacity to produce child- and family-level outcomes at a cost savings, as described earlier in this chapter. As such, MST is currently being used within managed care organizations and several research studies are under way to extend the applicability of MST in ways that are consistent with the general goals of managed care. Regarding the current use of MST in managed care, for example, a large private provider is using MST as the foundation of its extensive home-based services. Serving youths who have been taken into state custody, this provider has negotiated a capitated reimbursement rate with the state that is higher than the cost of home-based services, but lower than the cost of residential services. In addition, the provider is held to outcome criteria at a 9-month follow-up so that funds must be returned to the state if targeted outcomes are not achieved. Hence, the provider organization has a strong financial incentive to use interventions that can reduce out-of-home placements while achieving desired clinical outcomes.

Three MST research projects with implications for managed care have recently been funded. The first addresses the mental health and substance abuse needs of a very "high use" group of youths and families referred across mental health, juvenile justice, and social welfare. The aim of this project is to develop an MST-based continuum of care (i.e., less intensive MST outpatient services, MST home-based, MST-friendly foster care, a small MST-friendly residential component) in which all clinicians, administrators, and staff are on the same philosophical and conceptual wavelengths—consistent with the values and principles of MST. In the context of a randomized design, youths and families assigned to the MST condition will receive their mental health and substance abuse services from this continuum for the duration of the project. Key outcomes will pertain to the psychosocial functioning of the youths (e.g., in school, not arrested) and cost savings. If successful, the results of this project would have strong implications for the development of services aimed at "deep end" users within managed care networks.

Similarly, the two other managed care related research projects, using quasi-experimental designs, are attempting to develop continua of MST-based services for predefined groups of youths and families. In one project, the neighborhood with the highest combination of negative social indicators (i.e., high crime, high rates of out-of-home placement, high unemployment) in the state is being identified and will be targeted to partner in the development of empirically based and ecologically oriented strategies to address one or two of the most important family-related needs as defined by the neighborhood residents. The other project targets inner-city middle schools with high rates of violence, drug use, expulsions, and dropouts. Here, empirically based and ecologically oriented prevention and intervention strategies will be integrated into the school, with extensive family involvement, in an attempt to ameliorate these difficulties. Again, if successful, the project will have important implications for addressing the needs of geographically defined groups of high-end users (consistent with public sector managed care needs).

SUMMARY

Based on the conceptual underpinnings of the theory of social ecology, MST is specified through nine treatment principles and is generally provided via a home-based model of service delivery. As such, MST has been effective in addressing serious mental health problems in youths and their multineed families by targeting known correlates of serious problem behaviors in the natural ecology and removing barriers to service access. Studies are currently under way to develop MST-based service networks that are consistent with the general goals of managed care—achieving desired clinical outcomes at cost savings.

Acknowledgments
Preparation of this chapter was supported by the National Institute on Drug Abuse, Grants R01DA08029 and R01DA10079, and the National Institute of Mental Health, Grant R01MH51852.

REFERENCES

Borduin, C. M., Henggeler, S. W., Blaske, D. M., & Stein, R. (1990). Multisystemic treatment of adolescent sexual offenders. *International Journal of Offender Therapy and Comparative Criminology, 35,* 105–114.

Borduin, C. M., Mann, B. J., Cone, L. T., Henggeler, S. W., Fucci, B. R., Blaske, D. M., & Williams, R. A. (1995). Multisystemic treatment of serious juvenile offenders: Long-term prevention of criminality and violence. *Journal of Consulting and Clinical Psychology, 63,* 569–578.

Bronfenbrenner, U. (1979). *The ecology of human development.* Cambridge, MA: Harvard University Press.

Brunk, M., Henggeler, S. W., & Whelan, J. P. (1987). A comparison of multisystemic therapy and parent training in the brief treatment of child abuse and neglect. *Journal of Consulting and Clinical Psychology, 55,* 311–318.

Cuffel, B. J., Snowden, L., Masland, M., & Piccagli, G. (1996). Managed care in the public mental health system. *Community Mental Health Journal, 32,* 109–124.

Haley, J. (1976). *Problem solving therapy.* San Francisco: Jossey–Bass.

Henggeler, S. W. (1993). Multisystemic treatment of serious juvenile offenders: Implications for the treatment of substance abusing youths. In L. S. Onken, J. D. Blaine, & J. J. Boren (Eds.), *Behavioral treatments for drug abuse and dependence: National Institute on Drug Abuse Research Monograph 137* (NIH Publication No. 93-3684, pp. 181–199). Rockville, MD: U.S. Department of Health and Human Services.

Henggeler, S. W. (1997). The development of effective drug abuse services for youth. In J. A. Egertson, D. M. Fox, & A. I. Leshner (Eds.), *Treating drug abusers effectively* (pp. 253–279). New York: Blackwell.

Henggeler, S. W., Borduin, C. M., Melton, G. B., Mann, B. J., Smith, L., Hall, J. A., Cone, L., & Fucci, B. R. (1991). Effects of multisystemic therapy on drug use and abuse in serious juvenile offenders: A progress report from outcome studies. *Family Dynamics of Addiction Quarterly, 1,* 40–51.

Henggeler, S. W., Melton, G. B., Brondino, M. J., Scherer, D. G., & Hanley, J. H. (1997). Multisystemic therapy with violent and chronic juvenile offenders and their families: The role of treatment fidelity in successful dissemination. *Journal of Consulting and Clinical Psychology, 65,* 821–833.

Henggeler, S. W., Melton, G. B., & Smith, L. A. (1992). Family preservation using multisystemic therapy: An effective alternative to incarcerating serious juvenile offender. *Journal of Consulting and Clinical Psychology, 60,* 953–961.

Henggeler, S. W., Melton, G. B., Smith, L. A., Schoenwald, S. K., & Hanley, J. H. (1993). Family preservation using multisystemic treatment: Long-term follow-up to a clinical trial with serious juvenile offenders. *Journal of Child and Family Studies, 2,* 283–293.

Henggeler, S. W., Pickrel, S. G., & Brondino, M. J. (in press). Multisystemic treatment of substance abusing and dependent delinquents: Outcomes, treatment fidelity, and transportability. *Mental Health Service Research.*

Henggeler, S. W., Rodick, J. D., Borduin, C. M., Hanson, C. L., Watson, S. M., & Urey, J. R. (1986). Multisystemic treatment of juvenile offenders: Effects on adolescent behavior and family interactions. *Developmental Psychology, 22,* 132–141.

Henggeler, S. W., Rowland, M. D., Pickrel, S. G., Miller, S. L., Cunningham, P. B., Santos, A. B., Schoenwald, S. K., Randall, J., & Edward, J. E. (1997). Investigating family-based alternative to institution-based mental health services for youth: Lessons learned from the pilot study of a randomized field trial. *Journal of Clinical Child Psychology, 26,* 226–233.

Henggeler, S. W., Rowland, M. D., Randall, J., Ward, D. M., & Santos, A. B. (1997). *Multisystemic therapy vs. hospitalization of youth presenting psychiatric emergencies: Preliminary short-term clinical outcomes.* Paper presented at National Institute of Mental Health Conference on Improving the Condition of People with Mental Illness: The Role of Services Research. Washington, DC.

Henggeler, S. W., Schoenwald, S. K., Borduin, C. M., Rowland, M. D., & Cunningham, P. B. (1998). *Multisystemic treatment of antisocial behavior in children and adolescents.* New York: Guilford Press.

Henggeler, S. W., Schoenwald, S. K., & Pickrel, S. G. (1995). Multisystemic therapy: Bridging the gap between university- and community-based treatment. *Journal of Consulting and Clinical Psychology, 63,* 709–717.

Kendall, P. C., & Braswell, L. (1985). *Cognitive behavioral therapy for impulsive children* (2nd ed.). New York: Guilford Press.

Kiesler, C. A. (1982). Mental hospital and alternative care: Non-institutionalization as potential policy for mental patients. *American Psychologist, 37*, 349–360.

Minuchin, S. (1974). *Families and family therapy.* Cambridge, MA: Harvard University Press.

Munger, R. L. (1993). *Changing children's behavior quickly,* Lanham, MD. Madison Books.

Schoenwald, S. K., Ward, D. M., Henggeler, S. W., Pickrel, S. G., & Patel, H. (1996). Multisystemic therapy treatment of substance abusing or dependent adolescent offenders: Cost of reducing incarceration, inpatient, and residential placement. *Journal of Child and Family Studies, 5*, 431–444.

Sondheimer, D. L., Schoenwald, S. K., & Rowland, M. D. (1994). Alternative to the hospitalization of youth with a serious emotional disturbance. *Journal of Clinical Child Psychology, 23*(Suppl.), 7–12.

Stokes, T. F., & Baer, D. M. (1977). An implicit technology of generalization. *Journal of Applied Behavior Analysis, 10*, 349–367.

Thornberry, T. P., Huizinga, D., & Loeber, R. (1995). The prevention of serious delinquency and violence: Implications from the program of research on the causes and correlates of delinquency. In J. C. Howell, B. Krisberg, J. D. Hawkins, & J. J. Wilson (Eds.), *A sourcebook: Serious, violent, & chronic juvenile offenders* (pp. 213–237). Newbury Park, CA: Sage.

Weithorn, L. A. (1988). Mental hospitalization of troublesome youth: An analysis of skyrocketing admission rates. *Stanford Law Review, 40, 773*–778.

22

School-Based Interventions for Aggressive Children
PrimeTime as a Case in Point

JAN N. HUGHES and TIMOTHY A. CAVELL

OVERVIEW

PrimeTime is a school-based secondary prevention program that integrates empirically supported treatment components into a unified intervention. We use our experience with PrimeTime to illustrate recommended practices in school-based interventions. First, however, we present a rationale for schools as logical sites for the delivery of psychological health services, especially prevention services, and place PrimeTime within the context of educational and health care restructuring. Next we articulate our conceptualization of the development of conduct problems that underlies the PrimeTime intervention and describe the intervention components. We strive to make clear the connections between our theory of the development of conduct problems, our theory of change, and our intervention components. We evaluate the empirical support for PrimeTime by first reviewing the empirical support for each of the four separate interventions, based on published literature, and then reviewing the first round of outcome data for the integrated intervention. In evaluating these data, we assess support for the efficacy of the intervention as well as support for the underlying theoretical conceptualization. We conclude with a discussion of practical issues in implementing school-based prevention programs, including eliciting school support and obtaining operating funds.

JAN N. HUGHES and TIMOTHY A. CAVELL • Department of Educational Psychology, Texas A & M University, College Station, Texas 77843-4225.

Handbook of Psychotherapies with Children and Families, edited by Russ and Ollendick. Kluwer Academic/Plenum Publishers, New York, 1999.

Schools as Health Service Delivery Sites

The importance of schools as sites for mental health prevention and intervention efforts is captured in the maxim, "Schools are where children are." In addition to serving as convenient locations for finding children, schools are important developmental contexts. Children spend a large part of their waking hours in school, where they develop relationships with peers and adults that shape their interpersonal competence and views of self and others, learn skills that promote competence and autonomy, and relate to cultural values, beliefs, and mores that may or may not be similar to those of their family.

In 1987 the National Mental Health Association's Commission on the Prevention of Mental–Emotional Disabilities concluded that school-based mental health programs offer the best opportunity to impact the psychological well-being of children. Since then, numerous commissions and task forces have reached the same conclusion (Healthy People 2000, 1990; National Education Goals Panel, 1994; National Health/Education Consortium, 1990; Paavola et al., 1995). Several reasons are marshaled in support of schools as logical sites for the delivery of psychological health services. Because families are familiar with schools and view schools as community resources, they tend to view psychological services provided through the schools as less stigmatizing and more acceptable. School-based services are more physically accessible than are clinic-based services. Teachers are often the first to notice developmental deviations that may signal the need for early intervention services, which may prevent the need for subsequent services that are more intensive and costly. Schools provide an existing, community-based infrastructure for the delivery of integrated health, educational, and social services for children most in need of comprehensive and integrated services, resulting in cost efficiencies. Because schools are the most stable caregiving system in many children's lives, they can support coordination of care across time. Finally, school-based programs offer the possibility to intervene with populations of children during developmental transitions, such as entrance to schools or transition to middle school, known to be especially important to children's developmental pathways.

Contributing to a renewed commitment to school-based prevention is the increased public awareness of the widespread risk and dysfunction among our nation's youth and of huge gaps in the provision of mental health services (Knitzer, Steinberg, & Fleisch, 1990; Schorr & Schorr, 1988). Of the approximately 15–19% of children aged 4–17 who have a diagnosable mental disorder that results in functional impairment (Doll, 1996), only a small percentage receive treatment (Duchnowski, Johnson, Hall, Kutash, & Friedman, 1993). When treatment is available, it is often inappropriate, restrictive, and expensive (Saxe, Cross, Silverman, & Batchelor, 1987). Only a small segment of children with diagnosable psychiatric problems are classified by schools as having an emotional disturbance, and these children are unlikely to receive psychological treatment as part of their special education program (Duchnowski, 1994). Many other children's behavioral dispositions and adverse life circumstances place them at elevated risk for academic and social failure.

Increased awareness of children's poor educational outcomes (e.g., *A Nation at Risk: The Imperative for Educational Reform,* 1983) and of the interrelatedness of health and educational outcomes led to a call for comprehensive and coordinated education, health, social, and human services within a restructured educational system (National Education Goals Panel, 1994; National Health/Education Consortium, 1990). In response, many states have attempted to address the related problems of inadequate health care for children and poor educational outcomes with plans that extend health care to uninsured children, that emphasize prevention and health promotion over inpatient care, and that include school-based or school-linked health and mental health services (Carlson, Tharinger, Bricklin, DeMers, & Paavola, 1996; Tharinger et al., 1996).

Childhood Aggression as an Example of the Need for School-Based Prevention

In the absence of intervention, aggressive elementary children are likely to continue along deviant developmental pathways (Robins, 1979; Stattin & Magnusson, 1989; West & Farrington, 1977). Furthermore, their risk status becomes more unbending as they become caught up in reciprocal systems of negative transactions. Early disruptive and controlling behavior leads to peer rejection and reduced opportunities to learn and to practice prosocial skills. Their interactions with teachers are often likely to be characterized by high levels of criticism and control and low levels of support and responsiveness (Coie & Koeppl, 1990; Itskowitz, Navon, & Strauss, 1988; Walker & Buckley, 1973), contributing to their lowered academic motivation and effort and low sense of belonging to school (Hawkins & Weis, 1985). Socially rejected and academically behind their peers, in middle school these children form deviant peer groups that further increase their alienation from school and identification with antisocial beliefs, values, and behaviors (Dishion, Andrews, & Crosby, 1995; Dishion, Capaldi, Spracklen, & Li, 1995). Affiliation with antisocial peers is a strong proximal antecedent to delinquency and substance abuse during adolescence (Kandel, 1973; Keenan, Loeber, Zhang, Stouthamer-Loeber, & Van Kammen, 1995).

This progression from early aggression to subsequent academic, social, and behavioral problems is not invariable. In recent years, researchers have identified numerous factors that buffer aggressive children from continuing along antisocial trajectories. Supportive relationships with parents (Eron, 1987; Steinberg, 1986), effective parenting discipline and monitoring practices (Haapasalo & Tremblay, 1994; Patterson, Reid, & Dishion, 1992), supportive relationships with teachers (Pianta, Steinberg, & Rollins, 1995), academic achievement (Schonfeld, Shaffer, O'Connor, & Portnoy, 1988), friendships with prosocial peers (Dishion, Capaldi, et al., 1995), safe neighborhoods (Guerra, Eron, Huesmann, & Tolan, 1997), and schools that have effective discipline practices and high academic expectations (Guerra et al., 1997) reduce the aggressive child's risk for further escalation of externalizing symptoms. Secondary prevention programs that impact these factors would be expected to reduce the aggressive child's risk for antisocial behaviors.

Despite the seriousness of childhood aggression, few services are available to aggressive children and their families because they often fall outside the care of current systems responsible for the well-being of children. Although the education system serves all children, aggressive children are typically recognized by school systems as socially maladjusted, which is not considered a handicapping condition under the Individual with Disabilities Education Act (P.L. 101-476) or under Section 504 of the Rehabilitation Act of 1973 (P.L. 93-112). Thus, such children and their families are unlikely to receive additional services that are available to children who meet special education criteria. Even if an aggressive child qualifies for special education services, psychological and other "related services" are rarely provided (Duchnowski, 1994) and existing service arrangements rarely address the multidetermined nature of aggression.

Private psychological treatment is outside the financial means of many families. When available, health care delivery systems usually construe intervention too narrowly to benefit most aggressive children. Family and individual therapy, parent training, and other mental health services offered by social service agencies are usually not available to families with aggressive children unless there is evidence of pathological parenting (abuse or neglect). And again, the quality of services provided often falls short of the needs of such families, as they do not address the multidetermined nature of aggression or provide ecologically valid treatments.

The juvenile justice system has a special responsibility to serve the needs of delinquent youth. But by the time children enter this system, the developmental "window of opportunity" for instituting a targeted prevention program will likely have ended. Granted some children may enter the system earlier, but their access comes at the cost of having started their criminal activity earlier and having a more serious prognosis. To the extent such treatments isolate aggressive youth or increase their association with aggressive and delinquent peers, they are likely to have harmful effects (Dishion & Andrews, 1995).

In summary, existing systems offer very limited and fragmented services to aggressive children and their families. Henggeler is doubtful that traditional clinical practices will be effective in stemming the downward trajectory of aggressive and delinquent youth: "Indeed, juvenile justice and mental health solutions are often unrealistic, exacerbate youths' clinical problems, and are delivered via financially strapped social service systems" (1996, p. 139). The challenge for these systems is to coordinate services that are easily accessible, cost-effective, timely, ecologically valid, and designed to address the multiple and interactive determinants of aggression, delinquency, and substance abuse. We offer PrimeTime as an example of a selective intervention program designed to offset the downward trajectory of aggressive children.

THE PRIMETIME MODEL

The PrimeTime Program is based on an organizational-developmental framework of risk and resilience (Cicchetti & Toth, 1992; Egeland, Carlson, & Sroufe, 1993). This perspective assumes (1) that children develop through the interaction of dispositional and environmental factors in the context of supportive caregiving, (2) that early experiences are critically important and children are active participants in the developmental process, and (3) that developmental change is reflected in the reorganization of available structures for transacting with the environment. Childhood aggression is recognized as an often unyielding form of maladaptive behavior that requires attending to both child and environmental variables when attempting to deflect (and hold) these transactions in a more prosocial direction. Altering the developmental trajectory of young aggressive children, therefore, requires an appreciation for the stability and the complexity of their behavior as well as how it is received and reacted to by the environment. Moreover, effective interventions must lead to a *reorganization* of the internal structures and skills that aggressive children use to transact with the environment.

Typically, the confluence of dispositional and environmental risk factors is thought to function as a formidable obstacle to efforts at altering the downward spiral of aggressive children. From an organizational-developmental framework (e.g., Cicchetti & Richters, 1993; Stattin & Magnusson, 1996), however, future transactions and reorganizations may also represent treatment opportunities or possible turning points (Rutter, 1996) in the lives of aggressive children. Taking advantage of such opportunities requires a realistic model for how to shift future transactions and reorganizations in therapeutic directions (McCord, 1996). In designing the PrimeTime model of school-based intervention, we tried to fashion a theoretically coherent intervention model that combined innovative and cost-effective treatment components. We began with the notion that both the child and the environment should be targeted if we were to succeed in shifting the transactions between them in a more prosocial direction. Also, in line with recent empirical and theoretical work on the etiology of childhood aggression (Greenberg, Speltz, & DeKlyen, 1993; Richters & Waters, 1991; Shaw & Bell, 1993), we drew from both social learning and attachment theories to design our model of intervention.

From a social learning perspective, environmental targets typically include the degree to which parents and teachers respond contingently to a child's use of prosocial or antisocial behavior. Child-based targets, on the other hand, generally include children's use of prosocial skills to meet their needs and to resolve interpersonal conflict. The empirical literature offers modest support for both parent training and child skills training as interventions for aggressive children (Kazdin, 1993), and there is some evidence that treatment programs that combine the two approaches may yield greater gains than programs that use them in isolation (e.g., Kazdin, Seigel, & Bass, 1992).

Compared with the vast treatment literature stemming from social learning theory, the application of attachment theory to treating aggressive, school-age children is less straightforward. Attachment-related phenomena are clearly implicated in childhood aggression, as evidenced by recent studies linking insecure or disorganized attachment to disruptive and aggressive behavior in children (Greenberg et al., 1993; Lyons-Ruth, 1996). However, a main effects role for attachment variables does *not* appear to be the case (Greenberg et al., 1993). Rather, attachment difficulties and their representational and affective sequelae are thought to interact with dispositional and environmental variables to determine the child's acquisition and use of antisocial behavior. In fact, it would seem that attachment-related phenomena interact with those variables that are most often targeted by social learning interventions. First, the success of parents' efforts (and presumably those of teachers) to socialize aggressive children may depend on the extent to which these children have come to experience a sense of felt security and autonomy in their relationships with caregivers (Kochanska, 1995; Richters & Waters, 1991; Shaw & Bell, 1993). Second, efforts to train aggressive children to use prosocial skills may depend on the degree to which children's internal models of self and others are not hindered by the defensive exclusion of discrepant but therapeutic information (Bowlby, 1980), or by the selective inclusion of congruent but countertherapeutic information (Crick & Dodge, 1994). An overly positive view of self or one's relationships with others has been shown to be directly related to children's aggression (Hughes, Cavell, & Grossman, 1997). Similarly, the tendency to infer hostile intent under ambiguous social conditions or to believe in the positive consequences of aggressive actions has also been shown to be directly related to childhood aggression (Dodge, 1986).

For the most part, we have placed greater emphasis on this second possibility in designing our intervention. We hypothesized that skills training for aggressive children should be coupled with efforts to relax and improve negatively-biased internal working models that guide the on-line processing of social information. It is believed that "the process of changing young children's perspectives on human relationships requires experiencing supportive relationships" (Crittenden, 1992, p. 592). Based on the reasoning that supportive adult relationships have the potential to mollify and improve aggressive children's maladaptive views of self and others, our skills training component did not begin until several months after we initiated efforts to bolster the quality of their relationships with significant adults. Our intervention model is perhaps best captured by three general hypotheses.

> *Interventions for aggressive children will be effective to the extent that changes in children's internal working models and social cognitive skills promote positive transactions with the environment.*

The construct of the working model of the self in relation to others is a useful heuristic for understanding the processes by which past interactions with significant others are carried forward into future relationships (Erickson, Korfmacher, & Egeland, 1992; Sroufe & Fleeson, 1986). Aggressive children's maladaptive internal models of self and others can bias the motivational and perceptual processes that lead to negative interactions with others in their environment (Crick & Dodge, 1994). Child-focused intervention components must address both types of cognitive processes. Past social cognitive skills interventions have typically addressed the latter but not the former.

> *Therapeutic changes in the internal working models and social cognitive skills of aggressive children are enhanced by children's participation in corrective attachment relationships and in social cognitive skills training.*

In order for aggressive children to form more benign representations of self and others, specific skills training must be supplemented by interventions designed to relax and improve internal working models. Although the malleability of children's working models is presently unknown, participation in relationships that offer opportunities for corrective attachment experiences is considered especially important (Lieberman, Weston, & Pawl, 1991).

> *For aggressive children, corrective attachment relationships provide the following conditions over time: (1) communication of accurate emotional understanding and acceptance, (2) strict limits on antisocial behavior, and (3) modeling of prosocial norms.*

Past attempts to change the social and interpersonal ecologies of aggressive children have generally focused on only one of these dimensions at a time (Hughes & Cavell, 1994), owing perhaps to the difficulty in establishing and maintaining a relationship that would provide all three conditions. And yet our model (see Figure 1) would

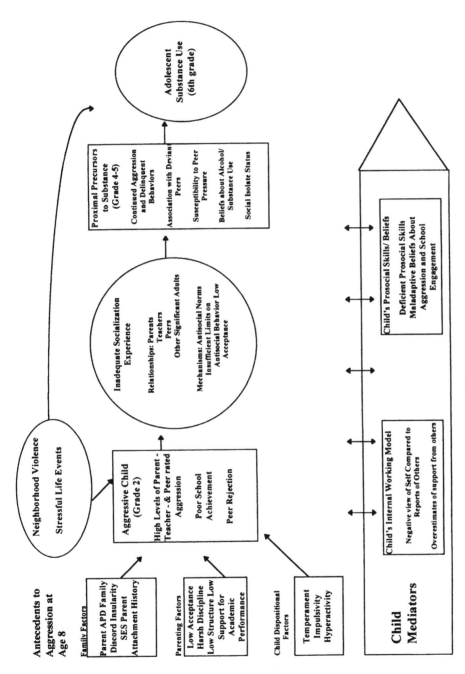

Figure 1. A theoretical model of the pathway taken by young aggressive children to adolescent substance abuse.

posit that effective socialization of aggressive children is unlikely unless these children participate in significant relationships with adults who are prosocial and who can both accept them and contain them (Cavell, in press; Lykken, 1995; Richters & Waters, 1991). Communicating understanding and acceptance is needed to challenge pathogenic working models; however, aggressive children tend to behave in ways that make them hard to understand and hard to accept (Greenberg et al., 1993). Strict limits on antisocial behavior are needed to challenge the contingencies that shaped and currently reinforce aggression and other coercive acts; unfortunately, aggressive children are not easily contained (Patterson et al., 1992). Exposure to prosocial models is needed to counter beliefs in the positive value of aggression and other antisocial acts; however, aggressive children often live in homes and neighborhoods where antisocial beliefs are seen as normative (Hawkins, Catalano, & Miller, 1994).

We call our program PrimeTime for three reasons: (1) we intervene at a *prime* or critical time in children's lives in order to prevent negative outcomes such as delinquency before these maladaptive patterns of behavior become too firmly entrenched, (2) we promote *prime* or quality interactions between aggressive children and significant adults, and (3) we endeavor to *prime* or prepare children for skills training by providing mentoring relationships designed to correct maladaptive working models of self and others.

The PrimeTime intervention model combines teacher and parent consultation with therapeutic mentoring and problem-solving skills training (PSST). Parents and teachers received regular consultation designed primarily to enhance their interactions with and perceptions of these troubling children. In our work with parents and teachers we placed less emphasis on teaching behavioral management skills. Consultants assisted with concerns about discipline in the home or with questions about classroom management; however, the thrust of their efforts was to be an emotionally supportive presence in the lives of these parents and teachers. There were several reasons for deemphasizing specific skills training for parents and teachers. First, because PrimeTime was a secondary prevention program, neither parents nor teachers had initially asked for our assistance; to impose on them a prescribed, skills-based agenda seemed to run counter to many of the fundamental rules of effective consultation (Hughes, 1992). Second, we were cautious about assuming a priori that deficits in behavior management skills explained the negative interactions that teachers and parents may have experienced with these difficult children (Webster-Stratton & Herbert, 1994; Witt & Martens, 1988). Finally, previous efforts to conduct school-based parent training with this same target population had revealed that only a minority of eligible parents were willing to participate (Grossman, 1993).

Because parents of aggressive children often feel overwhelmed and distressed, and because teachers are responsible for an entire classroom of children, our efforts to provide supportive relationships also included a therapeutic mentoring component. Mentors receive training and ongoing supervision in how to establish and maintain relationships that offered emotional acceptance, behavioral limits, and prosocial norms. In Year 2 of our program, these intervention components are combined with the 9-month-long PSST program. Skills training for PrimeTime children is deferred until the second year of the program based on the premise that children participating in corrective attachment relationships will be more likely to benefit from such training.

TREATMENTS AND MECHANISMS OF CHANGE

Each of the four intervention components comprising PrimeTime has garnered at least a modicum of empirical support. By sequencing, coordinating, and implementing these interventions in accordance with our theoretical model, we hoped to enhance the generally small treatment effects reported for the separate interventions. In this section, we review the empirical support for the separate interventions.

Teacher Consultation

Psychological consultation to teachers is a common service delivery approach within school psychology (Conoley & Conoley, 1992; Zins, Kratochwill, & Elliott, 1993). Although various models of teacher consultation have been described, common to these approaches is a collaborative, systematic problem solving process in which a psychological consultant attempts to provide assistance to a teacher concerning a work-related problem. Thus, consultation is an indirect model of delivering psychological services to children, in which teachers are responsible for implementing agreed-upon approaches.

As a general approach for delivering psychological services to children, consultation can incorporate diverse interventions. Most empirical studies of consultation effectiveness have evaluated behavioral consultation (Gutkin, 1993). In behavioral consultation, the consultant engages teachers in a series of interviews that focus on the steps of applied behavior analysis: behavioral specification of child problems, assessment of antecedent and consequent stimuli associated with specific child behaviors; baseline assessment of child behaviors; development and implementation of interventions; and evaluation of the intervention (Kratochwill & Bergan, 1990). Studies evaluating the effectiveness of behavioral consultation typically use single-case designs (most often AB designs) and document improvements in the targeted behaviors. For example, Kratochwill, Elliott, and Busse (1995) reported an average effect size of 0.95 for 23 behavioral consultation cases.

Despite the consistent finding of improvements in student behaviors resulting from behavioral consultation, evidence that consultation improves long-term functioning of children is largely lacking (Hughes, 1994b). Indeed, the prevailing research paradigm in behavioral consultation is unconcerned with the developmental significance of changes resulting from consultation. Elliott and Busse (1993) state that "an effective treatment can be defined in terms of problem resolution. Thus, if a problem is defined as the discrepancy between the present behavior or situation and the desired behavior or situation then the ability of a treatment to eliminate that discrepancy defines the level of treatment effectiveness" (p. 180).

A variant of teacher consultation involves in-service training and supervision to teachers concerning classroom management practices. In these approaches, teachers are instructed to implement behaviorally oriented classroom management strategies to reduce student disruptive and aggressive behaviors. Numerous early studies demonstrated that teacher-administered behavior modification techniques such as planned ignoring, contingent use of praise and other reinforcers, and response cost for negative behaviors resulted in decreases in disruptive behaviors (e.g., Becker, Madsen, Arnold, & Thomas, 1967; O'Leary & Becker, 1967). Again, these researchers typically ignored issues of generalization and maintenance of change and of the social validity of measured outcomes (Hughes, 1994b).

Although behaviorally oriented consultation often produces short-term changes in targeted student behaviors, its emphasis on control-oriented approaches may have an unintended negative impact on children's learning and positive engagement in school activities (Jason, Ferone, & Anderegg, 1979). Classrooms characterized by lower levels of teacher control, higher supportive relationships with students, and teaching practices that promote student autonomy are associated with greater student academic motivation and effort and sense of belonging to school (Goodenow, 1993; Solomon, Watson, Battistich, Schaps, & Delucchi, 1992). Thus, short-term gains in behavior may be offset by negative shifts in student motivation or a drop in the commitment to prosocial values and behaviors.

An alternative model of consultation focuses on improving the student–teacher relationship (Pianta, 1996, 1999). The importance of a positive teacher–student relationship on a child's concurrent and subsequent school adjustment is supported by a number of studies (Birch & Ladd, 1997; Howes, Hamilton, & Matheson, 1994; Howes, Matheson, & Hamilton, 1994; Pianta, 1994; Werner & Smith, 1982). For example, Pianta et al. (1995) found that a close relationship with one's kindergarten teacher deflected adjustment difficulties in second grade. Furthermore, the magnitude of the deflection was strongest for children whose relationships with kindergarten teachers were initially characterized as conflicted. In a 3-year longitudinal study of aggressive second- and third-grade children, Hughes and colleagues (Hughes, Cavell, & Jackson, 1999), found that a positive teacher–student relationship was associated with lower rates of teacher- and peer-rated aggression. To date, no published studies have evaluated the impact of consultation that targets the student–teacher relationship

Taken together, outcome studies of behavioral consultation and developmental studies of the role of a supportive teacher–student relationship on aggressive children's academic and behavioral adjustment suggest that consultation with teachers of aggressive children should focus on both containing the child's disruptive and aggressive behavior and promoting a warm and supportive teacher–student relationship. Thus, best practices in teacher consultation with aggressive children tend to parallel best practices in parent-directed interventions.

Parent Consultation

We describe our involvement with parents as *consultation* and not *training*, yet our consultants draw heavily from the parent training literature to guide their efforts. This literature has been dominated by the behavior management parent training (BMPT) approach, an approach that emphasizes parents' effective use of discipline to counter children's noncompliance (Barkley, 1987; Eyberg, 1988; Forehand & McMahon, 1981; Patterson, Chamberlain, & Reid, 1982; Webster-Stratton, 1987). The lack of research examining other approaches continues to be a shortcoming of the parent training literature (see Cavell, 1996; Sheeber & Johnson, 1994). A recent review of the parent training outcome literature estimated that 89% of the investigations used a behavioral approach (Rogers-Wiese, 1992).

Reviews of the parent training literature (e.g., Cavell, in press; Dumas, 1989; Kazdin, 1993, 1997; Miller & Prinz, 1990) note that early single-case studies offered clear support for BMPT (e.g., Patterson & Brodsky, 1966). Impressive initial results soon gave way, however, to findings from group outcome studies that both supported (e.g., Patterson et al., 1982) and failed to support (e.g., Bernal, Klinnert, & Schultz, 1980) the short-term efficacy of BMPT. A recent meta-analysis (Serketich & Dumas, 1996) found that only 26 of 117 controlled outcome studies met minimal inclusion criteria (i.e., training in differential reinforcement or time-out, children with elevated problem behavior, five subjects in each condition, one child behavior outcome measure). Two-thirds of these studies involved individually administered parent training, the average number of sessions used was just under ten, and the mean age of the target child was 6 years. From these 26 studies were computed 36 different comparisons and investigators found an overall mean effect size of 0.86 ($SD = 0.36$). This finding is encouraging but should be interpreted with caution because control subjects received an alternative treatment in only 4 of the 36 comparisons. In fact, Serketich and Dumas (1996) found that over the past 25 years only 22% of BMPT outcome studies used adequate control groups. They conclude that "the results of the meta-analysis largely provide support for the effectiveness of [BMPT] in comparison to no intervention" (p. 181).

The handful of studies that have assessed the long-term impact of BMPT (1 to 14 years) report generally positive results (Baum & Forehand, 1981; Long, Forehand, Wierson, & Morgan, 1994; Patterson & Fleischman, 1979; Webster-Stratton, 1990). However, few BMPT outcome studies actually report follow-up data (Serketich & Dumas, 1996), and the conclusions that can be drawn are limited by a lack of comparison data from subjects who were untreated or who received contrasting treatments (Kazdin, Mazurick, & Bass, 1993). Follow-up studies also suffer from differential dropout rates between target and comparison subjects (Forehand & Long, 1991). Studies with positive results (Forehand & Long, 1991; Long et al., 1994) can also be contrasted with studies in which treatment gains were lost at follow-up (Dumas, 1989).

Sizable numbers of children are nonresponders to BMPT. When Webster-Stratton (1990) assessed *clinically* significant changes in her 3-year follow-up study, 53.7% of mothers and 74.5% of fathers rated their child's behavior as falling within the normal range. She concluded that the "results are similar to other parent training studies, which have suggested that 30% to 50% of treated families fail to maintain clinically significant improvements" (p. 148). A recent study by Forgatch (1991) offers reasons why a substantial number of children may not benefit from BMPT. Participating were 50 families who received an average of 19 treatment sessions each. As expected, improved parenting practices led to decreases in child antisocial behavior. However, parents' use of monitoring was more predictive of treatment gains than was their use of discipline, and neither positive reinforcement nor problem solving was related to a reduction in child antisocial behavior. Only 25 (50%) families improved their use of discipline, only 8 (16%) improved their monitoring skills, and only 5 (10%) improved both their discipline and their monitoring. These findings raise questions about the extent to which participation in BMPT leads consistently to positive changes in targeted parenting practices.

Among the risk factors associated with a poor response to BMPT include characteristics of the child (e.g., severity of problem behavior) and the parents (e.g., depression and antisocial traits) as well as stressful family circumstances such as divorce, marital discord, poverty, and social isolation (Dumas, 1989; Webster-Stratton & Hammond, 1990). Risk factors that predict a poor response to BMPT also predict a greater chance of dropping out of therapy. The average percentage of parents who drop out of BMPT has been estimated to be about 28% (Forehand, Middlebrook, Rogers, & Steffe, 1983). The likelihood of families dropping out increases steadily as the number of child, parent, and family risk factors increases (Kazdin et al., 1993). Parents with older children (i.e., $6^{1}/_{2}$ to $12^{1}/_{2}$ years old) are also more likely to drop out of treatment prematurely (Dishion & Patterson, 1992).

The limited number of studies assessing the generalization of BMPT typically show that treatment benefits carry over to untargeted problem behaviors and to untreated siblings. However, generalization of treatment benefits to other settings such as classrooms has been less consistent (see McNeil, Eyberg, Eisenstadt, Newcomb, & Funderburk, 1991). Parents who participate in BMPT programs tend to rate the training experience as a positive one. Consumer satisfaction data suggest that parents prefer performance-oriented (e.g., skill rehearsal exercises) and group discussion formats over formats that rely solely on the use of lectures and written material or self-administered videotapes.

In many respects, data supporting the use of BMPT are impressive. However, a careful review of the BMPT outcome literature also makes clear that we know very little about the use of parent training as a school-based intervention for aggressive children (Kazdin, 1997). If schools are to become useful points of mental health service delivery, then the attention of parent training researchers must shift from the clinic to the schools. The handful of studies that have been conducted suggest important differences in the populations targeted by clinic-based and school-based parent training efforts (Braswell et al., 1997; Cunningham, Bremner, & Boyle, 1995; Dumas, 1996; Grossman, 1993). A commonly stated reason for conducting school-based interventions is that many parents of children at risk are not active consumers of clinic-based mental health services. Unfortunately, few data speak to how parents in clinic-based programs differ from parents who are identified by, participate in, and ultimately complete school-based parent training programs (see Cunningham et al., 1995). It does appear that parents of at-risk children identified through large screening programs are less likely to avail themselves of opportunities for parent training, even when these services are offered in the schools (Braswell et al., 1997; Grossman, 1993). For example, Braswell et al. (1997) offered parents of disruptive children 18 and 12 hours of parent training in Years 1 and 2 of their intervention, respectively. However, in Year 1, only 18.7% participated in at least 14 hours of training and in Year 2 only 11.6% participated in at least 6 hours of training.

One way to counter such high attrition rates is to make it easier or more rewarding for parents to attend school-based parent training sessions. For example, parents in the NIMH-funded FAST Track program (Conduct Problems Prevention Research Group, 1992) are actually paid for their participation in parent training sessions and both transportation and child care are provided. Hughes (1994a) was able to boost parent participation by making "scholarships" to a children's after-school program contingent on attendance at parent training sessions. An alternative approach to countering high attrition in this population of parents is to offer parent-related services in the home. Even then, however, there is no guarantee that parents will avail themselves of these services. Some parents of aggressive children—usually those who are isolated, impoverished, or impaired—can make it very difficult to conduct face-to-face visits and can effectively avoid the more demanding and perhaps therapeutic aspects of intervention (Cavell & Hughes, 1997). In sum, the current parent training literature offers a number of useful guidelines to practitioners working with families in school-based interventions; however, the extent to which clinic-based parent training programs fit within school settings has yet to be determined.

Problem-Solving Skills Training

Teaching aggressive children problem solving skills is based on the common finding that aggressive children display deficits and distortions in social cognition. Compared with nonaggressive children, aggressive children tend to attribute hostile intent to peers in situations in which the intent is ambiguous, fail to accurately interpret others' affective reactions or cognitive perspective, selectively attend to and remember hostile cues, generate more aggressive and fewer prosocial solutions to provocation, respond impulsively to social challenges, underestimate their level of aggressiveness and overestimate their competence, and minimize or deny negative feelings (e.g., Crick & Dodge, 1994; Hughes et al., 1997; Lochman & Dodge, 1994). Furthermore, these social cognitive deficits and distortions are predictive of children's behavioral responses in social problem situations (Crick & Dodge, 1994). Presumably, aggressive children's antisocial responses are a result, in part, of these deficits in self-control and social information processing.

PSST evolved from behavioral social skills training (SST), which is also based on the view that aggressive children lack skills necessary for successful peer interactions. However, whereas SST teaches specific behavioral solutions to social situations, PSST teaches more general problem-solving steps that are employed with greater flexibility and across a number of social situations. The shift from SST to PSST was a result, in part, of the failure of SST to improve aggressive children's social adjustment, despite improvements in targeted social skills (Bierman, Miller, & Stabb, 1987; Ollendick & Hersen, 1979; Spence & Marzillier, 1981).

Typically, PSST involves training in self-control techniques and problem-solving skills. Children are first taught to "stop and think" in anger-provoking situations and then to engage in a series of problem-solving steps: defining the problem, setting a goal, generating alternatives, evaluating consequences of different alternatives, selecting a response, and evaluating its effectiveness. Discussions, exercises, modeling, and role-plays of hypothetical social situations are used to teach targeted skills.

With some exceptions, PSST interventions have yielded positive effects on measures of problem solving and small gains on measures of social adjustment (Beelmann, Pfingsten, & Lösel, 1994). Lochman and his colleagues (Lochman, 1992; Lochman, Coie, Underwood, & Terry, 1993; Lochman & Curry, 1986) have demonstrated positive effects from school-based PSST with aggressive elementary children. Treatment consisted of 18 small group sessions of 45–60 minutes' duration, and a subset of treated boys received additional "booster" sessions as well as parent training the following year. At the end of the first year of treatment, treated boys improved relative to control boys on measures of disruptive/aggressive class-room behavior, parent-completed measures of aggression, and self-esteem (Loch-man & Curry, 1986). Three years after treatment, treated boys displayed lowered levels of self-reported substance use, improved self-esteem, and lower levels of be-havioral deviance, but did not differ in classroom behavior (Lochman, 1992). This study was the first to document long-term improvement on socially consequential outcomes resulting from school-based PSST with aggressive children.

The effectiveness of clinic-based, individually administered PSST with seri-ously aggressive children was demonstrated by Kazdin, Bass, Siegel, and Thomas (1989). This more costly and intensive treatment with involved parents as "coteachers" resulted in significant behavioral improvement lasting up to 1 year after treatment. Despite these gains, a majority of treated children continued to ex-hibit clinically elevated levels of aggressive and disruptive behavior. The authors concluded that more comprehensive treatments would probably be necessary to enhance these treatment gains.

Recently, PSST programs with aggressive children have addressed the social ecology of childhood aggression by involving socially competent children in PSST groups (Hudley & Graham, 1993; Prinz, Blechman, & Dumas, 1994). Concern with potential harmful effects of providing skills training in the context of deviant-only groups is warranted on the basis of recent research by Dishion and Andrews (1995), who found that at-risk adolescents provided group skills training actually increased their behavior problems and tobacco use 1 year posttreatment, relative to adolescents in a parents-only treatment or in two control treatments. Hudley and Graham (1993) evaluated an attribution-training intervention for mixed groups of socially competent and aggressive African-American children. Children were instructed in how to accurately detect others' intent, how to ask questions to discover intent in ambiguous situations, and how to respond when uncertain of the intent. Treated children not only improved on measures of attribution but also were rated as less aggressive by their teachers following treatment. Unfortunately, follow-up data were not reported. Prinz et al. (1994) evaluated Peer Coping Skills Training (PCS) with aggressive children in Grades 1–3. PCS is different from PSST in its emphasis on teaching children how to cope with social challenges through information exchange (e.g., asking questions and stating clearly what they want and how they feel) rather than through problem-solving scripts. PCS is similar to PSST in its emphasis on prosocial skills, including communication skills, affec-tive coping skills, and problem-solving skills. Six months following the yearlong intervention, children receiving PCS showed significantly higher teacher-rated prosocial coping and significantly lower teacher-rated aggression, relative to chil-dren in the control condition. However, treated children were still within the clin-ical range on measures of aggression and did not improve on posttreatment measures of peer acceptance.

In summary, PSST interventions warrant a judgment of "promising" (Kazdin, 1993). Before this judgment can be upgraded to "effective," evidence that training consistently results in long-term and clinically significant improvement on so-cially consequential outcomes is needed. The development of more effective skill training approaches will likely follow research that identifies processes that me-diate child responsiveness to the intervention (e.g., the specific skills or beliefs that mediate behavioral improvement) as well as child (e.g., temperament, attachment history) or ecological (e.g, school discipline practices, neighborhood violence) variables that moderate intervention effectiveness. Unfortunately, most outcome studies in PSST have failed to test whether the putative mechanisms of change are responsible for behavioral improvement or under which of the conditions the intervention is effective.

Mentoring

Mentoring as a tool for intervening with troubled children has become increasingly popular in recent years (Blechman, 1992). Mentors have been used as paratherapists for children of divorce and as role models for high-risk minority youth (Cowen, Zax, & Laird, 1966; Taylor, 1982). Despite the surge of interest in mentoring, there remains a disturbing lack of empirical research on the topic (Stein, 1987). Without a well-grounded "technology" of mentoring, the promise inherent in this approach will never be fully realized (Blechman, 1992). The few empirical studies that exist raise doubts about the viability of mentoring programs as a prevention tool. In a review of 19 published outcome studies that assessed the effects of "adult companionship" as a primary treatment strategy for children, treatment effects were found to be minimal (Stein, 1987). These programs were based on the belief that a relationship with an untrained but interpersonally warm and empathic adult would have a therapeutic effect on disadvantaged or maladaptive children. Blechman (1992) has argued that mentoring programs are being promulgated prematurely, before we have adequate knowledge of how they may work, if at all. For example, recent funding initiatives by the U.S. Office of Juvenile Justice to provide millions of dollars to support mentoring programs are based largely on quasi-experimental studies that have yet to be subjected to the peer review process. Blechman (1992) also noted that "existing mentoring programs rarely have articulated underlying scientific principles or specified program operations at a level of detail necessary for program evaluation" (p.160). There also is no consensus about how mentors should be recruited, trained, and evaluated, or about how mentoring programs should be integrated with other mental health interventions.

Multicomponent Programs

Given the multidetermined nature of aggression and the interplay of child characteristics with the social settings in which the child is embedded, it is unlikely that any single-focus intervention will deflect aggressive children from antisocial pathways. Consistent with this conclusion, recent efforts to evaluate school-based interventions for aggressive children combine two or more interventions. The most ambitious of these initiatives is the multisite FAST Track program mentioned earlier (Conduct Problems Prevention Research Group, 1992). This multiyear prevention program includes parent training, a classroomwide communication and affective skills curriculum, PSST, peer pairing with socially competent children, and academic tutoring. The intervention is provided within a highly resourced environment, with parents paid for their participation and staff receiving extensive consultation and support. Preliminary findings from this project are promising, with treated children making modest gains on measures of social problem solving, peer acceptance, academic achievement, and observed prosocial and aggressive behavior (Coie, 1997). The long-term effects of this program are presently not known. It is also unknown whether the changes brought about by comprehensive but resource-rich intervention programs will generalize to settings where the resources are more constrained.

AN INITIAL TEST OF THE PRIMETIME MODEL

We recently completed a controlled outcome study assessing the impact of the PrimeTime intervention program on a sample of aggressive school-age children (Cavell & Hughes, 1997). The project began in the fall semester of Year 1 and concluded at the end of the spring semester of Year 2. In the fall of Year 1, children who were nominated and rated by teachers as aggressive were blocked by grade and randomly assigned to the PrimeTime condition or to a minimal treatment condition known as Standard Mentoring (SM). Additional baseline assessments were also completed at this time. Interventions began in the spring semester of Year 1 and continued through the end of the spring semester of Year 2 (for a total of 16 months). Posttreatment assessment occurred in May of Year 2, and follow-up assessment occurred 1 year later. The measurement design assessed treatment outcome as well as variables thought to mediate change in outcome (i.e., social cognition and quality of mentoring) and variables that could possibly moderate intervention responsiveness (i.e., child narcissism and parental attachment history).

Subjects

Second- and third-grade teachers in six elementary schools were asked to identify children who met a behavioral description of an aggressive child: picks on other children, starts fights, teases, tells mean lies about others, or excludes others from their group. Parental consent for screening was obtained for 68 (75%) children, all of whom met the screening criterion of a score at or above the 84th percentile on the Aggressive Scale of the teacher-report Child Behavior Checklist (CBC, Achenbach, 1991). Children were blocked by grade and randomly assigned to PrimeTime or to the SM condition. A total of 62 children (31 in PrimeTime and 31 in SM) completed the pretreatment assessment. The average age of children in the PrimeTime was 7.55 (SD = 0.84), and that of children in SM was 7.54 (SD = 0.74). No significant differences between the groups at pretreatment on demographic variables were found.

Measures

Three types of outcomes were assessed: problem behavior, acceptance by others, and self-concept. Measures of problem behavior and acceptance were completed by teachers, parents, and classmates. Child measures were obtained via individually administered interviews conducted at schools by undergraduate or graduate psychology students. Peer measures were completed in classroom groups; parents and teachers completed their measures at home and at school, respectively.

Treatment Conditions

PrimeTime

This intervention is based on previous work by both attachment theorists (e.g., Ainsworth, Bowlby, Main, & Sroufe) and social learning researchers (e.g., Bierman, Coie, Dodge, & Patterson). In Year 1 of the PrimeTime program, children were provided three treatment components designed principally to enhance the emotional support they receive from parents, teachers, and a therapeutic mentor. These components were in place throughout the duration of the intervention, except for teacher consultation, which was not possible during the summer months. At the start of the fall semester of Year 2, PrimeTime children began participating in a PSST group.

Teacher consultants met with teachers once each month and their primary tasks were (1) to provide emotional support to teachers struggling to manage these difficult children and (2) to assist teachers in developing alternative classroom strategies to counter children's disruptiveness. Parent consultants met with parents in their homes once each month to provide emotional support as well as training in relevant skills and knowledge. Consultants' primary task was to develop a supportive and accepting relationship with parents.

PrimeTime mentors were undergraduate psychology or education students enrolled in an undergraduate field experiences course. An attempt was made to select mentors who scored most favorably on a set of measures designed to screen for problems in socioemotional functioning (e.g., attachment style, agreeableness, symptomatology); however, our pool of candidates was so small that only three candidates were excluded. Mentors received 18 hours of training designed to enhance their understanding of childhood aggression and their capacity to develop and maintain an accepting, emotionally supportive relationship with an aggressive child. Visits took place outside of school hours for at least 1 hour/week for the entire 16 months of the program. Small group supervision occurred weekly and mentors maintained logs of each mentoring contact. Mentors attempted to provide children with corrective attachment experiences characterized by accurate understanding, emotional acceptance, and firm limits on antisocial behavior. Mentors were free to pursue a variety of activities, but were given suggestions about activities that would promote significant, emotional interactions (e.g., working on a scrapbook) versus activities that may preclude such interactions (e.g., video games, movies). During the last 4 months of the relationship, mentor supervision focused extensively on termination issues, and at termination mentors gave to their mentees a scrapbook documenting their time together.

PSST took place during school hours in two 30-minute sessions per week for a total of 46 sessions. Lessons in the PSST manual targeted skills known to differentiate aggressive and nonaggressive children (e.g., empathy, attention to social cues, interpretation of intentions, generating competent solutions, anticipating outcomes of solutions).

Standard Mentoring

Initially, mentors for SM children were recruited from a campus service organization that frequently provides mentors to local school children. Unfortunately, the level of contact between these "standard mentors" and target children was unacceptable for even a minimal treatment condition. Therefore, beginning in the fall of Year 2, mentors in the SM condition were education and psychology majors enrolled for the same amount of course credit as PrimeTime mentors. Standard mentors and their mentees met for a minimum of 1 hour/week outside of school hours. Standard mentors attended a 2-hour orientation focusing primarily on safe and appropriate mentoring activities. Regularly scheduled supervision was not provided but standard mentors completed log sheets after each visit. Mentors in the two conditions did not differ on any of the screening measures.

Results

Treatment Outcome

Overall the findings provided only partial support for the efficacy of the PrimeTime intervention. Analyses of change over time revealed an expected decrease from baseline to posttreatment in teachers' ratings of externalizing problems for children in the PrimeTime condition. These gains were no longer evident at follow-up, however. Parents tended to see little if any change in PrimeTime children's functioning, either at posttreatment or at follow-up. Peers, on the other hand, regarded PrimeTime children as less aggressive at follow-up. Other significant changes over time were unexpected: By follow-up, PrimeTime children rated themselves as less competent academically and physically.

Some of the changes noted for PrimeTime children were also exhibited by children in our control condition. By follow-up, SM children's peer-rated aggression had decreased significantly and their self-ratings of academic and physical competence had fallen. Other within-group changes were unique to SM children. Parents reported significant decreases from pre- to posttreatment and from pretreatment to follow-up in their children's levels of externalizing problems. On the other hand, SM children reported significant declines from baseline to follow-up in the quality of the relationships they had with fathers and with teachers.

Significant within-group gains experienced by children in our SM condition suggest that it was not only a credible control condition but also an active comparison treatment. Direct comparisons between the two conditions support the viability of the SM program. At follow-up, SM children were rated by parents as having fewer externalizing problems than PrimeTime children. Mean CBC scores for SM children both at posttreatment and at follow-up were below 60 T.

In the absence of a no-treatment control condition, it is unclear how one should interpret these findings. Should they be taken as evidence that neither treatment was particularly effective at reducing the problem behavior of aggressive children? Significant improvements in children's peer-rated aggression scores would suggest otherwise. Our findings also suggest that both treatments effectively prevented further escalation of problem behavior in this sample of highly aggressive, at-risk children. It is clear from our results that PrimeTime children did not fare better than control children.

Treatment Process and Mechanisms of Change

Analyses that examined hypothesized mediator and moderator variables helped to clarify the mixed picture that emerged from our outcome findings. We had predicted that children in the PrimeTime condition would show greater improvement in their social cognitive skills than SM children and that social cognitive variables would mediate the relation between treatment and outcome. Our expectations were partially confirmed in that PrimeTime children displayed less hostile attributions at posttreatment than SM children, and their level of hostile attributions predicted teacher-rated aggression at follow-up. These positive findings were offset, however, by an increase at posttreatment in PrimeTime children's beliefs in the positive consequences of aggression. The seriousness of this unexpected, iatrogenic effect was revealed in our mediational analyses. For PrimeTime children only, beliefs in the benefits of aggression were significant predictors of teacher-rated aggression at posttreatment. Taken together, these findings suggest that our intervention, and perhaps PSST specifically, resulted in both gains and losses for PrimeTime children.

Because of the multifaceted nature of our intervention, we cannot say whether this negative effect resulted specifically from PSST, but it seems unlikely that other treatment components (e.g., consultation with parents and teachers, mentoring) would produce this kind of result. The fact that skills training groups comprised only aggressive children further increases our suspicion that PSST was the source of this unwanted change. Recent studies have highlighted the potential dangers associated with the aggregation of deviant youth (Dishion &Andrews, 1995). Weekly sessions of PSST—some of which were devoted to promoting group cohesion among these groups of aggressive children—may have inadvertently created a deviant social climate for children in the PrimeTime condition.

In addition to children's social cognitions, we also hypothesized that the quality of mentoring relationships would serve as a mechanism of change. PrimeTime mentors were viewed more positively by their mentees than were SM mentors. This is not surprising given that PrimeTime mentors had a longer opportunity to build a relationship and were extensively trained and continuously supervised. More importantly, PrimeTime children's perceptions of the mentoring relationship predicted posttreatment changes in teacher-rated externalizing problems, and mentor ratings of the relationship predicted these scores at follow-up for children in both conditions. Further supporting our conceptual model was evidence linking the quality of mentoring to children's response to PSST. PrimeTime children who began their skills training with a positive view of the mentoring relationship were less likely to endorse positive beliefs about aggression at posttreatment even when controlling for pretreatment levels of aggression. The relation between quality of mentoring and posttreatment beliefs about aggression was significant despite the apparent role that PSST played in boosting PrimeTime children's beliefs about the value of aggression. In fact, because of the iatrogenic nature of PSST in our study, a positive mentoring experience may have functioned more as a buffer against deviancy training and less as a priming mechanism for later skills training. The buffering effect of pre-PSST mentoring is supported by Steinberg's (1986) finding that authoritative parenting appeared to guard children against susceptibility to deviant peer pressure, particularly in that group of children who were poorly supervised and "hanging out" with peers after school. Because children with authoritative parents are more likely to internalize parental norms, Steinberg reasoned that these children were less likely to be influenced by peers with deviant norms. Collectively, the findings from our mediational analyses lend strong support to the use of therapeutic mentors for aggressive children—an essential feature of the PrimeTime model.

Moderators of Change

Perhaps most intriguing from our analyses were findings suggesting the presence of significant moderator variables. These analyses revealed that peer-rated narcissism (Narc) and parents' attachment history (based on scores from the Parental Acceptance–Rejection Questionnaire, PARQ) may be useful parameters by which to predict aggressive children's response to treatment. We learned that aggressive children who were judged by peers as less "stuck up" responded particularly well to our SM condition. In fact, these children seemed to fare better than all other target children. A similar finding emerged with respect to our other moderator variable: SM children whose parents reported a fairly benign attachment history had the lowest peer aggression scores of any subgroup of children. Both of our moderator variables reflect protective factors for young aggressive children in that each is a potential indicator of the child's capacity to respond positively to new interpersonal relationships. If replicated, these findings would suggest that weekly contact with an untrained but supportive mentor is an inexpensive yet highly effective treatment for these sorts of aggressive children.

In contrast to the gains exhibited by low-Narc and low-PARQ SM children, these two groups of children did not seem to benefit from the PrimeTime condition. Of particular concern was the degree to which low-PARQ children in the PrimeTime condition were regarded by peers as aggressive at follow-up (i.e., > 1 *SD*). Though it would seem from these findings that PrimeTime is an unsuitable intervention for children with low-Narc or low-PARQ scores, we suspect that these children—*because* they may have been less impaired relationally (or perhaps less defended emotionally)—were even more vulnerable to the influence of deviant peers in our PSST groups. Assuming that alternative PSST formats (e.g., mixed groups of deviant and nondeviant children) can eliminate or reduce such iatrogenic effects (Kazdin, 1993), we would predict that PrimeTime programs using nonharmful PSST can actually be beneficial to these two groups of children as well.

There was some indication from our moderator analyses that the PrimeTime treatment model was a better fit for children who were at risk relationally, either because peers viewed them as narcissistic or because their parents reported a history of parental rejection. Given the attachment focus of the PrimeTime model, a greater treatment response by high-Narc or high-PARQ children in this condition would not be unexpected. We suspect that any differential gains realized by these PrimeTime children compared with their SM counterparts are likely the result of our mentoring program with its extensive training and supervision. By providing relationally at-risk children with a wholly new relationship that was successfully begun, successfully maintained, and successfully ended, we may have been able to provide some degree of benefit for a group of children who clearly did not benefit from SM.

For the next phase of our project (PrimeTime-2), treatment procedures will be revised to reflect the lessons learned from this preliminary study. Most significant is that PSST groups will include prosocial children in equal or greater numbers than those of deviant children. A second change is a control condition in which the "mentoring" is done only during the school lunch period twice a week. Because SM was a fairly potent treatment for a subset of aggressive children, we tried to create a control condition that would more closely approximate an inert or attention control treatment.

Future Directions with Attention to Health Care Delivery

Despite the intuitive appeal of early identification and prevention as an alternative to costly and inefficient remedial services and the growing body of empirically supported prevention programs (see Durlak, 1995, for a review of school-based prevention programs), systematic prevention programs are rarely used in schools. Exemplary prevention programs (Greenberg, Kusche, Cook, & Quamma, 1995; O'-Donnell, Hawkins, Catalano, Abbott, & Day, 1995; Stolberg & Gourley, 1996) are usually university-affiliated demonstration projects, as is the case with Prime-Time. A key challenge facing the child and adolescent psychologist is the implication of empirically supported prevention programs to typical schools. Rather than viewing demonstration projects as separate from, and therefore as irrelevant to, community practice, we should attempt to replicate characteristics of successful demonstration projects in school settings. Tolan (1996) suggests that partnerships between community providers and university training programs that characterize successful demonstration projects can be replicated in many community settings. Universities benefit from such arrangements because they provide opportunities for trainees (and faculty) to gain valuable experience in innovative models of service delivery. University involvement and ongoing supervision of trainees increase the likelihood that the intervention is based on a sound conceptualization of the problem, consistent with the empirical literature on effectiveness, and delivered in accordance with clearly specified intervention principles and methods. Ideally, university involvement extends to program evaluation activities, including monitoring and assessing treatment integrity and outcome effectiveness. Such collaborative partnerships between universities and schools are not to be confused with the common practice of schools serving as placements for specific training experiences with little dialogue regarding models of service delivery transpiring between university trainers and school personnel. Rather, the university collaborates with the school in every aspect of program planning, implementation, and evaluation, including facilitating partnerships with other agencies and funding sources.

Success in securing funds to support prevention programs depends more on perseverance and collaborative skills than on research skills. The Memphis City Schools Mental Health Center (Hannah & Nichol, 1996) is an excellent example of securing and combining funds from many diverse public and private agencies to provide a range of prevention programs within the context of a comprehensive, school-based mental health clinic. On a smaller scale, partnerships with local businesses and community service groups and charities can provide essential support for prevention efforts. A number of directories (e.g., the *Foundation Directory*, published annually by the Foundation Center and available in most universities) and on-line sources of information on grants (e.g., http://www.grantscape.com; http://www.nih.gov/grants; http://fdncenter.org) provide invaluable information on funding for education and children's mental health.

Being well-informed of regulations and laws that impact schools is an essential responsibility of the school-based interventionist. For example, several provisions of the 1997 Amendments to the Individuals with Disabilities Education Act (P.L. 105-17) create new opportunities for funding prevention services. Now, at state discretion, children under the age of 9 may receive services for developmental delays in physical, cognitive, communications, social or emotional, or adaptive development without requiring a special education label. The new IDEA also requires consideration be given to behavioral issues and behavioral plans when a child's behavior interferes with eduation, and that consultation be provided to the regular education teacher regarding behavioral interventions. Although heavily regulated by state and federal laws, schools are operated under the control of local school boards. These boards have a wide measure of discretion in the provision of school-based psychological services, including prevention, and in terms of the school's participation in interagency agreements and public/private partnerships. Thus, psychologists may want to advocate with local school boards for enhanced prevention services and for partnerships with other agencies.

The government's increased role in the provision of health care to children has implications for school-based prevention efforts. Many states have responded to the unmet health care needs of children with state initiatives to provide medical coverage for uninsured children. These programs use either state funding or a combination of state funds and Medicaid or private funds to extend insurance coverage to additional groups of children not eligible for Medicaid. Particularly noteworthy is the emphasis included in these state plans in linking health care to educational restructuring efforts (see Spring 1995 special issue of *The Future of Children*). For example, Florida's Healthy Kids, Inc. program combines private and public funds to provide a package of health benefits, including prevention and health promotion to school children who are eligible for free or reduced lunch. One of the program's major strengths is its administrative simplicity. It uses school districts to define its client base and eligibility for free or reduced school lunch to set sliding premium rates. With less than 5% of its overall budget going toward administration and impressive performance on health criteria in its first 3 years, several states are adopting similar programs (John F. Kennedy School of Government, 1997). With the recent infusion of federal dollars available to states for increasing health services to children, psychologists should be advocating within their state mental health authorities and legislatures for the inclusion of preventive health and mental health services.

Summary

Childhood aggression is a multidetermined problem that is often resistant to secondary prevention efforts. Although results from the initial outcome study of the PrimeTime program fall short of our expectations, our findings make a valuable contribution to the conceptual basis underlying prevention programs for aggressive children. By following the tenets of prevention science, we not only demonstrated the adequacy of our conceptualization of childhood but also identified specific changes needed in how we should implement the intervention to boost benefits. Through our analyses of processes thought to mediate treatment effectiveness, we learned that group-based skills training with this population resulted in specific harmful changes in children's beliefs about aggression. We believe these harmful effects attenuated the benefits children received from the mentoring and consultation. We learned that mentors who receive training and supervision develop more supportive relationships with these challenging children. Our moderator analyses taught us that weekly contact with an untrained, supportive adult is an effective and low-cost intervention for a subset of aggressive children who are low in peer-rated narcissism and whose parents report more positive attachment histories. For the subset of aggressive children who are more relationally at risk and who are viewed by their peers as "stuck up," a more intensive intervention is called for.

We have translated these lessons into a revised intervention model. A test of the efficacy of this model is under way, with support of NIDA and the Hogg Foundation. We hope our efforts contribute to the search for an effective response to the rising tide of juvenile delinquency and substance abuse. We also hope that our discussion of PrimeTime serves to illustrate the value and the challenge of school-based interventions.

REFERENCES

Achenbach, T. M. (1991). *Manual for Child Behavior Checklist 14–18 and 1991 Profile.* Burlington, VT: University of Vermont, Department of Psychology.

Barkley, R. A. (1987). *Defiant children: A clinician's manual for parent training.* New York: Guilford Press.

Baum, C. G., & Forehand, R. (1981). Long term follow-up assessment of parent training by use of multiple outcome measures. *Behavior Therapy, 12,* 643–652.

Becker, W. C., Madsen, C. H., Jr., Arnold, C. R., & Thomas, D. R. (1967). The contingent use of teacher attention and praise in reducing classroom behavior problems. *The Journal of Special Education, 1,* 287–307.

Beelmann, A., Pfingsten, U., & Lösel, F. (1994). Effects of training social competence in children: A meta-analysis of recent evaluation studies. *Journal of Clinical Child Psychology, 23,* 260–271.

Bernal, M. E., Klinnert, M. D., & Schultz, L. A. (1980). Outcome evaluations of behavioral parent training and client centered parent counseling for children with conduct problems. *Journal of Applied Behavioral Analysis, 13,* 677–691.

Bierman, K. L., Miller, C. L., & Stabb, S. D. (1987). Improving the social behavior and peer acceptance of rejected boys: Effect of social skill training with instructions and prohibitions. *Journal of Consulting and Clinical Psychology, 55,* 194–200.

Birch, S. H., & Ladd, G. W. (1997). The teacher–child relationship and children's early school adjustment. *Journal of School Psychology, 35,* 61–79.

Blechman, E. A. (1992). Mentors for high-risk minority youth: From effective communication to bicultural competence. *Journal of Clinical Child Psychology, 21,* 160–169.

Bowlby, J. (1980). *Attachment and loss: Vol. III. Loss.* New York: Basic Books.

Braswell, L., August, G. J., Bloomquist, M. L., Realmuto, G. M., Skare, S. S., & Crosby, R. D. (1997). School-based secondary prevention for children with disruptive behavior: Initial outcomes. *Journal of Abnormal Child Psychology, 25,* 197–208.

Carlson, C. I., Tharinger, D. J., Bricklin, P. M., DeMers, S. T., & Paavola, J. C. (1996). Health care reform and psychological practice in schools. *Professional Psychology: Research and Practice, 27,* 14–23.

Cavell, T. A. (1996, August). *Responsive Parent Training: A preliminary trial.* Paper presented at the 14th Biennial Meeting of the International Society for the Study of Behavioral Development, Quebec City, Quebec, Canada.

Cavell, T. A. (in press). *Working with parents of aggressive children: A practitioner's guide.* Washington, DC: American Psychological Association.

Cavell, T.A., & Hughes, J. N. (in press). Secondary prevention as context for assessing change processes in aggressive children. *Journal of School Psychology.*

Cicchetti, D., & Richters, J. E. (1993). Developmental considerations in the investigation of conduct disorder. *Development and Psychopathology, 5,* 331–344.

Cicchetti, D., & Toth, S. L. (1992). The role of developmental theory in prevention and intervention. *Development and Psychopathology, 4,* 489–493.

Coie, J. D. (1997). *Initial outcome evaluation of the prevention trial.* Paper presented at the Biennial Meeting of the Society for Research in Child Development, Washington, DC.

Coie, J. D., & Jacobs, M. R. (1993). The role of social context in the prevention of conduct disorder. *Development and Psychopathology, 5,* 263–275.

Coie, J. D., & Koeppl, K. G. (1990). Adapting intervention to the problems of aggressive and disruptive children. In S. R. Asher & J. D. Coie (Eds.), *Peer rejection in childhood* (pp. 309–337). London: Cambridge University Press.

Commission on the Prevention of Mental–Emotional Disabilities. (1987). *The prevention of mental–emotional disabilities.* Alexandria, VA: National Mental Health Association.

Conduct Problems Prevention Research Group. (1992). A developmental and clinical model for the prevention of conduct disorder: The FAST Track program. *Development and Psychopathology, 4,* 509–528.

Conoley, J. C., & Conoley, C. W. (1992). *School consultation: Practice and training* (2nd ed.). Boston: Allyn & Bacon.

Cowen, E. L., Zax, M., & Laird, J. D. (1966). A college student volunteer program in the elementary school setting. *Community Mental Health Journal, 2,* 319–328.

Crick, N. R., & Dodge, K. A. (1994). A review and reformulation of social information processing mechanisms in children's social adjustment. *Psychological Bulletin, 115,* 74–101.

Crittenden, P. M. (1992). Treatment of anxious attachment in infancy and early childhood. *Development and Psychopathology, 4,* 575–602.

Cunningham, C. E., Bremner, R., & Boyle, M. (1995). Large group community-based parenting programs for families of preschoolers at risk for disruptive behaviour disorders: Utilization, cost effectiveness, and outcome. *The Journal of Child Psychology and Psychiatry, 36,* 1141–1159.

Dishion, T. J., & Andrews, D. W. (1995). Preventing escalation in problem behaviors with high-risk young adolescents: Immediate and 1-year outcomes. *Journal of Consulting and Clinical Psychology, 63,* 538–548.

Dishion, T. J., Andrews, D. W., & Crosby, L. (1995). Antisocial boys and their friends in early adolescence: Relationship characteristics, quality, and interactional process. *Child Development, 66,* 139–151.

Dishion, T. J., Capaldi, D., Spracklen, K. M., & Li, F. (1995). Peer ecology of male adolescent drug use. *Development and Psychopathology, 7,* 803–824.

Dishion, T. J., & Patterson, G. R. (1992). Age effects in parent training outcomes. *Behavior Therapy, 23,* 719–729.

Dodge, K. A. (1986). A social information processing model of social competence in children. In M. Perlmutter (Ed.), *Cognitive perspective on children's social and behavioral development* (pp. 77–125). Hillsdale, NJ: Erlbaum.

Doll, B. (1996). Prevalence of psychiatric disorders in children and youth: An agenda for advocacy by school psychology. *School Psychology Quarterly, 11,* 20–46.

Duchnowski, A. J. (1994). Innovative service models: Education. *Journal of Clinical Child Psychology, 23*(Suppl.), 13–18.

Duchnowski, A. J., Johnson, M. K., Hall, K. S., Kutash, K., & Friedman, R. M. (1993). The alternatives to residential treatment study: Initial findings. *Journal of Emotional and Behavioral Disorders, 1,* 17–26.

Dumas, J. E. (1989). Treating antisocial behavior in children: Child and family approaches. *Clinical Psychology Review, 9,* 197–222.

Dumas, J. E. (1996). Why was this child referred? Interactional correlates of referral status in families of children with disruptive behavior problems. *Journal of Clinical Child Psychology, 25,* 106–115.

Egeland, B., Carlson, E., & Sroufe, L. A. (1993). Resilience as process. *Development and Psychopathology, 5,* 517–528.

Elliott, S. N., & Busse, R. T. (1993). Effective treatments with behavioral consultation. In J. E. Zins, T. R. Kratochwill, & S. N. Elliott (Eds.), *Handbook of consultation services for children* (pp. 179–203). San Francisco: Jossey–Bass.

Erickson, M. F., Korfmacher, J., & Egeland, B. R. (1992). Attachments past and present: Implications for therapeutic intervention with mother–infant dyads. *Development and Psychopathology, 4,* 495–508.

Eron, L. (1987). The development of aggressive behavior from the perspective of a developing behaviorism. *American Psychologist, 42,* 435–442.

Eyberg, S. (1988). Parent–child interaction therapy: Integration of traditional and behavioral concerns. *Child and Family Behavior Therapy, 10,* 33–45.

Forehand, R., & Long, N. (1991). Prevention of aggression and other behavior problems in the early adolescent years. In D. J. Pepler & K. H. Rubin (Eds.), *The development and treatment of childhood aggression* (pp. 317–330). Hillsdale, NJ: Erlbaum.

Forehand, R. L., & McMahon, R. J. (1981). *Helping the noncompliant child: A clinician's guide to present training.* New York: Guilford Press.

Forehand, R., Middlebrook, J., Rogers, T., & Steffe, M. (1983). Dropping out of parent training. *Behaviour Research and Therapy, 21,* 663–668.

Forgatch, M. S. (1991). The clinical science vortex: A developing theory of antisocial behavior. In D. J. Pepler & K. H. Rubin (Eds.), *The development and treatment of childhood aggression* (pp. 291–315). Hillsdale, NJ: Erlbaum.

Goodenow, C. (1993). Classroom belonging among early adolescent students: Relationships to motivation and achievement. *Journal of Early Adolescence, 13,* 21–43.

Greenberg, M. T., Kusche, C. A., Cook, E. T., & Quamma, J. P. (1995). Promoting emotional competence in school-aged children: The effects of the PATHS curriculum. *Development and Psychopathology, 7,* 117–136.

Greenberg, M. T., Speltz, M. L., & DeKlyen, M. (1993). The role of attachment in the early development of disruptive behavior problems. *Development and Psychopathology, 5,* 191–214.

Grossman, P. B. (1993). *Attachment style and history of parents of aggressive children: Effects on response to intervention.* Unpublished doctoral dissertation, Texas A&M University, College Station.

Guerra, N. G., Eron, L. D., Huesmann, L. R., & Tolan, P. H. (1997). A cognitive-ecological approach to the prevention and mitigation of violence and aggression in inner-city youth. In D. P. Fry & K. Bjoerkqvist (Eds.), *Cultural variation in conflict resolution: Alternatives to violence* (pp. 199–213). Hillsdale, NJ: Erlbaum.

Gutkin, T. B. (1993). Conducting consultation research. In J. E. Zins, T. R. Kratochwill, & S. N. Elliott (Eds.), *Handbook of consultation services for children* (pp. 227–248). San Francisco: Jossey–Bass.

Haapasalo, J., & Tremblay, R. E. (1994). Physically aggressive boys from ages 6 to 12: Family background, parenting behavior, and prediction of delinquency. *Journal of Consulting and Clinical Psychology, 62,* 1044–1052.

Hannah, F. P., & Nichol, G. T. (1996). Memphis City Schools Mental Health Center. In M. C. Roberts (Ed.), *Model programs in child and family mental health* (pp. 173–192). Mahwah, NJ: Erlbaum.

Hawkins, J. D., & Weis, J. G. (1985). The social development model: An integrated approach to delinquency prevention. *Journal of Primary Prevention, 6,* 74–97.

Hawkins, J. D., Catalano, R. F., & Miller, J. Y. (1994). Risk and protective factors for alcohol and other drug problems in adolescence and early adulthood: Implications for substance abuse prevention. *Psychological Bulletin, 112,* 64–105.

Healthy People 2000. (1990). *National health promotion and disease prevention objectives.* DHHS Publication No. (PHS) 91-50212. Washington, DC: U.S. Government Printing Office.

Henggeler, S. W. (1996). Treatment of violent juvenile offenders—we have the knowledge: Comment on Gorman-Smith et al. (1996). *Journal of Family Psychology, 10,* 137–141.

Howes, C., Hamilton, C. E., & Matheson, C. C. (1994). Children's relationships with peers: Differential associations with aspects of the teacher–child relationship. *Child Development, 65,* 253–263.

Howes, C., Matheson, C. C., & Hamilton, C. E. (1994). Maternal, teacher, and child care history correlates of children's relationships with peers. *Child Development, 65,* 264–273.

Hudley, C., & Graham, S. (1993). An attributional intervention to reduce peer-directed aggression among African-American boys. *Child Development, 64,* 124–138.

Hughes, J. N. (1992). Social psychology of consultation. In F. J. Medway & T. P. Cafferty (Eds.), *School psychology: A social psychological perspective* (pp. 269–303). Hillsdale, NJ: Erlbaum.

Hughes, J. N. (1994a). *Prevention of conduct problems and school failure in aggressive/disruptive low-achieving students: Final report submitted to Texas Education Agency.* Available from author, Department of Educational Psychology, Texas A&M University, College Station, TX 77843-4225.

Hughes, J. N. (1994b). Back to basics: Does consultation work? *Journal of Educational and Psychological Consultation, 5,* 77–84.

Hughes, J., & Cavell, T. A. (1994). Enhancing competence in aggressive children. In G. Cartledge & J. F. Milburn (Eds.), *Teaching social skills to children: Innovative approaches* (3rd ed., pp. 199–236). New York: Pergamon Press.

Hughes, J. N., Cavell, T. A., & Grossman, P. B. (1997). A positive view of self: Risk or protection for aggressive children? *Development and Psychopathology, 9,* 75–94.

Hughes, J. N., Cavell, T. A., & Jackson, T. (1999). Influence of teacher–student relationship on child-hood aggression: A prospective study. *Journal of Clinical Child Psychology, 28,* 173–184.

Individuals with Disabilities Education Act of 1990, 20 U.S.C. Section 1400 et seq. (1990).

Itskowitz, R., Navon, R., & Strauss, H. (1988). Teacher's accuracy in evaluating students' self-image: Effect of perceived closeness. *Journal of Educational Psychology, 80,* 337–341.

Jason, L. A., Ferone, L., & Anderegg, T. (1979). Evaluating ecological, behavioral, and process consultation interventions. *Journal of School Psychology, 17,* 103–115.

John F. Kennedy School of Government. (1997, July). Innovations in American government: 1996 Award Recipients. On-line document (http://ksgwww. harvard. edu/~innovat). JFK School of Government, Harvard University.

Kandel, D. (1973). Adolescent marijuana use. Role of parents and peers. *Science, 181,* 1067–1070.

Kazdin, A. E. (1993). Treatment of conduct disorder: Progress and directions in psychotherapy research. *Development and Psychopathology, 5,* 277–310.

Kazdin, A. E. (1997). Parent management training: Evidence, outcomes, and issues. *Journal of the American Academy of Child and Adolescent Psychiatry, 36,* 1349–1356.

Kazdin, A. E., Bass, D., Siegel, T., & Thomas, C. (1989). Cognitive-behavioral therapy and relationship therapy in the treatment of children referred for antisocial behavior. *Journal of Consulting and Clinical Psychology, 57,* 522–535.

Kazdin, A. E., Mazurick, J. L., & Bass, D. (1993). Risk for attrition in treatment of antisocial children and families. *Journal of Clinical Child Psychology, 22,* 2–16.

Kazdin, A. E., Siegel, T. C., & Bass, D. (1992). Cognitive problem-solving skills training and parent management training in the treatment of antisocial behavior in children. *Journal of Consulting and Clinical Psychology, 60,* 733–747.

Keenan, K., Loeber, R., Zhang, Q., Stouthamer-Loeber, M., & Van Kammen, W. B. (1995). The influence of deviant peers on the development of boys' disruptive and delinquent behavior: A temporal analysis. *Development and Psychopathology, 7,* 715–726.

Knitzer, J., Steinberg, Z., & Fleisch, B. (1990). *At the schoolhouse door: An examination of programs and policies for children with behavioral and emotional problems.* New York: Bank Street College of Education.

Kochanska, G. (1995). Children's temperament, mothers' discipline, and security of attachment: Multiple pathways to emerging internalization. *Child Development, 66,* 597–615.

Kratochwill, T. R., & Bergan, J. R. (1990). *Behavioral consultation in applied settings: An individual guide.* New York: Plenum Press.

Kratochwill, T. R., Elliott, S. N., & Busse, R. T. (1995). Behavior consultation: A five-year evaluation of consultant and client outcomes. *School Psychology Quarterly, 10,* 87–117.

Lieberman, A. F., Weston, D. R., & Pawl, J. H. (1991). Preventive intervention and outcome with anxiously attached dyads. *Child Development, 62,* 199–209.

Lochman, J. E. (1992). Cognitive-behavioral intervention with aggressive boys: Three-year follow-up and preventive effects. *Journal of Consulting and Clinical Psychology, 60,* 426–432.

Lochman, J. E., Coie, J. D., Underwood, M. R., & Terry, R. (1993). Effectiveness of social relations intervention program for aggressive and nonaggressive, rejected children. *Journal of Consulting and Clinical Psychology, 61,* 1053–1058.

Lochman, J. E., & Curry, J. F. (1986). Effects of social problem-solving training and self-instructional training with aggressive boys. *Journal of Clinical Child Psychology, 15,* 159–164.

Lochman, J. E., & Dodge, K. A. (1994). Social-cognitive processes of severely violent, moderately aggressive and nonaggressive boys. *Journal of Consulting and Clinical Psychology, 62*(2), 366–374.

Long, P., Forehand, R., Wierson, M., & Morgan, A. (1994). Does parent training with young noncompliant children have long-term effects? *Behaviour Research and Therapy, 32,* 101–107.

Lykken, D. T. (1995). *The antisocial personalities.* Hillsdale, NJ: Erlbaum.

Lyons-Ruth, K. (1996). Attachment relationships among children with aggressive behavior problems: The role of disorganized early attachment patterns. *Journal of Consulting and Clinical Psychology, 64,* 64–73.

McCord, J. (1996). Family as crucible for violence: Comment on Gorman-Smith et al. (1996). *Journal of Family Psychology, 10,* 147–152.

McNeil, C. B., Eyberg, S., Eisenstadt, T. H., Newcomb, K., & Funderburk, B. (1991). Parent–child interaction therapy with behavior problem children: Generalization of treatment effects to the school setting. *Journal of Clinical Child Psychology, 20,* 140–151.

Miller, G. E., & Prinz, R. J. (1990). Enhancement of social learning family interventions for childhood conduct disorder. *Psychological Bulletin, 108,* 291–307.

National Education Goals Panel. (1994). *The national education goals report: Building a nation of learners.* Washington, DC: U.S. Government Printing Office.

National Health/Education Consortium. (1990). *Creating sound minds and bodies: Health and education working together.* Washington, DC: Author.

O'Donnell, J., Hawkins, J. D., Catalano, R. F., Abbott, R. D., & Day, L. E. (1995). Preventing school failure, drug use, and delinquency among low-income children: Long-term intervention in elementary schools. *American Journal of Orthopsychiatry, 65,* 87–100.

O'Leary, K. P., & Becker, W. C. (1967). Behavior modification of an adjustment class: A token reinforcement program. *Exceptional Children, 33,* 637–642.

Ollendick, T., & Hersen, J. (1979). Social skills training for juvenile delinquents. *Behavior Research and Therapy, 17,* 547–554.

Paavola, J. D., Cobb, C., Illback, R. J., Joseph, H. M., Torruella, A., & Talley, R. C. (1995). *Comprehensive and coordinated psychological services for children: A call for service integration.* Washington, DC: American Psychological Association.

Patterson, G. R., & Brodsky, G. (1966). A behavior modification program for a child with multiple problem behaviors. *Journal of Child Psychology and Psychiatry, 7,* 277–295.

Patterson, G. R., Chamberlain, P., & Reid, J. B. (1982). A comparative evaluation of a parent-training program. *Behavior Therapy, 13,* 638–650.

Patterson, G. R., & Fleischman, M. J. (1979). Maintenance of treatment effects: Some considerations concerning family systems and follow-up data. *Behavior Therapy, 10,* 168–185.

Patterson, G. R., Reid, J. B., & Dishion, T. J. (1992). *Antisocial boys.* Eugene, OR: Castalia.

Pianta, R. C. (1994). Patterns of relationships between children and kindergarten teachers. *Journal of School Psychology, 32,* 15–32.

Pianta, R. C. (1999). *Enhancing relationships between children and teachers.* Washington, DC: American Psychological Association.

Pianta, R. C., Steinberg, M. S., & Rollins, K. B. (1995). The first two years of school: Teacher–child relationships and deflections in children's classroom adjustment. *Development and Psychopathology, 7,* 295–312.

Prinz, R. J., Blechman, E. A., & Dumas, J. E. (1994). An evaluation of peer coping-skills training for childhood aggression. *Journal of Clinical Child Psychology, 23,* 192–203.

Richters, J. E., & Waters, E. (1991). Attachment and socialization: The positive side of social influence. In M. Lewis & S. Feinman (Eds.), *Social influences and socialization in infancy* (pp. 185–214). New York: Plenum Press.

Robins, L. N. (1979). Follow-up studies. In H. C. Quay & J. S. Werry (Eds.), *Psychopathological disorders of childhood* (pp. 483–513). New York: Wiley.

Rogers-Wiese, M. R. (1992). A critical review of parent training research. *Psychology in the Schools, 29,* 229–236.

Rutter, M. (1996). Transitions and turning points in developmental psychopathology: As applied to the age span between childhood and mid-adulthood. *International Journal of Behavioral Development, 19,* 603–626.

Saxe, L., Cross, T., Silverman, N., & Batchelor, W. F. (1987). *Children's mental health: Problems and treatment.* Durham, NC: Duke University Press.

Schonfeld, I. S., Shaffer, D., O'Connor, P., & Portnoy, S. (1988). Conduct disorder and cognitive functioning: Testing three causal hypotheses. *Child Development, 59,* 993–1007.

Schorr, L. B., & Schorr, D. (1988). *Within our reach: Breaking the cycle of disadvantage.* New York: Anchor.

Serketich, W. J., & Dumas, J. E. (1996). The effectiveness of behavioral parent training to modify antisocial behavior in children: A meta-analysis. *Behavior Therapy, 27,* 171–186.

Shaw, D. S., & Bell, R. Q. (1993). Developmental theories of parental contributors to antisocial behavior. *Journal of Abnormal Child Psychology, 21,* 493–518.

Sheeber, L. B., & Johnson, J. H. (1994). Evaluation of a temperament-focused, parent training program. *Journal of Clinical Child Psychology, 23,* 249–259.

Solomon, D., Watson, M., Battistich, V., Schaps, E., & Delucchi, K. (1992). Creating a caring community: Educational practices that promote children's prosocial development. In F. K. Oser, A. Dick, & J. L. Patry (Eds.), *Effective and responsible teaching: The new synthesis* (pp. 383–396). San Francisco: Jossey–Bass.

Spence, S. H., & Marzillier, J. S. (1981). Social skills training with adolescent male offenders II. Short-term and generalized effects. *Behavior Research and Therapy, 19,* 349–368.

Sroufe, L. A., & Fleeson, J. (1986). Attachment and the construction of relationships. In W. W. Hartup & Z. Rubin (Eds.), *Relationships and development* (pp. 51–71). Hillsdale, NJ: Erlbaum.

Stattin, H., & Magnusson, D. (1989). The role of early aggressive behavior in the frequency, seriousness, and types of later crimes. *Journal of Consulting and Clinical Psychology, 57,* 710–718.

Stattin, H., & Magnusson, D. (1996). Antisocial development: A holistic approach. *Development and Psychopathology, 8,* 617–646.

Stein, D. (1987). Companionship factors and treatment effects in children. *Journal of Clinical Child Psychology, 16,* 141–146.

Steinberg, L. (1986). Latchkey children and susceptibility to peer pressure: An ecological analysis. *Developmental Psychology, 22,* 433–439.

Stolberg, A. L., & Gourley, E. V., III. (1996). A school-based intervention for children of divorce: The children's support group. In M. C. Roberts (Ed.), *Model programs in child and family mental health* (pp. 75–89). Hillsdale, NJ: Erlbaum.

Taylor, L. (1982). The effects of a non-related adult friend on children of divorce. *Journal of Divorce, 5,* 67–76.

Tharinger, D. J., Bricklin, P., Johnson, N. F., Paster, V., Lambert, N. M., Feshbach, N., Oakland, T. D., & Sanchez, W. (1996). Education reform: Challenges for psychology and psychologists. *Professional Psychology: Research and Practice, 27,* 24–33.

Tolan, P. H. (1996). Characteristics shared by exemplary child clinical interventions for indicated populations. In M. C. Roberts (Ed.), *Model programs in child and family mental health* (pp. 91–108). Hillsdale, NJ: Erlbaum.

Walker, H. M., & Buckley, N. K. (1973). Teacher attention to appropriate and inappropriate classroom behavior: An individual case study. *Focus on Exceptional Children, 5,* 5–11.

Webster-Stratton, C. (1987). *The parents and children series.* Eugene, OR: Castalia.

Webster-Stratton, C. (1990). Long-term follow-up of families with young conduct problem children: From preschool to grade school. *Journal of Clinical Child Psychology, 19,* 144–149.

Webster-Stratton, C., & Hammond, M. (1990). Predictors of treatment outcome in parent training for families with conduct disordered children. *Behavior Therapy, 21,* 319–337.

Webster-Stratton, C., & Herbert, M. (1994). *Troubled families—problem children.* New York: Wiley.

Werner, E. E., & Smith, R. S. (1982). *Vulnerable but invincible: A longitudinal study of resilient children and youth.* New York: McGraw-Hill.

West, D. J., & Farrington, D. P. (1977). *The delinquent way of life.* London: Heinemann.

Witt, J. C., & Martens, B. K. (1988). Problems with problem-solving consultation: A reanalysis of assumptions, methods, and goals. *School Psychology Review, 17,* 211–226.

Zins, J. E., Kratochwill, T. R., & Elliott, S. N. (Eds.). (1993). *Handbook of consultation services for children.* San Francisco: Jossey–Bass.

23

Psychological Interventions for Children with Chronic Physical Illness and Their Families
Toward Integration of Research and Practice

DENNIS DROTAR

The importance of and necessity for psychological interventions with children with chronic physical illness stem from several sources. First, chronic physical illness affects large numbers of children and families. Depending on how a chronic condition is defined, estimates of affected children vary from 5% to 30% (Newacheck & Taylor, 1992). For the purpose of this chapter, a chronic or ongoing health condition is defined as one that lasts a year or longer and requires specialized treatments, technologies and/or causes limitations of function, activities, or social roles, compared with physically healthy peers (Stein, Bauman, Westbrook, Coupey, & Ireys, 1993). Second, a chronic illness and its treatment place significant physical and psychological burdens on children and families that affect the quality of their lives, including their mental health. Although children demonstrate a wide range of psychological adjustment patterns to their chronic conditions (Drotar, 1981; Drotar & Bush, 1985), the heightened risk to the child's mental health associated with chronic conditions is relatively well documented. For example, population-based studies such as the Ontario Health Study have reported a threefold risk of mental health and social problems among children with chronic physical illness, especially among those who also have physical disabilities (Cad-

DENNIS DROTAR • School of Medicine, Case Western Reserve University, Cleveland, Ohio 44106-6038.

Handbook of Psychotherapies with Children and Families, edited by Russ and Ollendick. Kluwer Academic/Plenum Publishers, New York, 1999.

man, Boyle, Szatmari, & Offord, 1997). Meta-analyses have also indicated an elevated risk for mental health disorders, especially internalizing problems, among children with a chronic illness (Lavigne & Faier-Routman, 1992).

The psychological impact of chronic illness transcends the individual child and affects the entire family, including siblings and parents. Cadman, Boyle, and Offord (1988) noted a twofold increase in risk for emotional disorders, especially depression and anxiety, among siblings of children with chronic illness. In addition, the high level of emotional distress that is experienced by mothers of children with chronic illness, who bear the lion's share of the child's caregiving burden, has been a robust finding (Hausenstein, 1990; Jessop, Riessman, & Stein, 1989). Finally, over and beyond the effects of a chronic illness on child and family mental health, are the significant health problems and economic costs that are raised by a child's and family's lack of compliance with difficult medical regimens, which is a frequent problem (LaGreca & Schuman, 1995).

Taken together, the weight of the empirical evidence suggests that mental health interventions are needed to reduce the level and burden of psychological problems that are experienced by children with chronic physical illness and their families and prevent some of these problems from occurring. The purpose of this chapter is to present an integrated view of research and practice concerning psychological interventions in childhood chronic illness. Readers who are interested in the general topic of chronic illness and its psychological consequences on children and their families might wish to consult early influential work such as Pless and Pinkerton (1975) and Hobbs and Perrin (1985), or more recent descriptions (Eiser, 1990; Garrison & McQuiston, 1989; Siegel, Smith, & Wood, 1991; Thompson & Gustafson, 1995).

THEORETICAL APPROACHES THAT APPLY TO PSYCHOLOGICAL INTERVENTIONS FOR CHILDREN WITH CHRONIC HEALTH CONDITIONS

Several theoretical perspectives are very relevant to understanding the nature of psychological risk in childhood chronic illness and in designing interventions to reduce such risk. For example, the risk and resistance models developed by Wallander, Varni, Babani, Banis, and Wilkox (1989) and elaborated by Thompson and his colleagues (Thompson & Gustafson, 1996; Thompson, Gustafson, Hamlett, & Spock, 1992) have been highly influential in guiding research on childhood chronic illness. In these models, risk factors include disease and disability-related stressors imposed by severity of illness or handicap and handicap-related problems, major life events, and daily stressors. The impact of these risk factors is moderated by three basic types of resistance factors: (1) stable intrapersonal factors, e.g., personality; (2) stress processing or coping ability; and (3) social-ecological influences, such as the quality of family relationships, and support. Substantial empirical support has been obtained for the role of these risk and resistance models in studies of the relationship of parent and family functioning to psychological outcomes of children with a range of chronic conditions (Drotar, 1997; Thompson & Gustafson, 1996).

The Double ABCX Model of Family Adaptation (McCubbin & Patterson, 1982), which focuses on processes by which families adapt to a crisis, such as the diagnosis of a chronic illness or handicap, is clearly applicable to childhood chronic illness. Salient features of this model include the concept of "pileup" of demands on family resources and the identification of family coping strategies. It should be noted that the concept of the diagnosis of a chronic illness as a crisis has also been an influential framework for the model of medical crisis counseling that has largely focused on adults with chronic illness, but also has clinical application to children and their families (Polin, 1991, Shapiro & Koocher, 1996).

An extension of the Double ABCX Model, the Family Adjustment and Adaptation Response (FAAR) model (Patterson, 1988), emphasizes the meanings that family members attribute to stressors, e.g., the family's subjective definition of demands and capabilities. In a time of crisis, such as the diagnosis of a chronic illness in a child, family members may reduce stress and restore adaptation by (1) acquiring new adaptive resources and/or coping behaviors, (2) reducing the pileup of demands, or (3) changing the way they perceive their potentially stressful situation.

According to the FAAR model, families use many resources and capabilities for meeting demands, including financial, personal (e.g., self-esteem, knowledge, and skills), family systems resources (e.g., cohesion, organization, and communication skills), and community resources (e.g., schools, churches, medical care, and social support). Coping behaviors, which are a major family resource in the FAAR model, are defined as actions that family members take to reduce demands or acquire resources, changing the meaning of a situation to make it more manageable. The FAAR model assumes that some families are much more vulnerable than others to the impact of chronic stress. For example, specific family relationship resource problems such as conflicted patterns of interaction may develop into chronic strains. On the other hand, families with very high levels of resources are assumed to be resilient to most stresses. The FAAR model has received some support with pediatric populations, such as children with cystic fibrosis (Patterson, 1985).

Conceptualizing Interventions for Children with Chronic Health Conditions

While empirical studies of mental health interventions for children and chronic illness have not generally been guided explicitly by theory (Bauman, Drotar, Leventhal, Perrin, & Pless, 1997), there are interesting potential applications of the above models (Drotar, 1992). For example, in both FAAR and Varni–Wallander models, psychological intervention is defined as resource or support that is designed to reduce the negative effects of stressors or demands of a chronic illness or other risk factors, such as family conflict, and thus enhance the child's psychological adjustment. Such resources may include information about the child's condition, generalized support and advocacy, or direct help with financial resources as well as targeted psychological interventions designed to ameliorate or prevent psychological distress among children or family members (Drotar & Bush, 1985). Patterson (1988) has described one important role of intervention as helping family members acquire "resistance capabilities," which may include specific coping behaviors, positive appraisals of their child's chronic condition, or support groups. In the Varni, Wallander, and Thompson models, risk factors such as severity of disability and illness-related psychosocial stressors are assumed to be fixed and hence not amenable to direct intervention. On the other hand, resistance resources such as intrapersonal factors (e.g., problem-solving ability), social-ecological factors (e.g., social support), and coping strategies are potentially modifiable targets of intervention (Thompson & Gustafson, 1996; Wallander *et al.*, 1989).

Hobfoll's (1988, 1989) theoretical perspectives on psychological stress are also very relevant to interventions for chronic childhood illness. In his model, stress is conceptualized as a reaction to the environment in which there is a threat of loss of resources, or the lack of resource gain following the investment of resources. Successful interventions are hypothesized as reducing the level of stress experienced by the child and family by preventing loss of critical psychological resources, e.g., personal esteem and sense of mastery, to which children and families with chronic illnesses are vulnerable (Hobfoll, 1989) and/or by reducing the vicious cycles of problematic communication and problem solving that can occur in some highly stressed families (Drotar, 1997).

PRESENTING PSYCHOSOCIAL PROBLEMS EXPERIENCED BY CHILDREN WITH CHRONIC HEALTH CONDITIONS AND THEIR FAMILIES

The heterogeneity in physical problems and illness severity encountered among children with chronic physical illness raises significant challenges for designing psychological interventions. Although very different chronic illnesses present common core challenges and burdens to children and families that often need to be addressed in interventions (Stein & Jessop, 1982), the specific expressions of illness-related demands of psychological distress can vary significantly as a function of the specific condition and situational context of treatment (Quittner et al., 1996), the stage of the child's illness (Rolland, 1987), and/or the child's developmental level (Garrison & McQuiston, 1989). Consequently, both generic and illness-specific effects of children's chronic health conditions need to be considered in designing and evaluating interventions.

A second issue that needs to be considered in planning psychological interventions for this population concerns the marked heterogeneity in the type and severity of psychological adjustment problems experienced by children with chronic illness that are encountered in clinical practice: Children with chronic illness present with a wide range of disorders that are classifiable by the *Diagnostic and Statistical Manual* (DSM-IV) (American Psychiatric Association, 1994) as well as other problems that bring them to clinical attention, e.g., problems adjusting to changes or deterioration in health, problems with pain, difficulties with adherence to treatment, and so forth. To give readers a feel for some of the adjustment problems that are experienced by children with chronic physical illness and their families, several typical problems are described next.

Depression

Kate, a 12-year-old with cancer, presented with chronic tiredness and vague pains not explainable by the severity of her illness. Kate had not attended school for more than a year and gradually lost interest in peers and outside activities. Feeling that her peers did not accept her because of her illness, she had given up trying to tell them about it. At home, her parents had gradually given up efforts to involve her in activities. Kate's problems benefited from both individual and family discussions that clarified her isolation and the parents' feeling of grief.

Problems with Compliance

Alex, a 16-year-old, was admitted to the hospital for evaluation and intervention concerning his emotional problems and control of his diabetes. His control of his diabetes has been quite problematic. Alex noted that family problems played a role in his problems, including serious conflict with his parents about his diabetes and a number of adolescent issues. In addition to these problems with his family, Alex often struggled with accepting diabetes and the demands of his treatment. He also had a strong fear of needles and described his getting up in the morning and worrying about taking his insulin and felt trapped in a vicious cycle where he would begin by omitting one dose in the morning, which would sometimes progress to several insulin doses, as he began to feel discouraged by his lack of progress.

Parent–Child Relationship Problems

The demands of a chronic illness can sometimes place significant strain on parent–child relationships as shown by Jay, a 16-year-old young man with cystic fibrosis who was referred for evaluation of poor school achievement. Psychological evaluation indicated that Jay was not really an underachiever, as his parents had suggested, but rather was in conflict with his parents about their excessively high standards for his achievement. His parents' standards were based on their wish that he become a "supernormal" adolescent, in contrast to one who is affected with a serious illness. His parents minimized the severity of his condition and not only expected him to behave as if he did not have a chronic illness, but actually achieve at a much higher level than his physically healthy sister.

BARRIERS TO MENTAL HEALTH INTERVENTIONS FOR CHILDREN WITH CHRONIC HEALTH CONDITIONS

The management of psychological problems associated with chronic illness needs to be closely integrated in the clinical setting where these problems are managed. Children with chronic health conditions are generally cared for in large medical settings, which vary widely in their level of staffing, comprehensiveness of care provided, and access to mental health specialists. The structure and organization of medical care as well as the physical demands of caring for a child with a chronic physical illness can seriously interfere with families' access to mental health services for their children with chronic health conditions. For example, Cadman et al. (1987) found that among children with chronic physical illness who also had a diagnosable mental health disorder, only one in four received mental health services.

There are several potential barriers to effective mental health referral and interventions for children with chronic physical illness (Sabbeth & Stein, 1990). For example, a child's physical illness can generate intense emotions for parents that heighten their need to deny the magnitude and implications of the child's psychological problems. Parents may also feel that the medical team will question the quality of their care if their child is identified as having a psychological problem. Problems with insurance and physical limitations also may make it very difficult for children with a chronic illness to receive mental health care. Moreover, relatively few mental health professionals have had specialized training to conduct psychological interventions with children with a chronic physical illness. Such limitations in training may increase mental health professionals' hesitancy to see such children or limit parents' interest in treatment.

Barriers to mental health intervention can also be created by the medical team. For example, some pediatricians may be hesitant to refer children for mental health treatment because they are concerned about labeling them and do not want to cause the family additional distress. In addition, the medical staff may not be familiar with the range of behavioral norms for children with medical conditions (Sabbeth & Stein, 1990).

EFFICACY OF PSYCHOLOGICAL INTERVENTION IN CHILDHOOD CHRONIC ILLNESS

Another set of barriers to effective mental health interventions for children with chronic illness and their families is raised by limitations in knowledge concerning the efficacy of interventions. Controlled empirical trials of psychological interventions with children with chronic physical illness are very difficult to design and implement. Children with chronic health conditions and their families are burdened by a great many stressors that may make it difficult for them to be recruited and maintained in intervention research. In addition, the numbers of children with specific chronic illness in any one setting are relatively small, and multisite studies are very difficult to implement (Drotar, 1994). Recently, Bauman et al. (1997) evaluated peer-reviewed articles that were published in English between 1979 and 1993 that met the following criteria: (1) primary focus on children with chronic health condition or their family members, (2) described a planned psychosocial intervention, (3) evaluated a program for psychological or social outcomes, (4) had a sample size of 15 or greater in the experimental group, and (5) included a comparison group. Computer searches generated 266 articles, of which only 15 met the above criteria. Education was the most frequent intervention method that was provided, but social skills training, support, and peer counseling were also represented.

Methodological problems such as inadequate descriptions of programs and participants, use of heterogeneous, single-site samples, lack of statistical power, and lack of statistical correction for multiple comparisons were identified. However, the good news in this review was that 11 of the 15 studies described significant effects of interventions on children's behavior and mental health. Effective interventions tended to focus on specific individuals, e.g., child or parents, and were targeted on specific targets, e.g., enhancing support and communication. Examples of models of intervention that were found to be effective are described in this section.

Enhancing Level of Support Provided to Mothers

Several studies have documented the effectiveness of targeted support for mothers of children with chronic health conditions. One of the best-known examples of these programs, The Pediatric Ambulatory Care Treatments (PACT) program, assessed the impact of a program that was designed to provide integrated biomedical and psychosocial care to children with a wide range of different chronic illnesses. In addition to comprehensive medical care, PACT provided coordination of health services and social/community resources, education of child, and family background of chronic condition and training in self-care skills. The intervention model included an initial home visit by pediatric nurse practitioner and general pediatrician and at least one contact a month thereafter in person or by telephone for a period of at least 6 months (Stein & Jessop, 1984).

Results of this study showed that at 6- to 12-month follow-up as hypothesized, children who received the comprehensive care program had better psychological adjustment than children who received medical standard care (Stein & Jessop, 1984). In addition, mothers who received the comprehensive care program had fewer psychiatric symptoms and greater satisfaction with care. These findings were maintained on a 5-year follow-up and, in fact, were even stronger than they were on initial follow-up (Stein & Jessop, 1991). However, these interventions did not affect the impact of the illness on the child's family or the child's functional status.

Ireys, Sills, Kolodner, and Walsh (1996) tested the efficacy of a comprehensive social support intervention including informational support (e.g., sharing information), affirmational support (e.g., identification of competency and giving positive feedback), and emotional support (e.g., listening to concerns) that was provided by mentors who were mothers of adults who had juvenile rheumatoid arthritis since childhood. Mothers who received the intervention demonstrated greater improvement on several measures of support relative to controls. The total number of reported mental health symptoms decreased in the experimental group and remained the same in the control group.

Family-Centered Intervention Models

Family-centered intervention models, which involve multiple family members, have also received empirical support. For example, Lewis, Hatton, Salas, Leake and Chiofalo (1991) and Lewis, Salas, de la Sota, Chiofalo and Leake (1990) tested the efficacy of a child-centered and family-focused intervention on the adjustment of parents and children with epilepsy in a randomized, controlled clinical trial. The counseling model was designed to help mothers deal with their anger and resentment and grief concerning their children's conditions, to increase their knowledge about caring for their child, reduce anxieties related to having a child with a seizure disorder, and also improve their decision-making skills. The intervention reduced parents' anxiety levels but effects on children's adjustment were less powerful.

In another study, Pless et al. (1994) tested the efficacy of a family-centered nursing intervention that focused on helping families manage the impact of the chronic illness on the family, address parental concerns related to their children's behavior and school performance, parenting issues, helping the family change their perceptions about their situation, improve their problem solving, enhance emotional support, and acquire the resources and services that would best meet their needs. Intervention was associated with less anxiety and depression, and greater scholastic confidence and global self-worth among children with different chronic conditions.

Training in Social Skills and Problem Solving

Owing to the impact of their condition on physical appearance, school attendance, and so forth, many children with chronic health conditions are exposed to stigma and social stressors, which can be very distressing. These children need to learn effective ways to cope with these problems. Varni, Katz, Colegrove, and Dolgin (1993) evaluated the efficacy of a social skills training program for children with cancer combined with school reintegration services versus a group that received only the school integration services. Social skills training included problem identification, assertiveness training, and coping with verbal and physical teasing associated with changes in physical appearance. At 9-month follow-up, children who received the social problem-solving skills training reported less internalizing and externalizing problems and greater classmate and teacher/social support than children in the comparison group.

Enhancing School Reintegration

From the child's vantage point, one of the most problematic features of a chronic illness is the potential disruption on school attendance and socialization experiences. Katz and his colleagues (Katz, Varni, Rubenstein, Blew & Hubert, 1988) have developed a program designed to help children newly diagnosed with cancer return to school as quickly as possible. The program included arranging conferences with school personnel to help them understand basic facts about the child's illness and medical treatment, planning for absences, anticipating peers' reactions to the child, and formulating an individualized educational plan. Classroom presentations provided peers with information about their illness, medical procedures, and common side effects such as hair loss. Contact with school personnel and parents also took place after the child returned to school. Compared with pretest measures, children who received the intervention (and their parents) reported fewer internalizing and behavioral problems, more social confidence, less self-reported depressive symptoms, greater perceived social confidence, and had better adjustment to school as rated by their teachers.

Education and Stress Management

Many children with chronic illness have special needs for information and management of the specific stresses associated with their conditions. Perrin, Maclean, Gortmaker, and Asher (1992) assessed the effectiveness of a combined education and stress management program among school-age children with asthma. Their approach to education was based on a developmental model of children's concepts of illness and focused on helping children learn about their asthma and symptoms. Children also learned about methods of prevention and treatment, medications, and so forth. Stress management included relaxation training, which emphasized deep breathing through guided imagery and muscle relaxation. In addition, contingency coping exercises targeted specific difficulties each child had encountered in coping with their asthma and alternative choices of action, including strategies for coping. Children who were randomized to the intervention group had fewer behavior problems and internalizing symptoms compared with controls.

Evans et al. (1987) studied the effects of health education on self-management skills, self efficacy, and school attendance of children with asthma from 12 elementary schools. This program focused on enhancing the child's responsibility for recognizing his or her symptoms and taking appropriate management steps. Follow-up that was obtained 1 year after the program ended showed that the experimental group had better asthma management skills, higher grades in school, and fewer episodes of asthma and of shorter duration and more influence on parents' asthma management decisions than controls.

DILEMMAS RAISED BY INTEGRATING RESEARCH-BASED MENTAL HEALTH INTERVENTIONS IN CLINICAL CARE

Despite their promising results, the above intervention programs have not been routinely integrated into practice settings, which is a common dilemma in child mental health services (Kazdin, Bass, Ayers, & Rodgers, 1990). In pediatric settings, the large number of children who are affected with chronic health conditions outstrips the resources that are generally available for mental health services. Consequently, psychologists and other mental health practitioners must disperse their collaborative efforts across a large number of pediatric subspecialties and their intervention resources across a large number of children and adolescents with different chronic conditions. Consequently, with some exceptions, they cannot dedicate the time that is needed to develop an integrated program of research and practice that is focused on a specific chronic illness population.

A second reason for the lack of integration of empirically based treatments in practice settings is that children with chronic health conditions present with heterogeneous, multifaceted problems that are difficult to manage with protocol-driven interventions and require highly individualized approaches. For example, consider Jerry, a 16-year-old, who had a history of cancer at ages 5–7 and was now considered a survivor. However, when this unfortunate young man also developed diabetes, his endocrinologist expressed concern about his potential emotional reaction. Jerry lived with his mother and older brother. His parents had been divorced for several years. Although he saw his father, he felt estranged from him. Jerry's mother was quite protective of him and very vigilant about his every move. There was a family history of affective disorder, including depression. Jerry was painfully shy and had trouble initiating activities with male and female peers because he was very fearful of rejection from others. He eventually shared his painful memories about how he had been traumatized by his experience of cancer. For example, as a younger child, he felt quite rejected by his peers' negative reactions to him because of his hair loss. Jerry made some progress in managing his feelings more adaptively in short-term cognitive–behavioral treatment. However, a year later he developed a major depression, for which he needed psychiatric consultation and medication, which facilitated improved functioning.

NEW DIRECTIONS

Although progress has been made in developing mental health services for children with chronic health conditions in some pediatric settings (Drotar, 1995) and empirically based mental health interventions for this population (Bauman et al., 1997), much more needs to be done (Pless & Stein, 1994). Promising future directions include testing new models of interventions that are tailored to the wide range of problems seen in practice, documenting the social validity of mental health interventions for children with chronic illness, identifying key moderators of the impact of psychological interventions, assessing children's access to mental health intervention as well as the costs and benefits and efficiency of these interventions, and developing programs of integrated research and practice with specific chronic illness populations.

Testing New Models of Psychological Intervention

Cognitive–behavioral interventions, which have been shown to be effective with physically healthy, psychologically distressed children (Kendall & Southam-Gerow, 1997), have clear application to children with chronic health conditions who demonstrate anxiety and depression. Hains, Davies, Behrens, and Biller (1997) described the utility of cognitive–behavioral intervention in a case series of adolescents with cystic fibrosis. The three key elements of this treatment approach were (1) a conceptualization phase in which adolescents were taught the theoretical basis for cognitive restructuring and problem solving and to identify negative, self-defeating cognition; (2) a skills acquisition and rehearsal phase in which these adolescents were taught to question their self-defeating thoughts by examining evidence and problem-solving strategies to stress; and (3) an acquisition phase in which the youths were given the opportunity to practice skills in anticipation of future or potential stressors. This intervention model was associated with decreases in anxiety and negative coping techniques concerning problems related to cystic fibrosis, and perceived functional disability as well as increases in positive coping (Hains et al., 1997). These data suggest that this intervention warrants evaluation in a larger sample, ideally in the context of a randomized control study.

Another example of a promising new intervention that may eventually have wide applicability for children with chronic health conditions is massage therapy (Field, 1995). In a recent report, Field et al. (1997) reported that children with juvenile rheumatoid arthritis who received a daily 15-minute massage by one of their parents for over 30 days experienced immediate lowering of anxiety and decrease in pain and pain-limiting activities over 30 days compared with controls who experienced a relaxation session. These data suggest that massage therapy may offer a cost-effective treatment that clearly warrants further study.

Documenting the Social Validity of Mental Health Interventions for Children with Chronic Illness

The target problems and/or perceived need for mental health intervention that are identified by children with chronic illness may not coincide with those of their parents or practitioners. Consequently, an important, but neglected, set of questions in clinical intervention with pediatric populations concerns the following: Do those children and families who have received psychological treatments find them acceptable and applicable to their problems? Do they regard them as relevant to their lives and effective in managing problems that distress them?

In an interesting study of the social validity of family interventions, Wysocki et al. (1997) found that adolescents rated the acceptability of an education and support group lower than their parents did and lower than a behavior family systems approach (Robin & Foster, 1989), which is a promising approach to enhance adherence to medical regimens for adolescents with diabetes (Wysocki, White, Bubb, Harris, & Greco, 1995).

Unfortunately, very little is known about the quality of care and/or patient/ family satisfaction with psychological services for children with chronic conditions (for exceptions, see Baine, Rosenbaum, & King, 1995; Krahn, Eisert, & Fifield, 1990). The impact of such parameters as timeliness and access of psychological intervention on the reduction of psychological symptoms and patient, family, and provider satisfaction should be assessed. Shapiro, Walker, and Jacobson (1997) have developed a measure of children's satisfaction with mental health services that could be adapted for use with pediatric chronic illness populations.

Documenting Access, Costs, and Efficiency of Mental Health Intervention

Another critical, but unanswered, question is the access to psychological services among children with chronic health conditions, who struggle with significant barriers that limit their access to psychological services despite high levels of need (Sabbeth & Stein, 1990) and may have special problems with access to both health and mental health services under managed care (Newacheck et al. 1996).

Clinical practitioners appreciate that a given model of psychological intervention may have a very different impact on individual differences in children with chronic health conditions and their families. However, little is known about how such factors as comorbid problems and associated risk and protective factors influence the outcomes of psychological interventions with children with chronic illness. In an example of the kind of data that are needed, Jessop and Stein (1991) determined which subgroups benefited most (relative to controls) and which benefited least from a pediatric home care program that had been shown to be effective in prior research (Stein & Jessop, 1984). These authors found that maximal benefits of intervention were evident when the family's illness burden was small and their coping resources (social, educational, financial, and personal) were low. Their findings suggested that the conventional treatment priority of allocating intervention resources to the families whose children have the greatest medical burden may not be the most beneficial strategy.

The above example also suggests how empirical data may inform more effective allocation of psychological interventions. The economic costs and benefits of mental health interventions have been neglected for children with chronic health problems (for an exception, see Pinto & Hollandsworth, 1989), but should be studied, especially given the realities of resource allocation under managed care (Newacheck et al., 1996).

Developing Integrated Programs of Research and Practice for Children with Chronic Health Problems

Although integrated programs of research and practice for children with chronic health conditions are all too rare in many pediatric settings, some pediatric psychologists have developed such models. One example is Kazak and Meadow's (in press) comprehensive service, teaching, and research program in the division of oncology at the Childrens Hospital of Philadelphia. This program features a wide range of clinical services such as primary psychosocial care, strong links with community resources, school consultation, psychological consultation and evaluation, and specialized services such as support groups for parents, siblings, and adolescent and young adult survivors of cancer. Ongoing research in this program focuses on assessment and evaluation of clinical interventions, including prospective outcomes of psychological and pharmacological intervention protocols for reducing distress in pediatric leukemia (Kazak et al., 1996). The scientific information that has been generated by this team is characterized by clinical relevance and rigorous evaluation, which is a very difficult combination to achieve. I would hope that other programs would follow their lead.

SUMMARY

The development of psychological interventions for children with chronic health conditions and their families has been informed by progress in theories concerning risk and resilience factors and empirical tests of various intervention models. Intervention approaches that have received empirical support include those that are designed to enhance the following outcomes: maternal support and coping, family problem solving, support and coping, children's social skills, problem solving, and stress management, and children's reintegration into school following hospitalization. Despite their promising results, integration of such interventions into practice settings has generally not occurred and remains an important goal for the future.

Other important future directions involve improving the quantity and methodological quality of research on psychological interventions for children with chronic health conditions. In particular, new research is needed to test models of interventions that can be applied to the wide range of clinical problems that are seen in practice, document the social validity of mental health interventions for children with chronic illness and their families, identify key moderators of the impact of psychological interventions, assess children's access to mental health interventions, and document the costs, benefits, and efficiency of such interventions.

ACKNOWLEDGMENT

The assistance of Anne Brennan in processing this chapter is gratefully acknowledged. Preparation of this manuscript was funded in part by a Cleveland Foundation grant: The Center for Chronic Illness.

REFERENCES

American Psychiatric Association. (1994). *Diagnostic and statistical manual of mental disorders* (4th ed.). Washington, DC: Author.

Baine, S., Rosenbaum, P., & King, S. (1995). Chronic childhood illnesses: What aspects of care giving do parents value? *Child: Care, Growth, and Development, 21,* 291–304.

Bauman, L. J., Drotar, D., Leventhal, J. M., Perrin, E. C., & Pless, I. B. (1997). A review of psychosocial interventions for children with chronic health conditions. *Pediatrics, 100,* 244–251.

Cadman, D., Boyle, M. L., & Offord, D. R. (1988). The Ontario Child Health Study: Social adjustment and mental health of siblings of children with chronic health problems. *Journal of Developmental and Behavioral Pediatrics, 9,* 117–121.

Cadman, D., Boyle, M., Szatmari, P., & Offord, D. R. (1987). Chronic illness, disability and mental and social well-being. *Pediatrics, 79,* 805–812.

Drotar, D. (1981). Psychological perspectives in childhood chronic illness. *Journal of Pediatric Psychology, 6,* 211–228.

Drotar, D. (1992). Integrating theory and practice in psychological interventions with children with a chronic illness. In J. Akamatsu, M. E. P. Stephens, S. E. Hobfoll, & J. H. Crowler (Eds.), *Family health psychology* (pp. 175–192). Washington, DC: Hemisphere Press.

Drotar, D. (1994). Psychological research with pediatric conditions: If we specialize, can we generalize? *Journal of Pediatric Psychology, 19,* 403–414.

Drotar, D. (1995). *Consulting with pediatricians: Psychological perspectives.* New York: Plenum Press.

Drotar, D. (1997). Relating parent and family functioning to the psychological adjustment of children with chronic health conditions: What have we learned? What do we need to know? *Journal of Pediatric Psychology, 22,* 149–165.

Drotar, D., & Bush, M. (1985). Mental health issues and services. In N. Hobbs & J. H. Perrin (Eds.), *Issues in the care of children with chronic illness* (pp. 514–550). San Francisco: Jossey–Bass.

Eiser, C. (1990). *Chronic childhood illness: An introduction to psychological theory and research.* London: Cambridge University Press.

Evans, D., Clark, N. M., Feldman, C. H., Rips, J., Kaplen, D., Levison, M. J., Wasilewski, Y., Levin, B., & Mellins, C. (1987). A school health education program for children with asthma aged 8–11 years. *Health Education Quarterly,* Fall, *14,* 267–279.

Field, T. (1995). Massage therapy for infants and children. *Journal of Developmental and Behavioral Pediatrics, 16,* 105–111.

Field, T., Hernandez-Reif, M., Seligman, S., Krasnegor, J., Sunshine, W., Rivas-Chacon, R., Schanberg, S., & Kuhn, C. (1997). Juvenile rheumatoid arthritis benefits from massage therapy. *Journal of Pediatric Psychology, 22,* 607–617.

Garrison, W. T., & McQuiston, S. (1989). *Chronic illness during childhood and adolescence. Psychological aspects.* Newbury Park, CA: Sage.

Hains, A. A., Davies, W. B., Behrens, D., & Biller, J. A. (1997). Cognitive behavioral interventions for adolescents with cystic fibrosis. *Journal of Pediatric Psychology, 22,* 669–687.

Hausenstein, E. J. (1990). The experience of distress in parents of chronically ill children. Potential or likely outcome? *Journal of Clinical Child Psychology, 19,* 356–364.

Hobbs, N., & Perrin, J. M. (Eds.). (1985). *Issues in the care of children with chronic illness.* San Francisco: Jossey–Bass.

Hobfoll, S. E. (1988). *The ecology of stress.* Washington, DC: Hemisphere Press.

Hobfoll, S. E. (1989). Conservation of resources: A new attempt at conceptualizing stress. *American Psychologist, 44,* 513–524.

Ireys, H. T., Sills, E. M., Kolodner, K. B., & Walsh, B. R. (1996). A social support intervention for parents of children with juvenile rheumatoid arthritis results of a randomized trial. *Journal of Pediatric Psychology, 21,* 633–641.

Jessop, D. J., Riessman, L. K., & Stein, R. E. K. (1989). Chronic childhood illness and maternal mental health. *Journal of Developmental and Behavioral Pediatrics, 9,* 147–158.

Jessop, D. J., & Stein, R. E. K. (1991). Who benefits from a pediatric home care program? *Pediatrics, 88,* 497–505.

Katz, E. R., Varni, J. W., Rubenstein, C. L., Blew, A., & Hubert, N. (1992). Teacher, parent, and child evaluative ratings of school reintegration intervention for children with newly diagnosed cancer. *Children's Health Care, 21,* 69–75.

Kazak, A. E., & Meadows, A. (in press). Integrating psychosocial research and practice in a pediatric cancer treatment center. In D. Drotar (Ed.), *Handbook of research in pediatric and clinical child psychology.* New York: Plenum Press.

Kazak, A. E., Penati, B., Bryer, B. A., Himelstein, B., Brophy, P., Waibel, M. K., Blackall, G. F., Daller, R., & Johnson, K. (1996). A randomized controlled prospective outcome study of psychological and pharmacological intervention protocol for reducing distress in pediatric leukemia. *Journal of Pediatric Psychology, 21,* 615–632.

Kazdin, A. E., Bass, D., Ayers, W. A., & Rodgers, A. (1990). Empirical and clinical focus of child and adolescent psychotherapy research. *Journal of Consulting and Clinical Psychology, 57,* 138–147.

Kendall, P. C., & Southam-Gerow, M. A. (1996). Long-term follow up of a cognitive-behavioral therapy for anxiety-disordered youth. *Journal of Consulting and Clinical Psychology, 64,* 724–730.

Krahn, G. L., Eisert, D., & Fifield, B. (1990). Obtaining parental perceptions of the quality of services for children with special needs. *Journal of Pediatric Psychology, 15,* 761–774.

LaGreca, A. M., & Schuman, W. B. (1995). Adherence to prescribed medical regimens. In M. C. Roberts (Ed.), *Handbook of pediatric psychology* (pp. 53–83). New York: Guilford Press.

Lavigne, J. V. L., & Faier-Routman, J. (1992). Psychological adjustment to pediatric physical disorders: A meta-analytic review. *Journal of Pediatric Psychology, 17,* 133–157.

Lewis, M. A., Hatton, C. L., Salas, I., Leake, B., & Chiofalo, N. (1991). Impact of the children's epilepsy on parents. *Epilepsia, 32,* 365–374.

Lewis, M., Salas, I., de la Sota, A., Chiofalo, N., & Leake, B. (1990). Randomized trial of a program to enhance the competencies of children with epilepsy. *Epilepsia, 31,* 101–109.

McCubbin, H. L., & Patterson, J. M. (1982). Family adaptation to crises. In H. L. McCubbin, A. E. Cauble, & J. M. Patterson (Eds.), *Family coping and social support* (pp. 96–115). Springfield, IL: Thomas.

Newacheck, P. W., Stein, R. E. K., Walker, D. K., Gortmaker, S. L., Kuhlthau, K., & Perrin, J. H. (1996). Monitoring and evaluating managed care for children with chronic illnesses and disabilities. *Pediatrics, 98,* 952–958.

Newacheck, P. W., & Taylor, W. R. (1992). Childhood chronic illness: Prevalence severity, and impact. *American Journal of Public Health, 82,* 364–371.

Patterson, J. M. (1985). Critical factors affecting family compliance with cystic fibrosis. *Family Relations, 34,* 79–89.

Patterson, J. M. (1988). Families experiencing stress: I. The family adjustment and adaptation response model. II. Applying the FAAR model to health-related issues for intervention and research. *Family Systems Medicine, 6,* 202–237.

Perrin, J. M., Maclean, W. E., Gortmaker, S. L., & Asher, K. A. (1992). Improving the psychological status of children with asthma: A randomized controlled trial. *Journal of Developmental and Behavioral Pediatrics, 13,* 241–247.

Pinto, R. P., & Hollandsworth, J. G. (1989). Using videotape modeling to prepare children psychologically for surgery: Influence of parents and costs versus benefits of providing preparation services. *Health Psychology, 8*(1), 79–95.

Pless, I. B., Feeley, N., Gottlieb, L., Rowat, K., Dougherty, G., & Willard, B. (1994). A randomized trial of a nursing intervention to promote the adjustment of children with chronic physical disorders. *Pediatrics, 94,* 70–75.

Pless, I. B., & Pinkerton, P. (1975). *Chronic childhood disorder: Promoting patterns of adjustment.* Chicago: Year Book Medical.

Pless, I. B., & Stein, R. E. K. (1994). Intervention research: Lessons learned from research on children with chronic disorders. In R. J. Hagerty, L. R. Sherrod, N. Garmezy, & M. Rutter (Eds.), *Stress, risk, and resilience in children and adolescents: Processes, mechanisms and interventions* (pp. 317–354). London: Cambridge University Press.

Polin, I. (1990). *Medical crisis counseling. Short-term therapy for long-term illness.* New York: Norton.

Quittner, A. L., Tolbert, V. E., Regoli, M. J., Orenstein, D. M., Hollingsworth, J. L., & Eigen, H. (1996). Development of the role-play inventory of situations and coping strategies for parents of children wtih cystic fibrosis. *Journal of Pediatric Psychology, 21,* 209–235.

Robin, A. L., & Foster, S. L. (1989). *Negotiating parent–adolescent conflict. A behavioral family systems approach.* New York: Guilford Press.

Rolland, J. S. (1987). Chronic illness and the life cycle: A conceptual framework. *Family Process, 26,* 203–221.

Sabbeth, B., & Stein, R. E. K. (1990). Mental health referral: A weak link in comprehensive care of children with chronic physical illness. *Journal of Developmental and Behavioral Pediatrics, 11,* 73–78.

Shapiro, D. E., & Koocher, G. P. (1996). Goals and practical considerations in outpatient medical crises intervention. *Professional Psychology: Research and Practice, 27,* 109–120.

Shapiro, J. P., Walker, L. J., & Jacobson, B. J. (1997). The Youth Client Satisfaction Questionnaire: Development, construct validation, and factor structure. *Journal of Child Clinical Psychology, 26,* 87–98.

Siegel, L. J., Smith, K. E., & Wood, T. R. (1991). Children medically at risk. In F. R. Kratochvil & R. J. Morris (Eds.), *The practice of child therapy* (2nd ed., pp. 328–366). New York: Pergamon Press.

Stein, R. E. K., Bauman, L., Westbrook, L. E., Coupey, S. M., & Ireys, H. J. (1993). Framework for identifying children who have chronic conditions: The case for a new definition. *Journal of Pediatrics, 122,* 342–347.

Stein, R. E. K., & Jessop, D. J. (1982). A noncategorical approach to chronic childhood illness. *Public Health Reports, 97,* 354–362.

Stein, R. E. K., & Jessop, D. J. (1984). Does pediatric home care make a difference for children with chronic illness? Findings from the pediatric ambulatory care treatment study. *Pediatrics, 73*, 845–853.

Stein, R. E. K., & Jessop, D. J. (1991). Long-term mental health effects of a pediatric home care program. *Pediatrics, 88*, 490–496.

Thompson, R. J., Jr., & Gustafson, K. E. (1996). *Adaptation to childhood chronic illness.* Washington, DC: American Psychological Association.

Thompson, R. J., Jr., Gustafson, K. E., Hamlett, K. W., & Spock, A. (1992). Psychological adjustment of children with cystic fibrosis: The role of child cognitive processes and maternal adjustment. *Journal of Pediatric Psychology, 17,* 741–755.

Varni, J. W., Katz, E. R., Colegrove, R., Jr., & Dolgin, M. (1993). The impact of social skills training on the adjustment of children with newly diagnosed cancer. *Journal of Pediatric Psychology, 18,* 751–767.

Wallander, J. L., Varni, J. W., Babani, L., Banis, H. T., & Wilcox, K. T. (1989). Family resources as resistance factors for psychological maladjustment in chronically ill and handicapped children. *Journal of Pediatric Psychology, 14,* 157–173.

Wysocki, T., Harris, M. A., Greco, P., Harvey, L. M., McDonnell, K., Danda, C. K., Bubb, J., & White, N. H. (1997). Social validity of support group and behavior therapy interventions for families of adolescents with insulin-dependent diabetes mellitus. *Journal of Pediatric Psychology, 22,* 635–649.

Wysocki, T., White, N. H., Bubb, J., Harris, M. A., & Greco, P. (1995). Family adaptation to diabetes: A model for intervention research. In J. S. Wallander & L. J. Siegel (Eds.), *Advances in pediatric psychology: Vol. 2. Adolescent health problems: Behavioral perspectives* (pp. 289–304). New York: Guilford Press.

24

Integrated Approaches to Acute Illness

KATHLEEN L. LEMANEK and APRIL DAWN KOONTZ

Acute minor illness is defined as routine, health problems (e.g., respiratory and gastrointestinal infections) and common occurrences of physical trauma experienced by all children (Carey, 1992). Related to acute illness are stressors that may be felt by both children and their families. For children, these stressors may include discomfort of the illness and its treatment, emotional reactions to the illness (e.g., fear, anger), restricted activity (e.g., peer contacts, diet), altered sensory input, and modified relationship with family members (e.g., greater leniency) (Carey, 1992; Sibinga & Carey, 1976). For families, stress may generate from the illness and its treatment (e.g., additional responsibility and expense, obstacles with employment) or be associated with personal and situational variables that negatively affect responses to the illness (e.g., parental depression, marital conflict) (Carey, 1992; Sibinga & Carey, 1976).

Although reports by health care providers and parents of negative reactions to an acute illness are common, the empirical literature describing these reactions and management strategies is minimal. Based on provider and parent reports, both internalizing behaviors (e.g., dependency, withdrawal) and externalizing behaviors (e.g., irritability, defiance) may be evident in children with an acute illness (Carey, 1992; Cunningham, 1989). Behaviors reflecting fears and anxieties, anger, guilt, sadness, and misconceptions are most often seen in parents (Carey, 1992; Cunningham, 1989).

In terms of management, the pediatric literature outlines strategies to limit negative reactions to the illness and to enhance recovery from it. Carey (1992) rec-

KATHLEEN L. LEMANEK • Department of Psychology, Columbus Children's Hospital, Columbus, Ohio 43205.   APRIL DAWN KOONTZ • Clinical Child Psychology Program, University of Kansas, Lawrence, Kansas 66045.

Handbook of Psychotherapies with Children and Families, edited by Russ and Ollendick. Kluwer Academic/Plenum Publishers, New York, 1999.

ommends that, overall, the discomfort, trauma, and restrictions of illness management be kept to a minimum to decrease the stress associated with an acute illness. Therefore, attention should be directed toward managing the illness itself, the child, and the family (Carey, 1992; Sibinga & Carey, 1976). Similar guidelines describing negative reactions and guidelines for management are not, however, readily available in the child psychology literature.

The fact that greater attention, albeit meager, is given to acute illness in the pediatric literature is not surprising, as children with an acute illness are most often seen initially in primary care or family practice settings. A larger number of children are being seen by pediatricians and family practitioners for health monitoring, management of acute medical problems, identifying and managing developmental and behavioral problems (e.g., learning problems, aggression), and providing preventive guidance to parents (AAP Committee on Psychosocial Aspects of Child and Family Health, 1993; Crawford, 1997; Drotar, 1997). However, in both of these settings, informal and formal collaboration between health care providers and mental health professionals are increasingly common in terms of practice, research, and training (Drotar, 1997).

Referrals to mental health professionals in outpatient settings typically center on such acute problems as negative behaviors (e.g., noncompliance, tantrums), toileting difficulties (e.g., enuresis, encopresis), developmental delays, school concerns, personality issues (e.g., lack of self-esteem), and, to some degree, psychosomatic complaints (e.g., recurrent abdominal pain, tics) (Finney, Riley, & Cataldo, 1991; Kanoy & Schroeder, 1985; Walker, 1979). A range of interventions and services are provided by mental health professionals in these settings, including brief therapy, crisis intervention, and intermittent contact on an "as-needed" basis, in addition to running parent education classes and therapeutic groups for children and parents (e.g., social skills) and serving as advocates to community agencies (e.g., schools, courts) (Drotar, Benjamin, Chwast, Litt, & Vajner, 1982; Schroeder & Mann, 1991). Efforts are also being directed at improving regimen adherence and enhancing parent–provider interactions (Armstrong, Fischetti, Romano, Vogel, & Zoppi, 1992; Finney, Friman, Rapoff, & Christophersen, 1986). Unfortunately, the data on how mental health professionals can contribute to alleviating the stress associated with acute illness, in collaboration with both parents and health care providers, are limited. The premises and the practices evident in primary care and family practice settings, as well as the role already played by mental health professionals in these environments, can, however, furnish guidelines for working with children with an acute illness and their families.

THEORETICAL OVERVIEW

Two basic premises emerge in the care of children with an acute illness and their families. The first is the acknowledgment that biological and psychological variables are interrelated and need to be considered in their care. The second is the focus on the contribution of family factors to children's health and illness. Various theoretical models encompass these basic premises and can be extended to acute illness, including the biopsychosocial model (Engel, 1977), the transactional model (Fiese & Sameroff, 1989), and the ecological model (Kazak, 1989).

Engel (1977, 1980) proposed the biopsychosocial model to replace the bio-medical model. In this model, a hierarchy of systems is presented with the lowest system being subatomic particles and the highest system being the biosphere. Each system is considered a whole with its own unique characteristics, but also a part of the next higher system. The person is, for example, the highest level of the organismic hierarchy and the lowest unit of the social hierarchy. This model also suggests that disruption of one system will affect the functioning of other systems, particularly those closest to it. Engel indicates that clinical practice and research starts at the person level but occurs within a two-person system, the physician–patient relationship. Physicians following this model will not only critically ana-lyze the cell and the organ systems but also the inner experiences (e.g., feelings, sensations, thoughts) and the reported and observed behaviors of their patients for diagnostic and management purposes. Furthermore, the reciprocal effects (both disrupting and stabilizing) of the patients' illness on their social environment, and the environment (including relationships and events) on the illness should be con-sidered by physicians. Although this model pertains primarily to health care providers, similar models are applicable to mental health providers.

The transactional and ecological models (e.g., Fiese & Sameroff, 1989; Kazak, 1989) delineate a series of bidirectional interactions between parents and children that are set within concentric rings representing different ecologies or envi-ronments. The influence of children and family members on one another within social and cultural contexts can be examined, particularly during age-related de-velopmental tasks or transitions that involve organization and stress (Fiese, 1997). Such tasks or transitions can include occurrences of acute illness. Factors such as the type and course of an illness, the developmental period in which the illness occurs, the time since recovery, and positive expectations may contribute to chil-dren's level of adaptation (Kazak & Nachman, 1991). In turn, the illness itself may affect family members' perceptions and their level of functioning (Kazak & Nach-man, 1991). According to these models, interventions can be implemented at mul-tiple points in order to achieve a positive outcome. To date, these models have been used most often to predict maladaptive outcomes in research rather than to furnish intervention guidelines for clinical practice (Fiese, 1997; Kazak & Nach-man, 1991).

As stated by Kazak (1997), family members' history with illness and ideas about illness and health are critical ingredients of adaptation when children de-velop an illness, acute or chronic, serious or relatively time-limited. In addition, the goals of pediatric family psychology research and clinical practice should be to foster competencies and to identify vulnerabilities (Kazak, 1997). Because of the nature of an acute illness, these goals need to be fulfilled within the context of a collaborative relationship between health care providers and mental health pro-fessionals. Drotar (1993) has delineated factors related to successful collaboration between these providers. One factor pertains to the individuals' skills in linking assessment information to precise treatment recommendations that can be imple-mented by specific practitioners. These skills may also involve a respect for col-leagues and interpersonal skills (Stabler, 1988). A second factor focuses on beliefs and expectations about the efficacy of collaboration in terms of the necessity and ability of another professional in assisting in the management of a clinical or re-search problem. A final factor concerns the ratio of rewards to limitations on collaboration evident in health care settings (Drotar, 1997; Stabler, 1988). These factors, as well as the mutual influence of biological and psychological factors within different ecologies, will need to be considered when implementing specific intervention procedures for acute illnesses.

INTERVENTION PROCEDURES

Interventions for acute illnesses usually target children who are at some degree of risk of responding negatively to the illness (Gordon, 1983). The following questions should be answered before implementing specific intervention procedures: (1) "who" is the focus of the intervention (i.e., children, families, and/or health care system), (2) "what" behaviors should be targeted for change, and (3) "when" should the intervention occur (Pless & Stein, 1994). These practices are consistent with general intervention research and pediatric family psychology research. The specific intervention procedures are also adapted from those employed in behavior therapy and family therapy.

Russo and Varni (1982) place the behavioral techniques frequently used in research and practice in behavioral pediatrics into three categories: (1) operant and social learning procedures, (2) cognitive and behavioral self-regulation procedures, and (3) biofeedback and physiological self-regulation procedures. The majority of techniques within each category fit within an integrated approach to the care of children with an acute illness. Operant and social learning procedures include such techniques as direct social and token reinforcement (e.g., stars), response cost and time-out, and modeling. Relaxation training (e.g., deep muscle), cognitive restructuring, behavioral rehearsal, and systematic desensitization are techniques categorized as cognitive and behavioral self-regulation procedures. These techniques are within the repertoire of most mental health professionals working in primary care or family practice settings, or those referred to by physicians in these settings (La Greca, Stone, Drotar, & Maddux, 1988). Biofeedback is utilized to a lesser degree and depends on the training of the mental health professional and the equipment available in each setting. A precise description of these procedures can be found in texts by Kanfer and Goldstein (1997) and Kazdin (1980). In general, the mechanism of change underlying these procedures are based on the main learning paradigms of operant conditioning, classical conditioning, and observational learning. Such sources as Bandura (1977) and Catania (1997) can be consulted to obtain a detailed account of how these learning paradigms "explain" behavior change.

The second category of procedures falls under the rubric *family therapy*. Goldenberg and Goldenberg (1983) categorize different family therapies into four groups: (1) psychodynamic, (2) communication and strategic, (3) structural, and (4) behavioral. The focus and procedures of the communication and strategic and behavioral family therapies appear suited to caring for children with an acute illness and their families. These therapies tend to follow a solution-focused approach to intervention where presenting problems are actively discussed, solutions are generated, and collaboration occurs between therapists, family members, and other systems (Anderson & Goolishian, 1991; Selekman, 1997). The foundation of this approach is on enhancing parental problem-solving and coping strategies relative to addressing specific skill deficits (Selekman, 1997). Parents then serve as models for children with respect to coping with stress and, in general, an optimistic problem-solving style (Seligman, 1995). In addition, the family's interactional processes that maintain the presenting problems are emphasized within these therapies. Specific intervention tasks and procedures include, for example, the victory and compliment boxes, the structured family fighting task, reframing, paradoxical intervention, and skills training (e.g., communication, child management). A detailed description of these tasks and procedures can be found in such sources as de Shazer (1988), Goldenberg and Goldenberg (1983), and Selekman (1997). Further information about family psychology and mechanisms of change can be obtained in texts by Goldenberg and Goldenberg (1990) and Gurman and Kniskern (1981).

PROBLEM AREAS AND RESEARCH SUPPORT

Pediatric Headaches

Headaches are a frequently overlooked complaint in the area of pediatric acute illness. However, recent research highlights the gains that have been made in assessment and intervention with this type of illness. Though the literature cites numerous potential etiologies for the occurrence of headaches in children, the majority of headaches fall into two basic categories: vascular headaches or "migraines" and muscle contraction or "tension" headaches (Singer & Rowe, 1992). The distinction between these types of headaches in children is sometimes difficult. However, experts agree that vascular headaches are more disabling for both adults and children than tension headaches. Although this section focuses on pediatric migraines, the same nonpharmacological coping strategies can be used with tension headaches.

To diagnose a pediatric migraine, the presence of recurrent headaches separated by pain-free periods of time should be ascertained by a health care provider. Additionally, Prensky (1984) suggests at least three of the following six symptoms be present to make a more precise diagnosis: (1) an aura (visual, motor, or sensory); (2) unilateral head pain; (3) throbbing sensation in the pain location; (4) associated nausea, vomiting, or abdominal pain; (5) alleviation of symptoms after sleep; and (6) positive family history of migraines. A health care provider should take a headache history that includes detailed information regarding the onset of symptoms, descriptive information about the symptoms, location, frequency, duration, time of day, information regarding the disruption of the daily activities, and any associated symptoms (Singer & Rowe, 1992); this history should also be obtained from both parents (when possible), the child, and siblings. Additionally, the observation of human behavior (child, child–parent dyad, marital dyad, and so forth) is an invaluable source of information and should be included in the assessment process.

Although the presence of stress in children's lives is frequently denied, it is one of the most common factors precipitating headaches in children. Usually, migraines are induced by such stressors as changes in daily habits (e.g., sleeping, eating, consumption of drugs or alcohol), previous head trauma, heavy exertion, bright or flashing lights, and hormonal changes (e.g., menstruation) (Singer &

Rowe, 1992). Specific stressors can be identified when taking the headache history. Therefore, one treatment intervention is simply to have children avoid the stressors that precipitate their migraines. Unfortunately, a strategy of avoidance is not always feasible for most children and their families.

A goal of most interventions is to teach children to minimize their headache complaints and to assume primary responsibility for their own care. Consistent with this goal are two interventions frequently used to manage pediatric migraines, namely, biofeedback and relaxation training. These interventions have been shown to reduce the frequency and severity of both migraine and tension headaches in children (Wanranch & Keenan, 1985). Under the direction of a mental health professional, children are typically taught progressive muscle relaxation, abdominal breathing, and visual imagery exercises. Biofeedback is added to help children monitor and voluntarily control their physiological responses. Though biofeedback and relaxation training can be used separately, most studies have shown the combination of the two to be a more effective intervention (Engel & Rapoff, 1990; Engel, Rapoff, & Pressman, 1992; Hermann, Kim, & Blanchard, 1995).

Without training in these techniques, however, parents are left to their own devices as how best to treat their symptomatic child. Engel (1991) investigated the ways in which children communicate their headache pain to their mothers, how mothers respond to the headache occurrences, and how those responses may serve to elicit or maintain future headache occurrences. Of the 20 children who participated in the study, it was noted that 16 had a positive family history of headache disorders. All of the children and their mothers (independently) were asked to keep a headache diary for 17 weeks to record the frequency, peak intensity, and how they tried to alleviate the headache. Engel (1991) found that (1) children typically communicate their headache verbally, (2) girls requested and took more medication for their headaches than boys, in addition to reporting lower activity levels and more rest time than their male counterparts, and (3) mothers were more likely to respond to older children's headache by ignoring it and to younger children's headache with medication. Thus, mothers and other caretakers may benefit from learning how to assist their children in relaxing as a more constructive way to respond to the headaches. Relaxation training practiced on a daily basis and during times of stress may act as a prophylactic against future headache episodes. Additionally, by training parents in relaxation techniques, they can model coping behaviors for headaches.

Allen and McKeen (1991), in their study of a home-based multicomponent treatment program incorporating thermal biofeedback and behavioral reinforcement ($N = 21$), found that treatment outcome was closely related to how often the treatment was practiced at home and how supportive the parents were of using an adaptive coping strategy (i.e., biofeedback) versus reinforcing maladaptive pain behaviors. With only three clinic visits, those who were compliant with treatment recommendations reported a substantial decrease in frequency and intensity of headaches and maintained these reductions at 3- and 8-month follow-ups. These results suggest that an integrative treatment package combining both biofeedback and environmental support is an effective and cost-effective intervention for acute headache pain. This package may result in fewer clinic visits and less analgesic medication over both the short and long term.

Abdominal Pain

Abdominal pain is the most common complaint among children between the ages of 6 and 15 (Apley & Naish, 1958; Poole, 1984; Valman, 1981). Similar to headaches, recurrent abdominal pain (RAP) is thought to be stress related, where the contribution of physical and psychological variables is difficult to separate (Schaefer, Millman, & Levine, 1994). As such, a detailed medical and psychological history from referred children and their parents is necessary to design an effective intervention plan.

The criteria for diagnosing RAP in children and adolescents include (1) three or more episodes of abdominal pain, (2) 3-month duration of abdominal pain complaints, (3) disruption of daily activities, and (4) absence of an identifiable organic etiology (Apley, 1975; Apley & Naish, 1958). Some researchers and clinicians use the above criteria (Ernst, Routh, & Harper, 1984; Routh & Ernst, 1984), whereas others have shortened the duration criterion to 1 month (Walker, Garber, & Greene, 1991). In a study of 1000 school-age children in Great Britain, the pattern of onset was similar for both boys and girls until age 8, suggesting that the underlying factors may be similar (Apley & Naish, 1958). The incidence peaked markedly for females at age 9 (25%). Males, on the other hand, exhibited an increase in reports of abdominal pain from age 5 to 10, with a later peak at age 14. A more recent study (Sharrer & Ryan-Wenger, 1991) of 250 children aged 8–12 revealed an incidence of 10% for RAP, which is consistent with previous incidence reports (Apley & Naish, 1958; Poole, 1984). However, Sharrer and Ryan-Wenger (1991) found the occurrence of RAP to be similar for males and females, differing only in peak ages. Males in their study had the highest prevalence rate at age 8, while females had their peak rate at age 9. Interestingly, 21 of the 25 children with RAP also reported experiencing other potentially stress-related problems, with the most frequent being headaches (60%). Moreover, in the Sharrer and Ryan-Wenger (1991) study, children with RAP had significantly higher mean stress scores for frequency and severity, and total stress scores than the non-RAP group, indicating that children with abdominal pain perceive their stress to be more severe than other children. The most common stressors reported were family factors (e.g., parents arguing in front of them, parents not spending enough time with them) and physical factors (e.g., feeling sick all the time). Furthermore, children with RAP reported fewer and less effective coping strategies available to them than did the children without abdominal pain. This finding suggests that training in coping skills should be an integral component of any successful intervention for children with abdominal pain.

Although the research on the assessment of RAP, children's coping, and potential stressors that may exacerbate abdominal pain is rather thorough (Ernst et al., 1984; Routh & Ernst, 1984; Walker & Greene, 1989), the intervention research is lacking. Much of the literature in this area suggests that RAP is psychogenic rather than physical. In addition, experts view the family system as a "maintainer" of the psychosomatic behavior of children (Routh & Ernst, 1984; Wood, 1993; Wood et al., 1989). These perspectives suggest that effective interventions for RAP should consist of varying combinations of parent training, family therapy, positive reinforcement for nonpain behavior, and techniques to reduce anxiety (e.g., relaxation training). Lask and Fosson (1989) recommend parent training in behavior management to deal with the illness and education on how to maintain appropriate expectations for children as a starting point for intervention rather than either marital or family therapy. Supporting this recommendation is a recent study by Sanders, Shepard, Cleghorn, and Woolford (1994) who developed a cognitive–behavioral intervention that focused on both the parents and the children with RAP. During six sessions, the intervention included educating parents about RAP, teaching them behavioral management and distraction techniques, and instructing the children in self-talk and relaxation skills. This integrative intervention was superior to standard pediatric care in reducing the occurrence of abdominal pain at 6- and 12-month follow-ups. However, more research is needed in the area of integrated intervention for pediatric abdominal pain.

Preparing Children for Outpatient Surgery

Until recently, children were frequently hospitalized for several days following a minor surgery, such as placement of tubes in the ears or removal of tonsils. The literature on hospitalization in children documents fear and anxiety in children and parents as common reactions (Brown, 1971; Melamed & Siegel, 1975; Peterson & Shigetomi, 1981; Schepp, 1991). There is in addition a plethora of literature on the importance of preparing children and their families for hospitalization (Azarnoff, 1976; Elkins & Roberts, 1983; Melamed & Siegel, 1975; Peterson & Shigetomi, 1981; Siegel, 1976, 1983). However, at a time when managed care abounds, there are fewer and fewer children being hospitalized for minor surgeries. Same-day surgery (also termed *outpatient surgery*) is no longer the exception to the rule. Unfortunately, the literature describing how children are prepared for these brief, but intense and invasive encounters with the medical setting, procedures, and personnel is scant. The available literature does suggest, however, that with proper presurgical preparation, children will be less resistant to the induction of anesthesia, have a higher tolerance for the stress of the surgery, have a shortened recovery period, and will be less likely to have long-lasting behavioral problems in response to the surgery (Campbell, Scaife, & Johnstone, 1988; Visintainer & Wolfer, 1975; Zuckerberg, 1994).

Typical surgical preparation programs for children include educating the parents and children about the procedure, using filmed models demonstrating the procedure, teaching and rehearsing coping skills for children to use prior to the surgery, and allowing children to engage in medical play with dolls (Bolig, Yolton, & Nissen, 1991; Chan, 1980; Gaynard, Goldberg, & Laidley, 1991; Melamed & Siegel, 1975; Peterson & Shigetomi, 1981). Parents also seem to prefer to have comprehensive information regarding their children's impending surgery (Kain, Wang, Caramico, Hofstadter, & Mayes, 1997; Schepp, 1991). For example, Schepp (1991) found that by telling mothers what events to expect, they actually experienced less anxiety and reported less effort expended trying to cope with the stressful events. Communicating honestly about the procedure and allowing parents to make informed decisions may, thus, give them a sense of control, establish rapport with the surgical team, and decrease their anxiety, which in turn may decrease their children's anxiety about the surgery.

Depending on the age of the children, simply giving them information about the upcoming surgery will probably not be an effective stress-reducing technique and may, in fact, exacerbate the underlying anxiety. Providing the preparatory and procedural information in combination with showing children how to successfully adapt to the surgical procedure seems to be a more effective approach (Melamed & Siegel, 1975). The well-cited film, "Ethan has an operation," created by Melamed and Siegel (1975), shows a filmed model of a child successfully overcoming his anxiety about such stressors as anesthesia induction and being separated from his mother. The film also includes information about hospitals and medical staff, while the child model discusses his worries and anxiety about the medical situation he is in. Information provided by peer models may, thus, be more helpful to pediatric patients in terms of facilitating their understanding and coping because they are more apt to identify with a peer model who has mastered the experience. The research in the area of filmed peer modeling clearly demonstrates its effectiveness in reducing children's anxiety regarding surgery (Faust & Melamed, 1984; Melamed & Siegel, 1975; Peterson, Schultheis, Ridley-Johnson, Miller, & Tracy, 1984). However, filmed modeling is seldom used in clinical practice despite its effectiveness in research trials (Peterson & Ridley-Johnson, 1980).

Teaching children coping skills also appears to reduce their anxiety during surgical experiences (Peterson & Shigetomi, 1981). Most attempts to help children cope with hospitalizations and/or surgery focus on a combination of interventions, such as relaxation, distraction, and self-talk. For example, Peterson and Shigetomi (1981) trained pediatric patients ($2\frac{1}{2}$ years to $10\frac{1}{2}$ years) to engage in a combination of coping strategies, including progressive muscle relaxation, deep breathing exercises while saying the word *calm* during exhalation, imagining a quiet and happy scene (i.e., distraction), and using comforting phrases such as "I will be all better in a little while" and "Everything is going to be alright." As part of the hospital preparation program, the parents in this study were encouraged to participate by helping their children make the happy scene as vivid as possible (e.g., adding details like sights, sounds, smells, and so on), encouraging their children to do the self-talk exercises out loud, and practicing the relaxation exercises with them. Results demonstrated that children who received coping skills training experienced less distress and were more cooperative during the hospitalization than children who did not receive the training.

Although it is unclear which of these strategies are most responsible for alleviating children's distress, interventions that include combinations of these coping techniques are consistently proven to be effective (e.g., Jay, Elliott, & Varni, 1986). Furthermore, parents should be involved in the preparation as much as possible, not only by their presence during the anesthesia induction but also as an active "coach." Parents may then continue to reinforce and support their children's coping behaviors and to facilitate their children's overall presurgical and postsurgical adjustment.

Adherence to Medical Regimens

Nonadherence to medical regimens is probably one of the most pervasive problems pediatricians and family practitioners face with pediatric populations. Unfortunately, health care providers greatly overestimate the number of parents who adhere to medical recommendations for their children (Finney, Hook, Friman, Rapoff, & Christophersen, 1993).

In the area of acute illnesses, nonadherence to treatment regimens occurs in children suffering from otitis media (ear infections) and streptococcal pharyngitis (strep throat) (e.g., Colcher & Bass, 1972; Mattar, Markello, & Yaffe, 1975; Schwartz-Lookinland, McKeever, & Saputo, 1989). Otitis media is particularly problematic when medical recommendations are not adhered to because hearing impairment can occur. A domino effect may develop for children in that inadequate hearing can lead to language skills deficits. These deficits can potentially result in behavioral problems, which can then contribute to children being labeled throughout their school career as problem students or slow learners (Wald, 1983). Thus, the treatment of otitis media should address adherence issues at the point of implementation.

Factors that affect adherence to short-term regimens for acute illness are multidimensional. The treatment providers should take into account children's developmental level (cognitively, emotionally, and behaviorally), the role the family will play in helping children adhere, the child–parent, parent–provider, and child–provider dyadic relationships, the complexity of the treatment regimen, and the family's ability to carry out the treatment regimen successfully before implementing a treatment plan. Moreover, because multiple factors contribute to treatment adherence, providers will need to tailor interventions that meet the specific needs of the patients' or families' difficulties. Because of the complexity of factors affecting adherence, multicomponent programs appear to be the most effective interventions with pediatric populations.

Education alone may be an appropriate intervention for short-term medication regimens (e.g., Colcher & Bass, 1972), but the degree to which families have the knowledge and skills that are necessary to carry out the treatment regimen effectively has to be considered. Yet, even when parents have the knowledge and skills, education may still not be sufficient for successful adherence, especially for aversive or complex treatment regimens (La Greca & Skyler, 1991). To successfully adhere to some treatment regimens, parents' efforts may be facilitated by additional procedures that support and reinforce proper medical care.

Additional support for families to facilitate caretaking of children with an acute illness can include such measures as visual cues (i.e., reminders), self-monitoring, written instructions, telephone reminders, and reinforcement schedules for children's adherent behavior with the medical regimens. Reminders have been effective in increasing adherence to both appointment keeping and medication schedules. For instance, in a study using children with otitis media ($N = 1983$), Casey, Rosen, Glowasky, and Ludwig (1985) found that telephone reminders increased adherence to follow-up medical appointments. However, even with the reminder, the adherence rate in their study was only 56%. Therefore, simply calling parents to inform them of their children's next appointment may not be sufficient to ensure adherence to medical appointment keeping. A more promising strategy may be a "reminder package" that includes both mailed and telephone reminders along with a parking pass (Friman, Finney, Rapoff, & Christophersen, 1986). This package was tested in an ambulatory pediatric clinic and resulted in an increase in the percentage of appointments kept and a decrease in the percentage of appointments broken. These findings alone speak to the cost-effectiveness of using reminders.

Other reminders, such as visual cues, have also been effective in increasing adherence to a medical regimen. More specifically, an investigation on adherence to a 10-day oral medication regimen for acute otitis media found that visual cues increased adherence in both adults and children (Lima, Nazarian, Charney, & Lahti, 1976). In their study, the researchers used two visual cues: One cue was a clock on the prescription label of the medication bottle with the administration times circled and the second was a fairly large red sticker to post in their home. Although both adults and children in the reminder group were more adherent to taking their medicine, children in the intervention group demonstrated adherence levels that were twice as high as those of the control group. Therefore, it would behoove clinicians working with an children who have an acute illness to include visual and verbal reminders in their intervention plans to promote adherence to both appointment follow-ups and taking medication.

CASE EXAMPLES

Pediatric Headache

Maria G. was a 12-year-old girl, who was physician-referred to the staff pediatric psychologist. According to her physician, Maria had been seen on six separate occasions over the last 4 years complaining of debilitating headaches that were preceded by an aura and accompanied by nausea. Though the physician had initially prescribed medication to alleviate Maria's headache symptoms, he suggested that the pediatric psychologist might assist in designing a nonpharmacological treatment. Treatment goals centered on stopping the headaches entirely or, at least, eliminating the necessity of medication.

Maria and her mother were both interviewed in regard to the family history of headaches and possible triggers to the headaches. There was a positive history of headaches on the mother's side of the family. Maria stated that her headaches usually occurred the first week of a new school year and sometimes after the winter break. An assessment battery indicated that Maria tended to internalize her difficulties and was seen by others to be anxious and to have a propensity toward worrying. Maria and her mother also reported a lot of tension in the household. Mr. G. was a contracted employee for the city, and the family finances were usually tightest during the fall and winter. During times of unemployment, Mr. G. became more punitive of his daughter, particularly with regard to her grades at school. Mrs. G. then gave her daughter extra attention to compensate for the harshness of Mr. G. When Maria complained of severe headaches, the fighting in the family temporarily stopped. However, Mrs. G. noted that she secretly felt her husband was to blame for the headaches.

The intervention for alleviating Maria's headaches consisted of several distinct components. The first component was training in progressive muscle relaxation and thermal biofeedback. An adjunct relaxation technique, for use in the classroom, was a guided visualization script that Maria memorized. When Maria felt a headache coming on, she simply closed her eyes and imagined herself swinging on the porch swing at her grandmother's house on a quiet summer evening. She imagined feeling a soft breeze, hearing the rustling of leaves, and smelling a sweet scent of roses that surrounded the porch. The visualization only took 2–5 minutes, depending on how much time she allowed herself to experience each soothing sensation. The second component of treatment related to family and parenting issues. Mr. and Mrs. G. received instruction on disciplinary strategies and how to attend to nonpain behaviors, as well as referral to a marriage counselor. Both parents agreed to minimize their fighting in front of Maria, to agree on disciplinary rules for Maria, and to take Maria to school on days that she complained of headaches. The third component of the intervention involved the school system. The school principle, school nurse, and Maria's teacher were also contacted and agreed not to let Maria go home when complaining of headaches; however, she was allowed to go to the nurse's office for 10 to 20 minutes to practice her relaxation exercises. Finally, Maria, her family, her physician, and the pediatric psychologist agreed to evaluate the psychological intervention plan at the end of 6 months before deciding whether to add medication to the regimen.

Follow-up information was collected from Maria and her family 6 months and 1 year following treatment. Maria did not experience any headaches requiring hospitalization or medication during this time. She reported regularly performing her relaxation exercises, especially when she feels a headache beginning to develop.

Adherence to Short-Term Medical Regimen

Mark is a 3-year-old boy with no atypical physical features or cognitive abilities. Mark lives with his mother and attends a full-day preschool program. He is being followed by a speech-language pathologist because of a delay of 6 months in expressive language skills, although his receptive language skills are adequate. During an office visit to his primary care provider, Mark was diagnosed with bilateral otitis media (BOM) (ear infections) based on a physical examination and maternal reports of Mark complaining that his ears hurt, a runny nose and cough, greater irritability, and problems sleeping. A previous diagnosis of BOM was given 1 year earlier, also requiring medical intervention. In addition, Mark's mother commented that she was having difficulty managing Mark's behavior since his father and she separated 6 months earlier. She reported increased verbal and physical aggression (e.g., calling her names, hitting other children) and noncompliance.

Mark was prescribed a 10-day course of antibiotics (amoxicillin), 5 ml every 8 hours. Factors considered in designing an integrated approach to care included mild language delay, recent environmental stress (separation of parents), and current problems with compliance at home. A multicomponent program consisting of educational, organizational, and behavioral strategies was implemented in order to offset problems in adherence to the medical regimen. The primary care provider described the medical regimen, along with a rationale for the medication and the importance of adherence. A written instruction sheet was given to Mark's mother on ear infections and the purpose and dosage of the medication. The provider also discussed with Mark's mother how she would implement the regimen at home and at school (e.g., same time every day), as well as what problems she anticipated in giving Mark the medication (e.g., refusals). The following behavioral program was developed, stemming from previous collaborations with mental health colleagues: (1) A medication calendar was placed on the refrigerator with the time of the evening dose specified to serve as a cue to adhere to the regimen; (2) Mark's mother also took her vitamin at the time Mark took his medication; (3) each day Mark took his medication without crying or refusing, his mother praised his adherence, and they placed a sticker on the calendar; (4) if Mark did not take his medication he was placed in time-out; medication was reintroduced until taken; and (5) a special outing was scheduled if Mark took his medication for 10 days. Mark's mother was instructed to contact the primary care provider if repeated problems occurred with the medication or with adherence. A pediatric nurse then called Mark's mother 4 and 8 days into the regimen to monitor the status of Mark's ear infection and his success with taking the medication, as well as to address concerns of his mother. Because Mark would be taking his morning and afternoon doses at school, a similar instruction sheet and behavioral program were given to his preschool teacher. The sheet and program were presented by Mark's mother, but consultation would be available from a mental health provider if issues arose at school about its implementation. Conjoint sessions with a mental health provider would be scheduled depending on the frequency and intensity of current behavioral concerns and his mother's skill in behavior management. Improvements or continued problems with language development and in behavior would be reviewed during future pediatric appointments.

Telephone contact with Mark's mother indicated no significant difficulties in taking his medication, with only two time-outs given and eight stickers earned at day 8 of the regimen. However, a mental health professional had to contact Mark's preschool teacher because of the use of multiple time-outs before he took his medication. A modification in the time-out procedure eliminated further problems after day 4 of the regimen.

This case illustrates the use of educational (e.g., written handouts), organizational (e.g., telephone contact), and behavioral strategies (e.g., visual reminders, reinforcement) to foster adherence to a short-term medication regimen. Multiple systems were involved in this brief exchange, such as parent–child, parent–physician, and parent–child–teacher. The mental health provider would serve as an indirect consultant in terms of providing advice or protocols for patient management, but not directly contacting the patient or his family (Roberts, 1986).

FUTURE RESEARCH AND SUMMARY

As in most areas of psychology, additional research is required to determine what interventions work, with which children, under what settings, and at what point in the management of the illness. With respect to an integrated approach to acute illness, greater attention should be directed toward developing general and specific intervention guidelines for different ecologies (i.e., health care settings, homes, and schools). In addition, the utility of different models of adaptation and theories underlying intervention procedures will need to be explored. Deterrents to pursuing an integrated approach to acute illness relate to clinical research and practice, and collaboration between multiple providers, including case managers. With respect to collaboration between health care providers and mental health professionals, identified hindrances involve differences in training, theoretical models, and working styles, and limited support for this activity (Drotar, 1997; McDaniel, Campbell, & Seaburn, 1995). Such factors may also affect working relationships among family systems, school systems, and managed care companies.

The significance of collaboration is evident when one considers the impact of managed care on clinical practice. For example, a larger number of patients need to be seen because of decreased reimbursement for outpatient care (Drotar, 1997). Assessing presenting complaints and outlining a care plan need to be accomplished within 10 to 15 minutes, leaving little time for discussion of psychosocial concerns related or unrelated to the illness (Bergman, Dassel, & Wedgewood, 1966; Crawford, 1997). Increased accessibility of mental health professionals, especially in primary care and family practice settings, may ensure services are available to children and their families (Drotar, 1997). However, these services will need to employ documented efficacious and efficient interventions based on clinical research. In this vein, Kazak (1997) has offered guidelines to increase the flexibility when carrying out research in pediatric family psychology: (1) frame questions from a family systems orientation; for example, consider ways in which families intervene with children when examining intervention efficacy for compliance with treatment recommendations (e.g., relaxation exercises, dietary restrictions); (2) follow a multi-informant approach to assess interrelationships among family members and individuals outside the family; (3) expand the perimeters of systems to include children, family members, and hospitals because of fluctuating health care policies and strategies; and (4) explore in more detail the effect of ethnic and economic differences on interactions between systems, including the family and health care settings. She has also emphasized the importance of delineating how research findings can be translated to interventions for individual children and their families.

Patient-focused research may be one method to establish the link between research and clinical practice. One attempts to answer the question "Is this intervention working for this child?" within patient-focused research (Howard, Moras, Brill, Martinovich, & Lutz, 1986). This type of research is in contrast to examining whether the intervention works under controlled conditions (efficacy method) and whether it works in actual practice (effectiveness method) (Howard et al., 1986; Seligman, 1986). Assessment of a child's ongoing response to intervention to monitor progress is a core feature of this method of research. This feature is identical to tenets of empirical assessment of childhood disorders and single-case methodology (Hersen & Barlow, 1981; Ollendick & Hersen, 1993). Future research should, therefore, actively incorporate ongoing assessment and replicated single-case studies to provide documentation of empirically validated interventions with children. A single-case research design is actually the first phase in a "phased studies approach" of treatment outcome research described by La Greca and Varni (1993). Such single-case studies on innovative treatments lead to single-site group designs, which then move to multisite randomized controlled group designs. These issues and concepts have largely been ignored in terms of an integrated approach to the care of children with an acute illness and their families.

Specific problem areas and populations will no doubt employ both general and unique intervention procedures. How to tailor these interventions to individual children and their families is the next question to be addressed in future research. A variety of illness variables (e.g., severity), child variables (e.g., comorbidity with other conditions), family variables (e.g., family experience of distress, involvement in treatment), and health care variables (e.g., number of visits allowed for mental health services) may influence treatment outcome (Kazak, 1997; Kazdin, Bass, Ayers, & Rodgers, 1993, 1990). These variables will need to be examined in future studies, both within and across illnesses, to answer the above question. In addition, the beneficial and harmful, short- and long-term effects of specific interventions on individual systems will need to be considered and explored in future research and practice (Pless & Stein, 1994). Analysis of these effects will also need to include the cost of the intervention with respect to, for example, health care utilization, professional and family time, and generalization to other problem areas.

Mental health providers are being required by consumers (including insurance and managed care companies) to empirically validate the overall effectiveness of interventions and to determine the cost–benefit ratio of different interventions (Howard et al., 1986). Reimbursement of treatment services typically emphasizes those that are short-term and empirically validated (Sloan, 1997). Also influencing direct services to children is the relationship among mental health professionals, families, and managed care companies, especially case managers. Selekman (1997) and Sloan (1997) have delineated guidelines for assisting families in working with managed care companies. The first guideline focuses on educating families about relevant aspects of the managed care environment, such as the need for medical necessity to authorize visits, the emphasis on symptom stabilization and not insight, the role of case managers in the treatment process, and the levels of care for specific diagnoses. Identifying changes from the time the agency is contacted to the first scheduled appointment is the second guideline. The third guideline centers on problem solving with clients and case managers in terms of negotiating realistic treatment goals and treatment plans. Developing and maintaining collaborative, rather than conflictual, relationships between families and case managers is the final guideline. These guidelines will need to be more clearly communicated to families, training programs, practitioners, and administrators to obtain integrated services for children and their families.

The literature on an integrated approach to the care of children with an acute illness is virtually nonexistent. The theoretical approach outlined in this chapter draws together several models that emphasize biological and psychological variables, as well as the interface between different ecologies, such as the family and the health care setting. The problem areas and populations described in this chapter were chosen to highlight specific interventions that could be conceptualized as an integrated approach to acute illness. However, future research will need to more directly examine the utility of this approach within and across illnesses and settings. Both the medical and the psychological literatures emphasize how the illness, the child, and the family impact one another in terms of adaptation to an illness. Advancements in research and practice in acute illness will also continue to emphasize collaboration and communication among these systems.

REFERENCES

Allen, K. A., & McKeen, L. R. (1991). Home-based multicomponent treatment of pediatric migraine. *Headache, 31,* 467–472.

American Academy of Pediatrics Committee on Psychosocial Aspects of Child and Family Health. (1993). The pediatrician and the "new morbidity." *Pediatrics, 92,* 731–733.

Anderson, H., & Goolishian, H. (1991, October). *"Not knowing": A critical element of a collaborative language systems therapy approach.* Plenary address presented at the annual conference of the American Association for Marriage and Family Therapy, Dallas.

Apley, J. (1975). *The child with abdominal pain* (2nd ed.). Oxford: Blackwell.

Apley, J., & Naish, N. (1958). Recurrent abdominal pain: A field survey of 1,000 school children. *Archives of Diseases of Children, 33,* 165–170.

Armstrong, P., Fischetti, L. R., Romano, S. D., Vogel, M. S., & Zoppi, K. (1992). Position paper on the role of behavioral science faculty in family medicine. *Family Systems Medicine, 10,* 257–264.

Azarnoff, P. (1976). The care of children in hospitals: An overview. *Journal of Pediatric Psychology, 1,* 5–6.

Bandura, A. (1977). *Social learning theory.* Englewood Cliffs, NJ: Prentice–Hall.

Bergman, A. B., Dassel, S. W., & Wedgewood, R. (1966). Time-motion study of practicing pediatricians. *Pediatrics, 38,* 254–263.

Bolig, R., Yolton, K. A., & Nissen, H. L. (1991). Medical play and preparation: Questions and issues. *Children's Health Care, 20,* 225–229.

Brown, M. J. (1971). Pre-admission orientation for children and parents. *Canadian Nurse, 67,* 29–31.

Campbell, I. R., Scaife, J. M., & Johnstone, J. M. S. (1988). Psychological effects of same-day surgery compared with inpatient surgery. *Archives of Diseases of Children, 63,* 415–417.

Carey, W. B. (1992). Acute minor illness. In M. D. Levine, W. B. Carey, & A. C. Crocker (Eds.), *Developmental and behavioral pediatrics* (2nd ed., pp. 295–296). Philadelphia: Saunders.

Casey, R., Rosen, B., Glowasky, A., & Ludwig, S. (1985). An intervention to improve follow-up of patients with otitis media. *Clinical Pediatrics, 24,* 149–152.

Catania, C. (1997). *Learning* (4th ed.). Englewood Cliffs, NJ: Prentice–Hall.

Chan, J. M. (1980). Preparation for procedures and surgery through play. *Pediatrician, 9,* 210–219.

Colcher, I. S., & Bass, J. W. (1972). Penicillin treatment of streptococcal pharyngitis: A comparison of schedules and the role of specific counseling. *Journal of the American Medical Association, 222,* 657–659.

Crawford, P. (1997). Psychological consultation in family medicine. In D. Drotar (Ed.), *Consulting with pediatricians. Psychological perspectives* (pp. 196–203). New York: Plenum Press.

Cunningham, A. S. (1989). Beware overtreating children. *American Journal of Diseases of Children, 143,* 786–788.

de Shazer, S. (1988). *Clues: Investigating solutions in brief therapy.* New York: Norton.

Drotar, D. (1993). Influences on collaboration activities among psychologists and physicians: Implications for practice, research, and training. *Journal of Pediatric Psychology, 18,* 159–172.

Drotar, D. (1997). *Consulting with pediatricians. Psychological perspectives.* New York: Plenum Press.

Drotar, D., Benjamin, P., Chwast, R., Litt, C., & Vajner, P. (1982). The role of the psychologist in pediatric outpatient and inpatient settings. In J. M. Tuma (Ed.), *Handbook for the practice of pediatric psychology* (pp. 228–250). New York: Wiley.

Elkins, P. D., & Roberts, M. C. (1983). Psychological preparation for pediatric hospitalization. *Clinical Psychology Review, 3,* 275–295.

Engel, G. L. (1977). The need for a new medical model: A challenge for biomedicine. *Science, 196,* 129–136.

Engel, G. L. (1980). The clinical application of the biopsychosocial model. *American Journal of Psychiatry, 137,* 535–544.

Engel, J. M. (1991). Behavioral assessment of chronic headaches in children. *Issues in Comprehensive Pediatric Nursing, 14,* 267–276.

Engel, J. M., & Rapoff, M. A. (1990). Biofeedback-assisted relaxation training for adult and pediatric headache disorders. *Occupational Therapy Journal of Research, 10,* 283–299.

Engel, J. M., Rapoff, M. A., & Pressman, A. R. (1992). Long-term follow-up of relaxation training for pediatric headache disorders. *Headache, 32,* 152–156.

Ernst, A. R., Routh, D. K., & Harper, D. (1984). Abdominal pain in children in symptoms of somatization disorder. *Journal of Pediatric Psychology, 9,* 77–86.

Faust, J., & Melamed, B. G. (1984). Influence of arousal, previous experience, and age on surgery preparation of same-day surgery and in-hospital pediatric patients. *Journal of Consulting and Clinical Psychology, 52,* 359–365.

Fiese, B. H. (1997). Family context in pediatric psychology from a transactional perspective: Family rituals and stories as examples. *Journal of Pediatric Psychology, 22,* 183–196.

Fiese, B. H., & Sameroff, A. J. (1989). Family context in pediatric psychology: A transactional perspective. *Journal of Pediatric Psychology, 14,* 293–314.

Finney, J. W., Friman, P. C., Rapoff, M. A., & Christophersen, E. R. (1986). Improving compliance with antibiotic regimens for otitis media: Randomized clinical trials in a pediatric clinic. *Journal of Diseases of Children, 139,* 89–95.

Finney, J. W., Hook, R. W., Friman, P. C., Rapoff, M. A., & Christophersen, E. R. (1993). The overestimation of adherence to pediatric medical regimens. *Children's Health Care, 222*, 461–467.

Finney, J. W., Riley, A. W., & Cataldo, M. F. (1991). Psychology in primary care: Effects of brief target therapy on children's medical care utilization. *Journal of Pediatric Psychology, 16*, 447–462.

Friman, P. C., Finney, J. W., Rapoff, M. A., & Christophersen, E. R. (1985). Improving pediatric appointment keeping with reminders and reduced response requirement. *Journal of Applied Behavior Analysis, 18*, 315–321.

Gaynard, L., Goldberg, J., & Laidley, L. (1991). The use of stuffed, body-outline dolls with hospitalized children and adolescents. *Children's Health Care, 20*, 216–224.

Goldenberg, H., & Goldenberg, I. (1990). *Counseling today's families.* Pacific Grove, CA: Brooks/Cole.

Goldenberg, I., & Goldenberg, H. (1983). Historical roots of contemporary family therapy. In B. B. Wolman & G. Stricker (Eds.), *Handbook of family and marital therapy* (pp. 77–89). New York: Plenum Press.

Gordon, R. S., Jr. (1983). An operational classification of disease prevention. *Public Health Reports, 98*, 107–109.

Gurman, A. S., & Kniskern, D. P. (Eds.). (1981). *Handbook of family therapy.* New York: Brunner/Mazel.

Hermann, C., Kim, M., & Blanchard, E. B. (1995). Behavioral and prophylactic pharmacological intervention studies of pediatric migraines: An exploratory meta-analysis. *Pain, 60*, 239–256.

Hersen, M., & Barlow, D. H. (1981). *Single-case experimental designs. Strategies for studying behavior change.* New York: Pergamon Press.

Howard, K. I., Moras, K., Brill, P. L., Martinovich, Z., & Lutz, W. (1986). Evaluation of psychotherapy: Efficacy, effectiveness, and patient progress. *American Psychologist, 51*, 1059–1064.

Jay, S. M., Elliott, C. H., & Varni, J. W. (1986). Acute and chronic pain in adults and children with cancer. *Journal of Clinical and Consulting Psychology, 54*, 601–607.

Kain, Z. N., Wang, S. M., Caramico, L. A., Hofstadter, M., & Mayes, L. C. (1997). Parental desire for perioperative information and informed consent: A two-phase study. *Anesthesia & Analgesia, 84*, 299–306.

Kanfer, F. H., & Goldstein, A. D. (1997). *Helping people change: A textbook of methods* (4th ed.). Boston: Allyn & Bacon.

Kanoy, K. W., & Schroeder, C. S. (1985). Suggestions to parents about common behavior problems in a pediatric primary care office: Five years of follow-up. *Journal of Pediatric Psychology, 10*, 15–30.

Kazak, A. E. (1989). Families of chronically ill children: A systems and social-ecological model of adaptation and challenge. *Journal of Consulting and Clinical Psychology, 57*, 25–30.

Kazak, A. E. (1997). A contextual family/systems approach to pediatric psychology: Introduction to the Special issue. *Journal of Pediatric Psychology, 22*, 141–148.

Kazak, A. E., & Nachman, G. S. (1991). Family research on childhood chronic illness: Pediatric oncology as an example. *Journal of Family Psychology, 4*, 462–483.

Kazdin, A. E. (1980). *Behavior modification in applied settings.* Homewood, IL: Dorsey Press.

Kazdin, A. E. (1993). Psychotherapy for children and adolescents: Current progress and future research directions. *American Psychologist, 48*, 644–657.

Kazdin, A. E., Bass, D., Ayers, W. A., & Rodgers, A. (1990). Empirical and clinical focus of child and adolescent psychotherapy research. *Journal of Consulting and Clinical Psychology, 58*, 729–740.

La Greca, A. M., & Skyler, J. S. (1991). Psychological management of diabetes. In C. J. H. Kelnar (Ed.), *Childhood diabetes* (pp. 295–310). London: Chapman & Hall.

La Greca, A. M., Stone, W. L., Drotar, D., & Maddux, J. E. (1988). Training in pediatric psychology: Survey results and recommendations. *Journal of Pediatric Psychology, 13*, 121–139.

La Greca, A. M., & Varni, J. W. (1993). Editorial: Interventions in pediatric psychology: A look toward the future. *Journal of Pediatric Psychology, 18*, 667–679.

Lask, B., & Fosson, A. (1989). *Childhood illness: The psychosomatic approach.* New York: Wiley.

Lima, J., Nazarian, L., Charney, E., & Lahti, C. (1976). Compliance with short-term antimicrobial therapy: Some techniques that help. *Pediatrics, 57*, 383–386.

Mattar, M., Markello, J., & Yaffe, S. (1975). Pharmaceutical factors affecting compliance. *Pediatrics, 55*, 101–108.

McDaniel, S. H., Campbell, T. L., & Seaburn, D. B. (1995). Principles for collaboration between health and mental health problems in primary care. *Family Systems Medicine, 13*, 283–299.

Melamed, B. G., & Siegel, L. J. (1975). Reduction of anxiety in children facing hospitalization and surgery by use of filmed modeling. *Journal of Consulting and Clinical Psychology, 43*, 511–521.

Ollendick, T., & Hersen, M. (1993). Child and adolescent behavioral assessment. In T. Ollendick & M. Hersen (Eds.), *Handbook of child and adolescent assessment* (pp. 3–14). Boston: Allyn & Bacon.

Peterson, L., & Ridley-Johnson, R. (1980). Pediatric hospital responses to survey on pre-hospital preparation for children. *Journal of Pediatric Psychology, 5,* 1–7.

Peterson, L., Schultheis, K., Ridley-Johnson, R., Miller, D. J., & Tracy, K. (1984). Comparisons of three modeling procedures on the presurgical and postsurgical reactions of children. *Behavior Therapy, 15,* 197–203.

Peterson, L., & Shigetomi, C. (1981). The use of coping techniques to minimize anxiety in hospitalized children. *Behavior Therapy, 12,* 1–14.

Pless, I. B., & Stein, R. E. K. (1994). Intervention research: Lessons from research on children with chronic disorders. In R. J. Haggerty, L. R. Sherrod, N. Garmezy, & M. Rutter (Eds.), *Stress, risk, and resilience in children and adolescents: Processes, mechanisms, and interventions* (pp. 317–353). London: Cambridge University Press.

Poole, S. (1984). Recurrent abdominal pain in childhood and adolescence. *American Family Physician, 30,* 131–137.

Prensky, A. L. (1984). Differentiating and treating pediatric headaches. *Contemporary Pediatrics, 1,* 12–45.

Roberts, M. C. (1986). *Pediatric psychology: Psychological interventions and strategies for pediatric problems.* New York: Pergamon Press.

Routh, D. K., & Ernst, A. R. (1984). Somatization disorder in relatives of children and adolescents with functional abdominal pain. *Journal of Pediatric Psychology, 9,* 427–437.

Russo, D. C., & Varni, J. W. (1982). Behavioral pediatrics. In D. C. Russo & J. E. Varni (Eds.), *Behavioral pediatrics: Research and practice* (pp. 3–24). New York: Plenum Press.

Sanders, M. R., Shepard, R. W., Cleghorn, G., & Woolford, H. (1994). The treatment of recurrent abdominal pain in children: A controlled comparison of cognitive-behavioral family intervention and standard pediatric care. *Journal of Clinical and Consulting Psychology, 62,* 306–314.

Schaefer, C. E., Millman, H. L., & Levine, G. F. (1994). *Therapies for psychosomatic disorders in children.* Northvale, NJ: Aronson.

Schepp, K. G. (1991). Factors influencing the coping effort of mothers of hospitalized children. *Nursing Research, 40,* 42–46.

Schroeder, C. S., & Mann, J. (1991). A model for clinical child practice. In C. S. Schroeder & B. N. Gordon (Eds.), *Assessment and treatment of childhood problems: A clinician's guide* (pp. 375–398). New York: Guilford Press.

Schwartz-Lookinland, S., McKeever, L. C., & Saputo, M. (1989). Compliance with antibiotic regimens with hispanic mothers. *Patient Education and Counseling, 13,* 171–182.

Selekman, M. D. (1997). *Solution-focused therapy with children. Harnessing family strengths for systemic change.* New York: Guilford Press.

Seligman, M. E. (1986). Science as an ally of practice. *American Psychologist, 51,* 1072–1079.

Seligman, M. E. (1995). *The optimistic child: A revolutionary program that safe-guards children against depression and builds lifelong resilience.* Boston: Houghton Mifflin.

Sharrer, V. W., & Ryan-Wenger, N. M. (1991). Measurements of stress and coping among school-aged children with and without recurrent abdominal pain. *Journal of School Health, 61,* 86–91.

Sibinga, M. S., & Carey, W. B. (1976). Dealing with unnecessary medical trauma to children. *Pediatrics, 57,* 800–803.

Siegel, L. J. (1976). Preparation of children for hospitalization: A selected review of the research literature. *Journal of Pediatric Psychology, 1,* 26–30.

Siegel, L. J. (1983). Hospitalization and medical care of children. In E. C. Walker & M. C. Roberts (Eds.), *Handbook of clinical child psychology* (pp. 1089–1108). New York: Wiley.

Singer, H. S., & Rowe, S. (1992). Chronic recurrent headaches in children. *Pediatric Annals, 21,* 369–373.

Sloan, D. M. (1997, July). Are students being prepared for the managed health care market? *American Psychological Association Graduate Student Newsletter,* 17–19.

Stabler, B. (1988). Pediatric consultation-liaison. In D. K. Routh (Ed.), *Handbook of pediatric psychology* (pp. 538–566). New York: Guilford Press.

Valman, H. B. (1981). Recurrent abdominal pain: ABC of 1 to 7. *British Medical Journal, 282,* 1949–1951.

Visintainer, M. A., & Wolfer, J. A. (1975). Psychological preparation for surgical pediatric patients: The effect on children's and parents' stress responses and adjustment. *Pediatrics, 56,* 187–202.

Wald, E. R. (1983). The middle ear in early years. *Emergency Medicine, 15,* 94–111.

Walker, C. E. (1979). Behavioral intervention in a pediatric setting. In J. R. McNamara (Ed.), *Behavioral approaches to medicine: Application and analysis* (pp. 227–266). New York: Plenum Press.

Walker, L. S., Garber, J., & Greene, J. W. (1991). Psychosocial correlates of recurrent childhood pain: A comparison of pediatric patients with recurrent abdominal pain, organic illness, and psychiatric disorders. *Journal of Abnormal Psychology, 102,* 248–258.

Walker, L. S., & Greene, J. W. (1989). Children with recurrent abdominal pain and their parents: More somatic complaints, anxiety, and depression than other patient families? *Journal of Pediatric Psychology, 14,* 231–243.

Wanranch, H. R., & Keenan, D. M. (1985). Behavioral treatment of children with recurrent headaches. *Journal of Behavior Therapy and Experimental Psychiatry, 16,* 31–38.

Wood, B. L. (1993). Beyond the "psychosomatic family": A biobehavioral family model of pediatric illness. *Family Process, 32,* 261–278.

Wood, B., Watkins, J. B., Boyle, J. T., Nogueira, J., Zimand, E., & Carroll, L. (1989). The "psychosomatic family" model: An empirical and theoretical analysis. *Family Process, 28,* 399–417.

Zuckerberg, A. (1994). Perioperative approach to children. *Pediatric Anesthesia, 41,* 15–29.

25

An Ecological Perspective on Pathways of Risk, Vulnerability, and Adaptation
Implications for Preventive Interventions

ROBERT D. FELNER

Prevention has become a central goal among those concerned with a wide array of human conditions (Cowen, 1996; Felner, Jason, Mortisugu, & Farber, 1983). At the start of the 1990s, the Secretary of Health and Human Services called prevention the nation's number one health and social priority (Healthy People 2000, 1990). The reasons for prevention's emergence as a central priority on the national health agenda are quite clear. Simply put, after-the-fact, reconstructive approaches have proven to be inadequate to the task of reducing the crushing levels of social and health problems confronting the nation.

There are several reasons for this failure. Primary among these is the scope of the problems we confront. Most estimates are that 15–20% of all children and families, or approximately 35–50 million people in the United States, are in need of intensive mental health services (Joint Commission on Mental Health and Mental Disabilities, 1961; President's Commission on Mental Health, 1978). Social ills are also at epidemic levels. There will never be adequate levels of economic or human resources to address these overwhelming levels of need if we rely on reconstructive and individually focused models of intervention (see Albee, 1959; Sarason, 1981).

Preventive interventions have shown their potential to be both far more effective and cost efficient than those that attempt to reverse existing dysfunction (see Schorr, 1988; Committee for Economic Development, 1991). Studies have sug-

ROBERT D. FELNER • Department of Education, University of Rhode Island, Kingston, Rhode Island 02881.

Handbook of Psychotherapies with Children and Families, edited by Russ and Ollendick. Kluwer Academic/Plenum Publishers, New York, 1999.

gested that for every dollar spent on prevention, cost savings of between $3 and $10 may be realized in reduced demand for after-the-fact service. Adding to the cost efficacy of prevention is that, beyond providing for cost savings, prevention programs also yield additional tax revenues. For example, the Committee for Economic Development (1991), a group led by executives in the private sector, has shown that the prevention of school failure and drop-out would result in significantly higher levels of taxes paid by those who avoid these outcomes. This combination of prevention's cost efficacy and the enormous societal needs we confront constitutes a clarion call for an emphasis on prevention.

For prevention to fulfill its promise and to be fully incorporated into the fabric of social policy requires that we reexamine and rethink the guiding frameworks for solving social problems that have been used in the past (Seidman & Rappaport, 1986). A central goal of this chapter is to assist in moving us closer to the attainment of a science of prevention. This science of prevention must be built on a conceptual framework that enables us to overcome inefficient, ineffective, victim-blaming models of service delivery in which ambiguity in the concepts and terminology of prevention impedes the development of a cumulative knowledge base.

In the pages that follow, I attempt the further articulation of such a framework and greater clarity in the operationalization of key variables. Perhaps the best place to start is with what appears to be a very innocent question. That is, what do we mean by the concept of "prevention"—and in what ways is it distinct, with unique features and foci, vis-à-vis other forms of intervention? This chapter considers the ways in which a developmental perspective provides a sound basis for addressing the issues of concern in prevention. Of particular concern is the articulation of the ways in which the design of prevention efforts must be guided by understandings of developmental processes, and directly targeted to the modification of critical elements of developmental pathways (e.g., conditions of risk, acquisition of vulnerabilities). I then build on a more specific model of development—the *transactional–ecological* framework—that was previously proposed as especially well suited to the needs of a unique science of prevention. In a final section, the ways in which we may move from these conceptual considerations and related literatures to applications at both policy and programmatic levels are discussed. Here, I consider what we have learned from field trials about the characteristics of effective prevention efforts, and the ways in which these understandings are congruent with the theoretical perspectives I have offered.

PREVENTION: DEFINITIONAL ISSUES AND THE QUESTION OF UNIQUENESS

Intentionality and Prevention as a Science

Cowen (1980) argues that a defining characteristic of sound prevention programs is that they are *intentional*. Intentionality implies that in prevention efforts the strategies selected and the targets of change should follow directly from theory and research concerning "pathways" to disorder and adaptation (Felner & Felner, 1989). In prevention the immediate goal and focus of intervention is the modification of those *processes that lead to the emergence of maladaptation* so as to reduce the onset of the target problem(s) (Felner & Lorion, 1985; Lorion, Price, &

Eaton, 1989). To meet the criteria of intentionality, those involved in the design of a program must first specify those causal processes that are to be changed. Intervention strategies should then be selected that will influence the levels of these processes in ways that first reduce risk or promote resilience and, ultimately, reduce the onset of disorder.

Put otherwise, good prevention practice is good science. A program that meets the criteria of intentionality can be viewed as a test of hypotheses about etiologically significant pathways to disorder. Indeed, systematically mounted prevention programs may be seen as the only *acceptable and ecologically valid* experimental tests of such hypotheses. Consider that there are only two experimental ways to test hypotheses about the causes of disorder (Felner, Silverman, & Adan, 1989, 1992; Mednick, Griffith, & Mednick, 1981). One is to attempt to create conditions in the lives of people to induce disorder. This option is obviously unacceptable. The other option is to locate people who are naturally exposed to those conditions hypothesized to contribute to disorder. We can then systematically modify these conditions in desired directions to show that when such changes are made, the desired reductions in dysfunction follow. The latter approach is synonymous with prevention.

If we accept that prevention efforts must meet the standards of intentionality, we must now ask what we mean by prevention vis-à-vis other forms of intervention. Of central concern is the question of whether conceptual distinctions between prevention and other forms of intervention add to our ability to develop more effective intervention efforts at all levels.

Blended and Unique Prevention Models

Currently, there are two quite different views concerning whether prevention is a unique intervention approach. One position is the "blended approach." This view holds that prevention is merely an extension of other types of intervention. It emphasizes the commonalities and downplays the distinctions among prevention and other forms of intervention. By contrast, the second perspective, which sees preventive interventions as involving a "unique approach," holds that prevention is a distinct element in the continuum of care.

Blended views of prevention trace their roots to the public health model. In this model the term *prevention* encompasses the full range of traditional medical and human service interventions. *Tertiary prevention* focuses on individuals already displaying serious disorder and seeks to reduce the associated disruption for both the target individual and significant others. *Secondary prevention* focuses on persons showing early signs of disorder, with the goals of reducing the intensity, severity, and duration of dysfunction. Such interventions seek to identify specific individuals who are "at risk" as a result of showing "preclinical" manifestations of the focal disorder(s) (Lorion et al., 1989). *Primary prevention* seeks to reduce the incidence of new cases of disorder. It is targeted to entire populations, not to particular individuals (Cowen, 1983).

Proponents of the blended position (e.g., Lorion et al., 1989; Sameroff & Fiese, 1989) argue that the overlap among these prevention types, especially primary and secondary prevention, should be embraced. Lorion et al., (1989) state, "rather than emphasizing the theoretical distinctions between primary (i.e., incidence-focused) and secondary (i.e., prevalence-focused) preventive efforts . . . their overlapping value for emotional and behavioral disorders [should] be appreciated" (p. 64). This argument builds on the public health model's linear view of the evolution of dysfunction. In a linear model, disorders are seen to move sequentially from onset through clinical syndrome such that the timing of the "onset" of dysfunction is something that can be readily identified. Sameroff and Fiese (1989) note that current data do not support this discrete onset element of a linear view of onset for most socioemotional disorders. Rather, they note that early forms of developmental functioning have been linked to a variety of outcomes, depending on the contexts in which they occur (see Sameroff, Seifer, Barocas, Zax, & Greenspan, 1987). Thus, conditions that in a linear model would be seen to mark "onset" in actuality, can be employed to predict the ultimate emergence of specific dysfunction only in a probabilistic and nonspecific way.

Prevention as a Unique Approach

In contrast to the blended position, others argue that such blending obscures important distinctions among intervention types and perpetuates old problems under new labels. For example, Cowen (1983) states, "To lump such diversity under a unified banner of 'prevention' is sheer slight of hand. . . . Calling such things prevention . . . only dilutes and obscures a set of conceptually attractive alternatives to past ineffectual mental health ways" (p. 12). I am not arguing here for assigning a lesser importance to other forms of intervention, but rather that the development of a sound knowledge basis for both prevention and other forms of intervention will be hindered by inadequate attention to their differences.

To develop the precision necessary for a science of prevention a fundamental shift must occur in our language. I, along with others (see Gordon, 1983; Seidman, 1987), recommend the abandonment of the traditional public health phraseology. Instead, what is required are terms that are more descriptive and conceptually suited to the approaches being implemented. Adopting this perspective, tertiary prevention becomes *treatment,* secondary prevention becomes *early intervention,* and primary prevention assumes the sole mantle of *prevention.*

There are several additional bases for assigning a unique status to prevention in addition to the nonapplicability of the linear, onset-based public health model. A second defining feature of particular import is the level of analysis regarding the targets of prevention. Prevention efforts are by definition mass or population focused. This does not mean that prevention efforts must target all persons in the population at large. Gordon (1983) has proposed a framework for the organization of prevention trials that may be especially helpful here. This organization is based on how the targeted groups are selected. "Universal" interventions are those that are designed for all segments of a population. "Selected" interventions are targeted to subpopulations that are characterized by shared exposure to some epidemiologically established risk factor(s). Groups of individuals exposed to "risky situations" (Price, 1980), such as the children of teenage mothers or of parents with a serious social/emotional problem, and persons experiencing major life transitions or other conditions of risk, are among the populations to which selected interventions would be targeted. Finally, "indicated" interventions are targeted to specific individuals who are already displaying preclinical levels of disorder and who have been identified through screening procedures.

In our reformulated model of prevention, both universal and selected interventions would continue to be included under the rubric of prevention. In the remainder of this chapter, preventive or *population-level interventions* refer to these interventions. But, indicated interventions *would not* continue to be included under the flag of *prevention*. Instead, we can see that such efforts are now more appropriately labeled *early intervention*.

A third defining feature of prevention concerns the focus of change efforts. In treatment or early intervention, change efforts center on reversal or amelioration of conditions that have already emerged in specific individuals. By contrast, because prevention is before the fact, it cannot have as its first-order targets of change the disorders it seeks to reduce. Instead, prevention directly targets the enhancement, disruption, or modification, as appropriate, of the unfolding process (and conditions) that lead to well-being or to serious mental health or social problems. That is, "preventive intervention(s) involve the systematic alteration and modification of processes related to the development of adaptation and well-being or disorder, with the goals of increasing or decreasing, respectively, the rate or level with which these occur in the [target] population" (Felner & Lorion, 1985, p. 93).

The above leads to a fourth defining feature of prevention. Integral to preventive interventions is a focus on promoting the acquisition of strengths, well-being, and positive developmental outcomes (Cowen, 1994). By focusing on promoting strengths, preventive interventions lead to a significant reduction in the degree to which exposure to conditions of risk may precipitate the onset of disorder. The positive developmental outcomes that promotion-focused efforts yield are also important in their own right. Throughout the remainder of this chapter, the term *prevention* should be understood to mean prevention and promotion.

Given these views, an adequate framework for a science of prevention must enable us to develop interventions that are consistent with these defining features and values. More specifically, it must (1) enable "preventionists" (Price, 1983) to address the evolution of dysfunction in a more differentiated fashion than is provided for by linear models, (2) facilitate the understanding of target problems and "disorders" in ways that do not *require* personal-level explanations for the cause or maintenance of the disorders and social problems, (3) allow for the identification of conditions to be changed that impact entire sectors of the population, and (4) guide the systematic targeting of conditions that may be developmentally quite distant from the actual onset of disorder among members of the target population.

To attain such specificity we need greater precision and agreement in our definitions of the central concepts that mark potential points for intervention in developmental pathways to disorder. Of particular concern are the ways in which we define risk, vulnerability, resilience, protective conditions, and onset. Failure to draw clear distinctions among these concepts may lead to ambiguity and confusions that hamper the systematic accumulation of a body of knowledge for prevention science (Mrazek & Haggerty, 1994).

Points of Intervention in Developmental Pathways: Disentangling Vulnerability, Risk, Protective Factors, and Onset

Most current perspectives on disorder start with a fundamental "diathesis–stress" perspective. This model holds that individuals may have either genetically based or otherwise acquired vulnerabilities to the onset of disorder. These vulnerabilities are the diathesis side of the equation. They "set" the person's threshold of susceptibility to environmental conditions (e.g., stress) or hazards (e.g., high levels of disorganization, restrictive opportunity structures, or danger) that may precipitate the onset of disorder.

For the purposes of prevention the concept of *risk* is defined epidemiologically. It is a conditional statement about the probability that any member of a given population or subpopulation will develop later disorder. Often overlooked in discussions of risk is that the designation of being a member of an "at-risk" group says little about any specific member of that group other than that he or she has been exposed to the condition(s) of risk under consideration. If the conditional probabilities of disorder in a population are "X," it is not that all members of that group possess "X" levels of predisposition or "riskness" for disorder (Richters & Weintraub, 1990). Many members of the risk group will be free of all signs of difficulties, while others will develop significant adaptive difficulties. A risk designation is no more than an actuarial statement about the members of a selected group. Thus, assessment efforts to guide the targeting of prevention programs are based on knowledge of the probabilistic ways in which conditions of risk disrupt developmental processes in the lives of all persons in a cohort. There is no need to know the extent to which these processes have been disrupted for specific individuals. It is more accurate to speak of *conditions of risk* or *populations "at risk"* rather than *"high-risk" individuals*. Unfortunately, the term *risk* has been frequently applied to individual characteristics and/or to imply that all individuals in a "high-risk" group are somehow more fragile or *vulnerable* than all of those in lower-risk groups.

Why has this conceptual slippage occurred? Certainly part of the problem stems from the practice of individual-level variables, especially when aggregated for a population or group, being spoken about as risk markers (see Hawkins, Catalano, & Miller, 1992). For example, children who are shy, show signs of behavioral problems in the classroom, or have lower levels of self-esteem are often designated "at risk." I feel that this terminology creep is simply unwise and often confusing. *Actuarial statements cannot be made about particular individuals,* even those who have characteristics that, at the population level, do relate to probability statements.

To address this slippage, there are several corollaries of my definition of risk that may be helpful. First, conditions of risk are primarily environmental in nature (although being part of a population group that may have some genetic risk characteristics would also qualify as long as we remember we are talking about a population-level attribute). Second, environmental conditions can have two quite distinct roles—as predisposing conditions and as precipitating/compensatory conditions. When environmental conditions act in a predisposing fashion, *vulnerabilities*, which in our definition are always *person-level variables*, are *acquired*. Vulnerabilities may be acquired from either problematic interactions with environmental conditions that are present or the lack of exposure to important developmentally promoting conditions and resources (Rutter, 1989). For example, poor early parent–child interactions may lead to the development of vulnerabilities and delays in a number of areas of child functioning. Strengths and *personal competencies* may also be acquired from developmental contexts—this time positive— and are again person-level variables. Failure to accurately understand that these person-level characteristics are, in fact, "first-order" developmental *outcomes* (i.e., acquired vulnerabilities and competencies/strengths) has, in the past, led to their being incorrectly labeled as individual-level risk conditions or as early signs of "onset" of specific disorders (Figure 1). Competencies, strengths, and vulnerabili-

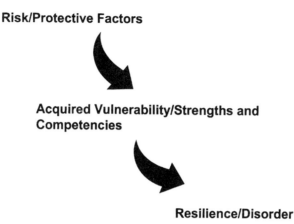

Figure 1. Risk/protective factors.

ties will influence the probability that an individual will be resilient in the face of stress and other risk conditions. But, as we have seen, they are not markers of individual risk nor are they typically direct and inevitable markers of the onset of disorder. I must pause here to note that to talk about building resiliencies in individuals also muddies these concepts. Resilience is an outcome, defined by a person's or population's response to challenge and stress. Discussions of building "resiliencies" lose this essential defining element and obscure important differences between such outcomes and aspects of developmental pathways that produce them (e.g., strengths, vulnerabilities, environmental resources).

When environmental circumstances act as precipitating conditions, rather than predisposing ones, they interact with *existing* vulnerabilities and competencies to trigger the onset of more serious dysfunction. Similarly, protective conditions in the environment may act in a compensatory fashion, reducing the likelihood that existing vulnerabilities will be "activated" when the person experiences conditions of risk (Figure 2). For example, acquired vulnerabilities may make an individual susceptible to the development of disorder during major life changes. But, if these changes occur in a context in which the person receives additional support and external coping resources, such difficulties may still not be triggered, even if the person brings relatively high levels of acquired vulnerabilities to the situation.

Implicit in this view of unfolding pathways to disorder is that exposure to conditions of risk or the acquisition of vulnerabilities is not synonymous with the onset of disorder. Neither is exposure to protective factors or the acquisition of competencies synonymous with health and resilience. Rather, these are the sequential and interactive elements of *developmental trajectories* to dysfunction and well-being that are the appropriate direct targets for change by prevention programming. Framed this way, prevention initiatives may include several strategies that *target root causes and contributing factors* to dysfunction, all of which would qualify as before-the-fact. They include attempts at (1) reducing levels of conditions of risk or increasing levels of protective factors; (2) efforts to directly, or indirectly through the previous step, reduce the incidence rates of person-level vulnerabilities or the enhancement of personal competencies and strengths; and (3) altering

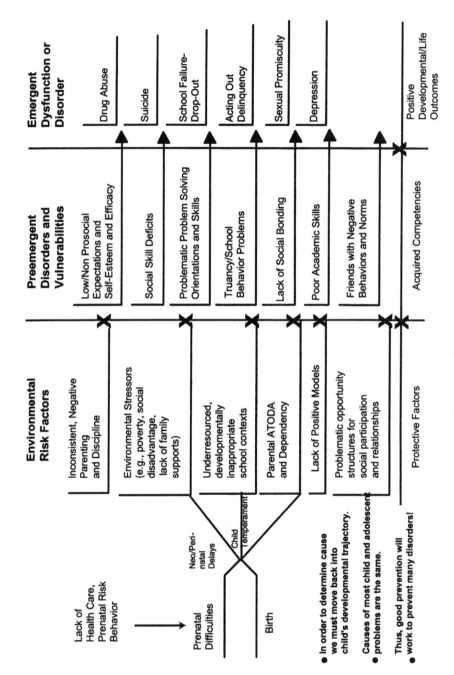

Figure 2. Pathways to disorder.

levels of conditions of risk and of protective factors that have been shown to *inter-act* with acquired vulnerabilities and strengths to trigger the onset of more serious disorder or to produce resilience in the face of serious challenge (Figure 2).

This conceptualization of developmental pathways has direct implications for the evaluation of prevention programs. The initial assessments of the efficacy of prevention efforts may take place far sooner than is often thought to be possible. Illustratively, for some prevention efforts, especially those dealing with children, it may be a number of years before the primary conditions and disorders we seek to reduce are likely to develop. By adopting a perspective based on the above understandings of developmental pathways, it is possible to obtain relatively rapid assessments of the degree to which the program and its effects are "on course" and show support for having the desired long-term effects. This can be done by assessing the degree to which the initiative has produced changes, in the desired directions, in key conditions that are earlier in the developmental pathway, even when they are far from the expected onset of dysfunction.

Given these understandings about those aspects of developmental pathways that are the direct and indirect, intermediate, targets of change, we turn to the question, what are the appropriate long-term goals of prevention? The answer we select is critical as it defines those specific conditions earlier in developmental pathways with which we will be concerned. For example, it answers the question of conditions of risk for what? Vulnerability to the development of what? It is to these concerns that we now turn.

Intervention Goals, Outcome Specificity, and Pathways to Disorder

Outcome Specificity

When we consider the question of what the appropriate goals for prevention are, a critical issue is whether a given prevention program should have as its goal(s) the reduction of highly specific disorders or *whether it should be focused on multiple outcomes.*

Historically, a major dimension on which most prevention efforts can be categorized reflects two quite different assumptions about the specificity and uniqueness of developmental pathways. Single-outcome-focused programs, such as those targeted to substance abuse, delinquency, school failure, depression, teen suicide, and teen pregnancy, reflect a specific disease prevention model that rests heavily on classic medical paradigms of disorder. These paradigms hold that dysfunction is caused by specifiable disease agents or germs that interact with individual vulnerabilities that in turn can also be specified.

A contrasting perspective to this position is one that holds that there is a need for a comprehensive, multicausal, and nonspecific developmental pathways/root causes-focused approach (see Felner & Felner, 1989). This model recognizes that (1) most of the disorders we seek to prevent have a large number of common risk factors, (2) that conditions that protect against one disorder generally also protect against many others, and (3) that there are nonspecific personal vulnerabilities that increase a person's susceptibility to the onset of a wide array of dysfunction. The pathways to most of the social, emotional, and adaptive difficulties with which we are concerned are generally complex and shared by more than one disorder. Hence, for a wide range of developmental outcomes and sociopathologies, it appears that efforts to identify specific and unique etiological "causal" agents are not appropriate.

Current data are highly supportive of this view and come from a number of converging research traditions. Studies of the adaptive impact of a wide array of developmental circumstances have shown that there are common developmental antecedents, such as family resources and interaction patterns, economic and social deprivation, other life stresses, powerlessness, and an array of nonspecific protective resiliency factors (e.g., social support, sense of self-efficacy, hope), that all relate to the probability that persons in a population will develop an extraordinary assortment of mental and physical disorders (Felner, Farber, & Primavera, 1983; Kellam & Brown, 1982; Kellam, Brown, Rubin, & Ensminger, 1983; Sameroff & Fiese, 1989; Silverman, 1989). Converging with this developmental evidence, other authors who have focused on epidemiology of serious disorders (see Cantwell & Baker, 1989; Dryfoos, 1990; Jessor & Jessor, 1977; Kellam et al., 1983; Rutter, 1989) have pointed to the high levels of comorbidity among such disorders and further underscored the fact that they appear to share a common constellation of antecedent developmental experiences and root causes in their emergent pathways.

The nonlinear and overlapping nature of pathways to disorder is further underscored by a third set of studies on the stability of the developmental course of such difficulties. Cantwell and Baker (1989), for example, examined the "stability" of clinical levels of disorder in childhood and adolescence and found that, 4 years after the time of initial diagnosis, for some disorders 100% of those who were diagnosed as previously showing clinical levels of dysfunction were symptom free. Additionally, among those children who had an initial diagnosis and who still had a diagnosable condition at the follow-up, across conditions only 30–50% were still found to have the original condition, while the remainder manifested quite different clinical conditions than had been originally diagnosed. Summarizing the findings pertaining to high levels of comorbidity of disorder, Rutter (1989) reviewed recent studies of child psychiatric epidemiology and concluded, "Perhaps the most striking finding to emerge from all developmental epidemiological studies undertaken up to now has been the extremely high levels of comorbidity" (p. 645). Similarly, in discussing commonalities across root causes and the need to consider broadly focused prevention approaches rather than focusing on specific outcomes, Sameroff and Fiese (1989) state that, "Whereas clear linkages have been found between some 'germs' and specific biological disorders, this has not been true for behavioral disorders" (p. 24). Less technically, but more succinctly, Lisbeth Schorr (1988) has summarized the interconnectedness among social problems by noting, "Rotten outcomes cluster."

To this point I have emphasized sets of interrelated but still discrete issues and understandings that need to be woven together in the creation of a science of prevention. What is now required is an integrative theoretical framework that allows us to accomplish this weaving. It is to a presentation of that framework we turn next.

TRANSACTIONAL–ECOLOGICAL MODELS OF PREVENTION

The transactional–ecological (T-E) model is a framework that the author of this chapter (Felner & Felner, 1989; Felner, Silverman, & Adix, 1991; Felner et al., 1992) and others (Seidman, 1987) have argued contains the requisite levels of comprehensiveness to address the range of issues raised above, while also providing for the degree of specificity required by intentionality. This T-E model obtains from a conceptual synthesis of two other highly complementary frameworks, the transactional (see Sameroff & Fiese, 1989) and ecological (see Bronfenbrenner, 1979) models of development. Full discussion of each of these approaches is beyond the parameters of this chapter, but I attempt to capture the key features of each for prevention.

The transactional model has been articulated by Sameroff and his colleagues (Sameroff & Chandler, 1975; Sameroff & Fiese, 1989) and others (Lorion et al., 1989) as a guide for preventive efforts. The model emphasizes the dynamic, reciprocal interactions between the individual and his context, with bidirectional influence being a fundamental element (Sarason & Doris, 1979). For example, the interactions between an infant and his parent, or between a youth and her peers, are thought to be a result of the child's influence on the parent or group, and the reciprocal effect of the environmental influence on the child.

A transactional perspective then is one element of a science of prevention that has as its focal targets for change those developmental processes that lead to disorder. But, it is not sufficient for addressing the full range of conditions that must be considered by preventive interventions. The transactional model is still at best dyadic (Seidman, 1987). It can only deal with those proximal environments in which the person directly participates. Further, because the transactional model always views the sources of influence as bidirectional (Sarason & Doris, 1979), there are some proximal contexts on which individual behavior has little influence (e.g., schools) for which it is not well suited for providing directions for intervention. To address these limitations and provide for a comprehensive model of prevention, several authors (Felner & Felner, 1989; Felner, Yates Felner, & Silverman, 2000; Seidman, 1987) have advocated for the joining of an ecological model of development (Barker, 1968; Bronfenbrenner, 1979) to the transactional one.

Combining the ecological and transactional perspectives to create a T-E model broadens the focus of each in some ways that are important for prevention. Consistent with transactional perspectives, an ecological view holds that developmental trajectories are shaped by "progressive, mutual accommodation between an active, growing human being and the changing properties of the settings in which the developing person lives" (Bronfenbrenner, 1979, p. 21). But, an ecological framework also provides for the consideration of critical additional elements of human contexts. It offers a comprehensive and integrative means of viewing the interactions between the various parts of total ecological and psychological systems, not only between individuals and their proximal environments. Thus, it better allows for the design of setting- and population-focused interventions. In particular, the ecological perspective allows for the consideration of influences that shape the dynamic relationships *between* systems, and the ways in which being part of these multiple systems influences human development.

There are at least three important ways in which the synthesis of ecological and transactional models enables us to address these concerns. First, it enables us to consider the etiological significance of conditions with which the person comes into direct contact but *on which their behavior does not have a significant bidirectional influence.* Included in this category of conditions are broader "social regularities" (Seidman, 1987), or "social structural conditions," such as the density and distribution of poverty and social disadvantage (Jencks & Peterson, 1991;

Schorr, 1988; Wilson, 1987), shifting economic conditions that influence motivation (W.T. Grant Foundation, 1988), and the regularities or structures of such primary developmental contexts as schools (Sarason, 1982).

Of particular interest for prevention are those systemwide conditions that distort, in pathogenic ways, all of the dyadic transactions that take place within their reach. These conditions may occur at several different system levels. The smallest system level of this type is what have been termed *microsystems* (Bronfenbrenner, 1979), or *settings-level* (Seidman, 1987) systems. These systems are the primary developmental contexts in which people live. They include such contexts as schools, religious congregations, the family, the worksite, and peer groups. The regularities of these settings may be only influenced slowly, if at all, by the dyadic interactions that take place within them (Sarason, 1982). For example, the overwhelming flux and disorganization that accompanies the transition to a high school "fed" by multiple middle schools is a condition that may seriously disrupt many of the dyadic patterns that are taking place within the school and peer groups (Felner & Adan, 1988). Similarly, the social regularities of a school or workplace, its resource patterns, and other formal system regularities may go far to shape the nature of the interpersonal interactions that take place within it (Felner et al., 2000). But, in neither case will the dyadic interactions rapidly or necessarily impact the system regularities that are shaping them.

At the level of *macrosystems* (i.e., social structural conditions and regularities) (Bronfenbrenner, 1979), there are again conditions on which the individual's behavior has little effect. But, as before, these conditions have significant adaptive implications for individual behavior, both directly and through their impact on the other system relationships that a person experiences. For example, because of societal changes the earning potential of a high school graduate has dropped over 40% in the past two decades (W.T. Grant Foundation, 1988). This is a structural condition over which the individual has little control. But this shift may have profound effects on the nature of those behaviors students view as adaptive. When this condition is coupled, for example, with others that indicate to youth that they have little hope for attending college—even if they complete high school—this fundamental shift in the economic meaning of graduation may make alternative, societally undesirable behaviors, such as early school leaving, early parenthood, and/or involvement in illicit activities to earn money, appear to be intelligent and attractive choices.

A second enhancement for prevention that derives from joining ecological views to transactional ones is that this synthesis allows for consideration of the ways in which interactions between individuals and any specific setting are influenced by differences and similarities *between that setting and others that make up their life context* (i.e., it allows for consideration of *transcontextual* effects). These relationships between microsystems have been labeled *mesosystems* (Bronfenbrenner, 1979). The need to consider transcontextual influences rests on the understanding that persons have a number of primary settings which comprise the ecological map of their life context. Each of these settings has unique demands that shape the nature of the transactions required by them. The solutions, skills, and abilities required by one context may, when applied in other settings, be complementary, antagonistic, and/or irrelevant. For example, the skills and interaction styles required to be adaptive in an inner-city environment may, when applied to a school setting, be maladaptive or irrelevant. Such conditions may result in children from inner-city environments being mislabeled as lacking in social competence or other abilities when, in fact, the actual problem is not that these children are deficient; rather, there is a poor match in the skills required among the different developmental contexts that make up their lives (e.g., Eccles & Midgley, 1988).

These mesosystemic relationships also add to our efforts to design effective prevention programs in another way. In particular, they bring attention to conditions that surround prevention programs that may require change in order for particular prevention efforts to be fully effective. Such conditions may play a limiting role in the impact of a prevention program and, if not adequately considered, may lead to false conclusions that a program effort is ineffective when, in fact, *it is a necessary but not sufficient element of a more complete prevention strategy.*

There are a number of instances where this may occur. For example, the impact of a preventively focused life skills curriculum will certainly be attenuated if the school context in which it functions does not provide adequate academic experiences to enable the students to develop necessary skills in those related areas. Even with the best decision-making skills, the choices available, and the motivation to make prosocial ones, will be limited by a student's inability to read. Similarly, programs to develop self-sufficiency skills for families who need them may fail if they do not consider that other systems that impact these families, such as the social welfare system, may provide disincentives for participation. Likewise, parent training programs may enable parents to gain important knowledge and skills, but the degree to which they apply this new knowledge in their interactions with children may be influenced by conditions in other systems in their lives. As the most highly trained developmental psychologists can tell you, when it has been a "bad day" outside the home, the quality of their parenting may be sharply diminished. Such "bad days" are, unfortunately, the stark day-to-day reality for single parents with few economic resources, those in negative job surroundings, those in poverty, and other groups with chronic stressors. These conditions will all certainly reduce the degree to which newly acquired parenting skills are translated to action. Thus, an ecological analysis of the interrelated systems of the lives of those we seek to impact is critical for ensuring that change efforts are adequately comprehensive and that research on them does not lead to the incorrect conclusion that prevention elements that may be necessary, but not sufficient, do not have utility for prevention of disorder.

Third, a comprehensive prevention model must provide for consideration of the impact of settings on individuals *with which they do not come into direct contact.* Bronfenbrenner (1979) has referred to these as *exosystems.* For instance, a child may never have direct contact with the neighborhoods and conditions in which her parents or grandparents were raised, or with the workplaces of her parents. But traumas suffered in these earlier developmental contexts (Garbarino, 1992), values learned in them (Sarason, 1981), or conditions within the workplaces, must all be part of a broader analysis of influences that contribute to the nature of the parent–infant interactions that occur (Seidman, 1987). T-E-based prevention initiatives would seek to understand developmental transactions by attempting to identify the presence of variables in the work settings of concern that have been linked to parent–child and familial difficulties (e.g., poor supervisor/worker communications; high stress levels; high levels of job instability and underemployment). These setting-level regularities would then be directly targeted by introducing systemwide conditions (e.g., improved supervisor relationships; on-site, childcare centers that promote parent involvement; linking parents to appropriate employment opportunities) that reduce workers' stresses and enhance well-being and family support resources. These changes would then be expected to radiate to the family/microsystem-level interactions of all workers in the setting.

To briefly summarize, joining an ecological perspective to a transactional one to create a T-E model expands our focus to include the ways in which person–setting interactions are impacted by relationships between settings, as well as the broader, macrosystemic contexts in which they may be nested. Equal weight is given to understanding dyadic transactions and to the analysis of the impact of and interactions among various settings, mesosystems, and macrosystems that may significantly influence developmental pathways. Such understandings will enable preventive interventions to move closer to the view of Seidman (1987), who states that, in prevention, "At both the setting and mesosystem level, the direct targets are the behavioral regularities and or relationships characterizing each respective level; individual effects are only an indirect result of the intervention" (p. 9).

There is an important corollary of the above features of the T-E model that makes it particularly useful for generating interventions that are congruent with the values and goals that we have set out for prevention as well as expanding the ways we can conceptualize possible approaches to intervention. The T-E model affords us the ability to view the behaviors that are to be prevented in ways that do not require the assumption that there are deficits or defects in the persons/population targeted—a core factor in victim blaming—for a condition to be targeted. Clinical–individual models require that we define target behaviors in terms of the existence of pathology and disorder *in* the individual. At transactional levels of analysis the person is still, at least in part, seen as responsible for problematic transactions and disorder. Neither of these theoretical frameworks allows us to consider the ways in which the target "disorders" may, in fact, be adaptive solutions to contextual conditions that are disordered. However, by utilizing the lens of a T-E perspective, many of the target conditions with which we are concerned can be seen to be the result of highly appropriate and adaptive efforts in disordered contexts. To state otherwise, "what might appear to be deviant outcomes may be those that any healthy child [or person] would exhibit in the environments and systems that define their lives . . . what might have been seen as disorder or disease may be better understood as a result of the child's appropriate, predictable, and highly adaptive attempts to adjust to contexts and conditions that require responses which are incompatible with those in other contexts in which they live. That is, . . . what might have been seen as a disorder or disease may be better understood as the [person's] appropriate, predictable, and highly adaptive attempts to adjust to contexts and conditions [that are developmentally inappropriate or disordered]" (Felner & Felner, 1989, p. 21).

Applying this view to prevention programs, the first questions that must be asked in the design of any prevention effort are: "In what ways were the conditions (e.g., behavior, belief system) that we wish to prevent adaptive at the time they developed?" and "Are there factors that are being experienced by the population that make the condition continue to be adaptive?" A basic assumption of this model is that any adaptive pattern, however problematic, originated as an attempt to positively adapt to conditions that existed at the time.

Given this assumption, efforts to understand or change any developmental pathway or outcome cannot take place independent of a consideration of the full set of historical, familial, economic, social, and political contexts that provide meaning to a person's life experiences. Such an approach will allow us to see that many of the problems we seek to reduce through prevention efforts are simply intelligent, effective attempts at adaptive solutions to disordered contexts. For example, social welfare policies that punish recipients for earning income, acquiring savings and attempting to accumulate equity (Moynihan, 1986) may lead recipients to behave in ways that society views as inappropriate (e.g., not saving; not seeking employment). Instead, the recipients are actually showing intelligent and adaptive problem-solutions in the face of disordered contextual demands. To avoid the confusion that places the locus of such difficulties inside the person, we might better refer to these and other positive adaptations to disordered contexts—that are dysfunctional in later or other developmental settings—as *sociopathology* rather than *psychopathology,* with the latter's inherent individual focus. This view further sharpens our focus on the characteristics of contexts that systematically distort normal developmental pathways to produce what appear to be deviant outcomes, but that are, in fact, better understood as positive adaptive efforts to dysfunctional contexts when considered in their full ecological–developmental context.

Given our model and its central features, let us now consider its application to current prevention efforts and to the building of next-generation prevention models.

From Theory to Practice: Creating Comprehensive, Developmentally Sequenced Interventions

Until now our focus has been on prevention theory, as well as theory and research relating to the evolution of sociopathologies and other problems of human well-being. Before closing, let us turn to an examination of what we know about proven prevention efforts and the ways in which it expands on, illustrates, and otherwise guides the further translation of the issues discussed above to concrete application.

It is beyond the scope of this chapter to review the full range of prevention efforts that have been shown to be effective. Recent reviews of research on prevention programs (see Bond & Wagner, 1988; Dryfoos, 1990; Felner, DuBois, & Adan, 1991; Felner et al., 2000; Price, Cowen, Lorion, & Ramos-McKay, 1988) point to a number of features that are common to prevention efforts that have been found to have strong empirical support. These elements are summarized in Table 1. As should be apparent, they are highly consistent with the perspective on prevention that I have offered above.

Given the general characteristics of effective prevention programs, let us next consider the ways in which these principles may be manifested in actual practice. First, the characteristic of comprehensiveness is an overarching one that is further defined and addressed by each of the other features in Table 1. That is, comprehensive programming will reflect a multisystem–multilevel perspective, attend to the timing, dosage, and fidelity of the intervention, focus on natural settings and systems, and strive to be scientific and replicable. It must also be made clear that to simply instruct most professionals or members of a community to attempt to

Table 1. Common Features of Effective Prevention Programs

- Recognize that there is no solution to addressing a target outcome
- Reflect understanding that high-risk behaviors are interrelated and that there are high levels of comorbidity among many focal outcomes
- Take a comprehensive, integrative strategy at each developmental level
- Attempt to create "developmental ladders" for target population with provision of developmentally appropriate strengthening experiences and reduction of developmentally hazardous conditions being primary foci for change efforts at each level
- Recognize importance of timing—start as early in the developmental pathway as possible and continue
- Target entire population or selected groups, not just indicated individuals
- Efforts are comprehensive, have adequate dosage, intensity, fidelity, and duration. Long-term efforts that continue throughout and across life stages. "One shots" and brief nonintegrative add-on "programs" are avoided
- Primary targets for first-order change are the conditions and elements of developmental pathways that may lead to disorder and that enhance strengths and well-being rather than focusing on the specific problematic outcome per se

create a "comprehensive prevention strategy and system" may be so overwhelming that they will be left with little sense of where to start.

To facilitate this task, what is required is an organizing heuristic or framework that is consistent with and builds on the T-E perspective and that provides a systematic approach to breaking this larger task down into more manageable "bite-sized" ones. Here, the concept of a "developmental ladder" is one that we think is especially useful (Felner, Silverman, & Adix, 1991). This approach makes explicit that comprehensive prevention approaches must be both "horizontally comprehensive," i.e., comprehensive at particular life stages and critical risk periods, and "vertically comprehensive," reflecting a life span perspective. The latter aspect builds on the understanding that the *timing* of preventive interventions is critical. A developmental ladder-based prevention system attempts to get each member of the target population through each life stage and developmental transition undamaged, and having been exposed to the requisite developmentally enhancing experiences to be prepared to master the tasks of the next phase of his or her life.

A developmental ladder approach to developing a comprehensive prevention system for a community provides a highly specific and easily applied framework for thinking about what needs to be done to address the health and social problems and well-being of a community. Now, rather than asking, "What elements of a prevention system need to be in place for our entire community?" (clearly a question that will rapidly become unfocused given the diversity of needs at different ages and levels), those involved can ask, for example, "For families with children aged 0–3, 3–5, in elementary school, having an elderly parent, and so forth, what conditions are particularly hazardous during 'X' or 'Y' developmental phase?" "What experiences are especially important to provide?" and "What resources are necessary?" A community can then examine whether, for each developmental phase, the requisite actions, conditions, and resources are in place.

A developmental ladder approach also addresses an additional key requirement of effective prevention efforts. Prevention programs have been shown to have the capacity to create enduring positive consequences and to reduce vulnerability to the development of later problems in the face of life's challenges (see Felner, Silverman, & Adix, 1991; Price et al., 1988). But, it is also the case that effective efforts at one life stage may be eroded if severe conditions of risk are confronted at later stages or necessary developmental experiences are lacking. Further, the effectiveness of programming later in life may be undermined by difficulties and vulnerabilities acquired previously. Illustratively, the research on the Perry Preschool Project (Schweinhart & Weikart, 1988) and Project Head Start (McKey et al., 1985) has demonstrated the potential enduring effects of preschool programming in obtaining a wide range of desired outcomes. These same data also reveal, however, that at least some of the gains may be lost if the preschool experience is surrounded or followed by schooling, familial, or community conditions that do not adequately allow the child to take full advantage of his or her newly acquired competencies.

Hence, there is a need both for comprehensive programming within life stages as well as for ongoing, complementary programming across each life stage, including "booster sessions" as discussed below. Inherent in the use of a developmental ladder strategy for prevention programming is just such integrated, ongoing prevention efforts. That such programming is required should not be taken as evidence that prevention programs at any one stage are not effective. To reach such a conclusion based on these data would be a little like saying that just because a person may develop problems later in life there are no positive benefits to having positive parent–child interactions during infancy. Rather, just as is the case for such naturally occurring positive developmental conditions, adequate prevention efforts at each life stage are necessary, but not always sufficient conditions for obtaining the outcomes we seek.

In employing a developmental ladder perspective, although the programming may be organized by the age of the target cohort of youth, it should be understood that, as discussed above, T-E programs will by definition focus on both these individuals and at least one of their primary developmental system contexts. Thus, in the case of children and youth this means that initiatives that target those at particular ages must implicitly, if not explicitly, also target, at a minimum, primary caregivers (i.e., parents, teachers) in the relevant environments to meet the assumptions of a T-E approach to prevention.

Reforming Policy and Practice at the Federal, State, and Local Levels

In our quest to achieve more effective prevention programs, knowing what works and having an adequate framework to guide these efforts are, unfortunately, still not sufficient conditions to ensure that these more effective strategies will actually emerge. The understandings of what it takes for effective and well-conceived programming are generally not reflected either in the nature of state and federal funding initiatives or in the practices of field professionals. Prevention initiatives funded by federal and state agencies are often organized more by the accident of who funds them and/or focused on highly specific outcomes (e.g., teen births, substance abuse, conduct disorders, depression), than based on the understandings discussed above. For example, state and federal agencies currently fund separate initiatives to prevent teenage pregnancy, child abuse, substance abuse, school failure, youth suicide, school aggression, gang membership, illiteracy, pre-

and perinatal complications, and welfare dependency, to name but a few of these fragmented and often uncoordinated efforts. Even among efforts that focus on a common single outcome (e.g., substance abuse) there may be multiple state and/or federal agencies, each of which has its own separate initiative. At best these are typically only loosely coordinated. At worst they may fight over turf and create needless and wastefully duplicative programs.

Such fragmentation is a very poor use of resources, typically leaving each initiative with just enough resources to not be effective. As we have seen, this organization is also the opposite of what we would do if our efforts were based on theory and research. A major priority of policymakers in many states, as well as of several federal initiatives (see Virginia Department of Mental Health, Mental Retardation, and Substance Abuse, 1988; the U.S. Center for Substance Abuse Prevention's Community Partnership Program), is to develop a more integrative approach given the growing recognition of the interrelatedness of the problems of concern, the need to reduce fragmentation for the cost efficient expenditure of resources, and the growing understanding that such disjointed services are neither effective nor appropriate. Comprehensive family support programs (see Moynihan, 1986; Schorr, 1988; Weiss & Jacobs, 1988) and the Schools of the Future (Holtzman, 1992), with their emphasis on positive development and meeting the needs of whole families, are more effective policy metaphors than are the traditional categorical approaches.

Creating the required enduring shifts in the thinking of funding agencies and staff in educational settings and human service agencies about what they are doing, and translating that to action, will not be easy tasks. To ask those who have been working in these agencies and policy systems to change what they do may be difficult and met with resistance even among those who are favorably inclined. Those working within existing systems will be limited in their ability to frame what they do by their personal and professional socialization experiences (Sarason, 1981). Instead of simply criticizing prevention professionals, researchers must offer these individuals new ways of "thinking about what they are thinking about." The T-E perspective offered above is one such step. Further, the prevention field in general, and prevention researchers in particular, must attend to the development of an infrastructure and technology transfer capacity that will allow for the effective dissemination to and implementation of what we have learned by those who live in our communities.

Much has been made in recent years of the need for those in local communities to be fully involved in generating the solutions to the social and health problems they face. This call should not be mistaken for a move to an abdication of professional involvement. Rather, much can be gained, by all involved, through focused, careful collaborations among policymakers, educational/social program professionals, and, importantly, community members. In this vein, Rappaport (1977) cited the need to recast the role of the mental health professional to that of "community collaborator" rather than expert. In such collaborations, the definitions of problems and issues to be addressed, and of the resources required to address them, can and must be provided and shaped by the community members. Prevention professionals, providers, and policymakers can then serve as partners by identifying a range of strategies and community change models that have been attempted and their strengths or weaknesses. These groups must then work together to take those state-of-the-art efforts that are identified as most appropriate to the needs that have been defined, and mold them to local community conditions, through a dynamic ongoing process between providers and constituents.

This chapter has presented a framework that can guide the development of the next generation of prevention efforts and serve as a foundation on which to build a systematic knowledge base for a science of prevention. As prevention moves toward its next generation of efforts, the contributions of those who provide the shoulders on which we stand in gaining our current vision should not be underestimated or underappreciated. Given this perspective and their "boost," it is hoped that the perspective provided in this chapter further changes the ways in which we "think about what we are thinking about" in the continued evolution of a science of prevention, and moves us further from the bounds of the procrustean, individually focused bed in which it was born.

REFERENCES

Albee, G. W. (1959). *Mental health manpower trends.* New York: Basic Books.

Barker, R. G. (1968). *Ecological psychology: Concepts and methods for studying the environment of human behavior.* Stanford, CA: Stanford University Press.

Bond, L. A., & Wagner, B. M. (1988) Familes in transition: Primary prevention programs that work. In *Primary prevention of psychopathology,* Vol. II (pp. 343–354). Newbury Port, CA: Sage Publications.

Bronfenbrenner, U. (1979). *The ecology of human development: Experiments by nature and design.* Cambridge, MA: Harvard University Press.

Cantwell, D. P., & Baker, L. (1989). Stability and natural history of DSM-III childhood diagnoses. *Journal of the American Academy of Child and Adolescent Psychiatry, 28,* 691–700.

Committee for Economic Development. (1991). *The unfinished agenda: A new vision for child development and education.* New York: Author.

Cowen, E. L. (1980). The wooing of primary prevention. *American Journal of Community Psychology, 8,* 258–284.

Cowen, E. L. (1983). Primary prevention in mental health: Past, present, and furture. In R. D. Felner, L. A. Jason, J. N. Moritsugu, & S. S. Farber (Eds.), *Preventive psychology: Theory, research, and prevention* (pp. 11–25). New York: Pergamon Press.

Cowen, E. L. (1994). The enhancement of psychological wellness: Challenges and opportunities. *American Journal of Community Psychology, 22,* 149–179.

Dryfoos, J. G. (1990). *Adolescents at risk: Prevalence and prevention.* London: Oxford University Press.

Eccles, J. S., & Midgley, C. (1989). Stage–environment fit: Developmentally appropriate classrooms for young adolescents. In R. E. Ames & C. Ames (eds.), *Research on motivation in education* (Vol. 3, pp. 139–186). New York: Academic Press

Felner, R. D., & Adan, A. M. (1988). The school transitional environment project: An ecological intervention and evaluation. In R. H. Price, E. L. Cowen, R. P. Lorion, & J. Ramos-McKay (Eds.), *Fourteen ounces of prevention: A casebook for practitioners* (pp. 111–122). Washington, DC: American Psychological Association.

Felner, R. D., DuBois, D. L., & Adan, A. M. (1991). Community-based intervention and prevention: Conceptual underpinnings and progress toward a science of community intervention and evaluation. In C. E. Walker (Ed.), *Clinical psychology: Historical and research foundations* (pp. 459–510). New York: Plenum Press.

Felner, R. D., Farber, S. S., & Primavera, J. (1983). Transitions and stressful life events: A model for primary prevention. In R. D. Felner, L. A. Jason, J. N. Moritsugu, & S. S. Farber (Eds.), *Preventive psychology: Theory, research, and prevention* (pp. 191–215). New York: Pergamon Press.

Felner, R. D., & Felner, T. Y. (1989). Prevention programs in the educational context: A transactional-ecological framework for program models. In L. Bond & B. Compas (Eds.), *Primary prevention in the schools* (pp. 13–49). Beverly Hills: Sage.

Felner, R. D., Jason, L. A., Moritsugu, J. N., & Farber, S. S. (1983). An overview of preventive psychology. In R. D. Felner, L. A. Jason, J. N. Moritsugu, & S. S. Farber (Eds.), *Preventive psychology: Theory, research, and practice.* New York: Pergamon Press.

Felner, R. D., & Lorion, R. P. (1985). Clinical child psychology and prevention: Toward a workable and satisfying marriage. *Proceedings: National Conference on Training Clinical Child Psychologists, 41–95.*

Felner, R. D., Silverman, M., & Adan, A. M. (1989). Primary prevention: Relevance of principles for the prevention of youth suicide. *Report of the Secretary's Task Force on Youth Suicide: Vol. 3. Prevention and intervention in youth suicide* (pp. 23–30). DHHS Publication No. ADM 88-1623. Washington, DC: U.S. Government Printing Office.

Felner, R. D., Silverman, M., & Adan, A. M. (1992). Risk assessment and prevention of youth suicide in educational contexts. In R. Maris, A. Berman, J. Maltsberger, & R. Yufit (Eds.), *Assessment and prediction of suicide* (pp. 420–447). New York: Guilford Press.

Felner, R. D., Silverman, M., & Adix, R. (1991). Prevention of substance abuse and related disorders in childhood and adolescence: A developmentally based, comprehensive ecological model. *Family and Community Health, 14,* 12–22.

Felner, R. D., Yates Felner, T., & Silverman, M. M. (2000). Prevention in mental health and social intervention: Conceptual and methodological issues in the evolution of the science and practice of prevention. In E. Seidman & J. Rapaport (Eds.), *Handbook of community psychology.* New York: Plenum Press.

Gordon, R. S. (1983). An operational classification of disease prevention. *Public Health Reports, 98,* 107–109.

Hawkins, J. D., Catalano, R. F., & Miller, J. (1992). *Communities that care: Action for drug abuse prevention.* San Francisco: Jossey–Bass.

Healthy People 2000: National health promotion and disease prevention objectives. (1990). Department of Health and Human Services Publication, U.S. Government Printing Office.

Holtzman, W. H. (Ed.). (1992). *School of the future.* Austin, TX: American Psychological Association and Hogg Foundation.

Jencks, C., & Peterson, P. E. (Eds.). (1991). *The urban underclass.* Washington, DC: Brookings Institution.

Jessor, R., & Jessor, S. L. (1977). *Problem behavior and psychosocial development: A longitudinal study of youth.* New York: Academic Press.

Joint Commission on Mental Illness and Health. (1961). *Action for mental health: Final report of the joint commission on mental illness and health.* New York: Basic Books.

Kellam, S. G., & Brown, C. H. (1982). *Social, adaptational and psychological antecedents of adolescents psychopathology ten years later.* Baltimore: Johns Hopkins University Press.

Kellam, S. G., Brown, C. H., Rubin, B. R., & Ensminger, M. E. (1983). Paths leading to teenage psychiatric symptoms and substance abuse: Developmental epidemiological studies in Woodlawn. In S. B. Guze, F. J. Earls, & J. E. Bartlett (Eds.), *Child psychopathology and development.* New York: Raven Press.

Lorion, R. P., Price, R. H., & Eaton, W. W. (1989). The prevention of child and adolescent disorders: From theory to research. In D. Schaffer, I. Phillips, N. B. Enzer, M. M. Silverman, & V. Anthony (Eds.), *Prevention of mental disorders, alcohol and other drug use in children and adolescents: OSAP Prevention Monograph-2* (pp. 55–96). DHHS Publication No. ADM 89-1646. Washington, DC: U.S. Government Printing Office.

McKey, R., et al. (Eds.). (1985). *The impact of Head Start on children, families, and communities.* DHHS Publication No. OHDS 85-31193. Washington, DC: U.S. Government Printing Office.

Mednick, S. A., Griffith, J. J., & Mednick, B. R. (1981). Problems with traditional strategies in mental health research. In F. Schulsinger, S. A. Mednick, & J. Knop (Eds.), *Longitudinal research: Methods and uses in behavioral science* (pp. 3–15). The Hague: Nijhoff.

Moynihan, D. P. (1986). *Family and nation.* New York: Harcourt Brace Jovanovich.

Mrazek, P. J., & Haggerty, R. J. (1994). *Reducing risks for mental disorders: Frontiers for preventive intervention research.* Washington, DC: National Academy Press–Institute of Medicine.

President's Commission on Mental Health. (1978). *Report to the President.* Vol. 1. Stock No. 040-000-0390-8. Washington, DC: U.S. Government Printing Office.

Price, R. H. (1980). Prevention in mental health. In R. H. Price, R. F. Ketterer, B. C. Bader, & J. Monahan (Eds.), *Prevention in mental health: Research, policy, and practice* (pp. 9–20). Beverly Hills: Sage.

Price, R. H. (1983). The education of a prevention psychologist. In R. D. Felner, L. A. Jason, J. N. Moritsugu, & S. S. Farber (Eds.), *Preventive psychology: Theory, research, and practice.* New York: Pergamon Press.

Price, R., Cowen, E. L., Lorion, R. P., & Ramos-McKay, J. (Eds.). (1988). *Fourteen ounces of prevention: A casebook for practitioners.* Washington, DC: American Psychological Association.

Rappaport, J. (1977). *Community psychology: Values, research, and action.* New York: Holt, Rinehart & Winston.

Richters, J., & Weintraub, S. (1990). Beyond diatheses: Toward an understanding of high-risk environments. In J. Rolf, A. S. Masten, D. Cicchetti, K. H. Nuechterlein, & S. Weitraub (Eds.), *Risk and protective factors in the development of psychopathology* (pp. 67–96). London: Cambridge University Press.

Rutter, M. (1989). Isle of Wight revisited: Twenty-five years of child psychiatric epidemiology. *Journal of Child and Adolescent Psychiatry, 28,* 633–653.

Sameroff, A. J., & Chandler, M. J. (1975). Reproductive risk and the continuum of caretaking casualty. In F. D. Horowitz, M. Hetherington, S. Scarr-Salapatek, & G. Siegal (Eds.), *Review of child development research* (Vol. 4) (pp. 187–244). Chicago: University of Chicago Press.

Sameroff, A. J., & Fiese, B. H. (1989). Conceptual issues in prevention. In D. Schaffer, I. Phillips, N. B. Enzer, M. M. Silverman, & V. Anthony (Eds.), *Prevention of mental disorders, alcohol and other drug use in children and adolescents: OSAP Prevention Monograph-2* (pp. 23–54). DHHS Publication No. ADM 89-1646. Washington, DC: U.S. Government Printing Office.

Sameroff, A. J., Seifer, R., Barocas, R., Zax, M., & Greenspan, S. (1987). I.Q. scores of 4-year-old children: Social–environmental risk factors. *Pediatrics,* 343–350.

Sarason, S. B. (1981). *Psychology misdirected.* New York: Free Press.

Sarason, S. B. (1982). *The culture of the school and the problem of change* (2nd ed.). Boston: Allyn & Bacon.

Sarason, S. B., & Doris, J. (1979). *Educational handicap, public policy, and social history: A broadened perspective on mental retardation.* New York: Free Press

Schorr, L. B. (1988). *Within our reach: Breaking the cycle of disadvantage.* New York: Doubleday.

Schweinhart, L. J., & Weikart, D. P. (1988). The High/Scope Perry Preschool Program. In R. H. Price, E. L. Cowen, R. P. Lorion, & J. Ramos-McKay (Eds.), *Fourteen ounces of prevention: A casebook for practitioners* (pp. 53–66). Washington, DC: American Psychological Association.

Seidman, E. (1987). Toward a framework for primary prevention research. In J. A. Steinberg & M. M. Silverman (Eds.), *Preventing mental disorder: A research perspective* (pp. 2–19). DHHS Publication No. ADM 87-1492. Washington, DC: U.S. Government Printing Office.

Seidman, E., & Rappaport, J. (Eds.) (1986). *Redefining social problems.* NY: Plenum Press.

Silverman, M. M. (1989). Commentary: The integration of problem and prevention perspectives: Mental disorders associated with alcohol and drug use. In D. Schaffer, I. Phillips, N. B. Enzer, M. M. Silverman, & V. Anthony (Eds.), *Prevention of mental disorders, alcohol and other drug use in children and adolescents: OSAP Prevention Monograph-2* (pp. 7–22). DHHS Publication No. ADM 89-1646. Washington, DC: U.S. Government Printing Office.

VDMHMRSA. (1988). *A plan for prevention services: Phase I: Prenatal to age 18.* Commonwealth of VA: DMHMR.

Weiss, H. B., & Jacobs, F. H. (1988). Introduction: Family support and education programs—challenges and opportunities. In H. B. Weiss & F. H. Jacobs (Eds.), *Evaluating family programs* (pp. 3–36). New York: Aldine de Gruyter.

Wilson, W. J. (1987). *The truly disadvantaged: The inner city, the underclass, and public policy.* Chicago: University of Chicago Press.

W. T. Grant Foundation. (1988). *The forgotten half: Non-college youth in America.* New York: Author.

26

A Pragmatic Perspective toward Treating Children with Phobia and Anxiety Problems

WENDY K. SILVERMAN and WILLIAM M. KURTINES

> I fear it will always be as if we are walking on infirm or swampy ground and this is good because if the ground were firm, we'd have no reason to go anywhere.
>
> CHARLES SANDERS PEIRCE (1905/1955)

Included along with the invitation to us to contribute a chapter to the *Handbook of Psychotherapies with Children and Families* was the editors' brief description of the book's aims and content, and its various parts. In describing the chapters that would appear in this part of the book, Part IV, the editors wrote, "Part IV will present empirically validated interventions that integrate specific components of different theoretical orientations. These are not 'theoretically pure' approaches, but rather, are a *pragmatic* [italics ours] mix of different aspects of various approaches."

We were delighted that the editors used *pragmatic* in describing the interventions that would be included in this part of the book. We were delighted because *pragmatic* is the word that we have been using in describing our own attitude and perspective toward treating children who suffer from phobic and anxiety disorders (Silverman & Kurtines, 1996a,b, 1997). Along with delight, however, was a feeling of curiousness. Curiousness because in using and writing about pragmatics and about "being pragmatic," we have meant something very specific by "pragmatic." We thus wondered, were all of the contributors to this section on "Integra-

WENDY K. SILVERMAN and WILLIAM M. KURTINES • Child and Family Psychosocial Research Center, Florida International University, Miami, Florida 33199.

Handbook of Psychotherapies with Children and Families, edited by Russ and Ollendick. Kluwer Academic/Plenum Publishers, New York, 1999.

tive Approaches" pragmatic in the way that we view ourselves as pragmatic? Perhaps they are; perhaps they are not. We hastily add that examining this question is not the point of this chapter (although the reader may wish to examine this question subsequent to reading this section of the book). What is the point of the chapter is to delineate and to clarify what we mean by "being pragmatic." In doing so, we hope to show that "being pragmatic" means far more than being practical or expedient. We hope to show that "being pragmatic" means having an attitude and perspective that is useful for working with all children (and adults) who are in distress, including children who suffer from phobic and anxiety disorders.

In orienting the reader to our views about pragmatism, we first provide some general background about the pragmatic tradition in Western thought. We also briefly highlight recent developments that have occurred within psychology as well as outside of psychology that pose challenges to the role of theory. We explain how the pragmatic tradition is a particularly reasonable tradition from which we can draw a response to these developments. We follow this discussion with a description of our "transfer of control" treatment approach for use with children who have problems with phobias and anxiety, and we explain how this approach is a pragmatic one. In addition, we provide a summary of research findings from a recently completed treatment outcome study that evaluated the efficacy of this approach. We end the chapter with a brief discussion of future clinical research directions, with attention to managed care.

DEVELOPMENTS WITHIN AND OUTSIDE OF PSYCHOLOGY THAT POSE CHALLENGES FOR "THEORY"

The pragmatic tradition is a particularly useful tradition to draw on at this time in light of developments that have occurred within psychology as well as outside of psychology. These developments pose serious challenges to the notion of having "a theory" of child psychotherapy, in terms of both practice and research.

Within psychology, the main development that poses a serious challenge to theory is the incredible growth of different psychotherapeutic orientations and approaches. As Sol Garfield (1994) explained: "Psychotherapeutic orientations and approaches have been a growth industry, and some of the differences in theoretical views at times have been quite amazing" (p. 123). This growth and diversity within the field represents a significant challenge to the conceptual hegemony of the major theoretical approaches (e.g., psychoanalytic, behavioral, family systems, client-centered).

Another main development within psychology that poses a serious challenge to theory is clinicians' increased identification with and affiliation to "eclecticism" and "integrationism." Eclecticism has been used to refer to the approach in which practitioners "use what works" and do not feel constrained by individual schools of psychotherapy or singular approaches to treatment in so doing (Garfield, 1994). Integrationism reflects an attempt to integrate diverse approaches by identifying commonalities among different treatments with a goal of seeking theoretical integration, to recognize common factors that transcend individual treatments, and to identify different techniques that might be used together to provide a comprehensive model of therapy (Garfield, 1994). It should be apparent how the growth of eclecticism and integrationism poses a challenge to traditional ways of thinking about theory in child psychotherapy practice and research: Namely, if almost "everyone" is eclectic or integrative, then what need or value is there for having a theory that guides one's psychotherapeutic activities?

Outside of psychology, the main development that poses a serious challenge to theory has taken a variety of forms, and has been described using terms such as *postmodern, poststructural,* and *postpositivist.* In a postmodern vein, knowledge is not viewed as universal, objective, and cumulative. Postmodernists offer, instead, an alternative view of knowledge—a view that emphasizes the local and particularistic nature of knowledge—whereby knowledge is not discovered but is "sociolinguistically created" (Gergen, 1991). It should be apparent how postmodernism poses a challenge to traditional ways of thinking about theory in child psychotherapy research and practice. Namely, within the postmodern vein, privilege or priority is not granted to one particular point of view (i.e., to one theory) and all things are open to question, even the notion that objective "foundations" of knowledge (e.g., foundational knowledge about child psychotherapy theory and research) can ever even be realized (see Silverman & Kurtines, 1997, for further discussion of the implications of postmodernism on theory in child psychosocial intervention).

Given these developments, within and outside of psychology, that challenge the notion of a theory of child psychotherapy, or that there is a set of foundational assumptions by which to enact child psychotherapy, we have found the pragmatic tradition to be one that allows us to draw a reasonable response (at least reasonable to us) to the challenge raised. It is a reasonable response because it does not lead us down either one of the following two paths: It does not lead us down the modernist path of essentialist or foundational pursuits (Amundson, 1996). That is, it does not lead us to pursue the "truth" about theory in child psychotherapy research as we are not guided by the hope (or one may even say the delusion) that eventually we will get it "just right." It also does not lead us down the postmodernist path of relativism or nihilism (a frequent charge launched against postmodernism) (McSwite, 1997). That is, it does not lead us to view all ideas as being as "good" or as "bad" as another, or that "nothing really matters, and if it did, so what?!" The path that our pragmatic tradition *does* lead us on is described next.

THE PRAGMATIC TRADITION AND ITS IMPLICATIONS ON VIEWS ABOUT THE ROLE OF THEORY

We turn to the pragmatic tradition as the path or as the bridge, between the modernist view of knowledge as foundational (universal, objective, and cumulative) and the importance of "scientific" knowledge in generating it, and the postmodernist view of knowledge as contingent (local and particular, and possibly relativistic) and the role of "narrative" knowledge in generating it. Specifically, we have adopted from the pragmatic tradition a view of knowledge as contextual in significance.

A view of knowledge as contextual in significance does not begin with a priori assumptions about whether knowledge is universal and objective *or* local and particular. Rather than beginning with foundational assumptions about knowledge, the pragmatist begins with the concrete problems of specific human beings in particular contexts. The pragmatic tradition begins with concretely experienced human problems because the pragmatist adopts a problem-solving orientation. Moreover, the pragmatist adopts an approach to problem solving that is contextual as well as pragmatic. The pragmatist, for example, thinks that the solution to problems cannot be separated from the practical effects or consequences of the solutions because what is a successful solution in one context may be a more or less successful solution in another context.

With respect to the role of theory then, our pragmatic perspective yields a "bottom-up" view of the role of theory in psychosocial treatment. This bottom-up view stands in contrast to the more traditional "top-down" view that theoretical concepts and constructs derive their meaning and significance from the theoretical frameworks or approaches in which they are embedded. In the area of child psychosocial treatment, for example, concepts and constructs related to clinical processes (behavioral, affective, cognitive) have been traditionally associated with particular theories and approaches (behavioral, psychodynamic, cognitive). On this "top-down" view, concepts and constructs derive their meaning and significance from the theoretical frameworks in which they are embedded. Our pragmatic and problem-solving orientation, in contrast, adopts a "bottom-up" view that is rooted in the concrete and specific problems that concepts and constructs are used to solve. From this view, the theoretical concepts and constructs that we use in working with children in distress do not derive their meaning and significance from the theoretical frameworks or approaches in which they are embedded; they derive their meaning and significance from the "contexts" in which they are used. That is, we consider the meaning of constructs and concepts of all types and at all levels (e.g., theoretical and metatheoretical as well as clinical procedures, research methods) to be derived from the problems they address and their significance (i.e., utility and validity) to be derived from their success in solving these problems.

Our pragmatic orientation to theory further means that although we do not advocate a particular theory, we are not opposed to particular theories of therapy that focus on particular processes, clinical procedures, or research methods. Being pragmatic, we sometimes think that it is useful to focus on particular processes, procedures, and methods, just as we also think that theories are often useful things to have. However, we are opposed to the idea that any one particular theory provides the one right way to think about clinical and research issues or that any particular type or variety of research methods or therapeutic techniques provides the one right way of working with children in distress.

This is not to say, however, that we are eclectic or integrative. We think that sometimes it may be useful to be eclectic or integrative but sometimes it may not be. As noted above, sometimes it may be useful to focus on a particular theory. Moreover, what particularly attracts us to pragmatism, rather than to eclecticism and integrationism, is that pragmatism offers an intellectual frame with a rich philosophical, historical tradition. Consider this question: Is there a philosopher or thinker who espoused a philosophy of "integrationism" or a philosophy of "eclecticism"? In contrast, American in origin, pragmatism encompasses a long and distinguished tradition that contains some of the most prominent thinkers in American philosophy, including Charles Peirce, William James, and James Dewey. In addition, with the emergence of the postmodern movement, pragmatism has re-emerged as one of the most significant influences in contemporary thought (e.g., see Rorty, 1979, 1992). We think that being rooted in a tradition as rich as pragmatism gives this perspective a real intellectual edge over eclecticism and integrationism, which lack such roots and in general, overall, lack a coherent conceptual frame (Garfield, 1994).

SPECIFIC PROBLEMS AND POPULATION

Now that we have provided the background to our pragmatic perspective, and have explained how our pragmatic perspective frames our views about the role of theory in child psychotherapy, the most important (i.e., pragmatic) question is, how is it useful in psychotherapy with children? To date, we have examined this question in the context of helping children who suffer from distress related to excessive problems with fear and anxiety. In this section of the chapter we describe how it has been useful (see Silverman & Kurtines, 1996a,b, for more detailed discussion).

In *developing* our interventions, our pragmatic orientation has helped to organize the way that we, as theoreticians, think about the conceptual issues that we face in developing our treatment approaches. Our pragmatic orientation shows itself in the basic transfer-of-control approach (described below), and in how we conceptualize specific change-producing procedures and strategies. This pragmatic orientation is useful because it places *no* limits on the nature or type of approach that we adopt, other than the pragmatic constraint that it work. Being pragmatic, we thus have been able to draw on the most recent development in child psychotherapy research, and to integrate and combine in useful ways the most efficacious procedures identified by such research, and to modify and adapt these procedures for use with this particular population in particular contexts.

The transfer-of-control approach that we have developed, for example, explicitly recognizes that phobic and anxiety disorders in children are complex, multifaceted, and multidetermined. We draw on the major theoretical traditions for our conceptualization of the basic, interrelated types of processes—behavioral, cognitive, and affective—that are at the core of our approach. In addition, consistent with our pragmatic orientation, our efforts in developing our transfer-of-control approach focused on delineating the links between the types of interrelated maladaptive processes or symptoms that provide the basis for a diagnosis of an anxiety disorder and the types of interventions (therapeutic procedures and strategies) that can be used to modify those processes or symptoms.

More specifically, the transfer-of-control approach holds that effective long-term psychotherapeutic change in children involves a gradual "transfer of control" where the sequence is generally from therapist to parent to child. The therapist is viewed as an expert consultant who possesses the knowledge of the skills and methods necessary to produce therapeutic change, and who then transfers the use of these skills and methods to the parent, and subsequently, from parent to child.

In treating children with phobic and anxiety disorders, the primary focus of the transfer of control is on "controlling" the occurrence and successful implementation of key change producing procedures. The approach further assumes that the most critical task of a child phobic or anxiety treatment program is allowing for the adequate transfer of control from the therapist to the child.

KEY CHANGE-PRODUCING PROCEDURE

Exposure

We adopt exposure as the key therapeutic ingredient or change-producing procedure in all of our childhood anxiety interventions for the simple (and pragmatic) reason that a large and growing body of research evidence shows it to be the most effective way to reduce phobic and anxious symptomatology (Barlow, 1988). Although there are varying views among theorists and investigators as to why exposure works, all of these views involve in various ways the modification of behavioral, cognitive, and affective processes (see Barlow, 1988). The forms of direct therapeutic exposure that we have found useful in our interventions involve the child confronting anxiety-provoking objects or events (*in vivo* and imaginal) in a gradual or graduated manner.

Facilitative Strategies

We also have developed and/or adapted a variety of therapeutic strategies for facilitating the occurrence of exposure that draw on two of the major theoretical approaches, behavioral and cognitive. We note here that at present we have adapted behavioral and cognitive strategies for facilitating the occurrence of exposure. Over time, we may choose to adapt and to evaluate other potential strategies that may be useful in facilitating the occurrence of child exposure.

The first strategy we have thus adapted was contingency management. Based on behavioral processes of change, contingency management emphasizes the training of parents in the use of appropriate contingencies to facilitate the child's exposure or approach behavior toward feared objects or situations. A key element of contingency management is contingency contracting. The second strategy that we adapted, self-control, is based on cognitive processes of change. Self-control strategies emphasize the training of the child in the use of appropriate cognitive strategies to facilitate exposure or approach behavior toward feared objects or situations. A key element of self-control training is cognitive restructuring and self-reward.

USING A TRANSFER-OF-CONTROL APPROACH FOR IMPLEMENTING AN EXPOSURE-BASED INTERVENTION

The transfer-of-control approach provides guidelines for the general sequence for the administration of the behavioral and cognitive strategies that we use. It is built on the links that exist between key maladaptive processes of anxiety disorders (i.e., behavioral, cognitive, affective), related contextual processes (e.g., relational, institutional) that give rise to and/or maintain these processes, and the key change-producing procedure (i.e., exposure) and related therapeutic facilitative strategies (e.g., contingency management and self-control training) that have an impact on these maladaptive processes with our particular population. Hence, the transfer of control involves first the training of parents in contingency management and in using these skills to encourage the child's exposure (parent control). This is followed by a gradual fading of parental control while the child is taught to use self-control strategies to encourage his or her own exposure (child control). Consequently, parental (or external) control is gradually reduced while the child learns cognitive self-control strategies in contexts specific to his or her anxiety problems.

Because being pragmatic for us also means being contextualistic, we recognize that, in some cases or contexts, the therapist may find that it is either sufficient or necessary to work with single and direct lines only. For example, in the case of a child with severe developmental delays the therapist may find it useful to work directly with the parent, i.e., a line from therapist to parent. In certain contexts, such as a school-based setting, the therapist may find it necessary to work with a single and direct line (i.e., a line from therapist to child), because parents are usually unavailable for participation in school-based intervention programs.

In *implementing* our interventions, our pragmatic orientation shows itself in the therapeutic stance that we bring into each therapy session, and in how we use specific change producing procedures and strategies during therapy. The therapeutic stance that we adopt when working with children with phobias and anxiety problems has three basic dimensions. It is *problem-focused and present-oriented, structured,* and *directive.*

The problem-focused and present-oriented dimension is generally rooted in our pragmatic orientation, although there is nothing in this orientation that rules out adopting an insight and past-oriented stance when it is useful to do so. The structured and directive dimensions are more rooted in the specific nature of the population and problem. Specifically, the transfer-of-control approach itself provides a "natural" structure to how therapy is conducted in that it guides the sequence of the change-producing procedures (from therapist to parent to child), thereby rendering a structured approach more useful. We adopt a therapeutic stance that is directive rather than nondirective because of the nature of the problem with which we work: Phobic and anxiety problems tend to be linked to external antecedent conditions, and the most effective change-producing procedures involve exposures to the conditions that elicit the phobic/anxious response. Our therapeutic stance is consequently directive because the most effective change-producing procedure involves systematic and direct arranging of exposures to fear/anxiety-producing stimuli.

Now that we have provided a description of our transfer-of-control approach and have shown how its development was driven by our pragmatic perspective, in the subsequent sections we provide a more detailed account of the treatment itself. The treatment described is the most "basic" transfer-of-control approach, i.e., whereby the therapist transfers control to parent (via contingency management) followed by a transfer-of-control from parent to child (via self-control training). As noted above, however, the basic approach might vary and might require ongoing modification depending on the context/case in which the therapist works. However, our approach is a start in developing a treatment approach that "works" for children with phobic and anxiety disorders.

DESCRIPTION OF INTERVENTION

Individual and Conjoint Sessions

We usually conduct separate parent and child individual sessions (each 30 and 45 minutes in length, respectively) followed immediately by a conjoint meeting (15 minutes) with the therapist. In the conjoint meetings, the focus is on resolving parent–child difficulties (e.g., interaction patterns) that may interfere with program participation. Our treatment program runs for 10 weeks: The first 3 weeks are the education phase, the next 5 weeks are the application phase, and weeks 8 to 10 are the relapse prevention phase—with participants still applying what they have learned. In practice, however, the clinician can adapt our program, as necessary. For example, shorter treatment sessions can be used over a longer period of time.

Phases Overview

As noted, the first phase of our treatment program is education. During the education phase, the parent sessions focus on providing the information and the skills necessary for parents to control or manage their child's anxious behaviors, and on how to gradually transfer control to their child. The child sessions during the education phase focus on providing the information and the skills necessary for children to make the gradual transition from an external agent of control (parent) to self-control.

In the application phase of the program, the focus is on implementing the transfer of control. As noted, in treating fear and anxiety problems, this specifically focuses on "controlling" the occurrence, and successful use of our key change-producing procedure, namely, child exposure or approach behavior. In the application phase, the parents and the children actually use the methods that were explained to them in the education phase. Specifically, contingency management, followed by self-control procedures are used to facilitate the child exposures.

In the relapse prevention phase, strategies are presented to handle and prevent the recurrence of child avoidant behaviors. This phase is important to help ensure a complete final transfer of control so that in the event of relapse both the child and parent will be able to successfully manage the event, especially if they are no longer being seen by the therapist. A more detailed description of the major aspects of the education, application, and relapse prevention phases of the program is given below (see also Silverman & Kurtines, 1996a, and Silverman, Ginsburg, & Kurtines, 1995).

Education Phase

Five main concepts are presented during the education phase. First, an overview of the program is presented, including the importance of exposure. Second, the program's conceptualization of fear and anxiety is presented. Third, the fear/anxiety hierarchy is devised. Fourth is explaining basic principles of contingency management, and fifth is explaining basic principles of self-control procedures. The latter two concepts are explained only briefly during the education phase, as the actual use of these principles (during the application phase) renders it much easier for children and parents to understand them.

Overview of Program. We emphasize that there is nothing "magical" about the program. For treatment to "work," the children and parents must practice all that they learn—just as they would any other skill, such as basketball or piano. We explain that the children will not necessarily be "cured." Rather, they will learn skills needed to decrease their anxiety and fear so that these feelings no longer interfere with their lives.

Next, the importance of exposure or approach behavior is emphasized. Families are told that when individuals stay away from (or avoid) what makes them feel afraid or anxious, their anxiety is maintained because they do not have the opportunity to learn that "there is nothing to lead you to feel afraid or anxious." To learn this, it is necessary to approach what is feared, or do what is avoided. We give numerous examples, as well as the analogy of "getting back on a bicycle after falling off," which is readily understood.

Conceptualization of Excessive Fear and Anxiety. In presenting the program's conceptualization of fear and anxiety, we explain that there are three ways in which anxiety is manifested: (1) bodily reactions, such as increased heart rate, stomachaches, and sweating; (2) thoughts or talking to oneself, such as "I might get hurt" and "No one likes me"; and (3) actions or behaviors, such as avoiding feared objects or events. Our treatment targets each of these manifestations.

To help explain the above, the therapist poses questions to both the child and parent. Examples include: "When you feel afraid, how do you know it?" or "What happens to you when you feel scared?" The therapist also prompts, as necessary, to facilitate understanding. Examples include: "What do you do when you are near something that you are afraid of—get closer or run away?," "What happens to your body?," and "What are you thinking?" The therapist and child also together draw figures on the blackboard or paper to illustrate how bodily reactions, thoughts, and behavior interrelate.

To help the children in identifying their feelings of fear to various objects and/or events, the children are also taught how to complete self-monitoring forms, or what are called Daily Diaries in the program. They are asked to keep track every time during the week that they experienced excessive feelings of anxiety—the situations, their degree of anxiety using a four-point scale, their thoughts, and whether they approached or avoided the situation or object.

Fear Hierarchy. Both children and parents are informed early on that the child will learn how to handle his or her fears or anxiety through exposure—"facing your fear." Most children as well as parents are relieved to hear that the program takes a gradual approach to exposure, thereby creating step-by-step success experiences.

The gradual exposure tasks are designed along a fear hierarchy. Each hierarchy consists of 10 to 15 specific situations or objects that range from only slightly fearful to extremely fear provoking. Although the expectation is conveyed that the child is to progress up the hierarchy, we make clear that the child is the one who ultimately determines the rate of progress.

Principles of Contingency Management. Basic principles of learning principles, with an emphasis on contingency management training, are explained to the children and parents during the education phase. Emphasis is placed on explaining to children and parents the concept of reinforcement and the proper delivery of reinforcement. We differentiate between different types of rewards (i.e., social, tangible, activity), and highlight how our program encourages use of social and activity rewards. We explain to both children and parents that rewards are provided contingent on completion of desired behaviors, and that in this program, the desired behaviors are child approach or exposure to the fearful object or situation. The importance of consistency and follow-through is explained to parents as well as potential difficulties that parents encounter that prevent effective follow-through. The advantages of using contracts that explicate the specific rewards that are to be delivered contingent on the emittance of specific behaviors are explained.

Principles of Self-Control. Basic principles of cognitive self-control are explained to the children and parents during the education phase, following the explanation of the contingency management procedures. Emphasis is placed on explaining to children and parents the concepts of self-observation, self-evaluation, and self-reward. We differentiate between different types of self-statements, and highlight how our program encourages the use of not using negative self-statements (i.e., "the power of nonnegative thinking"), in light of current research findings (Kendall & Chansky, 1991). We explain to both children and parents that positive child self-rewarding statements also should be used contingent on completion of desired behaviors, and that in this program, the desired behaviors are child approach or exposure to the fearful object or situation. The importance of parental support and encouragement for children's appropriate use of cognitive self-control procedures is explained to parents as well as potential difficulties that parents encounter that prevent effective parental delivery of support and encouragement.

Application Phase

Three main activities occur during the application phase. First, in-session and out-of-session activities (i.e., exposures) are conducted. To help facilitate the occurrence of the exposures, contingency management procedures are applied. After successful occurrence of exposures using contingency management, these procedures are faded out and are followed by the use of self-control procedures.

In-Session and Out-of-Session Activities. The main in-session and out-of-session activities that are implemented during the application phase are the exposure tasks. The exposure tasks represent one of the various steps that have been listed on the fear hierarchy. It is emphasized to the child that in implementing these tasks, the emphasis is on trying and in doing one's best.

Graduated exposure tasks also are implemented in-session in the presence of the therapist. This allows for the therapist to provide corrective feedback, to display appropriate adaptive responses for modeling, and to serve as a source of encouragement and positive reinforcement.

Contingency Management Procedures. As noted earlier, we use contingency management procedures to help in initially obtaining parental control of the child's avoidant behaviors. An important aspect of contingency management is the use of contingency contracts. Specifically, in each session a detailed contract is written between the child and parent, with the assistance of the therapist, that explicitly states the specific exposure task that the child is to attempt as the in-session and as the out-of-session exposure (e.g., what to do, when to do it, how long to do it) and the consequence that follows for successful completion or attempt of the task (e.g., specific reward, when it is to be delivered).

Self-Control Procedures. On attaining some degree of parental control of child exposure behavior via contingency management procedures, we begin to initiate child control of this behavior via the use of self-control procedures. As noted, the main focus of our child self-control procedures is on the use of children's thoughts and self-statements and their role in inhibiting successful child exposure. In applying self-control, we teach children to use the STOP acronym, where S stands for Scared, T stands for Thoughts, O stands for Other thoughts or Other things I can do to handle my fear, and P stands for Praise myself for successful handling of my fear and exposure (e.g., "I'm really proud of myself" and "I am a brave boy/girl").

Relapse Prevention Phase

Two main concepts are presented during the relapse prevention phase. First, the importance of continued practice or of continuing child exposure is emphasized. Second, how to interpret and construe "slips" is emphasized.

Importance of Continued Exposure. It is explained that the more the child engages in continued exposure, the less likely it is that he or she will have a relapse. It is explained that much of what the child has accomplished is largely the result of the practice exposure exercises and that, like any accomplishment, "if you don't use it, you lose." Examples are provided from other skills that the child may have learned in his or her own life, such as sport or an instrument, and how if the child does not continue to practice or to expose him- or herself to this sport or instrument the child will lose the skill needed to successfully perform that sport or instrument.

Interpreting Slips. It is explained that no matter how much the child may practice and continue to engage in exposure, it is likely, nevertheless, that a relapse or a "slip" will occur. It is emphasized that this is a common occurrence. The analogy of a person on a weight loss program who may have successfully lost 20 pounds but then eats a piece of cake at a party may have different ways of interpreting the "slip." We analyze this case in detail with the child and the parent. Via this analysis, it becomes evident that the most adaptive interpretation is that "this is a single event. It does not mean that everything is blown or ruined. And I need to pick myself back up and get back on the positive track I was on." Emphasis is placed on the parents' role in handling slips and how many children will look to the parents and take the cues from them in interpreting the slips.

RESEARCH SUPPORT FOR EFFICACY

We have recently completed two controlled clinical trials for children with phobic and anxiety problems, and the findings from our studies provide support for the exposure-based transfer-of-control treatment approach described above (Silverman, Kurtines, Ginsburg, Weems, Lumpkin, et al., in press a; Silverman, Kurtines, Ginsburg, Weems, Rabian, et al., in press b). Because of space constraints, in this part of the chapter, we detail only the second of these two treatment studies.

This study examined the efficacy of this treatment approach using a group format. We viewed a group treatment format to be a particularly useful format in light of the growth of HMOs and problems with third-party payments that have created increased pressure on the mental health practitioner to offer services that are not only efficacious, but also cost and time efficient.

Practically, a group format offers several additional advantages. First, group treatment is a more efficient use of therapists' time and is a less expensive format for clients than individual treatment. Second, developing a cost/time-effective treatment for prevalent disorders, such as anxiety, has the potential to make treatment available to children who might not otherwise receive it. Third, a group format for children who present with different primary anxiety diagnoses, such as social phobia, overanxious disorder, and generalized anxiety disorder (the disorders targeted in our study), is consistent with clinical reality as most children present with a range of disorders.

In addition, we view a group treatment format as providing the therapist with an additional pathway (i.e., therapist to peers to child) and allowing for the therapist to make use of natural group processes to facilitate the transfer of control (e.g., peer reinforcement). In addition, use of multiple pathways in group treatment provides the child with opportunities for even more complex and difficult exposures than are typically possible in individual treatment. That is, in group treatment the child engages in activities that require not only that she or he be exposed to social evaluation (which may be particularly important for the child with social phobia, generalized anxiety disorder, and overanxious disorder), but also that she or he actively participate in the social evaluation of another child (i.e., a bidirectional and reciprocal transfer of control). Moreover, exposure to social evaluative situations is intrinsic to the group format itself (see Ginsburg, Silverman, & Kurtines, 1995a).

We evaluated the therapeutic efficacy of the group treatment format using a randomized clinical trials design with two conditions: a group treatment condition and a wait-list control condition. A total of 56 children aged 6–17 years (34 boys, 22 girls) and their parents participated in the study. Using proportional random assignment, 37 (66%) of the participants were assigned to the group treatment condition and 19 (34%) to the wait-list condition. All children met criteria for a primary DSM-III-R diagnosis of Overanxious Disorder, Generalized Anxiety Disorder, or Social Phobia, based on a structured interview administered separately to the child and parent (i.e., the Anxiety Disorders Interview Schedule for Children; ADIS-C/P, Silverman & Nelles, 1988).

The results of this outcome study provided strong evidence for the group treatment format. Differences in the recovery rates for participants in the group treatment format versus the wait-list control condition were dramatic. This was observed first with respect to diagnosis: 63% of the children in group treatment were recovered at posttreatment (i.e., no longer met diagnostic criteria) compared with only 12% in the control condition. Treatment maintenance was equally impressive: There was a consistent trend for treatment gains to continue well after treatment ended. For example, there was no evidence at any of the follow-up points (3, 6, and 12 months) for the occurrence of relapse among any of the recovered participants. Even the children who had continued to meet diagnostic criteria at posttreatment showed a pattern of improvement in terms of severity and interference ratings.

This pattern of improvement in terms of diagnosis and clinical severity and interference (at posttreatment and throughout the follow-ups) was evident as well by both the child- and parent-completed measures. Specifically, there was a pattern of significant condition by time interactions (i.e., group treatment condition showing improvements over the wait-list control condition over time). This was observed on the most important child self-report measure of anxious symptomatology, the Revised Children's Manifest Anxiety Scale. This pattern of the differential effectiveness of the group treatment condition over the wait-list control condition (i.e., significant condition by time interactions) was even more dramatic for the parent-completed measures (e.g., the Child Behavior Checklist internalizing, sub-scale, parents' global ratings of severity). Moreover, not only did parents in the group treatment report gains for their children, but parents in the wait-list control condition reported that their children were worse, or had deteriorated, at the postwait assessment.

Finally, the pattern for all of the child- and parent-completed measures indicated a continued reduction in degree and severity of anxious symptoms from posttreatment to 3-month follow-up, with improvement leveling off at that time but still being maintained at 6- and 12-month follow-up.

CASE EXAMPLE

Presenting Problem

Henry, an 11-year-old Caucasian boy, was brought to our Center by his mother because of his extreme distress reactions pertaining to parental separation. Henry's mother described that almost all events that entailed his separation from her would lead to severe protest and anxious reactions. The only exception to this, fortunately, was separation that surrounded school attendance: Henry could apparently manage going to school because he was a good student and he enjoyed attending school. However, events other than going to school, such as if the mother wanted to leave the house to run some errands, were "impossible." Her son would repeatedly ask questions about her plans for the day, whether she was planning to go out somewhere; if so, where; and, could he go with her. If he knew in advance that his mother was intending to go out somewhere, Henry would report that his "stomach hurt," and he generally appeared tense and nervous. On her leaving the house, Henry fussed and pleaded with her not to go or to take him with her.

In addition, Henry refused to go to other activities if his mother did not go with him. Although he played with other children his age, he preferred that they play in his house rather than theirs; and he refused to camp out with his Boy Scout troop, unless either his mother or father accompanied the troop. Similarly, although Henry enjoyed playing soccer, the only way that he would play in the local children's soccer sports organization is if his father served as a coach. The father consequently did coach for several years but now he wanted "a break" from coaching for at least a couple of seasons. Henry therefore was currently not playing soccer.

Henry's mother reported that her son "never liked to be alone," and that even as a toddler his protest about separation appeared to her to be much worse than what she recalled experiencing with her two other children. They, she noted, were 10 and 12 years older than Henry. She wondered whether having Henry "late in her life" led her to treat him "differently than the others" as he was "the baby in the family." She noted how she found that she "worried" much more about Henry than she had with her other children because he was "the baby" and because he seemed "to need her" more than the others. Mother acknowledged, however, that her perceptions were somewhat tainted because while she was raising her other children she also worked full-time and thus she "did not have the time to worry." With Henry, however, she was now home full-time and could spend more of her time worrying.

Assessment and Diagnosis

Henry and his mother were administered respective child and parent versions of the Anxiety Disorders Interview Schedule for Children (Silverman & Nelles, 1988). They also completed several questionnaires. As noted, Henry's mother reported that his nervousness and upset about separation from her was interfering in various aspects of his and the family's life, and she provided several examples (e.g., making it difficult for her to leave the house, limitations placed on where he played with friends, participation in sports unless father coached, father not wanting to coach).

Based on Henry's and his mother's responses to the interviews, Henry was assigned a diagnosis of Separation Anxiety Disorder. On the interviews, both Henry and his mother reported that his concerns about separation were a "7" on the 8-point fear thermometer. His scores on the questionnaires were also elevated.

Treatment

Henry was enrolled in the Center's exposure-based treatment program in which parent and child were seen individually and then briefly together. The program, based on the transfer-of-control model, involved first teaching Henry's mother the principles of contingency management and then teaching both Henry and his mother child self-control strategies. These strategies were then applied in graduated exposure tasks that involved Henry gradually participating in events that required him to separate from his mother.

Exposure tasks were both imaginal and *in vivo* and were based on a hierarchy that varied the duration of time that Henry needed to be away from his mother. Initial *in vivo* steps on the hierarchy ranged in duration from 1 to 5 minutes. These exposures were completed successfully. However, as the duration of time for the exposures became longer, Henry did not complete the exposures.

In examining the reasons for the failure to complete the exposures, the therapist learned that Henry's mother was ambivalent about Henry moving up the hierarchy. Mother indicated concern that "maybe something could happen" while she was away from her son and she noted the high rates of burglary in her neighborhood.

To deal with these concerns, subsequent treatment sessions addressed some of the common obstacles encountered with treating children with anxiety disorders. For instance, emphasis was placed on reviewing with Henry's mother the importance of parental modeling of courageous behavior. In part, this was accomplished by discussing common parental "protective behaviors" and her own concerns about child–parental separation. In addition, treatment focused on helping Henry and his mother think of alternative ways of handling their anxieties, including specific steps they could take to help ease the burden of separation. This included arranging for "telephone checks" that were to be gradually faded out over time, and giving Henry advanced warning about subsequent maternal leave so that he could be more prepared. This approach helped to empower the family and enabled them to have an action plan for handling Henry's (and mother's) anxieties. All of these methods were helpful and subsequent contracts were successfully carried out, including the one that required him to sleep over at a friend's house—a task on the hierarchy Henry had noted initially as being "impossible."

In the final phase of the transfer of control, wherein self-control strategies were used (using self-reward and fading out parental rewards) Henry practiced using STOP. He examined the specific cognitions that played a role in maintaining his fear (e.g., "my mother will leave and never come back"). He learned to recognize when he was afraid or worried, to employ more adaptive coping thoughts and behaviors, and to praise himself for doing so.

Posttreatment and Follow-Up

At posttreatment assessment, readministration of the interview schedules revealed that Henry no longer met criteria for Separation Anxiety Disorder and there was no longer any interference in his daily functioning. In addition, his scores on the questionnaires decreased markedly. These gains were maintained at 3- and 12-month follow-up assessments.

FUTURE RESEARCH, WITH ATTENTION TO MANAGED CARE

We believe that the pragmatic perspective described in this chapter, as well as its application in developing and implementing a treatment procedure for use with children who suffer from phobic and anxiety disorders, is particularly timely and important in light of the current climate of managed care, HMOs, and problems in obtaining in third-party payments. Specifically, in this climate, practitioners no longer have the luxury of keeping patients in long-term treatment. Practitioners have a limited number of sessions and they need "to deliver" within this very restricted window of time. As a consequence, practitioners need to figure out the types of child emotional and behavioral problems that they can effectively reduce using short-term treatment. Ideally, this decision should be based on findings obtained from well-conceived, well-designed, and well-executed research studies.

Evidence is growing that child phobic and anxiety problems constitute one set of child problems that can indeed be reduced using a time-limited, "pragmatically derived," exposure-based treatment approach, as described in this chapter. This is good news given the growth of managed care and HMOs. In addition, we discussed in this chapter that the pragmatic perspective that guided the development of our intervention has an intellectual frame that is based on the work of some of the most prominent thinkers in American philosophy, such as Peirce,

James, and Dewey. Thus, practitioners have this intellectual frame to fall back on as they think through and reconcile critical issues regarding the role of theory in child psychotherapy, as pressure continues to mount on them to do what is useful and what works in a short amount of time.

In our future research at the Center, we have shifted our attention to removing the main obstacles that impede the pathways for a successful transfer of control. In this frame, we have received funding from the National Institute of Mental Health to conduct another clinical trials that will attempt to render the pathways more clear and direct by systematically targeting parent–child relational processes and parental anxiety/phobic disorders/symptoms in a dyadic format. It is hypothesized that treatment outcome (and maintenance) will be enhanced because training that improves these processes will serve to unblock the pathways, thereby maximizing the likelihood that the change-producing procedure will occur (and be maintained).

In particular, when relational processes such as child management, parent–child communication, and parent–child problem solving are maladaptive, pathways of transfer of control may be obstructed. For example, when parents and children are given an "out of session" exposure task and a problem arises that the child and the parent cannot solve, the opportunity for a transfer of control from therapist to the parent to the child is lost. In addition, if the problem is serious enough, the exposure may not be completed and the opportunity for a therapeutic gain may be lost.

Similarly, interventions that target the reduction of parent symptoms are likewise hypothesized to enhance treatment outcome effectiveness (and maintenance) because symptom relief in parents is likely to render pathways of transfer of control more clear and direct. Specifically, parents who suffer from anxiety and phobic symptoms may display avoidant behavior, distorted cognitions, and subjective distress. These symptoms may make it difficult for the parents to be actively involved in their child's treatment program. For example, parents who display avoidant behavior may not be able to engage in activities (e.g., transport the child) that facilitate their child's exposure to objects or situations that they themselves find anxiety or fear provoking. Working with children and parents in dyads to improve their relational processes and parental symptomatology is just one example of where we see our future clinical research activities heading.

ACKNOWLEDGMENT

Preparation of this chapter was supported in part by NIMH Grant 54690.

REFERENCES

Amundson, J. (1996). Why pragmatics is probably enough for now. *Family Process, 35,* 473–486.

Barlow, D. H. (1988). *Anxiety and its disorders: The nature and treatment of anxiety and panic.* New York: Guilford Press.

Garfield, S. L. (1994). Eclecticism and integration in psychotherapy: Developments and issues. *Clinical Psychology: Science and Practice, 1,* 123–137.

Gergen, K. J. (1994). Exploring the postmodern: Perils or protentials? *American Psychologist, 49,* 412–415.

Ginsburg, G. S., Silverman, W. K., & Kurtines, W. M. (1995a). Cognitive-behavioral group therapy. In A. R. Eisen, C. A. Kearney, & C. E. Schaefer (Eds.), *Clinical handbook of anxiety disorders in children* (pp. 521–549). Northvale, NJ: Aronson.

Ginsburg, G. S., Silverman, W. K., & Kurtines, W. M. (1995b). Family involvement in treating children with phobic and anxiety disorders: A look ahead. *Clinical Psychology Review, 15,* 457–473.

Kendall, P. C., & Chansky, T. E. (1991). Considering cognition in anxiety-disordered children. *Journal of Anxiety Disorders, 5,* 167–185.

McSwite, O. C. (1997). Postmodernism and public administration's identity crisis. *Public Administration Review, 55,* 174–181.

Peirce, C. S. (1955). What pragmatism is. In J. Buchler (Ed.), *Philosophical writings of Peirce.* New York: Dover Publications. (Original work published 1905)

Rorty, R. (1979). *Philosophy and the mind as the mirror of nature.* Princeton, NJ: Princeton University Press.

Rorty, R. (1992). *Consequences of pragmatism: Essays 1972–1980.* Minneapolis: University of Minnesota Press.

Silverman, W. K., Ginsburg, G. S., & Kurtines, W. M. (1995). Clinical issues in the treatment of children with anxiety and phobic disorders. *Cognitive and Behavioral Practice, 2,* 93–117.

Silverman, W. K., & Kurtines, W. M. (1996a). *Anxiety and phobic disorders: A pragmatic approach.* New York: Plenum Press.

Silverman, W. K., & Kurtines, W. M. (1996b). Transfer of control: A psychosocial intervention model for internalizing disorders in youth. In E. D. Hibbs & P. S. Jensen (Eds.), *Psychosocial treatment of child and adolescent disorders: Empirically based strategies for clinical practice* (pp. 63–82). Washington, DC: American Psychological Association.

Silverman, W. K., & Kurtines, W. M. (1997). Theory in child psychosocial treatment research: Have it or had it? A pragmatic alternative. *Journal of Abnormal Child Psychology, 25,* 359–366.

Silverman, W. K., Kurtines, W. M., Ginsburg, G. S., Weems, C. F., Lumpkin, P. W., Carmichael-Hicks, D. (in press a). Treating anxiety disorders in children with group cognitive behavioral therapy: A randomized clinical trial. *Journal of Consulting and Clinical Psychology.*

Silverman, W. K., Kurtines, W. M., Ginsburg, G. S., Weems, C. F., Rabian, B., & Serafinin, L. T. (in press b). Contingency management, self-control, and education support in the treatment of childhood phobic disorders: A randomized clinical trial. *Journal of Consulting and Clinical Psychology.*

Silverman, W. K., & Nelles, W. B. (1988). The Anxiety Disorders Interview Schedule for Children. *Journal of the American Academy of Child and Adolescent Psychiatry, 27,* 772–778.

Part V

Research in Child Psychotherapy

27

Child Therapy Outcome Research
Current Status and Some Future Priorities

JOSEPH A. DURLAK and KATE A. McGLINCHEY

This chapter is divided into two major sections. In the first section, we present an overview of the breadth and results of child outcome research. In the second section, we focus on several priorities for future research and identify some exemplary studies that have addressed these priorities. Our general intent is to highlight the diversity of the large outcome literature that has been produced within the past 30 years, emphasize that child interventions have been successful, and identify some directions for future research.

AN OVERVIEW OF CHILD OUTCOME RESEARCH

Breadth of Outcome Research

The reader is likely to be surprised at the extent and diversity of child therapy outcome research. Table 1 contains representative reviews of child therapy research and is divided into two sections. The first section identifies reviews of control group designs in which a control group of some type (no treatment, waiting list, or attention placebo) is used to assess the impact of treatment. This control group literature targets a variety of pathologies and treatments including juvenile delinquency (Lipsey, 1992), sexual abuse (Reeker, Ensing, & Elliott, 1997), mental retardation (Arnold, Myette, & Casto, 1986), attention-deficit hyperactivity disorder (DuPaul & Eckert, 1997), and preschoolers with different types of develop-

JOSEPH A. DURLAK and KATE A. McGLINCHEY • Department of Psychology, Loyola University of Chicago, Chicago, Illinois 60626.

Handbook of Psychotherapies with Children and Families, edited by Russ and Ollendick. Kluwer Academic/Plenum Publishers, New York, 1999.

Table 1. Representative Reviews of Child Therapy Research

Review	Number of studies	Target problem, therapy, or population	Mean ES if applicable
		Control group designs	
Arnold Myette & Casto (1986)	30	Preschoolers with mental retardation and language problems	0.59
Barth (1979)	24	Home-based reinforcement	
Batts (1987)	40	Teacher consultation	0.66
Beelmann, Pfingsten, & Lösel (1994)	49	Social competence training	0.47
Casey & Berman (1985)	64	Behavioral and emotional problems	0.71
Casto & Mastropieri (1986)	74	Preschoolers with developmental disabilities	0.68
Durlak, Fuhrman, & Lampman (1991)	64	Behavioral problems	0.56
Durlak, Wells, Cotton, & Johnson (1995)	516	Behavioral and emotional problems	
Dush, Hirt, & Schroeder (1989)	48	Self-control therapies	0.32
Forness & Kavale (1996)	53	Learning disabilities	0.21
Houts, Berman, & Abramson (1994)	66	Enuresis	
Lipsey (1992)	397	Juvenile delinquents	0.17
Lyman & Campbell (1996)	34	Inpatient and day treatments	
McGlinchey & Durlak (1997)	178	Internalizing disorders	0.42
Medway & Updyke (1985)	42	Teacher consultation	0.71
Ottenbacher & Petersen (1985)	38	Preschoolers with organic impairments	0.97
Pfeiffer & Strzelecki (1990)	34	Inpatient treatment	
Reeker, Ensing, & Elliott (1997)	15	Group treatments for sexually abused children	0.79
Schneider (1992)	79	Social skills training	0.80
Serketich & Dumas (1996)	26	Behavioral parent training	0.86
Shadish et al. (1993)	163	Marital and family therapies	0.51
Weisz, Weiss, Alicke, & Klotz (1987)	105	Behavioral and emotional problems	0.79
Weisz, Weiss, Han, Granger, & Morton (1995)	150	Behavioral and emotional problems	0.71
White (1985–1986)	65	Preschoolers with developmental disabilities	0.65
		Single-subject designs	
DuPaul & Eckert (1997)[a]	63	Children with ADHD	1.16
Hermann, Kim, & Blanchard (1995)[a]	41	Pediatric migraine	
Kavale, Mathur, Forness, Rutherford, & Quinn (1997)[a]	64	Social skills training	
Scotti, Evans, Meyer, & Walker (1991)	242	Youth with developmental disabilities	
Scruggs, Mastropieri Cook, & Escobar (1986)	16	Preschoolers with developmental disabilities and conduct problems	
Stage & Quiroz (1997)	99	Disruptive school children	0.78

Note. Some reviews included studies of adolescents as well as children.
[a] These reviews also included some control group designs.

mental disabilities (Casto & Mastropieri, 1986; Ottenbacher & Petersen, 1985; White, 1985). Treatment modalities include various individual and group outpatient therapies (Durlak, Wells, Cotten, & Johnson, 1995), family and marital therapies (Shadish et al., 1993), teacher consultation (Batts, 1987; Medway & Updyke, 1985), and inpatient and day treatment programs (Lyman & Campbell, 1996; Pfeiffer & Strzelecki, 1990).

Reviews of single-subject designs are noted in the second section of Table 1. Single-subject designs evaluate treatment effects for individual children using some form of time-series analysis such as a reversal or multiple-baseline protocol. Single-subject designs have not received the attention they deserve in outcome research. Well-done single-subject designs are the logical equivalent of randomized controlled trials and should not be overlooked (Task Force on Promotion and Dissemination of Psychological Procedures, 1995). Moreover, many single-subject interventions contain excellent examples of customized treatments for children with organic impairments, serious behavior problems, and various developmental disabilities including autism. Therefore, this literature is highly relevant not only for reaching conclusions about treatment effectiveness, but also for clinicians wanting practical information on how to implement interventions for individual clients.

Because of such factors as different inclusionary and exclusionary criteria, when the review was conducted and its target years, there is not as much overlap among the reviewed studies in Table 1 as one might think. For example, the two reviews of social skills and social competence training that contain a total of 128 studies (Beelmann, Pfingsten, & Lösel, 1994; Schneider, 1992), only have 22 studies in common, and the two reviews that each evaluate 30 inpatient programs (Lyman & Campbell, 1996; Pfeiffer & Strzelecki, 1990) only share 4 studies.

Furthermore, all of the child outcome literature is not captured in Table 1. For example, there have been several hundred additional single-subject designs targeting children with various behavioral and emotional problems. Over 300 single-subject studies involving children have appeared in one publication outlet alone, the *Journal of Applied Behavior Analysis,* between 1968 and 1990 (see Gresham, Gansle, & Noell, 1993; Peterson, Homer, & Wonderlich, 1982). Drug therapies or combinations of drug plus psychological treatments are also not represented. There have been 341 *reviews* of interventions for ADHD children (Swanson, McBurnett, Christian, & Wigal, 1995). Finally, the unpublished literature is largely untapped. We estimated that around 670 unpublished dissertations involving control group designs were conducted between 1960 and 1990, an average of about 22 per year (Durlak et al., 1995).

When one considers that outcome research on children did not begin in earnest until the mid-1960s, the number of evaluated interventions is remarkable. Considering published studies, we estimate there have been at least 2400 reports evaluating therapeutic interventions for children. Of these, there are over 200 studies of family therapy, over 200 studies of parent training (see Dembo, Sweitzer, & Lauritzen, 1985; Serketich & Dumas, 1996; Wiese & Kramer, 1988), over 75 studies of teacher consultation, approximately 1175 additional control group designs assessing other types of individual or group child therapies, and over 700 single-subject interventions.

Within this vast group of reports, at a minimum, there have been 600 studies of nonbehavioral forms of treatment, 1000 samples have had clinically relevant problems, 250 samples demonstrate some form of comorbidity, 400 interventions have directly involved parents or teachers as change agents, and 225 treatments lasting 20 sessions or more have been evaluated. We mention these latter features because child therapy research has been criticized for lacking these characteristics (e.g., Hibbs, 1995; Kazdin, 1997; Weisz, Weiss, & Donenberg, 1992). Although the characteristics and experimental quality of outcome studies vary considerably depending on the specific research area, when one views child outcome research in its full context, the field does not deserve the criticism that it lacks relevance to real-world clinical problems and settings.

It is impossible to do justice to 2400 outcome studies in this brief chapter. The reviews listed in Table 1 contain good discussions of the strengths and limitations of research conducted in different domains. Therefore, we focus on three general issues: (1) Is child treatment effective? (2) Which problems have been treated? (3) Are some treatments more effective than others?

Is Treatment Effective?

The mean effect sizes obtained in several meta-analyses of different literatures evaluating control group designs are also presented in Table 1. In general, these outcome data are impressive. As a comparison, Lipsey and Wilson (1993) found that 156 meta-analyses of interventions in the psychological, educational, and social science literature involving approximately 9400 different studies yielded an overall mean effect of 0.47 (SD = 0.28). Most of the mean effects in Table 1 compare favorably to this grand mean and several are substantially higher (e.g., 0.97, Ottenbacher & Petersen, 1985; 0.79, Reeker et al., 1997; 0.80, Schneider, 1992; 0.86, Serketich & Dumas, 1996; 0.71, Weisz, Weiss, Han, Granger, & Morton, 1995), suggesting that child treatments tend to produce outcomes that are generally equal to and sometimes greater than those produced by many treatments for adults.

In the second section of Table 1, some authors reported mean effect sizes obtained from single-subject designs (1.16, DuPaul & Eckert, 1997; 0.78, Stage & Quiroz, 1997). Because such effects are computed on within—rather than between-subject data, the data from control group and single-subject designs are not directly comparable. Nevertheless, the findings from the narrative and meta-analytic reviews of single-subject studies also consistently attest to the positive impact of child interventions. In summary, current outcome data clearly put to rest earlier concerns about the efficacy of child therapy (Levitt, 1963). Child therapy is clearly effective.

Which Problems Have Been Treated?

Virtually all types of presenting problems including several different combinations of comorbid difficulties are represented in the literature and have responded to treatment, although the amount of research conducted on different problems varies. In general, we have much more information on the efficacy of interventions for different forms of externalizing behavior (e.g., aggression, noncompliance, and school disruption) than for internalizing difficulties (e.g., social withdrawal, phobias, anxiety, and depression). There has also been relatively little research on children with psychotic or autistic disorders, chronic medical conditions, or a combination of academic and psychological problems. In the latter case, although there have been many school-based interventions, there are few evaluations of treatments for children placed in special education classes because of serious emotional problems.

Which Treatments Are More Effective?

Offering conclusions about the superiority of one type of treatment over another might create some controversy, but research findings converge to suggest that, in general, more structured treatments such as behavioral and cognitive–behavioral therapies have obtained better results than less structured nonbehavioral treatments. This finding has appeared for individual and group interventions targeting various problems including juvenile delinquency (see Casey & Berman, 1985; Lipsey, 1992; Weisz, Weiss, Alicke, & Klotz, 1987; Weisz et al., 1995), for school consultation (Batts, 1987), and in a limited way for family therapy (Shadish et al., 1993). Significant differences do not always emerge between treatments, however (Beelmann et al., 1994; Medway & Updyke, 1985). Another way to characterize the outcome literature is to say that if the collective findings from a particular research domain point to the superiority of any treatment, the superior approach invariably emphasizes behavioral or cognitive–behavioral rather than nonbehavioral techniques. It is noteworthy that no review has indicated a clear superiority for nonbehavioral over behavioral treatments.

Another way to assess the value of different therapies is to determine which particular treatments have been evaluated carefully enough so that we can say they are efficacious. There is no single or absolute standard for judging the scientific evidence surrounding a treatment, but two reports using slightly different evaluative criteria are relevant. The Task Force on Promotion and Dissemination of Psychological Procedures (1995) determined that the only "empirically well-established" child treatments were behaviorally oriented. These treatments included behavior modification for developmentally disabled individuals, behavior modification for enuresis and encopresis, and behavioral parent training programs for children with oppositional behavior. Similarly, Kadzin and Weisz (1998) reviewed the most carefully evaluated and successful child treatments. With perhaps one exception, all of the 34 outcome studies they discussed involved behavioral or cognitive–behavioral interventions. In other words, child therapies that have received the strongest empirical support and thus inspire the most confidence in their efficacy are behavioral or cognitive–behavioral in nature.

There are two main qualifications to current outcome research, however. First, there have not been enough studies of nonbehavioral approaches (particularly psychodynamic treatments) to make meaningful comparisons in several areas. Whereas severe externalizing problems, and problems associated with ADHD, autism, mental retardation, and other forms of developmental disabilities have been successfully treated using behavioral and cognitive–behavioral treatments, evaluations of nonbehavioral interventions for such problems are rare or completely nonexistent. For example, Shadish et al. (1993) found only one study of psychodynamic family therapy.

Unfortunately, recent trends suggest that the imbalance in studying certain forms of child treatment is not being rectified. Some of our own unpublished analyses indicate a substantial drop in outcome research on all types of nonbe-havioral treatments during the 1980s. Among all outcome studies appearing from 1990 through the end of 1997, we would estimate that behavioral and cogni-tive–behavioral treatments outnumber all other forms of interventions combined by probably 50 to 1. Therefore, some nonbehavioral treatments will probably never receive the attention they need in order to judge their scientific merit.

A second important qualification regarding current research is that small cell sizes usually require collapsing specific types of treatments into broad categories (e.g., behavioral and nonbehavioral) for analytic purposes. This precludes assess-ing the more important question of which specific therapeutic techniques are ef-fective under different clinical circumstances and what important interactions might occur among client, problem, and treatment variables. For instance, there are many different strategies that can be used within a broad treatment category such as behavioral or cognitive–behavioral and the relative impact of specific pro-cedures in different situations requires careful scrutiny.

FUTURE RESEARCH DIRECTIONS

As Kazdin (1997) has indicated, we do not need more research; we need *better research,* that is, investigations that help us understand how therapy changes clients, whom it helps, and for how long and under what conditions. Kazdin (1997) and others (Hibbs, 1995; Weisz et al., 1992) have offered several suggestions to im-prove child therapy research. We cannot discuss every issue but will focus on 12 that we wish to highlight as priorities for future research. Nine of these twelve are listed at the top of Table 2 along with 13 studies appearing within the past 5 years that are exemplary in their attention to these priorities. These studies are also ex-emplary in terms of their experimental rigor. Although not every study contains every characteristic, collectively the reports in Table 2 feature random assignment to conditions, relatively large subject samples, careful screening and assessment of presenting problems, psychometrically sound outcome measures, attempts to as-sess both the specificity and generality of treatment effects using multiple methods and measures, and they have had low attrition even during follow-ups. Each study has also reported positive therapeutic results, although not on every outcome mea-sure or for every experimental condition. Therefore, these investigations can serve as useful models for future work recognizing, of course, that no single approach is appropriate for all situations. Some of the study features noted in Table 2 have been addressed more recently in outcome research (e.g., such as studying populations with clinically relevant problems and comorbidity; see Durlak et al., 1995), but their importance deserves continued attention from researchers.

Underserved Populations

Low-income families and members of different ethnic and cultural minority groups frequently do not receive the therapeutic services they need. Furthermore, because estimates suggest that as many as 70% of clinically distressed children and adolescents never receive any formal treatment (Kazdin, 1991), there is a need to reach out to at-risk groups and effectively recruit them for interventions. Sev-

Table 2. Exemplary Studies

	Subject characteristics					Treatment characteristics			
Authors	Underserved population	Parent involvement	Family variables	Comorbid	Clinical population	Treatment fidelity	Follow-up	Practical significance	Treatment moderators
Aronen (1993)	High-risk sample	Yes					10 yr	Yes	Yes
Barkley et al. (1992)		Yes	Yes	Yes	Yes	Yes	3 mo	Yes	Yes
Barrett et al. (1996)		Yes	Yes	Yes	Yes	Yes	1 yr	Yes	Yes
Costantino et al. (1994)	Low SES and minority			Yes		Yes		Yes	
Cunningham et al. (1995)	High-risk sample	Yes	Yes		Yes	Yes	6 mo	Yes	Yes
Frankel et al. (1997)	Some minority (10%)	Yes		Yes	Yes	Yes		Yes	
Henggeler et al. (1992)	Low SES and minority	Yes	Yes		Yes	Yes	Unclear	Yes	
Kazdin et al. (1992)	Low SES and minority	Yes	Yes	Yes	Yes	Yes	1 yr	Yes	Yes[a]
Kendall (1994)				Yes	Yes	Yes	3 yr[b]	Yes	
Lochman et al. (1993)	Low SES and minority			Yes		Yes	1 yr		
Smyrnios & Kirby (1993)		Yes	Yes		Yes		4 yr	Yes	
Strayhorn & Weidman (1989, 1991)	Low SES and minority	Yes			Yes	Yes	1 yr	Yes	Yes
Webster-Stratton (1994)	Low SES	Yes	Yes	Yes	Yes	Yes	Unclear	Yes	Yes

[a] Subsequent publications from this treatment program explored potential treatment moderators (Kazdin, 1995; Kazdin & Crowley, 1997).
[b] A separate publication (Kendall & Southam-Gerow, 1996) presented 3-year follow-up data for this sample.

eral investigators have demonstrated that interventions can effectively serve members of historically underserved populations (see Table 2). For example, techniques usually used with white middle class populations can be successfully modified for or applied to low-income and minority populations (e.g., Costantino, Malgady, & Rogler, 1994; Lochman, Coie, Underwood, & Terry, 1993; Strayhorn & Weidman, 1991). Two studies illustrate that families with at-risk children can be involved in interventions when efforts are made to reduce barriers for participation by, for instance, scheduling home visits or offering flexible times for group meetings (Aronen, 1993; Cunningham, Bremner, & Boyle, 1995).

Parent Involvement

The value of actively involving parents in treatment is evident given the important role parents play in children's lives. Although the general effectiveness of parent training has been established with white middle- and upper-class parents, there is a need to extend the range of populations who can benefit from this type of intervention. To this end, several studies in Table 2 demonstrate that parent training can be successful for parents who are low SES, single, or members of various ethnic and cultural groups (Kazdin, Siegel, & Bass, 1992; Strayhorn & Weidman, 1989, 1991; Webster-Stratton, 1994).

Family Variables

There is a need to examine how treatment changes aspects of family functioning and how family functioning affects outcomes. On the one hand, dysfunctional family processes might hinder treatment progress; on the other hand, if intervention can positively modify the family environment, then outcomes might be enhanced and sustained over time. In addition to specific measures of individual child adjustment, a majority of the researchers in Table 2 have examined family processes related to cohesion or conflict, behavioral interactions and communication, and levels of marital adjustment. Interventions have usually been more successful in changing the target child's adjustment than improving family functioning, suggesting a need for modifying treatments to more directly address dysfunctional family processes (Barkley, Guevremont, Anastopoulos, & Fletcher, 1992; Henggeler, Melton, & Smith, 1992; Kazdin et al., 1992; Smyrnios & Kirkby, 1993).

Clinical Distress and Comorbidity

It is important to determine the range of dysfunction that can be effectively treated by different interventions. In particular, are treatments effective for those with clinical-level problems and does it help those with comorbid difficulties? These two issues are often related because many youths have multiple rather than singular problems. Assessments to detect the possible presence of comorbidity are not routinely conducted, however. Many of the study samples in Table 2 clearly qualify as clinically distressed; they either met formal criteria for one or more clinical disorders or the assessment procedures confirmed the severity of symptomatology. For instance, Henggeler et al. (1992) treated a sample of juvenile offenders with criminal histories, and Kazdin et al. (1992) selected a sample of antisocial children who were above the 90th percentile on standardized measures of aggression and/or delinquency. To their credit, many of the researchers listed in Table 2 also made the effort to evaluate multiple presenting problems and included subgroups with comorbidity in their treatment samples.

Treatment Fidelity

In general, treatment fidelity (sometimes called *adherence, integrity,* or *implementation*) involves the extent to which prescribed treatment procedures are faithfully conducted and additional, extraneous elements are kept to a minimum. Although only a small minority of child outcome studies have monitored treatment fidelity, data are nevertheless accumulating that levels of treatment fidelity influence outcome and that insufficient fidelity is a rival explanation for negative results or for findings favoring one treatment over another in comparative outcome research (Durlak,1998). Moncher and Prinz (1991) discuss different ways to monitor treatment fidelity; these include training therapists to a criterion level, examining therapist reports of their practices, providing ongoing supervision, using detailed treatment manuals or protocols, and rating selected treatment sessions for adherence. The last method, which is the most rigorous, was used by Barkley et al. (1992), Barrett, Dadds, and Rapee (1996), and Kendall (1994).

Follow-Up

Most child therapy studies do not report any follow-up, and when they do, the follow-up periods are less than 6 months. Therefore, the long-term durability of treatment gains is often unknown. In contrast, most of the studies in Table 2 reported some positive follow-up data, and the duration of the follow-up periods was impressive; in seven studies, follow-up was at least 1 year and in three cases it was as long as 3, 4, or 10 years (Aronen, 1993; Kendall & Southam-Gerow, 1996; Smyrnios & Kirkby, 1993).

Practical Significance

Almost all of the studies in Table 2 made some effort to assess the practical significance of their findings, that is, they tried to determine the clinical as well as the statistical significance of outcomes. In most cases, they were able to demonstrate that treatment produced a meaningful change in children's lives. For instance, Kendall (1994) found that the behavior of 60% of the treated subjects dropped to within normal limits following intervention, and 64% of treated cases no longer met criteria for a diagnosis. As another example, Henggeler et al. (1992) reported there were about 50% fewer arrests among members of the treatment group compared with controls and a 33% lower rate of recidivism.

Treatment Moderators

Outcome studies need to go beyond simply demonstrating that a treatment is effective and examine what variables moderate treatment outcome. It is extremely unlikely that a treatment will have the same effect on all participants. Several studies in Table 2 investigated how treatment outcome varied as a function of such variables as gender, age, socioeconomic status, degree of problem severity, presence of concurrent learning difficulties and/or academic dysfunction, parental psychopathology, and levels of marital and family distress (Barkley et al., 1992; Barrett et al., 1996; Kazdin, 1995; Kazdin & Crowley, 1997; Strayhorn & Weidman, 1991). It is premature to reach general conclusions about these variables based on so few studies, but unless more investigators conduct similar outcome assessment on these and other variables, there will be insufficient data to synthesize findings across studies and reach conclusions about the most important factors that influence outcomes.

A large sample size is important in the search for treatment moderators. The small n's that are often produced when a total treatment group is subdivided for additional analyses greatly reduces statistical power. Nonsignificant findings for different moderators that have been reported in many individual studies and in several meta-analyses have been plagued by low statistical power and thus are not convincing evidence of "no effect."

We want to highlight three additional areas that we hope become priorities in the next generation of research studies.

Training, Clinical Skills, and Outcomes

Despite comments to the contrary (Weisz et al., 1992), there is little specific information on the amount and quality of training and supervision provided to therapists in different outcome studies. Treatment manuals, which are beginning to appear more frequently in child and family research, are no guarantee of therapeutic proficiency. Even highly structured manualized interventions require clinical judgment and sensitivity regarding the timing and delivery of different interventions.

There are also few data on the relationship between different clinical skills and therapeutic outcomes and how change agents can best acquire the competence needed to implement different therapeutic techniques. We would include the ability to form a good therapeutic relationship as one aspect of clinical competence but know of no systematic research determining how training helps therapists in this regard. Unfortunately, professional training programs have been remiss in evaluating the specific clinical skills of their graduates or determining how different training practices contribute to clinical competence.

Therefore, there is a lack of data in the child clinical literature on the processes whereby training contributes to clinical competence which, in turn, is linked to outcomes. For instance, we know much more about what skills parents and teachers can use to modify child behavior effectively than about how to develop skillful parent and teacher trainers and consultants. Work by Kratochwill, Elliott, and Busse (1995) is one notable exception. For instance, data collected over a 5-year period indicated that successive groups of graduate students acquired knowledge of consultation principles through classwork, were able to help teachers implement successful school-based interventions while functioning as their consultants, and, finally, that teachers were highly satisfied with the services provided by the student consultants.

It is naive to believe that therapists will be equally adept at implementing all treatment approaches, or that variations in skill proficiency will not occur across client populations, presenting problems, and over time and different treatment modalities (e.g., individual versus group administration). We need information on how clinical competence and presumably therapeutic outcomes fluctuate across these different circumstances and how to train therapists most effectively and efficiently to accomplish different tasks.

Cost Analyses

Cost analyses can be one useful criterion for gauging the value of different therapies and making decisions about how to allocate limited resources. Good cost analyses provide data relevant to two important questions: (1) What are the relative costs and benefits of a particular therapy program? (2) Among the many possible alternatives, which approach is preferred because it produces better outcomes for the same cost, or similar outcomes for a lower cost? Good cost analyses emphasize both costs and benefits and may help to deflect managed health care companies away from their focus on treatment duration toward issues about treatment quality. Is it worthwhile treating this child or family using this particular technique? (as opposed to "What will it cost?").

There have been few cost analyses of child or adult therapy (see Shadish, Ragsdale, Glaser, & Montgomery, 1995, for a few limited examples in the family therapy literature), but some good models exist among prevention programs for children and adolescents (Durlak, 1997). We emphasize one caution about cost analysis, however, and that is the tendency to include only costs and benefits that can be directly expressed or easily converted into monetary figures. Evaluations must consider children and families as more than just "economic units." Cost analyses of therapy programs should include the psychological benefits of intervention. The main goals of therapy are humanitarian: to reduce personal pain and suffering and to improve psychological well-being. If these items are excluded, then the cost analysis is incomplete and biased against therapy. Several methods exist to include nonmonetary cost and benefits (see Durlak, 1997, for discussion and examples). Furthermore, cost analyses should include follow-up data, because if therapy is effective, its most important gains might not be evident until some time after treatment has ended. In fact, if children can consolidate or internalize important principles learned during the intervention, there might be a steady increase in benefits during follow-up. This has been demonstrated in some prevention programs (Durlak, 1997).

Cunningham et al. (1995) deserve credit for reporting data indicating that community-based group training of parents was six times less costly than clinic-based individual parent training. This comparison would have been even more favorable for community training, however, if the analyses were more extensive and included personal benefits because the community group training resulted in greater reductions in child problems and better maintenance of gains during follow-up.

Developmental Level

It has become axiomatic that a child's developmental level should be considered in the conduct of treatment and the analysis of effects, yet this is one area where rhetoric far exceeds practice. Authors have observed that "therapies have not been modified to make them developmental-stage specific" (Lourie, 1987, p. 85) and "what appears to be missing, at least in the case of children, is clear acknowledgment of the important role of developmental level as a foundation for determining how variables interact and what path therapy might most productively follow" (Selman, 1980, p. 255). Developmental level refers to a range of social–cognitive abilities that include components of social-information processing (such as attributions and interpretation of social cues), empathy, role-taking skills, communication ability, causal understanding, and social judgment. Holmbeck and Kendall (1991) offer a good discussion and examples of the relevance of various social–cognitive skills to treatment.

Abilities related to a child's developmental level are likely to influence what attributions children make about their problems, how well they understand the tasks and goals of therapy, and how effectively they can internalize, apply, and retain what they learn in treatment. Unfortunately, only a few investigators have analyzed the relation between such abilities and treatment responsiveness. For instance, in one study 6-year-olds who were functioning at the level of concrete operations benefited from treatment while children in the preoperational stage did not (Schleser, Cohen, Meyers, & Rodick, 1984). In another investigation, children who made more internal attributions of personal control profited more from self-control training while those with more externally oriented attributions showed more improvement when reinforcement was provided by others (Bugenthal, Whalen, & Henker, 1977). Age is a poor proxy variable for developmental level because children of the same age can differ substantially in their social–cognitive abilities.

SUMMARY

A substantial data base now exists in the child therapy area, involving over 2400 outcome studies conducted on a wide range of clients, problems, and treatments. Outcome data clearly confirm that child therapy is effective although there is much we still need to learn. Some priorities for future research are determining the success of interventions for historically underserved populations, making a positive impact on the family environment as well as the individual child, assessing how well treatment works for children with serious and comorbid problems, monitoring treatment integrity, assessing the factors that moderate outcome including the child's developmental level, and establishing the long-term, practical benefits of intervention. We also need more data on how to train therapists most effectively and efficiently, and how the costs and benefits of different treatments compare.

REFERENCES

Arnold, K. S., Myette, B. M., & Casto, G. (1986). Relationships of language intervention efficacy to certain subject characteristics in mentally retarded preschool children: A meta-analysis. *Education and Training of the Mentally Retarded, 21,* 108–116.

Aronen, E. (1993). The effect of family counseling on the mental health of 10–11 year-old children in low- and high-risk families: A longitudinal approach. *Journal of Child Psychology and Psychiatry, 34,* 155–165.

Barkley, R. A., Guevremont, D. C., Anastopoulos, A. D., & Fletcher, K. E. (1992). A comparison of three family therapy programs for treating family conflicts in adolescents with attention-deficit hyperactivity disorder. *Journal of Consulting and Clinical Psychology, 60,* 450–462.

Barrett, P. M., Dadds, M. R., & Rapee, R. M. (1996). Family treatment of childhood anxiety: A controlled trial. *Journal of Consulting and Clinical Psychology, 64,* 333–342.

Barth, R. (1979). Home-based reinforcement of school behavior: A review and analysis. *Review of Educational Research, 49,* 436–458.

Batts, J. W. (1987). *The effects of teacher consultation: A meta-analysis of controlled studies.* Unpublished dissertation.

Beelmann, A., Pfingsten, U., & Lösel, F. (1994). Effects of training social competence in children: A meta-analysis of recent evaluation studies. *Journal of Clinical Child Psychology, 23,* 260–271.

Bugenthal, D. B., Whalen, C. K., & Henker, B. (1977). Causal attributions of hyperactive children and motivational assumptions of two behavior-change approaches: Evidence for an interactionist position. *Child Development, 48,* 874–884.

Casey, R. J., & Berman, J. S. (1985). The outcome of psychotherapy with children. *Psychological Bulletin, 98,* 388–400.

Casto, G., & Mastropieri, M. A. (1986). The efficacy of early intervention programs: A meta-analysis. *Exceptional Children, 52,* 417–424.

Costantino, G., Malgady, R. G., & Rogler, L. H. (1994). Storytelling through pictures: Culturally sensitive psychotherapy for Hispanic children and adolescents. *Journal of Clinical Child Psychology, 23,* 13–20.

Cunningham, C. E., Bremner, R., & Boyle, M. (1995). Large group community-based parenting programs for families of preschoolers at risk for disruptive behaviour disorders: Utilization, cost effectiveness, and outcome. *Journal of Child Psychology and Psychiatry, 36,* 1141–1159.

Dembo, M. H., Sweitzer, M., & Lauritzen, P. (1985). An evaluation of group parent education: Behavioral, PET, and Adlerian programs. *Review of Educational Research, 55,* 155–200.

DuPaul, G. J., & Eckert, T. L. (1997). The effects of school-based interventions for Attention Deficit Hyperactivity Disorder: A meta-analysis. *School Psychology Review, 23,* 5–27.

Durlak, J. A. (1997). *Successful prevention programs for children and adolescents.* New York: Plenum Press.

Durlak, J. A. (1998). Why program implementation is important. *Journal of Prevention and Intervention in the Community, 17,* 5–19.

Durlak, J. A., Fuhrman, T., & Lampman, C. (1991). Effectiveness of cognitive-behavior therapy for maladapting children: A meta-analysis. *Psychological Bulletin, 110,* 204–214.

Durlak, J. A., Wells, A. M., Cotton, J. K., & Johnson, S. (1995). Analysis of selected methodological issues in child psychotherapy research. *Journal of Clinical Child Psychology, 24,* 141–148.

Dush, D. M., Hirt, M. L., & Schroeder, H. E. (1989). Self-statement modification in the treatment of child behavior disorders: A meta-analysis. *Psychological Bulletin, 106,* 97–106.

Frankel, F., Myatt, R., Cantwell, D. P., & Feinberg, D. T. (1997). Parent-assisted transfer of children's social skills training: Effects on children with and without attention-deficit hyperactivity disorder. *Journal of the American Academy of Child and Adolescent Psychiatry, 36,* 1056–1064.

Gresham, F. M., Gansle, K. A., & Noell, G. H. (1993). Treatment integrity in applied behavior analysis with children. *Journal of Applied Behavior Analysis, 26,* 257–263.

Henggeler, S. W., Melton, G. B., & Smith, L. A. (1992). Family preservation using multisystemic therapy: An effective alternative to incarcerating serious juvenile offenders. *Journal of Consulting and Clinical Psychology, 60,* 953–961.

Hermann, C., Kim, M., & Blanchard, E. B. (1995). Behavioral and prophylactic pharmacological intervention studies of pediatric migraine: An exploratory meta-analysis. *Pain, 60,* 239–256.

Hibbs, E. D. (Ed.). (1995). Psychosocial treatment research [Special Issue]. *Journal of Abnormal Child Psychology, 23*(1), 1–156.

Holmbeck, G. N., & Kendall, P. C. (1991). Clinical-childhood-developmental interface: Implications for treatment. In P. R. Martin (Ed.), *Handbook of behavior therapy and psychological science: An integrative approach* (pp. 73–99). New York: Pergamon Press.

Houts, A. C., Berman, J. S., & Abramson, H. (1994). Effectiveness of psychological and pharmacological treatments for nocturnal enuresis. *Journal of Consulting and Clinical Psychology, 62,* 737–745.

Kavale, K. A., Mathur, S. R., Forness, S. R., Rutherford, Jr., R. B., & Quinn, M. M. (1997). Effectiveness of social skills training for students with behavior disorders: A meta-analysis. *Advances in Learning and Behavioral Disabilities, 11,* 1–26.

Kazdin, A. E. (1991). Effectiveness of psychotherapy with children and adolescents. *Journal of Consulting and Clinical Psychology, 59,* 785–798.

Kazdin, A. E. (1995). Child, parent, and family dysfunction as predictors of outcome in cognitive-behavioral treatment of antisocial children. *Behaviour Research and Therapy, 33,* 271–281.

Kazdin, A. E. (1997). A model for developing effective treatments: Progression and interplay of theory, research, and practice. *Journal of Clinical Child Psychology, 26,* 114–129.

Kazdin, A. E., Bass, D., Ayers, W. A., & Rodgers, A. (1990). Empirical and clinical focus of child and adolescent psychotherapy research. *Journal of Consulting and Clinical Psychology, 58,* 729–740.

Kazdin, A. E., & Crowley, M. J. (1997). Moderators of treatment outcome in cognitively based treatment of antisocial children. *Cognitive Therapy and Research, 21,* 185–207.

Kazdin, A. E., Siegel, T. C., & Bass, D. (1992). Cognitive problem-solving skills training in the treatment of antisocial behavior in children. *Journal of Consulting and Clinical Psychology, 60,* 733–747.

Kazdin, A. E., & Weisz, J. R. (1998). Identifying and developing empirically supported child and adolescent treatments. *Journal of Consulting and Clinical Psychology, 66,* 19–36.

Kendall, P. C. (1994). Treating anxiety disorders in children: Results of a randomized clinical trial. *Journal of Consulting and Clinical Psychology, 62,* 100–110.

Kendall, P. C., & Southam-Gerow, M. A. (1996). Long-term follow-up of a cognitive–behavioral therapy for anxiety-disordered youth. *Journal of Consulting and Clinical Psychology, 64,* 724–730.

Kratochwill, T. R., Elliott, S. N., & Busse, R. T. (1995). Behavioral consultation: A five year evaluation of consultation and client outcomes. *School Psychology Quarterly, 10,* 87–117.

Levitt, E. E. (1963). Psychotherapy with children: A further evaluation. *Behaviour Research and Therapy, 60,* 326–329.

Lipsey, M. W. (1992). Juvenile delinquency treatment: A meta-analytic inquiry into the variability of effects. In T. D. Cook, H. Cooper, D. S. Cordray, H. Haitmann, L. V. Hedges, R. J. Light, T. A. Louis, & F. Mosteller (Eds.), *Meta-analysis for explanation: A casebook* (pp. 83–127). New York: Russell Sage Foundation.

Lipsey, M. W., & Wilson, D. B. (1993). The efficacy of psychological, educational, and behavioral treatment: Confirmation from meta-analysis. *American Psychologist, 48,* 1181–1209.

Lochman, J. E., Coie, J. D., Underwood, M. K., & Terry, R. (1993). Effectivenss of a social relations intervention program for aggressive and nonaggressive, rejected children. *Journal of Consulting and Clinical Psychology, 61,* 1053–1058.

Lourie, I. S. (1987). New approaches in mental health services for adolescents. *The Clinical Psychologist, 40,* 85–87.

Lyman, R. D., & Campbell, N. R. (1996). *Treating children and adolescents in residential and inpatient settings.* Newbury Park, CA: Sage.

McGlinchey, K. A., & Durlak, J. A. (1997). *Therapy outcome research on child and adolescent internalizing disorders.* Unpublished manuscript.

Medway, F. J., & Updyke, J. F. (1985). Meta-analysis of consultation outcome studies. *American Journal of Community Psychology, 13,* 489–505.

Moncher, F. J., & Prinz, R. J. (1991). Treatment fidelity in outcome studies. *Clinical Psychology Review, 11,* 247–266.

Ottenbacher, K., & Petersen, P. (1985). The efficacy of early intervention programs for children with organic impairment: A quantitative review. *Evaluation and Program Planning, 8,* 135–146.

Peterson, L., Homer, A., & Wonderlich, S. (1982). The integrity of independent variables in behavior analysis. *Journal of Applied Behavior Analysis, 15,* 477–492.

Pfeiffer, S. I., & Strzelecki, S. C. (1990). Inpatient psychiatric treatment of children and adolescents: A review of outcome studies. *Journal of the American Academy of Child and Adolescent Psychiatry, 29,* 847–853.

Reeker, J., Ensing, D., & Elliott, R. (1997). A meta-analytic investigation of group treatment outcomes for sexually abused children. *Child Abuse and Neglect, 21,* 669–680.

Schleser, R., Cohen, R., Meyers, A., & Rodick, J. D. (1984). The effects of cognitive level and training procedures on the generalization of self-instructions. *Cognitive Therapy and Research, 8,* 187–200.

Schneider, B. H. (1992). Didactic methods for enhancing children's peer relations: A quantitative review. *Clinical Psychology Review, 12,* 363–382.

Scotti, J. R., Evans, I. M., Meyer, L. H., & Walker, P. (1991). A meta-analysis of intervention research with problem behavior: Treatment validity and standards of practice. *American Journal on Mental Retardation, 96,* 233–256.

Scruggs, T. E., Mastropieri, M. A., Cook, S. B., & Escobar, C. (1986). Early intervention for children with conduct disorders: A quantitative synthesis of single-subject research. *Behavioral Disorders, 11,* 260–271.

Selman, R. L. (1980). *The growth of interpersonal understanding: Developmental and clinical analyses.* New York: Academic Press.

Serketich, W. J., & Dumas, J. E. (1996). The effectiveness of behavioral parent training to modify antisocial behavior in children: A meta-analysis. *Behavior Therapy, 27,* 171–186.

Shadish, W. R., Montgomery, L. M., Wilson, P., Wilson, M. R., Bright, I., & Okwumabua, T. (1993). Effects of family and marital psychotherapies: A meta-analysis. *Journal of Consulting and Clinical Psychology, 61,* 992–1002.

Shadish, W. R., Ragsdale, K., Glaser, R. R., & Montgomery, L. M. (1995). The efficacy and effectiveness of marital and family therapy: A perspective from meta-analysis. *Journal of Marital and Family Therapy, 21,* 345–360.

Smyrnios, K. X., & Kirkby, R. J. (1993). Long-term comparison of brief versus unlimited psychodynamic treatments with children and their parents. *Journal of Consulting and Clinical Psychology, 61,* 1020–1027.

Stage, S. A., & Quiroz, D. R. (1997). A meta-analysis of interventions to decrease disruptive classroom behavior in public education settings. *School Psychology Review, 26,* 333–368.

Strayhorn, J. M., & Weidman, C. S. (1989). Reduction of attention deficit and internalizing symptoms in preschoolers through parent–child interaction training. *Journal of the American Academy of Child and Adolescent Psychiatry, 28,* 888–896.

Strayhorn, J. M., & Weidman, C. S. (1991). Follow-up one year after parent–child interaction training: Effects on behavior of preschool children. *Journal of the American Academy of Child and Adolescent Psychiatry, 30,* 138–143.

Swanson, J. M., McBurnett, K., Christian, D. L., & Wigal, T. (1995). Stimulant medications and the treatment of children with ADHD. In T. H. Ollendick & R. J. Prinz (Eds.), *Advances in clinical child psychology* (Vol. 17, pp. 265–322). New York: Plenum Press.

Task Force on Promotion and Dissemination of Psychological Procedures. (1995). Training in and dissemination of empirically-validated psychological treatments: Report and recommendations. *The Clinical Psychologist, 48,* 3–23.

Webster-Stratton, C. (1994). Advancing videotape parent training: A comparison study. *Journal of Consulting and Clinical Psychology, 62,* 583–593.

Weisz, J. R., Donenberg, G. R., Han, S. S., & Kauneckis, D. (1995). Child and adolescent psychotherapy outcomes in experiments versus clinics: Why the disparity? *Journal of Abnormal Child Psychology, 23,* 83–106.

Weisz, J. R., Weiss, B., Alicke, M. D., & Klotz, M. L. (1987). Effectiveness of psychotherapy with children and adolescents: A meta-analysis for clinicians. *Journal of Consulting and Clinical Psychology, 55,* 542–549.

Weisz, J. R., Weiss, B., & Donenberg, G. R. (1992). The lab versus the clinic: Effects of child and adolescent psychotherapy. *American Psychologist, 47,* 1578–1585.

Weisz, J. R., Weiss, B., Han, S. S., Granger, D. A., & Morton, T. (1995). Effects of psychotherapy with children and adolescents revisited: A meta-analysis of treatment outcome studies. *Psychological Bulletin, 117,* 450–468.

White, K. R. (1985–1986). Efficacy of early intervention. *Journal of Special Education, 19,* 401–416.

Wiese, M. R., & Kramer, J. J. (1998). Parent training research: An analysis of the empirical literature 1975–1985. *Psychology in the Schools, 25,* 325–330.

28

Child Psychotherapy Process Research
Suggestions for the New Millennium

ROBERT L. RUSSELL

Unfortunately, process research, in the adult and especially in the child area, has not progressed to a stage where it can focus its intellectual and monetary resources on just a few remaining minor but irksome issues. Instead, process research, in each of its myriad of forms, remains tentative, slipshod, or merely exploratory without systematic development and painstaking verification. In fact, process researchers have tended to skirt the foundational tasks of precisely defining the proper scope and content of their domain of research. Correlatively, process research is most often characterized by the use of simplistic or inappropriately borrowed methodologies and procedures to tackle rather local, not vital, questions and concerns. Of course there are exceptions, but given this general state of affairs, it is not surprising that progress in process research is slow, results from process research are unconfirmed or unconfirmable, and the practical utility of process research is nearly nil in terms of its current impact on common treatment practices. Over 50 years old, process research is still in its infancy, however prodigal it may appear in reviews by its apologists and most productive investigators.

With the approach of the new millennium, we have the right, if not the sober scholastic duty, to ask if process research will mature to the extent that is required to make good on its many promissory notes and seemingly fruitful beginnings. In the foreseeable future, will it tell us with any precision what essentially comprises successful therapies? In the foreseeable future, will it be able to identify and meticulously describe therapist techniques and client reactions that predict a successful course of treatment? In the foreseeable future, will it be able to impose

---

ROBERT L. RUSSELL • Department of Psychology, Loyola University Chicago, Chicago, Illinois 60626.

Handbook of Psychotherapies with Children and Families, edited by Russ and Ollendick. Kluwer Academic/Plenum Publishers, New York, 1999.

phase, stage, or sequential order on the therapist–patient interaction, circumscribing mechanisms of developmental change and treatment progress? And will it be able to do all of this, taking into account patient and therapist characteristics, types of disorders, and levels of pathology in ways that can speak to the frontline practitioner and to his or her cost-conscious consumer, never mind the ever more mettlesome quality control managers? The answers to these questions, I contend, depend almost entirely on defining the primary tasks of process research in terms unabashedly informed by knowledge and techniques developed in those systematic areas and disciplines focused on the development of interpersonal communication and the language sciences.

In this brief chapter, I want to outline some basic questions that child process research should address and I want to highlight a few innovative methods by which their pursuit can meaningfully proceed. In this respect, then, I will not be reviewing the field as a whole or summarizing what we have learned so far (see Shirk & Russell, 1996). Instead, I will try to formulate a few principles or tenets that can orient researchers as we seek answers to a few basic questions—actually questions that process researchers have been asking, albeit sometimes only implicitly, from the very start. If my comments appear critical, I should confess and state openly that I do not feel that there is a significant body of sophisticated process investigations in the child area today. Further, and perhaps surprisingly to some, I do not feel real progress in child psychotherapy process research is attainable by simply aping the content and methods of the supposedly more advanced adult process literature. Real scientific progress, I contend, will require a type of investigative effort and commitment that the field has yet to witness in either the child or adult literatures. Finally, by way of introduction, I should also make apparent that the critical edge that I am now advancing uncovers as many problems in some of my own research as in the bulk of the studies making up the tradition I would hope to change.

BASIC TENETS

Of what is psychotherapy comprised? Rightly, a long tradition of researchers and reviewers has answered this question by stating that psychotherapy is comprised of communications, including behaviors that, in the framework of treatment, are taken as communicating something, even if not intended by the participant speakers to do so (Kiesler, 1966). Psychotherapy should be conceived, then, as principally comprised of symbolic exchanges—they are the basic stuff that give form and content to what we call psychotherapy. Researchers have tended to hit on this insight without much difficulty and then erroneously proceed to study "the stuff" of therapy without first deciding if it is like any other stuff in the world and without curiously and studiously exploring if any one else had run up against it and decided to make it a topic of serious study. Such a strategy has often resulted in what might be termed unfortunate and embarrassing consequences.

For example, imagine becoming interested in the stuff some shamans give to their possessed patients in the form of an elixir. You might naturally formulate a reasonable first question: Of what is this elixir-stuff comprised? You and a small set of colleagues then proceed to independently devise ways to measure, categorize, rate, and otherwise describe it, without first exploring if others had already decided to study it or stuff very much like it and had already devised, tested, and refined true analytic methods for use in answering just the question you had formulated. After much time, effort, and money, someone reviews the investigations of this stuff and is compelled, by a fair and sober estimate, to describe numerous incommensurate category, rating, and measurement systems (all quite modest in scope in that they contain few differentiations along usually only one dimension), along with a set of noncumulative findings. Progress has been slow and what results that have been produced find little to corroborate them in other fields of investigation. The elixir-stuff remains virtually unknown and is left unsituated as an object in the matrix of the many branches of science that might be able to help to determine its nature.

Inevitably, however, someone ponders if other fields of investigation might have findings that would lend support to those few garnered in the insulated pursuit of the identity of the stuff shamans use. Analytic and clinical chemistry and the material and biological sciences are consulted. Interestingly, there is already a table of elements (over 100 such elements compared to the 5 or 10 categories or rating scales you and your colleagues have used) and numerous tried-and-true analytic methods to apply to determine the constituents of any stuff—and, importantly, at various levels of complexity. Interestingly, you also find out that such progress had been won only with laborious, meticulous, and often frustrated investigations over an entire career or a tradition of careers spanning hundreds of years. Very few studies of convenience (done in pursuit of nontheoretically motivated hunches, of quick results and publications, and so forth) can be found in this literature and the few that do exist are seldom found to contribute to the cumulative research record. Over against these traditions long established in other disciplines, the mock tradition begun with the formulation of a reasonable first question about the makeup of the elixir-stuff begins to look, well, underdeveloped at best, misguided and embarrassing at worst. Divorced from any real scholarship, the research tradition spins out of control from its reasonable starting point, and accumulates findings that are of limited value and have only a locally sustainable significance.

Of what is psychotherapy comprised? If the answer to this question is, on the general level, symbolic transactions or communication, then process researchers have a choice to make: proceed straightaway to its investigation, or curiously and studiously find out if others might have run up against symbolic transactions, or communication, in other disciplines, and have progressed through long and arduous effort in its investigation, both theoretically and empirically. Historically, the choice has been almost unanimous: Generation after generation of process researchers have plunged headlong into study after study of the process of therapy as communication, blithely ignoring and remaining almost entirely ignorant of work in disciplines whose primary focus is to study symbolic transactions, communication, and language. This near unanimity is partially understandable, given that it seems that our graduate programs take it as their mission to perpetuate, rather than supercede and topple, traditions, and they rarely require or even enable their students to seriously study language and communicative development, never mind the detailed microprocesses of treatment. What this means, of course, is that the field's progress rests in the hands of frank novices and the rare autodidacts who obtain at least a measure of real insight into language and communication. Is it any wonder that the field of process research does not have a reasonably sophisticated answer to the basic question: Of what is psychotherapy comprised?

If we turn to the other literatures concerned with symbolic exchange—linguistics, communication, developmental pragmatics, literary criticism, ethnomethodology, and so forth—some basic tenets can be garnered to orient and inform process research. For example, it is commonly understood that whatever unit of symbolic communication is chosen for the object of study it should be conceived as conveying multiple meanings that routinely subserve multiple functions, as having intended meanings that differ from their actual effects, and as being totally dependent on its communicative and extracommunicative context: Without context, it is nearly impossible to disambiguate an utterance's meaning, the speaker's intent, and the impact it has had on the hearer. These tenets have been articulated for quite some time, and studied with the exactitude associated with linguistics proper and the tradition of analytic philosophy. In contrast, process research has proceeded in the main as if units of communication have one exclusive meaning or one exclusive function. This implicit assumption is implemented in the typical nominal coding systems that have somehow earned disciplinewide bragging rights by virtue of their mutually exclusive definitions of their 5 to 12 constituent categories (see Russell & Stiles, 1979). One can imagine a student of language remarking something to the effect that if it were possible to meaningfully boil down all of that which took place in communication to a few mutually exclusive categories our human lot would hardly be different from that of our distant cousins far down on the phylogenetic scale. The truth of the matter is that communication is multiply complex; programs or traditions of research that do not have this as a basic orienting tenet at the outset will end up producing simplistic and spacious findings much like those characterizing the bulk of process research.

To dramatize the point a bit, linguists (i.e., phonologists/phoneticists) have long been interested in discovering just those features that are necessary and sufficient to describe and differentiate the smallest bits of meaningful sounds in language. They have used both qualitative and quantitative methods in their investigations. It is clear that over 20 simultaneously applied features are needed to distinguish the smallest meaningful sounds from each other. Given that this much complexity is evident when dealing with mere bits of sound, can you imagine seriously claiming that fewer features would be needed to distinguish the communicative intents, meanings, and functions of whole sentences? As bizarre as this claim may appear when put in context, most of process research has been carried out with use of far fewer categories or features, even when dealing with such immeasurably more complex units of language as whole narratives!

To make the absurdity of this practice as apparent as possible, anthropomorphize the tradition of process research as a renowned professor. His or her first sentence in a well-attended invited address might be: "Although, lamentably, it has taken our colleagues in linguistics over 200 years and over 20 features to describe and differentiate such sounds as /b/, /p/, /d/, etc., I have been able, investigating independently and without recourse to previous work, to describe and differentiate entire life stories with the use of only five mutually exclusive categories." That the audience at this imaginative lecture produces few groans of incredulity speaks volumes about the normative knowledge base of the discipline. Abstractionism, reductionism, or even parsimony, when employed in an intellectual vacuum, cannot be expected to achieve results on par with those won by painstaking erudition and a cumulative record of tough empirical tests of well-motivated hypotheses.

The pragmatic upshot of taking the alternative viewpoint, that is, in supposing that any unit of communication is multiply complex, is that methods have to be devised that at least seem commensurate with the tenet of complexity. If, as a modest beginning, what the therapist says and what the client says is taken as at least a large portion of that from which therapy is comprised, then their sayings ought to be viewed as carrying multiple meanings and multiple functions. In other words, utterances are complex and to capture their multiple meanings and multiple functions requires the creation of multidimensional measurement systems. Further, it is because the degree to which any utterance conveys specific meanings and functions varies, these systems ought to be, not mutually exclusive nominal category systems, but ordinal rating systems. The same utterance, or set of utterances, for example, can be intended to inform, persuade, humor, and even impress and offend you, among a host of other plausible intents, and the relative degree of each of these functions can be made to vary, depending on the circumstances surrounding its use.

Once investigators of psychotherapy process embrace the notion of complexity as an irrefutable fact of communication, then the work of identifying and studying the constituents of psychotherapy can begin in earnest. The first problem, of course, for the construction of ordinal rating systems that are applied to each unit of communication in the therapy, is to attempt to achieve acceptable levels of content validity. One needs to obtain circumspect coverage of the domain of communication in therapy to answer the question "Of what is therapy comprised?" Not insignificant here is the problem created by an irksome paradox: to find out of what psychotherapy is comprised, one must construct rating systems that have adequate levels of content validity. But to aim for and achieve content validity depends on prior knowledge of the domain that is to be investigated. If an investigator knows little about the processes of symbolic exchange in general, what means can be summoned to surmount the paradox and obtain valid knowledge about treatment processes? Most theories of the process of psychotherapy are not formulated in the terminological frameworks used to describe and explain basic discourse processes and language functioning. Instead, they are formulated in the various terminologies associated with distinct therapeutic orientations. To use such terminologies to find out of what therapy is comprised already presupposes what researchers should hope to find out. If there is anything distinct about the process of psychotherapy, quantitatively or qualitatively, from ordinary processes of discourse, is it not reasonable to suppose that such processes would build on or modify or otherwise transform what goes on in any act of communicative exchange?

Such considerations recommend basing the construction of rating scales for the series of initial investigations into the processes of psychotherapy on our knowledge of symbolic exchange processes per se. In other words, initial attempts to answer the question "Of what is psychotherapy comprised?" should be couched in terms that are necessary to describe any act of interpersonal communication. It is, after all, inconceivable that therapeutic discourse would share absolutely no commonalities with the everyday discourses from which it has presumably emerged. To reiterate, then, rating systems ought first to be based on knowledge of general processes of communication inherent in any act of discursive interaction. Only when they are shown to be insufficient does it make sense to amend, modify, add, or otherwise transpose scales that might plumb further the idiosyncratic character of therapeutic, as distinct from ordinary, discourse (see Labov & Fanshel, 1977).

If the above suggestions were to be followed, the pursuit of content validity, and the tenet of complexity, would dictate that numerous rating scales would be constructed in terms applicable to instances of communication per se. Each of the many units of communication identified in the therapy session, treatment, or other fragment of the case(s), would be rated on all of the scales. Understand that now the researcher will be confronted with hundreds of units of communication each rated on scores of scales. This produces an abundance of data. Technically, the question becomes how to evaluate these data (a matrix comprised of number of units by number of features represented by the rating scales). Is there a way to boil this down to ascertain the structure or underlying organization of discourse in therapy? In other words, is there a way to identify quantitatively the main constituents out of which therapeutic discourse is comprised?

Before suggesting a technique for the analysis of such data, it is important to supplement the tenet of complexity with another, namely, that any adequate characterization of the process of psychotherapy has to account for its processive character—the fact that, as discourse, it begins, transpires, and ends in time. The values of any given constituent can and do change as discourse progresses—at various rates, in various clusters, in various interrelationships with each other. In other words, the values associated with units of communication comprising a discourse take systematic shape over time, not only in terms of their typical fluctuations within typical ranges, but also in relation to each other. This is true both within one person's speech and across the interactive communication of two or more people. With guidance from the tenet of complexity, one can bet that the temporal systematicity of discourse will not be confined or represented along one and only one dimension, but will itself be complex, and require the identification of multiple dimensions of organization.

Consequently, the technique used to assess discourse data must be able to deal with their complexity of meanings, functions, and intensities at the same time as it deals with their temporal organization. One way to view discourse, in fact, is as the primary form in and by which human beings, individually and collectively, organize shared meanings in and across time. Our techniques of analysis should then be able to inform us what values or intensities of meanings and functions systematically covary across the various durations of discourse investigated. This means that the matrix of the number of units to be investigated (in order of their appearance in the discourse) by the number of features represented by and evaluated along the numerous rating scales should be decomposed into the underlying dimensions that best account for how the values of the features covary over the temporally organized units in the discourse. Put as a question: Do all of the values of each of the many scales used to assess every unit of discourse covary in unison across the discourse (very unlikely), or do they form several distinct patterns of covariation across the discourse.

P-TECHNIQUE: A PROMISSORY APPROACH

A technique especially suited to this sort of analysis is called P-technique. It has been described as one of the best analytic techniques for the investigation of psychotherapeutic processes, and it would seem that this is an apt description

(Cattell & Luborsky, 1950; Mintz & Luborsky, 1970). Basically, P-technique is a form of factor analysis that can be applied to the type of matrix described above. With several precautions, it can be applied to such matrices when they derive from the ratings of an individual's discourse ($N = 1$, in an intrasubject matrix) or from the chained or interleaved discourse of several individuals ($N > 1$, in a combined intra- and intersubject matrix). Like other forms of factor analysis, it can be used to discover the underlying dimensions or factors that best explain the variation in the observed matrix of values. In other words, it can be used to discover what values of which features tend to covary with each other over the temporally organized units chosen for investigation. In a nutshell, it discovers the underlying dimensions (i.e., factors) in terms of which the discourse has been constructed. For example, in a study of adult therapy, Czogalik and Russell (1994a) discovered that the discourse of clients was organized around four dimensions: Continuing Objective Information Exchange, Performing Painful Self-formulating Work, Negotiation of the Therapeutic Relationship, and Depicting Nonsignificant Others. These were the factors around which the discourse of the clients seemed to be organized. Moreover, even though the clients' discourse was organized around these factors or dimensions, the extent to which each utterance reflected each of these dimensions could be quantitatively determined, using factor scores. Consequently, the ebb and flow of values on these factors could be described and assessed, both within and across clients, by plotting the factor values in special "discoursagraphs," or what had been described by the misnomer, "chronograph." Such graphs present the heartbeat of the discourse for visual inspection and analysis much as an electrocardiogram presents a picture of heart functioning across a span of time. Used wisely, this technique can go a long way in the search for the answer to the first basic question: "Of what is psychotherapy comprised?"

Before confronting a second basic question, several points need to be made about the use of P-technique. The field of process research, in the child and adult areas, has advanced far enough to be dissatisfied with such broadband questions as "Of what is psychotherapy comprised?" We have learned to append prefixes and suffixes to this question, such as: for this patient, with this diagnosis, in this treatment, at what stage, and so forth (see Russell, Bryant, & Estrada, 1996, 1997). We have become suspect of the meaning and usefulness of such grand central tendencies, and, instead, search for ways to dismantle them to secure more precise knowledge about families of treatment processes and mechanisms. Because P-technique can be used on data collected on single individuals or on data chained together from multiple individuals, and because the results can be systematically compared, it provides a way to build a bridge from the particularities of single cases to the more common, general processes undergirding all discourse based treatments. It can satisfy both idiographic and nomothetic research demands. In fact, it can provide a base of knowledge that is a synthesis of the two traditions—an idiothetic basis for process research.

This suggests our third tenet, to supplement the tenet of complexity and the tenet characterizing discourse as processive. This third tenet is meant to highlight the multiplicity of discourse pathways leading to change. Different individuals or groups of individuals, even with the same disorder and the same therapist dispensing the same treatment, may engage, sustain, and/or transform the client–therapist discourse differently over time. Transformative discourse may take more than one form, and this is especially relevant with children, where development is so rapid and diversity in competencies so readily apparent. Consequently, it would seem wise to assess patterns of discourse and change in the discourse patterns individually as well as collectively, and to do so with methods that can preserve unique and general patterns of conversational interaction. In fact, one can argue that averaging unique patterns of discourse organization and change to produce broad central tendencies may obscure real change processes and wrongly produce findings that characterize processes that actually do not exist for anyone. P-technique can be used to build general models based on individual ones, so that characterizations can be generated at various levels of abstraction, each taking into account and modeling possibly different discourse organizations and patterns of change in them over time.

Further, because P-technique is a form of factor analysis, and because techniques have been advanced that allow it to be used to build, test, and confirm process models, P-technique can contribute to establishing a body of cumulative and confirmed findings, at various levels of abstraction. To date, no other method has been used that can provide the advantages inherent in the correct use of exploratory and confirmatory P-technique for building a confirmable (i.e., validated) body of knowledge about treatment processes. In the area of process research, replication and validation are only beginning to take place, and whatever analytic means that can be used to facilitate wider concern for the generality of findings should be received quite favorably.

For example, in a demonstration study by Russell, Bryant, and Estrada (1997) methods were introduced to assess and differentiate child clients' discourse that had occurred in sessions which had been independently rated as high or low in quality. Using exploratory P-technique on utterances that had been contiguously linked across the three high-quality child sessions, a three-factor model was derived. In the high-quality sessions, children's discourse was organized around the provision of information, cognitively appraising self or experience in the present, and the expression of positive affect and evaluations. What this means is that each of the variables with high loadings on one of these factors tended to have scale ratings that varied in systematic relation to each other over the many utterances comprising the high-quality sessions, and not with, or to a lesser extent than, the variables comprising the other factors.

Was the discourse in the low-quality sessions similarly organized? In short, no. Only when a much simpler and more general model was derived from the original model for the high-quality sessions, did the discourse of the two session types begin to resemble each other. But even then, there remained large and reliable differences in the basic organization of the children's discourse participation in the two session types.

Importantly, the use of P-technique analyses, both exploratory and confirmatory, not only allows one to assess the fit of given models across session types, but also allows one to simplify and prune models so as to discover if there is reasonable approximation of the discourses to each other at various levels of generality. Moreover, when there are differences, use of these types of analytic strategies allows one to specify in detail how the discourses differ from each other. If applied to the discourse of therapists in high- and low-quality sessions, for example, one would be in a position to learn what features of the discourse in the low-quality sessions would need to change to begin to approximate that used in the high-quality sessions. In other words, P-technique can also be a powerful tool for training.

In summation, then, three principles have been advanced to orient researchers in their quest to answer a basic question about what constitutes the process of psychotherapy. The principles relate to the complex character of language behavior, the fact that discourse is situated in time, and that individuals can and do take different discourse pathways to achieve similar psychotherapeutic gains. One analytic strategy that seems to respect these three principles has been advanced here, namely, P-technique. This technique has the added advantage of being able to discover, model, and confirm basic underlying structures of the discourse comprising therapy. In other words, it can be used in both analytic (e.g., What is the basic discourse structure of dynamic therapy?) and comparative (e.g., In what ways do the discourses of analytic and cognitive therapies differ?) process studies—the latter design also being relevant for the task of identifying processes that are associated with successful and unsuccessful therapies.

Even with the advantage of sustained research that is oriented as recommended above, the answer to our initial question would be limited. Knowing of what therapy is comprised, does not tell us how much of this or that ingredient needs to be provided and at what points in the process to optimize client outcomes. Historically, the question concerning levels or doses of treatment or treatment techniques and the question concerning timing or phasing have been posed somewhat separately. Moreover, in the adult and in the child literature, answers to these questions have been formulated on the basis of more molar and not microanalytic data. For example, the question of dose has been formulated in terms of number of sessions, or in terms of the frequency or relative frequency of occurrence of nominal therapist technique categories. In this paradigm, the salience or strength of a treatment would be related to number of sessions or the relative number of, say, interpretations or reflections. Clearly such formulations abide little with the three tenets for process research described above. They do not capture the complexity of the discourse processes comprising therapy, the temporal character of therapeutic conversations, or the fact that there are multiple pathways to change, requiring very different "dosages," "dispensed" over very different periods of time.

Use of P-technique can also help us to reframe our question about strength of treatment in terms of discourse. We can ask: How much of certain discourse factors need to be present for sessions to be deemed of high quality versus of low quality? Or, how much of a certain discourse factor tends to be present in successful therapies in contrast to less successful therapies? If we are to take the idea seriously that therapy is comprised of discourse, then it only makes sense to ask how much of certain discourse processes facilitate client change. But now, with the use of P-technique, the answer to this question can be formulated in ways that are informed by our basic process tenets. For example, because P-technique is a form of factor analysis, factor scores can be assigned to each utterance. In other words, each utterance can be described in terms of the quantitative degree to which it embodies or represents each of the factors. Basically, the higher the factor score for a particular utterance, the more salient are those variables that loaded highly on the relevant factor. In effect, one can plot and graph the factor scores across the utterances comprising the discourse to construct a "discoursagram" (i.e., a visual document much like those used for electrocardiograms), to capture

the heartbeat of the discourse, with all of its ebb and flow at the utterance by utterance level (Czogalik & Russell, 1994b). Because factor scores have a mean of
zero and a standard deviation of one, it is easy to formulate a more precise question about the magnitude of discourse dosages: To what degree must the discourse
of therapy deviate from its central tendency or normative basis, and on which factors, taken singly or in conjunction, so as to optimize positive change?

Note that even this seemingly more complex question is in actuality an unacceptable simplification, as it does not also incorporate information about the timing of the interventions or client responses. We want to know not only how far
from central tendencies must a discourse sway to be therapeutic, but also at what
opportune moment, or during which phase of a session or treatment. This means
that, at the level of discourse, the question of "dosage" should not be separated
from the question of timing, especially interactive or conversational timing—a tru-
ism we can all relate to from a practice point of view.

In a demonstration paper addressing the dose and timing question, Russell
and Bryant (1998) attempted to differentiate high- and low-quality child therapy
sessions on the basis of dose, rendered at the level of discourse, and timing, characterized as percent of the children's discourse for a particular session. Building
on their previous P-technique papers examining child participation in treatment,
Russell and Bryant used optimal discriminant analysis to try to discover an optimal zone of discourse participation. Without going into the statistical details, the
authors built models that simultaneously (1) identified utterances with factor
scores that deviated from the mean at progressively larger magnitudes and (2) optimally differentiated the relevant distributions of high- and low-quality utterances (i.e., the utterances meeting the various factor-score criteria) in terms of
location in the sampled sessions. One factor having to do with discourse attentiveness achieved a statistically significant result when its factor score exceeded
0.4, and it reached its highest level of statistical significance when it exceeded 0.6.
The classification model was: if time of utterance with high values of discourse attentiveness was < 0.21 (i.e., occurred in the first fifth of a session) then utterance
was from a low quality session, if > 0.21 then utterance was from a high-quality
session. A second factor having to do with cognitive processing of information
also reached statistical significance, but only when its factor values were more
than a standard deviation larger than the mean. The classification model was: if
time of utterance with high values on cognitive processing < 0.82 (i.e., occurred in
the first four-fifths of a session) then the utterance was from a high-quality session;
if time of utterance was > 0.82 then utterance was from a low-quality session.
These models correctly classified over 85% of utterances that had been sampled
from high-quality sessions, but only about 36% of utterances that had been sampled from low-quality utterances.

Taken together, these results suggested that if children's discourse tends to
have above-average intensities on discourse attentiveness (i.e., attending to the
discourse) and cognitive processing of information in the middle three-fifths of
sessions, the sessions are likely to be of high quality. Conversely, if children's discourse is high on discourse attentiveness only in the first fifth of a session, and
high on cognitive processing only in the last fifth of a session, then the session is
likely to be of low quality. These findings make good clinical sense as they capture
information about the clinically significant intensities and phasings of the chil-

dren's involvement and participation in the sessions. But beyond the particulars of this study, the methods introduced enable researchers to refine their analyses of discourse processes in treatment by incorporating information about dosage and timing to pinpoint optimum zones of clinical engagement.

CONCLUSION

Several critical tenets have been underscored to properly orient child psychotherapy process research for the future. The tenets have to do with basic parameters of any conversational interaction—that it is complex, occurs in time, and that change in the discourse, in the direction of some criterion defined in terms of clinical significance, is likely to be achieved, not through one, but through various discourse pathways. One method of analysis was highlighted that tends to incorporate these tenets, namely, P-technique. With its use, not only can the field progress with its first order of business—to find out of what therapy is comprised—but it can begin to delve into questions having to do with dose and phase at the microanalytic level of analysis. However, as Russell and Czogalik (1989) have argued, even P-technique analyses should be viewed as only a middle step in the process of identifying, through quantitative means, key types of conversational exchange in the process of therapy. Such key exchanges can then be used to establish a corpus of process data on which more sophisticated, rule-based analyses can begin. Ultimately, if we are to understand therapy as a form of conversation, then gaining an understanding of the rules that undergird it, in contradistinction to the statistical regularities that describe it, must be the paramount goal for process researchers.

In conclusion, if we take seriously the proposition that therapy, even child therapy, is essentially a form of communication, then it is at that microanalytic level of analysis that we should reap the most gains in our research programs and in relating our findings to the problems faced by practitioners. This is true because the latter must be concerned with what happens in the therapy hour on an utterance-by-utterance basis, and with the many nuances that can transpire at that level. In short, child process research should aid in developing more sensitive listeners and more catalytic speakers, so that the ailing children can return as rapidly as possible to their normal developmental trajectories.

REFERENCES

Cattell, R. B., & Luborsky, L. (1950). P-technique demonstrated as a new clinical method for determining personality and symptom structure. *Journal of General Psychology, 42,* 3–24.

Czogalik, D., & Russell, R. (1994a). Therapist structure of participation. An application of P-technique and chronographic analysis. *Psychotherapy Research, 4,* 75–94.

Czogalik, D., & Russell, R. (1994b). Key processes of client participation in psychotherapy: Chronography and narration. *Psychotherapy: Theory, Research, Practice, and Training, 31,* 170–182.

Kiesler, D. J. (1966). Some myths of psychotherapy and a search for a paradigm. *Psychological Bulletin, 65,* 110–136.

Labov, W., & Fanshel, D. (1977). *Therapeutic discourse: Psychotherapy as conversation.* New York: Academic Press.

Mintz, J., & Luborsky, L. (1970). P-technique factor analysis in psychotherapy research: An illustration of a method. *Psychotherapy: Theory, Research, and Practice, 7,* 13–18.

Russell, R. L., & Bryant, F. (1998). *Are there optimal zones of child participation in therapy?: Quantity and phase in high and low quality sessions.* Paper presented at the Chicago Society for Psychotherapy Research.

Russell, R. L., Bryant, F., & Estrada, A. U. (1996). Confirmatory p-technique analyses of therapist discourse: High versus low quality child therapy sessions. *Journal of Consulting and Clinical Psychology, 64,* 1366–1376.

Russell, R. L., Bryant, F., & Estrada, A. U. (1997). *Child participation in high versus low quality therapy sessions: An application of optimal discriminant analysis with p-technique.* Manuscript submitted for publication.

Russell, R. L., & Czogalik, D. (1989). Strategies for analyzing conversations: Frequencies, sequences, or rules. *Journal of Social Behavior and Personality, 4,* 221–236.

Russell, R. L., & Stiles, W. B. (1979). Categories for classifying language in psychotherapy. *Psychological Bulletin, 86,* 404–419.

Shirk, S. R., & Russell, R. L. (1996). *Change processes in child psychotherapy: Revitalizing treatment and research.* New York: Guilford Press.

29

Epilogue

SANDRA W. RUSS and THOMAS H. OLLENDICK

The chapters in this handbook give a sense of the high quality of theory, clinical practice, and research in the field of intervention with children and families today. After reviewing the chapters, we think that the trends in the field that we identified in the Preface and in Chapter 1 will continue and will be strong directions for research and practice in the future. Those trends were (1) the use of a developmental framework, (2) research on empirically supported treatments, (3) focus on specific problems and populations, (4) integration of treatment approaches, and (5) importance of situational and contextual factors in planning and implementing interventions. What follows are our observations about each of these trends and their future.

Certainly the emphasis on a developmental framework will continue. Toth and Cicchetti (Chapter 2) eloquently discussed the developmental psychopathology framework, which has become a dominating framework in the field. It is interesting to see the similarities between Anna Freud's principles of development and the basic tenets of contemporary developmental psychopathology (Mayes & Cohen, 1996). Her concept of developmental lines and organizational hierarchies is consistent with developmental psychopathology's organizational perspective of child development and focus on the quality of the integration within and among biological and psychological systems of the individual (Sroufe & Rutter, 1984). This developmental framework has a long history and, now in a more sophisticated and testable form, is evident in many of the chapters throughout the book.

Research in the area of empirically supported treatments should be of top priority for all treatment approaches. The behavioral and cognitive–behavioral approaches already have an impressive list of research-supported treatments. Other approaches must develop a research base or they will no longer be viable forms of

SANDRA W. RUSS • Psychology Department, Case Western Reserve University, Cleveland, Ohio 44106-7123.   THOMAS H. OLLENDICK • Child Study Center, Virginia Polytechnic Institute and State University, Blacksburg, Virginia 24061-0355.

Handbook of Psychotherapies with Children and Families, edited by Russ and Ollendick. Kluwer Academic/Plenum Publishers, New York, 1999.

treatment. This state of affairs would be a loss to the field. As Fonagy stated, the psychodynamic approach is a broad comprehensive one that is then tailored to the individual child. Based on this multidimensional approach, the therapist is flexible in choosing the intervention, sometimes from moment to moment. The advantage of this approach is difficult to investigate empirically, but it can be done. For example, a recent study with adults investigated the interventions of expert therapists in psychodynamic–interpersonal and cognitive–behavioral therapies (Wiser & Goldfried, 1998). The study investigated the associations among types of interventions within the therapy hour and amount of affective experiencing. The research paradigms exist for carrying out research on interpersonal approaches. As Russell describes in Chapter 28, research paradigms from other disciplines can also be useful and should be explored.

The trend of investigating specific problems and populations is also evident in these chapters, as is the need to focus on specific underlying processes. For example, both Shirk (Chapter 19) and Durlak and McGlinchey (Chapter 27) discuss the need for investigating the effect of specific techniques on specific cognitive, affective, and interpersonal processes. Also, many authors expressed dissatisfaction with the current DSM-IV classification system. We need to go beyond this rather simplistic diagnostic system. As Toth and Cicchetti put it, it is only when psychotherapists are aware of the possible diversity in etiology, process, and outcomes with similar diagnostic categories that optimal treatment will be possible. Also, by investigating the effect of specific interventions on specific cognitive, affective, and personality processes, we can learn about optimal treatment techniques. By placing specific process research within a developmental psychopathology framework, we can identify protective factors in child development. By understanding protective factors, we can then develop effective intervention and prevention programs. Although this handbook did not focus on prevention, Chapter 25 by Felner gives us a taste of what can and should be done in that area.

Experimentation with thoughtful integration of different treatment approaches should continue. Shirk's chapter presents a new framework for conceptualizing integrated approaches and should be very useful for the field. As we pointed out in Chapter 1, the risk of integrating different approaches is that we lose the research base for the individual techniques unless that research is also carried out with the integrated approach. Hughes and Cavell (Chapter 22) present a carefully done evaluation study of an integrated treatment with aggressive children. Because aggression in children is multidetermined, a single-focused intervention is not optimal. Hughes and Cavell present a thoughtful and sophisticated integration of approaches based on attachment theory and social learning theory. Their results suggest how complex the process of combining theories and approaches really is.

Some disorders lend themselves to the integration of approaches better than others. For example, very young children with Oppositional Defiant Disorder benefit from the combination of play and behavioral management techniques in the Parent–Child Interaction Therapy of Rayfield, Monaco, and Eyberg (Chapter 17). And multisystemic therapy (Randall and Henggeler, Chapter 21) flexibly combines a variety of techniques with seriously disturbed youth. Once these integrated treatment packages have been demonstrated to be effective, then the next step would be a systematic component analysis of the different elements of the intervention. As

Russ pointed out in her introductory comments to the Special Section on Developmentally Based Integrated Psychotherapy with Children: Emerging Models in the *Journal of Clinical Child Psychology* (1998) the field needs research at both the micro and macro levels, both in the laboratory and in the clinical setting. There needs to be specific research on specific processes with specific populations. Simultaneously, the field needs experimentation combining different theoretical models and techniques. By integrating, we take the best change mechanisms from different approaches for different problems and populations.

Finally, the contextual framework for considering interventions will become more essential as we become a more diverse society. Howard, Barton, Walsh, and Lerner (Chapter 3) stress the importance of tailoring the intervention to the population. They call for multiple levels of assessment and intervention. Their focus is not on the DSM-IV diagnosis, but rather the lack of fit of the child with the context. Optimal intervention should enhance the fit between the child and the environment.

The concepts and frameworks within the field of intervention with children and families have multiplied and become increasingly complex. Hopefully, this is a temporary stage in this relatively young science. As the field evolves, overarching principles of child development and change processes in development should emerge and give clarity to selecting intervention approaches with children and families.

REFERENCES

Mayes, L., & Cohen, D. (1996). Anna Freud and developmental analytic psychology. In A. Solnit, P. Neubauer, S. Abrams, & A. S. Dowling (Eds.), *The psychoanalytic study of the child* (Vol. 51, pp. 117–141). New Haven: Yale University Press.

Russ, S. (1998). Introductory comments to special section on developmentally based integrated psychotherapy with children: Emerging models. *Journal of Clinical Child Psychology, 27,* 2–3.

Sroufe, L. A., & Rutter, M. (1984). The domain of developmental psychopathology. *Child Development, 55,* 17–29.

Wiser, S., & Goldfried, M. (1998). Therapist interventions and client emotional experiencing in expert psychodynamic–interpersonal and cognitive–behavioral therapies. *Journal of Consulting and Clinical Psychology, 66,* 634–640.

Author Index

Subject Index

Abdominal pain, 469–470
Adherence to regimens, 471–473
Aggressive behavior in children
  description of, 281–282
  multisystemic treatment of, 411–413
  rational-emotive behavioral treatment of, 290–300
  school-based interventions, 419–446
Antidepressant medications, 209–210
Antiepileptic medications, 213
Antimanic medications, 210–211
Antipsychotic medications, 207–209
Anxiety in children
  brief psychodynamic treatment of, 219–237
  cognitive-behavioral treatment of, 126–130
  pragmatic treatment of, 505–521
  prevalence of, 222
Anxiolytic medications, 211–213, 345–366
Assessment, and
  behavior analysis, 184–187
  brief psychodynamic psychotherapy, 231–234
  client-centered therapy, 109–110
  cognitive-behavioral therapy, 123–124, 262–264
  family therapy, 141–144
  multisystemic therapy, 411–414
  parent–child interaction therapy, 339–340
  parent training, 158–161
  psychodynamic psychotherapy, 94–96
  psychopharmacological approaches, 201–204

Behavior analysis
  case formulation in, 184–187
  history of, 183–184
  managed care and, 194–195
  mechanisms of change, 187–193
  research support of, 193–194
  theoretical overview of, 181–183
Behavior modification, 4–6, 181–197

Brief psychodynamic psychotherapy
  and expressive play, 229
  insight and, 228–229
  managed care and, 234–235
  mechanisms of change, 228–230
  principles of, 223–228
  research and, 230–231

Case formulation
  behavior analysis, 184–187
  brief psychodynamic psychotherapy, 231–234
  client-centered therapy, 109–110
  cognitive-behavioral play therapy, 392–402
  cognitive-behavioral therapy, 123–124, 268–274
  family therapy, 141–144, 317–322
  interpersonal psychotherapy, 249–250
  multisystemic therapy, 411–414
  pragmatic therapy, 517–519
  parent–child interaction therapy, 329–330
  parent training, 158–161
  psychoanalytic psychotherapy, 94–96
  psychopharmacological approaches, 201–204
  rational-emotive behavior therapy, 291–293
Child psychotherapy
  and contextual factors, 6, 11, 22– 24, 45–62
  cost analyses, 535
  current trends in, 8– 11
  and development, 535
  developmental framework for, 6–7, 15–38
  evidence-based practice, 7–9, 553–555
  history of, 4–6
  outcome research in, 525–540
  process research, 541–552
  treatment fidelity, 533
  treatment integration, 10–11, 18–19, 59–60
  treatment moderators, 533–534
  and treatment specificity, 9–10
  underserved populations, 530–532